P9-BTL-922

Date Due

Courtesy of Ford Division, Ford Motor Company, Dearborn, Michigan.

To produce a full-color advertisement for a magazine, you, as an advertising manager, will oversee the work of many different people—the copywriter who writes the ad, the photographer who takes the product shot, the production artist who puts all the elements of the ad together, and last but not least, the printer, who prepares a chromolin or proof for the ad. The chromolin shows you what the ad will look like when it is printed. On this proof, you check that the copy, art, and photograph are correctly placed and that the colors are true.

(a)

To print a color ad, the colors are first separated into four colors—yellow, magenta, cyan, and black—by photographing the original art for the ad, as seen in Figures (a), (b), (d), and (f). These colors are called "process colors" and represent the ink colors used in four-color printing.

After the colors are printed in yellow, cyan, magenta, and black from four corresponding printing plates, they are combined as seen in Figures (c), (e), and finally, (g). As you can see, the inks blend to provide an optical illusion of full, natural color.

(b)

(c)

(d)

(e)

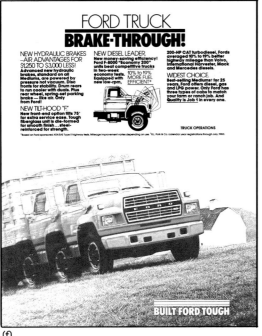

(f)

(g)

(a)

The optical illusion in four-color printing is achieved by combining the photographic screens, which are made up of many dots, as shown in Figure (a). Screens must be placed at angles for each of the four colors. When the dot patterns are placed at the proper angles, as seen in Figure (b), a correctly registered ad results.

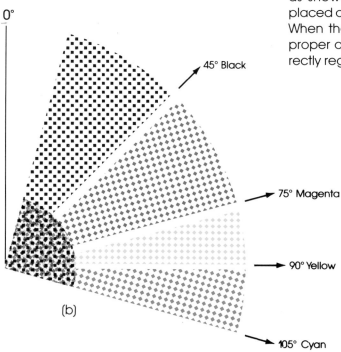

0°

45° Black

75° Magenta

90° Yellow

105° Cyan

(b)

# Advertising:

### 3rd Edition

## Planning, Implementation, & Control

David W. Nylen
Professor of Marketing
Stetson University

Published by

### S59 SOUTH-WESTERN PUBLISHING CO.

CINCINNATI    WEST CHICAGO, IL    DALLAS    PELHAM MANOR, NY    LIVERMORE, CA

# PREFACE

## Author's Intent

I have written this book for current and prospective business managers who want to know how to use advertising as a tool in marketing the products of their companies. Although the book contains some description of advertising as an institution, the primary focus lies in providing the manager of advertising with a specific process to follow in developing effective advertising programs. The heart of this process is the preparation and implementation of an advertising plan. As explained below, the book is organized according to the logical steps to advertising-plan preparation.

An effort has been made to make this book authoritative. Theory has been introduced where it helps to explain practice, but the thrust of the book clearly is to present the practice of advertising as it is carried on today. In support of the effort to make the book authoritative, I have again called upon active practitioners to supplement my own experience as I updated the text. I am particularly indebted to Robert A. Cronenwett, Manager of Consumer Advertising and Sales Promotion Services for ITT Corporation and to Earl Bahler, Senior Vice President with Ogilvy and Mather Direct. In addition, I have again received outstanding cooperation from many businesses and friends who have supplied counsel and illustrative materials.

## Organization

**Part 1** provides background understanding of advertising management that is an essential prerequisite to building the advertising plan. Its major purposes are to explain:

- How advertising relates to other marketing functions
- How to build and utilize an organization of advertising people
- How to find and build productive working relations with advertising specialists
- How to approach the process of planning
- How advertising relates to and influences the consumer decision process.

**Part 2** is devoted to consumer, product, and market analyses that furnish objectives for the advertising programs to follow. Its major purposes are to explain:

- How to conduct a consumer analysis
- How to analyze the product
- How to analyze the market
- How to make the positioning decision and define advertising objectives.

**Part 3** describes the process by which advertising programs are developed to fulfill advertising objectives. Its major purposes are to explain:

- How to establish the advertising budget at the appropriate level
- How to select advertising media that will reach target consumers
- How to direct the creation of advertising
- How to design a sales-promotion program

iii

- How to prepare an advertising program for the purpose of introducing a new product.

**Part 4** shows how to control advertising effectiveness and assure legal and social responsibility. Its major goals are to explain:

- How to set standards for desired performance
- How to measure actual or projected performance
- How to know when to take corrective action.

## Special Features

*State of the Art Coverage.* There have been numerous changes made in this third edition so as to reflect changes that have taken place in practice. There have been some exciting advances in advertising research, many of them stimulated by technological innovations such as the laser scanner and split-cable technology. There have also been major changes in the media with the emergence of the new electronic media and the revitalization of direct marketing. The area of advertising regulation has also changed dramatically in the last five years and further modifications apparently lie just ahead. All of these changes and more have been incorporated into this third edition.

*Questions for Discussion.* These were prepared with the stated objectives for each chapter in mind. They are meant to reinforce the key concepts studied in the chapter.

*Problems.* A case problem is included at the end of each chapter in order to lead the student to apply the knowledge gained through studying the chapter.

## Instructional Aids

I have designed the Instructor's Manual in order to help the teacher of the course in Advertising to prepare for class with a minimal amount of time invested in the text. I intend to make it possible for the instructor to review the textual material directly from the Manual and to get a good feel for what the student has read without the need to continually refer to the text. Each chapter of the Manual follows the same pattern and presents seven different sets of information:

1. I begin with a paragraph which describes the *purpose* and *motivation* of the chapter.
2. A chapter *outline* is presented.
3. The *learning objectives* as spelled out in the text are repeated.
4. The *chapter summary* is also repeated as it stands in the text.
5. The *key terms* as presented in the text are reproduced with definitions.
6. *Teaching suggestions,* based on my own experience in preparing the material for class presentation, are included. These vary in length from chapter to chapter. It is hoped that instructors may find them useful in their attempts to expand on various important concepts and ideas in the classroom.
7. *Suggested answers* to all end-of-chapter questions and problems follow the *teaching suggestions.*

David W. Nylen

# CONTENTS

## *Part Three*_____

# PROGRAMS FOR REACHING
# ADVERTISING OBJECTIVES

## *Part Four*_____

# CONTROL AND EVALUATION OF THE ADVERTISING PROGRAMS

# Part One
## FRAMEWORK FOR THE ADVERTISING PLANNING PROCESS

The purpose of this book is to describe how to manage an advertising effort. The process to be described is applicable to both products and services, to manufacturers or retailers, to profit and nonprofit firms.

The book is directed to people who are or who aspire to be advertising managers. These are the people responsible for planning, implementing, and controlling advertising programs—basic elements of the management process.

We begin in Part 1 the description of the advertising management process by providing some background on how the advertising process actually works in practice and something about the people involved in the process.

By the time you have completed Chapters 1–5 you should understand the following things:

1. How advertising relates to other marketing functions such as personal selling and merchandising.

2. How to build an organization of advertising people and how to utilize them in carrying out the advertising process.

3. How to find and build productive working relations with the needed advertising specialists who are outside the advertising manager's organization.

4. How to approach the process of planning; that is, how to plan for planning.

5. How advertising relates to and influences the consumer purchase decision process.

# CHAPTER 1

## *Advertising as a Marketing Management Tool*

**LEARNING OBJECTIVES**

In studying this chapter you will learn:

- The size of and the growth in the advertising industry.

- The leading national advertisers and the percentage of sales that they spend on advertising.

- The various types of jobs available in the advertising industry.

- The use of advertising objectives and the interaction of advertising with other marketing variables.

- The advertising manager's role in planning, implementing, and controlling the advertising function.

A study estimated that the average consumer is consciously aware of and thus influenced by 76 advertisements a day. That means nearly 28,000 advertisements a year or a million and a half in a lifetime.[1] With these numbers, most of us come to the study of advertising with more than a little experience and knowledge. Advertising practitioners often complain, with some justification, that most people fancy themselves to be advertising experts and freely criticize advertisers' efforts. However, it is advertising expertise as a consumer, not as an advertiser, that most people possess. While this knowledge provides useful perspective, the advertising practitioner's knowledge also includes an understanding of the use of advertising to sell products.

This chapter explains the use of advertising as a tool or technique for

---

[1]Raymond A. Bauer and Stephen A. Greyser, *Advertising in America* (Boston: Division of Research, Graduate School of Business Administration, Harvard University, 1968), p. 176.

marketing products. Information is provided on the overall dimensions of the advertising industry to give a feeling for its characteristics in relationship to the total economy. The focus of the discussion then turns to the individual firm and considers the relationship of advertising to other tools that contribute to the marketing of the company's products. More specific consideration of the characteristics of the job of the advertising manager, through whose eyes this study of advertising will be viewed, completes the chapter coverage.

## Dimensions of the Advertising Industry

Any discussion of the size, growth, and location of the advertising industry should be preceded by a definition of advertising.

### Advertising Defined

Advertising is so familiar to most Americans that the term has intuitive meaning. Most definitions of advertising, of which there are many, agree upon three aspects of the term:

1. *Advertising is a paid message* as contrasted, for example, to publicity which is free.
2. *Advertising appears in the mass media.* (**Mass media** are public advertising carriers such as television, radio, magazines, and newspapers.) By contrast, personal selling by a salesperson is a paid message that does not appear in a public medium.                                                                              *mass media*
3. *Advertising attempts to inform or to persuade people about a particular product, service, belief, or action.* For marketers, the dominant use of advertising is to sell products and services. There are also political advertisements and public service advertisements with slightly different objectives.

The working definition used in this book is developed from these three aspects. Hence, **advertising** is a paid message that appears in the mass media for the purpose of informing or persuading people about particular products, services, beliefs, or actions.                                                                              *advertising*

### The Size of the Advertising Industry

The advertising industry is substantial, but most people overestimate its size because they have such frequent contact with the industry's product — advertising.

Total advertising expenditures in 1982 in the United States were $66 billion.[2] That certainly sounds like a huge expenditure, yet it constitutes only a minor part of the total economy. In 1982, for example, total advertising expenditures were only 2.0 percent of GNP. (Gross National

---

[2]"U.S. Advertising Volume," *Advertising Age* (May 30, 1983), p. 42.

Product is the total value of all final goods and services produced by our economy.)

Another comparison provides additional perspective. A report based on an analysis of tax returns and published by the Federal Trade Commission revealed that for all manufacturing firms the average media advertising expenditure was only 1.2% of sales.[3] This means that only a little over one cent of each sales dollar becomes advertising expense, far less than for many other expense categories and probably far less than most people would guess. At $66 billion, total advertising expenditures are slightly larger than the sales revenue of the domestic iron and steel industry ($51 billion) and the electrical equipment industry ($54 billion). However, a single company, General Motors (sales of $60 billion) is nearly as large as the entire advertising industry and Procter and Gamble ($73 billion of sales) is larger.[4]

### The Growth of Advertising

Over the past twenty years advertising dollar volume in the United States has shown consistent growth. Exhibit 1-1 seems to indicate that advertising expenditures are rising at an increasing rate. However, Exhibit 1-1 also shows that advertising volume has grown only at the same rate as GNP. The recent sharp increases in advertising expenditures reflect, in part, inflationary price rises that also affect other segments of the economy.

### Concentration of Advertising

Discussion of the average advertising investment by all industries and of the aggregate advertising expenditure in the United States tends to obscure the highly uneven distribution of these expenditures. Advertising expenditures are highly concentrated, both by firm and by industry.

LEADING NATIONAL ADVERTISERS. One measure of the concentration of advertising is the proportion of total advertising expenditures accounted for by the heaviest advertisers. *Advertising Age* annually estimates advertising expenditures of the 100 leading national advertisers in eight measured media. Measured media are ones for which there are commercial services available that collect expenditure data. They include newspapers, magazines, television, radio, and outdoor advertising.

In 1982 expenditures in these media by the top 100 advertisers amounted to $8.3 billion. This was more than the total expenditures by all other advertisers in these same media. The proportion of advertising by the top 100 was particularly heavy in network television (accounting for

---

[3]"FTC Tells Line-of-Business Data," *Advertising Age* (October 19, 1981), p. 43.
[4]Industry data from *The Value Line* (New York: Arnold Bernhard and Co., Inc., 1983).

U.S. advertising expenditures in total and as a percentage of GNP, 1963-1982.                EXHIBIT 1-1

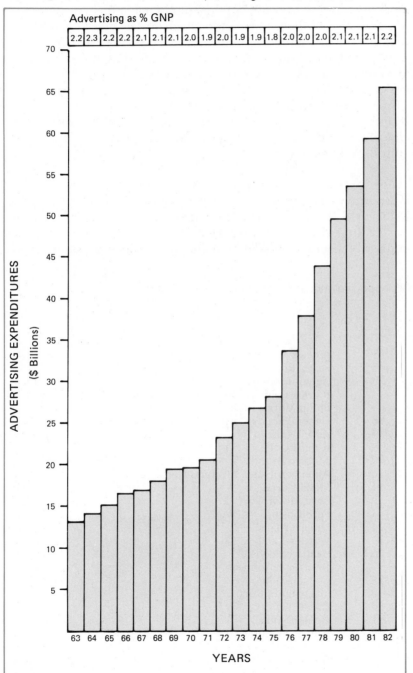

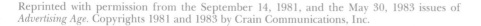
Reprinted with permission from the September 14, 1981, and the May 30, 1983 issues of *Advertising Age.* Copyrights 1981 and 1983 by Crain Communications, Inc.

78% of total television expenditures) and in magazines, network radio, and outdoor advertising (over 50% of the grand total in these media).

The first 25 of the leading national advertisers and their 1982 expenditures, in both measured and unmeasured media, are listed in Exhibit 1-2. The list is dominated by large, well-known firms, but notice that the firms tend to be marketers of high-volume, branded, consumer goods. Drugs, toiletries, foods, cigarettes, soaps, and automobiles are conspicuous on the list. By contrast, there are very large firms in other product fields to whom advertising is apparently less important. Occidental Petroleum, United Technologies, and Caterpillar Tractor, for example, do not appear among the top 100 advertisers.

PERCENTAGE OF SALES SPENT ON ADVERTISING. The relationship between heavy advertising and type of product is confirmed by the figures in Exhibit 1-3 which show the percentage of sales invested in advertising by some leading product groups. Heaviest users of advertising include manufacturers and retailers of high-volume, branded consumer goods.

**EXHIBIT 1-2**      The 25 leading national advertisers, 1982.

| Rank | Company | Expenditure ($ millions) |
|:---:|:---|:---:|
| 1 | Procter & Gamble | $726.1 |
| 2 | Sears, Roebuck & Co. | 631.2 |
| 3 | General Motors Corp. | 549.0 |
| 4 | R. J Reynolds Industries | 530.3 |
| 5 | Philip Morris Inc. | 501.7 |
| 6 | General Foods Corp. | 429.1 |
| 7 | AT&T Co. | 373.6 |
| 8 | K mart Corp. | 365.3 |
| 9 | Nabisco Brands | 335.2 |
| 10 | American Home Products Corp. | 325.4 |
| 11 | Mobil Corp. | 320.0 |
| 12 | Ford Motor Co. | 313.5 |
| 13 | PepsiCo Inc. | 305.0 |
| 14 | Unilever U.S. | 304.6 |
| 15 | Warner-Lambert Co. | 294.7 |
| 16 | Beatrice Foods Co. | 271.0 |
| 17 | Johnson & Johnson | 270.0 |
| 18 | Colgate-Palmolive | 268.0 |
| 19 | McDonald's Corp. | 265.5 |
| 20 | Coca-Cola Co. | 255.3 |
| 21 | General Mills | 244.4 |
| 22 | Anheuser-Busch Cos. | 243.4 |
| 23 | H. J. Heinz Corp. | 235.7 |
| 24 | Batus Inc. | 235.0 |
| 25 | Warner Communications | 232.2 |

EXHIBIT 1-3

Percentage of sales invested in advertising for selected heavily advertised industry sectors, 1982.

| Industry | Percentage |
| --- | --- |
| Retail Mail-Order Houses | 15.7 |
| Phonograph Records | 13.0 |
| Toys & Sporting Goods | 10.5 |
| Perfumes & Cosmetics | 8.4 |
| Drugs | 8.2 |
| Distilled Beverages | 7.9 |
| Retail Furniture Stores | 7.2 |
| Soap & Detergents | 6.8 |
| Motion Picture Producers | 6.4 |
| Retail Jewelry Stores | 6.3 |

Reprinted with permission from the August 15, 1983 issue of *Advertising Age*. Copyright 1983 by Crain Communications, Inc.

The social and economic consequences of the concentration of advertising expenditures by company and by product class is a matter of dispute. Some maintain that it reflects an undesirable concentration of economic power in these firms and industries, resulting in high prices to support advertising budgets. Others see it as evidence of healthy rivalry between firms, leading to product innovation and lower prices.

Of greater immediate importance, the great unevenness in advertising expenditures suggests that the usefulness of advertising varies by product class. This evidence can be important to advertising managers who must appraise the impact that advertising will have on product revenues.

ADVERTISING VOLUME IN OTHER COUNTRIES. Advertising expenditures in the United States are concentrated among a relatively small number of firms and product groups. Additionally, the large-scale use of advertising is concentrated among only a few countries, with the United States by far the leading spender. In 1981 total advertising expenditures in the non-Communist world exceeded $118 billion.[5] Advertising expenditures in the United States accounted for $61 billion or more than half of the free world total. Six nations—the United States, Japan, the United Kingdom, West Germany, France, and Canada accounted for more than 78 percent of world advertising.

The concentration of advertising among a few nations reflects more than the larger population in these nations. Per capita advertising expenditures in the United States were $266, higher than in any other nation. Ranked next were Bermuda, Switzerland, Finland, Norway, and Australia. It is apparent from this list that advertising expenditures tend to be heavier in free-market nations and more affluent nations where consumers have more discretionary income.

[5]"International Ad Spending, 1981, By Country," *Advertising Age* (June 20, 1983), p. 72.

## Advertising Industry Jobs

The description of the advertising industry's size, growth, and concentration omits an important dimension of the business—the people who work in it. Advertising people may be specialists who concentrate on one dimension of advertising, or they may be generalists who manage whole advertising programs.

ADVERTISING SPECIALISTS. Advertising is a field in which there is great specialization. The practice of advertising is too demanding in training and experience for anyone to become expert in all phases. Instead, people who work in advertising tend to specialize along functional lines, and they tend to work for firms that are equally specialized. There are so many specialties in advertising that they cannot all be considered here, but the major categories will be described.

*media sales representative*

*Media Sales Representatives.* **Media sales representatives** (frequently called "media reps") sell advertising time and space. The firms that market advertising time and space are the media themselves—radio and television stations, newspapers, magazines, and others. The specialists who sell advertising are called media representatives. They may work directly for the medium whose time or space they sell or they may work for separate firms of sales agents that represent a number of media.

Media representatives call on potential buyers of advertising—generally advertising agencies and advertiser firms—explaining the merits of the product, taking orders, and handling buyer-seller communication.

*media buyer*

*Media Buyers.* The specialist who is the counterpart of the media sales representative is the **media buyer.** Most of these specialists work for advertising agencies, although some are retained by advertisers and some work for firms of media specialists who offer media buying services to both advertising agencies and advertisers.

The media buying specialist helps decide what media should be used for a product, purchases the media, and controls and evaluates the performance of the media purchased.

*copywriter*
*art director*

*Advertising Creators.* To the general public, a job in advertising means creating advertising. This most glamorous of advertising functions is the specialty of copywriters and art directors. **Copywriters** write the words used in print or broadcast commercials. **Art directors** design and illustrate print advertisements and they design the viewed action in television commercials. Most of these creative specialists work for advertising agencies or for advertisers, but some are free-lancers, selling their services to agencies or advertiser firms.

*producer*

*Advertising Producers.* The specialists who work closely with the designers of advertisements are the **producers** who bring the advertisement from the design stage to the physical form required by the media. Producers generally specialize either in print advertising or broadcast advertising.

Some production specialists work for printers, engravers, and film studios. Others work for advertising agencies or advertisers, coordinating the production activities between the creators and the producers.

*Advertising Researchers.* Measurement of the effectiveness of advertising and measurement of the size of media audiences are two of the very important functions performed by **advertising researchers.** However, many advertising researchers work for independent research services, gathering information that is then sold to advertisers and agencies.

*advertising researcher*

ADVERTISING MANAGERS. The advertising jobs described thus far have all been highly specialized, focusing on one aspect of advertising. The generalists in the advertising industry are the **advertising managers.** Their function is to plan the advertising effort and to implement and control the plan using the advertising specialists. These managers may work for advertiser firms, where they are usually titled advertising manager or advertising director. Advertising agencies also employ managers of advertising to plan, direct, and control the advertising programs of their clients. These managers are usually called **account executives,** account representatives, client representatives, or some similar title.

*advertising manager*

*account executive*

Another important advertising management position is that of brand manager. **Brand managers** (sometimes called product managers) are most often found in larger, multi-product, consumer-goods firms. They are assigned responsibility for a single brand, including overseeing all marketing efforts for their brand with the emphasis often on advertising and related sales promotions.

*brand manager*

## Advertising Planning and the Total Marketing Process

Effective use of advertising requires planning. Decisions about the message contained in advertisements and about the audience to which the advertisements are directed cannot be made separately for each advertisement. For most advertisers such an approach would take too much time. More important, there would be a danger that the individual ads would not be coordinated and thus would lack the focus that is necessary for the individual ads to reinforce one another.

The advertiser needs to develop an **advertising plan** — a detailed schedule of coordinated advertising activities to be carried out for a product. The advertising plan defines how the advertising will be focused and then coordinates decisions as to the content of the advertisements, to whom the advertisements are to be directed, and the magnitude of the advertising effort. The advertising plan is discussed in detail in Chapter 4.

*advertising plan*

### The Use of Advertising Objectives

Coordination of advertising activities is achieved by setting advertising

*advertising objectives*

objectives that provide common direction or focus to all advertising programs. **Advertising objectives** are goals which must be attained if advertising is to contribute to the successful marketing of a product. In a general sense, the objective of advertising is to sell goods or services of the advertiser company. However, such an objective is too vague to be of value to the advertiser attempting to coordinate the various elements of the advertising plan. What is needed is a series of more specific objectives which, if fulfilled, will result in increased sales.

The advertising program should begin with an understanding of the product and the situation that it faces. Specific objectives then can be set for the advertising. These objectives should provide focused direction in answering the following questions:

1. To what persons or to what groups of consumers is the advertising to be directed?
2. What information is to be included in the advertisements?
3. What should be the magnitude of the total advertising effort?

Advertising objectives provide coordinating guidelines for the various elements or activities of the total advertising plan. With objectives set, the advertiser can specify in advance how each element in the advertising program will contribute to reaching these goals.

To illustrate how objectives aid in focusing the elements of the advertising plan, think for a moment of the coordination problems faced by an automobile manufacturer. Typically, the advertising program for an automobile is costly, utilizes a variety of advertising media, and contains hundreds of different advertisements. Coordination problems are enormous. For example, the campaign may use combinations of very diverse media such as television and outdoor advertising. The expression of the advertising message is necessarily very different in these two media, but a clearly stated objective can help to make the two messages consistent with each other. Furthermore, the objective can help the messages in the two media reinforce each other, the outdoor ad acting as a reminder of the television ad.

Consider the problem of coordinating media purchases. Typically, with a large advertising budget, the automobile marketer would place advertising in several different media. Suppose that an objective of the automaker was to concentrate the advertising messages on adult men. Part of the budget might be devoted to sponsoring football telecasts — programs with heavy male viewership. With the same objective in mind, what second medium would complement the first? One possibility would be male-oriented magazines such as *Esquire* and *Sports Illustrated*. These magazines have predominantly male readership and they are a good complement to television because those who are less frequent television viewers tend to be heavy magazine readers. Again, it is the advertising objective that has provided a guideline for the coordination of these different elements of the advertising program.

## The Interaction of Advertising with Other Marketing Variables

Advertising is one of the important tools that the marketer has for selling a company's product, but it is by no means the only tool. The marketer may also use a personal sales force, attempt to have dealers or retailers sell the product, design superior benefits into the product, or offer it for an advantageous price. Sales might be stimulated with special packaging or by offering other incentives such as trading stamps, money-back guarantees, or cents-off coupons.

The particular combination of marketing tools decided upon for a product is called the product's *marketing mix*. It includes the advertising, pricing, packaging, distribution technique, product design, and sales promotion to be used for the product. It is in the *marketing plan* that a product's marketing mix for a period is specified. What the marketer seeks is to combine all of the elements of the marketing mix so that they complement or reinforce one another.

INFLUENCES ON THE ROLE OF ADVERTISING. The interdependence of advertising and other elements of the marketing mix means that the objectives assigned to advertising will depend in part upon decisions made concerning other marketing elements. Advertising is often given the responsibility for supporting some other marketing element. For example, if the marketer decides to reduce price, advertising support may be required to notify consumers of the reduction. A decision to run a contest for a product would probably require advertising to announce the contest to consumers. Advertising objectives define the support that advertising is expected to provide to other elements of the marketing mix.

The other elements in the marketing mix not only influence what advertising is asked to do, but also the amount of money available for advertising. For each unit of product, the producer expects to take in a certain amount in sales revenue. Part of this revenue must be allocated to pay for the cost of manufacturing the product. The margin left over is available for profit and for marketing expense. If a profit target is deducted, the amount remaining is available for marketing activities. From this pool of marketing funds, the marketer must pay for all the marketing mix elements. A decision to increase one element in the mix leaves less money for other elements, with the result that the other elements must be reduced. Thus, if a decision were made to increase the size of the sales force, it would decrease funds available for other activities such as advertising.

THE VARYING ROLE OF ADVERTISING. The role of advertising in the marketing mix depends on what advertising is asked to do and on the role assigned to other elements of the mix. Some common determinants of the role of advertising are described below.

*Push vs. Pull.* In total dollars both soap and automobiles are among the most heavily advertised products. In 1982 Procter & Gamble spent $726 million on advertising while General Motors' expenditures were $549 million (see Exhibit 1-2). However, when the percentage of sales spent on advertising is examined for these two companies, quite a different picture emerges. Procter & Gamble spent 5.8 percent of sales on advertising while General Motors only spent 0.9 percent.[6] Considering that both firms manufacture consumer products, why is there such a disparity in the amount of advertising per dollar of sales?

Part of the reason lies in differences in the marketing mix typically used by firms in these industries. Advertising is the dominant element in the marketing mix of the soap manufacturers. They are able to afford relatively large sums for advertising because the other elements in their marketing mix are inexpensive. Product costs are low, the discounts given to retailers are modest, and personal selling expense per unit sold is low. The soapers' marketing mix not only permits the concentration of funds in advertising, it also influences the task assigned to advertising. Since soap is sold predominantly through low-margined, self-service retail stores, with no retail salesperson to sell the soap, advertising's objective is to pre-sell consumers before they arrive at the store. This is termed a *"pull" marketing operation* **"pull" marketing operation;** advertising's task is to pull the merchandising through retail outlets.

In the marketing of automobiles, advertising is a less dominant element in the marketing mix and it is assigned a different task. Personal selling by dealer organizations is probably the key element in the automotive marketing mix and it requires a substantial portion of marketing funds in the form of trade margins given to the dealer and other services provided. This leaves a smaller proportion of the marketing fund for advertising. At the same time, the importance of the dealers and their personal selling results in different objectives for advertising. With its emphasis on personal selling to move products to consumers, automobile marketing can *"push" marketing operation* be termed a **"push" marketing operation;** advertising's task is to get the consumer to the dealer's showroom so that the personal selling phase can take place.

*Number and Accessibility of Customers.* The extent to which advertising is used also depends on the number of people to be reached and their accessibility. If the number of customers is relatively few and the unit sales per customer is large, then personal selling is usually used in place of heavy advertising. For example, grocery wholesalers spend about 0.2 percent of sales on advertising while retail food stores spend over six times that amount.[7] The reason for the great difference in amount is not difficult to

---

[6]Data from *Advertising Age* (September 8, 1983), pp. 84, 127.
[7]"Advertising-to-Sales Ratios, 1982," *Advertising Age* (August 15, 1983), p. 20.

see. The wholesale grocer sells primarily by having the salesperson call on the retailer. This personal approach can be utilized because the wholesale grocer has relatively few customers, each of whom purchases in great volume. Advertising is not an important marketing element for the wholesaler and, to the extent that it is used, its usual objective is to pave the way for the salesperson. Food stores, by contrast, use advertising as an important device to draw in traffic. The usual objective of food-store advertising is to support special offers of lower-priced merchandise.

*Difference in Target Market.* The level and objective of advertising can vary dramatically, even within a product class, depending upon the target market to which the advertising is directed. A striking example is the contrast in advertising spending patterns between Pfizer, Inc., and Richardson-Vicks. Both companies derive a substantial proportion of their sales from pharmaceutical and related health-care products. In 1982, Pfizer spent $65.7 million on advertising and had sales of $3.5 billion. By contrast, Richardson-Vicks spent nearly twice as much on advertising, $129.3 million, but only had one-third as much sales revenue, $1.1 billion.[8]

The great difference in advertising spending between these two companies is a result of differences in the target markets toward which they aim their marketing efforts. Pfizer tends to focus its marketing efforts on a target market of druggists and doctors in an effort to get them to recommend and prescribe Pfizer brands. Because the number in their target market is relatively small, Pfizer allocates most of its marketing dollars on a highly specialized sales force that calls directly on physicians and druggists. The relatively small amount of marketing dollars that are allocated to advertising of Pfizer drug products is spent on pharmaceutical and medical journals with the objective of "opening the door" for the sales force.

Richardson-Vicks, by contrast, markets its health-care products not to physicians and druggists, but directly to consumers. Since their target market of consumers is much larger and highly dispersed, it is not practical for Richardson-Vicks to reach them directly with a sales force. Instead, Richardson-Vicks concentrates its marketing dollars on advertising to the consumer target market.

This is but another example of the way in which advertising interacts with other elements in the marketing mix. For Richardson-Vicks, advertising is the primary marketing tool with the objective of directly acting on consumers to create brand preference. For Pfizer, advertising is secondary to personal selling. The objective of the advertising is to pave the way for the sales force whose task is to obtain physician and druggist recommendation of Pfizer brands.

---

[8]Sales and advertising expenditure estimates from *Advertising Age: 100 Leading National Advertisers* (September 8, 1983), pp. 124, 134.

*corporate or
institutional
advertising*

*Product vs. Institutional Objectives.*  In some cases, the objectives defined for advertising are not to sell particular products, but to create favorable attitudes toward the entire company. This type of advertising is often called **corporate advertising** or **institutional advertising.** When institutional rather than product sales objectives are set for advertising, it results in a very different audience for the advertising and very different information in the ads themselves. While the target for product advertising is usually the prospective purchaser of the product, the target audience for corporate advertising may be the financial community, government officials, educators, or the general public. The information included in corporate ads is also very different from that used in product advertising. If, for example, the advertising were directed to enhancing the firm's reputation with the financial community, then the advertising content would focus on financial strength and earnings growth of the firm.

ITT Corporation has for some ten years conducted a corporate advertising campaign. A major objective of this advertising has been to clear up the confusion between ITT and AT&T.[9] A television commercial from that campaign is shown in Exhibit 1-4.

*Variation Over the Product Life Cycle.*  Both the level and the objectives of advertising vary over the life cycle of the product class. Each category of products goes through a life cycle that looks like Exhibit 1-5. Sales grow slowly during introduction, but as the product category becomes better known with competition entering the market, the sales growth accelerates. During maturity, weaker competitors are squeezed out and sales growth declines as the product category achieves broad acceptance. Decline occurs when a new class of products enters to usurp the market of the older product class.

How does advertising tend to vary over the product life cycle?

1. During introduction, the objective of advertising is to develop awareness of the new product class and encourage consumers to try the new product. Advertising expenditures per unit sold tend to be very high.
2. During growth, as competitors enter the market, advertising begins to focus on communicating the difference between the advertiser's brand and newly entering competitors. Advertising budgets decline per unit sold, but increase sharply in total as sales rise.
3. During maturity, with competition consolidating, marketers use advertising to position the brand within a unique segment of consumers by demonstrating that the brand is particularly useful for the group. The advertising budget continues to decline per unit sold and level out or even decline in total.
4. In the decline phase, with a new product class drawing customers away, advertising becomes more defensive, tending to use reminder-style adver-

---

[9]"How ITT Shells out $10 Million or So a Year to Polish a Reputation," *The Wall Street Journal* (April 2, 1982), p. 1.

A television commercial from ITT Corporation's corporate campaign.      **EXHIBIT 1-4**

OPERATOR (VO): Hello, this is information--may I help you?

MAN: Hello, operator. Let me have the number of ITT.

OPERATOR (VO): That is "A" as in Alfred, "T" as in Thomas, "T" as in Thomas?

MAN: No, not AT&T--ITT.

"I" as in I gotta get this number . . .

"T" as in Thomas, "T" as in Thomas.

OPERATOR: (VO): They sound very similar.
MAN: ITT and AT&T may sound alike . . .

but they're two different companies. They're totally unrelated.

ITT is a telecommunications company, all right. One of the biggest in the world. But ITT also makes Wonder Bread . . .

and it's Sheraton, and Hartford Insurance, and Scotts Lawn Products, and Koni Shock Absorbers, and microprocessors, and terminals, and pumps . . .

and publishing and --
(Sound of disconnect)
Hello, Operator? Operator?

OPERATOR (VO): Hello, this is information--may I help you?

Source: ITT Corporation.

EXHIBIT 1-5          The product life cycle.

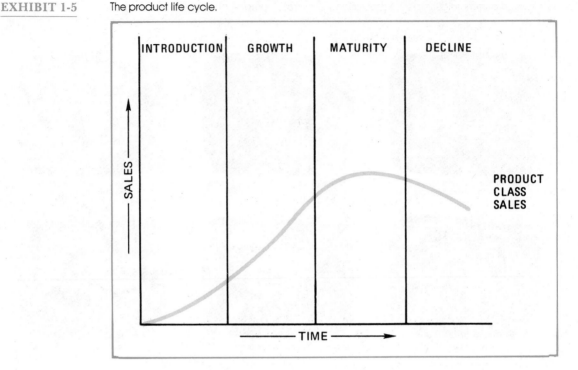

tising directed to current users in an attempt to retain their loyalty. As the decline proceeds, advertising budgets tend to be cut sharply as the marketer milks profit from the brand.

## Overview of the Advertising Manager's Job

With an understanding of the nature of advertising plans and of the interaction of advertising with other marketing mix elements, it is now possible to describe the advertising manager's job in relation to these functions. It is from the point of view of the manager of advertising that this book is presented. The objective is to describe the process by which an advertising manager can plan, implement, and control an advertising program.

### Planning the Advertising

Planning the advertising is the advertising manager's most important responsibility because success in carrying out other functions depends on a carefully developed advertising plan.

ANALYSIS OF PROBLEMS AND OPPORTUNITIES. The advertising manager's planning responsibility begins with analysis of the situation facing the product to be advertised. Both the product and the market must be examined closely to determine what problems and opportunities face the product.

DEFINITION OF OBJECTIVES. Advertising objectives define the task that the advertising is to accomplish. They are of critical importance to the success of the advertising plan. If the objectives are improperly defined, all the advertising work that follows will be misdirected. Advertising objectives are defined so as to focus the advertising effort on resolving the problems and realizing the opportunities facing the product.

The advertising objectives must also be coordinated with other elements in the marketing mix. As discussed earlier, both the volume and the task of advertising are influenced by other marketing elements. In defining the advertising objectives, the advertising manager must work with the other marketing managers to ensure that the advertising objectives are consistent with other marketing tools.

DEFINITION OF ADVERTISING PROGRAMS. With advertising objectives defined, the advertising manager is responsible for formulating the advertising programs that will achieve the objectives. Through the advertising plan, the advertising manager determines what message the advertising will contain, how it will be presented, to whom it will be directed, and what the cost of all advertising activities will be.

## Implementing the Advertising Plan

Having determined what advertising activities will help to achieve the advertising objectives for a particular product, the advertising manager is also responsible for directing the implementation of the advertising plan. Implementation activities include the writing of copy, designing of ads, production of advertising materials (printing, filming, and recording), and the purchase of media time and space.

In most cases, the advertising manager calls upon creative specialists to create the advertising that meets the specifications laid down in the advertising plan. Media-buying specialists are utilized to purchase the time and space schedules specified by the plan. This is not to say that advertising managers never create ads or never purchase media time or space. In many instances they do, particularly in smaller firms.

## Control of the Advertising

A third major responsibility of the advertising manager is to exercise control over the advertising program. To exercise control the advertising manager must establish standards as to what constitutes satifactory advertising performance. Then actual performance must be measured and compared to desired performance, and necessary corrective action taken if actual performance fails to meet the standards.

Standards of desired advertising performance can be derived directly from advertising objectives if they have been properly stated. If the objectives state in specific, measurable terms what advertising is expected to accomplish, then advertising performance can be judged in terms of the degree of fulfillment of the objectives.

With standards set in measurable terms, it then becomes necessary to measure actual performance. Performance measurement programs, frequently established with the aid of marketing research specialists, usually involve a number of testing and monitoring devices. There may be tests to measure performance of creative materials, measures of the effectiveness of media purchases and overall measure of the results of the total advertising plan.

The advertising manager must next take corrective action if the advertising plan is not achieving objectives. This may call for redesigning some or all elements of the advertising plan or redirection of faulty implementation of the advertising plan. The results of the performance measurements may indicate that the original objectives were wrong or unrealizable and in need of redefinition. In any event, the analysis and replanning required is a basic responsibility of the advertising manager.

All three functions of advertising managers — planning, implementing, and controlling — will be examined in more detail in the succeeding parts of this book.

*CHAPTER SUMMARY*

Advertising can be defined as paid messages in public media designed to inform and persuade people about the advertiser's product, service, or cause. The economic characteristics of advertising might be measured in a number of ways. In dollar volume, advertising qualifies as a major industry; it is growing with the economy, and it is highly concentrated. In terms of employment, the advertising industry is characterized by great specialization and fragmentation. The generalist who directs the activities of these specialists is the advertising manager, who has the responsibility of setting advertising objectives and developing a plan of advertising that will accomplish those objectives. The objectives and the plan must be coordinated with other marketing mix elements with which advertising interacts. The advertising manager has the further responsibility of directing implementation of the advertising plan and controlling its effectiveness in meeting the stated objectives.

Mass media
Advertising
Media sales representative
Media buyer
Copywriter
Art director
Producer
Advertising researcher

Advertising manager
Account executive
Brand manager
Advertising plan
Advertising objectives
"Pull" marketing operation
"Push" marketing operation
Corporate or institutional advertising

1. Considering the definition of advertising presented in this chapter, should the following items be classified as advertising? Explain why or why not.

   a. A newspaper message urging the election of a candidate for Congress.
   b. A radio message asking listeners to contribute to the Community Fund.
   c. A television message describing a particular program to be telecast on that station later in the week.
   d. A message in the *Wall Street Journal* by a firm to describe its earnings record and prospects.

2. Suppose a company received charges for the items listed below. Which ones should be charged to the advertising budget? On what basis should the decision be made?

   a. Advertising space in the newspaper.
   b. Charges for talent appearing in a television commercial.
   c. Charges from a public relations firm for preparing a news release concerning a new product.
   d. Charges for redesign of a package.
   e. Charges for ball-point pens with the company emblem to be given away by salespeople.

3. The percentage of sales spent on advertising by different kinds of retailers varies substantially. For example, furniture stores and household appliance stores spend four to six times as much as do grocery stores for advertising.[10] What accounts for the difference in spending levels between these types of stores?

4. United States Steel is the fourteenth largest industrial firm in the U.S., yet it is not included in the list of the 100 largest U.S. advertisers. What reasons might account for this?

---

[10]"Advertising-to-Sales Ratios, 1982," *Advertising Age* (August 15, 1983), p. 20.

5. Some critics of advertising have charged that heavy advertising is symptomatic of highly concentrated, noncompetitive industries. Does a review of the heavy advertiser industrial classifications in Exhibit 1-3 tend to support this contention?

6. Advertising expenditure figures for East Germany do not appear in the discussion of nations that are heavy advertisers. Considering the nature of the East German economy, what role is advertising likely to play? Are per capita advertising expenditures likely to be high or low?

7. Why do so many advertising specialists work for independent advertising specialty firms rather than for manufacturing firms that are the actual users of advertising?

8. Is there anything wrong with establishing an advertising objective such as the following: The objective of the advertising plan in the coming year is to increase sales by 15 percent.

9. Suppose that a company marketing a popular detergent makes a major change in the package design to modernize its appearance. In what ways will this decision influence advertising plans?

10. What are the major elements in the marketing mix for an automobile dealer? Explain how advertising is likely to interact with each of the other marketing mix elements.

11. Suppose a firm is preparing a corporate advertising campaign to influence investment analysts and, hopefully, increase the price of the company's stock. Would it be appropriate for the ads to focus on one of the company's products?

---

PROBLEM

One of the world's most unusual marketing companies is Jeffrey Martin, Inc., founded by Martin Himmel in 1960 with Compoz, the night-time sleep aid as the first product.[11] With the success of Compoz, Mr. Himmel built his business by acquiring what he terms "undermarketed brands" which he repackaged, repriced, and backed with heavy advertising. By 1982, Jeffrey Martin had sales of $58 million with its leading brand, Topol smokers' tooth polish, making up 41 percent of sales. Other brands included Ayds appetite suppressant, Doan's Pills, Bantron smoking deterrent, Cuticura medicated soap, and Porcelana fade cream. Jeffrey Martin products were sold primarily through drug stores and mass merchandisers with Topol also sold through food stores. When the product line had only two products, they were sold through brokers, but with the expansion of

---

[11]This case is based on information in Pat Sloan, "Jeffrey Martin Wants More Brands to Promote," *Advertising Age* (September 5, 1982), pp. 4, 44.

the product line a direct sales force of about 40 was established. The most unusual aspect of Jeffrey Martin's marketing program was its advertising, which, according to its president, was the firm's number one priority. In 1982, the leading advertising measurement service reported that the firm's advertising expenditures were $52 million, nearly equivalent to its sales. Apparently this level of advertising, which was placed by an in-house agency, was achieved by negotiating large discounts for unsold advertising time. Jeffrey Martin was a heavy user of daytime television, cable television and network radio.

1. Would you characterize Jeffrey Martin as using "push" or "pull"?

2. What is the objective of Jeffrey Martin advertising?

3. Why is the amount of advertising used by Jeffrey Martin so great?

# CHAPTER 2

*Organizing the*
*Advertising Department*

**LEARNING OBJECTIVES**

In studying this chapter you will learn:

- To whom the advertising manager reports in various organizations.

- The various organizational levels at which advertising decision-making takes place.

- The four most common advertising department organizational patterns.

- The considerations involved in deciding upon the division of advertising work between staff specialists and outside specialists.

- About the relationships that the advertising department should develop with other departments.

The advertising manager's work is affected by a number of organizational decisions which will be considered in this chapter. The advertising department's placement in the company's total organizational structure will be examined first. Then the problem of division of work within the department will be considered, followed by a look at the qualifications that department members should have. Finally, relations between advertising and other departments will be covered.

## The Position of Advertising in the Company Organizational Structure

One decision to be made in organizing the advertising department concerns its position in the company's total organizational structure. This decision will be looked at in terms of two subproblems. First, to what executive officer should the advertising manager report? Second, at what level in the company's organization should the advertising department be placed?

22

Should it be placed high in the organization near the chief executive or should it be lower, close to the operating units?

## Determining to Whom the Advertising Manager Should Report

There is substantial variation in the officer to whom the advertising manager reports. Sometimes the difference in supervisor reflects only different titles for similar jobs; sometimes differences represent dissimilar positions. The function of the officer to whom the advertising manager reports reflects the company's belief about the best location of advertising in the organization.

REPORTING PATTERNS IN PRACTICE.  One survey among 267 industrial firms indicated that in nearly 85 percent of these firms, advertising was placed in some form of marketing department as a subfunction of marketing. The advertising department supervisor usually reported directly to the chief marketing officer.[1] The reporting pattern, which is found in both industrial and consumer goods firms, might take the form of pattern A as shown in Exhibit 2-1.

There are two major alternatives to having the advertising department directly subordinate to the director of marketing. One alternative is to have advertising separated from other marketing functions, with the advertising manager reporting directly to top management, perhaps to the chief executive officer. This is represented by pattern B in Exhibit 2-1. The other alternative is to have the advertising manager report to a sales manager whose major responsibility is supervision of the field sales force. This organization, shown as pattern C in Exhibit 2-1, more often occurs in industrial product companies.

GUIDELINES FOR DETERMINING A REPORTING PATTERN. No one of these three reporting patterns is best for all situations, but a few guidelines can be suggested for the manager who is trying to select the best reporting relationship for the advertising department.

*Reporting to the Marketing Director.* If the company's advertising is devoted to increasing the sales of individual products or brands, then the advertising department should report to a director of marketing. This reporting pattern offers two advantages. First, coordination of product advertising with the other marketing elements is enhanced because the marketing director supervises the other marketing functions. Second, the marketing director, by training and experience, is qualified to control and evaluate the advertising effort.

---

[1] David L. Hurwood and Earl L. Bailey, *Advertising, Sales Promotion, and Public Relations — Organizational Alternatives* (New York: The National Industrial Conference Board, Experiences in Marketing Management, No. 16), pp. 24–25.

**EXHIBIT 2-1**          Alternative reporting patterns for the advertising department.

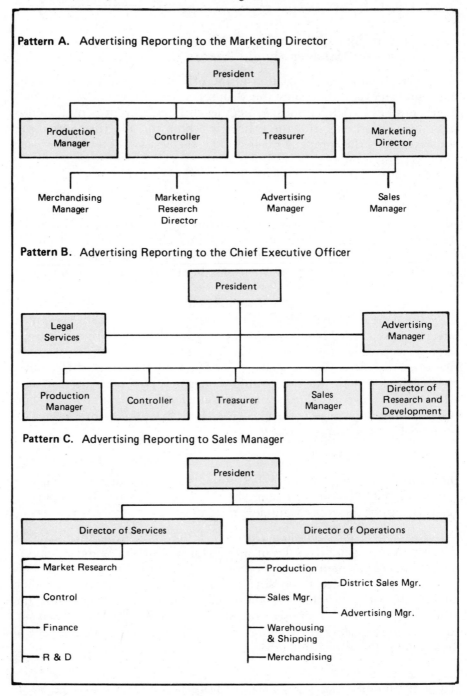

**Pattern A.**  Advertising Reporting to the Marketing Director

**Pattern B.**  Advertising Reporting to the Chief Executive Officer

**Pattern C.**  Advertising Reporting to Sales Manager

*Reporting to the President.*  There are some companies whose advertising is not devoted to promoting the sale of individual brands but, as discussed in Chapter 1, is intended to develop favorable attitudes toward the total company. See, for example, the MidCon Corporation advertisement in Exhibit 2-2. This advertisement is designed to enhance the general reputation of the company among investors and the financial community. If a firm's advertising effort is solely or primarily designed to enhance the firm's general reputation or its community relations, then it might be desirable for the advertising manager to be outside the marketing chain of command and to report directly to the president.

A disadvantage with this arrangement is that the president may have little training or experience in the management of advertising. This places a greater burden of responsibility on the advertising manager. If the company does use advertising to promote specific products, the direct-to-the-president reporting pattern is probably undesirable since it would make coordination of advertising with other marketing mix variables more difficult.

*Reporting to the Sales Manager.*  If personal selling is the dominant element in the marketing program and the role of advertising is primarily to aid salespeople, then it is desirable to have the advertising department subordinate to the manager of the sales effort. Advertising in such instances may be designed primarily to get leads for the salespeople or to build sufficient awareness of the firm or product so that the salespeople can gain access to prospect firms.

A problem that sometimes arises under this alternative is that the sales manager has greater interest in and commitment to the sales function than to advertising. The sales manager's experience and concerns are likely to be in sales rather than advertising. This problem can be overcome by an organizational structure in which all marketing functions, including advertising and sales management, report to an overall director of marketing who is charged with the responsibility for creating a balanced mix of all marketing functions.

It should be noted that in some firms the advertising manager reports to a person called "sales manager," but despite the title, this position supervises all marketing functions and serves as a marketing director.

## Determining the Organizational Level of the Advertising Department

The second problem in determining the advertising department's position in the organizational structure is to decide on the organizational level at which advertising decision making should take place. If advertising decisions are made high in the organization structure, then the advertising function is said to be *centralized*. If advertising decisions are made lower in the organization structure, close to the operating units, then the advertising function is termed *decentralized*.

# Our commitment couldn't be more clear.

MidCon's commitment to supply natural gas to mid-America is stronger than ever.

We recently expanded our scope of operations into the St. Louis area by acquiring Mississippi River Transmission Corporation. This adds 1,500 more miles of main transmission line and increases our delivery capacity by a billion cubic feet of gas per day.

You already know Natural Gas Pipeline Company of America, MidCon's largest subsidiary. With its 12,500 miles of pipeline, Natural is one of the nation's largest transmission companies. Thanks to the financial commitments made and risks taken years ago, Natural is now able to sell its gas at a cost lower than most other pipelines.

Our pipelines link key U.S. gas-

producing fields with major domestic gas markets, including the heavily populated metropolitan areas of Chicago and St. Louis. These two interstate transmission firms make MidCon owner of one of the largest and strongest natural gas pipeline operations in the country.

While pipelines presently account for most of MidCon's earnings and its over $3 billion in assets, there's more. Our other subsidiaries are engaged in oil and gas exploration and production, contract drilling, coal mining and marketing, and other energy-related ventures.

To get the full story, just contact Investor Relations Department, MidCon Corp., 701 East 22nd Street, Lombard, Illinois 60148 (312) 691-2557.

# MIDCON CORP.

Natural Gas Pipeline Company of America • Mississippi River Transmission Corporation • Exeter Drilling Company •
MCN Exploration Company: Harper Oil/Buckhorn Petroleum/Texoma Production • MidCon Ventures, Inc. • Industrial Fuels Corporation.

When advertising is centralized, there is usually a single group of advertising specialists located, in the larger firms, at the main office and placed near the top of the management hierarchy. Organization chart A in Exhibit 2-3 shows this centralized structure. Decentralized advertising, by contrast, probably means an advertising department (or departments) responsible to the operating product division, perhaps located at the production site rather than the home office. For a firm with multiple divisions producing different products, the tendency under a decentralized arrange-

Centralized vs. decentralized placement of the advertising function.                    **EXHIBIT 2-3**

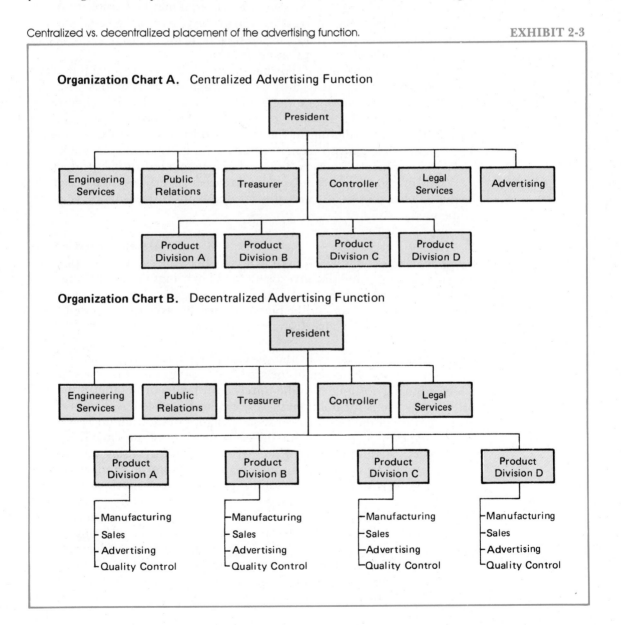

**Organization Chart A.** Centralized Advertising Function

**Organization Chart B.** Decentralized Advertising Function

ment is to have a separate advertising department for each division. This decentralized structure is represented by organization chart B in Exhibit 2-3.

CENTRALIZED ADVERTISING FUNCTION. The choice between the centralized and decentralized patterns, like the determination of the reporting relationship, is dependent on the mission of the advertising. A **centralized advertising department** offers the advantage of substantial specialization. By pooling advertising resources and demands, it may be feasible to retain full-time specialists in such areas as copywriting, advertising research, and display design. These specialists would then be made available as needed to work on problems of each operating division.

One disadvantage of the centralized advertising department is that the department may have difficulty in coordinating its activities with the differing needs of the operating product divisions. Also, the advertising department would be less aware of each division's problems and would be less helpful in contributing to the product divisions' planning processes. This would be a major problem if the advertising program were not a general corporate effort but were designed to promote individual products.

Controlling the activities of a centralized advertising department is facilitated because it is centrally located and responsibility is easily pinpointed.

DECENTRALIZED ADVERTISING FUNCTION. The **decentralized advertising department** has its strength in areas where the centralized approach is weak. Decentralizing the advertising function brings the advertising decision maker in closer contact with other marketing decisions on a company's products. The result should be better informed advertising decisions and better coordination of advertising with other marketing decisions for each product.

A potential weakness in the decentralized pattern is the absence of company-wide coordination of the advertising program. One result may be a loss of buying economies in the purchase of media or in other purchases offering discounts for bulk purchases. A related problem is the uneven or erratic picture of the firm that consumers might receive from uncoordinated advertising campaigns by several different divisions of the same firm.

Supervision and control of the decentralized advertising department are likely to be by marketing-trained managers. Control standards can be related to advertising's contribution to specific product performance.

CENTRALIZED/DECENTRALIZED COMBINATION. A combination of centralized and decentralized advertising departments is sometimes seen, although only in larger firms. Under this setup one or more decentralized advertising departments would be attached to the various product divisions while a centralized advertising unit would serve as staff advisor to the decentralized units and would also coordinate company-wide advertising programs. This organizational pattern sometimes occurs in large, multi-product, consumer-goods firms that utilize a brand management system. As will be discussed later, the brand manager serves as advertising manager for a particular product, but frequently has a centralized advertising staff group to draw upon for advice.

## Internal Organization of the Advertising Department

The advertising manager is responsible for building an effective structure for the department. If the advertising department is small, as many are, then internal organizational problems will be slight. Many advertising departments are single-person units, in which case all departmental responsibilities are borne by the advertising manager. In fact, there are many cases in which advertising management is a part-time responsibility, the advertising manager having responsibility for other marketing functions in addition to advertising.

### Tools for Defining the Organizational Structure

As the advertising department's responsibilities increase, the advertising manager will need assistance and the department will add personnel. As soon as the department becomes more than a one-person operation the advertising manager must decide how the work should be divided among members of the department.

Regardless of the size of the advertising department, there are two indispensable managerial tools that should be used to define the organizational structure. One is the organization chart; the other is the position description. The *organization chart* pictures the titles of the jobs within the department and the relationships among jobs. A *position description,* perhaps the more valuable of the two tools, should be prepared for each job in the department, even for a one-person department. The position description lists in detail the responsibilities of the position. It is useful in reaching agreement with a subordinate concerning work expectations. Exhibit 2-4 shows a typical position description for an advertising manager.

### Guidelines for Dividing the Advertising Work

Work requirements and personnel will determine the pattern of work division in an advertising department. There are several common objectives or guidelines that the advertising manager should attempt to follow in making this organizational decision.

GAINING BENEFITS OF SPECIALIZATION. Advertising is a highly technical field. Specialization is essential if employees are to attain maximum

EXHIBIT 2-4        Typical advertising manager position description

## MANAGER–ADVERTISING
### *Wyandotte Chemicals Corporation*

BASIC FUNCTION: Responsible, in accordance with established corporate and divisional policies, practices, and procedures, for the formulation and execution of advertising policy, plans, and programs designed to increase the effectiveness of the marketing effort of the Industrial Chemicals Group.

ORGANIZATIONAL RELATIONSHIP

| | |
|---|---|
| Accountable to: | Director of Sales |
| Exerts direct supervision over: | One employee |
| Type: | Asst. to Manager–Advertising |
| Approximate number of people for whom responsible: | Three |

SPECIFIC RESPONSIBILITIES

1. Formulate and recommend advertising programs for the I.C. Group.
2. Direct and administer the scheduling, planning, and production of approved advertising programs.
3. Direct the activities of the I.C. Group advertising agency in the execution of approved advertising and sales promotion programs.
4. Responsible for the creation, production, and execution of direct-mail programs, literature, and related sales promotion materials and activities in accordance with approved sales objectives and programs.
5. Responsible for making certain that all advertising copy is checked and approved for legal and technical correctness and for compliance with company policy.
6. Responsible for obtaining approval on trade advertising from the Director of Sales and/or respective Marketing Managers. Responsible for obtaining the approval of the Vice President–Operations and/or Director of Sales on all corporate copy.
7. Responsible for maintaining contacts with representatives of advertising media.
8. Responsible for the preparation of the annual advertising budget. Submit budget for approval by Director of Sales and Vice President–Operations.
9. Audit all invoices for advertising costs.
10. Responsible for control of inventories of advertising material.
11. Responsible for the analysis of competitive advertising. Advise Director of Sales and Marketing Managers of new uses, claims, or services for products competitive with I.C. Group products.

12. Responsible for evaluating and reporting effectiveness of individual advertising campaigns, as well as overall advertising program.
13. Responsible for distribution of all advertising material.
14. Responsible for maintaining up-to-date Addressograph mailing records on customers and selected prospects.
15. Prepare and submit annual budget to Director of Sales for controllable departmental operating expenses.
16. Responsible for proper selection of key personnel and for developing the abilities and performance of subordinate personnel by training, counseling, and example.
17. Responsible for the appearance of new or revised product labels, packages, and shipping containers. Obtain approval of Marketing Managers for any change necessary.
18. Responsible for the proper processing of inquiries resulting from advertising efforts.

FUNCTIONAL RELATIONSHIP

1. Collaborate with Marketing Manager and District Field Sales groups, as well as other sales personnel in the formulation of sales and promotional programs.
2. Maintain contacts with salespeople, distributors, and customers to secure suggestions for new ideas relative to advertising and sales promotion activities.
3. Collaborate with Technical Service Department in the preparation of new or revised product labels, packages, and shipping containers.
4. Collaborate, in accordance with company policies, with the Public Relations Department in handling publicity on products, processes, and personnel.
5. Work with, and participate in, industry or professional group conventions or conferences to keep fully informed on general industry trends, sales and promotion methods, and competitive advertising activities; report all matters of interest in these areas to the Director of Sales and to the Marketing Managers of the various divisions.

Source:  Reprinted, by permission of the publisher, from *Job Descriptions in Marketing Management* (AMA Research Study No. 94) by JoAnn Sperling, pp. 180–181 © 1969 by AMACOM, a division of American Management Associations, New York. All rights reserved.

experience and thereby develop superior skills. The advertiser should attempt to gain these superior skills by dividing the work in the advertising department so that specialization is possible. For example, the advertising work might be divided along functional lines so that each departmental worker could specialize in performing one particular step in the advertising process. One worker might specialize in writing copy, another in design, and another in the purchase of media.

Work may also be divided along product lines. By assigning all advertising responsibility for a particular product to one member of the department, that person can become a specialist in that product.

ATTAINING COOPERATION. While specialization tends to increase the skills of the individual worker, there is always the danger that the isolation of functions will result in a loss of cooperation between jobs. If creative personnel, for example, were divided into two groups — one specializing in print advertising and the other in broadcast — coordination between creative materials in the two media might suffer. If a product used both broadcast and print media, some special arrangement would have to be adopted to assure that the creative materials were complementary.

One solution to the coordination problem lies in grouping under one person those functions that must be coordinated. For example, if members of the advertising department in a multi-product firm specialized by product, it would aid coordination if jointly advertised products were assigned to the same person. Variations of a basic product sold under a family brand name, called *line extensions*, frequently need this type of advertising coordination. If a leading cough syrup marketer were also to bring out a lozenge and a nasal spray, they might well be jointly advertised. It would aid coordination, in this case, if all three products were assigned to the same member of the advertising department.

FOCUSING ON VITAL FUNCTIONS. Some companies make heavy use of particular kinds of advertising. The division of work in an advertising department should attempt to isolate and focus attention on these important responsibilities.

The large marketers of soaps and cleaners, for example, find that television is an extremely important medium in their advertising programs. As a consequence, they purchase great quantities of television time. Because of the importance of these purchases, these companies are likely to have a separate person or group charged with coordinating and overseeing this function for all products. Separation of the television buying function permits specialization and also clearly marks the responsibility for the task.

MEETING NEEDS OF PERSONNEL. The division of work within the advertising department should not overlook the personal needs of the members of the department. Many people get satisfaction from gaining specialized knowledge and developing skill in its application. However, in time, overspecialization can make a job boring, can create a feeling of isolation, and can rob the individual of perspective.

Greater self-fulfillment often occurs when jobs are broadened. Often this can be accomplished by making a department member responsible for an entire process, from beginning to end, rather than only one step in the process. An advertising researcher, for example, might be made responsible for an entire research project — design of the study, directing the data gathering, analyzing the results — rather than specializing only in writing questionnaires for various projects. Responsibility for the larger job, if the individual feels capable of handling it, increases the feeling of contribution and encourages a more creative use of individual talents.

## Advertising Department Organizational Patterns

There are four patterns of organization in advertising that are commonly observed. They are division of work by function, by product, by geographic location, and by customer. No one of these patterns represents a best organization for all circumstances, but they do suggest alternatives that the advertising manager can measure against the department's particular needs.

FUNCTIONAL ORGANIZATION.  Under a **functionally organized advertising department** the work is divided by advertising subfunction. In its simplest form, for example, the advertising manager might have a subordinate who is a creative specialist and another who is a media specialist. These subordinates would contribute their specialized skills to the advertising program of each product advertised by the company.

*functionally organized advertising department*

With more subordinates, the functional division of responsibilities can be considerably expanded. For example, part A of Exhibit 2-5 shows a form of functional division in which each subordinate specializes in one form of advertising. The public relations manager would specialize in nonpaid promotion, the sales promotion manager in special offers such as contests or premiums, the trade advertising manager in advertising to retailers and wholesalers, and the mass media advertising manager in consumer advertising in media such as television, magazines, and newspapers.

Many other divisions of the advertising work are possible in the functional pattern. The benefits to be gained from functionally dividing the work are derived from specialization which can result in increased skills from narrowly focused efforts. The problems likely to arise are ones of coordinating the functional specialties for the benefit of the product and the possibly adverse morale effects of a narrowly defined job.

Functional specialization is seen frequently in centralized advertising staff groups that serve as advisers to other product-oriented advertising groups.

PRODUCT ORGANIZATION.  In a **product-organized advertising department,** each subordinate of the advertising manager is assigned responsibility for the entire advertising program for a particular product. The subordinate thus becomes a specialist in that product. Sometimes a group of products rather than a single product is assigned to each subordinate. When this is done, benefits from specialization will increase if the products assigned to a particular subordinate are similar to each other. Part B of

*product-organized advertising department*

EXHIBIT 2-5     Advertising department organizational alternatives.

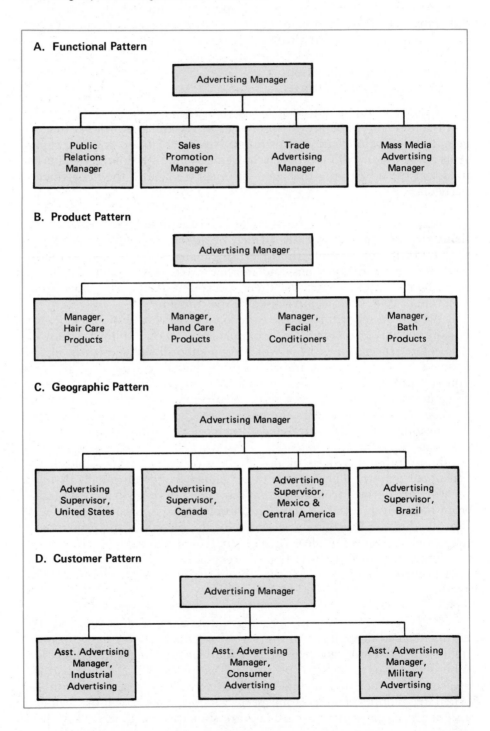

**A. Functional Pattern**

Advertising Manager

- Public Relations Manager
- Sales Promotion Manager
- Trade Advertising Manager
- Mass Media Advertising Manager

**B. Product Pattern**

Advertising Manager

- Manager, Hair Care Products
- Manager, Hand Care Products
- Manager, Facial Conditioners
- Manager, Bath Products

**C. Geographic Pattern**

Advertising Manager

- Advertising Supervisor, United States
- Advertising Supervisor, Canada
- Advertising Supervisor, Mexico & Central America
- Advertising Supervisor, Brazil

**D. Customer Pattern**

Advertising Manager

- Asst. Advertising Manager, Industrial Advertising
- Asst. Advertising Manager, Consumer Advertising
- Asst. Advertising Manager, Military Advertising

Exhibit 2-5 shows a product pattern for a hypothetical company marketing four kinds of cosmetic products — hair care products, hand care products, facial conditioners, and bath products. A separate advertising manager is assigned to each product group.

One form of product specialization used most often by large consumer package goods firms is the brand manager system. Originated by Procter & Gamble in 1927, the brand manager is assigned responsibility for all planning and marketing activities for a particular product.[2] Procter & Gamble's brand manager organization is illustrated in Exhibit 2-6.

The advantages of the brand manager system are that each brand is assured attention so that it does not become on "orphan," the brand manager becomes a specialist in the assigned product, and the brand manager is in a position to provide coordination of the various marketing mix elements for a particular product. Brand managership can provide a broad and challenging job experience. It has provided a training ground for many young people who have later become top marketing executives.

Procter & Gamble's brand-manager organization.                                    EXHIBIT 2-6

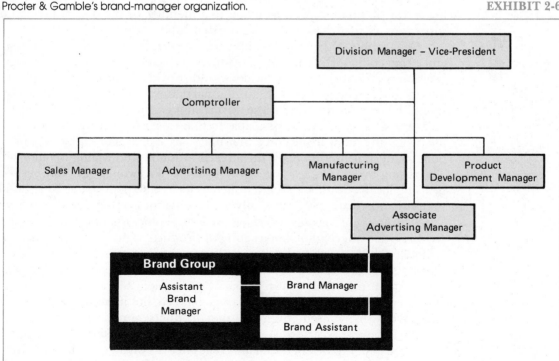

Source:    Reprinted from the June 9, 1973 issue of *Business Week* by special permission, © 1973 by McGraw-Hill, Inc.

---

[2]"The Brand Manager: No Longer King." *Business Week* (June 9, 1973), pp. 58–66.

In the 1950s and 1960s many firms switched to the brand manager system, but since then some disillusionment with the approach has appeared.[3] One problem has been the uncertainty of the brand manager's authority over functional marketing departments. The brand manager is responsible for coordinating the marketing activities for the product and is held accountable for its performance. At the same time, for example, the brand manager can request, but can't order, a certain level of sales force effort for the product since direct authority over the sales force is likely held by the sales manager. The same ambiguous relationship is present in other marketing areas. As a result, brand managers spend a great deal of time on internal persuasion rather than focusing externally on the marketplace needs of their brand. Some feel that brand management encourages narrow, short-term focus. Brand managers tend to have short tenure; they strive for short-term gains that will rate an advancement to a more senior position.

*geographically organized advertising department*

GEOGRAPHIC ORGANIZATION. In a **geographically organized advertising department,** the work of the department is divided along geographic lines. The company's total distribution area is subdivided and each resulting sector or subdivision is assigned to a member of the department who supervises all advertising activities for that subdivision.

Geographic organization might be appropriate if there were important geographic differences in consumer characteristics or product usage. Division of the work geographically would provide a specialist in local conditions for each area. If this organizational pattern is utilized, consideration should be given to locating these advertising executives in the geographic areas for which they are responsible so that they can observe the advertising program and its results on a first-hand basis. The geographic organizational pattern is useful only if the advertiser is able and willing to tailor the advertising program to each geographic area. This would be accomplished by using locally originated media, such as local newspapers and local radio stations, and creating different advertisements for each distinctive area.

A prominent instance in which the geographic organization pattern is used is in the international marketing of products. The wide differences in national cultures make local knowledge essential to effective communication with consumers in foreign markets. An example of a geographic organization pattern is shown in part C of Exhibit 2-5 on page 34. There are other applications of the geographic pattern, but in most instances only intensively distributed, high-volume products generate enough sales volume to be able to afford separate advertising supervisors by geographic area. The geographic approach also relies heavily on an overall advertising plan and strong home-office supervision to maintain a coordinated advertising program.

---

[3]*Ibid.*, p. 58.

CUSTOMER ORGANIZATION.  A **customer-organized advertising department** may be desirable if a product appeals to distinctively different classes of customers and if each class requires a different advertising approach. Such a pattern assigns advertising responsibility for each customer class to a different member of the advertising department.

A firm that sells its product for both industrial and consumer use (for example, a manufacturer of a paper product used both as a household paper towel and as an industrial wiper) might well use a customer pattern. A company marketing a drug product both directly to the general public through mass advertising and to the public through recommendation by the medical profession would need two different advertising programs. Dividing the work so that one departmental subordinate supervises each program would be desirable.

An example of a customer pattern of work division is shown in part D of Exhibit 2-5. Such a pattern calls for coordination between the customer divisions. The advertising plan is ideal for achieving this coordination.

## Staffing the Advertising Department

In addition to deciding how the work of the advertising department should be divided, people must be selected to staff the department. The number and qualifications of staff members depend in part upon the organizational pattern selected. The staffing decision should follow and support the decision made concerning the division of work in the department.

Another consideration that affects the type of staff members needed is the amount of operational work to be carried out within the advertising department. This decision is considered next.

### Choosing Between Staff Specialists and Outside Specialists

Advertising departments vary widely in the extent to which the implementing or operational work of advertising is carried on by personnel within the department. At one extreme are those departments that delegate all operational work to specialists outside the firm, retaining only supervisory responsibilities within the department. In these firms responsibility for *planning* the advertising program is generally retained by the advertising department. However, advertising agencies, marketing researchers, printers and engravers, and film production houses are given responsibility for *carrying out* the advertising programs.

At the other extreme are advertising departments (usually in firms that are heavy advertisers) that are staffed with their own specialists to carry out much of the advertising plan. These firms might have on their staff creative specialists — copywriters, designers, and production technicians — media buyers, and marketing researchers. However, even firms with extensive staffs of specialists find substantial need to utilize independent specialists.

ECONOMIC CONSIDERATIONS. The choice between placing full-time specialists on the staff of the advertising department and using outside specialists is dictated in part by the scale of the advertising operation. Unless an advertiser has sufficient work to keep a copywriter occupied full time, it is probably more economical to purchase a writer's services by the hour from an advertising agency. For the same reason, most advertisers do not own printing plants, film studios, or photoengraving shops since they could use only a fraction of the capacity of such facilities. Unless their requirements are unusually heavy, most firms can more economically meet their needs by hiring these services when they are needed.

CONTROL CONSIDERATIONS. If a firm's requirements are large enough to justify economically the use of the staff specialists, there is yet another set of considerations affecting the choice of inside versus outside specialists. The major advantage to having staff advertising specialists is not economy, but the added control over the advertising process that they provide. Easier control is possible because the specialist is physically closer and directly subordinate to a departmental manager. In addition, the staff specialist's attention is focused on the needs of only one advertiser. This can be a particularly important advantage for a company requiring large quantities of specialized or technical advertising materials. Some industrial advertisers, for example, even though their dollar volume of advertising is modest, find it advantageous to have a staff copywriter and a staff designer because of the great volume of specialized brochures, technical literature, and sales aids required.

AVAILABILITY. Offsetting the advantage of greater control through the use of staff specialists is the difficulty of attracting high caliber specialists to advertising department staff jobs. The best copywriters and designers, for example, are attracted to the better advertising agencies where both the prestige and salary are high. Additionally, they have the opportunity for greater variety in their work since they handle assignments from a variety of companies. What this means is that the advertiser must determine the caliber of advertising specialists needed in terms of the work to be done and then determine the availability of the appropriate personnel.

## Qualifications of Advertising Department Personnel

When the advertising department organizational pattern has been selected and a decision made concerning the balance between inside and outside specialists, it is then possible to specify the qualifications that members of the advertising department should have.

QUALIFICATIONS OF THE ADVERTISING MANAGER. The most important function that the advertising manager must perform is to plan advertising programs. Planning requires analytical skills—the ability to define problems, gather relevant data, and set objectives. These planning skills are the most important qualifications needed by an advertising manager.

A second skill that is essential to success in advertising management is leadership ability or the ability to get the enthusiastic cooperation of others. The advertising manager relies on other people such as accountants and product engineers for much of the information upon which the advertising plan is built. Cooperative relations with other marketing managers such as the sales manager and marketing research manager are essential so that advertising plans are coordinated with other departmental plans. The advertising manager must also be able to bring out the best in the many advertising staff members who will participate in preparing and implementing the advertising plan. Advertising is not a one-person job; it requires a manager who can build and coordinate a team.

The third qualification that the advertising manager should possess is advertising skill. If, in addition to managing the advertising program, the advertising manager is expected to perform some of the operating work (such as writing copy or designing layouts), then advertising skills in those special fields are needed. In the advertising fields that are delegated to specialists, the advertising manager still needs substantial knowledge, but of a different kind—not the know-how for performing the specialties, but what to ask for and what information and direction to provide in order to get superior performance.

QUALIFICATIONS OF ADVERTISING STAFF. The qualifications required in advertising staff members will vary greatly with the way in which the work is divided in the department. If, for example, the advertising work is divided by product as in a brand manager setup, then qualifications needed by the staff will be much like those specified for the advertising manager. This is because each staff member is, in effect, the advertising manager for an assigned product.

However, when a specialized central advertising staff is formed and organized by function, the primary requirement for staff members is specialized skill in the function for which they are assigned responsibility.

## Developing Relationships with Other Departments

The advertising department relies heavily on assistance from organizations outside the advertising department. It also must coordinate its activities with functions managed by other departments. Consequently, in addition to dividing the work and providing qualified staff members, the advertising manager must build a pattern of productive relations between the advertising department and other departments.

These outside organizations fall into two broad categories — those organizations that are external to the company and other departments within the company. Those organizations external to the company with which the advertising department commonly works include advertising agencies, research firms, design studios, and producers of promotional and packaging materials. Relations with these external firms are extremely important and will be considered in detail in the chapter which follows.

Two important characteristics typify the relationship of the advertising department to other departments in the company. First, the relationship is usually nonauthoritative; the advertising manager has no authority over other departments, and as a consequence must rely on influence or persuasion to accomplish departmental goals. Second, since the advertising department is usually in the position of requesting assistance rather than supplying it to other departments, it is in the interest of the advertising department to take the initiative in forming effective relations with other departments.

The requirements of the relationships with other departments vary depending in part on whether the department is responsible for one of the marketing subfunctions or is outside the marketing field.

## Relationships with Marketing Departments

In relationships with other marketing departments, the stress is on coordination of activities rather than on assistance. A notable exception is the relationship to the marketing research department which will be considered separately in the next section.

Coordination of advertising department activities with other marketing activities is heavily dependent upon clear, two-way communications. The keystone of this communication by the advertising department is the advertising plan; the plan is the basic sourcebook describing what the advertising department intends to do and why. It is not sufficient communication, however, simply to send a copy of the advertising plan to other marketing departments. There must be participation and communication during the preparation of the plan and intensive follow-up on its completion and implementation. A strong personal communications network with other marketing departments is an essential supplement to the building of effective coordination.

## Relationships with the Marketing Research Department

Unlike other marketing departments, the marketing research department is one that provides specialized services to the advertising department. Effective use of marketing research requires an understanding of how the marketing researcher can contribute to the advertising program. It also requires an understanding of the contribution that the advertising manager must make in the research process.

CONTRIBUTIONS OF MARKETING RESEARCH. The advertising manager will find a natural ally in the marketing research department. The primary mission of a *marketing research department* is to provide information to improve planning and decision making. The special skills of the marketing research department will be needed both in preparing the advertising plan and in controlling the advertising effort.

*Planning Assistance.* Marketing research plays an important part in helping the advertising manager to define the problems and opportunities facing the product. The advertising plan outline, which will be considered in detail in Chapter 4, calls for intensive analysis in three areas — the nature of the consumer, the attributes of the product, and the characteristics of the market. Marketing research can help gather data in each of these areas. For example, in consumer analysis, there are research techniques that can help uncover the often difficult-to-fathom needs and goals that underlie the purchase of a product. In analysis of the product, marketing research can prepare tests to determine consumer reaction to proposed changes in a product. In market analysis, marketing research can gather data to help predict future sales of the product class.

Marketing research can also contribute to the selecting of advertising programs to reach advertising objectives. In preparing the media program, for example, if the advertising manager were attempting to choose between television and radio, marketing research could devise a test of the relative effectiveness of the two media for the product. Various message contents might also be tested. The choice between different advertising budget levels likewise lends itself to testing. In each of these program areas, marketing research can develop information to guide the decision maker.

*Control Assistance.* Marketing research can also make an important contribution to controlling the advertising program. The actual achievements of each one of the advertising programs must be measured and compared to the objectives or standards set for the program and necessary corrective action taken.

Marketing research is well equipped to set up the necessary measurement devices. The researchers might, for example, measure the effectiveness of the advertising copy by conducting a series of surveys to discover changes in consumers' awareness of the advertising and changes in their knowledge about the product. They might measure the media program by gathering data on the actual number and characteristics of people reading or viewing the media vehicles in which the product's advertising appeared. Each of the advertising programs is likely to be measured in several different ways. Marketing research can make a contribution in devising and conducting these measurements.

RESPONSIBILITY IN RESEARCH PROJECTS. Marketing research is a specialized area requiring considerable technical expertise. In the more technical areas, the advertising manager must rely upon the skills of the researcher, but there are other phases of research where the researcher relies upon the advertising manager's knowledge. The key to a productive relationship with the marketing research department lies in understanding how responsibility should be shared in a marketing research project. These responsibilities can best be explained by tracing the steps of a marketing research project and considering how responsibility for each step is divided.

*Defining the Problem.* A marketing research project begins when the advertising manager sees an impending difficulty or an upcoming decision for which there is inadequate information. The advertising manager should then initiate a request for research assistance.

The researcher's first step will be to gather preliminary information that will clarify the specific problem or question that the research is to answer. The advertising manager's responsibility here is to describe the problem and its context as completely as possible and provide any relevant information, such as data from prior studies. With the available preliminary information, the researcher and the advertising manager must collaborate to define the question that the research is to answer.

*Designing the Research Study.* With the problem defined, the research next moves to the more technical phase of deciding how the needed information will be gathered. These decisions result in the research design. The research design, because it is largely a technical job, is primarily the responsibility of the research director rather than the advertising manager. The decisions that must be made include selection of the data gathering method, which might be a telephone survey, personal interviews, or perhaps an experiment. A questionnaire or other data-collection instrument must be designed, and the method for selecting the sample of consumers for the research study must be decided.

*Considering the Research Proposal.* The research design, together with the problem statement and cost and time estimates, are prepared in written form by the research department. This research proposal, as it is called, is submitted to the advertising manager who must approve it before the actual research is conducted. The proposal gives the advertising manager an opportunity to consider whether or not the research is likely to yield the information required to solve the problem and whether or not the information will be worth the cost.

*Collecting the Information.* If the research proposal is approved, the research project returns to the research department for implementation. The research department, often using outside interviewing firms, supervises administration of the questionnaires and assembly of the results.

*Analyzing the Information.* The data gathered from the research must be edited and arranged in such a way as to facilitate interpretation. The advertising manager should participate with the researcher in this interpretation. The final result of this analysis should be a decision as to the action needed to solve the problem that had initially dictated the need for the research project. Although guided in this decision by the researcher, the ultimate responsibility for a decision belongs to the advertising manager.

## Relationships with Nonmarketing Departments

The advertising department, both in originating and in carrying out the advertising plan, relies upon the counsel and assistance of a great many nonmarketing departments. For example, a legal department may give advice on advertising claims, a product development group may provide technical product information, production departments may provide cost and output estimates, and the accounting department may supply cost measurements.

Gaining the willing cooperation of these departments depends, in part, upon well-developed personal relationships. But it also stems from making requests in a clear, concise manner with adequate justification of the need. It is also important that the relationship not be abused by requests for assistance that are unnecessary. A simple follow-up with the assisting department, showing how the information was used and the result obtained, will do much to dispel any suspicion of abuse of the relationship.

---

*CHAPTER SUMMARY*

The advertising manager needs to structure a relationship with the advertising staff and with other departments that will help in carrying out advertising planning, implementing, and controlling responsibilities.

The most common practice is for the advertising department to be subordinate to a marketing director who coordinates all marketing functions. The advertising function may be centralized, permitting a pool of advertising specialists, or it may be decentralized to improve coordination with product planning. The work within the advertising department should be divided among staff members so as to gain the benefits of specialization, enhance internal cooperation, focus attention on the most important jobs, and make the work satisfying. Widely used approaches to dividing the work include functional, product, geographic, and customer patterns.

In selecting an advertising manager, managerial skills such as analytical ability and leadership ability should be emphasized. Qualifications of advertising staff members depend upon whether they are to have managerial responsibilities or technical advertising jobs. Where economically feasible, having advertising specialists on the staff gives greater control, but top quality specialists may shun the narrowness of a company staff job.

The advertising manager must build relationships with other departments with which advertising must coordinate and from which assistance will be needed. Building these relationships requires that the advertising manager establish good two-way communication with the other departments. The marketing research department plays a particularly important role in providing planning information. Effective use of marketing research requires that the advertising manager understand the marketing research process and the times and places in which a managerial contribution is necessary.

*KEY TERMS*

Centralized advertising department
Decentralized advertising department
Functionally organized advertising department
Product-organized advertising department
Geographically organized advertising department
Customer-organized advertising department

*QUESTIONS FOR DISCUSSION*

1. In some companies that use a brand manager organization pattern, the brand managers report to a supervisor of brands who, in turn, reports directly to the marketing director, rather than to the advertising manager. These firms also have an advertising department headed by an advertising manager. In such an organization, what would be the responsibility of the advertising manager?

2. Conglomerates are formed through acquisition by the parent company of a number of businesses with largely unrelated product lines. The acquired firms are given substantial operational independence, but receive policy direction and staff assistance from a small corporate management group. In such an organization, should the advertising department be centralized or decentralized?

3. What pattern of dividing up the work of the advertising department would likely be found in the following types of companies:
   a. A department store in a large city?
   b. An international airline?
   c. A large consumer magazine?
   d. A multi-product food company?
   e. A large integrated oil company?

4. Suppose that you were the advertising manager for a firm marketing a line of exterior and interior house paints on a regional basis. You are the only member of the advertising department. When your company acquires a firm manufacturing a line of marine paints, the advertising for this line is also assigned to your department, and the president authorizes you to hire an assistant. What qualifications would you set for this assistant? Would you specify an advertising specialist or a management person? What factors would govern this decision?

5. Suppose that the following advertisement appeared in the help wanted section of a local newspaper:

> Wanted: Advertising manager to head four-member advertising department. Must be a shirt-sleeve, no-nonsense executive prepared to write copy, prepare layouts, and negotiate media schedules. Experience in printing or photo-engraving desirable. Company is in women's fashion goods, so good taste and design sense are essential.

Evaluate this company's concept of the job of the advertising manager.

6. An advertising manager when requesting research assistance in solving a problem often has preconceived notions about what the research results will show. One of the most valuable contributions that a marketing researcher can make is to view the facts unemotionally and make an objective recommendation. Isn't there a danger that in collaborating closely with the advertising manager the researcher will adopt the advertising manager's preconceptions and lose objectivity? How can the advertising manager safeguard against this danger?

---

*PROBLEM*

You have just been hired as advertising manager for a large appliance distributor, Beck and Co. Beck buys and warehouses appliances from manufacturers and then sells them to about 300 independent retail appliance dealers. Beck carries two major appliance lines—one a premium quality, nationally advertised line, the other a less well-promoted line that sells primarily on price. In addition to national advertising, the manufacturers of both lines work through the distributor with an end to offering advertising assistance to the dealers in the form of in-store signs, direct-mail pieces, outside-store signs, advertising mats, and cooperative advertising (a shared advertising-expense program).

Beck has a six-person sales force headed by a sales manager. The salespeople solicit new dealer accounts for Beck and do both sales and merchandising work with existing dealer accounts. The advertising manager reports to the sales manager. Beck has a small advertising budget of its own which is used to advertise for leads on dealers that might want to handle the Beck line. The major share of the advertising manager's time, however, is spent in working with salespeople and their dealer accounts in order to help them develop advertising programs for the dealers. As a collateral duty, the advertising manager is also responsible for Beck's limited public-relations program.

As your first task, the president of Beck and Co. has asked you to prepare your own position description. Using the position description shown in Exhibit 2-4 as a guide, develop a position description that:

1. describes the basic function of the job
2. defines the organizational relationship
3. lists specific responsibilities. (It should be possible to list at least six or eight.)

# CHAPTER 3

## LEARNING OBJECTIVES

In studying this chapter you will learn:

- The various services offered by advertising agencies.

- How advertising agencies are organized.

- The criteria that should be used in deciding what agency to select.

- The ground rules that the advertising manager should follow in developing effective working relations with the agency.

- The way advertising agencies are compensated.

Although there are many advertisers who create and place their own advertising, most major advertisers utilize the services of one or more advertising agencies for parts of their advertising program. The success of advertising depends on the contribution made by these specialists. Thus, it is important that the advertising manager carefully select the agency and establish working relationships that will maximize the agency's ability and incentive to perform.

## Advertising Agency Functions and Organization

Before considering the responsibilities of agency selection and formation of productive relations, it is essential to understand the nature of advertising agencies — their functions and their organizational structure.

### Functions Performed by the Advertising Agency

According to the bureau of the Census, there were 9,559 advertising firms with payrolls in the United States in 1982.[1] These agencies range from very small enterprises to giant international firms. The largest of these advertising agencies in 1982 was Young & Rubicam, placing $2.5 billion in advertising and employing over 7,000 persons worldwide.[2] A list of the largest 25 U.S. advertising agencies is shown in Exhibit 3-1. Although a few of the large agencies develop reputations among the general public, most remain anonymous.

Despite the variation in the size of agencies, the range of services tends to standardize once the agencies reach moderate size.

CREATIVE SERVICES. **Advertising agencies** are in business to create     *advertising agency*
advertisements, and their success hinges on this skill. Agency creative personnel conceive the basic idea for an advertisement, they write the words or

Largest 25 U.S. advertising agencies, 1982 (In millions of dollars)                    EXHIBIT 3-1

| Agency | Gross Income | Billings | Employees |
|---|---|---|---|
| 1. Young & Rubicam | $ 376.6 | $2,511.7 | 7025 |
| 2. Ted Bates Worldwide | 356.1 | 2,374.0 | 5041 |
| 3. J. Walter Thompson Co. | 347.1 | 2,315.2 | 7443 |
| 4. Ogilvy & Mather | 315.0 | 2,151.0 | 7010 |
| 5. McCann-Erickson Worldwide | 276.1 | 1,841.4 | 5850 |
| 6. BBDO International | 238.3 | 1,605.5 | 3583 |
| 7. Leo Burnett Co. | 221.2 | 1,487.4 | 3498 |
| 8. Saatchi & Saatchi Compton | 186.5 | 1,302.6 | 1140 |
| 9. Foote Cone & Belding | 178.1 | 1,195.9 | 3888 |
| 10. Doyle Dane Bernbach | 175.9 | 1,235.0 | 2986 |
| 11. SSC&B: Lintas Worldwide | 175.0 | 1,153.0 | 3713 |
| 12. D'Arcy-MacManus & Masius | 167.3 | 1,113.5 | 3504 |
| 13. Grey Advertising | 148.1 | 987.7 | 3789 |
| 14. Benton & Bowles | 127.6 | 885.7 | 2763 |
| 15. Marschalk Campbell-Ewald | 119.0 | 793.6 | 1964 |
| 16. Dancer Fitzgerald Sample | 96.4 | 666.0 | 2764 |
| 17. NW Ayer Inc. | 83.9 | 587.0* | 1252 |
| 18. William Esty Co. | 82.0 | 550.0 | 636 |
| 19. Marsteller Inc. | 81.2 | 541.5 | 1648 |
| 20. Needham, Harper & Steers | 79.0 | 526.8 | 1913 |
| 21. Wells, Rich, Greene | 79.0 | 527.0 | 720 |
| 22. Bozell & Jacobs | 70.3 | 514.6 | 1360 |
| 23. NCK Organization | 69.8 | 433.5 | 1184 |
| 24. Kenyon & Eckhardt | 64.9 | 436.9 | 2676 |
| 25. Ketchum Communications | 54.3 | 362.0 | 1100 |

Reprinted with permission from the March 16, 1983 issue of *Advertising Age*. Copyright 1983 by Crain Communications, Inc.

---

[1]U.S. Bureau of the Census, *Statistical Abstract of the United States: 1982-83* (103rd ed.; Washington: U.S. Government Printing Office, 1982), p. 814.
[2]"U.S. Agency Income Profiles," *Advertising Age* (March 16, 1983), p. 10.

copy that will appear in the ad or be spoken by an actor, and they design the layout for a print ad or the filming sequence for a television commercial. Advertising agencies do not produce the advertisements themselves — that is, they do not take photographs, draw illustrations, prepare engravings, make recordings, or make films. They contract for these services for their clients, provide direction concerning the end product desired, and control the process until the product is finished.

Advertising agency creative services are most frequently used in creation of print and broadcast advertising, although agencies sometimes provide creative services in related areas. For example, agencies are sometimes asked to prepare package designs, letterhead designs, point-of-purchase designs (displays used inside the store), or selling aids. They are frequently asked to write copy for packages or labels, prepare scripts for sales meetings, and suggest product names.

MEDIA SERVICES. A second basic function offered by advertising agencies is the placement of advertising in the media. This service includes analysis and recommendation of media and media schedules, purchase of the advertising time or space, and placement of the advertising materials with the media. In addition, agencies are generally charged with the responsibility for controlling the media program, including both budgetary control and control of actual media performance as compared to planned performance. Most advertising agencies employ their own media specialists to perform these services, although some specialized media services may be partially or entirely subcontracted under agency supervision.

*media buying service*      In recent years **media buying services** have been formed that specialize in planning and implementing media buys. Although these services will purchase any form of media, they specialize in large purchases of television time, probably the most complex of all media buys. Media services may purchase under advertising agency direction or, more often, directly for the advertiser. Media buying services, through specialization, claim to generate significant media buying economies for their clients.

RESEARCH SERVICES. Most advertising agencies, the major exceptions being very small or highly specialized agencies offer a variety of marketing research services. Key agency research services center on research that contributes to or tests advertising effectiveness. Advertising agencies do not, in most instances, actually conduct the research themselves. They do, however, design research projects, subcontract them, supervise their implementation, and provide the advertiser with research analysis and recommendations based on the findings.

MERCHANDISING SERVICES. Many advertising agencies offer materials and counsel in a wide variety of other marketing areas that might be lumped under the term "merchandising." Agency staffs often plan and implement sales promotions directed either to consumers or to

the trade. A **sales promotion** is a limited term, special-incentive offer          *sales promotion*
designed to accomplish a specific, usually short-term objective; for exam-
ple, contests, coupons, or premiums offered to the consumer, free-goods
offers, display programs, or price incentives offered to the trade.

Agency staffs frequently prepare selling aids utilized by salespeople
and prepare many collateral materials that supplement an advertising campaign. These include mailings to alert the trade to the advertising campaign, in-store display materials, and even presentations to the sales force.

Another class of merchandising service, more akin to research, is sur-
veillance of competitive activity, which may involve field checks, store
audits, trade interviews or reviews of trade literature. All are designed to keep
an advertiser informed of changes in competitors' marketing activities.

In addition to these services, agencies frequently have marketing
experts on their staffs who are available to analyze pricing problems, distribution problems, and product design.

ADVERTISING PLANNING. Advertising agencies, except perhaps for
the smaller ones, are well equipped to handle or participate in the advertising planning process. Frequently, as part of its service, an agency will
assume full responsibility for advertising plan preparation under the
supervision of the client's advertising manager.

## Organization of Advertising Agencies

To the uninitiated, advertising agency organization is deceptive,
largely because most agencies have not one, but two organizational
structures—one, quite visible; the other, less so. The first structure—the
visible one—is the functional organization. It is of lesser importance to the
advertising manager, serving mainly as an agency internal administrative
and control device. The second structure—the one less visible to the
outsider—is a task group built to formulate the advertising programs of
each client of the agency.

THE FUNCTIONAL ORGANIZATION. Certainly the most common
formal organizational structure used by advertising agencies is a functional
pattern. There is an understandable reason for this. Advertising agency
jobs are far more specialized than those in the advertising departments of
most companies and there is a natural tendency to group these specialists
together in departments. This allows them to share skills and information
and makes supervision easier.

The functional organization serves mainly as a device for internal
administration. Personnel policies and practices are administered through
the functional organization, as is professional training. Quality control and
budgetary control may be exerted through the functional organization, but
these two control responsibilities are also commonly administered through
the task-group organization.

**EXHIBIT 3-2**        Typical advertising agency's functional organization.

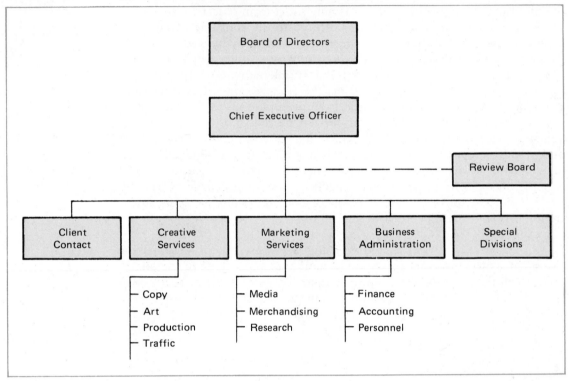

One typical functional grouping is shown in Exhibit 3-2. This grouping will form the basis for a brief review of the responsibilities normally given to each functional area.

*client contact unit*

*Client Contact.* Responsibility for liaison between the advertising agency and the client organization rests with the **client-contact unit.** The unit receives and supervises client requests and serves as the channel through which agency work and recommendations flow to the client. It directs advertising planning within the agency, drawing upon other functional areas for necessary planning assistance. Client contact is also responsible for coordinating the implementation of advertising plans for those areas assigned to the advertising agency. Client-contact personnel — account executives and their supervisors — have managerial responsibilities. In many ways their job is parallel to that of the advertising manager of a company. The *account executive* serves as the advertising manager's counterpart or direct representative within the advertising agency.

*creative services unit*

*Creative Services.* The **creative-services unit** is responsible for writing, designing, and supervising production of advertisements and related materials. This is the unit that produces the agency's principal product. Creative members also contribute to the advertising planning process. They frequently participate in defining objectives for the advertising and have the major responsibility for defining creative directions that will achieve those objectives.

The creative function is divided into specialized subfunctions. The copy department includes *copywriters* who write the words used in print and broadcast commercials or write other collateral materials. In the art department *art directors* are responsible for design and illustration in print advertisements and for designing video action in television commercials. Art directors also design other materials that supplement the advertising program. The **production departments**—usually specialized by print or broadcast media—contract for and supervise the physical preparation of the advertising materials. **Traffic departments** are concerned with the internal routing and scheduling of creative work and with the delivery and scheduling of the advertising materials used by the media.

*production department*

*traffic department*

*Marketing Services.* Media, merchandising, and research subgroups are included in the **marketing-services unit.** The **media department,** usually the largest in personnel numbers, is responsible for planning the media program and negotiation for and purchase of the media in which its clients' advertisements appear.

*marketing services unit*

*media department*

**Merchandising departments** include marketing specialists who plan sales promotions, conduct marketing studies, and gather data for marketing decisions. These departments frequently include specialists in particular product fields such as grocery specialists or fashion-goods specialists.

*merchandising department*

The research department serves by designing and supervising advertising research and general marketing research. It contributes to the planning process by recommending research approaches to pressing problems. It also aids the planning process on a more general level by contributing an analysis and interpretation of available information about the product and its market. Advertising effectiveness research is usually directed by research department members.

*Business Administration.* Internal administration of agency affairs is the central concern of the **business administration unit,** whose function is usually financial, and whose manager often is a financial officer. Advertising agencies have both very important cash flow requirements and complex accounting needs. The cash flow problems arise from the fact that agencies themselves make the media purchases—often running into the millions of dollars—for their clients and must, in turn, bill and collect from their clients. This practice, along with the complexity of large media purchases and the need to service many clients, each frequently having several products, creates a need for sophisticated accounting systems.

*business administration unit*

Advertising agencies have very little in the way of tangible assets, their stock-in-trade being the skills of their employees. Attracting and retaining top-grade personnel is obviously vital to the success of an agency.

*Special Functions.* There are other special functions that may be separated in the functional advertising agency organization. Some agencies have divisions that handle specialized types of advertising. For example, a large agency might have a division to handle small accounts or a division specializing in new products. Some advertising agencies also have divisions that concentrate on the solicitation of new clients.

Many larger agencies have branch offices in various cities and countries. As a result, there is sometimes a form of geographic organizational pattern used in conjunction with the functional pattern. The branch offices themselves are usually organized on a functional basis like a separate agency, although the smaller offices may not have a full range of functional specialties.

*account group*

ACCOUNT-GROUP ORGANIZATION. In addition to the formal, functional organizational structure, most advertising agencies superimpose an account-group organization. The **account group** is a team made up of members from the various functional areas who work together on a particular account.

*Account-Group Structure.* The account-group organization is frequently not formally stated. If it were charted, it would probably resemble a series of wheels—one for each team. In the center of the wheel would be the client, the product, and probably the client contact members who coordinate account group efforts. Arranged around the center would be the individuals (not departments) assigned to service that account, including copywriters, art directors, media buyers, researchers, and other specialists. Exhibit 3-3 illustrates this organizational form. The full account group will sometimes meet formally to consider major problems, but more often the association is informal.

Frequently subgroups form within the main account group to handle recurring problems that do not concern all of the specialists in the main group. For example, the creative members often come together to work on the creation of advertising for a particular product. This subteam would likely include those copywriters, art directors, and production personnel assigned to the product.

*Responsibilities of the Account Group.* The account-group organization has as its purpose the creation of an advertising program for a product. Thus the account group is the most important organizational group to the advertising manager.

The success of the account group depends not only on the skill of the individual members, but also on their ability to work together and coordinate their efforts effectively. The client contact member of the team must play a leading role in developing this organizational effectiveness.

The account group also serves as a control center within the agency. Agencies usually account for costs by client or product and determine the profitability of each product account and hence of each account group. Account profitability is important to the advertiser as well as to the agency. The level of service that the agency can offer will decline if an account

Organization of an agency account group          EXHIBIT 3-3

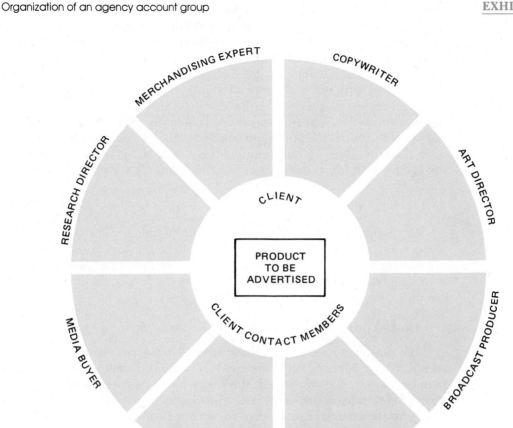

proves to be unprofitable. The quality of the agency's product is also controlled on a group basis. Advertising plans and their implementation are reviewed and remedial action is taken mainly on a product or account-group basis.

REVIEW BOARDS. A form of control used by many advertising agencies is the review board made up of senior agency personnel. Two frequently used types are **plans boards,** which review the advertising plan to be recommended to the client firm, and **creative review boards** that appraise creative output.

*plans board*
*creative review board*

The success of this review process is open to some question. One problem is that the reviewers usually come into the planning or creative process too late to contribute effectively to the end result. By the time the review boards appraise the materials, the account groups are undoubtedly committed to a course of action, and timetables have become compressed. Consequently, the account group becomes defensive of its product and sees review board criticism as ill-informed carping. A more effective use of senior agency talent is to incorporate such personnel into the account groups.

Another form of review control utilized by some advertising agencies is a legal review of proposed advertising or, in some cases, a review by medical authorities. Outside counsel is frequently used for these reviews. For certain product categories (pharmaceuticals, for example), this form of control has become very important and is a valuable service performed by the agency both for its own protection and for its clients' protection.

## Should an Agency be Retained?

Once the functions and organization of advertising agencies are understood, the next step is to determine if the services of such agencies are necessary to the advertiser's program. A company must determine if it is more advantageous to provide advertising services itself or to contract out those services through an advertising agency.

### Do-It-Yourself Advertising

It is possible to obtain specialized advertising services without retaining an advertising agency. There are two somewhat different approaches that may be taken—one rather old, the house agency approach, and a more recent development, the "a la carte" approach.

*house agency*

A **house agency** is an advertising agency formed by an advertiser for the purpose of handling the advertiser's own products. Sometimes the house agency also handles the products of a few other small clients, but its dominant concern is with the products of its parent company. House agencies have been around for many years, but they are few in number and account for only a small portion of total advertising volume.

The American Association of Advertising Agencies (Four A's) has since 1976 tracked the movement of advertising accounts in and out of house agencies. They report a definite trend toward movement of accounts away from in-house agencies.[3] In explaining this trend, the president of the Four A's suggested that in-house agencies are "the height of false economy. House agencies are primarily peopled by either young folks getting experience so they can move to a bona fide agency, or those who have been in the bona fide agency world and were flushed out somewhere along the way."[4]

*a la carte advertising approach*

The **a la carte advertising approach** is a more recent phenomenon in which the advertiser contracts with independent specialists for various

---

[3]"Accounts Continue Move Outside," *Advertising Age* (August 9, 1982), p. 6.
[4]*Ibid.*

agency-type services. It is possible, for example, to engage a specialist to purchase media, a specialist to create ideas for advertisements, and a specialist to produce finished advertisements. Usually several such specialists would be involved for any particular campaign, so coordination must be provided by the advertising manager.

There appear to be several factors motivating a do-it-yourself approach. One of these is financial. The advertiser hopes to gain the commission normally accruing to the advertising agency and provide advertising services at lower cost than could an independent advertising agency. Another factor is the desire that the advertiser's products receive fuller attention than would be possible in an agency that serves many different clients. And, finally, some advertisers have unusual advertising requirements which they feel a multi-client advertising agency could not handle or would not be interested in handling.

## Advantages of Retaining an Agency

Unless the advertiser is very small or very specialized, an advertising agency probably should be retained. The advantages of retaining an agency are many. Multi-client (as opposed to house) agencies tend to attract top advertising specialists because they pay better, they offer their people the stimulating competition of working with the best specialists, and they offer them the chance to work on a variety of client accounts. Agencies can provide specialized talent for less than could advertisers who hire their own advertising specialists. The agencies' ability to do so is a result both of the system by which they are compensated (see page 65 on agency compensation) and their ability to spread the cost of talent across several clients' accounts.

In addition, an agency can better coordinate the various specialists involved in the project. Coordination difficulties may be a problem especially in the a la carte approach to do-it-yourself advertising. John O'Toole, president of Foote, Cone and Belding advertising agency, notes this problem: "It's difficult enough to bring about coordination when you have the players all under one roof. Dealing with a team whose members are all over the telephone directory adds at least another dimension of frustration."[5]

Finally, the advertising agency can provide a cost savings for the advertiser. It is not at all clear that either the house agency or the a la carte approach to do-it-yourself advertising generates less expenditure on the part of advertisers. The basic services provided by an agency must be performed, and transferring the responsibility from agency to advertiser may not greatly affect the costs involved if adequate controls over the agency are maintained. Maxwell Dane of Doyle Dane Bernbach, Inc., quite perceptively pointed out that the real economies in advertising come from the way the 85 percent is spent, not from shaving a percentage point from

---

[5]Quoted in *The 4A Newsletter* (October 5, 1970), pp. 8–9.

the 15 percent commission.[6] The real issue may be who can best advise the advertising manager on the most effective way of spending the advertising dollar.

## Selection of an Advertising Agency

Once a decision is made to utilize the services of an advertising agency, the selection process itself begins and an initial screening of possible agencies is undertaken. The final selection process centers on the account group and how it relates to the advertiser's objectives.

### Responsibility for Agency Selection

The selection of an advertising agency is an important decision for any company, and, in practice, it is usual for top management to participate in making the choice. This participation can be helpful and can contribute to a successful, long-term relationship with the agency, but top managers should work within specific guidelines.

First, the selection of an agency should be based on objective criteria that recognize the nature of an advertising agency's contribution and the importance of an effective client-agency relationship. Agency contributions, to be effective, must be the products of imaginative, enthusiastic minds. This is true not only of the advertisements suggested, but also of the media, research, merchandising, and planning efforts. Selecting an agency that can make imaginative and enthusiastic contributions should be based not on the personal affinities of top managers, but on objective criteria. Top managers should contribute to and adhere to such objectivity if they participate in the agency selection process.

In addition, top management should recognize the primacy of the advertising manager in the selection process. Advertising agencies like to maintain cordial relationships with top management, but agency personnel rarely work regularly with executives above the advertising manager level. It is with advertising managers and their subordinates that the advertising agency works on a daily basis and it is between them that an effective relationship must grow. Further, it is the advertising manager who will be held responsible for the quality of the agency's contribution. Because of these responsibilities, the advertising manager should be given a dominant role in the agency selection.

### The Selection Process— Initial Screening

In considering how to select an advertising agency, it will be assumed that the client firm, the advertiser, is taking the initiative in searching for an agency. It is true, however, that the opposite often occurs. In an effort to

---

[6]From a speech by Maxwell Dane, quoted in *The 4A Newsletter* (January 4, 1971), p. 8.

grow, advertising agencies solicit new accounts, often rather aggressively. While these solicitations are flattering and a source of interesting background information, they do not in themselves provide an adequate basis for a decision to retain or change advertising agencies. When that decision is to be made, the advertiser should control the gathering of information about prospective agencies, and as part of the analysis, should compare the attributes of a number of agencies.

Since there are so many advertising agencies of so many types, it is clearly necessary to find some means of narrowing the alternatives. A logical approach is to establish selection criteria that will serve to form a preliminary list of agencies that appear to fit the particular needs of the advertiser. Criteria are suggested below as guides to developing a preliminary agency list.

AGENCY SIZE. Large budget advertisers tend to go to large agencies and small advertisers to small agencies for a number of reasons. Most large agencies set a minimum billing requirement because they do not feel able to handle small accounts profitably. Small budget advertisers tend to avoid large agencies because they fear inattention in competition with large accounts. The account group approach used by most agencies may partially offset this problem since each such group is like a small agency. Large agencies can maintain a greater number of different specialists on their staffs, and because their pay scales tend to be higher, some feel that they attract the highest caliber talent.

PRODUCT CONFLICTS. An advertising agency generally will not handle products that are competitive with each other. This rule has arisen to prevent any conflict of interest or breach of confidence between the agent and client who share confidential information. The practical effect of the rule is to eliminate a number of agencies from consideration including, unfortunately, those most experienced in the product class being considered. Exactly how broadly the product class should be defined in determining product conflicts is a matter of controversy that can ultimately be settled only by the agency and the clients directly involved.

SPECIAL SKILLS. Agencies themselves sometimes specialize in particular kinds of products. Some specialize rather broadly in industrial goods or consumer goods. Others have narrower specialties such as financial advertising or medical advertising. If an agency that specializes in a certain type of product is selected, the advantage is its experience and familiarity with the field; the disadvantage is that it may lack the fresh perspective of a newcomer to the field.

Along the same lines, the product to be advertised may require particular staff specialists — doctors, dietitians, fashion experts, or simply people experienced in the marketing of the product. If the account is large enough, an agency can afford to hire these experts to work just on that particular product. But if the advertising budget is not large, an agency that already has these specialists should be found, so that the expense can be shared among several clients.

A decision must be made as to the breadth of service required from the agency. Some agencies offer the full range of services reviewed earlier in this chapter. Others offer fewer services, concentrating instead on what they consider to be their strengths, usually creative and media services, leaving other responsibilities to the advertiser's organization.

AGENCY LOCATION. Effective agency-client relations require clear and frequent communication, which is, in turn, aided by the proximity of advertiser and agency. Advertising agencies, particularly the larger ones, tend to cluster in the large cities. If geographic criteria are set, large numbers of agencies will be screened out.

The advertiser must also decide whether domestic or international agency branch offices are necessary. For some kinds of products, it is desirable to have agency personnel available to handle local problems in different areas. The availability of foreign branches is important for advertisers who need local knowledge in designing and placing international advertising.

AGENCY RECORD. Some advertisers feel that a good measure to apply to a prospective advertising agency is the agency's own performance record. Has the agency shown growth? Has it been successful? Has it had stable relations with its clients? If the answer to any of these questions is no, some investigation of the cause may be in order before the agency is considered further.

Other criteria will doubtless suggest themselves in each individual agency selection situation. If the occasion for agency selection has been brought about by dissatisfaction with the currently retained agency, the criteria for selecting a new agency should take into account the underlying cause of that dissatisfaction and attempt to eliminate it in the selection of a new agency. Unfortunately, agency changes are too often made without a good understanding of why the relationship has been unsuccessful. An agency change in such situations is merely treatment of a surface symptom that soon recurs with the new agency.

## The Selection Process — Final Selection

Application of the foregoing criteria should result in the development of a short list of prospective agencies which can then be studied to determine the final selection.

APPROACHING THE AGENCIES. The preliminary screening can usually be done from publicly available information sources such as the *Standard Advertising Register,* an advertising agency directory, and advertising trade magazines such as *Advertising Age.* However, for the final selection, it is necessary to contact the prospective agency and to get information from them directly.

The approach to prospective agencies should be frank and business-like. The advertiser should explain the nature of the prospective assignment, including some description of the product, the market, and the likely budget. The advertiser should ask the prospective agency if it could accept such an assignment and if it would like to participate in the final selection process.

The advertiser should attempt to keep the search for a new agency as confidential as possible, although this often proves difficult. If news of the agency search leaks out, the advertiser may be deluged with unsolicited requests to participate from agencies not on the preliminary list. Opening the selection to all interested agencies defeats the purpose of the preliminary screening and makes thorough, analytical examination of each agency impossible.

USE OF A QUESTIONNAIRE. In approaching the prospective agencies the advertiser should make very clear what action the agency is expected to take if it has an interest in the advertising account. Some advertisers, for example, ask agencies to fill out a questionnaire concerning the agency, its personnel, facilities, and ways of approaching its work. Such an approach, unfortunately, reveals more about the agency's flair for answering questionnaires than it does about their long-term effectiveness in creating advertising programs. The answers are more likely to represent the efforts of agency top management, revealing little about the thinking or the skills of the agency members who would be assigned to the advertiser's product.

REQUESTING SPECULATIVE PRESENTATIONS. Another approach to final screening — and another one to be discouraged — is to ask the agency to prepare a **speculative presentation.** This requires that the agency prepare the basic elements of the advertising campaign that might be used if the account were won. In fairness, the advertiser asking for such presentations should pay for them, a substantial cost if several agencies are involved.

*speculative presentation*

Many agencies, especially the more successful ones, will not participate in such speculative competitions. From the advertiser's point of view, the speculative presentation approach starts the relationship off in a most undesirable way. Good advertising starts with patient research and analysis, and full disclosure of information between advertiser and agency. Since these conditions can hardly be met in a speculative presentation, the result is to encourage an inadequate foundation for the advertising program.

PREFERRED CRITERION — THE ACCOUNT GROUP. A weakness of both the questionnaire approach and the speculative presentation approach is that they fail to evaluate the personnel who would regularly work on the advertiser's account. If the advertiser wishes to explore the likely effectiveness of the prospective agency's work and the effectiveness of the relationship with it, the search must go beyond the agency as a whole to the particular people who will be working actively on the advertising for the product. This means that the advertiser, at this point, needs to analyze the personnel (account executives, creative personnel, etc.) who would be assigned to the account group.

*Analyzing the Account Group.* How can the advertiser analyze the account group? What information is needed? First, of course, the advertiser needs to know who would actually be working to develop the company's advertising.

Second, it is important to know how much time this group would have available. Unless the account is very large, the advertiser should expect the group to be working on several product accounts at once. This is essential as a means of spreading the cost and also desirable as a means of enriching the work experience and, hence, the creativity of the group. On the other hand, it is essential that the team have adequate time to do a thorough job on each account, and it is probably desirable that the group not be dominated by a large account that demands preferential treatment at the expense of time needed for other product accounts.

Third, it would be helpful to get some feeling as to how well the group works together, since cooperation, compatibility, and coordination are vital to success. Has the group had experience in working together? Does there appear to be good leadership? Do the members enjoy mutual respect?

Fourth, it would be helpful to view examples of the work of the group so that their actual performance might be evaluated. This should reveal something about how they go about their jobs—it should indicate whether or not they are thorough, analytical, creative, and self-critical.

Fifth, and finally, the advertising manager needs to know something about the compatibility of this agency's team with his or her advertising department team. Do the agency team members have the intellect to be challenging associates? Do they have the courage necessary to represent their points of view? Do they have the flexibility to accept new points of view? The advertising manager needs self-knowledge and insight into the advertising department staff in order to define the qualities needed in the agency group. The advertising manager should seek an agency team that is strong rather than one that will be easily dominated.

*Interviewing the Account Group.* Obtaining the desired information from the account group—much of it quite qualitative—is not easy. Perhaps the best approach is simply to ask the agency for a meeting with the account group members to view some of their work on other products. In this way it is possible to meet the team; to see, from viewing their work, how they go about their jobs; and to develop a feeling for how well they work together by observing how well they interact. Questions can be asked about time availability, and some feeling should emerge about their compatibility with the advertising department team.

The trick to carrying out this process successfully is for the advertiser to convince the agency to provide access to the working level people in the

account group rather than to the senior heads of the functional departments who are most frequently used as "presenters" of the agency's story.
The people who really matter to the advertiser are the ones who will do the
daily work on the advertising programs. Final selection of an advertising
agency must rest upon an evaluation of the capabilities of this account
group.

## Advertiser/Agency Relationships

An orderly and objective approach to selection of an advertising
agency can do much to set a pattern for the relationship that follows. There
is, however, more to advertiser-agency relations than this. The nature of
day-to-day working arrangements and the nature of advertising agency
compensation are two further elements of the client-agency relationship.

### Structuring the Relationship with the Advertising Agency

The responsibility for building the advertiser's working relationship
with the advertising agency rests with the advertising manager. The advertising manager sets the direction or basic ground rules for the relationship
which are then applied by the subordinates who work with the agency.

The advertising manager should recognize that it is the advertiser
rather than the agency that dominates the relationship. This dominance
results from the advertiser's power to award or take away product assignments and the advertiser's "power of the purse" which gives ultimate
authority for all advertising decisions. This does not mean that the agency
plays no role in forming the working relationship, but usually the agency
accepts the leadership of the advertiser if it is offered.

OBJECTIVES OF THE RELATIONSHIP. The crucial agency-advertiser
relationship develops between the working levels in both organizations,
between the account group assigned to the advertiser's product and the
advertising manager's organization. The purpose of the relationship is
not to make happy workers or generate friendships (although either may
result), but rather to gain greater productive efficiency. The advertising
manager should define relationship objectives, but, in general, should
encourage three kinds of behavior.

First, the advertiser wants the agency team to work hard, long, and
conscientiously on the firm's advertising. It is important that the agency
team be enthusiastic, involved, and motivated.

Next, the advertiser wants agency team efforts to be creative and
imaginative. The relationship should be such that the members of the team
feel free to explore new approaches and experiment with new forms.

Finally, the advertiser wants agency team members to feel free to state
their views, to suggest their ideas, to disagree, and above all, to be honest in
stating what they believe, even if their ideas are unpopular.

SOME RELATIONSHIP GROUND RULES. Creating a relationship that will achieve the motivational objectives just outlined requires substantial personal leadership skill on the part of the advertising manager. Some useful ground rules can be suggested as a supplement to personal leadership in developing effective working relations with the advertising agency.

*Admit the Agency to Full Partnership.* Do not treat the agency as a vendor trying to sell something. Instead, treat the members of the agency team as partners with a stake in the success of the product. As a practical matter this means that the advertiser should be eager to share all available information on the product with agency team members. The agency, of course, needs complete information if it is to aid in developing a sound advertising program. This practice has an important motivational effect also. The advertiser that refuses to supply information to an agency has implied a lack of trust.

*Be Demanding of the Agency Team.* In seeking a motivated agency team, the advertiser should not set low standards in either quantity or quality. On the contrary, a healthier relationship is created when the advertiser sets high and consistent standards both for the advertising department and for the agency. The advertiser must be prepared to reward good performance and must also recognize reasonable limits to demands.

*Respect the Agency's Area of Expertise.* The reason for retaining an advertising agency is to gain the benefits of its specialized skills. It makes sense, then, to delegate to the agency personnel responsibility for those areas in which they specialize. When a problem arises that is in the agency's special field, it should be defined by the advertiser, ground rules or decision boundaries should be established, and the problem should be given to the agency to work on. When the agency presents a solution that falls within the boundaries initially established, the advertiser should accept it as the solution of the best expert available.

*Reward Superior Performance.* The greatest reward for any agency person is acceptance of work done — production of the creative ideas, purchase of the media schedule, acceptance of the plans. The most discouraging of situations can arise if the work of the advertising specialist is rejected, particularly if the rejection comes from personnel not equipped either by training or experience to evaluate the work. This can occur if nonmarketing senior executives are placed in the advertising approval chain of command or if the advertising manager delegates these approval powers to inexperienced subordinates. The advertising manager should feel a responsibility for protecting the agency's efforts from such unwise intrusion.

*Be Responsive to the Agency Profit Position.* Advertising agencies derive their income from commissions paid by the media on time and space purchases made by the agency and from fees charged to the advertiser. Expenses, however, are rather independent of income, depending largely on the work load assigned by the advertiser. Thus, if an advertiser's demands for a product assignment become excessive, costs can soon outstrip revenues, resulting in a negative profit position on that product assignment.

It is not in the advertiser's interest for the agency to lose money on the company's assignments. When this occurs, the agency account group comes under internal pressure to reduce cost, and this can only be done by their spending less time on the account. This places the account team's objectives in conflict with the advertiser's goals, and the relationship can quickly break down.

The advertising manager can avoid this problem by maintaining an awareness of the agency's profit position on the account. Most advertising agencies collect cost and revenue figures by product account, and most are more than willing to review this information with clients. The advertiser should make it a regular practice to review this information and set some standard of reasonable profit that the agency should realize. One guide to reasonable profit is provided by the American Association of Advertising Agencies in yearly reports on advertising agency costs and profits. They reported, for example, that average net profit among reporting agencies was .85 percent of sales (gross purchases or billings) in 1982 and about 3.4 percent of gross income (fees and commissions).[7]

If the advertiser finds that an account is unprofitable or excessively profitable to the agency and if the result cannot be attributed to the account group's level of efficiency, then the advertiser should take steps either to change agency revenue (through a change in fees, addition or subtraction of products assigned) or to change the work load demanded of the account team.

*Regularly Evaluate the Agency Account Group.* In addition to reviewing the financial status of the account, the advertiser should, on a regular basis, formally evaluate the performance of the account group. This idea merely represents an application to the agency team of a standard practice used by a manager with subordinates. The benefits to be derived are very similar. Evaluation lets the agency team know where they stand in the eyes of their client. It brings out into the open any problems, allowing frank discussion and suggestions for solutions. The evaluation should, of course, be reviewed with agency personnel and should provide a means for the agency to present to the advertiser its perceptions of the problems it faces in working with the advertiser.

Borden, the food and chemical company, installed an agency evaluation system several years ago. It rates agency performance twice a year on such criteria as market performance of assigned products, creativity, and cooperation.[8] Exhibit 3-4 shows the scorecard used in the evaluation.

---

[7]"4A's Member Agencies' Costs and Profits," *Advertising Age* (July 25, 1983), p. 84.
[8]Nancy Giges, "Reviewing the Review: Borden Likes Systems of Agency Evaluation," *Advertising Age* (April 18, 1977), pp. 3, 112.

EXHIBIT 3-4    Borden agency-evaluation report.

## AGENCY PERFORMANCE EVALUATION SUMMARY

### AGENCY _____

#### Biannual Review Dated _____

Product Line _____

| WEIGHT | ITEM PERFORMANCE EVALUATION | | | | | | ITEM POINT SCORE (Item Weight × Evaluation) | TOTAL SCORE |
|---|---|---|---|---|---|---|---|---|
| | % Impm't Goal | | | | | | | |
| **I. 60** | **Share of Market Performance** (Range: 0 – 100% = Optimum) | | | | | | | |
| | 60 (a) Percent Improvement Achieved (Memo) Actual Data: Subtotal | % | % | % | % | % | ___ ___ | XXX |
| **II. 20** | **Creativity** (Range: 0 – 100%; 100% = Optimum) | | | | | | | |
| | 6 (a) Marketing Strategy Formulation | % | % | % | % | % | | |
| | 4 (b) Conceptual Ability (Defining & Solving Problems) | | | | | | | |
| | 4 (c) Creative Ability in TV | | | | | | | |
| | 4 (d) Creative Ability in Print | | | | | | | |
| | 1 (e) Advertising Research Ability (Media & Copy) | | | | | | | |
| | 1 (f) New Product Development Subtotal | | | | | | | XXX |
| **III. 20** | **Cooperation** (Range: 0 – 100%; 100% = Optimum) | | | | | | | |
| | 10 (a) Overall Performance | % | % | % | % | % | | |
| | 5 (b) Service (Deadlines, Cost Control) | | | | | | | |
| | 5 (c) Goal Achievement Efforts Subtotal | | | | | | | XXX |
| **IV.** | **Total Individual Product Line Performance** (100 Points = Optimum) | | | | | | % | % |
| | A. Planned Relative Profit Importance of Marketing Strategies | | | | | | % | |
| | B. Total Agency Performance Score (100 Points = Optimum) | | | | | | % | % |

Courtesy: Borden Inc.

## Advertising Agency Compensation

Agency compensation is somewhat unusual, rather complex, and the subject of some controversy. Understanding the compensation system will enable the advertising manager to evaluate and adjust the compensation received by the agency. An advertising agency has two basic sources of income — commissions on purchases of media and fees received directly from clients.

AGENCY COMMISSIONS. The largest source of agency compensation is commissions, and it is paid not by the agency's clients, but by the media. When an agency purchases media time or space for a client, the medium pays a commission or a percentage of the purchase price to the advertising agency. This practice has its origin in the early history of advertising agencies when they served as sales agents for the media. The agencies developed the technique of creating advertisements as a way of inducing advertisers to buy space in the medium they were selling. The agency business was gradually transformed into a service business for advertisers rather than for media, but the commission system remains.

Media commissions realized by advertising agencies are 15 percent of the gross amount of the media purchase, except for outdoor advertising which gives 16⅔ percent. Most of the major media (including radio, television, newspapers, magazines, and outdoor) are commissionable. That is, they offer commissions to what they regard as legitimate advertising agencies. An advertiser can, of course, purchase time or space directly from a medium, but the advertiser is not ordinarily granted any commission. One incentive for retaining an agency, therefore, is the fact that the bulk of the charges for the agency's services are paid for by the commissions that are not ordinarily recoverable by the advertiser.

Agency billing practices are simple in concept, yet become rather complex in practice. If an agency buys $1,000 worth of time or space for an advertiser, the agency is billed by the medium for $1,000 commissionable. The agency pays the medium $1,000 less 15 percent or $850, and bills its client the full $1,000. The difference of $150 is income to the agency. In practice, the agency actually bills the advertiser in advance of receiving the bill from the medium so that cash will be available to pay the medium. Adjustments in the bill to the advertiser have to be made later to reconcile the estimated and actual media costs. Bills are also affected by the availability of cash discounts and discounts given for frequent or continuous use of a medium. These discounts are generally passed on to the advertiser.

Some media purchases, direct mail, for example, made by agencies are not commissionable. Agencies also purchase materials and services for advertisers on which no commission is offered. The most important case is the cost of producing the advertising. On these purchases the agency marks up the cost of the purchase by 17.65 percent to yield commission equivalent to 15 percent of the gross amount.

AGENCY FEES. Charging fees to advertisers as a supplement to commission income has become an increasingly widespread agency practice. As the advertising agency business has matured, it has broadened the services offered. Agencies have also felt that their general cost of doing business has risen. These two factors have led to declining profit margins that agencies have sought to offset by charging fees. Two types of fees charged are those that are supplementary to media commissions and those that replace the commission system.

Supplementary fees can arise in a number of ways. An agency may be asked to work on a project for which there is no commissionable advertising, such as designing a new package label. For such a project the agency would probably charge a fee based on a flat hourly rate for the time spent on the task, plus out-of-pocket expenses. Most agencies have standard hourly rates that are designed to absorb allocated overhead plus return a profit. A supplementary fee might also arise if the commissions realized by the agency on a product were not sufficient to cover the agency's costs in handling the account. This is the case discussed in the previous section concerning the advertiser's responsibility for being responsive to the agency profit position. One case where supplementary fees are frequently necessary is when an agency is asked to work on new products. These usually require a great deal of preparatory work during a period when commissions are small or nonexistent. In this situation the fee might be negotiated not on an hourly basis, but as a monthly fee designed to match anticipated agency costs.

The other type of fee arrangement is one that replaces rather than supplements media commissions. The amount of the fee is usually a subject of negotiation. It is in some way based on an estimated cost (personnel and materiel) that the agency will incur in servicing an account to the client's specifications. Allowance is made in the fee for a profit above cost. The agency, of course, takes advantage of all commissions available on media purchases and credits them to the fee to be paid to the agency by the advertiser.

COMMISSIONS VS. FEES. The all-fee compensation arrangement just discussed has been suggested by some as a desirable substitute for the commission approach to compensating advertising agencies. Many charges have been leveled against the commission system, but one central contention is that the compensation from commission is not directly related to the amount of effort and cost expended on the account by the agency. Certain types of accounts are notorious for their servicing demands. Generally they are accounts that use many different advertisements separately placed in many different individually purchased media. A women's wear account or a regional beer brand are good examples. Other accounts are regarded by agencies as natural money-makers. They utilize a single campaign over a long period of time in heavily purchased national media. Major proprietary drugs or cigarette brands (more so before they left television) are good examples. Some accounts require and get more service than is justified by the commissions earned by the agency. This excess service is at the expense of others who get less than their fair share of service.

Another charge made against the commission system is that because agency income increases with media expenditures, there is pressure for agencies to recommend ever-larger advertising budgets. This is a potentially serious problem since the advertiser needs to have the objective, professional participation of the agency in this vital decision. It is difficult in practice to determine the force of this pressure, since it is mixed with agency personnel's very natural belief in the power of advertising. The feeling that agency personnel have a conflict of interest in budgetary recommendations can affect the relationship of mutual confidence between the advertiser and the agency.

The fee method has been suggested as a substitute approach to overcome the problems of the commission system. The arguments for a fee approach appear to be logical—the fee approach directly relates income received to effort and cost expended, and it relieves the agency of some of the pressure to recommend larger advertising budgets. It also brings the entire question of the agency's profit position into the open, where it can be considered in an objective, businesslike manner.

Today many advertising agencies offer to work with their clients on either a commission or a negotiated fee basis. A 1982 survey by the Association of National Advertisers (ANA) showed that while 52 percent of the agencies surveyed used a traditional commission system, 29 percent used a fee system and 19 percent used some variation of the commission system.[9] The percentage of agencies relying on traditional commissions for their compensation has declined substantially from 68 percent in 1976 to the 52 percent reported in 1982. However, an *Advertising Age* survey of agency chief executives revealed that most believe that the 15 percent commission system will continue to survive as the dominant form of agency compensation.[10]

### Relationships with Other Outside Organizations

The discussion thus far has been limited to consideration of the relationship of the advertiser with only one type of outside organization— the advertising agency. The advertising manager and staff, however, normally come in contact with various other outside specialists who are retained by the firm, sometimes for a single job and sometimes on a continuing basis. Among these are marketing research firms, designers (of packages or point-of-sale materials, for example), representatives of specialized media (direct mail, novelties), public relations firms, and legal counselors.

---

[9]"The 15% Media Commission Is On the Way to Becoming a Relic in the Ad Agency Compensation Plans," *Marketing News,* (June 10, 1983), p. 9.
[10]Merle Kingman, "To Fee or Not to Fee," *Advertising Age* (August 29, 1983), p. M-24.

*CHAPTER*
*SUMMARY*

Services offered by advertising agencies include creation of advertisements, purchase of media time and space, design of research projects, merchandising assistance, and marketing planning. These services are usually provided to advertiser clients by an account team of agency specialists assigned to the advertiser's product. The advertiser should evaluate these agency services and decide whether to opt for an in-house or an a-la-carte approach or whether to retain an outside agency. In selecting an advertising agency, the advertiser should first form a preliminary list of agencies that meet screening requirements such as size, location, and services. Final selection should be based on evaluation of the capabilities of the account group that would be assigned to the advertiser's product.

Responsibility for building productive work relations with the advertising agency belongs to the advertising manager, who should set demanding and objective standards and yet be sensitive to the needs of the agency and its workers. The system by which agencies are compensated also affects the relationship. The major part of agency compensation is derived from commissions earned on media purchases for its clients. This compensation system is said to distort the agency-client relationship, yet the system is only slowly giving way to a fee approach.

*KEY TERMS*

Advertising agency
Media buying service
Sales promotion
Client contact unit
Creative services unit
Production department
Traffic department
Marketing services unit
Media department

Merchandising department
Business administration unit
Account group
Plans board
Creative review board
House agency
A la carte advertising approach
Speculative presentation

*QUESTIONS*
*FOR*
*DISCUSSION*

1. Suppose that an advertiser wished to have the tasks in the following list performed. Which of the tasks should an advertising agency be able to perform? What kind of specialist in the agency would actually do the work?

   a.  Design a new label.
   b.  Design a research study to evaluate a new product design.
   c.  Think of a name for a new product.
   d.  Take a photograph for an advertisement.
   e.  Think of a contest idea.
   f.  Select an actor for a television commercial.

2. Advertising agency research departments are particularly skilled and experienced in researching advertising problems. Consequently they should be adept at designing and directing research aimed at evaluating the effectiveness of an advertising program. However, is it desirable that an advertising agency be able to evaluate the effectiveness of its own work?

3. Suppose a company were considering changing the price of one if its products. Would it be desirable for the company to consult with its advertising agency before making a decision? If the advertising manager decided that it was desirable to ask the agency's opinion on this problem, to whom should the question be directed?

4. How should an advertiser, satisfied with its current agency, respond to an offer of a free, no-obligation, speculative presentation by a competitive agency?

5. If you were an advertising manager, how would you resolve the agency/advertiser problems that are listed below?

   a. The advertising agency is perpetually late in meeting assignments.
   b. There have been several resignations and requests for transfers among members of your agency account team.
   c. The agency claims that it is losing money in servicing your product.
   d. Agency personnel seem too quick to agree with any suggestion or idea that you have.
   e. Account team members seem preoccupied with problems of another, larger client to which they are also assigned.

6. What position should an advertising manager take if a superior does not personally like the advertisements recommended by the advertising agency?

7. On purchases made on behalf of a client on which there are no commissions offered, agencies commonly mark up the purchase price by 17.65 percent to provide compensation for the agency. Show why this would yield income to the agency that is equivalent to the 15 percent earned on a commissionable purchase.

8. Suppose an advertising agency, compensated under the normal commission system, made the following purchases in connection with one client's products. What would be the agency's gross income?

   | | |
   |---|---:|
   | a. Television time | $80,000 |
   | b. Production of two television commercials (cost) | 27,000 |
   | c. Out-of-pocket cost for test of the two television commercials | 600 |
   | d. One-month posting of outdoor posters | 10,000 |
   | e. Photograph for use in outdoor ads | 1,000 |
   | f. Postage charges for direct mail advertisements | 500 |

9. One of the charges made against the commission system is that it distorts the agency's judgment in the selection of media. Why might this be true?

---

*PROBLEM*

Recently, General Foods, one of the largest U.S. advertisers (Maxwell House, Jell-O, Birds-Eye, and other leading brands), decided that their advertising needs required a fifth advertising agency.[11] A committee of senior marketing executives was established to select the new agency. After a preliminary screening based on size, location, and account conflicts, a list of six agencies was selected.

Each of the six agencies was visited and given the questionnaire shown here. Responses to the questionnaire were hundreds of pages long. After analysis of the questionnaire results, two agencies were selected as finalists. These two agencies were then asked to prepare an advertising program for a Good Seasons salad dressing product. The winning advertising agency was then selected by the committee using a simple numerical rating system. The winning agency was awarded $24 million in advertising billings.

How would you evaluate General Foods' approach to selecting an advertising agency?

---

[11]This problem is based on Nancy Giges, "How General Foods Picked Its Fifth Agency," *Advertising Age* (July 14, 1980), pp. 45, 48.

# General Foods' Agency Search Questionnaire

## A. General

**1.** Who holds the stock of your agency and what is its concentration?

**2.** What were total annual billings of your offices and of total agency for 1975 through estimated 1979?

**3.** How do you charge for your services?

**4.** Who are your five largest clients? What percent of total agency and New York office billings does each represent?

**5.** What is the average billing of all your accounts?

**6.** What percentage of your billings are for national brands? Regional brands? Retail or industrial?

**7.** Please list your current clients, broken down by package goods (food and nonfood) and indicate the length of time they have been with your agency. What percentage of your New York office billings do package goods represent?

**8.** What significant accounts have been added/lost over the past three years?

**9.** What percent of agency growth in each of the last five years was accounted for by existing clients (broken out by established and new assignments) and new clients?

**10.** What new products have you introduced over the past three years?

**11.** Please provide your most recent balance sheet and income statement.

## B. Organizational and Personnel

**1.** Briefly describe how your agency is organized.

**2.** Who are the key individuals who will work on our account? How much time will they spend? What have been their accomplishments?

**3.** Who are the senior general management and department management executives in your office? Please describe briefly the background of each one, including length of service and experience with your and other agencies and/or client organizations.

**4.** From where do you recruit your account executives? What percentage have MBAs?

**5.** Do you have formal training and development programs in place? If so, please describe them.

**6.** What is your average number of employees per $1,000,000 of billing in the creative, account management and media functions?

## C. Creative Policy/Philosophy

**1.** Do you have a creative process? Please describe the agency's responsibilities and the client's responsibilities in that process.

**2.** Do you have a copy strategy or copy work plan?

**3.** What methods do you use to check advertising effectiveness—both pre- and post-testing? Have you made studies of effectiveness research for your clients?

General Foods' Agency Search Questionnaire reproduced with the permission of General Foods Corporation. Maxwell House, Jell-O and Birds Eye are registered trademarks of General Foods Corporation.

# CHAPTER 4

## *The Advertising Plan*

The advertising manager is responsible for planning the advertising to be used, for implementing the planned advertising, and for controlling the advertising to assure that the advertising actually used conforms with company standards.

The advertising manager uses the advertising plan as a guide in carrying out these responsibilities. The advertising plan establishes advertising objectives and details the programs that will be used to achieve the objectives. The advertising plan also is used as a means of giving direction to those who will implement the plan, and serves as a control device by specifying the performance or results expected from the advertising and how these results will be measured.

## Characteristics of the Advertising Plan

The essential requirements of an advertising plan are that it be comprehensive, be based on the analysis of data, and be in written form.

### Plans Are Comprehensive

To be comprehensive an advertising plan should be broad in scope—it should consider all aspects of the product and the environments

72

(e.g., social, legal, competitive) in which it operates. Comprehensive also means detailed; the plan should contain full analysis and be a source book of relevant facts and decisions relating to the product.

The advertising plan must cover the past, present, and future of the product. Past product performance must be analyzed to define the problems, or opportunities, currently facing the product. These problems form the basis for the definition of objectives that the advertising must achieve in the coming period. The advertising plan specifies detailed, step-by-step programs designed to reach these objectives.

## Plans Are Data Based

A good advertising plan is based on factual data. An advertising plan begins with a definition of the problems facing the product. These problems can only be defined if data on the product and its environment are available for analysis.

Attempting to define problems without data simply results in an exposition of opinions, often colored by personal prejudices. Objectivity is gained when problem definition is based on facts. A fact-based advertising plan is also far more persuasive than one based on opinion.

## Plans Are Written

The idea that a mental outline of likely action can be substituted for a formal, written plan is a mistake. Putting the plan in written form has several advantages:

1. **To Make Reasoning Explicit.**  Writing the plan forces the advertising manager to make assumptions and reasoning concerning the plan explicit. Committing reasoning to paper serves to eliminate shaky assumptions and mental bypassing of knotty problems. Most people also find writing out an analysis or argument of great assistance in developing logical reasoning.
2. **To Permit Coordination and Delegation.**  Writing the plan makes it available to others. In all but the smallest organizations, the advertising program will affect various people inside the organization and some people outside the organization. As noted earlier, the advertising manager is responsible for coordinating advertising with other elements of the total marketing program. The advertising plan is a communications medium to facilitate this coordination. The advertising manager can use the written plan to facilitate delegation to subordinates. A well-written plan provides precise, permanent instructions and minimizes misunderstandings between manager and subordinates.
3. **To Provide a Permanent Record.**  Writing the plan provides a permanent record that stands as a basis against which actual performance can be compared and, as a performance standard, the written plan can be used in controlling the advertising program. The permanence of the written plan also makes it a useful element in the replanning process. Planning is not a one-time effort, but a cyclical process of planning, executing, evaluating, and replanning. An obvious starting point in evaluating and replanning is with the written plan from the previous period. Through comparison of

objectives with actual performance, new problems for the coming period can be defined.

## Use of the Advertising Plan

Preparation of a good advertising plan requires great personal effort and involves substantial expense for the company. However, both the effort and the expense are well worthwhile because of the many uses of the advertising plan. The advertising plan can serve the advertising manager in each major area of responsibility — planning, implementation, and control.

### The Plan as an Analytical Tool

The planning process for which the advertising manager is responsible involves setting objectives and defining programs to reach those objectives. However, these two planning steps, if they are to be successful, must be preceded by thorough analysis of factual data to define the problems facing the product. The advertising plan provides a framework within which this analysis takes place.

FORMAL ANALYSIS. Preparation of an advertising plan should be a regularly scheduled requirement. The usual practice is to require preparation of a complete new plan once a year. Frequently there are also formal reviews of the advertising plan on a quarterly basis. In any event, the requirement for annual plan preparation guarantees that the status of the product and its environment will be analyzed formally at least once a year.

COORDINATION OF ADVERTISING PROGRAM. The advertising plan serves to increase coordination of the advertising effort. Because all aspects of the advertising program are developed at the same time and place, the need for coordination is clearly seen. For example, if an advertising media schedule were proposed that cost more than the amount proposed in the advertising budget, this discrepancy would quickly become apparent. The same would be true of the coordination between the media schedule and the creative approaches. Because the selection of media and the design of advertisements would be worked out concurrently, necessary coordination could be established while the plans were in preparation so that the ads developed would be suited to the media selected.

COORDINATION WITH OTHER FUNCTIONS. Preparation of the advertising plan provides the advertising manager with a tool for coordination of advertising activities with other marketing functions. Coordination is best achieved through consultation with other marketing departments as the planning process proceeds. Consultation during the advertising planning process can be used to obtain agreement between advertising and other marketing areas on the problems facing the product and on the objectives of the product's advertising and marketing programs. Then communication and agreement can be sought again at the final stage when the programs to achieve the objectives are detailed.

## The Plan as an Implementation Tool

After the planning process is completed, the resulting plan document has continuing value. One way in which it serves is to assist the advertising manager and others to implement or carry out the advertising programs.

BASIS FOR APPROVAL.   The finished advertising plan serves as a basis for approval. The plan represents the advertising manager's proposal or recommendation for the advertising program that should be undertaken. This is usually forwarded to the senior marketing manager for approval and, in turn, may be forwarded to still higher levels for approval.

The importance and usefulness of the advertising plan in this approval process lies in the fact that it contains not only complete details on what advertising action is planned, but also the facts and analyses that lie behind the recommendations. Thus, the approving officer can evaluate whether or not the recommendations are based on fact and careful, thorough analysis. Examination of the finished advertising plan also permits evaluation of the soundness of the objectives set for the product and the programs' capability of reaching the objectives.

BASIS FOR DELEGATION.   The advertising plan is an ideal medium by which to delegate implementation to subordinates, other departments, and the advertising agency. Although the advertising manager is responsible for directing implementation of the advertising plan, in practice much of the actual work of carrying out the plan will be delegated to others.

Some of the implementation may be delegated to a subordinate, such as an assistant advertising manager, both for training and to free the advertising manager for other responsibilities. The advertising plan serves as a detailed set of instructions for the assistant to follow. By using the plan, the advertising manager can practice **management by exception.** This means *management by exception* that the assistant is encouraged to implement the written plan without constantly checking back with a superior unless some unforeseen circumstance requires an exception to the plan or a result turns out to be different from the one expected.

Much of the implementation of the advertising plan is typically delegated to advertising specialists in other departments of the company or entirely outside the company. For example, the purchase of the media time and space is frequently delegated to media buying experts in an advertising agency. Here again the advertising plan plays a vital role. The plan will contain an explanation of what is to be purchased and background information on the requirements of the media program. By providing the media buyer with a copy of the plan, the advertising manager provides detailed instructions for implementation plus background information to aid the buyer's judgment in making purchasing decisions.

## The Plan as a Control Tool

Because advertising affects the entire marketing effort of the company, it is essential that the advertising manager exercise firm control over the advertising so that any shortcomings can be promptly corrected. The advertising plan serves the advertising manager in fulfilling this control responsibility by providing a source of control standards.

Specific performance standards can be established by the plan for each of the advertising programs. For example, the plan will contain a budget listing anticipated dollar expenditures for advertising over the coming period. Actual expenditures can be checked periodically against the budget to detect over- or under-expenditure. Purchases of advertising media such as television can also be controlled by setting standards specifying the number of people who are to be reached by the media purchased. Research services can then be used to measure the number of people who actually have been exposed to the media to see if the media were able to achieve the standard. The advertisements or creative materials themselves can also be controlled by incorporating into the plan certain scores to be achieved on specified copy tests. The prepared advertisements can be tested both before and during actual use to determine whether they meet attention-getting, believability, and memorability standards.

Advertising planning is not a one-time event, but a continuous process of planning, evaluating, and replanning. As a period draws to a close and a new plan must be prepared, the advertising manager uses the current plan as a starting point for the next plan. By comparing the projected accomplishments of the closing period with the actual accomplishments of the period, the advertising manager determines what remains to be done. The difference between planned and actual accomplishments reveals some of the problems which advertising must attack through the next advertising plan.

## Advertising Plans and the Total Planning Process

Planning is a way of life in modern business organizations — in advertising departments and throughout companies. As the discussion of the advertising plan proceeds through this book, it is well to keep in mind what other, non-advertising, plans are probably being developed and the relationship of these plans to the advertising plan itself.

## Types of Business Plans

In a company with a well-developed planning program, there are likely to be marketing plans, departmental plans, and corporate plans as well as various advertising plans.

ADVERTISING PLANS. In many firms there will be several different advertising plans at any one time. If a company has more than one advertised product, there will usually be a separate advertising plan for each product. Every product faces different problems and opportunities and thus analysis and planning need to focus on one product at a time rather than try to combine different product plans into a single plan. For example, a manufacturer that markets automobiles, trucks, and buses would find that each of these products has different consumers, different competitors, and different product characteristics. This means that each product has different advertising needs and, consequently, requires a separate advertising plan.

An exception to this practice of separate advertising plans for individual products would be acceptable if two or more products were so closely related that they faced identical markets. This situation most frequently occurs when a firm markets a line of products—a series of similar products varying in such characteristics as package size, flavor, or accessories. For example, a line of men's suits may be offered in a variety of patterns and materials. Despite this variety, the line of suits would likely have common customers and common competitors. Thus a single advertising plan for the entire line would be appropriate.

Another exception to the use of separate advertising plans for each product is a firm's use of corporate advertising that benefits several products. General Motors, for example, has conducted customer information advertising that explains automobile recall campaigns to consumers. An example of one of their advertisements is shown in Exhibit 4-1. Clearly an advertising effort of this type should be the subject of a single advertising plan even though several products are involved. This type of corporate advertising campaign should supplement, not substitute for, individual advertising plans for each product.

MARKETING PLANS. Another type of plan, and the one to which the advertising plan is most closely related, is the marketing plan. Although practice varies widely, a **marketing plan** is also usually prepared for each product, but its scope is wider than that of an advertising plan. Usually, the marketing plan includes programs for advertising, personal selling, research and product development, merchandising (pricing, packaging, sales promotion), and, perhaps, public relations. In many cases, the marketing plan is simply the combined plans from each of the functional marketing areas.

*marketing plan*

To assure that all the marketing areas will be coordinated in improving the position of the product, each of the individual functional plans making up one product's marketing plan should be derived from a single examination of the problems and opportunities facing that product. A logical approach to this examination is to first conduct an analysis of the product's situation, then to get agreement on the current status of the product among all functional marketing areas, and finally to ask each area to proceed with development of plans. Frequently the advertising manager is responsible for a major portion of this situational analysis.

**EXHIBIT 4-1**     An example of General Motors' corporate advertising that benefits several products.

**CUSTOMER INFORMATION FROM GENERAL MOTORS**

# RECALLS: WHY THEY OCCUR. HOW TO ANSWER ONE ON YOUR CAR.

When General Motors orders a recall, we believe we are providing an important service to our customers and showing again how GM stands behind its products.

Every car we manufacture has 14,000 or so parts which must be interchangeable. Although the reliability of parts in GM cars rivals that of the parts we supply for lunar rockets or for commercial jets, problems sometimes occur and probably always will.

You can't repeal the law of probability. Somewhere a machine tool may wear unexpectedly fast, or a material may have an invisible contamination. **General Motors tests its vehicles** for millions of the dirtiest, dustiest, roughest, coldest, hottest miles imaginable. We even put our newly developed vehicles and parts into thousands of taxis and other fleets in dozens of locations all over North America. The goal: to put on real-life mileage fast. But even this is not the same as billions of miles driven by customers through every possible road, climate and maintenance condition.

Then the law of probability comes into play, especially since we produce millions more vehicles for North America than any other manufacturer. Although all car and truck manufacturers—both foreign and domestic—have recalls, we're a little more noticeable because of our numbers.

If you receive a recall notice on your car, you may feel like taking a gamble and ignoring it. Please don't. Answer it promptly. Follow the instructions in the letter. Recalls are initiated to protect your safety or to keep your car in good running order.

**We publicize recalls** so car owners will be aware of them. By federal regulation, General Motors has to notify owners by letter and report to the government on the progress of a recall for 18 months. **We go beyond the federal requirements. GM dealers send follow-up letters to owners if no response is received the first time.** In addition, GM dealers can use our CRIS (Computerized Recall Identification System) to tell you instantly of any recall work necessary on a vehicle recalled during the last 7 years. This is important to know when buying a used car. Ask any GM dealer for this information.

**If you hear on television or radio of a recall which you think applies to your car, please follow these steps for your convenience.**
—First, wait until you receive a letter from us saying your car has been recalled. It may take some time before mailing lists can be compiled and parts can be distributed to the dealers.
—Then call your dealer and give him the recall campaign number supplied in the letter. He will arrange an appointment to have the repairs made. This could save you time and could help the dealer to schedule his busy service department.

**If you have read or heard in the media about a recall campaign, but don't receive a letter within a month,** ask your dealer to check the dealer bulletin or CRIS to see if your vehicle is affected. Give the dealer your vehicle identification number, which you'll find on your car's title, registration or warranty folder. It can also be found on the instrument panel just inside the windshield on the driver's side.

There are cases in which the auto manufacturers and the government differ over the seriousness of a problem. And these instances sometimes receive a great deal of publicity. But such situations are the exception.

**Almost all of our recalls are voluntarily started by General Motors before the government is involved.**

If your car needs to be recalled for any reason, please don't ignore the notice. Taking care of those problems in your car is good for you and good for us.

*This advertisement is part of our continuing effort to give customers useful information about their cars and trucks and the company that builds them.*

Chevrolet • Pontiac
Oldsmobile • Buick
Cadillac • GMC Truck

DEPARTMENTAL PLANS. In some companies the various marketing plans for each product are consolidated to form a **marketing department plan.** This plan may be consolidated with plans for other functional areas to form the company's total operating plan. Only the major goals, programs, and expectations are extracted from the individual plans, frequently in quantitative form. A common approach, for example, is to consolidate capital requirements together with revenue and expense targets for each product. This facilitates financial planning and control and helps top management determine if the combined plans for various products add up to a satisfactory sales, profit, and capital position for the company.

*marketing department plan*

CORPORATE PLANS. Looking at the total company, there is one additional plan to which the advertising plan should be related. Increasingly, companies are involved in corporate or strategic planning programs. Practice varies from company to company, but a frequent starting point in this overall company planning process is the definition of a corporate strategy. This is derived through careful analysis of the company's overall strengths and weaknesses and an analysis of the opportunities available in the marketplace. A **corporate strategy** results from a careful matching of a firm's strengths with market opportunities in order to define the businesses in which the firm will compete.

*corporate strategy*

Corporate strategy provides overall direction to the firm and objectives are formulated from it. These objectives are specific tasks that the company must accomplish if it is to compete effectively in the markets defined by the strategy. The objectives are communicated down the organizational hierarchy to appropriate functional departments. They serve as guides to insure that plans for individual products will contribute to the corporation's overall goals.

## The Planning Sequence

The relationship among these plans can best be understood if planning is viewed as a continuous process. Each of the plans that has been described is the product of an interrelated sequence of planning activities.

Corporate planning takes place at the highest level of the firm. Planning at this level considers the total company and takes a long-range point of view, probably five years or more. The process begins with evaluation of the total environment facing the firm and an analysis of the strengths and weaknesses of the firm. This leads to the determination of corporate strategy, followed by definition of corporate objectives. The results of this total process are consolidated into the corporate strategic plan which provides general guidance in the formulation of operating plans. This process is shown in Part A of Exhibit 4-2 on page 80.

Formulation of operating plans takes place at the departmental level and ordinarily encompasses a shorter time span, usually one year. Corporate strategy and objectives are used as general guidelines, but operating

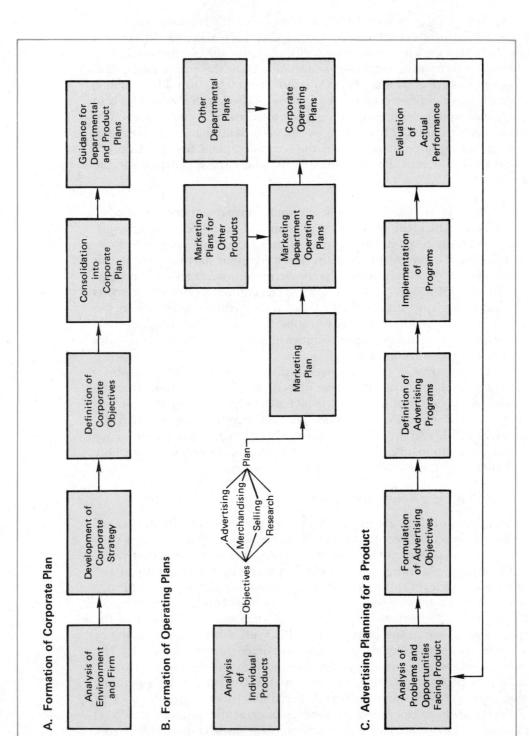

EXHIBIT 4-2    Business planning processes.

plans take a product-by-product approach rather than a total company approach. As shown in Part B of Exhibit 4-2, the process begins with analysis of the problems facing each individual product. This leads to specific objectives for each product which can then be assigned to each of the functional marketing areas. A plan to reach assigned objectives is then prepared by each marketing area (such as the sales department or the advertising department). The plans of each of these areas are consolidated to form the marketing plan for a product. Marketing plans for various products are combined to form marketing department operating plans, and plans from all of a company's departments are consolidated to form **corporate operating plans.**

*corporate operating plan*

Advertising planning on the level of the individual product should also be viewed as a continuing process. This planning process is shown diagrammatically in Part C of Exhibit 4-2 on page 80. The process begins with analysis of the problems and opportunities facing the product. Objectives for the product are then set, and from these objectives the advertising programs are defined. With the plan completed, it is then implemented. As the planning period nears an end, the success of the advertising programs is analyzed as a part of the product analysis for the next year's plan. The planning process thus begins again — new analysis, revised objectives, and new advertising programs.

## Time Span of the Advertising Plan

The advertising manager must select a time period which the advertising plan will cover. The most widely used practice is to prepare plans on a one-year basis, though this is not necessarily the most desirable practice. Two considerations that influence the length of the plan period are the length of other operating plans and the length of advertising commitments.

Many companies establish standard planning periods to insure that all product and departmental plans are on the same time basis. This makes it possible to consolidate the plans as shown in Part B of Exhibit 4-2.

If the advertising plan is to be consolidated with other plans, the usual one-year period will probably be used. However, there are occasions when the advertising plan should extend to longer time periods. If the advertiser makes a commitment to a program that will last more than a year, then the implications of that commitment should be considered over its full term.

Both creative and media programs may well represent commitments for more than one year. For example, advertisers frequently contract with celebrities who endorse a product in its advertising. Continued use of such personalities (Bob Hope's relationship with Texaco and Nancy Walker's with Bounty, for example) makes the association increasingly valuable and consequently the advertiser attempts to protect the built-up value with a long-term contract. This commitment has budgetary, creative, and media implications that are likely to extend beyond one year and the advertiser should explore these implications even if they do extend beyond the normal planning period.

## Content of the Advertising Plan

It was stated earlier that an advertising plan must be written and must be comprehensive. The content and organization of the plan will now be considered. Advertising plans vary greatly because of product needs, the style of the writer of the plan, and the capacity of the audience. Despite this, minimum content requirements can be specified and a pattern of organization suggested.

### Elements of an Advertising Plan

A complete advertising plan must contain four interrelated elements. They are considered in the order in which they would ordinarily be developed in preparing a plan.

ANALYSIS OF PROBLEMS AND OPPORTUNITIES. The advertising plan should logically begin with an analysis of the situation facing the product. This analysis must include both a look at the product itself and a study of the external environment it faces, including the competition, the structure of the market for the product, and the characteristics of prospective consumers. The analysis must be more than a recitation of facts in these areas. The facts must be analyzed in order to develop a specific list of problems and opportunities facing the product — problems which advertising must attack and opportunities which advertising must seize.

DEFINITION OF OBJECTIVES. The advertising plan must next specify objectives that will lead to solution of the problems and realization of the opportunities facing the product. The objectives are used to set direction for the advertising programs.

*product positioning*

*problem-solving objective*

Two types of objectives can usefully be defined. One type of objective is **product positioning.** It provides overall direction for the product by defining the particular niche in the market toward which the product will be aimed. The other type is the **problem-solving objective.** It specifies the tasks required to solve the problems facing the product.

PROGRAMS OF ACTION. The third essential element of the plan is the specification of programs for future action. The programs of action are guided by the objectives and define the steps that will be taken to meet the objectives. The determination of the advertising budget, selection of advertising media, and determination of the advertising message are considered in this section of the advertising plan.

CONTROL AND EVALUATION. The fourth element in an advertising plan, and one that cannot be too heavily stressed, is a program of control and evaluation of the advertising effort. There are two important areas in which control must be exerted. First, the effectiveness of the advertising programs in reaching their goals must be monitored; thus, specific standards of acceptable performance must be stated in the plan. One of the standards of performance frequently used is the advertising budget, which represents the allowable level of spending. Standards for media programs are often set in terms of the target number of prospects to be contacted by the media selected.

The plan must also indicate how actual performance is to be measured so that comparisons can be made with the standards. In the case of budget control, performance would be measured by recording actual expenditures as they occurred. In the case of the media program, achievement of standards is often measured through use of rating services and audience studies that give the number and characteristics of people reached by the advertising.

The second area of the advertising program that requires control is the legality and propriety of the advertising effort. Again, the advertiser must establish standards — legal standards from a study of applicable laws and standards of good taste based on management's sense of propriety. Proposed advertising must then be measured or evaluated, preferably before commitments are made, to see that it conforms to these standards.

## Organization of the Advertising Plan

The organization of an advertising plan should be logical and clear, suited to its audience, and useful and convenient to those who work with it.

One suggested organizational structure for an advertising plan is shown in Exhibit 4-3. It arranges the sections of the plan in the sequence in which they should be developed, moving from an analysis of past performance, to a statement of current problems and opportunities, and finally to objectives and programs for the future.

The advertising plan outline shown in Exhibit 4-3 is one that has been used extensively in actual practice. While it is not the only organization possible, it is a structure that works. Thus, it provides a useful starting place for the advertising manager in organizing the advertising plan.

The plan structure in Exhibit 4-3 also provides the basis for the organization of Parts 2-4 of this book. After the decision-making frameworks are established in Part 1, the balance of the book will concentrate on the process of preparing and implementing an advertising plan. This focus of attention is appropriate because the advertising plan is central to the responsibility of the advertising manager. It is the basis for the most important decisions, it defines goals, it outlines the work that will be implemented throughout the year, and it is the basis for controlling advertising programs and thus advertising effectiveness.

EXHIBIT 4-3          Suggested organization of an advertising plan.

---

### I. Analysis to Define Problems and Opportunities
    A. Consumer analysis
        1. Definition of consumer needs and motives
        2. Determination of consumer characteristics
    B. Product analysis
        1. Determination of product characteristics
        2. Analysis of marketing history of the product
    C. Market analysis
        1. Sales analysis
        2. Analysis of competitive sales
        3. Analysis of environmental influences

### II. Positioning the Product and Setting Advertising Objectives
    A. Positioning the product
    B. Advertising objectives

### III. Programs for Reaching Objectives
    A. Budget program—setting the advertising budget
    B. Media program—selecting the media
    C. Creative program—determining the advertising message
    D. Other programs—sales promotion, new products, etc.

### IV. Control and Evaluation of the Advertising Program
    A. Evaluation of advertising effectiveness
    B. Evaluation of legal and social acceptability

---

## CHAPTER SUMMARY

An advertising plan is a comprehensive, data based, written document that establishes advertising objectives and specifies programs that will be used to achieve the objectives. Its preparation is a fundamental responsibility of the advertising manager, although parts of the work may be delegated to subordinates or specialists in the company or in an advertising agency. The advertising plan provides a framework for analyzing the problems facing the product and the advertising program. The advertising plan serves also as a set of specific directions to those charged with carrying out the advertising program. Finally, the advertising plan contains standards which the advertising is to meet and against which actual performance can be compared. In an organization that has a company-wide planning process, the advertising plan is just one of many plans in the planning hierarchy. The advertising manager is responsible for integrating the advertising plan into the company's total planning process.

The organization and style of an advertising plan should be determined by the needs of the organization. However, to be complete, it must contain four elements: (1) an analysis of the problems and opportunities facing the product to be advertised, (2) a definition of the objectives that the advertising must achieve to meet the problems and opportunities, (3) programs of action that will lead to achieving the objectives, and (4) a program for controlling and evaluating the advertising program as it progresses.

---

*KEY TERMS*

Management by exception
Marketing plan
Marketing department plan
Corporate strategy

Corporate operating plan
Product positioning
Problem-solving objective

---

*QUESTIONS FOR DISCUSSION*

1. This chapter specifies that a primary responsibility of the advertising manager is to prepare the advertising plan. However, the content and uses of the advertising plan imply a number of additional responsibilities. What are the additional responsibilities that might appear in the position description of an advertising manager?

2. Some advertising managers delegate responsibility for preparation of the entire advertising plan to the company's advertising agency. This does not, however, relieve the advertising manager from ultimate responsibility for the quality of the plan. Suggest steps that the advertising manager might take to maintain control over the agency's planning efforts.

3. Suppose instead of delegating to an agency the responsibility for the entire advertising plan, the advertising manager asks only that they prepare the creative program — the actual advertisements to be used in the coming year. What information should the advertising manager provide to the advertising agency to enable them to carry out this assignment?

4. In preparing an advertising plan, the advertising manager frequently finds it necessary to consult people in other departments for information. For each of the following information needs, whom might the advertising manager consult?

   a. The reaction of retailers carrying the product to last year's advertising campaign.
   b. Interpretation of recent Federal Trade Commission rulings on permissible practices in consumer contests.
   c. Factory sales of the product by package size; retail sales of the product by package size.
   d. Improvements to the product that might be expected in the coming year.

5. Suppose an advertising manager were responsible for the advertising for 25 diverse products and had five assistant advertising managers. How might the use of advertising plans help the advertising manager handle this very complex managerial job?

6. One type of advertising plan that usually covers a time period substantially longer than one year (often three to five years) is the plan for a new product. Why would this longer-term plan be desirable for a new product?

7. Some advertising managers prepare an advertising plan in two separate parts. Part one contains the analysis of problems and opportunities plus the advertising objectives. This part is presented to management for approval before part two, which contains the advertising programs, is prepared. What advantage do you see in this approach?

*PROBLEM*

Recently Domino Sugar was analyzing the disappointing first two years' sales results of its Domino Liquid Brown Sugar.[1] The new product's sales had fallen far short of the projected 12 percent of the $80 million market despite over $1 million in advertising and good national distribution.

Domino used a secret process to liquify brown sugar, resulting in a concentrated product only half as much of which was needed for cooking and baking as compared to regular brown sugar. The product, which was the only one of its type on the market, was advertised as a cooking ingredient to be used in place of granulated brown sugar. Because it was in liquid form, the product formed no lumps and was easy to blend in with other ingredients. Because only half as much was needed, the liquid product was less expensive.

Opinions in the company varied as to why the product was not successful. One executive noted that shortly after introduction the price of regular brown sugar dropped by half. Another speculated that home bakers are traditionally conservative and tend to reject new products. However, analysis of sales indicated that sales of the product had recently picked up in some traditionally heavy-use brown-sugar markets, including the Great Lakes and New England regions. Another thought advanced was that perhaps lumps just were not that much of a problem to home bakers.

The price of regular brown sugar has recently begun to rise again and with that the company is considering restaging the brand. Placing yourself in the position of the advertising manager preparing the background section of the advertising plan for Liquid Brown Sugar, what problems and opportunities can you define that face the product?

---

[1]This problem is based on Leah Rozen, "What Happened to Liquid Sugar?" *Advertising Age* (May 26, 1980), pp. 3, 66.

# CHAPTER 5

## The Role of Advertising in the Consumer Decision Process

### LEARNING OBJECTIVES

In studying this chapter you will learn:

- The three key variables in the consumer decision process.

- The role of advertising in consumer behavior.

- The major steps in the consumer decision process.

- The various uses of the consumer decision model.

Throughout most of this book, advertising will be viewed through the eyes of the advertising manager. To make effective decisions, the advertising manager must be able to see advertising from the point of view of the consumer.

In this chapter a conceptual scheme will be presented that is designed to allow us to look at advertising through the consumer's eyes and to show us how it enters into the purchase decision process. Perceiving the consumer's point of view helps predict the consumer's response to advertising.

## Key Variables in the Consumer Decision Process

An understanding of consumer purchasing behavior can be gained by looking first at three major variables in the purchase decision: (1) the nature of consumer needs, (2) the role played by products, and (3) the role of advertising in the purchase decision.

### Nature of Consumer Needs

Just as advertisers set objectives to guide advertising programs, so too do consumers have objectives that they attempt to satisfy through the purchase of a product or service. We shall term these objectives "needs."

NEEDS, GOALS, AND PROBLEMS. The total "package" of needs that influences consumer shopping behavior and the use of the advertising is highly complex. Needs vary in their depth, origins, and importance.

*underlying needs*

The deepest lying and most permanent category of needs we shall call **underlying needs.** Protection from a hostile environment (warmth, shelter) is an example of an underlying need. Underlying needs are inborn rather than learned and they are highly resistant to change.

*consumer goals*

In an effort to satisfy these underlying needs, consumers establish a second level of needs called **consumer goals.** Consumer goals are tangible, achievable targets that the consumer sets up as steps to fulfillment of underlying needs. For example, in order to satisfy the underlying need for protection from the elements, an individual might set the goal of becoming a homeowner. For any particular underlying need, the individual may set a series of goals. The goals that are seen by an individual to be need-satisfying are greatly influenced by social and cultural forces.

*consumer problems*

Finally, a third level of needs can be thought of as the **consumer problems** or obstacles that the consumer faces and must overcome if goals are to be achieved. Continuing the previous example, if the individual wishes to become a homeowner, it may be necessary to build a savings account or acquire home-building skills that would help to acquire a home. It is at the problem level that the consumer utilizes products. In this example, woodworking tools might serve to repair or construct the home.

Underlying needs, goals, and problems make up the total need structure of the individual consumer. As is common among advertising practitioners, for convenience we shall frequently refer to this complex need

*consumer needs*

structure simply as **consumer needs.**

CONSUMER MOTIVATION. The behavior of consumers is motivated or activated by needs, goals, and problems. Consumers come to the marketplace searching for products that will fulfill their needs and goals and will help to solve their problems.

Looked at in this way, it can be seen that the behavior of consumers in purchasing products is not random or haphazard, but purposeful activity designed to satisfy needs. Marketers and others sometimes mistakenly view patterns of consumer behavior and conclude that consumers are confused, inconsistent, and irrational. What this too often means is not that the consumer is inconsistent, but that the observer has misjudged the need the consumer is trying to satisfy.

For example, consumerists have for years argued that it was irrational for consumers to purchase advertised brands of aspirin when the same chemical compound was available at a lower price in unadvertised private labels. Is this a case of consumer irrationality or a case of not understanding consumer needs? If the most important goal of a consumer in purchasing aspirin is to be sure that the product provides reliable, top quality medication, is it not entirely rational to buy an advertised brand in which the consumer has confidence rather than to buy a price brand to save a few pennies at the perceived risk of nonfulfillment of the primary goal?

When consumer behavior does not conform to the pattern expected by the advertiser, a more helpful approach is to assume that the consumer's behavior is purposeful and then attempt to understand what need is motivating the behavior.

CATEGORIES OF CONSUMER NEEDS.  Since consumer needs are a major factor influencing consumer purchase behavior, it is important for the advertiser to know what kinds of needs consumers are likely to have. Considerable work has been done in the behavioral sciences in an attempt to understand and categorize the basic needs that motivate people. Various behavioral schools have uncovered and explored different basic need categories, three of which are of great interest to advertisers: (1) utilitarian needs, (2) social needs, and (3) psychological needs.

*Utilitarian Needs.* Perhaps the most common, most prosaic, and most fundamental class of needs that a person has is a need to cope with the surrounding environment. People live in a hostile, competitive world and many of their efforts are devoted simply to staying alive, staying healthy, and keeping comfortable. This category of practical needs for getting along in the physical world will be termed **utilitarian needs.**

*utilitarian needs*

There are a number of needs that might be categorized as utilitarian; for example, the need for shelter, the need for nourishment, and the need for security. In seeking to satisfy these needs, consumers establish tangible goals and experience various practical problems, but eventually these needs translate, for example, into demand for a house to meet the shelter need, for vegetables to meet the need for nourishment, and for a watchdog for security.

The idea that people are motivated by utilitarian needs is basic to two different schools of individual behavior. One of these is the *Gestalt theory of psychology* that sees people as rational, problem-solving creatures. The Gestalt school includes among this group of needs people's urge not only to cope with the world around them, but also a need to know and understand the nature of their environment. Another school of thought to which utilitarian needs are central is the demand theory of economics. The economist sees people striving to allocate their limited resources among available goods and services. The rational economic person is presumed to act so as to solve practical problems in the environment and to maximize physical well-being.

*Social Needs.* In addition to getting along with the physical world, a person also has social needs. People feel the need to be accepted by other people and by groups of people. They want to feel that they belong and get along with others.

**Social needs,** like utilitarian ones, lead individuals to set specific goals that will result in acceptance by others. These goals, in turn, translate into demands for products that will help the individual to achieve acceptance by others. For example, the selection of clothing styles by young people probably reflects, in great measure, a desire to conform to group dress standards and thus promote group acceptance. Social groups set standards for

*social needs*

acceptable behavior and acceptable products. If an individual desires to be accepted by a group, that individual is likely to conform to group standards.

*Psychological Needs.*  The third category of needs is concerned with people's efforts to develop and project themselves as individuals. This category is called **psychological needs.** The concept of psychological needs has been most fully developed by the clinical psychologists. From this source, marketers have borrowed such concepts as the self-image and ego defense. People establish in their minds an idealized picture of the type of person they want to be — their self-images. They attempt to behave in ways that are consistent with their individual self-images and that enhance their self-esteem. By their behavior, individuals attempt to project or communicate their self-images to other people. At the same time, people defend themselves against any real or imagined attack by others that would lessen their self-esteem or the individual images that they project to others. This is termed ego defense.

*psychological needs*

One form of behavior by which people attempt to project their individual self-images is the purchase and ownership of products. In other words, people buy products not just for what they do, but also for what they say about the purchaser. The choice of automobile is believed to be greatly influenced by psychological needs. The purchase of a luxury car expresses the buyer's wealth, status, and self-importance. Purchasing economy sedans, by contrast, enables consumers to project themselves as careful, frugal, sensible people. Although interpretations by researchers vary, other types of automobiles permit expression of other self-images. High performance cars connote a "swinger" whereas a pickup truck means "honest worker."

DOMINANCE OF NEEDS.  Three categories of needs have been described — utilitarian, social, and psychological — which raise two questions. Is consumer behavior dominated by one of these categories of needs or do all three influence behavior? If all three influence consumer behavior, which one is dominant?

*Single vs. Multiple Needs.*  Through many years of development, each different category of needs was the basis for an alternate explanation of behavior. Thus the need categories were seen as competitive. Marketers, when they borrowed knowledge from the behavioral scientists, tended to focus on one single school of thought and hence tended to view consumers as dominated by one of these classes of needs. As a result, marketers argued about people's basic needs — were consumers emotional or rational, were they influenced by internal drives or by social influences?

In later years several behavioral scientists advanced the notion that the three needs categories are not competitive, but represent the range or mix of needs found in individuals.[1] These theorists, in other words, suggested

---

[1] I. Sarnoff and D. Katz, "The Motivational Bases of Attitude Change," *Journal of Abnormal and Social Psychology,* Vol. 49 (January, 1954), pp. 115–124; D. Katz, "The Functional Approach to the Study of Attitudes," *Public Opinion Quarterly,* Vol. 24 (Summer, 1960),

that people are not dominated by a single type of need, but that all three categories of needs motivate their behavior.

*Salience of Needs.* If people are actually motivated at one time or another by needs in all three categories, which group of needs is most important? The answer seems to be that the relative importance or salience of different needs varies from time to time, from person to person, and from situation to situation.

The salience of a particular need is influenced by the degree to which it is already fulfilled. To a starving person, the need for nourishment takes precedence over all other needs. The well-fed person, by contrast, finds that the nourishment need recedes, and another need, perhaps a social acceptance need, takes its place as the more salient need. Some theorists have suggested that there is a natural hierarchy of needs—that people first strive to satisfy their more utilitarian needs and with these met they are able to concern themselves with the higher social and psychological needs.[2]

Need salience will also vary from person to person. For example, people have different levels of aspiration so that what is required to fulfill their needs will vary. To one person self-fulfillment might mean being president of a large corporation; to another the goal might be to run one's own small business. Need salience also depends upon the individual's situation. Dormant needs may come to the forefront when an opportunity for satisfaction presents itself. Advertising sometimes works in this way. While it does not create consumer needs, it sometimes points out an opportunity to satisfy a need which will, in turn, raise the potency of that need. A special discount sale advertisement, for example, may serve to trigger or raise the salience of a consumer's need to economize.

## The Role Played by Products

Consumer needs are the motivating force that bring consumers to the marketplace. Products represent the other end of the market equation. They are the need-satisfying solutions offered by marketers.

PRODUCTS ARE MEANS, NOT ENDS. Products offered by marketers do not represent a need for which the consumer is striving. Rather, products represent means to satisfy the need. Consumers buy products because of the need-satisfying benefits that they provide.

This distinction between viewing products as means rather than as ends in themselves has an important implication for marketers. It is a mistake for marketers to view their products (or their competitors' products)

---

pp. 163–204; Milton Rokeach, *The Open and Closed Mind* (New York: Basic Books, Inc., 1960), pp. 64–66; Herbert C. Kelman, "Processes of Opinion Change," *Public Opinion Quarterly*, Vol. 25 (Spring, 1961), pp. 57–58; Raymond A. Bauer, "The Obstinate Audience: The Influence Process from the Point of View of Social Communication," *American Psychologist*, Vol. 19 (May, 1964), pp. 319–328.

[2] A. H. Maslow, "A Theory of Human Motivation," *Psychological Review*, Vol. 50 (1943), pp. 370–396.

only in physical terms. A restaurant, for example, is much more than a building, some fixtures, and a menu. Consumer reaction to a product is much more understandable if the marketer views the product as the consumer does — as a potential means to satisfying a need. If, for example, a restaurant is sought by consumers as a means for satisfying a social interaction need, they may select a restaurant by its patrons rather than on the basis of its menu or the comfort of its seats. The perceptive restauranteur would try to understand and influence consumer reaction through the social environment dimension of the restaurant rather than through changing the menu or the prices.

PRODUCTS SERVE MULTIPLE NEEDS. The marketer seeking to determine the underlying need served by a product will frequently find that the product serves multiple needs, even for the same person. For example, the hostess who serves dinner guests filet mignon and a fine French wine is undoubtedly contributing to the fulfillment of some utilitarian need — maintenance of health and strength or satisfaction of appetite. But undoubtedly the particular choice of menu was also designed to enhance her social standing with the guests. The same point might be made for a choice of automobile, clothing, or dwelling. Each of these products would seem to satisfy a utilitarian need, but in addition they are used as means of self-expression and social acceptance.

With the increasing affluence of consumers in our society, there appears to be an increasing expectation on the part of consumers that products should serve multiple needs. Affluent consumers still have to satisfy utilitarian needs — they need nourishment, shelter, and the protection of clothing. But with increased economic well-being, the style or the means of satisfying these needs becomes an important means of satisfying social and psychological needs. Thus, the decision to purchase clothing may be stimulated by a utilitarian need, but it is likely that the style of clothing chosen will be influenced by a need for self-expression or by conformity to the social dress standards of a peer group.

Just as consumers use products to serve multiple needs, so too will we find that products have multiple attributes. One of the tasks confronting the advertiser is to understand the multiple needs of the consumer and the relative priorities of those needs and to be sure that the various attributes of the product coincide with them.

## The Role of Advertising

In attempting to examine the purchase decision process through the consumer's eyes, two important variables — consumer needs and products — have been examined. A third critical variable is *advertising*, the function of which is to serve as a link between the advertiser's product and the consumer's need.

CONSUMERS AS INFORMATION SEEKERS. When consumers come into

the marketplace seeking to satisfy needs, they are normally faced with a considerable number of product alternatives from which to choose. The purchasing decision facing consumers is one of finding a satisfactory "match" between the needs they are trying to satisfy and products that offer the most satisfactory sets of benefits for satisfying those needs. This matching process is carried out by gathering and processing information about alternative products and the satisfactions that they offer.

It is important to note that the consumer's role in gathering and processing information is an active one, not a passive one. Consumers seeking to satisfy a need do not wait passively for product information to reach them. Instead they actively search for it.

CONSUMER INFORMATION SCREENING.    In the course of their efforts to satisfy needs, consumers are exposed to a great mass of information. Some of this information is the result of deliberate information-seeking by consumers, and at the same time, consumers are exposed to much of it without any particular effort on their part. A consumer preparing to shop for new clothing may search the morning newspaper for apparel advertisements that will provide guidance in forming a shopping itinerary. In the course of reading the newspaper, however, that consumer will also be exposed to a variety of advertisements for groceries, automobiles, and other products which the consumer does not seek at the moment. On the same morning, the shopper might be exposed to a variety of radio commericals, outdoor signs, and advertisements within the stores themselves. Thus consumers often receive far more information than they can effectively use in their search for a product.

Behavioral scientists have demonstrated that individuals are very adept at screening out unwanted information. There is less agreement, however, on the criteria by which individuals screen the information to which they are exposed. Out of this mass of information, how do they decide which to accept and which not to accept?

Among the screening criteria that have been suggested is one that has both research substantiation and is in accord with the observations of many advertising practitioners.[3] This suggestion is that consumers select information in terms of its usefulness. Information is useful if it presents a means to satisfy a need that a consumer has. Information is not useful if it is irrelevant to a current or anticipated need. However, it is also true that one of the problems faced by the advertiser is that information derived from advertisments may be considered irrelevant by consumers because advertisements are a biased source.[4] Consequently, what this **information usefulness concept** means to the advertiser is that if advertising is to be

*information usefulness concept*

---

[3]For a review of evidence relating to the usefulness criterion see David O. Sears and Jonathan L. Freedman, "Selective Exposure to Information: A Critical Review," *Public Opinion Quarterly*, Vol. 31 (Summer, 1967), pp. 194–213.

[4]Robert E. Smith and William R. Swinyard, "Information Response Models: An Integrated Approach," *Journal of Marketing* (Winter, 1982), pp. 81–93.

accepted by consumers, it must contain information that is both relevant and credible. To create advertising that is relevant, the advertiser must have an understanding of consumer needs. To create advertising that is credible, the advertiser must develop and present verifiable information about the benefits offered by the product.

*marketing concept*

The information usefulness concept is parallel to the marketing concept, a proposition that has wide acceptance among marketing theorists and practitioners. The **marketing concept** holds that to be successful in the marketplace, producers must design products to meet consumer needs rather than try to reshape consumer needs to fit existing products.

A final question should be raised concerning the information screening process. What happens to information that is not accepted by consumers? How do they avoid it? One device that consumers use is to avoid exposure to information not likely to be useful to them by avoiding the source of that information. People not engaged in business are unlikely to read *Business Week* and people disinterested in home improvement are likely to avoid *Better Homes and Gardens*. This selective pattern of exposure avoids considerable irrelevant information. There is, of course, still a great deal of irrelevant information to which consumers are exposed. Much of this is not perceived by the consumer, or it "goes in one ear and out the other." Information that is perceived but proves irrelevant is more quickly forgotten than is relevant information. Finally, there is some evidence that information that is not useful, in the sense that it conflicts with existing beliefs or with planned action, may be disbelieved, downgraded in importance, or even distorted to fit existing beliefs.

SOURCES OF CONSUMER SHOPPING INFORMATION. When consumers seek information about products, they can utilize stored information or seek new information. Stored information is often available because consumers frequently accept and retain information that, although not useful for a current need, is seen as potentially useful in the future.

*word-of-mouth communication*

If a need arises for which the stored information is insufficient, the consumer becomes active in seeking further sources of information. New information may be obtained from commercial sources or from private sources. Private sources include information gained from family, friends, or expert acquaintances. This information, usually oral, is termed **word-of-mouth communication.** Another private source is one's own past experience with products and their satisfaction of needs. Private sources of information are particularly valued by consumers because they are viewed as objective.

Commercial sources also provide new information. From the advertising manager's point of view, the most important commercial source is advertising, although consumers use other commercial sources as well. Salespeople are an important commercial information source, as is publicity. The advertising manager is responsible for coordinating a product's advertising with these other sources to insure that consistent information is communicated to consumers.

CONSUMER ATTITUDES TOWARD ADVERTISING.  It is difficult for the manager who works daily at an advertising job to maintain a perspective on the attitudes that consumers have toward advertising and the way that consumers use advertising in their daily lives. To be sure, consumers can point out both good and bad aspects of advertising. However, in a comprehensive consumer study conducted in 1975, Bartos and Dunn found that consumer opinion toward advertising tended to be favorable. When sample members were asked how they felt about advertising, 56 percent responded favorably while 41 percent responded unfavorably. This was a better rating than was given to labor unions, big business, and the federal government.[5] More important, perhaps, than this overall attitude is evidence concerning the role that consumers see advertising as playing in their decision process. When asked in this same study why they had a favorable attitude toward advertising, the leading reason cited was the information that advertising provided as an aid in the selection of products.[6]

Surveys conducted during newspaper strikes consistently suggest that newspaper advertising is one of the most highly valued parts of the medium because it aids the shopping process. During a 1971 newspaper strike in Rockford, Illinois, a typical survey response reported was "I miss the Rockford newspapers, especially the news and the ads."[7] Forty-nine percent of the respondents in that survey reported that the lack of newspaper advertisements affected their shopping. During the 1978 newspaper strike in New York City, nearly half of all regular readers said that they most missed the newspaper features and advertising because they "read the newspaper primarily for them."[8]

It appears from the evidence that consumers have a potentially favorable attitude toward advertising in proportion to the usefulness of the information that it contains. It is clearly in advertisers' interests to see that the content of their advertising is perceived as useful to prospective consumers.

CAN ADVERTISERS CREATE NEEDS?  Some critics contend that advertising is a persuasive weapon with dangerous potential because it permits users to create consumer needs. If the product which the manufacturer wishes to market is one which does not fulfill an existing consumer need, these critics contend that advertising can be used to manipulate the consumer, creating a need that the advertiser's product can then fulfill. John Kenneth Galbraith, for example, in his book *The Affluent Society* says of

---

[5]Rena Bartos and Theodore F. Dunn, *Advertising and Consumers — New Perspectives* (New York: American Association of Advertising Agencies, n.d.), p. 104.

[6]*Ibid.*, p. 44.

[7]"Newspapers Retain Readers' Loyalty in 2 Surveys Made During Absence," *Editor and Publisher* (January 23, 1971), pp. 7–8.

[8]"One of Our Media Is Missing," (New York: Newspaper Advertising Bureau, Inc., February, 1979), p. 25.

advertising and salesmanship, "Their central function is to create desires — to bring into being wants that previously did not exist."[9]

If this were true, how simple it would make the advertising manager's job. If advertising could, at the will of the advertiser, create needs in the consumer, then the advertising manager would not need to be concerned with determining consumers' needs. Instead, the advertiser would simply "make up" a need to be fulfilled by the product and instill it in the consumer's mind.

Those who believe that advertising has the power to create needs either explicitly or implicitly consider the consumer to be a purposeless, mindless subject awaiting instructions before acting. In contrast, the consumer is actually purposeful, active, and aggressive. The consumer already has needs and takes the initiative in satisfying those needs. Advertising that attempts to change the consumer's needs is ineffective because the consumer rejects information that is not useful in satisfying already existing needs. It is the consumer, not the advertiser, who decides what information is useful and hence will be acted upon.

The idea that advertising can be used to create needs is appealing because it would greatly simplify the job of the advertiser. But the evidence against this notion is massive and convincing, both from the world of the practicing advertiser and from the theorists.

*Evidence from Advertisers' Experience.* Almost every advertiser has had experience, directly or indirectly, with a product that simply could not win consumer acceptance despite persistent advertising. The failure rate of new products, variously estimated at 90 percent and over, is recurrent evidence of advertising's inability to force people to buy products that do not fit their needs. One of the lessons that every advertiser must sooner or later learn is that advertising, despite its great public visibility, is a tool of very limited power. It seems to work best when it is working with, rather than counter to, consumers' existing interests. It is ineffective when it attempts to "argue" with consumers. Meat extenders were introduced with heavy advertising in the early 1970s and met with immediate success. At the time meat prices were temporarily at extremely high levels. A year later meat prices declined, along with the consumer need satisfied by meat extenders. Sales of meat extenders dropped to almost nothing in spite of continued advertising because the consumer need could again be satisfied by meat.

Low-calorie beer had been around for years, but advertising had never found a meaningful consumer need to address and the product had limited sales. Miller Brewing Company brought out Lite and advertised that fewer calories "make it less filling." The advertising addressed a real consumer need and the result was a huge success for Lite. Exhibit 5-1 shows a commercial from the Miller Lite series.

---

[9]John Kenneth Galbraith, *The Affluent Society* (New York: The New American Library, 1958), p. 126.

A commercial from the Miller Lite series.          **EXHIBIT 5-1**

BOOG: For years now we've been kidding Jim here about his eyesight.

The fact is that Jim has the eyes of an eagle.

JIM: Thanks, Boog.

BOOG: Why, he was one of the first guys to spot Lite Beer from Miller.

He saw right away that Lite tastes great . . .

and is less filling.

JIM: Sure, all you have to do is read the label.

JIM: It says Lite has 1/3 less calories than their regular beer.

BOOG: I think you want this, Jim.

JIM: As I was saying, it's as plain as the nose on your face.

ANNCR: (VO) Lite Beer from Miller. Everything you always wanted in a beer. And less.

BOOG: I don't believe this!

Courtesy: Miller Brewing Co. and Backer & Spielvogel, Inc.

*Evidence from Research.* Research evidence supports the belief that advertising must work with existing needs rather than attempt to create them. Probably the most quoted, most respected research on advertising's effects is Neil Borden's *The Economic Effects of Advertising* which reports the results of dozens of actual advertising campaigns for a wide variety of products.[10] One of the basic findings of this research concerns the issue of need creation by advertising. Borden concludes from the many case histories examined that advertising works best when it offers something that meets existing needs. "Advertising creates needs only in the sense that it makes consumers aware that a product offers a satisfactory solution to a need."[11] Borden goes on to observe that individual needs are shaped by much more profound, deeper lying, slow-changing sociological forces, compared to which advertising is a minor force. Some forty years later, Albion and Farris, in an evaluation of research since Borden's work, conclude:

> Borden's discussion of the effects of advertising on the demand for an industry's product and the demand for aggregate consumption of goods and services is still relevant forty years later. Advertising may be of help in increasing the demand for a particular product, and it may have helped create attitudes and desires compatible with increased consumption at the expense of savings, but only within a social and economic environment conducive to that increase.[12]

A second area of supporting research comes from the study of mass communication's effectiveness in changing social and political attitudes. Joseph Klapper analyzed the results of a great many individual studies of the effects of mass communications campaigns.[13] He concluded that mass communication does not ordinarily result in changed attitudes in the audience, but is more likely to work when it serves to reinforce existing attitudes and beliefs. He also found that persons are far more responsive to communications that show how to satisfy existing needs rather than those that attempt to develop new needs.

## Advertising and the Consumer Decision Process

Consumer goals, the product, and advertising are three important variables in the consumer decision process, but there are many more considerations in this process. The role of these additional variables will be considered next as we look at a more comprehensive model of advertising's role in consumer behavior.

---

[10]Neil H. Borden, *The Economic Effects of Advertising* (Chicago: Richard D. Irwin, 1942).
[11]*Ibid.*
[12]Mark S. Albion and Paul W. Farris, *The Advertising Controversy* (Boston: Auburn House Publishing Company, 1981), p. 179.
[13]Joseph T. Klapper, *The Effects of Mass Communications* (Glencoe, Ill.: The Free Press, 1960).

## A Model of the Consumer
## Decision Process

The model to be presented describes the process that a consumer goes through in making a purchase and the role that advertising plays in that purchase decision.

THE SIR FORM. The model of the consumer decision process is in *the SIR form,* the initials standing for Stimulus, Intervening Variables, and Response. This model form is widely used in the behavioral sciences to describe individual behavior. The diagram in Exhibit 5-2 shows the basic form of this model.

The stimulus can be some suggestion from a source outside the individual that the individual should behave or respond in some particular fashion. However, when signals are received, the individual does not immediately respond as directed by the stimulus. Instead, the individual processes or interprets the stimulus in terms of the situation. This modification process is represented by the middle box in Exhibit 5-2, the intervening variables.

After interpreting the stimulus, an individual responds or behaves in some manner. This is represented by the third box, response. The response is likely to be different from the one suggested by the stimulus because the stimulus has been modified by the intervening variables which serve the individual's self-interest. Because of their effect on consumer response, these intervening variables are of great interest to those who wish to predict individuals' responses to stimuli.

BASIC ELEMENTS OF THE CONSUMER DECISION MODEL. The consumer decision process model is diagrammed in Exhibit 5-3. Although more complicated than Exhibit 5-2, this model retains the basic three-element SIR form.

The stimulus in the model is a communication concerning the attributes of the advertiser's product. The type of communication of concern here is an advertisement for the product. There are, of course, other stimuli to which the consumer is exposed, including both other commercial and personal sources of product information and the same range of communications sources for each competitive product.

The center box contains the intervening variables representing the decision-making process that takes place unseen in the consumer's mind. It

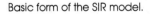
Basic form of the SIR model.

EXHIBIT 5-2

**EXHIBIT 5-3**          The consumer decision process model.

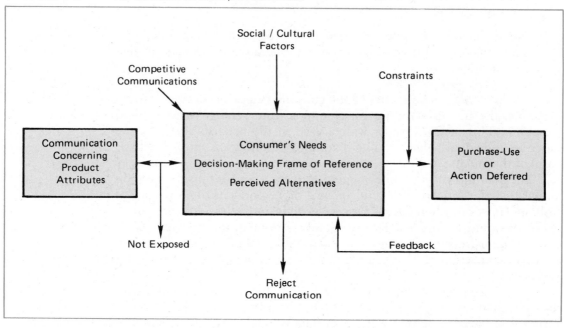

processes the information received from the stimulus and utilizes it to form a decision. Three components of this decision are consumer's needs, the list of alternative product solutions that the consumer perceives as being available, and the process by which the consumer matches the goal with perceived alternatives to make a product selection.

The third box represents the consumer's response which may range from a decision to purchase and use the advertiser's product, to a decision to take no immediate action, or to a decision to purchase a competitive product.

OTHER VARIABLES AND RELATIONSHIPS. In Exhibit 5-3 the major groups of variables in the model are represented by boxes while the lines that attach the boxes represent relationships between the variables. To the three major variables—stimulus, intervening variables, and response—the model in Exhibit 5-3 adds an additional set of variables termed social and cultural factors. These variables represent environmental forces external to the individual that influence the individual consumer's decision processes.

One other important relationship has been added to the model in Exhibit 5-3. That is the return relationship between the response variable and the decision process variable. This relationship is added to make the model a closed system meaning that the purchase process is a cyclical or continuing process in which the outcome of one decision feeds back information that influences subsequent purchase decisions.

## The Consumer Decision Process

Using the model in Exhibit 5-3 the major steps in the consumer decision process will now be described.

Because the model is a closed system, or circular process, it is possible to enter the model at any variable and trace the effect of a change in that variable on the total decision process. However, the particular interest here is to determine how an advertisement influences a consumer decision. Thus, the description of the steps in the decision process suggested by the model will begin with the stimulus of an advertisement.

STEP ONE: THE ADVERTISEMENT DIRECTS INFORMATION TO THE CONSUMER. An advertisement is a communication to consumers concerning the need-fulfilling benefits of the advertiser's product. Most products have a number of benefits that might be offered to consumers as need-fulfilling attributes. The advertiser selects one of these product attributes to be the subject of the advertisement. The content of the advertisement, then, is a promise by the advertiser that if the consumer selects this product, it will satisfy a particular need. This advertising content is a variable in the stimulus box.

Communications are directed to consumers through various communication media. In the case of advertising, the media are the paid or commercial ones such as television, radio, newspapers, or magazines.

STEP TWO: CONSUMER EXPOSURE IS SELECTIVE. A great many advertising messages miss their targets because consumers avoid the media in which they appear. In the model, this possibility is indicated by the "not exposed" line.

Consumers select the media to which they will pay attention by the relevance of the medium's content to their needs. Thus financiers tend to read *The Wall Street Journal* and some young women about to be married read *Brides* magazine. The astute advertiser utilizes this tendency by placing advertising in those media most likely to meet the needs of prospective consumers.

STEP THREE: CONSUMERS HAVE NEEDS. Consumers have a variety of needs which have been categorized as utilitarian, social, and psychological. In attempting to satisfy these needs, consumers set a series of specific goals toward which they strive. Along the way they encounter problems that must be solved to achieve the goal. When a particular need, goal, or problem becomes salient (of primary importance), the consumer is motivated to satisfy it.

STEP FOUR: CONSUMERS SEEK ALTERNATIVES. When a need becomes salient, the consumer seeks products representing the means to achieving the need. In some cases the consumer is able to summon from memory a set of alternative product solutions. This set of perceived alternatives would be based on past experience with products and from advertisements or other information gathered in anticipation of the need.

If consumers are unable to summon forth a satisfactory set of alternatives, they become active seekers of information concerning potential solutions to the salient need. Thus these consumers actively seek and read advertisements likely to suggest a solution. This is symbolized in the model by the double-headed arrow between the stimulus box and the intervening variable box, indicating that the communication is a two-way process. This information-seeking continues until an adequate set of perceived alternatives is built.

Thus, advertisements are judged by consumers in terms of the relevance and usefulness of their information to the need that the consumer is trying to satisfy. If the information is judged useful, the message is accepted by the consumer and the product becomes one of the perceived alternatives shown in the intervening variables section of the model. If the communication is perceived as relevant to a future need — not the one now salient — it may still be accepted if the information appears useful for future needs. This information is stored in the memory. Advertisements to which the consumer is exposed but which are not relevant to currently salient or anticipated needs are likely to be rejected. This is indicated in the model by the "reject communication" course.

STEP FIVE: CONSUMERS MATCH NEEDS TO PERCEIVED ALTERNATIVES. If a need is urgent and unsatisfied, the consumer is motivated to find a satisfactory solution. This is accomplished by matching the final set of perceived alternatives to the need and selecting the solution perceived as most satisfactory. Judgment as to what constitutes a satisfactory solution is arrived at by applying a series of "rules of thumb." In the model, these rules of thumb are the "decision-making frame of reference" shown bringing "perceived alternatives" and "consumer's needs" together.

The decision-making process is highly complex and only dimly understood since it cannot be seen or measured directly. The variables include what are often termed attitudes, beliefs, habits, traits, and prejudices. These variables, taken together, help the consumer to predict and evaluate the likely outcome of each of the perceived alternatives. These variables are in part inborn, but are primarily built up through experience and through information sources, both personal and commercial.

STEP SIX: EXTERNAL VARIABLES INFLUENCE THE DECISION PROCESS. The three sets of variables included in the middle or intervening variable box in Exhibit 5-3 on page 100 can be thought of as the consumer's decision processor. In addition, there are a variety of external variables, designated as "social/cultural factors" in the model, that influence all three sets of decision variables.

*social variables*      **Social variables** include influences from other individuals — friends, experts, and admired figures — and influence from groups such as the consumer's family, work group, or groups to which the consumer aspires to belong. The consumer looks to these other individuals and social groups for information about means to fulfill needs and for hints about what constitutes socially acceptable product choices.

**Cultural variables** are the traditional, learned responses to needs, goals, and daily problems that are shared by the members of a society. Consumers learn these traditional solutions from other members of the society in which they live and utilize them in forming their own choices.

*cultural variables*

Social and cultural variables influence all three of the variables (needs, decision-making frame of reference, perceived alternatives) shown in the middle box. While underlying needs are largely inborn, the goals established as steps to need fulfillment are strongly influenced by what is culturally traditional and by what is socially tested and acceptable. Social and cultural variables also influence the list of perceived alternatives by suggesting possible product solutions for inclusion and by discouraging other solutions that are deemed socially or culturally undesirable. Finally, the decision rules used by consumers in matching alternatives to needs are, in part, learned from social and cultural sources. Indeed, a culture can be viewed as a set of decision rules that are held in common by members of a society.

STEP SEVEN: THE DECISION MUST PASS CONSTRAINTS.    The outcome of the process of matching needs with alternatives is a decision concerning the preferred product solution. If the decision is a positive one, the consumer can be said to be motivated toward puchase of the product. However, before the decision can result in a purchase, there are a number of constraints or limitations to action that must be overcome by the consumer.

Two constraints of particular importance are economic constraints and availability constraints. If the consumer is motivated to buy a product, but does not have enough money, the decision is constrained. Equally, if the consumer cannot find the desired product or if it is temporarily out of stock, the decision is constrained. In both cases, the result is a modification of the action taken.

STEP EIGHT: RESPONSE RANGES FROM PURCHASE TO DELAY.    The consumer's decision motivates a response which is indicated by the third box in Exhibit 5-3. The response resulting from the advertising stimulus may take a variety of forms. The action hoped for by the advertiser is purchase, which may occur if a satisfactory match between alternative and need is found, if the need is sufficiently salient, and if the constraints can be overcome.

It is quite possible, however, that the response will be less than purchase of the product. In many cases, the response is deferral of action and formation of an intention to buy at some later time or a decision not to purchase at all. Deferred action may occur, for example, if the product solution is a satisfactory one, but the need is not a sufficiently salient one to demand immediate action. Deferred action may also take place if constraints block immediate purchase. Other lesser responses might also take place. The consumer may decide to defer immediate purchase or to purchase a competitive product, but still may develop a changed attitude or a change of knowledge about the product. Another possibility is a decision by the consumer that more information is needed before making a decision. To gain more information, consumers sometimes make a trial purchase to enable them to evaluate the product by direct experience.[14] Thus, the response resulting from the advertising stimulus, after processing by the intervening variables, can range from purchase action to a change in the consumer's state of mind.

STEP NINE: RESPONSE EXPERIENCE RESULTS IN FEEDBACK. The consumer decision process does not end with the purchase of a product or the other forms of response. The purchase and later use of a product results in experience which is a new input of information that is fed back to the consumer's decision-making mechanism.[15] This is indicated by the feedback line in Exhibit 5-3, page 100. Other responses that fall short of purchase also provide a form of information feedback to the consumer's decision processor.

The result of the feedback of experience is to modify the three sets of variables in the decision processor (needs, decision-making frame of reference, perceived alternatives), and hence future responses. This process is termed "learning." Needs are modified based on experience with the degree of satisfaction realized. Satisfying a need also means that another need becomes more salient. The list of perceived alternatives and their order of preference changes to reflect actual experience. Finally, the decision rules in the decision-making frame of reference are modified to reflect what was learned from the prior decision. Satisfying product experience tends to reinforce the decision rule used, and, as successive selections of the same product continue to give satisfactory results, the decision process hardens into a habitual response. Unsatisfactory experience, by contrast adds uncertainty to the decision rule, resulting in a more deliberative, information-seeking decision process.

## Uses of the Consumer Decision Model

The purpose in describing this model of consumer behavior is to give the advertising manager a way to look through the consumer's eyes when making advertising decisions. In the chapters to come, as the process of

---

[14]Robert E. Smith and William R. Swinyard, "Information Response Models: An Integrated Approach," *Journal of Marketing* (Winter, 1982), pp. 81–93.

[15]For a discussion of the role of advertising and sales promotion in consumer learning see Michael L. Rothschild and William C. Gaidis, "Behavioral Learning Theory: Its Relevance to Marketing and Promotions," *Journal of Marketing* (Spring, 1981), pp. 70–78.

preparing an advertising plan is discussed, there will be frequent occasions for referring back to this consumer model. However, before leaving consideration of the model, some specific lessons from the model will be previewed.

APPLICABILITY OF THE MODEL. The consumer decision model presented is widely applicable. Although not all people respond in the same way to stimuli, the process by which people arrive at a decision is similar.

*Industrial Buyer vs. Private Consumer.* A good deal of research has been done to understand industrial buying behavior.[16] The research indicates that there are significant similarities between the industrial and the consumer buyer and in the role that advertising plays in their buying behaviors. This suggests that our consumer decision model may be useful in both cases.

There are two considerations that indicate the applicability of the model to both groups. First, the differences between the industrial purchaser and the private consumer are apparently not as great as popularly imagined. Homemakers, for example, like industrial buyers, do much of their shopping as purchasing agents for their families. Close examination of homemakers' buying behavior has revealed them to be knowledgeable and economizing (in time as well as in money) buyers. On the other hand, studies have indicated that the industrial buyer is influenced by more emotional buying considerations than was once imagined. It is clear, for example, that a purchasing agent's behavior is sometimes influenced by a desire to maintain good social relations with particular salespeople. The purchasing agent's behavior may also be strongly influenced by a desire to please superiors and to avoid or resolve conflicts between the various persons in the organization who have a role in the purchase decision.[17]

Second, in addition to similarities in the needs that bring consumers and industrial buyers to the marketplace, there are similarities in the way that they attempt to satisfy those needs. Like the consumer, the industrial buyer goes through a decision-making process that includes gathering and processing information. The industrial decision-making process may be more formalized than the consumer's, with, in many cases, the process being prescribed by written policy, but this does not make the general model less applicable.

*Considered vs. Habitual Purchase.* The description of the model makes the decision process sound like a long, involved one. Some decisions are of this type, involving long consideration and much weighing of pros and cons. On the other hand, there are many purchases that are made with

---

[16]Jagdish N. Sheth, "Research in Industrial Buying Behavior — Today's Needs, Tomorrow's Seeds," *Marketing News* (April 4, 1980), pp. 14–15.

[17]Frederick E. Webster, Jr. and Yoram Wind, *Organizational Buying Behavior,* (Englewood Cliffs, N.J.: Prentice-Hall, 1972).

*habitual purchase*    little forethought. They are termed **habitual purchases.** Does the model apply to this type of purchase as well?

The model does appear adequate to describe the habitual purchase. A habitual purchase means that the consumer has accumulated a long string of satisfying experiences with a particular product, resulting in a strongly ordered or perhaps single item list of perceived alternatives. It also means that no further information search will be attempted and that the decision-making frame of reference has a rather firm and unchanged rule of thumb for satisfying this particular need. Advertising in such instances tends to be of a reminder type, designed to keep the advertiser's product in the consumer's list of perceived alternatives. The outdoor poster shown in Exhibit 5-4 is typical of such reminder ads.

In the absence, then, of new information, the decision process for this habitually purchased product is very rapid and very stable, to the point of appearing automatic and not well thought out. In fact, however, the habitual purchase is a great time saver for the consumer, allowing more time to be devoted to new or unusual purchase situations requiring more information and more consideration.

ADVERTISING DECISIONS FROM THE MODEL.   In Chapter 1, it was suggested that the advertising plan must develop answers to three questions — what message should be directed to consumers; to whom should the message be directed; and with what weight or intensity should it be presented? The model sheds some light on each of these questions.

*Advertising Content Decisions.*   An understanding of the process by

**EXHIBIT 5-4**        A reminder ad from Coca-Cola.

Courtesy:  The Coca-Cola Company.

which consumers select information to act on gives guidance in deciding on message content. Consumers accept and act on information that is useful to them in finding means to satisfy needs. This indicates that advertisements must contain information focused on the benefit that the consumer will derive from the product. How should this information be presented? The model indicates that an advertiser's message must compete for the consumer's overburdened attention. The presentation, therefore, must not only be distinctive and provocative, but must quickly show its relevance and demonstrate its credibility or run the risk of being rejected by the consumer.

*Advertising Media Decisions.* To whom should the message be directed? The model indicates that advertisements should be directed to those who have an unfulfilled need that the product could satisfy. To other people, the advertisement would be irrelevant and would be rejected. In using advertising media, then, greatest efficiency will be realized if media are used that are directed only to consumers with the relevant unsatisfied need.

Another guide to media selection can be derived by recalling that communication between marketer and consumer is a two-way process with consumers actively seeking information. In selecting media, the advertiser should attempt to place the advertisment in those media to which the consumer is likely to turn in a search for product information.

*Advertising Budget Decisions.* The consumer decision process model provides less direct evidence with a bearing on either the advertising weight or budget decisions. The model describes the behavior of a single consumer, whereas the budget decision is determined primarily by aggregate behavior.

The model does, however, suggest some determinants of advertising budget size. Since nonprospects will reject an advertising message as irrelevant to their needs, the advertising budget should not be wasted on trying to argue to nonprospects that they should need the product. The size of the budget, therefore, should vary in proportion to the number of prospects for the product.

The size of the budget will also vary with the number of messages directed to each prospect. The more frequent the messages, the higher the budget required. Under what conditions will multiple advertisements be required? In most cases the process of raising a product to the top of the list of perceived alternatives is a gradual one requiring successive advertisements. If there are frequent advertisements for competitive products, this may increase the number of advertisements needed. Information from advertisements that is stored in the memory can be forgotten and displaced by newer information. The greater the rate of forgetting and displacement by competition the more frequently is advertising needed. Finally, the more frequently the relevant consumer need arises, the more frequently advertisements can be useful in reminding the consumer of the potential solution offered by the product.

*CHAPTER*
*SUMMARY*
        The purpose in presenting a model of the consumer decision process is to provide the advertising manager with a consumer-oriented perspective so that advertising decisions *work with* rather than *conflict with* consumer actions.

        In the consumer decision process, three key variables are consumer needs, the product being offered, and the advertisement. The behavior of consumers is motivated by their needs, which can be categorized as utilitarian, social, and psychological. Products represent means by which these needs can be satisfied. Advertising is one source of information used by consumers to decide what product best helps to satisfy their needs. Consumers actively seek and process advertising information to aid in product choice. Only advertisements that offer relevant and credible information are accepted and given consideration. Advertising cannot create or change consumer needs, but must offer the means to satisfy needs.

        These three variables plus others can be related in an SIR model modified to provide feedback and the influence of social and cultural variables. The advertisement is the stimulus. Its effect is moderated by variables internal to the consumer through which the consumer processes the information to arrive at a decision. The decision may be to purchase the product or it may be to defer action. Results of the decision are fed back to modify the internal consumer variables.

        The model can be used as a guide to advertiser decision making and to trace the effect of a change in any variable in the system.

*KEY TERMS*

Underlying needs                    Information usefulness concept
Consumer goals                      Marketing concept
Consumer problems                   Word-of-mouth communication
Consumer needs                      Social variables
Utilitarian needs                   Cultural variables
Psychological needs                 Habitual purchase
Social needs

*QUESTIONS*
*FOR*
*DISCUSSION*

1. It was stated that products serve as means by which needs are satisfied. Suggest what needs might be satisfied by each of the following products; categorize each of the needs as utilitarian, social, or psychological:

   a. Mink coat.
   b. Deodorant.
   c. Cologne.
   d. Home heating oil.
   e. Cigarettes.

2. People tend to see in products those characteristics that are important to the use which the product will serve for them. Thus, different people see identical products as though they were different. Describe the characteristics that a person would perceive in an expensive wristwatch purchased for the following reasons:

    a. As a graduation gift for a nephew.
    b. As a navigation instrument.
    c. As a dress watch for personal use.

3. *Consumer Reports,* an authoritative independently edited buying guide, has been published since the 1930s yet has circulation of only about 2 million, despite aggressive promotion. This compares, for example, to circulation of over 19 million for *TV Guide* and over 18 million for the *Reader's Digest.* If consumers are concerned with obtaining useful and relevant information, what accounts for the relatively low level of popularity of this magazine?

4. Consumers obtain information about products from both commercial and private sources. The marketer can provide commercial information to consumers by advertising or by personal selling. However, word of mouth, a private source, is also highly influential in the purchase decision. Is there any way that an advertiser can create favorable word of mouth for a product?

5. Consumers develop, through experience, sources of information to which they turn in seeking products. For the following product requirements, to what sources of commercial information would the consumer likely turn?

    a. A home owner seeking an electrician.
    b. A doctor considering a new pharmaceutical product.
    c. An advertiser seeking a new advertising agency.
    d. A student seeking a used Moped.
    e. A restaurant chain purchasing agent seeking new kitchen equipment.

6. It has been suggested that one of the causes of social unrest in this country has been television advertising. According to this notion, television has presented highly attractive products in luxurious settings to vast numbers of underprivileged consumers. This has led these consumers to desire these products and living conditions and has produced dissatisfaction with the status quo. If true, would this not mean that advertising plays a role in creating consumer needs?

7. Newspapers have long been a favorite advertising medium of retailers. There are several factors that account for this, but what reason does the model of consumer behavior suggest for the appropriateness of newspapers as a retail medium?

8. Among the most heavily advertised products are headache remedies,

toothpastes, laundry detergents, cigarettes, and soft drinks. Does the discussion of consumer behavior suggest any reason why these products would require heavy advertising?

---

**PROBLEM**

The most dramatic change in the food marketing business in the past 20 years has been the increase in dining out.[18] In 1980 total expenditures in eating and drinking establishments were $85.8 billion; $27.4 billion of this was in fast-food establishments which are growing at a 10 percent annual rate.[19] Nearly one out of five meals is now eaten away from home. Continued rapid growth of fast-food outlets is anticipated.

Suppose you were the advertising manager for a major fast-food chain and your marketing research director pointed out the following trends:

a. Family income was expected to increase and discretionary income (the amount left over after purchase of necessities) to increase sharply.

b. About six out of ten women between ages 25 and 54 work and the proportion is expected to increase.

c. The custom of the family meal with all members present is rapidly disappearing. Even on weekends, families eat meals together only about half the time.

d. In recent years there has been a sharp increase in nutritional awareness among consumers. Nearly half of all consumers report active efforts to control weight and nearly half report actively avoiding foods that they consider bad for their health.

1. For each of the trends identified above, identify in the diagram in Exhibit 5-3 the variable that is changing. Trace step by step the chain of events that results from this trend. What is the likely effect on the sales of the advertising manager's fast-food firm?

2. For each of these trends, what changes should the advertising manager consider in the advertising for the fast-food service? Consider all three elements of the advertising program — the message, the media, and the budget.

---

[18]Material for this problem is drawn from Leo J. Shapiro and Dwight Bohmback, "Eating Habits Force Changes in Marketing," *Advertising Age* (October 30, 1978), pp. 27, 65, 66, 68.

[19]U.S. Bureau of the Census, Statistical Abstract of the United States: 1982-83 (103d edition), Washington, D.C., 1982.

The selected readings are arranged according to the parts of this text to which they pertain. The reader is also referred to current issues of several journals and trade periodicals that feature articles on topics in advertising. The most popular of these periodicals are *Advertising Age, Media and Marketing Decisions, The Journal of Marketing, The Journal of Advertising Research,* and *Marketing News.* Listings of specific articles are avoided since the subject matter is changing so rapidly that information referred to may be obsolete by the time that this book is published.

*How It Was in Advertising: 1776-1976.* Chicago: Crain Books, 1976. A highly readable and illustrated history of advertising in the U.S.

*Organizing for Marketing/Advertising Success in a Changing Business Environment.* New York: Association of National Advertisers, 1982. Reviews organizational structures of major advertisers based on direct interviews with company executives.

Kirkpatrick, Frank. *How to Get the Right Job in Advertising.* Chicago: Contemporary Books, 1982. Contains detailed descriptions of the organization and functions of modern advertising agencies.

Eldridge, Clarence. *The Role and Importance of the Marketing Plan* (no. 5 in a series of 16 booklets on marketing). New York: Association of National Advertisers, Inc., 1966. A clear and concise description of the planning process in marketing and advertising as practiced by major consumer products firms.

Webster, Frederick E. Jr. and Yoram Wind. *Organizational Buying Behavior.* Englewood Cliffs, N.J.: Prentice Hall, 1972. An extensive description of buying practices and buyer behavior in industrial and other business organizations.

Engel, James F. and David T. Kollat. *Consumer Behavior,* 3rd ed. Hinsdale, Ill.: The Dryden Press, 1978. A detailed description and model that reflects current understanding of consumer behavior.

# Part Two

## SETTING DIRECTION FOR THE ADVERTISING PROGRAM

Part 1 described some of the organizational and planning tools used by the advertising manager. With that background we turn now to the central theme of this book — the creation of an advertising plan that will serve to direct an advertising effort.

Advertising is a field that is full of trick phrases, cliches, and fads. Currently the most popular and overworked term in advertising is "positioning." But positioning is more than a fad — it is a hard-working, enduring concept of central importance in directing an advertising program.

Positioning sets sound market direction for a product and its advertising by defining how the product will compete. Our objective in Part 2 is to describe step by step the planning process that leads to the positioning decision.

Positioning the product is partly an analytical job and partly a creative art. Part 2 begins with the analytical task. To make a positioning decision the advertising manager must conduct three analyses: consumer, product, and market. The three analyses will be described in detail in Chapters 6–9.

The "art" portion of the positioning task is the creative combination of the information from these analyses to form the positioning. This process will be described and illustrated in Chapter 10.

By the time you have completed Chapters 6–10 these are the things that you should be able to do:

1. Conduct a consumer analysis that will tell you who your consumer prospects are and what problems they are trying to solve with products such as yours.

2. Analyze your product so that you know its strengths and weaknesses compared to competitive products.

3. Analyze the market to determine the environment in which your product will compete.

4. Combine this information to set basic direction for the advertising of your product; that is, make the positioning decision.

# CHAPTER 6

*Consumer Analysis—*
*Determining Consumer Needs*

**LEARNING OBJECTIVES**

In studying this chapter you will learn:

- What information is needed about consumers.

- Sources of information on consumer behavior.

- Problems in researching consumer behavior.

- Indirect research techniques used to gain insight into consumer behavior.

- The limitations of consumer needs research.

- What to look for in consumer needs research results.

The effective management of advertising requires preparation of an advertising plan that specifies what advertising is expected to accomplish, details the programs that will realize these goals, and provides for measurement of progress to determine whether or not the program has accomplished what it set out to do. The first objective of the advertising plan is to provide unifying direction to the advertising program. Two guidelines provide the needed direction: (1) most fundamental is the **positioning description** that specifies how the product is to compete; and (2) more immediate are **advertising objectives** that define problems and opportunities that the advertising is to address in the coming year.

*positioning description*

*advertising objectives*

To make effective decisions about product positioning and to set objectives, the advertising manager must develop and analyze information about the consumer, the product, and the market. Analysis in all three of these areas usually takes place simultaneously, but it is of at least symbolic importance that analysis of the consumer is considered first. Modern marketers acknowledge that the consumer should be the central figure influencing the design of marketing programs. The marketing concept, one of the most important principles guiding modern marketing, suggests that any marketing program should begin with an understanding of consumers.

Then, from an understanding of consumers and their needs, marketers must tailor products and information about products to suit consumer needs.

## Gathering Data on Consumer Needs

In the consumer analysis section of the advertising plan, essential positioning and objective-setting information is gathered and analyzed. Two classes of information that are needed might be classified as the "why" and "who" of consumers.

### Information Needed About Consumers

The first piece of information that the advertiser needs to know about consumers is why they purchase products such as the one to be advertised. Consumers purchase products to satisfy needs. If an advertiser wishes through advertising to position a product as a desirable fulfillment of some consumer need, the need must first be understood.

In practice, determining why consumers buy is very complex because of the difficulty in even defining "needs," because of the difficulties of collecting the information, and because there is great variety in the answers from person to person. It is too much to expect that a simple answer will be found to the question of why people purchase a particular product. Take, for example, the purchase of an automobile. What need does it serve? To some consumers, an automobile serves as simple transportation; to others it is a symbol of success; to most, it is a combination of these and other things. What the advertiser must know is the significant categories of needs for which products such as these are purchased. Look at the advertisement in Exhibit 6-1. It offers a consumer computer information service that will solve different problems for three members of the family. Many product categories face such variable consumer needs. The approach to determining this type of consumer information is the subject of this chapter.

The second piece of consumer information needed is to know the characteristics or the identity of the people who are prospects for the advertiser's product. Obviously if the advertiser is going to direct an advertising message with useful information for satisfying a need, it is essential to know who the people are who have that need. Again, the information is not easy to obtain; prospects for a product are not easily described. They vary in the intensity of their needs, in the nature of their needs, and in their personal characteristics. Solving this information-gathering problem will be the subject of the next chapter.

After determining who buys the product and why they buy it, the information that is gathered should be reanalyzed to uncover special problems and opportunities that face the product. This search for problems and

**EXHIBIT 6-1**        An advertisement directed to multiple consumer needs.

# LAST NIGHT, COMPUSERVE TURNED THIS COMPUTER INTO A TRAVEL AGENT FOR JENNIE, A STOCK ANALYST FOR RALPH, AND NOW, IT'S SENDING HERBIE TO ANOTHER GALAXY.

**NO MATTER WHICH COMPUTER YOU OWN, WE'LL HELP YOU GET THE MOST OUT OF IT.**

If you've got places to go, CompuServe can save you time and money getting there. Just access the Official Airline Guide Electronic Edition—for current flight schedules and fares. Make reservations through our on-line travel service. Even charter a yacht through "Worldwide Exchange."

If your money's in the market, CompuServe offers a wealth of prestigious financial data bases. Access Value Line, or Standard and Poor's. Get the latest information on 40,000 stocks, bonds or commodities. Then, consult experts like IDS or Heinold Commodities. All on line with CompuServe.

Or if, like Herbie, intergalactic gamesmanship is your thing, enjoy the best in fantasy, adventure, and space games. Like MegaWars, the ultimate computer conflict.

To get all this and more, you'll need a computer, a modem and CompuServe. CompuServe connects with almost any personal computer, terminal, or communicating word processor. To receive an illustrated guide to CompuServe and learn how you can subscribe, contact or call:

## CompuServe

Consumer Information Service
2180 Wilson Road, Columbus, Ohio 43228
**800-848-8199**
In Ohio, call 614-457-8650

Reprinted with permission of CompuServe Information Services, CompuServe, Inc.

opportunities will be continued in each of the three analysis sections of the plan—consumer, product, and market. An important end product of the analysis sections will be a list of the problems and opportunities facing the advertiser's product. From this list the advertising manager will be able to develop a list of advertising objectives that will direct the advertising programs toward overcoming the problems and realizing the opportunities facing the product.

## Sources of Information on Consumer Behavior

Information on consumer behavior might conceivably come from a variety of sources. Three sources warranting particular attention are secondary sources, observations from sales personnel, and original research.

SECONDARY SOURCES. Data originally collected for some other purpose but which the advertising manager might be able to use in planning is said to be **secondary source information.** The advantages in using secondary sources for information are low cost and the speed with which results can be obtained.

*secondary source information*

Secondary data on consumer behavior are, unfortunately, not often available for all product categories. Although a good deal of work has been done in consumer research, much of it is financed by companies for their own private use and, hence, is not published. There have been a few commercial researchers whose research results on particular products are available. Two leading examples are the work of Dr. Burleigh Gardner, reported by Pierre Martineau in *Motivation in Advertising*,[1] and the findings of the psychoanalyst Dr. Ernest Dichter in his book, *Handbook of Consumer Motivations*.[2]

There has also been a substantial amount of academic research in recent years into consumer behavior, much of it involving specific products. Certain products, such as automobiles, tend to make popular study topics. Published in scholarly journals, this material is sometimes a helpful source if the product studied matches the advertiser's product interest.

Other secondary sources, such as prior studies done by one's own firm, studies done by trade associations, and studies done by the media should, of course, be checked.

SALES FORCE AND TRADE OBSERVATIONS. Another often productive source of information on consumers is observation by salespeople and retailers, who have a firsthand opportunity to observe and listen to the

---

[1] Pierre Martineau, *Motivation in Advertising* (New York: McGraw-Hill Book Company, 1957).

[2] Ernest Dichter, *Handbook of Consumer Motivations* (New York: McGraw-Hill Book Company, 1964).

buyer in action. Some salespeople are not sufficiently sensitive to understand the buying process taking place before them, but others develop a detailed feeling for consumer needs as they relate to particular products.

If the advertiser's salespeople sell directly to the ultimate consumer of the product, as do retailers or some industrial product marketers, then feedback on perceptions of consumer behavior can be obtained directly from the company's own sales organization. Information can be solicited by means of direct interviews with salespeople or through questionnaires or reports administered by the sales managers.

When the advertiser's sales force does not come in contact with the consumer — such as in a firm that sells through wholesalers — information is less easily obtained. The usual approach is to utilize a small force of interviewers to call on a sample of retailers or distributors and solicit their judgments on the needs motivating consumers in the purchase of products such as those of the advertiser. The advertising manager, in fact, will often find it desirable to participate directly in making some of these trade inquiries in order to get a "feeling" for the market and the consumer.

*original research*

ORIGINAL RESEARCH WITH CONSUMERS. By far the most productive source of consumer motivation information is, in most cases, **original research.** A survey is directed to a sample of consumers asking them why they purchase products of a particular type. The advantage of original research, as compared to secondary research, is that the research can be designed to meet the specific requirements of the advertiser's product. A disadvantage of original research in this field is that the research tends to be expensive to conduct.

The advertising manager will usually need to utilize the assistance of a professional marketing researcher in the design and implementation of this form of consumer research. The researcher may be a member of the firm's marketing research department or an outside specialist. In either case, the general research procedure should be the same as that outlined in Chapter 2. The advertising manager should bring the research problem to the researcher, and jointly they should put it in researchable form. The researcher then designs the research project presenting it in the form of a research proposal. If the proposal appears to fill the advertising manager's requirements, the proposal is approved and the research proceeds under the direction of the researcher.

The design of research to probe consumer needs requires extraordinary skills, and advertising managers should utilize the skills of trained researchers in this field. Nonetheless it is important to have an idea of the difficulties facing research of this sort and the research techniques available to overcome these difficulties. This will enable advertising managers to evaluate the research proposed for their products.

## Problems in Researching Consumer Behavior

A central obstacle in doing research on consumer behavior is that consumers are frequently reluctant to divulge why they act in the ways that they do or they may not even be cognizant of their motives for buying a particular product. Consumers can hardly be approached and be asked to list the needs they are trying to satisfy. Instead, the usual procedure is to approach consumers who purchase products of the same class as the product to be advertised. They are then asked "why" they purchase that product. The hope is that they will express the need they are trying to satisfy.

RELUCTANCE TO ANSWER AND RATIONALIZATION.   Unfortunately people have difficulty in some cases in expressing why they purchase a particular product. It is important to understand the cause of this difficulty because it will help in understanding the research techniques used to determine consumer needs. In Chapter 5 it was suggested that one underlying need is to establish and maintain one's self-image. People establish in their minds an idea of the kinds of people they wish to be; they then strive to protect themselves from forces that represent them as other than those kinds of people. Consequently, when a researcher asks a consumer why a particular product was purchased, the consumer may refuse to respond if the true answer would be demeaning or would place the consumer in an unfavorable light. In many cases consumers do not refuse to answer the questions; instead they give an answer that they feel enhances their standing.

The research problem, then, is twofold. The advertiser seeking information on consumer needs must try to predict before doing research whether or not the purchase behavior is one about which consumers will talk. Then after the research is completed the responses must be examined to determine if they represent valid, underlying needs or simply surface rationalization.

RANGE OF CONSUMER NEEDS.   In attempting to evaluate the potential difficulty in gaining purchase motivation information, it is sometimes useful to think of consumer needs as ranging along a scale such as that shown in Exhibit 6-2.[3]

*Willing to Discuss.* At the left-hand side of the scale are the more utilitarian, everyday problems of coping with the physical world. The purchase of a hinge to repair a door, bread for children's sandwiches, or work pants for a worker are examples of purchases usually made to satisfy utilitarian needs. Usually consumers are willing and able to discuss, rather factually, the reasons behind purchases such as these.

*Reluctant to Discuss.* The center of the scale represents needs which, although consumers may be conscious of them, they hesitate to discuss them. They are needs which consumers feel may not be socially acceptable

---

[3]This way of thinking about consumer needs is suggested by George Horsley Smith, *Motivation Research in Advertising and Marketing* (New York: McGraw-Hill Book Company, 1954), pp. 18–24.

EXHIBIT 6-2        Range of consumer needs.

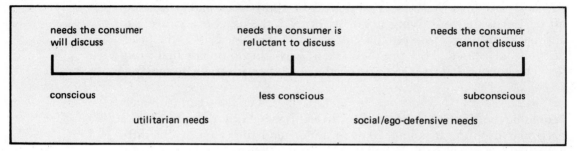

or may not project a favorable impression. Consumers, when asked about their motives, may refuse to answer, may be evasive, or may provide a self-enhancing but untrue answer. Marketers of pet food and pet care products face this problem in research among pet owners. It is known in the industry that many pet owners treat their pets like members of the family and attribute human characteristics to them. This reportedly accounts for pet owners' preference for dog food that looks like people food — products that make their own gravy and those that look like fresh hamburger. Many owners also insist that dog food have red, meat-like color even though dogs cannot perceive colors. Thus, pet products must not only serve the pet's hunger problem, but also the owner's need to treat the pet like a human. The advertisement for Mighty Dog® in Exhibit 6-3 shows how a dog food can be positioned to meet this pet-owner need. However, researchers have difficulty in getting pet owners to openly discuss these feelings toward their pets. Admitting a tendency to treat a pet like a human being would not enhance the consumer's self-esteem. Instead, pet owners tend to hide these feelings and attribute their own preferences to the pet.

*Unable to Discuss.* The right-hand side of the scale represents needs that are not conscious. Consequently, the consumer cannot discuss them. These are termed repressed needs; they are unacceptable socially and unacceptable to the individual. In the extreme, these represent pathological problems. It has been suggested, for example, that the gambler's subconscious wish to lose stems from a desire for self-punishment and that a compulsive bargain hunter is expressing a need to outsmart others.[4] Needs in this range of the scale are very difficult to uncover, but they are probably of less general interest to the marketer since it is difficult in many cases to determine how an advertiser can serve these needs.

### The Use of Indirect Research Techniques

The information problem of the advertiser lies with those needs or purchase motivations represented by the center of the scale. They tend

---

[4]*Ibid.*, p. 21.

Positioning to meet pet owners' needs.                    EXHIBIT 6-3

"Take it from me, Mighty Dog® makes hash out of other dog foods."

**Pure Beef.**
That's what makes
**Mighty Dog** taste so good.

**Beef Hash.**
Other brands combine meat
with soy and by-products.

"Surprisingly, many dog lovers don't know the difference between Mighty Dog® Beef for Dogs and brands like Alpo, Kal Kan and Cycle.

"Mighty Dog, you see, is pure beef, (like a steak). Those others combine meat with other ingredients, (like hash). In fact, meat by-products and soy flour can make up to 75% of their weight.

"And Mighty Dog is specially balanced and fortified to be 100% nutritionally complete.

"That's why, at dinnertime, my taste runs to Mighty Dog."

Carnation    **MIGHTY DOG®**
**The pure beef brand.**

Courtesy: The Carnation Co.

to be needs that were classified earlier as social and psychological. They are partially conscious, but reluctantly revealed by the consumer. What is required is a research technique that will go around the consumer's defenses, a technique that will penetrate surface rationalization and make the consumer willing to express true needs.

THE SOURCE OF INDIRECT TECHNIQUES. **Indirect research techniques** provide at least a partial solution to the problem of determining consumer goals that are hidden from view. There are a variety of indirect techniques that have been developed by researchers, but they have a common distinguishing characteristic: the intent of the questioner is hidden. Most of these marketing research techniques were developed from approaches used in clinical psychology where they are used in exploring behavioral problems. By keeping the purpose hidden in asking a question, the researcher hopes to avoid a defensive reaction by the respondent. With the fear of social embarrassment avoided and with no need to defend one's self-esteem, it is hoped that the respondent will be uninhibited and free to respond with true feelings.

The selection and application of indirect techniques and the interpretation of resultant findings require the use of a marketing research expert. In fact, marketing researchers themselves often rely on specialists in behavioral techniques when applying these research tools. Despite the need for specialized assistance, the advertising manager should have a good idea of the indirect techniques that are available and the nature of the results that can be expected when they are used.

*depth interview*

DEPTH INTERVIEWS. A **depth interview** is an unstructured interview in which the subject is asked to talk freely about a particular topic. After introducing the topic, the interviewer does not ask a series of questions as in a normal direct interview. Instead, the interviewer simply encourages the respondent, through nonevaluative comments, to continue talking about the topic. This approach is called the **nondirective technique.** The interviewer may, with probes or by showing interest, encourage the subject to expand certain statements. In no case does the interviewer show either approval or disapproval of the subject's responses. To do so might reveal the interviewer's purpose, placing the respondent on guard and raising his or her defenses.

*nondirective technique*

For example, a depth interview probing into the reasons behind the purchase of a mobile home might begin with a rather broad question such as this:

I'm interested in hearing about how you decided to purchase a mobile home. Could you just talk about it a little for me?

Suppose the respondent answers with:

Well, we just thought that with the kids all grown it would be a pretty convenient way to live.

The consumer may, in fact, have some rather mixed feelings about the purchase, including some concern about its social acceptability or the esteem attached to it. The interviewer would not ask directly about this, but would attempt to expand the interview by encouraging further conversation without evaluation. The interviewer's response might be:

Uh-huh, could you tell me more? *or,*
I see, what else was important? *or,*
You say you thought it would be convenient?

Hopefully, the respondent is encouraged by these comments and feels free to express his or her thoughts more openly.

Administration of depth interviews requires a highly skilled interviewer, trained and experienced in this specialty. The interviewer uses no formal questionnaire in a depth interview, but must know in which areas to probe for further information. The interviewer takes the respondent's comments by making detailed notes or by using a tape recorder.

Because each interview is lengthy (thirty minutes or more is not unusual) and requires specially trained interviewers, the depth interview technique is expensive to apply. Consequently, the number of interviews used in a study is typically small (on the order of thirty or forty interviews, for example). The research results obtained are highly qualitative and, in their raw form, highly disorganized. The researcher will usually analyze the interview results and point out responses that give special insight. The analyst skilled in this field tries to separate rationalizations from genuine motives and tries to find significant patterns of response. Although these efforts are helpful, usually the advertising manager will find it useful to read the transcripts of the interviews, which will help to build a "feel" for the product—the uses it serves and the language that consumers use in talking about this type of product and its use.

FOCUS GROUP INTERVIEWS. Depth interviews are carried out by an interviewer with one respondent at a time. An alternate form of indirect research is the **focus group interview** in which a sort of depth interview is *focus group interview* conducted between one interviewer (called a moderator) and a group of consumers. The consumers, usually 10–12 per session, are brought to a central location for the interview. The interview is conducted in a meeting room with every effort made to make the surroundings commodious and congenial in order to help the consumers to be relaxed. The sample for any one interview session is not a cross section of the population. Instead, an effort is made to gather a compatible group that will feel comfortable in conversation. Thus, respondents for any one session are likely to be from the same age group and work status; men and women are rarely mixed.

A trained interviewer is used to introduce the subject for group discussion and to give guidance concerning areas to be explored. The sessions are usually recorded for later analysis. The moderator does not use a formal questionnaire, but often has an interview guide that suggests areas of interest that should be explored. An example of an interview guide for research on English muffins is shown in Exhibit 6-4.

In the group interview sessions the interviewer uses the nondirective approach as in the depth interview. The group technique, however, depends upon a somewhat different process for overcoming the defenses that hide true needs. The depth interview with an individual develops frankness of response because of the privacy of the interview, rapport with the interviewer, and the interviewer's indirect, nonevaluative responses. The group interview, by contrast, depends upon the interaction of group members to suggest ideas to each other and to break down response barriers. If one group member gives a frank response, it often encourages other members to do the same. Thus, the role of the moderator is to encourage a free-flowing conversation, solicit participation from all respondents, listen carefully for meaningful insights, and encourage productive lines of conversation. The objective of the session is not to achieve consensus, but rather to draw out all points of view.

**EXHIBIT 6-4**    Focus group interview guide for English muffins.

---

### English Muffin Interview Guide

USE OF ENGLISH MUFFINS
  Situations where used
  Frequency of use
  Usage by various household members
  Types of uses
  Impact of flavor variety on usage patterns

SELECTION OF BRAND
  Brands used
  Degree of loyalty
  Criteria for selection
    Quality
    Availability
    Price
    Flavor variety
    Packaging
    Other factors
  Perceived differences among brands
  Substitution patterns

ATTITUDES TOWARD EXISTING BRANDS
  Satisfactory attributes
  Unsatisfactory attributes/sources of dissatisfaction
  Areas for improvement

REACTIONS TO NEW CONCEPTS
  Overall reactions
  Perceived likes/dislikes
  Product-related expectations
  Usage-related expectations
  Factors influencing likelihood of changing to new product

---

Group interviews are difficult to conduct and even with a skilled interviewer they often break down. Strident or strongly opinionated individuals sometimes take over the sessions, discouraging participation by other members.

A series of sessions must usually be conducted in order to get sufficient responses for analysis. The analysis is much like that prepared for depth interviews; emphasis is on patterns of responses and representative comments. As in the case of individual depth interviews, reading verbatim transcripts of focus group interviews may provide helpful insights to the advertising manager.

However, one of the great advantages of focus group interviews to the advertising manager is that they permit personal observation of the sessions. The interview facilities are generally equipped with one-way mirrors so that observers can see and hear the sessions without intruding on the discussion. The experience of hearing firsthand a consumer's discussion about needs and products can be invaluable. In addition, during the interview observers can often pass along to the interviewer questions that they wish to have explored further by the panel members.

PROJECTIVE QUESTIONS. A third type of indirect technique is the **projective question.** Here the intent of the interviewer is hidden, in this case by the form of the question. The term *projective* refers to the wording of the question which allows respondents to express their own feelings through another person. For example, instead of asking people why they attended a particular movie, they would be asked to describe why they thought other people attended that movie. Because the respondents in this case feel they are revealing nothing about themselves, they may answer frankly, attributing their own motives to other people.

*projective question*

Projective questions are sometimes used as probes in depth interviews and group interviews, but they are also used in more structured questionnaire approaches, sometimes mixed in questionnaires with direct question forms.

*Sentence Completion.* There are several well-known projective approaches that have been applied to marketing problems. The *sentence completion technique* presents an incomplete sentence and asks the consumer to finish it. For example, "People who drive sports cars _____." Notice that the question is indirect (the questioner's intent is hidden) and allows respondents to attribute their feelings to other people.

*Cartoon Test.* In a *cartoon test* the consumer is shown an illustration using simplified cartoon characters. One of the characters is shown making a statement or asking a question which is printed in the familiar cartoon balloon. The balloon over the other character's head is blank. The consumer is asked to fill in the second character's response. Again, the respondent is able to answer frankly by answering through another person. Exhibit 6-5 shows an application of this technique.

EXHIBIT 6-5          Application of a cartoon test to marketing research.

*Role Playing.* A role-playing approach requires a somewhat more involved interview. In this technique a situation is described for the consumer who is then asked to actually act out the behavior of some other person. The person or role that the consumer is to act out is described, but actually it is expected that consumers will project their own behavior into the situation. The consumer is able to act genuinely by hiding behind the role.

*Thematic Apperception Test.* The *thematic apperception test (TAT)* is a psychoanalytic test technique using an illustration of a situation, usually one involving people. In an automobile marketing application, for example, the picture might show a young couple in an automobile showroom looking at a new sports car with a salesperson standing nearby. Consumers are shown the picture and asked to tell what they think is going on in the picture. In telling the story, it is hoped that consumers will project their own feelings into the situation.

*association tests*

ASSOCIATION TESTS. Another form of indirect question is the **association test,** used primarily to reveal the connotations or attitudes attached to a product. In this test the consumer is read a list of words, and asked to respond after each word with the first word that comes to mind. Both the answer and the speed of response are usually recorded. Two devices are used here to avoid the consumer's defenses. First, the intent of the researcher is hidden by mixing the words or names that are being researched with other dummy words. The respondent has no way of knowing the researcher's direct area of concern. Second, by asking the respondent to answer quickly, a genuine response is often given before the consumer has a chance to worry about the social or psychological consequences of the response. Hence, the person's defenses are not erected.

The results of an association test are analyzed both in terms of the content of the responses and the delay before response. The associated words are analyzed to determine their connotations and to tabulate main categories of content. It is hoped that the responses will reveal how consumers think about the subject product—how they find it useful and whether or not they see it as a satisfactory solution. The time of response is analyzed to uncover emotional associations connected with the words. If consumers hesitate in responding or cannot respond (called a *blocked response*) the word is considered to have emotional content which the consumer would prefer not to discuss.

Association questions are often used as part of a structured questionnaire. This general approach is also used in depth interviews and group interviews. In these applications speed of response is not stressed, but the respondents are simply asked to discuss freely all thoughts that they associate with a particular product or other subject under investigation.

## Applying Information from Consumer Research

The advertising manager is likely to rely upon an expert in marketing research to design and carry out research into consumer needs and goals. However, when these research results are received, it is the responsibility of the advertising manager to apply them. To carry out this responsibility the advertising manager needs to understand the limitations of consumer research and what to look for in analyzing the results of such research.

### Limitations of Consumer Needs Research

There is probably no area in marketing research that is more complex than inquiry into the reasons why consumers buy products. Consumer responses must be analyzed carefully (usually by an expert). In addition, responses are difficult to quantify and may have limited value for projecting results onto the entire consumer group.

NEED FOR CAREFUL INTERPRETATION. Consumer needs research results must be interpreted carefully. Rationalizations must be separated from genuine needs—both are frequently present even when indirect techniques are used. Often consumers verbalize needs in imprecise, sometimes inconsistent, ways. In most cases a researcher trained in the behavioral field should be used to aid in interpreting the results. The advertising manager should be aware, however, that individual behavior is not a field in which there is a single unified body of knowledge to draw upon in interpreting research results. Instead, there are a number of behavioral schools, each of which would interpret consumer research findings differently. This lack of agreement among experts can be most disconcerting to the advertising manager who is paying the bill. The best point of view to take is that no one school of thought or no one expert is right or wrong. What the advertising manager requires is an expert whose training provides a helpful perspective for looking at consumer behavior.

INABILITY TO QUANTIFY RESULTS. Another characteristic of consumer needs research results is that they are difficult to quantify. The data collection methods rely upon free, open-ended responses by consumers. Consequently, the variety in answers is enormous. If the answers were to be quantified, different answers would have to be grouped. Not only would it be difficult to decide which answers were enough alike so that they could be grouped, but also much of the richness of detail would be lost in the grouping process.

To avoid losing the richness of the detailed findings, research results are sometimes presented in full, rather than condensed, form. At other times, a substantial number of the responses are quoted to indicate the range and variety of responses given. In addition to indicating responses most frequently made, attention is paid to those that are unusual and thought-provoking.

LIMITATIONS IN PROJECTING RESULTS. Research into consumer needs usually uses small samples; less than a hundred subjects is typical. The interviews tend to be time consuming, and to require interviewers with specialized skills. Both of these factors increase the research cost per interview and limit the number of interviews conducted. There is a danger in such small samples that a few extreme responses will distort the overall results. As a consequence the user of the research is uncertain of the representativeness of the results obtained.

The problem caused by small sample sizes is frequently intensified by the manner in which the samples are selected. For many indirect techniques, substantial cooperation is needed from sample members. In some cases, such as group interviews, sample members must be willing to come to a central location in order to be interviewed. The need for cooperative subjects tends to result in a sample that heavily favors certain available groups of people. The consequence may be that the results are not representative of the needs for all prospects.

Because of the small number of subjects and the lack of projectability, needs research results are used primarily to provide the advertising manager with a qualitative feeling for consumers' needs and attitudes. For this *qualitative research*    reason research of this type is commonly called **qualitative research.** In some cases the qualitative results can be quantified by using more direct question forms in large size samples once the appropriate questions have been established through qualitative research. Such studies might be conducted in connection with the search to identify prospects that is discussed in the next chapter.

## What to Look for in Consumer Needs Research Results

While an awareness of the limitations of consumer needs research is important, the value of the research findings should not be underestimated. The limitations, taken together, mean that the findings suggest categories of needs but do not reliably quantify their frequency of occurrence.

CONSUMER NEEDS. The central objective of consumer needs research is to discover the real needs that bring consumers to the market for products like those of the advertiser. The analysis of the data should therefore begin by extracting this information from the research data. The information sought goes beyond a simple listing of the uses to which the product is put, for this would be treating a product as an end in itself rather than as a means to an end. For example, it would not be terribly enlightening to find that the use to which most people put toothpaste is to brush their teeth. What advertisers really want to know is what need people are trying to satisfy by the whole tooth-brushing, tooth-cleaning ritual. Are they trying to avoid the discomfort of tooth decay and dental treatment, are they trying to avoid social rejection because of unpleasant breath, or is the ritual simply part of an effort to purge themselves of impurities?

SIGNIFICANT SUBGROUPS. In analyzing the research findings, the advertiser should not expect to find that all consumers are motivated to buy a particular product for the same reason. Most products can and do serve a variety of needs or solve a variety of problems. Consequently the total market is composed of consumers with many different needs. What the advertiser should seek in the research data, then, is a list of the significant needs for which consumers use the product. With this information, it should be possible to think of the total market for the product as being divided into subgroups of consumers. Each subgroup would be made up of those consumers who have a common need they are trying to satisfy. Such subgroups are termed consumer segments. One element of the positioning decision to be made in Chapter 10 is to select the segment to which the product and the advertising will be directed.

Results of recent research among users of non-fat dry milk (powdered milk) illustrate the diversity of needs satisfied by even a commonplace product. Research using projective questions (for example, "Why do you think people use non-fat dry milk?") found sharply differing reasons. For one group of consumers dry milk serves health needs. Because the product is low in fat, it serves as a nutritious beverage for people on low cholesterol diets. These consumers tend to be older men and women. Another group of consumers uses dry milk because it offers a low-cost substitute for fresh whole milk, thus serving an economy need. Consumers purchasing dry milk for economy reasons tend to head families with a large number of younger children. Still another group uses dry milk because of its convenience. In the positioning decision the advertiser must choose to which segment advertising is to be directed. Exhibit 6-6 shows a commercial for Carnation Instant Non-Fat Dry Milk positioning the product in the economy segment.

SEARCHING FOR PROBLEMS AND OPPORTUNITIES. In analyzing the results of consumer needs research the advertising manager should search for problems and opportunities that face the product. A problem is a barrier that prevents a product from realizing its potential. An opportunity is the opposite of a problem — it is a potential advantage which, if seized, will increase the potential of the product. Some examples of problems and opportunities may help to illustrate what to look for in the consumer needs research results.

One of the most rewarding opportunities to be found is a consumer need that is not satisfied by currently available products. For example, research among purchasers of microwave ovens discovered that a substantial number were dissatisfied with their purchase because the ovens were so large that they did not fit conveniently on a kitchen counter. This is a problem for current products but also a potential opportunity for a manufacturer able to produce a more compact product.

Any product class is made up of a mixture of heavy users and light or occasional users. In order to realize its potential a product must capture its fair share of heavy users. The consumer analysis may reveal whether or not a product has achieved this goal. A recent consumer study by a candy bar manufacturer revealed that it had an above-average number of adult purchasers and a below-normal proportion of children. This situation suggested a serious problem, perhaps correctable by advertising, because children are by far the heaviest consumers of candy bars.

The consumer analysis may also reveal consumer attitudes toward the advertiser's product, what they see as its use, and how it stacks up against competitive products. Thus, strengths and weaknesses may be revealed that represent opportunities to redirect a product. For example, research among automobile owners consistently reflects criticism of the durability and serviceability of automobiles, particularly those that are American made. Volvo has seized upon this as an opportunity and has for many years offered its automobiles as a more durable solution to the need for transportation. Exhibit 6-7 shows a current Volvo advertisement that focuses on this theme.

Consumer research findings may reveal confusion on the part of consumers about the advertiser's product and its use. The research could reveal that consumers are unaware of products like the advertiser's. Both problems seem to call for redirection of the advertising effort.

An ad positioning Carnation Instant Non-Fat Dry Milk in the economy segment.

EXHIBIT 6-6

*There he is folks.*

*America's number one . . .*

*milk consumer.*

*Fortunately, for our budget . . . we found an instant milk he'd drink.*

*We've been using Carnation Instant nonfat dry milk for years.*

*It's got all the . . .*

*calcium, protein and B-vitamins of whole milk -*

*Everything but the fat.*

*And it dissolves instantly . . . completely . . .*

*for a delicious, icy cold pitcher of milk.*

*Carnation Instant Milk. It costs less than 26¢ a quart -*

*and it's made for drinking!*

Courtesy: The Carnation Co.

**EXHIBIT 6-7**          An advertisement that offers Volvo as a solution to the automobile durability problem.

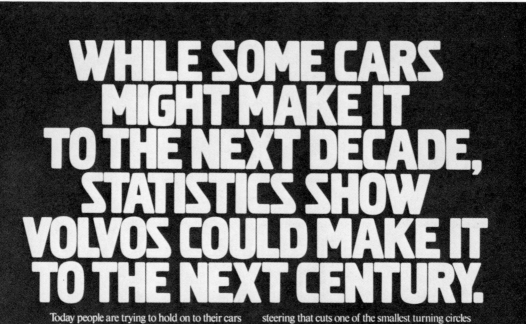

# WHILE SOME CARS MIGHT MAKE IT TO THE NEXT DECADE, STATISTICS SHOW VOLVOS COULD MAKE IT TO THE NEXT CENTURY.

Today people are trying to hold on to their cars longer than ever.

And while statistics show the average life expectancy of today's cars is eleven years, that figure pales in comparison to the life expectancy of today's Volvo.

Because statistics show the average life expectancy of a Volvo is over sixteen years.*

Which could mean over sixteen years of comfortable driving in seats equipped with adjustable lumbar supports that relieve tension and road fatigue.

Years of effortlessly maneuvering through parking lots due to power assisted rack and pinion steering that cuts one of the smallest turning circles of any car.

Years of clean air made possible by a Fresh Air Ventilation System that exhausts stale air from the passenger compartment, and helps prevent odors and fumes from ever getting inside.

If all this sounds like a sensible way to transport yourself to the next century, buy a Volvo.

Who knows?

By the year 2000 we may have a car that'll get you through that century, as well.

**VOLVO**
A car you can believe in.

*Based upon an actuarial analysis of 1981-1982 U.S. Registration Data conducted by Ken Warwick & Associates, Inc. Due to many factors including maintenance, driving conditions and habits, your Volvo may not last as long. Then again, it may last longer. Summary available at your Volvo dealer. © 1983 Volvo of America Corporation.

In order to provide direction to advertising programs, the advertiser must know what need the consumer seeks to satisfy through purchase of products like the one to be advertised. The difficulty in determining consumer needs stems from people's reluctance to reveal buying motives that may not put them in a favorable light. In order to get around consumers' reluctance to discuss their real reasons for purchasing products, researchers use indirect research techniques. These techniques try to create a situation in which consumers can talk about their reasons for purchase without fear of social embarrassment. These indirect techniques, although valuable, provide information that is difficult to interpret, difficult to quantify, and difficult to project. In analyzing results of research into consumer needs, advertisers should look for evidence concerning the real reasons why consumers purchase products like their own. In addition, advertisers should be alert to problems and opportunities that could influence their advertising efforts.

*CHAPTER SUMMARY*

Positioning description
Advertising objectives
Secondary source information
Original research
Indirect research techniques
Depth interview

Nondirective technique
Focus-group interview
Projective question
Association tests
Qualitative research

*KEY TERMS*

1. For each of the following products, comment on whether the reason for purchase is likely to be one that consumers would be willing to reveal or reluctant to discuss.

   a. Tires for a fleet of delivery trucks.
   b. Aerosol hair spray for men.
   c. A college education (by parents for their child).
   d. A lawn sprinkling system.
   e. Perfume.

2. A marketing researcher interested in the reasons why people live in mobile homes suspected, as discussed in the example in the chapter, that some mobile home owners are concerned that living in a mobile home lacks prestige. To investigate this possibility, mobile home owners were

*QUESTIONS FOR DISCUSSION*

contacted and asked to discuss the advantages and disadvantages of mobile home living. Although many advantages were listed, virtually no owners were able to think of any disadvantages. What should the researcher conclude?

3. Listed below are a number of pieces of information desired by an advertiser. For each one, write a projective question that would enable a consumer to answer accurately.

   a. The reason for buying life insurance.
   b. The reason for using instant coffee.
   c. The reason for buying private-label beer.
   d. The basis for selecting motel accommodations.

4. If an advertiser were attempting to discover the uses to which consumers might put a home computer, which would be the better research approach — depth interviews or group interviews?

5. Suppose that results from a small number of depth interviews suggest that one important reason for smoking cigars is to project manliness. Would it be possible to quantify this possibility in a large sample? What kind of question form might be used?

6. Three distinctly different types of products in the coffee market are ground coffee, instant coffee, and decaffeinated coffee. To what three different need groups might these three products appeal?

7. Suppose that research among purchasers of breakfast cereals revealed that these consumers were concerned about the high sugar content of many of these products, particularly those appealing to children. Does this represent a problem or an opportunity for marketers of breakfast cereals?

---

*PROBLEM*
    The National Highway Safety Administration decided to undertake a two-year, $5 million campaign to persuade automobile drivers and passengers to use seat belts.[5] The NHSA, a federal agency, was concerned at the fact that use of seat belts by drivers had declined to 11 percent from 25 percent six years earlier. The agency felt that if the program was successful, up to 15,000 lives a year could be saved.

    The NHSA planned to use a variety of means to communicate the buckle-up message, but the key element was to be television advertising. The agency hoped to place its commercials in prime-time network shows; dramatic and memorable commercials were planned. One, for example,

---

[5]This problem is based on Albert R. Karr "Will U.S. Push Sell the Public on Seat Belts?" *The Wall Street Journal* (August 13, 1981), p. 21.

would show a pumpkin flying through the air and smashing against a wall with the suggestion that this was what could happen in a collision to a motorist who had not used a seat belt.

When the advertising campaign was announced, some safety experts expressed doubt that it would be effective. It was noted that a dozen similar campaigns had already been tried with little evidence of their success. One critic contended that the program would not effectively reach young males and drunk drivers, the two groups most responsible for automobile accidents. An agency spokesperson, however, disagreed, stating that a more thorough effort was planned compared to past campaigns and that much greater emphasis would be placed on television.

1. What consumer need will the NHSA campaign be addressing?
2. Analyze the campaign approach and evaluate its chances for success. What changes would you recommend?

# CHAPTER 7 _____

## LEARNING OBJECTIVES

In studying this chapter you will learn:

- The information needed to identify who the prospects are for an advertiser's products.

- What a prospect profile is and how to construct it.

- The three important uses to which a prospect profile can be put.

- The various sources of information from which a prospect profile can be constructed.

Discussion of the consumer analysis section of the advertising plan has been divided into two sections. The last chapter described how to determine consumer needs, goals, and problems—vital information used in making the positioning decision. The needs analysis is qualitative; it gives a feeling about how consumers think, but it provides few hard numbers. By contrast, the second part of the consumer analysis to be described in this chapter is quantitative. Its objective is to identify prospects, defining in specific terms who is likely to buy the advertiser's product.

## The Need to Identify Prospects

Marketers are fond of saying that advertising should be used like a rifle and not like a shotgun. The thought is a good one. Not everyone is a prospect for an advertiser's products. Therefore, advertising should not be directed to everyone but focused on people who are likely purchasers. That is the purpose of this part of the consumer analysis—to get enough information about prospective purchasers so that advertising can be directed to reach them.

### Information Needed: An Overview

The end result needed from this part of the consumer analysis is clear.

We need to be able to say with some accuracy who the best prospects are for the advertiser's product. Generally this task is not too difficult to accomplish, but it is made easier if the process is divided into the following three steps.

WHO IS A PROSPECT? The first step is to decide who should be considered a prospect for the advertiser's product. For most products the number of consumers out of the total universe of consumers who are really likely to purchase a particular product is small. How does one differentiate between prospects and nonprospects? In terms of the consumer decision process discussed in Chapter 5, a prospect is a consumer with a need that might be satisfied by the advertiser's product. All others are nonprospects because advertising cannot make them need the product. As a practical matter it is not always easy to determine who has the relevant need. For that reason we will suggest, later in the chapter, some simplifying shortcuts to separate prospects from nonprospects.

DESCRIBING PROSPECTS. Once it has been determined who prospects are, the second step is to describe this group in terms that will permit the advertiser to reach them with advertising. What are the terms in which prospects should be described? In this case we can be quite specific since there are standard demographic specifications that advertisers have agreed to use so that results of different research projects are compatible.

SEGMENTING PROSPECTS. The first two information needs are relatively easy to fulfill; the third is somewhat more difficult. Having separated prospects out from all consumers, we would like now to be able to divide prospects into subgroups. Why is it desirable to do this? Aren't all prospects the same? Aren't they all of equal value to advertisers? The answer is usually no to both questions. As noted in the last chapter, different consumers may use particular products to satisfy a variety of needs. Recall the powdered milk example. Some consumers used the product for economy reasons, some for diet reasons, and others for convenience reasons. Thus, not all prospects for powdered milk are the same in terms of the need that they are trying to fulfill. These prospects may not be of equal value either. An advertiser may wish to specialize in serving the needs of one group of prospects rather than the whole group. For example, if one marketer had a vitamin-enriched, premium-priced dry milk, wouldn't the advertising be directed to the diet subgroup?

Students of marketing will recognize that these subgroups of consumers are termed **market segments** and that the process of dividing prospects into subgroups is called **segmenting the market.** The hard part of the task is to decide in what terms to subdivide or segment the prospect group and to find information that will permit one to do so. Once the segments have been defined there is a further step. The prospects in each segment need to be described in the same demographic terms used for the entire prospect group.

*market segments*
*segmenting the market*

### How Prospect Identification is Used

It is perhaps obvious at this point how prospect identification is used, but let us review the important applications of this information so that we are sure we know where we are going.

ANALYSIS OF PROBLEMS AND OPPORTUNITIES. As is true for other analysis sections of the advertising plan, an important use of prospect identification is to define problems and opportunities facing the advertiser's product. For example, identification of prospects tells the advertiser among what consumers the best sales opportunities can be found. Furthermore, by comparing this information to the company's actual sales pattern the advertiser can determine what sales opportunities are being missed.

POSITIONING THE PRODUCT. Prospect identification also enters into the positioning decision. If the analysis yields accurate information on the number and characteristics of consumers in each segment, it will help the advertising manager to decide toward which segment or segments to direct the product and its advertising.

MEDIA SELECTION. A final and obvious use of prospect identification lies in the selection of media to efficiently reach the most desirable prospects for the advertiser's product. As we will see in the media selection sections, information is available for most media that describes the characteristics of readers, viewers, or listeners of particular media. This information can be compared to the characteristics of the selected prospects to determine which medium most effectively reaches the chosen audience.

## Constructing a Prospect Profile

*prospect profile*

A convenient way to develop and present the prospect identification information needed by the advertising manager is to construct a prospect profile. A **prospect profile** is a table that presents the three pieces of information needed to identify prospects: (1) it defines who a prospect is and how many of them there are, (2) it describes prospects in demographic terms, and (3) it subdivides prospects into segments. As this section proceeds, we shall illustrate the construction of a prospect profile with a number of examples in consumer product fields. Since the problems in constructing a profile in nonconsumer products are somewhat different, it will be considered separately.

### Who Are the Prospects?

The starting point in constructing a consumer profile is to decide who among the total of all consumers is to be considered a prospect for the advertiser's product. We look first at the theoretically correct approach and then consider some of the shortcuts and compromises that are often necessary.

PROSPECTS ACCORDING TO THE CONSUMER DECISION PROCESS MODEL. According to the consumer decision process model discussed in Chapter 5, consumers purchase products as a means to satisfy needs. The more salient the need the more likely that consumers will allocate resources to purchase a solution. According to the model, then, a prospective purchaser of a product is any consumer with a strongly felt need that might be fulfilled by the advertiser's product.

In some cases it is practical to identify and count those consumers who are known to have a particular need. This approach is generally most useful with utilitarian problems rather than those that are social or psychological. As discussed in Chapter 6, social and psychological needs are less readily observed and less readily expressed by consumers. Thus, direct identification of consumers with particular nonutilitarian problems is often impractical.

CURRENT PURCHASERS. An easy and frequently useful way to determine who is a prospect is to find information on current consumers of products in the category of interest. This approach is easy because (1) there are many readily available sources of information on the number and characteristics of current users of products in a variety of categories, and (2) if this information is not available, the question can be answered by consumer research. For most product categories consumers will readily reveal whether or not they are users. Exhibit 7-1, as an example, shows the percentage of adults using a variety of cold remedies as identified by Mediamark Research in a national media and product usage survey. The survey revealed, for instance, that 29 percent of all adults had used medicated throat lozenges during the last 30 days. The 29 percent usage multiplied by the total adult population yields an estimate of just under 47 million current users of lozenges and, perhaps, 47 million prospects.

Percentage of adults using selected cold remedies.                                          **EXHIBIT 7-1**

| Product | % Users Last 30 Days | × | Adult Population | = | Total Adult Prospects |
|---|---|---|---|---|---|
| Medicated throat lozenges | 29% | × | 162,000,000 | = | 46,980,000 |
| Cough syrup | 27% | × | " | = | 43,740,000 |
| Nasal spray | 16% | × | " | = | 25,920,000 |
| Cough drops | 36% | × | " | = | 58,320,000 |
| Cold/sinus/allergy | 49% | × | " | = | 79,380,000 |

Source: *Pharmaceuticals* (Mediamark Research, Inc., 1982).

This approach is easy, but is it valid? Do current users accurately represent future prospects? For a well-established, mature product category (such as throat lozenges) the answer is probably yes. Although consumers may drift in and out of the user group, the characteristics of people using the product remain about the same. For the less well-known product—or for new products—using current consumers as an indicator of prospects may overlook substantial potential. For instance, when first introduced, personal computers were purchased by a small group of technically oriented and experimentally minded people. Later experience has revealed far wider application of the personal computer and a far larger prospect group. An estimation of the number of prospects based on the number of purchasers in the early years would have underestimated the market substantially.

PROSPECTS DEFINED BY RELATED CHARACTERISTICS. Another practical and useful way to identify and count prospects is through a readily observable characteristic that is necessarily related to the consumer's need or goal. The principle is easier to illustrate than to explain. For example, prospects for a yachting magazine would probably be people who own boats; the prospects for a denture cleanser would be people with dentures; the prospects for homeowner's insurance would be people who own homes. In each case prospects can be identified by a related characteristic that is readily observable. Sometimes the related characteristic is less direct. For example, who are the prospects for life insurance? Counting as prospects all persons who are living does not narrow the field very much. Suppose consumer research shows that life insurance is usually purchased by heads of households trying to satisfy the need to be good providers for their families. What are the easily observable related characteristics? Prospects are likely to be young, married, and to have a family.

The beauty of this approach is that the information needed to identify and count the number of prospects is often readily available. For example, in the consumer profile for vegetable gardeners shown in Exhibit 7-2, page 141, information was not available on current purchasers of garden products. Instead, a characteristic related to garden supplies purchasing was used. It was assumed that the best prospects for garden supplies were people who had gardens. Information was readily available showing that 43 percent of all U.S. households had gardens, giving a total of 30 million prospect households (43 percent with gardens × 70 million households = 30 million prospects at the time of the study).

DETERMINING APPROPRIATE HOUSEHOLD MEMBER. There is one further complication to be resolved in defining prospects for the advertiser's product. Until now we have spoken of the prospect as a household, but households don't buy products—people do, and advertising is directed to individuals rather than to households. Therefore, it is important to specify which member of the household is the prospect.

Profile of households with vegetable gardens.                                   EXHIBIT 7-2

| Characteristic | % Households with Vegetable Gardens |
|---|---|
| All households | 43 |
| Age | |
| 18–29 | 38 |
| 30–49 | 45 |
| 50 and over | 46 |
| Education | |
| College | 44 |
| High school | 42 |
| Grade school | 45 |
| Race | |
| White | 45 |
| Non-white | 39 |
| Occupation | |
| Professional | 46 |
| Business | 42 |
| Clerical and sales | 35 |
| Farmer | 74 |
| Manual labor | 42 |
| Non-labor force | 43 |
| Annual family income | |
| $15,000 and over | 48 |
| $10,000–$14,999 | 43 |
| $7,000–$9,999 | 41 |
| $4,000–$6,999 | 39 |
| Under $7,000 | 37 |
| Under $4,000 | 35 |
| Region | |
| East | 41 |
| Midwest | 52 |
| South | 44 |
| West | 34 |
| Garden size | |
| Over 2,500 sq. ft. | 28 |
| Under 2,500 sq. ft. | 15 |

Source: *Gardening in America* (Shelburne, VT: Gardens for All, Inc., 1977).

How is it decided who within the family is the prospect? Is it the person who purchases the product? Is it the user? It may be neither. If a woman buys dog food, certainly the user (the dog) is not the prospect, and if the woman made the purchase at the request of her husband, then the husband may be the prospect. The key issue is who specified the brand to be purchased. If the husband specifies the brand and his wife merely carries out his wishes, then the prospect is the husband. If the wife selects the brand, then she is the prospect. This definition of prospect relates directly to the consumer decision process outlined in Chapter 5. The role of advertising in this process is to influence which solution (brand) is selected to satisfy a particular need. Advertising must be directed to the person who selects the product, and this is not necessarily the person who purchases the product or the one who uses the product.

The results of a study on the family member who makes the purchase decision for a variety of familiar products is shown in Exhibit 7-3. Both husband and wife exert some influence in the purchase of most products shown in the table. However, the husband is clearly the key prospect for Scotch whisky, while the wife is the key prospect for cereals and peanut butter. (In the case of cereals it would be interesting to know the influence of children in the brand selection. Cereal manufacturers think their influence is high.)

## Describing Prospects

The result of defining who is a prospect permits the advertiser to determine how many people there are in the prospect group — how many people drink non-fat dry milk, how many households have gardens, etc. After the size of the prospect group has been established the advertising manager is ready to determine the characteristics of prospects so that they may be identified and reached through advertising media. The characteristics used to describe prospects should be the same as those used to describe the audiences of advertising media. This will permit the advertiser to compare media audiences with the characteristics of the prospect group to find a medium with an audience that matches or "delivers" advertising to the prospect group.

**EXHIBIT 7-3**      Husband vs. wife purchase influence (in percents).

|  | Purchased by: | | Direct influence | | | |
|---|---|---|---|---|---|---|
|  |  |  | Product | | Brand | |
|  | W | H | W | H | W | H |
| Cereals: | | | | | | |
|   Cold (unsweetened) | 84 | 16 | 74 | 26 | 71 | 29 |
|   Hot | 84 | 16 | 67 | 33 | 67 | 33 |
| Packaged lunch meat | 73 | 27 | 60 | 40 | 64 | 36 |
| Peanut butter | 81 | 19 | 70 | 30 | 74 | 26 |
| Scotch whisky | 35 | 65 | 18 | 82 | 18 | 82 |
| Bar soap | 85 | 15 | 65 | 35 | 64 | 36 |
| Headache remedies | 67 | 33 | 67 | 33 | 67 | 33 |
| Cat food (dry) | 66 | 34 | 75 | 25 | 81 | 19 |
| Dog food (dry) | 76 | 24 | 60 | 40 | 59 | 41 |
| Fast-food chain hamburgers | 68 | 32 | 55 | 45 | 55 | 45 |
| Catsup | 75 | 25 | 68 | 32 | 68 | 32 |
| Coffee: | | | | | | |
|   Freeze-dried | 68 | 32 | 57 | 43 | 62 | 38 |
|   Regular ground | 74 | 26 | 65 | 35 | 65 | 35 |
| Mouthwash | 72 | 28 | 56 | 44 | 56 | 44 |

Reprinted with permission from the March 17, 1975 issue of *Advertising Age*. Copyright 1975 by Crain Communications, Inc.

DEMOGRAPHIC DESCRIPTION. One means of describing prospects is through the use of *demographic data,* such as age, income, occupation, sex, and education. Through the years demographic classifications have become somewhat standardized although some classifications, like income classes, need to be updated often. The demographic classifications shown in Exhibit 7-4 on page 144 represent widely accepted classes for individuals.

Exhibit 7-2 shows a sample demographic profile of households with vegetable gardens which might be constructed for a marketer of garden supplies such as seeds, fertilizer, or implements. The prospect group is surprisingly large with 43 percent of all households maintaining a vegetable garden. There is some increase in gardening with age and income and gardening is heaviest in the Midwest and lightest in the West. One shortcoming of this profile is that the relative size of the various demographic classes that are used is not revealed.

This problem is overcome in the profile of travelers as shown in Exhibit 7-4, page 144. Like the other examples used here, this table presents only a partial profile showing a few of the available demographic classes. Notice that the second column in this profile shows the distribution of the total adult population so that the relative importance of various demographic classes can be seen. In addition, the percentages are arrayed vertically to show what percentage of total travelers come from each demographic subclass.

By comparing the percentage U.S. adults column with the percentage travelers column, one can quickly spot the heavy traveler groups and also determine how many prospects that group delivers to the total. Look, for example, at the distribution of travel by annual income. Clearly, adults with an annual income of over $35,000 travel more than the average. This group makes up 19 percent of the population, but accounts for 25 percent of the travel. Moreover, it is clear that the over-$35,000 group is large in size, making it a very important prospect group. This profile, which might have been constructed for the use of a travel agent or other marketer of travel services, shows that travel increases with income and education and is greatest among business and professional people.

Note that both the gardening and travel profiles were expressed as the percentage of each class participating in the activity of interest. Sometimes it is useful to express a profile in terms of the amount of a product used or consumed. This was done in the profile in Exhibit 7-5 which shows average weekly consumption of non-fat dry milk in quarts. Note how strongly consumption increases in large and relatively young families. These consumers clearly represent the heavy user group.

PSYCHOGRAPHIC DESCRIPTION. Consumer prospects may also be described using **psychographics**.[1] In this approach consumers are described with a series of dimensions that relate to activities, interests, and

*psychographics*

[1]See William D. Wells, (ed.), *Life Style and Psychographics* (Chicago: American Marketing Association, 1974).

144 PART TWO Setting Direction for the Advertising Program

EXHIBIT 7-4    Consumer profile of domestic travelers.

| Class | Total U.S. Adults | Total Travelers* |
|---|---|---|
| Total Consumers (000) | 161,718 | 92,248 |
| Descriptive Characteristics (%) | | |
| **Sex** | | |
| Men | 76,602 | 45,629 |
| Women | 85,116 | 46,619 |
| **Education** | | |
| Graduated College | 23,952 | 18,278 |
| Attended College | 27,422 | 18,499 |
| Graduated High School | 62,126 | 35,726 |
| Did Not Graduate H.S. | 48,219 | 19,745 |
| **Age** | | |
| 18–24 | 28,599 | 15,525 |
| 25–34 | 36,234 | 22,581 |
| 35–44 | 26,026 | 16,133 |
| 45–54 | 23,947 | 14,495 |
| 55–64 | 22,076 | 12,892 |
| 65 or over | 24,835 | 10,622 |
| **Employment Status** | | |
| Employed Full-Time | 83,022 | 52,594 |
| Employed Part-Time | 14,184 | 9,112 |
| Not Employed | 64,512 | 30,543 |
| **Employment Category** | | |
| Professional/Technical | 17,045 | 12,779 |
| Mgr./Admin./Clerical | 11,859 | 8,666 |
| Sales | 23,593 | 15,963 |
| Specialized and Supervisory Workers | 12,973 | 7,688 |
| Other employed | 31,735 | 16,609 |
| Not employed | 64,512 | 30,543 |
| **Income per annum** | | |
| $35,000 or over | 30,872 | 23,061 |
| $30,000–34,999 | 14,205 | 9,799 |
| $25,000–29,999 | 17,853 | 11,932 |
| $20,000–24,999 | 22,257 | 13,147 |
| $15,000–19,999 | 22,628 | 11,950 |
| $10,000–14,999 | 20,802 | 10,488 |
| $5,000–9,999 | 19,730 | 7,653 |
| $5,000 or less | 13,372 | 4,218 |

*A traveler is an adult who has taken a trip of over 100 miles one-way within the continental United States over the preceding 12 months.

Source: *Travel and Financial* (Mediamark Research, Inc., 1982).

Consumer profile of non-fat dry milk users.                                    EXHIBIT 7-5

| Characteristic | Average Weekly Consumption per Household of Non-Fat Dry Milk (in quarts) |
|---|---|
| Total U.S. | 5.72 |
| Region | |
| Northeast | 5.50 |
| North-Central | 6.27 |
| South | 5.55 |
| West | 5.60 |
| Income | |
| Under $4,000 | 4.89 |
| $4,000–$6,999 | 6.32 |
| $7,000–$10,000 | 6.15 |
| Over $10,000 | 5.43 |
| Family size | |
| 2 | 4.03 |
| 3 | 4.12 |
| 4 | 5.20 |
| 5 or more | 9.01 |

Source: Research and Development Division, American Dairy Association.

opinions. These factors are measured by asking prospects how they spend their time (activities), what they like to do (interests), and what they think about various issues (opinions). Prospects' responses are examined in a search for patterns that describe the common life-styles of significant groups of consumers.

One of the most far-reaching and widely used psychographic studies was the **Values and Life-Style (VALS) Program** conducted by Stanford Research Institute (now SRI International). The VALS Program, through a large-scale and detailed survey (800 questions and a national probability sample of 1600), developed detailed descriptions of nine life-styles, each with distinctive sets of values, attitudes, opinions, and beliefs.[2] The resulting VALS typologies are somewhat unique in that they are constructed first from inner values in the belief that these latter create consistent patterns of behavior or life-styles. The resulting life-styles, which are widely used in advertising, are summarized in Exhibit 7-6.

*values and life style (VALS) program*

[2] Arnold Mitchell, *The Nine American Lifestyles* (New York: Macmillan Publishing Co., Inc., 1983), Chap. 1 and the appendix.

How useful is psychographics? First, it should be noted that psychographics does not measure needs and thus is not as good a basis for segmenting as are needs, goals, and problems described in Chapter 6. However, life-styles do reflect or even result from needs and thus a group with a common need may also exhibit a common life-style. This suggests that life-style typologies can be used to describe segments and this is how they are commonly utilized in advertising. Life-style descriptions of prospects can be useful both in creating advertising and in media selection. As one advertising-agency manager put it, ".... life-style data provide a richer and more life-like picture of the target consumer than do demographics alone. They enable the writer or artist to form a better idea about the type

**EXHIBIT 7-6**    The VALS nine American life styles

| Typology | Description | Percent of Population |
|---|---|---|
| Achievers | Middle-aged and prosperous leaders; self-assured; materialistic; builders of the "American dream." | 22% |
| I-Am-Me | Transition state; exhibitionist and narcissistic; young; impulsive; dramatic; experimental; active; inventive. | 5% |
| Experiential | Youthful; seek direct experience; person-centered; artistic; intensely oriented toward inner growth. | 7% |
| Societally Conscious | Mission-oriented; leaders of single-issue groups; mature; successful; some live lives of voluntary simplicity. | 8% |
| Integrated | Psychologically mature; large field of vision; tolerant and understanding; sense of fittingness. | 2% |
| Survivors | Old; intensely poor; fearful; depressed; despairing; far removed from the cultural mainstream; misfits. | 4% |
| Sustainers | Living on the edge of poverty; angry and resentful; streetwise; involved in the underground economy. | 7% |
| Belongers | Aging; traditional and conventional; contented; intensely patriotic; sentimental; deeply stable. | 35% |
| Emulators | Youthful and ambitious; macho; show-off; trying to break into the system, to make it big. | 10% |

Source: Arnold Mitchell, *The Nine American Lifestyles* (New York: Macmillan Publishing Co., Inc., 1983), pp. 176–180.

of person he or she is trying to reach. They provide clues about what might or might not be appropriate to the life-style of the target consumer."[3]

Psychographics can also frequently be useful in media selection if the prospect groups have been described in terms of life-styles.[4] Some psychographic studies determine the media reading and viewing habits of each of the life-style groups. The VALS Program, for example, gathered extensive media data for each of the nine VALS typologies. If the advertiser knows from the consumer profile which life-styles dominate the prospect segment, media can then be selected that meet the media habits of the prospect segment. Similarly, some media, magazines for example, have surveyed their audiences to determine the life-style composition of their readers or viewers. Alternate media can then be compared to determine which ones deliver an audience with a life-style composition most like that of the prospect segment.

## Segmenting the Prospects

The third and final step in building a consumer profile is to separate the prospects into segments and to describe the characteristics of each segment.

SEGMENTATION CHARACTERISTICS. Not all consumers in a prospect group are of equal value to an advertiser. Some will be highly attracted to an advertiser's product, while others may find it less satisfactory than slightly different competitive products. It is useful to divide prospects into subgroups according to the type of product that is desired. Product advertising can then be directed to the subgroup most responsive to the company's product.

The process of dividing prospects into subgroups is termed **segmentation**. Each segment is a subgroup of prospects containing people who are alike in some respect, i.e., they have similar product needs. Prospect groups may be segmented along demographic, psychographic, social, cultural, socioeconomic, and various other lines. Such segmentation allows the advertiser not only to define the characteristics of the most likely prospect groups, but also to predict their product needs and to create advertising designed to position a particular product to appeal to those needs.

*segmentation*

The consumer needs research discussed in the last chapter should provide the advertiser with a definition of the significant consumer needs that could form a basis for segmenting consumers.

---

[3]Joseph Plummer, "Applications of Life Style Research to the Creation of Advertising Campaigns," in William D. Wells (ed.), *Life Style and Psychographics* (Chicago: American Marketing Association, 1974), p. 162.

[4]Douglas J. Tigert, "Life Style Analysis as a Basis for Media Selection," in William D. Wells, (ed.), *Life Style and Psychographics* (Chicago: American Marketing Association, 1974), pp. 173-201.

EXAMPLES OF SEGMENTATION ADDED TO THE PROSPECT PROFILES. To illustrate how segmentation enriches the prospect profile we return to the sample profiles shown in the previous section. Suppose that a marketer of organic fertilizers had defined the prospect group to include all vegetable gardeners. How should the prospect group be segmented? Exhibit 7-7 shows one obvious segmentation approach. The total vegetable gardener prospect group shown earlier in Exhibit 7-2 has been divided into two segments—gardeners who use organic methods and those who do not. Clearly this marketer would want to position the product against the

EXHIBIT 7-7          Vegetable garden prospect segments.

| Characteristics | %Households with Vegetable Gardens | %Households Using Organic Methods | %Households Not Using Organic Methods |
|---|---|---|---|
| All households | 43 | 25 | 18 |
| Age | | | |
| 18–29 | 38 | 22 | 16 |
| 30–49 | 45 | 27 | 18 |
| 50 and over | 46 | 26 | 20 |
| Education | | | |
| College | 44 | 33 | 11 |
| High School | 42 | 23 | 19 |
| Grade School | 45 | 22 | 23 |
| Race | | | |
| White | 45 | | |
| Non-white | 39 | | |
| Occupation | | | |
| Professional | 46 | | |
| Business | 42 | | |
| Clerical and Sales | 35 | | |
| Farmer | 74 | | |
| Manual Labor | 42 | | |
| Non-labor force | 43 | | |
| Annual family income | | | |
| $15,000 and over | 48 | 35 | 13 |
| $10,000–$14,999 | 43 | | |
| $7,000–$9,999 | 41 | | |
| $4,000–$6,999 | 39 | | |
| Under $7,000 | 37 | 16 | 21 |
| Under $4,000 | 35 | | |
| Region | | | |
| East | 41 | 27 | 14 |
| Midwest | 52 | 27 | 25 |
| South | 44 | 24 | 20 |
| West | 34 | 24 | 10 |
| Garden size | | | |
| Over 2,500 sq. ft. | 28 | 19 | 9 |
| Under 2,500 sq. ft. | 15 | 14 | 1 |

Source: *Gardening in America* (Shelburne, VT: Gardens for All, Inc., 1977).

organic segment. According to the profile this means that the advertiser should aim for better educated, higher income gardeners, especially those in the East and Midwest.

The profile constructed earlier for the use of travel agents (Exhibit 7-4) has been expanded in Exhibit 7-8 to show three segments—business travelers, vacation travelers, and travelers for other personal reasons. These three segments would demand quite different kinds of service and the travel agent might well wish to specialize in serving one segment. According to the profile, prospects who travel for business are less numerous than pleasure travelers, but their characteristics are quite distinctive, making them readily accessible through specialized audience media. Business travelers tend to be concentrated among upper income, better educated people, but they are particularly set off by their occupation, being most numerous among professional and administrative personnel. A travel advertisement for an airline is shown in Exhibit 7-9. To which of these segments—business, vacation, or personal—does this ad appear to be directed?

The non-fat dry milk prospect group has been segmented in Exhibit 7-10 into subgroups according to the reasons for which they use the product. The economy segment is made up of younger families with several children; in contrast, the diet segment is mostly made up of older people. The segment to which the advertiser should direct the advertising will depend on the characteristics of the product. Which need does the product best satisfy—diet or economy?

## Prospect Profiles for Nonconsumer Products

The approach to building a profile for products sold to businesses is generally the same as for consumer products, but two differences should be noted: (1) businesses as prospects, and (2) the description of prospect businesses.

BUSINESSES AS PROSPECTS. In constructing a profile for a product sold to businesses the prospect is usually designated as the business organization that would purchase the product. However, it is important to go one step further and learn what person within the prospect organization would actually select the product.

The person in an organization who makes the purchase decision will vary according to the kind and value of the product being sold. Janitorial supplies may be selected by a purchasing agent, but the purchase of heavy capital equipment may be decided by the president of the company. Especially in the case of major business purchases, several persons may have an important influence on product selection and each of them may have different motives which the advertiser must take into consideration.

THE DESCRIPTION OF PROSPECT BUSINESSES. The descriptive characteristics used in a prospect profile for consumer products are not applicable

**EXHIBIT 7-8**      Consumer profile of domestic travelers with prospect segments

| Class | Total U.S. Adults | Total Travelers* | Travel Segments | | |
| --- | --- | --- | --- | --- | --- |
| | | | Business | Vacation | Personal |
| Total Consumers (000) | 161,718 | 92,248 | 12,898 | 57,226 | 39,524 |
| **Descriptive Characteristics (000)** | | | | | |
| **Sex** | | | | | |
| Men | 76,602 | 45,629 | 8,779 | 26,895 | 18,780 |
| Women | 85,116 | 46,619 | 4,119 | 30,331 | 20,744 |
| **Education** | | | | | |
| Graduated College | 23,952 | 18,278 | 4,721 | 11,228 | 8,319 |
| Attended College | 27,422 | 18,499 | 3,108 | 11,435 | 8,188 |
| Graduated High School | 62,126 | 35,726 | 3,413 | 23,369 | 14,700 |
| Did not graduate H.S. | 48,219 | 19,745 | 1,657 | 11,195 | 8,317 |
| **Age** | | | | | |
| 18–24 | 28,599 | 15,525 | 1,755 | 9,573 | 7,135 |
| 25–34 | 36,234 | 22,581 | 3,770 | 14,190 | 9,670 |
| 35–44 | 26,026 | 16,133 | 3,131 | 9,911 | 6,471 |
| 45–54 | 23,947 | 14,495 | 2,381 | 9,170 | 6,500 |
| 55–64 | 22,076 | 12,892 | 1,435 | 8,249 | 5,270 |
| 65 or over | 24,835 | 10,622 | 427 | 6,133 | 4,477 |
| **Employment Status** | | | | | |
| Employed Full-Time | 83,022 | 52,594 | 10,581 | 32,401 | 21,949 |
| Employed Part-Time | 14,184 | 9,112 | 678 | 5,950 | 4,305 |
| Not Employed | 64,512 | 30,543 | 1,638 | 18,875 | 13,270 |
| **Employment Category** | | | | | |
| Professional/Technical | 17,045 | 12,779 | 3,312 | 7,921 | 5,644 |
| Managerial/Admin./Clerical | 11,859 | 8,666 | 2,677 | 5,277 | 3,534 |
| Sales | 23,593 | 15,963 | 2,429 | 10,206 | 6,783 |
| Specialized and Supervisory Workers | 12,973 | 7,688 | 1,174 | 4,805 | 3,163 |
| Other employed | 31,735 | 16,609 | 1,668 | 10,141 | 7,131 |
| Not employed | 64,512 | 30,543 | 1,638 | 18,875 | 13,270 |
| **Income Per Annum** | | | | | |
| $35,000 or over | 30,872 | 23,061 | 5,578 | 14,700 | 9,266 |
| $30,000–34,999 | 14,205 | 9,799 | 1,665 | 6,365 | 4,324 |
| $25,000–29,999 | 17,853 | 11,932 | 1,710 | 7,966 | 4,890 |
| $20,000–24,999 | 22,257 | 13,147 | 1,420 | 8,569 | 5,631 |
| $15,000–19,999 | 22,628 | 11,950 | 1,019 | 7,320 | 5,219 |
| $10,000–14,999 | 20,802 | 10,488 | 730 | 6,208 | 4,628 |
| $ 5,000– 9,999 | 19,730 | 7,653 | 407 | 4,008 | 3,497 |
| $ 5,000 or under | 13,372 | 4,218 | 368 | 2,090 | 2,069 |

*A traveler is an adult who has taken a trip of over 100 miles one-way within the continental United States over the preceding 12 months.

Source: *Travel and Financial* (Mediamark Research, Inc., 1982).

A travel ad directed to one of the travel segments.

EXHIBIT 7-9

# American announces the end of the line.

At American Airlines, we know business travelers have enough obstacles in their way without standing in lines at airports. That's why we invented no-stop check-in.℠ Now, thousands of authorized Travel Agents and every American Airlines ticket office can give you all your boarding passes for your entire trip before you get to the airport.

That means the end of waiting in lines. And with our pre-reserved seating, you can even choose your seat when you make your reservations. For more information and reservations, call your Travel Consultant or American today. American's no-stop check-in. Now we've taken out all the stops to get you through airports faster.

# American
## We're American Airlines. Doing what we do best.

Courtesy:  American Airlines

EXHIBIT 7-10        Non-fat dry milk prospect segments.

| Characteristic | Weekly Household Consumption of Non-Fat Dry Milk (in quarts) | | | | |
| --- | --- | --- | --- | --- | --- |
| | Total | Economy | Diet | Convenience | Other |
| Total U.S. | 5.72 | 2.63 | 1.37 | 0.69 | 1.03 |
| Region | | | | | |
| Northeast | 5.50 | 2.09 | 1.87 | 0.50 | 1.04 |
| North-Central | 6.27 | 3.26 | 1.13 | 0.82 | 1.06 |
| South | 5.55 | 2.44 | 1.22 | 0.67 | 1.22 |
| West | 5.60 | 2.86 | 1.18 | 0.84 | 0.72 |
| Income | | | | | |
| Under $4,000 | 4.89 | | | | |
| $4,000 to $6,999 | 6.32 | | | | |
| $7,000 to $10,000 | 6.15 | | | | |
| Over $10,000 | 5.43 | | | | |
| Family Size | | | | | |
| 2 | 4.03 | 1.13 | 1.69 | 0.52 | 0.69 |
| 3 | 4.12 | 1.65 | 1.32 | 0.45 | 0.70 |
| 4 | 5.20 | 2.03 | 1.35 | 0.52 | 1.30 |
| 5 or more | 9.01 | 5.32 | 1.08 | 1.08 | 1.53 |
| Age of housewife | | | | | |
| Under 25 | 3.91 | 2.70 | 0.35 | 0.39 | 0.47 |
| 25–34 | 7.70 | 4.93 | 0.77 | 0.77 | 1.23 |
| 35–44 | 6.62 | 3.64 | 1.19 | 0.93 | 0.86 |
| 45–54 | 5.62 | 1.74 | 1.91 | 0.73 | 1.24 |
| 55 and over | 4.21 | 1.14 | 1.68 | 0.46 | 0.93 |

Source:  Research and Development Division, American Dairy Association.

when the product is to be advertised to businesses. The descriptive characteristics used in business profiles should be those that help the advertiser identify prospect businesses so that media can be selected to reach the appropriate members in the business organization. In fact, a good approach to deciding on the descriptive characteristics to be used in a profile for business prospects is to examine circulation reports provided by business magazines typical of the field in which the product will be advertised.

There are four classes of descriptive information that will usually be needed. The geographic location of prospects should be described, usually in terms of regions defined by the U.S. Bureau of the Census. The type of business in which the prospect firm is engaged should be specified, usually in terms of the Standard Industrial Classifications (SIC) that have been established by the U.S. Office of Management and Budget. The SIC code assigns a two-digit number to each broad field of economic activity. For example, SIC code 25 covers businesses in the furniture and fixture industry; SIC code 26 covers paper and allied products. Digits are added to the code to form three-digit and four-digit codes that narrow the industry classification.

The size or volume of the prospect businesses should be described. This description may be in terms of sales volume, number of employees, or assets, depending upon the field of business. Finally, there should be an attempt to describe the characteristics of the person or persons who are influential in the purchase decision. The description might include job title, function, and demographic characteristics.

## Uses of the Prospect Profile

There are three important uses to which the prospect profile can be put: (1) as an aid in defining problems and opportunities facing the product, (2) as an aid in positioning the product, and (3) as an aid in selecting media.

### Defining Problems and Opportunities

A major purpose of all the analysis sections in the advertising plan is to define problems and opportunities facing the advertiser's product. The prospect profile should first be examined to determine what problems and opportunities are revealed. Some examples may suggest what to look for.

Some prospect profiles will reveal a group of prospects with underdeveloped potential. Look for example, at the consumer profile for non-fat dry milk in Exhibit 7-10, above. Clearly the 25 to 34 and 35 to 44 age groups are heavy users and are key groups in the market largely because they use dry milk as an economical way to nourish children. In older age groups consumption focuses on dietary use and falls off in total. In part, this decline in consumption is due to the smaller family size as children grow up and leave home. However, perhaps the older age group offers an unrealized opportunity to expand usage. If the standard quart and half-gallon packages are too large for the small household, a small size packet might increase usage and create a competitive advantage. This is the type of opportunity sometimes revealed by examination of a prospect profile.

Problems and opportunities are often revealed by comparing the prospect profile with the profile of the advertiser's own brand. Such a comparison could show, for example, that the advertiser's own sales are strongly clustered in a particular segment, which may or may not be the segment toward which the advertising message has been directed. For example, using the non-fat dry milk profile, if data were collected on the advertiser's non-fat dry milk sales which showed sales to be clustered in the diet segment, the advertiser might want to reposition the product to appeal to the economy segment, which is comprised of heavier users of non-fat dry milk.

A careful study of the prospect profile may reveal other differences, unusual patterns, or unexpected groupings. If a prospect profile is done each year, changes can be compared to determine emerging problems or opportunities.

## Positioning the Product

The prospect profile is one of several pieces of information that the advertiser will look at in positioning the product. The profile is particularly useful in suggesting the segment to which product advertising should be directed.

The travel prospect profile in Exhibit 7-8 showed that the pleasure travel segment has over four times more prospects than the business travel segment. Hence, pleasure travelers appear to be an attractive target. On the other hand, the business travel segment, although smaller, is nicely focused. Although the profile does not reveal it, business travelers tend to travel more frequently and to purchase travel services more heavily than pleasure travelers. These factors may make the business traveler an attractive target.

The non-fat dry milk profile in Exhibit 7-10 reveals similar distinct differences between segments. The economy segment is large and well focused. The diet segment is smaller, but it is also well focused in a very different group. More information would be needed before a choice could be made between these two segments. However, the profile does suggest that the two segments are so strongly different that they would require quite different advertising efforts.

## Selecting Media

After the positioning decision has been made, the prospect profile provides clear guidance in the selection of media. The profile provides a precise description of the characteristics of the target prospects that the advertiser's message is to reach. This description can be compared with the audience characteristics of available media to find a match between audience and prospect group.

If, for example, the advertiser decided to position the non-fat dry milk product in the diet segment of users (perhaps because the product offered special vitamin fortification), what media characteristics would be called for? The profile of the diet segment suggests that the media selected should be those with family audiences that are smaller and older in age.

## Sources of Information for the Prospect Profile

In the search for data for the prospect profile, the advertising manager must expect to be faced with imperfect and incomplete information. Many times a prospect profile will have to be compiled from many different sources. As incomplete as the information may be, it is likely to be a great advance over intuition. The risks and rewards in advertising are too great to justify reliance on intuition.

## Building Profiles from Existing Information

Many advertisers, especially those with limited research funds, build prospect profiles from existing sources of information. These sources will be considered first.

INDUSTRY SOURCES. There is a great deal of information on the characteristics of prospects available, often free, from industry sources. Two of the profiles shown earlier were constructed from readily available industry data. The non-fat dry milk profile was based on information from survey research published by the American Dairy Association, while the garden profile was based on the results of a survey sponsored by the National Association for Gardening.

Trade associations are frequently an excellent source of information because they often do surveys of consumer characteristics as a service to their members. Trade or business periodicals serving an industry often do the same thing, conducting research on product categories that are the subject of their publication. Consumer magazines and newspapers often offer profile information developed from surveys on various product classes. They usually conduct these studies to demonstrate how effectively their publication reaches a particular consumer group. For some kinds of products, particularly those sold to businesses, government publications provide excellent data on prospect characteristics. For example, advertisers of products or services sold to banks will find enormous amounts of information on bank characteristics from the Federal Reserve Board and Federal Deposit Insurance Corporations publications.

There are some cautions to be observed in using information from these industry sources because the information is generally gathered for a purpose other than the one to which the advertiser is putting it. As a result, the descriptive characteristics and the choice of segments may not be the ones that the advertiser would select. If the advertiser tries to piece together a profile from more than one source, the data from different sources often will not fully match because different definitions or descriptive characteristics are used. The advertiser should also be conscious of the reason why the source is providing the information. There are cases where the purpose is promotional, in which case the advertiser should be on guard against bias caused by selective presentation of findings.

SYNDICATED RESEARCH SERVICES. There are several research companies that regularly gather information on prospects for a variety of product classes and then offer the results for sale. The profile of travel prospects shown in Exhibits 7-4 and 7-8 were constructed from such information. A leading service offering this type of information currently is Mediamark Research, Inc. (MRI). In addition to showing prospect characteristics, these studies often provide information on the audience characteristics of various media. This permits matching of media characteristics with characteristics of the selected prospect group.

The information reported by these commercial report services is gathered in a number of different ways. Some services, MRI for example, approach a large sample of consumers with a direct questionnaire asking about their purchase and usage patterns for a great variety of products. Another approach is to maintain a panel on consumers who record their purchases of a variety of products in a diary. Purchases by all panel members as well as their socioeconomic characteristics are gathered, tabulated, and then provided to subscribers of the research service. Market Research Corporation of America (MRCA) is the leading supplier of this service. One difference in the information provided by this latter approach is that it shows purchases over a period of time with the result that trends in purchaser characteristics can be observed.

## Original Research — Segmentation Studies

An alternative source of data for the prospect profile is original research. This approach is more expensive and more time-consuming than use of existing data, but it may yield more satisfactory results.

ADVANTAGES OF ORIGINAL RESEARCH. Original research makes it possible to avoid difficulties that occur when existing data are used. Profiles developed from existing information are frequently incomplete because not all necessary data can be found. Many times definitions of prospects or segments are compromises based on the availability of data. Often profiles developed from existing information must be pieced together from several sources. Definitions and techniques may not be entirely compatible, making comparison difficult.

The basic advantage of original research is that it avoids the problems of incompleteness and lack of comparability. Because the research is designed specifically for constructing a consumer profile, all data can be collected at one time using comparable definitions.

SEGMENTATION STUDY RESEARCH APPROACH. Original research for prospect profile information generally utilizes some form of direct questioning of consumers. The sample sizes used are generally large, particularly in comparison to samples used in the consumer needs research which was discussed in Chapter 6. These research studies, often called **segmenta-**
*segmentation studies*     **tion studies,** usually take one of two forms — *a priori* and response-based.[5]

---

[5]James H. Myers and Edward Tauber, *Market Structure Analysis* (Chicago: American Marketing Association, 1977). See especially Chapter 6.

*A Priori Segmentation Studies.* In an ***a priori* segmentation study** the researcher knows or assumes in advance of the study what the segments are that are to be described. This information might be derived, for example, from the consumer needs research such as described in the last chapter. In doing such a segmentation study prospects are identified, separated into segments based on their responses to classification questions, and then asked questions that reveal their demographic characteristics. For example, in the case of the non-fat dry milk example prospects would be identified by asking if they use or have used in some specified time period non-fat dry milk. If from the needs research the segments were believed to be diet, economic, and convenience, prospects would be assigned to segments based on their response to the question, "Why do you use non-fat dry milk?" Finally, respondents would be asked a series of questions to determine their demographic characteristics.

*a priori segmentation studies*

*Response-Based Segmentation Studies.* **Response-based segmentation studies** by contrast, begin without the researcher's knowing or assuming what the prospect segments are. Instead, prospects are asked a longer series of questions about how they use the product, their product preferences, usage rates and benefits desired. At this point powerful statistical techniques are brought into play to sort through the many responses. These techniques are termed multivariate because they are capable of dealing with many variables at one time. The multivariate techniques, usually performed by computer routines, search through the many responses trying to find natural groups of prospects in terms of their responses to the questions. These natural groups are the segments.

*response-based segmentation studies*

Once the segments have been defined in this way, the prospects can be described on the basis of normal demographic characteristics so that media can be selected to reach them.

It should be noted that the statistical techniques group prospects according to their responses to questions. This does not guarantee that the prospects in the group will respond in a common way to particular products and advertising. This can be determined only by further testing.

---

In addition to understanding prospect needs, the advertiser must learn the identity of prospects so that media can be efficiently directed to reach them. The prospect profile provides a convenient way to develop the identity of prospects. It is constructed in three steps. The starting point is to decide who is a prospect and to determine how many there are. As nearly as is practically possible, prospects are defined as consumers with strongly felt needs that can be satisfied by the advertiser's product. Prospects are next described in terms of demographic characteristics. The descriptive characteristics used should be parallel to those used in describing media audiences in order to facilitate matching media with target

*CHAPTER SUMMARY*

prospects. The final step is to break the prospect group into subgroups or segments and describe each segment using the same demographic characteristics. Each segment should contain prospects that are alike with regard to the products and information to which they respond. This probably means that they share common needs.

The completed prospect profile is analyzed to reveal problems and opportunities facing the advertiser's product. It is also a useful aid in positioning the product and is used in selecting media that will efficiently reach the selected segment.

Data for construction of the prospect profile may come from secondary sources or from original research. Trade publications and industry sources provide inexpensive data for constructing prospect profiles in many product categories. Original research provides more complete and compatible information but at a higher cost.

---

*KEY TERMS*

| | |
|---|---|
| Market segments | Segmentation |
| Segmenting the market | Segmentation studies |
| Prospect profile | *A priori* segmentation studies |
| Psychographics | Response-based segmentation studies |
| Values and Life Style (VALS) Program | |

---

*QUESTIONS FOR DISCUSSION*

1. Prospects for a product are consumers with a need that can be satisfied by the product. What needs would the following products satisfy:

   a. Roofing shingles?
   b. Camera film?
   c. Original oil paintings?
   d. Industrial germicidal floor and wall cleaner?

2. For each of the above products, name the related characteristics that might identify prospects for each product.

3. Review in Exhibit 7-3 who makes and influences purchase decisions for dry cat food and dry dog food. What differences do you see? What underlying consumer need do you think accounts for the differences?

4. Identify the member of the family who is most likely to be the prospect for the following products:

   a. Razor blades.
   b. Electric razors.
   c. Breakfast cereals.
   d. New automobiles.
   e. Men's dress shirts.

5. Some years ago, a social researcher suggested that the automobile has five central meanings: (1) a practical means of transportation, (2) a sizable investment and a source of upkeep cost, (3) a source of social status, (4) a means of expressing personal mastery and control, and (5) a means of personality expression.[6] Based on these five meanings, how would you segment today's automobile market? For each segment suggest two or three car models that appear to satisfy the segment prospects' goal.

6. For each of the products listed below, which of the VALS life-style classes enumerated in Exhibit 7-6 do you feel would provide an above average proportion of prospects?

   a. Over-the-counter sleeping aids.
   b. Portable radio/tape players.
   c. Pickup trucks.
   d. American flags.

7. Suppose that you were advertising a drug product sold by prescription only and you had determined that the prospects were the prescribing physicians. What descriptive characteristics would you use in identifying these prospects?

8. Suppose the profile of the beer market developed by the advertising manager for Brand "B" contained the following data:

| Household Income | % Beer Drinkers | % Drink Brand "B" |
|---|---|---|
| $    0- 9,999 | 50 | 5 |
| 10,000-19,999 | 55 | 7 |
| 20,000 & over | 45 | 12 |

   Does this indicate that Brand "B" has a problem? What other information would you like to have?

9. The consumer profile for a child-care product indicates that the best prospects are mothers with young children, a medium-to-low family income, and some high school education. The market for the product appears to be national without great geographic variation. What media would appear to have matching audience profiles?

10. An advertising manager for a manufacturer of prefabricated vacation homes has requested that the marketing research manager assist in gathering data for construction of a consumer profile. The researcher has suggested that the profile be constructed from information contained in requests that have been received for a free booklet on house designs offered by company advertisements. The request coupons

---

[6]Pierre Martineau, *Motivation in Advertising* (New York: McGraw-Hill Book Company, 1957), pp. 68-73.

contain spaces for the consumer to indicate age, income, occupation, geographic location, family size, and number of children. Some 2,000 of these requests have been received. Do you think the results would provide reliable information? Explain.

---

*PROBLEM*        Some years ago, a midwestern dairy products manufacturer developed a new form of dry milk. Dry milks then on the market were 100 percent fat free, meaning that all the butterfat was removed during the drying process. The dairy company's new product idea was to leave 5 percent butterfat in the dry milk. When reconstituted, the milk would have 0.5 percent butterfat, slightly less than the 1 to 2 percent butterfat content of liquid low-fat milks that were popular at the time. Leaving some butterfat in the dry milk gave it a richer, creamier taste than non-fat dry milk when reconstituted. An advertisement for the new product is shown on page 161.

1. Review the prospect profile shown in Exhibit 7-10. To what segment do you think the new product should be directed?
2. Within the segment that you have selected, what member of the family would be the prime target for advertising?
3. What audience characteristics would you seek in the advertising media that you selected to reach your target audience?

A dry milk product containing a low level of butterfat.

# Instant milk isn't a bargain if your kids won't drink it.

But there is an instant milk your kids will drink. It's Milkman® Low-Fat Instant Milk. You see, Milkman is made with a kiss of cream.

Unlike non-fat instant milk, Milkman has a delicious touch of cream added, so it tastes richer, fresher, and better than instant milk ever did before.

Milkman with the kiss of cream. Your kids will drink it up. While you keep the cost of milk down.

## They'll love Milkman. It's got the kiss of cream.

# CHAPTER 8

Consumer analysis is designed to give the advertiser knowledge of the needs and goals that prospects are trying to satisfy. However, before selecting one of these needs and promising that the product will satisfy it, the advertising manager must determine what the product is capable of doing for the consumer. In other words, the decision as to which segment of the market advertising ought to be directed depends, in part, on the attributes of the product.

Thus, an important purpose in product analysis is to determine what problem-solving or need-satisfying attributes the product possesses. Because of the close relationship between product analysis and consumer analysis it is likely that the two will be done simultaneously, each suggesting leads for further investigation of the other.

In addition to determining the attributes of the product, the product analysis should continue the search for problems and opportunities. The advertiser needs to determine the shortcomings of the product so that improvements can be made and also to determine the advantages of the product, for these latter represent opportunities to improve sales.

## What Is A Product?

The advertiser's analysis of the product should begin with a clear understanding of what the product is. At first glance, the question "What is a product?" seems a simple one, usually summoning to mind a particular brand name, a package, and, perhaps, a recent advertisement. But the discussion in Chapter 5 of the consumer decision process and the role played by the product should alert the advertiser to the danger of such an oversimplified view. While it is useful to view the product through the manufacturer's eyes as an item with certain physical and technical attributes, it is also essential that the product be viewed as the consumer sees it, as a means of satisfying a need.

A second caution to be kept in mind is that a product has multiple characteristics. A product should be considered as a "bundle" of characteristics or attributes, each of which must be examined and understood prior to designing the advertising.

## Defining the Physical Product

A good way to begin the product analysis is by deciding the elements to be included in what is to be called the product. Defining the product is not as easy as it might at first seem. Suppose, for example, that the product to be advertised is a vacuum cleaner. The machine itself is clearly a part of the product, but what about the warranty on the vacuum? Is that part of the product? How about service facilities, accessories, free delivery?

A good guideline in defining the product is to include all attributes that offer a consumer benefit. This definition ensures that the product analysis will consider all features of the product that might provide an advertisable attribute.

The product includes, of course, the physical features such as design and ingredients that are manufactured into the product. Certainly the method of packaging must be considered to be part of the product. Packaging protects and identifies the product and it may also have value for other uses when the product is gone. For purposes of product analysis, price represents an important and promotable attribute of the product. If the cost structure is such that the product can be priced below the market, this is clearly an attribute with promotional value. The physical availability of the product or of service on the product are also promotable attributes.

DEFINING SIMPLE PRODUCTS. Probably the easiest type of product to define is one that is marketed in only one style, size, design, or color, for example, the Fox tennis racquet shown in Exhibit 8-1. Although this is a simple product, it has various advertisable attributes that are part of the physical product. In effect, the Fox advertisement lists ten attributes of this racquet, each of which could be a consumer benefit.

DEFINING MORE COMPLEX PRODUCTS. Moving beyond the simple product, however, product definition becomes more complex. Many products are offered in a variety of sizes, styles, prices, and packages. This variety is usually an attribute of the product because it allows the consumer more nearly to match the product to the need. More complex products frequently offer a variety of options and accessories to go with the physical product, plus, in many cases, services such as installation, service programs,

EXHIBIT 8-1        An ad offering a simple product with a variety of attributes.

Courtesy: FOX TENNIS RACQUETS CO., INC.

and financing. Exhibit 8-2 shows an advertisement for a complex service, Merrill Lynch's Cash Management Account. This complex offering includes:

1. a brokerage account
2. service by an account executive
3. Merrill Lynch research
4. automatic investment of idle cash
5. a choice of money-market accounts
6. a special VISA card
7. check-writing privileges
8. insurance protection on securities held
9. special loan privileges

SINGLE PRODUCT VS. PRODUCT LINE. Some marketers sell a line of products that are all related, but with each item having distinctive characteristics. A decision must be made as to whether or not the individual items are sufficiently similar to be included in a single product definition. For example, in the commercial in Exhibit 8-3, a single advertisement is used for a product line because it is clear that the products are closely related. A manufacturer of automobiles, on the other hand, might prefer to consider a compact model to be a product that is different from the luxury model even though they bear the same family brand name. This separation would appear especially sound if the items were to receive separate advertising campaigns.

DEFINING THE PRODUCT OF SERVICE, RETAIL, AND WHOLESALE FIRMS. Still more complex is the definition of the product offered by service, wholesale, and retail firms. It is important in these cases to take a broad view in order to encompass all of the attributes of the product.

The marketer of a service usually offers not just a single item, but many services all of which make up the product. Think, for example, of the services offered by a car rental firm. The firm offers particular makes and models of automobiles, available at a variety of locations, with a variety of prices and insurance options. All of these elements make up the product of the car rental firm.

It is essential that the product of the retail store also be thought of as a complex bundle of attributes. The product of a menswear store is more than suits and the product of a hardware store is more than nuts and bolts. The mix of products carried by a retailer is an important and promotable element of the product. However, the retailer may also find promotable attributes in location, parking facilities, credit terms, return policy, delivery service, specialized personnel, and many other services. It is the total of these elements — products, location, and services — that make up the product of the retail firm.

The product of the wholesale firm is similar to that of the retail firm. The product variety carried by the wholesaler is an important element. However, there are also other important elements to the product such as delivery, credit terms, advisory services, and special order services. All of

**EXHIBIT 8-2**     An advertisement offering a complex service.

# IF YOU'RE SATISFIED WITH A BANK MONEY MARKET ACCOUNT, MAYBE YOU'RE NOT DEMANDING ENOUGH.

## DO MORE WITH YOUR MONEY IN CMA®

Bank money market accounts are just that: bank accounts. What they can do with your money is limited. But with the Cash Management Account® financial service at Merrill Lynch, the breadth of investment options is far wider.

And with the economy clearly on the mend, *the greatest opportunities now are for investors, not savers.*

**You get an Account Executive, not just an account.** At the core of the CMA program is a Merrill Lynch brokerage account, individually serviced by a Merrill Lynch Account Executive who, in turn, is backed up by *the top-ranked research team on Wall Street.*

And that can be important, because although the bull market is likely to continue, we think the easy money has already been made. From now on, the key to success will be your skill in selecting the best growth opportunities *in certain sectors* of the market; and no one can help you do that better than the investment professionals at Merrill Lynch.

**The all-in-one financial service.** But it's not just your Account Executive who makes a CMA account so valuable.

Your idle cash is invested automatically, and earns dividends in a choice of money market funds — including one that gives you tax-free income, which you can't get in a bank money market account.

You also get a special VISA® card and check-writing privileges. At the end of each month, you receive a detailed statement of all the activity within your CMA account; it can save you a lot of hunting around at tax time.

And you have the reassurance of knowing that all securities held by Merrill Lynch in CMA accounts are protected for up to $10 million per customer.

**Loan rates that give bank rates some tough competition.** One final advantage of CMA: the extra resource of automatic variable-rate loans, up to the full margin loan value of your securities, at rates banks are not likely to match. *If you're currently paying your bank more than 12% for a loan, you're paying too much.*

No wonder customers now have over $60 billion working for them through the CMA program...and you can join them with a minimum investment of only $20,000 in cash, securities or a combination of the two.

And if you demand more of your money, you probably *should* join them.

For more information, including a prospectus containing all sales charges and expenses, call our Lincoln office at 402 474-5121. Read the prospectus carefully before investing or sending money.

And talk to a Merrill Lynch Account Executive. No one else can give you more help with more kinds of investments. No one else.

**THE MORE YOU DEMAND OF YOUR MONEY, THE MORE YOU NEED CMA.®**

Merrill Lynch Pierce Fenner & Smith Inc.

**A breed apart.**

A commercial that features a line of closely related products.

EXHIBIT 8-3

(MUSIC UNDER)
VACUUM (SINGS): I'VE GOT FIVE WAYS
TO LOVE

LOVE MY CARPET.
(SPEAKS) So do you!

Now, only Love My Carpet comes in five
terrific scents.

Introducing new Forest Fresh.

'Course Forest Fresh knocks

dog, cat, smoke and musty odors out of
the rug.

After all,

it's Love My Carpet.

Love My Carpet makes your whole room
smell fresh and clean

with a choice no one else can match. . .
five wonderful scents.

(SINGS) THAT'S WHY YOU'LL LOVE. . .

LOVE MY CARPET.
(MUSIC OUT)

Courtesy: Lehn & Fink Products Group, Sterling Drug, Inc.

these elements should be included within the scope of the product description as it comes to be evaluated in the product analysis.

## What is the Consumer's Perception of the Product?

To understand what a product is, it must be viewed not only from the manufacturer's viewpoint as has just been suggested, but also from the consumer's viewpoint. That is, the advertiser, in searching for promotable attributes, needs to know what characteristics of the product are actually perceived by the consumer.

CONSUMER'S VIEW VS. MANUFACTURER'S VIEW. The consumer looks at the product as something different than the physical attributes created by the manufacturer. The consumer views products in terms of their potential for satisfying needs. The consumer's view of a product is based on knowledge gathered from information sources such as advertising, word-of-mouth, and product experience. Over a period of time, products develop reputations in the consumer's mind regarding the kind of need each product will satisfy. The perceived product, then, is the need-satisfying value that consumers believe a particular product possesses. These perceptions are part of the mechanism by which the consumer matches alternative products to needs.

Sometimes the product attributes that consumers perceive as being useful for satisfying needs are the same attributes that the manufacturer sees as physical attributes of the product. The consumer, however, stores only a fraction of the physical attribute information, concentrating on information that seems useful. In addition, the consumer often develops knowledge about the symbolic value of products, sometimes from advertisements, but more often from social and cultural sources. In other words, consumers also value a product for what it symbolizes in the eyes of other people. Certain automobiles represent prestige and houses in certain sections of town symbolize success. The symbolic attributes of products are no less a part of the perceived product than are the physical characteristics.

*product (brand) image*

CORPORATE IMAGE, PRODUCT IMAGE. Sometimes the term **product image** or **brand image** is used to describe the sum of consumer perceptions, impressions, or predispositions toward a particular product. Similar terms are used to refer to consumer perceptions of an entire company (corporate image) or of an entire retail establishment (store image). There is, however, an unfortunate tendency to overuse the term "image" and to use it in an imprecise way by referring to a brand as having a "good" image or a "bad" image. It is much more useful to specify the dimensions of consumers' attitudes toward the brand through the use of expressions such as "an expensive brand," or "a brand for older people," or "a dependable brand."

Analyzing the
Attributes of the Product

In a broad sense what the advertiser needs to know about the product is the need it satisfies. To understand the product's characteristics, the advertising manager should analyze (1) the physical product to determine what characteristics have been manufactured into the product; (2) the product as perceived in order to determine what attributes the consumer sees in the product; and (3) past advertising for the product to determine the attributes that have been promised to consumers.

## Analysis of the Physical Product

In analyzing the physical product, particular attention should be paid to discovering characteristics in the product that are unique or that confer upon it a competitive advantage when compared to similar products. If the attributes of the product make it a superior solution to a consumer need, this is useful information that can be communicated to prospective consumers.

The physical product analysis should also attempt to uncover shortcomings of the product. For what needs does it constitute an unsatisfactory solution? In what ways do competitive products offer a superior solution? Product weakness may indicate market segments to which the product could not be effectively sold or may indicate directions for product development and improvement.

ATTRIBUTES OF THE PHYSICAL PRODUCT. The advertising manager who is developing an advertising plan for a product needs to be thoroughly immersed in all aspects of the product, observing how it is manufactured, how it is displayed, and how it is sold. The manager should sample the product and should try competitive products as well. The advertising manager should also read all available technical and research information concerning the product.

*Focusing on Product Differences.* The analysis should focus on the differences in the attributes contained in the product. In all but a handful of cases, the marketer's product is sold in competition with products of other manufacturers. Consequently, advertising must be able to demonstrate to consumers not only that the product will meet their needs, but that it will meet them better than will competitive products. The major objective of product analysis is to search for competitive advantages.

*Analyzing Consumer Products.* The characteristics of a product should be examined in the product analysis. Obviously these will vary depending upon the type of product. The product attributes to be examined when a brand of coffee is being considered are different from the pertinent characteristics of a machine tool. Yet in most cases the important characteristics that need to be examined can rather easily be listed for each particular product. The difficult part of the job lies in being sufficiently thorough in gathering and analyzing the product data.

Some of the areas that should be examined for a consumer product are as follows:

1. *Physical makeup.* What are the ingredients or components of the product? What does each ingredient contribute? What ingredients or features or accessories are different from competitors' products?
2. *Varieties.* What styles and sizes are available? What colors are offered? What flavors are sold?
3. *How does the product work?* Is it easier to use or operate than competing products? Is it more reliable? Is it safer? Is it faster acting or longer lasting?
4. *How is the product made?* Is the production process different? Is greater control exercised? Is the production process colorful or traditional?
5. *Cost and price.* Are the costs of the product above or below average? Are the margins offered above average? Are special price incentives offered?
6. *Package.* Is the package reusable? Does it have decorative value? Does the package have display value? Is the package acceptable to distributors? Is it convenient for users? Does it protect the product?
7. *Distribution.* Where is the product available? Is it easy to find? Is it in traditional outlets? Is it frequently out of stock?

Information necessary to answer these questions is usually available to advertising managers from within their own companies. The advertising manager may need the assistance of experts in the organization in evaluating this information. The ingredient analysis may require the skills of a chemist, engineer, or dietitian. The production process may require explanation by production specialists. Cost information will probably come from the controller who can explain the principal cost components. Distribution information is probably available from the sales department.

*Analyzing Industrial Products.* For an industrial product, a piece of productive machinery, for example, the questions asked attempt to determine the advantages that this machine offers. For example:

1. *Machine capacity.* What level of output can the machine deliver? At that output, what is the quality of the product? What is the waste or scrap?
2. *Output cost.* What is the cost per unit? How does the cost vary with levels of output? How does it compare with other available machines or with the machines it might replace?
3. *Installation.* How much does installation cost? How long is delivery time? How long is the training period for operators?
4. *Service.* What is the estimated service cost? What service facilities are available? Are parts readily available?
5. *Flexibility.* Is the machine adaptable to other products? To variations? Is changeover of the machine time-consuming, costly?

For analysis of a retail store, a wholesaler, or a service firm, the questions asked will again vary. Focus in these instances will be on the mix or variety of products offered and the mix of services made available to customers. Emphasis again should be on discovering advantages enjoyed over competition.

RESEARCH ON PHYSICAL PRODUCT CHARACTERISTICS. Research is often conducted on physical product attributes to determine consumer reaction to various product features. This research is often undertaken when a change in the product is being considered or when a new product is being evaluated for possible introduction. The purpose of the research in such cases is to learn how consumers might react to the product, or the change if it were made, and whether or not the change creates new perceived attributes.

Suppose, for example, that a scouring powder marketer was considering addition of a better bleaching ingredient to aid in stain removal. What the advertiser would like to know is whether or not the addition would change a consumer's perception of the product. If, without being prompted by advertising, consumers tried the revised product and freely commented that it seemed to be better at stain removal, this would give the advertiser confidence that the product change was perceived as an attribute by consumers.

*The Use Test.* One form that such research might take is called a **consumer use test** or **home use test.** In a use test a representative group of consumers is given a supply of the test product and asked to use it in the same way that they would use their regular product. Consumer evaluation of the product is obtained by asking them to fill out product evaluation forms during the course of the test, after the test, or both.

*consumer use (home use) test*

The test would usually include only prospective buyers of the product, those consumers who currently use a product in the same category as the test product. The sample may be one drawn especially for the test, or a permanent consumer panel might be used.

Controls should be used to assure that the consumer's evaluations are influenced only by the test product's characteristics, not by other variables that are not under test. For example, the brand name of the test product is usually not revealed so that the consumers will not be influenced by prior experience with the product or prior exposure to advertising for the brand. The product is usually put in a nondistinctive package so that it is not readily identifiable. Sometimes the consumers are given a second test product so that comparative evaluation can be made. This control product should also, of course, have its identity hidden. The use of a second product masks the tester's interest and thus serves to discourage the consumer from deliberately favoring the test product.

Use tests can contribute valuable insights into the nature of a product, but they do have limitations. Use tests tend to be expensive and time-consuming. The cost of the test product, delivery of the product to the respondents, and the interviewing procedure make the cost substantial. Research time is lengthened by the rather extensive preparation needed and by the necessity of leaving the product in use for a period of time. Control of use tests is frequently imperfect. Test participants sometimes recognize the test product despite the disguise. It is suspected also that they frequently do not use the product in a normal way since it is free and they know it is the subject of a test.

For these and other reasons the use test is not capable of evaluating small differences in products or consumer reactions. But the technique will reveal major attributes of the product and strong negative or positive reactions to a product change.

*preference tests*

*Preference Tests.* Less formalized test techniques are sometimes used to evaluate consumer reaction to an individual product attribute. In these less rigorous tests known as **preference tests,** the requirement that the product be placed in use in its normal environment is usually dropped. Instead, the attribute to be evaluated is pointed out to consumers and they are then asked their reaction or their preference with regard to several variants. This approach is frequently used to test such attributes as variation in flavor, color, or package design. For example, to test consumer reaction to a new cracker flavor, the researcher might set up a table or booth in a supermarket and invite shoppers to sample the product. Their reactions would be recorded.

The advertising manager should be cautious in interpreting results from preference tests. Two problems with these tests are (1) they assume that consumers can validly express a preference without normal use of the product, and (2) they assume that the expression of preference is somehow related to expected sales of the product. Furthermore, since the test consumer has been forced to notice and evaluate the attribute, there is no valid measure of the comparative importance of the product feature. For example, consumers may, when forced to choose, prefer a red vitamin tablet to a yellow one, but that reveals nothing about whether or not *any* color is an important attribute of this product. The sample used in these tests, as in the cracker example in the preceding paragraph, tends to be informal and may distort results.

*Testing Services and Industrial Products.* The discussion of use and preference tests has centered on consumer products, but similar research approaches can be utilized for services or for industrial goods. An industrial machine, for example, might be placed in a sample of prospect companies. Or a service might be evaluated by offering it to a sample group of consumers or businesses that were considered prospects. To the extent possible, these test situations should be controlled to prevent extraneous factors from influencing the appraisal of the test product's performance.

ANALYZING PRODUCT DEVELOPMENTS. The discussion of physical product analysis has thus far treated the product as though it were static or unchangeable. To the marketer, however, the product is one of the variables in the marketing mix that can be manipulated. Improvement of the product is competitively vital and is important to the advertising program. Although changes in the product may not be the direct responsibility of the advertising manager, product development is a vital advertising concern since changes in the product provide a different set of attributes to be communicated to target consumers. In the advertisement displayed in Exhibit 8-4, notice how the availability of a tablet form of Triaminic Cold Syrup provided an entirely new attribute to offer in the advertising of this product.

*Suggesting Product Shortcomings.* The product analysis should determine what shortcomings of the product require improvement. These shortcomings add to the list of problems and become inputs to the product development program. Product improvements that have already been developed should be analyzed to determine if the improvements provide new, promotable attributes.

*Evaluating Proposed Product Changes.* The product analysis should also evaluate product changes that are being developed for future introduction. In analyzing the product changes the advertising manager should continue to look for competitive advantage. Each proposed product change should be examined to determine whether or not it provides an attribute that offers a better solution to a consumer problem, and consequently, a basis on which to communicate with prospects.

Changes in the product can be analyzed by using the same approaches suggested for existing products. Facts on the product change are gathered and experts are utilized to interpret its advantages. Use testing and preference testing are appropriate for evaluation of consumer reaction to changes. Concept tests can be used to evaluate consumer reaction to product features before product development has taken place. In **concept tests,** proposed product changes are explained to a sample of consumers by means of short, descriptive paragraphs, drawings, or dummy advertisements. The consumers' reactions are then collected using short questionnaires or depth interview techniques. Exhibit 8-5 shows a dummy advertisement or **concept board** that was used in consumer research by an advertiser attempting to evaluate a proposed new automatic bagging feature for a lawn mower.

*concept test*

*concept board*

An already accomplished product change can be test-marketed by introducing the changed product in a limited geographic area, thus determining consumer response without the risk of a general introduction of the product. Consumer response can then be evaluated by measuring changes in sales occurring after introduction of the changed product.

If the analysis of impending product changes reveals that the change will create a new and distinctive product attribute, then this advantage should be added to the list of opportunities in the advertising plan. It may also occur that a change in a product, such as a reformulation for the purpose of using less expensive ingredients, will be perceived negatively by consumers. This becomes a problem that the advertising plan must address.

**EXHIBIT 8-4**     An advertisement offering a product improvement to consumers.

# Introducing a new way to take one of the most recommended liquid cold medicines in history.

**M**ORE doctors and pharmacists recommend Triaminic® Cold Syrup than any other cold liquid brand.* You can't beat it for relief

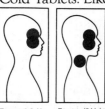

of cold symptoms.

Now you can get the same kind of relief in tablet form.

Triaminic® Cold Tablets, like our Syrup, give you prompt relief for the stuffy, runny nose of a cold.

We're also introducing Triaminicol® Multi-Symptom Cold Tablets. Like Triaminicol® Multi-Symptom Cold Syrup, our new Triaminicol Multi-Symptom Cold Tablets go to work on nasal congestion, frequent coughing and runny nose.

Each one contains a decongestant. Because one thing you expect from cold medicines is to let you breathe freer, fast. But none

Triaminic® Cold
Tablets
Stuffy nose
Runny nose
Postnasal drip

Triaminicol® Multi-
Symptom Cold Tablets
Nasal congestion
Runny nose
Frequent, annoying
cough

of them contain aspirin. Because we feel aspirin or other pain relievers are something you should take only when the symptoms require it.

Of course, there's the rest of our liquid cold medicines.

Triaminic-DM® Cough Formula effectively relieves an annoying, persistent cough and nasal congestion.

And Triaminic® Expectorant can break up congestion when you have a dry, hacking cough.

So don't overmedicate your cold with unnecessary ingredients. Know your symptoms better.

**A**ND try Triaminic Cold Tablets and Triaminicol Multi-Symptom Cold Tablets.

Not only can you get fast, effective cold relief.

Now, with our tablets you can take it with you, also.

18833

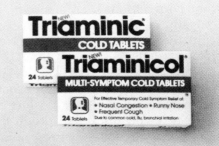

Why take more than you need.

A concept board for a new lawn mower feature.                  EXHIBIT 8-5

# THE CLEAN SWEEP MOWER
# WITH AUTOMATIC BAGGING

**Cuts, mulches and vacuums grass and leaves to eliminate bagging...
Automatic bagger holds 4 bushels of clippings in disposable bags.**

The self-propelled Clean Sweep Mower sweeps your lawn clean as it mows,
It chops clippings and leaves to reduce them in bulk and allow more
compact bagging. The catcher holds standard sized lawn and leaf bags
to eliminate transferring the clippings. When the catcher is full, the
bag is put in position to let you finish mowing faster and with less
extra work. The Clean Sweep Mower can also be used in the autumn to
automatically vacuum up and mulch leaves.

## Analysis of the Product as Perceived

The analysis of the physical properties of a product provides important clues as to the advertisable attributes of a product, but, by itself, it is a limited view. It is vital that the analysis of the physical product be joined by an analysis of the product as the consumer sees it.

INFORMATION NEEDED. Consumers retain only the characteristics of a product that they see as satisfying a need. The advertiser needs to know those specific physical and symbolic attributes that the consumer attaches to the product. Evaluations of the product by consumers are a rich source from which product problems and opportunities can be defined.

RESEARCHING PRODUCT PERCEPTIONS. Information on product perceptions is usually determined through original research. The information needed and the research techniques required are so specialized that it would be unreasonable to expect that appropriate data could be found from existing sources. However, original research on product perception can frequently be combined with the research on consumer needs discussed in Chapter 6. The research techniques required in the two cases are very similar and the subject of opinions about products is usually compatible with a discussion of consumer needs.

*Use of Indirect Questions.* The indirect question approach is useful in avoiding the frequent reluctance of consumers when asked to reveal their symbolic perceptions of products. There is some danger, in a direct question approach, that consumers will talk only about obvious physical features of the product.

Association tests, projective questions, depth interviews, and group interviews are all research techniques that can prove useful in probing consumer product perceptions. Exhibit 8-6 shows four of the TAT-type drawings used in research on perceptions of beer brands. Consumers were asked about each of the drawings, "What brand of beer do you think this person would drink?"

*Use of Semantic Differential.* Another research technique used to evaluate the perceived product is the **semantic differential,** a technique developed by social scientists to evaluate attitudes toward concepts and things. Marketing researchers have adapted the technique as a means of measuring consumer perceptions of products, companies, or stores.

*semantic differential*

In the semantic differential technique, consumers are asked to evaluate a product or company using a series of seven-interval rating scales each marked by a pair of descriptive polar adjectives. For example, adjectival pairs might be "strong/weak," "modern/old-fashioned," "female/male." Subjects are asked to mark each rating scale to indicate which of the two adjectives is descriptive of the product and, by the position on the scale,

TAT drawings used in research on beer brand perceptions.

EXHIBIT 8-6

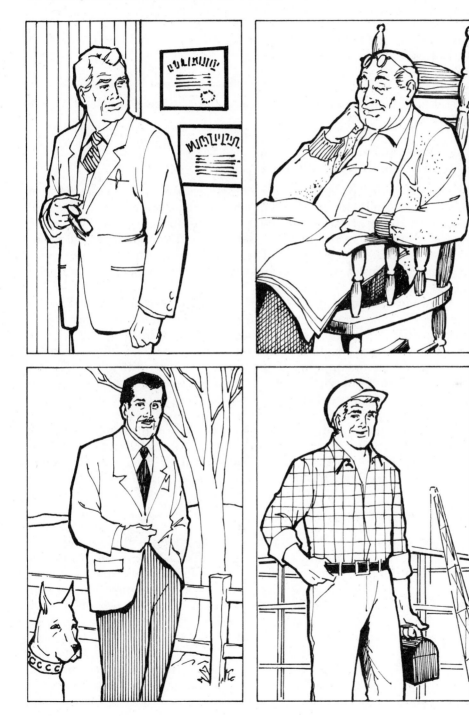

how well the adjective describes the product. For example, this rating

Modern ⌊_⌊_⌊_⌊_⌊_⌊_⌊___×_⌋ Old-fashioned

would mean that the product was strongly viewed as old-fashioned, while this answer

Best for men ⌊_⌊___×_⌊_⌊_⌊_⌊_⌋ Best for women

would indicate that the product was perceived as being just slightly more appropriate for men than for women.

### Evaluating Brand or Corporate Image

In analyzing a product, it is sometimes desirable to define the image of the brand, defining for a series of dimensions the attitudes consumers hold toward the product. Research to define brand image usually involves the use of attitude scales including the semantic differential discussed above. Exhibit 8-7 shows a set of abbreviated statements, with which consumers were asked to agree or disagree, and which are used to define the image of a food product.

Corporate image can be defined using similar approaches, although the attitude dimensions will be different. Exhibit 8-8 shows dimensions used by ITT Corporation in evaluating its corporate image.

The resulting product or corporate image should be analyzed to define problems and opportunities. Some attitudes are difficult to define as either problems or opportunities. For example, if a product is perceived as expensive, is this a problem (too costly) or an opportunity (prestigious)? The interpretation may depend on other factors such as the needs that the advertiser intends to address. In the case of ITT Corporation, the research revealed that many consumers confused ITT with AT&T (American Telephone and Telegraph Company). As a result, ITT launched a corporate advertising campaign. One of the commercials used is shown in Chapter 1.

### Analysis of Advertising Activity

The third analysis that contributes to an understanding of the products is an evaluation of the advertising that has been carried out for the product in the past. The consumer's knowledge and perceptions about a product are in some measure determined by the information that has been supplied to him or her by the marketer. A full understanding of the position that a product occupies in a consumer's mind is thus aided by analyzing past advertising efforts for the product.

ANALYSIS OF PAST ADVERTISING. This analysis should include an evaluation of what has been said about the product, the audience to which this information has been directed, and the intensity of the advertising effort.

Typical statements that might be used to test brand image of a food product. EXHIBIT 8-7

1. A brand I like.
2. A brand I would recommend to friends.
3. A brand I would serve guests.
4. A brand I would serve my family.
5. A brand I purchase for special occasions.

6. An expensive brand.
7. A brand to ask for when dining out.
8. A brand for cost-conscious people.
9. A low-price brand.
10. A healthful brand.

11. A brand for older people.
12. A brand my parents used.
13. A brand for young people.
14. A brand for children.
15. An old-fashioned brand.

16. A brand that no one uses any more.
17. A brand that "with it" people use.
18. A brand with an attractive package.
19. A brand that is available in most groceries.
20. A brand that is nutritious.

21. A brand with high quality.
22. A brand that is consistently good.
23. A brand for entertaining.
24. A dependable brand.
25. A fresh brand.

26. A brand I buy to reward myself.
27. A brand that reminds me of good times.
28. A natural brand.
29. A brand with a good reputation.
30. A brand I regularly keep on hand.

31. A brand I save for "company."
32. A brand for diet-conscious people.
33. A versatile brand.
34. A brand that is a good value.
35. A brand backed by a good company.

36. A brand I can't find in the supermarket.
37. A brand that has changed over the years.
38. A brand that is going downhill.
39. A brand that has improved over the years.
40. A brand for middle-class people.

Analysis of prior advertising should also evaluate the advertising's effectiveness and define deficiencies or problems encountered. Finding solutions to such problems leads to the definition of a key set of advertising objectives for the coming year's plan.

To understand the vital role of advertising effectiveness evaluation, it is essential to see its role in the total advertising planning process. Advertising planning is not a one-shot activity, but a cyclical process. The full

EXHIBIT 8-8     Dimensions used in evaluating corporate image, a section from ITT's corporate image survey.

---

5. **Now I would like to read you a list of characteristics. Please tell me which of these characteristics you associate with (name each company in turn: AT&T, GTE, IBM, ITT, RCA).**

High caliber management ...............................................................

Always improving quality of products and services ...........................

Leader in technology.....................................................................

Not as good an investment as most other companies ...........................

Committed to protecting the environment...........................................

Questionable connection with government and political situations...........

Has diverse business and markets ..................................................

So big that it seems too powerful .....................................................

Developing products to improve people's lives....................................

Fair to employees.........................................................................

Very profitable.............................................................................

Provides complete information about the company — both good and bad .

Good balance between profits and the public's interests.......................

Better place to work than most other companies .................................

Honest and forthright ....................................................................

Products and services that serve millions of people around the world ......

---

Source: Reproduced by permission of ITT Corporation.

process is pictured in Exhibit 8-9. The product analysis, together with the consumer and market analyses, make up the first step in the planning process. These analyses define problems and opportunities facing the product. The advertising analysis looks specifically at problems that have arisen while carrying out the advertising plan of the preceding planning period.

The definition of problems in step one leads directly to the definition of objectives for solving the problems, which is step two, and the spelling out of programs to achieve the objectives in step three. Step four, evaluation of effectiveness, is of particular relevance here. As we will discuss in Part 4, every plan should provide for collection of data to measure how well the advertising programs of step three are achieving the objectives of step two. The evaluation information collected by step four completes the cyclical process and is fed into the step-one analysis of the next planning period. Thus a vital source of information for the advertising analysis now being considered is information gathered by the evaluation measurements provided for in the preceding period's plan.

A thorough analysis of the advertising activity for a product should include consideration of each of the advertising programs — budget, media, and creative — plus other related programs such as sales promotion, public relations, and packaging, for which the advertising manager is responsible.

BUDGET ANALYSIS. Advertising expenditures for the product should be analyzed year by year for significant changes and trends. The budget should be viewed not only in terms of dollars, but also as a percentage of

sales — termed the **advertising to sales** or **A to S ratio** — in order to determine whether or not the advertising budget is growing faster or slower
than sales.

*advertising to sales*
*(A to S) ratio*

*Competitive Comparisons.* Comparison of the advertising expenditure
levels with industry standards can often point out potential problem areas.
Average advertising expenditures as a percentage of industry sales are
presented annually in *Advertising Age* for over 250 industrial classes. (See
Exhibit 1-3 for a sample from that listing.) In many industries, trade associations or trade publications present industry average-cost ratios, sometimes including advertising expenditures.

The advertiser's own advertising expenditures should be compared to
those of its competition. Competitive expenditures can be estimated for the
major media from a variety of sources. Media trade associations and syndicated services compile advertising expenditure data by company that are
then made available to advertisers. Some of the leading sources of expenditure information are, in order of media expenditure importance:

> *Broadcast Advertisers Reports* — spot television, network television, network cable
> television, and network radio expenditures.
> *Publishers Information Bureau* — consumer magazine and newspaper supple-
> ment expenditures as compiled by *Publishers Advertising Reports.*
> *Media Records* — newspaper expenditures.
> *American Business Press* — business publications expenditures.
> *Institute of Outdoor Advertising* — outdoor advertising expenditures.
> *Radio Expenditures Reports* — spot radio expenditures.

The advertising planning process.                                    **EXHIBIT 8-9**

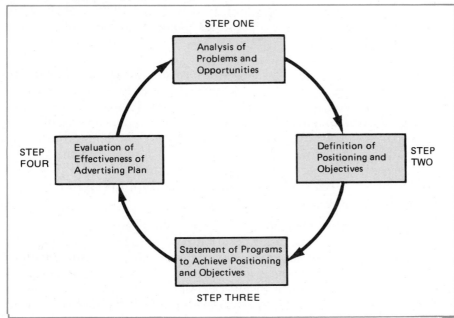

A sample page from a BAR (Broadcast Advertisers Reports, Inc.) Barcume Spot Television Report is shown in Exhibit 8-10.

Broadcast Advertisers Reports and Leading National Advertisers cooperate to produce the BAR/LNA Multimedia Report. This syndicated service leads the field in the compilation and publication of summarized expenditures for the more prominent companies and brands by using the sources indicated above. Advertising agencies and large advertisers usually subscribe to this service, and from these summary reports advertisers can prepare tables that show the advertising expenditures for major competitors. One such table for leading hotel chains is shown in Exhibit 8-11.

The small advertiser will find that the advertising expenditures of competitors are often too small to be reported by published sources. However, reasonable estimates can frequently be made in such instances by observing competitors' advertising schedules and applying published rates to them.

*Budget Breakdowns.* In addition to the comparison of the product's advertising budget to those of the competition, the advertiser's budget should be analyzed in terms of the allocation of funds within the budget. For example, tracing the proportion of the budget that has been devoted to media, to production of advertising materials, to research, and to sales promotion might reveal an unrealized shift in emphasis or a diffusion of effort.

*Budget Level Tests.* If the advertiser has conducted tests of different levels of advertising expenditure, the results should be analyzed in this section of the plan. Such tests are likely to have been scheduled as part of the effectiveness evaluation program to determine whether an increase or decrease in advertising expenditures would result in greater sales and profits.

MEDIA ANALYSIS. The task of *media analysis* is to classify advertising expenditures over recent years by media type in order to reveal any changes that may have taken place in media emphasis. Advertising expenditures should also be collected for major competitors, as was done in Exhibit 8-11, and compared to the advertiser's own media patterns. These contrasting media patterns will provide the advertiser with insight into the specific prospects competitors are attempting to reach. This, in turn, will be a factor in the advertiser's own decision as to which prospects to pursue to the greatest advantage.

*Scheduling Patterns.* The advertising scheduling pattern should also be examined. Advertising expenditures are rarely spread evenly through the year. Instead, the advertising schedule may conform to a seasonal pattern to reflect seasonal sales for the product. Or the advertising might be scheduled in a series of short bursts or pulses designed to improve its impact. A review of the media scheduling pattern should focus on identifying changes that have occurred in scheduling practices.

A sample page from a BAR (Broadcast Advertisers Reports, Inc.) Barcume Spot Television Report for the fourth quarter, 1983.                                             **EXHIBIT 8-10**

## SECTION 1 BRAND INDEX TO PARENT COMPANIES

| CLASS CODE | SEC 2 | SEC 3 | BRAND/PRODUCT | PARENT COMPANY | OCT | NOV | DEC | QTR | YEAR TO DATE |
|---|---|---|---|---|---|---|---|---|---|
| B612 | | 64 | CASCADE AIRWAYS AIR CRGO | CASCADE AIRWAYS INC | | | | | .8 |
| H411 | 169 | 292 | CASCADE DISHWSHR DETRGNT | PROCTER & GAMBLE CO | 477.6 | 429.2 | 381.1 | 1287.9 | 4172.3 |
| B316 | 18 | 47 | CASCADE TELECOMMUNCTNS | | 9.1 | 9.4 | 19.6 | 38.1 | 54.6 |
| T520 | | 358 | CASE PDTS-FARM EQUIPT | TENNECO INC | | | | | 48.0 |
| T610 | | 364 | CASE PDTS-LAWN & GARDEN EQUIPT | TENNECO INC | | | | | 56.3 |
| H235 | 158 | 264 | CASE-SET CASSETTE HOLDER | | | 1.9 | | 1.9 | 1.9 |
| G450 | | 217 | CASH CUBE PUZZLES | | | | | | 1.1 |
| B130 | 9 | 16 | CASHIER TRAINING COURSE | CASHIER TRAINING INSTITUTE | | | .7 | .7 | .7 |
| F132 | | 136 | CASINO CHEESES | DART & KRAFT INC | | | | | 2112.9 |
| T184 | 197 | 346 | CASSETTEN TAPE STR/AUTO | | | .7 | | .7 | .7 |
| T152 | | 343 | CASTLE PDTS-GAS ADDITIVE | | | | | | 9.7 |
| G450 | 126 | 217 | CASTLE ROCK-SNOW CAT PDTS | K-TEL INTERNATIONAL | | | 36.0 | 36.0 | 36.0 |
| H120 | 148 | 245 | CASTRO CONVRTBLE FURNTR | CASTRO CONVERTIBLE CORP | 55.1 | 37.7 | 23.1 | 115.9 | 472.0 |
| T211 | 197 | 349 | CASTROL MOTOR OIL | BURMAH OIL CO INC | 498.0 | 152.1 | 16.7 | 666.8 | 2241.0 |
| A117 | 197 | 5 | CATALINA APPRL-VARIOUS SPORTSWEAR | GULF & WESTERN INDS INC | | | | | 468.5 |
| A117 | | 5 | CATALINA APPRL-WOMENS SPORTSWEAR | GULF & WESTERN INDS INC | | | | | 11.6 |
| G211 | | 207 | CATENA DURA CHAIN | | | | | | 2.5 |
| F116 | 68 | 113 | CATES PICKLES | CATES CHAS F & SONS INC | | 80.8 | 8.6 | 89.4 | 218.1 |
| B210 | | 31 | CATHOLIC KNIGHTS INS-LIFE | | | | | | 6.8 |
| T531 | | 359 | CATTLE CROWDER SYSTEM | | | | | | .1 |
| F116 | | 113 | CATTLEMANS STEAK SAUCE | RECKITT & COLMAN LTD | | | | | 152.5 |
| A117 | | 3 | CAVALIER APPRL-VARIOUS JEANS | | | | | | 5.1 |
| T130 | 195 | 342 | CAVCO MFG HOMES | | 5.0 | | | 5.0 | 9.6 |
| H330 | | 280 | CBS CASSETTES | CBS INC | | | | | 147.7 |
| H320 | 163 | 275 | CBS SOFTWARE | CBS INC | 92.6 | 19.8 | | 112.3 | 1921.8 |
| H330 | 166 | 280 | CBS-FOX VIDEO DISCS | CBS/FOX INC | | | 1.0 | 1.0 | 1.0 |
| F171 | 97 | 166 | CDM COFFEE-VARIOUS | REILY WM B & CO INC | 3.0 | 6.4 | 2.1 | 11.5 | 35.1 |
| H525 | | 312 | CEASE FIRE FIRE EXTNGSHR | JUSTRITE MFG CO | | | | | 4.2 |
| D222 | 60 | 105 | CEDAR ROTH EMERGENCY KIT | | | 25.6 | | 25.6 | 25.6 |
| H512 | | 300 | CEDAR SIX WOOD SIDING | | | | | | 4.2 |
| H431 | 178 | 295 | CEILING BRIGHT CLEANER | | 2.4 | 43.0 | | 45.5 | 61.5 |
| G571 | | 244 | CEILING MASTERS BSNS PRP | | | | | | 7.8 |
| H330 | 166 | 280 | CELEBRATING XMAS RECORD | | | 1.9 | | 1.9 | 1.9 |
| H330 | | 280 | CELEBRATION RECORDING | | | | | | 14.1 |
| F125 | | 124 | CELESTE FROZEN PIZZA | QUAKER OATS CO | | | | | 831.3 |
| F171 | | 166 | CELESTIAL SEASONINGS-HERBAL TEA | CELESTIAL SEASONINGS & HERB TEA IN | | | | | 503.2 |
| H330 | 166 | 280 | CELIA LIPTON SMTHG RCDG | | | | .5 | .5 | .5 |
| D113 | 27 | 69 | CELISSE WOMENS FRAGRANCE | DANA PERFUMES CORP | | 46.6 | 375.0 | 421.6 | 616.5 |
| F320 | 120 | 201 | CELLA WINE | BROWN-FORMAN DISTILLERS CORP | 563.0 | 564.2 | 656.5 | 1783.7 | 2673.2 |
| F320 | 120 | 201 | CELLIER DES DAUPHIN WINE | UNION DES VIGNERONS DES COTES DU R | | 38.1 | | 38.1 | 106.3 |
| D125 | 38 | 80 | CELLINI MENS FRAG | FABERGE INC | | .5 | 1.4 | 1.9 | 2.4 |
| D141 | 41 | 84 | CELLOPHANE HAIR COLOR | SEBASTIAN INTERNATL INC | | 2.9 | 1.0 | 3.9 | 3.9 |
| T113 | 190 | 328 | CENTRAL AVE AUTO DLRS AS-VARIOUS | AREA AUTO DLRS ASSN | 4.8 | | 5.7 | 10.5 | 25.2 |
| B220 | 14 | 37 | CENTRAL INS-ALL FORMS | CENTRAL INSURANCE CO | 3.5 | 3.1 | .4 | 7.0 | 10.0 |
| D215 | 56 | 98 | CENTRUM VITAMINS | AMERICAN CYANAMID CO | 19.1 | 9.6 | 1.3 | 30.) | 360.5 |
| T113 | | 328 | CENTURY HOUSE DLR ASSN-VARIOUS | AREA AUTO DLRS ASSN | | | | | 26.7 |
| D121 | | 73 | CEPACOL MOUTHWASH | DOW CHEMICAL CO | | | | | 1.7 |
| H822 | | 305 | CERDIAK STOVES | | | | | | 6.1 |
| H232 | 154 | 260 | CERTAIN BATHROOM TISSUE | PROCTER & GAMBLE CO | 10.3 | 11.2 | 10.1 | 31.7 | 247.5 |
| H512 | 179 | 300 | CERTAIN-TEED INSLTN&SDNG | CERTAIN-TEED CORP | | | 1.0 | 1.0 | 49.8 |
| F150 | | 144 | CERTI-FRESH-FROZEN FISH | GEORGE WESTON LTD | | | | | 98.2 |
| F126 | | 127 | CERTI-FRESH-FRZN MEX SEAFD ENTREES | GEORGE WESTON LTD | | | | | .3 |
| H330 | | 280 | CERTIFIED GOLD RECORD | K-TEL INTERNATIONAL | | | | | .3 |
| F211 | 105 | 178 | CERTS MINTS-REGULAR | WARNER-LAMBERT CO | 92.3 | 64.4 | 45.4 | 202.1 | 1400.8 |
| F211 | 105 | 179 | CERTS MINTS-REGULAR & SUGAR FREE | WARNER-LAMBERT CO | 301.5 | 264.9 | 247.1 | 813.5 | 1888.8 |
| F211 | 105 | 179 | CERTS MINTS-SUGAR FREE | WARNER-LAMBERT CO | 14.8 | | | 14.8 | 15.1 |
| T300 | 199 | 353 | CESSNA AIRCRAFT-DLRS & LSSNS | CESSNA AIRCRAFT CO | 4.6 | | | 4.6 | 7.5 |
| T623 | | 367 | CHACON GARDEN SPRAY | | | | | | .6 |
| T184 | | 346 | CHAIN AID TIRE CHNG DVC | | | | | | 1.9 |
| G211 | 122 | 207 | CHAIN COLLECTION OFFER | NATIONAL MARKETING MAIL ORDER | | .1 | | .1 | 4.6 |
| G450 | | 217 | CHAIR PLANES TOY | | | | | | 5.5 |
| H525 | 183 | 312 | CHAMBERLAIN GRG DR OPNR | DUCHOSSOIS/THRALL GROUP | | 13.6 | 79.8 | 93.4 | 93.4 |
| F115 | | 112 | CHAMBOURCY FOOD-FLANBY DESSERT | NESTLE S A | | | | | 44.1 |
| F131 | | 132 | CHAMBOURCY FOOD-YOGURT | NESTLE S A | | | | | 6.7 |
| G221 | 124 | 209 | CHAMELEON SUNGLASSES | CORNING GLASS WORKS | 1.7 | 3.9 | | 5.5 | 119.6 |
| D113 | 27 | 69 | CHAMPAGNE FRAGRANCE | B A T INDUS PLC | | 22.4 | 55.2 | 77.7 | 281.2 |
| F310 | 117 | 196 | CHAMPALE MALT LIQUOR | IROQUOIS BRANDS LTD | | 83.9 | 191.0 | 274.9 | 275.4 |
| T130 | 195 | 342 | CHAMPION MOTOR HOMES | CHAMPION HOME BUILDERS | | 4.5 | | 8.2 | 8.2 |
| T154 | 197 | 346 | CHAMPION RADIAL CHAINS | FIRESTONE TIRE & RUBBER CO | 3.7 | 3.5 | | 3.5 | 8.5 |
| A131 | 6 | 9 | CHAMPION SNEAKERS | STRIDE RITE CORP THE | | 1.0 | 1.8 | 2.8 | 5.5 |
| T154 | 197 | 346 | CHAMPION SPARK PLUGS | CHAMPION SPARK PLUG CO | 10.6 | 94.1 | 1.8 | 106.5 | 121.8 |
| A115 | | 2 | CHAMPIONSHIP WRST T-SHRT | | | | | | 2.0 |
| F320 | | 201 | CHAMPS D'ORE WINE | VICEROY IMPORTS | | | | | .9 |
| A117 | | 5 | CHAMS APPRL-MENS SPORTSWEAR | HOPON/CHAMS DE BARON | | | | | 91.3 |
| A117 | | 5 | CHAMS APPRL-VARIOUS SPORTSWEAR | HOPON/CHAMS DE BARON | | | | | 350.8 |
| T154 | | 346 | CHANDALIGHT PODT LIGHT | | | | | | 43.7 |
| D125 | 38 | 80 | CHANEL PDTS-FRAGRANCE FOR MEN | CHANEL INC | | | 340.1 | 340.1 | 342.9 |
| D113 | 27 | 69 | CHANEL PDTS-FRAGRANCE FOR WOMEN | CHANEL INC | | | 1229.2 | 1229.2 | 2126.8 |
| D125 | | 80 | CHANEL PDTS-FRAGRANCE/MEN&WOMEN | CHANEL INC | | | | | 35.8 |
| D111 | | 65 | CHANEL PDTS-MOISTURE CREAM | CHANEL INC | | | | | 56.2 |
| H320 | 163 | 275 | CHANNEL MASTER-ANTENNA | AVNET INC | 2.7 | 1.8 | 2.5 | 7.0 | 19.0 |
| F320 | 120 | 201 | CHANTAINE WINE | | | 62.2 | 155.4 | 217.6 | 217.6 |
| D116 | 30 | 72 | CHANTEL COSMETICS-VARIOUS | | 2.6 | | | 2.6 | 2.6 |
| D216 | 57 | 100 | CHAP STICK LIP BALM | ROBINS A H CO INC | 3.2 | 1.7 | 32.0 | 36.9 | 1574.6 |
| D125 | 38 | 80 | CHAPS MENS FRAGRANCE | WARNER COMMUNICATIONS INC | 43.3 | 65.0 | 301.7 | 409.9 | 475.1 |
| H234 | 157 | 263 | CHARBEQUE ELEC GRILL | | | 7.0 | 64.1 | 71.1 | 92.4 |
| A117 | | 5 | CHARDON APPRL-VAR SPORTSWEAR | CHARDON INC | | | | | 12.7 |
| A116 | | 3 | CHARDON APPRL-VARIOUS JEANS | CHARDON INC | | | | | 8.8 |
| H330 | | 280 | CHARIOTS OF FIRE RECORD | | | | | | 1.8 |
| F212 | 109 | 183 | CHARLES CHIPS-POTATO CHIPS | CHARLES CHIP CO | 60.2 | 19.4 | 53.0 | 132.7 | 132.7 |
| H525 | | 312 | CHARLIE BAR DOOR SFTY DV | DUN & BRADSTREET CORP THE | | | | | 28.2 |
| B410 | | 50 | CHARLIE BROWNS ENCYCLPD | | | | | | 13.2 |
| D113 | 27 | 69 | CHARLIE PDTS-FRAGRANCE | REVLON INC | 35.2 | 6.7 | 166.6 | 208.4 | 237.3 |
| D116 | 30 | 72 | CHARLIE PDTS-VARIOUS COSMETICS | REVLON INC | | | 3.9 | 3.9 | 8.1 |
| D116 | 30 | 72 | CHARLIE PDTS-VARIOUS PDTS | REVLON, INC | | .3 | | .3 | .3 |
| H330 | 166 | 280 | CHARLIE PRIDE ALL MY BST | | | | 4.1 | 4.1 | 4.1 |
| A117 | | 3 | CHARLOTTE FORD APPRL-WOMENS SPORTSWR | | | 8.4 | 7.8 | 16.2 | 16.2 |
| G450 | | 217 | CHARLOTTE RUSSE DOLLS | | | | | | 25.4 |
| H232 | 154 | 260 | CHARMIN BATHROOM TISSUE | PROCTER & GAMBLE CO | 276.6 | 236.5 | 272.9 | 786.0 | 2327.5 |
| F211 | | 179 | CHARMS CANDY | CHARMS CO | | | | | 310.1 |
| A141 | 7 | 12 | CHAROL BODY SHPR CONTOUR | | 2.0 | | | 2.0 | 2.5 |
| H330 | 166 | 280 | CHART ACTION 83 RECORD | K-TEL INTERNATIONAL | 4.2 | | | 4.2 | 763.3 |
| B210 | 12 | 31 | CHARTERED LIFE UNDRWRT-LIFE | | | | 4.8 | 4.8 | 16.3 |
| F320 | 120 | 201 | CHATEAU LUZERNE WINE | KASSER DISTILLERS PDTS CORP | | 60.4 | 45.4 | 105.8 | 242.8 |
| H142 | 149 | 249 | CHATHAM REST WARMER | CHATHAM MFG CO | 178.6 | 165.2 | 202.7 | 546.5 | 555.4 |
| G112 | | 205 | CHATTANOOGA CHEW CHWG TB | CULBRO CORP | | | | | 314.8 |
| A111 | | 1 | CHAUVIN APPRL-MENS SHIRTS | | | | | | 53.9 |
| A115 | | 2 | CHAUVIN APPRL-MENS SWEATERS | | | | | | .1 |
| D125 | 38 | 80 | CHAZ PDTS-MENS FRAGRANCE | REVLON INC | | .4 | 4.9 | 5.3 | 7.5 |
| D121 | 30 | 74 | CHECK UP TOOTHPASTE-PASTE & GEL | MINNETONKA INC | 94.2 | 43.6 | | 137.8 | 397.0 |
| H412 | 171 | 293 | CHEER POWDERED DETERGENT | PROCTER & GAMBLE CO | 682.8 | 494.9 | 337.0 | 1514.7 | 6667.3 |
| F122 | 72 | 119 | CHEERIOS CEREAL | GENERAL MILLS INC | 590.3 | 461.1 | 871.4 | 1922.8 | 6717.0 |
| F122 | 72 | 119 | CHEERIOS HONEY NUT CRL | GENERAL MILLS INC | 221.1 | 309.5 | 539.7 | 1070.3 | 4042.6 |
| F221 | | 188 | CHEERWINE SOFT DRINK-REGULAR | CHEERWINE BOTTLING CO | | | .5 | | 87.5 |
| F125 | 79 | 124 | CHEF BOY AR DEE-CANNED PASTA PDTS | AMERICAN HOME PDTS CORP | 29.3 | 32.8 | 7.7 | 69.8 | 499.2 |

BARCUME - NATIONAL SPOT TV - FOURTH QUARTER, 1983                                           BROADCAST ADVERTISERS REPORTS, INC.

**EXHIBIT 8-11**    Advertising expenditures by major hotel chains

### FIRST QUARTER 1984

| | Magazines (LNA) | Newspaper Supplements (LNA) | Network Television (BAR) | Spot Television (BAR) | Network Radio (BAR) | Outdoor (LNA) | 6-media Total |
|---|---|---|---|---|---|---|---|
| Best Western International | $ 165.6 | | | $ 7.3 | | $120.8 | $ 293.7 |
| Hilton Hotels Corporation | 1,624.3 | $ 2.3 | | 361.4 | | 364.4 | 2,352.4 |
| Holiday Inns, Inc. | 1,122.2 | | $ 807.5 | 1,284.2 | $245.9 | 645.0 | 4,104.8 |
| Howard Johnson Motor Lodges | 15.4 | | | 87.6 | 136.0 | 243.8 | 482.8 |
| Hyatt Corporation | 1,414.9 | 24.0 | | 501.4 | | 142.1 | 2,082.4 |
| Inter-Continental | 161.7 | | | | | 30.0 | 191.7 |
| Mariott Corporation | 565.7 | 10.6 | | 277.9 | | 46.9 | 901.1 |
| Ramada Inns | 84.3 | | 2,125.8 | 155.1 | | 287.1 | 2,652.3 |
| Sheraton Corporation | 1,135.6 | 55.4 | 1,487.8 | 437.9 | | 148.4 | 3,265.1 |
| Westin International | 1,234.2 | 104.8 | | 81.7 | | | 1,420.7 |

Source:  Broadcast Advertisers Reports, Inc. (BAR) and Leading National Advertisers, Inc. (LNA) Multi-Media Service

*Geographic Patterns.* Advertising expenditures are seldom spread evenly across a product's distribution area. Instead, there is a tendency to place greater advertising expenditures in areas where there is a concentration of prospects. The actual distribution of advertising expenditures should be calculated and compared to the geographic pattern of the product's sales and the pattern of prospects for the product. The comparison may reveal areas of undeveloped potential or areas of unwarranted heavy expenditures.

*Effectiveness Evaluation.* If the advertising plan for the prior planning period contained a program of advertising-effectiveness evaluation, then data should have been collected on the performance of the media that were actually used in the previous period. If such data are available, a comparison of actual effectiveness to predicted effectiveness is possible. The comparison may well reveal shortcomings to be corrected in the next planning period.

Data on actual media audiences are gathered through sample surveys conducted by research firms which sell the results to advertisers. Reports on radio and television audiences are called **rating reports** while reports on the readership of magazines and newspapers are termed **audience studies.** The technical nature of these reports will be considered further in later chapters.

*rating reports*
*audience studies*

CREATIVE ANALYSIS. While the media analysis considers to whom the advertiser has been directing advertising messages, the *creative analysis* should focus on the content of those messages. What consumers know about a product and their perceptions of that product depend in part upon the advertising messages that have been directed to them.

*Analysis of Content.* The creative analysis should trace the content of the messages that have been directed to consumers so as to determine the length of time particular promises or appeals were presented, when shifts were made, when multiple appeals or overlapping appeals were used, and when the regular appeals were interrupted to promote limited-time offers such as reduced prices or contests.

In examining these changes in message content, attention should be paid not only to the literal copy content, but also to more subtle shifts such as the manner of presentation, which often conveys to the consumer important symbolic information about the product. A familiar example of the effect of presentation style can be seen in retail store advertisements. A store that uses crowded, jumbled ad layouts with large, heavy type conveys an impression of bargains, economy, perhaps lower quality. By contrast, a store that uses orderly layouts with substantial white space and a script typeface conveys an impression of high quality, prestige, and high prices. Changes in the manner of presentation also include such things as changes in the actors in a broadcast advertisement, shifts in the use of humor, and changes in the pace or urgency projected by the ads.

The source of information for this phase of the creative analysis should be readily available in any well-run advertising department. Copies of each advertisement that is used should be retained with notations as to the dates of usage.

*Effectiveness Evaluation.* The program of advertising effectiveness evaluation should also provide information on the effectiveness of some of the advertisements created or used during the previous period. It is possible to test such things as the ability of advertisements to attract attention, to communicate certain knowledge, and to change product perceptions. If such tests were run as part of the effectiveness evaluation program in the prior year, the results should be studied as part of the advertising analysis. These results are a rich source for defining creative problems and opportunities.

MERCHANDISING ANALYSIS. There are various other marketing activities that are so closely related to problems facing the advertising program that they should be included in the analysis of advertising activity. As in the case of the analysis of advertising that has already been discussed, the analysis of these related activities, termed *merchandising analysis,* should examine the significant changes that have taken place in the recent past.

*Price and Discount Structure.* What are some of the items that should be considered? Certainly it would be valuable to review price and discount structure changes that have taken place. Pricing changes affect the margins available for advertising expenditures. A change in price is also a change in the product's attributes. A lower price is an attribute with potential for use in advertising and may make the product attractive to a different segment of the market.

*Packaging.* Strengths and weaknesses in packaging and display materials used for the product should be analyzed. Packaging is designed to contain and protect the product, to identify it, and in some cases to be reusable after the product has been consumed. Distinctive attributes might be found in any of these functions. For example, Procter and Gamble found that the plastic tube used for Prell Shampoo afforded superior protection against breakage and used this attribute in its advertising for many years. Similarly, when it was discovered that aerosol propellants may be environmentally damaging, many products were shifted to mechanical sprayer bottles and the change advertised as an attribute. Reuse possibilities, likewise, are found in many packages. The metal box used for Sucrets Throat Lozenges has for many years been saved by consumers as a container for paper clips, pins, or change. This attribute is a small, but nonetheless important advantage built into the product. Exhibit 8-12 illustrates how reusable packaging can become the central benefit offered in an advertisement.

Distinctive in-store containers or racks sometimes provide a product attribute by making the product easier to locate or identify. Hanes Corporation is the industry leader in the sales of panty hose with its L'eggs brand.[1] This product is mass-marketed through supermarkets and drugstores and is packaged in distinctive egg-shaped containers which are displayed in an equally distinctive, tall, egg-shaped display rack. The L'eggs marketers feel that the display unit is such an important part of the package that it is pictured in newspaper and television advertisements for the product.

*Sales Promotions.* Effectiveness of sales promotions (special, limited-time offers to the consumer or trade) conducted during the year should be evaluated. These promotions are designed to achieve specialized objectives such as increasing display, building up dealer stocks, or stimulating consumer trial of the product. The success of the promotion should be evaluated in terms of the objective that has been set for it. In addition, the effect of the sales promotion on the regular advertising campaign should be considered. A sales promotion, such as a contest or a special price reduction, can interrupt and distract from the regular campaign if the two efforts are not well coordinated.

TOTAL PLAN EFFECTS. The individual programs of the advertising plan — budget, media, and creative — are each directed toward individual objectives in terms of which their effectiveness can be evaluated. It is also important, however, to analyze the overall effect of the combined programs. The important question here is whether or not the total advertising

---

[1]See "Our L'eggs Fit Your Legs," *Business Week* (March 25, 1972), pp. 96–97, 100.

Use of a unique package in an advertisement.                    EXHIBIT 8-12

# THIS CHRISTMAS, GIVE A GIFT THAT'S AS BEAUTIFUL EMPTY AS IT IS FULL.

## ONLY $4.29*
**THE DUNKIN' DONUTS CRYSTAL APPLE
WITH 30 MUNCHKINS DONUT HOLE TREATS**
(COMPARABLE RETAIL VALUE $6.99)

It's our beautiful crystal glass apple with 30 delicious Munchkins donut hole treats.
Not only will it be fun to empty, but once it is, your family and friends can find hundreds of ways to refill it.
Our glass apple is one gift you won't have to worry about being the wrong size or color.
Available only at participating Dunkin' Donuts shops while supply lasts.

*Suggested Retail Price     Offer not available in Canada.

**DUNKIN' DONUTS**
It's worth the trip.

plan is achieving the larger advertising objectives. These objectives should have been defined in the prior year's plan. They may include sales and profit as well as communication objectives.

How is achievement of these objectives measured? Ideally, the effectiveness evaluation program will have provided for continuing studies to gather information on the effectiveness of the advertising plan in achieving these overall, total-plan objectives. This information might include measurements of consumer purchases to evaluate sales effectiveness. The communications effectiveness of the advertisements might be evaluated by measuring consumer understanding of the advertising, or by measuring changes in attitudes toward the product. The information obtained from these measurements should be utilized in this section to determine the strengths and shortcomings of the total plan.

## Uses of Product Information

The purpose of the product analysis is to gain an understanding of the need-satisfying qualities of the product. The uses to which the results of the product analysis will be put are relatively obvious from the description of the information that is sought.

### Defining Problems and Opportunities

The product analysis should result in a substantial addition to the list of problems and opportunities that face the advertiser's product. In the sections on product analysis, stress was placed on the need to uncover attributes of the product that are unique or superior. These represent opportunities. Deficiencies noted in the product — both physical and in the way it is perceived — represent problems facing it.

### Positioning the Product

A second use of product analysis information will be in making the positioning decision. The consumer analysis focused on determining consumers' needs. In this chapter the stress has been on determining what need-satisfying attributes the product possesses. The positioning decision requires matching an attribute of the product with an existing consumer need. This decision helps the advertiser decide to what group to direct the message and what benefit or solution to promise in order to attract this group. Clearly a knowledge of existing product attributes is vital to this decision.

### Framing the Message

A third use of product analysis is to provide information to the creative personnel who must present the attributes of the product to consumers. A good product analysis gathers and interprets all available material on the product and puts it in a form that can easily be absorbed and utilized by the creative specialists when they prepare advertisements.

CHAPTER
SUMMARY

In defining the product to be analyzed, the advertiser should include all attributes of the product that offer a consumer benefit. These attributes should be viewed not only in physical terms, but should also include the consumer's perception of the need-satisfying capabilities of the product. The analysis of the product should focus on discovering attributes of the product that give an advantage over competition. Use testing is one approach to researching consumer reaction to product characteristics and changes. Understanding of consumer perceptions of the product often requires research using indirect question techniques and attitude scales. Analysis of past advertising for the product is an important part of the product analysis because information communicated by past advertising helps form consumers' perceptions of the product. In addition, the analysis of advertising activity evaluates the effectiveness of the past effort so that improvements can be made during the coming period.

Results of the product analysis are used in three ways in the advertising planning process. The analysis should result in definition of more problems and opportunities facing the product—both product design problems and advertising problems. Product analysis tells what attributes the product offers to consumers. This information is a vital element in deciding how to position the product. Finally, product analysis provides an important information source for those who create advertisements for the product.

KEY
TERMS

| | |
|---|---|
| Product (brand) image | Semantic differential |
| Consumer use (home use) test | Advertising to sales (A to S) ratio |
| Preference test | Rating reports |
| Concept test | Audience studies |
| Concept board | |

QUESTIONS
FOR
DISCUSSION

1. A product is almost always made up of several elements and may be a complex mix of characteristics. A city newspaper is an example of a rather complex product. Make a list of the elements that you feel make up the product sold by your local newspaper publisher. (Remember, a newspaper is sold to two kinds of prospects—readers and advertisers.)

2. One of the keys to successfully entering an established product category is to design a product with a unique product attribute. For each of the following product successes, what was the unique attribute offered?

   a. Taco Bell restaurants
   b. Prince tennis racquets
   c. Bufferin analgesic
   d. Sanka coffee
   e. Crest toothpaste

3. You have just received from the marketing research department a response to your request for a research plan to test consumer reaction to a new formula dishwasher detergent. The new formula is supposed to reduce the spots and cloudiness left on dishes by the previous formula. The research proposal suggests that the new formula product be distributed through the company store that sells the firm's products to employees for about half the usual price. Whenever an employee purchases the regular product, that employee will also be given a free package of the revised formula in a regular sized, but unlabeled, package, provided that he/she agrees to fill out and return a product preference questionnaire. The employees will be told that the blank package contains a revised formula, but will not be told how it differs. The questionnaire will ask for comparative preferences and will probe for the reasons for those preferences. What is your reaction to this proposal?

4. An adaptation of the semantic differential is sometimes used as a means of measuring consumer perceptions of a particular store. This approach requires that the user develop sets of polar (opposite) adjectives that will describe the dimensions of the consumers' perception of the store. For example, one set of scale adjectives might be:

   an up-to-date          ⌊_⌊_⌊_⌊_⌊_⌊_⌊_⌊_⌊_⌊          a traditional
   store                                                           store

   Suppose that you were planning research on the image of a downtown department store in a medium-sized city. Suggest the sets of adjectives that you would use to provide a description of the store's image.

5. You are the advertising director of a frozen food company that distributes its product in a three-state area. Sales for the year just ended were $500,000 with cost of goods sold, a variable cost, at 60 percent of sales. Administrative and selling expenses, not including advertising, were $100,000 and relatively fixed at volume up to $1,000,000. The advertising budget was $50,000. However, in one city you had authorized an advertising budget test using advertising at twice the regular level. You believe that the test city is reasonably representative of the total distribution area. In the test city, sales increased by 20 percent during the test.

In planning for the coming year's advertising budget, how would you interpret the test results?

6. The advertising manager of the First National Bank has carefully traced the advertising expenditures of competitors for the previous year as part of the advertising analysis for the bank's advertising plan. The manager is concerned at having discovered that, although the budget is larger than that of each of the two competitors, the First National Bank's advertising expenditures are not in proportion to its share of the market (in this case, share of deposits). The figures are as follows:

| Bank | Advertising $ | % of Total Advertising $ | Share of Market |
|---|---|---|---|
| First National | 50,000 | 42% | 60% |
| Bank "B" | 40,000 | 33 | 30 |
| Bank "C" | 30,000 | 25 | 10 |

Should the advertising manager be concerned? Explain.

7. As part of the program of advertising effectiveness evaluation, the advertising manager for a line of canned luncheon meats has a study conducted annually to measure the percentage of prospects who recall advertising for the company's products, the percentage who remember the central appeal in the advertising, and the percentage who plan to purchase the company's product next time. In the most recent study all three of the percentages showed an improvement, yet sales declined in the same period. What might lie behind this apparent contradiction? (The model of the consumer decision process in Chapter 5 may be helpful in considering this question.)

8. In analyzing the results of a 10-cents-off promotion conducted for the company's brand of artificial sweetener, the advertising manager finds that sales to consumers increased sharply during the two-month period of the promotion. However, after the promotion, sales dropped below normal for several months. The result was that the decline offset the increase during the promotion. What should the advertising manager conclude?

9. As the newly appointed advertising manager for a cough remedy you find that last year's heaviest sales were in January, February, and March for your product and for the industry. The pattern of advertising expenditures for your product shows the greatest expenditures were in November, December, and January, with a reduced effort in February and March. Does this indicate an error in the allocation of advertising funds by month?

*PROBLEM*          Marketing executives at Bristol-Myers were reviewing the results of the introductory marketing efforts for Small Miracle, a new hair-conditioning product, and trying to decide what action to take.[2]

Small Miracle was developed by researchers at Bristol-Myers. Hair conditioners are applied after shampooing to leave hair soft, shiny, and manageable. Small Miracle performed like other conditioners, but was unique in that it could last through several shampooings and thus did not need to be used every day.

Prior to marketing, the product was tested both qualitatively and quantitatively. In the qualitative tests, women shampooed and conditioned their hair while researchers observed through two-way mirrors. Depth interviews revealed that women with thick, curly hair were pleased with the product, but that women with fine, thin hair reported that the product stuck to their hair and created greasy clumps. The quantitative use-tests with over 1,000 women revealed that the new product was clearly preferred over all its competition by women with all types of hair.

Despite the conflicting initial test results, Small Miracle was put into test markets with advertising that claimed, "You can shampoo every day and condition twice a week." Advertising and promotion expenditures were the heaviest ever in the hair-conditioning product class. When early test-market results proved favorable, the new product was rolled out to the West Coast region. Advertising was continued at a heavy level, but copy was changed to testimonials eliminating the longer lasting claim used in the test markets. As the product was moved into additional markets, sales results were disappointing to the point that executives were seriously concerned. After examining sales results, some blamed the advertising and suggested a new agency. Others said that the problem was that not enough consumers had tried the product while others suggested that consumers were confused about the meaning of the product.

1. What is your evaluation of the product Small Miracle?
2. Why have initial sales results been disappointing?

---

[2]This problem was based on Nancy Giges, "No Miracle in Small Miracle," *Advertising Age* (August 16, 1982), pp. 1, 76.

# CHAPTER 9

## *Market Analysis*

### LEARNING OBJECTIVES

In studying this chapter you will learn:

- What market analysis is and how it is used in the advertising plan.

- The four types of market information needed for market analysis.

- Techniques used to determine the current size of a product market and to forecast future market growth.

- How to develop and analyze competitive sales information.

- What environmental factors are and how they influence market size, growth, and distribution.

- Sources of market analysis information.

The third major analysis that must be completed before preparing advertising programs is the *market analysis*. It is primarily concerned with projecting market sales. Like the consumer and product analysis, the market analysis provides vital information for positioning the product, for defining problems, and, in turn, for setting objectives. In the positioning decision a product attribute must be selected that is to be directed to a particular target segment of consumers. The market analysis provides information that is useful in deciding which segment offers the greatest potential. The market analysis also serves to define sales and competitive problems because it permits comparison of the advertiser's sales progress with that of competition. This problem definition, in turn, leads to the definition of objectives to improve performance.

In the sections that follow, we shall describe four types of market information needed for the market analysis:

1. Total market sales.
2. Advertiser's product sales.
3. Competitors' sales.
4. Environmental influences on sales.

Analyzing Total Market Sales

The natural way to initiate one's understanding of the opportunity offered by the market is to examine information describing the total market — its size, growth, and distribution by segment, geographic area, and season. Although the sales characteristics to be examined may vary somewhat from product to product, there are four characteristics that are basic:   (1) The absolute size of the market needs to be estimated to give an indication of its potential. (2) The expected growth of the market needs to be projected because growth influences the potential of the market. (3) The seasonality or distribution of sales over the year should also be projected as a guide to allocation of marketing effort. (4) The geographic distribution of sales should be projected because it specifies where the market is located. The process of developing information for each of these four characteristics will be considered in turn. First, however, we will consider how the market to be analyzed is defined or limited.

## Defining the Market

An essential preliminary to forecasting any of the sales characteristics described above is to define the market to be analyzed. The definition should state what products are to be included in the market and what geographic sales area is to be covered.

PRODUCTS INCLUDED. The first step in defining the market lies in deciding on the products to be included in the definition. Usually there is a generic group of products that should obviously be included in the product category. If the product to be advertised is a cough syrup, then clearly the product category would include all brands called cough syrups. But there are sometimes other products that are somewhat related and somewhat competitive. It is less clear which of these should be included in the product-category definition. For example, should cough drops be included in the same category as cough syrup? Or suppose the advertiser's product were a ground coffee. Should ground decaffeinated coffee be considered a part of the market? What about instant coffee? If instant coffee is included, should tea and instant tea also be included since, like ground coffee, they are used to make a beverage?

Deciding what products to include and what products to exclude from the definition of the market is sometimes of necessity rather arbitrary. Perhaps the best way to decide where the product-category dividing line should be drawn would be to borrow the consumer's point of view. Traditionally, product markets have been defined to include those products that consumers view as substitutes for one another. To this definition recent researchers have suggested two additional criteria: (1) the products to be considered in the same product class should be limited to those purchased for the same usage occasion, and (2) they should offer similar benefits.[1] Using this approach, the answers in the earlier examples are somewhat clearer. It seems unlikely that a confirmed coffee drinker would consider tea to be a substitute for coffee. And, likewise, an individual who felt that regular coffee caused wakefulness at night would probably not consider regular coffee to be an adequate substitute for decaffeinated coffee. Do cough syrup users consider cough drops to be a substitute product? Probably not. Cough drops are probably more often used as a supplementary product or for less serious problems.

GEOGRAPHIC AREA. In addition to defining the products to be included in the market definition, it is also necessary to specify geographic limits. The market to be analyzed should be limited to sales of the defined product category in the advertiser's distribution area. If an advertiser's product is distributed and advertised east of the Mississippi River, then the market should be defined as including only sales in that area. An international marketer, likewise, should develop a market definition that includes sales only in countries where the product is distributed.

## Determining the Size of the Total Market

With the market defined in terms of products and geographic area to be included, a first important estimate to be made is the size of the total market.

ESTIMATING MARKET SIZE. The market size estimate should be in current dollar or unit sales of the defined market. For many markets, estimates of sales can be obtained directly from published sources. These sources are described at the end of this chapter. Exhibit 9-1 shows a ten-year estimate of television receiver factory sales based on figures published by an electronics industry trade association. Retail sales could be estimated from these figures by applying a standard dealer markup. From such data advertising managers can project future sales.

If published figures of market size are not available a number of estimating approaches might be tried. Sometimes an estimate can be "built-up" by aggregating components of the market. For example, the size of the banking market in a city could be estimated by adding all the deposits from published statements of the major banks in the area.

Sometimes market size can be approximated by estimating the proportion of the population using the product and multiplying by the estimated usage rate. For example, in Chapter 7 it was estimated that 43 percent or 30 million homes had vegetable gardens. If the average expenditure for

---

[1]George S. Day, Allan D. Shocker, and Rajendra K. Srivastava, "Consumer-Oriented Approaches to Identifying Product-Markets" *Journal of Marketing* Vol. 43 (Fall, 1979), pp. 8–19.

EXHIBIT 9-1      Annual factory sales of television receivers, 1973–1982.

| Year | Units (000) | Dollars (000) |
|------|-------------|---------------|
| 1973 | 16,902 | $3,526,391 |
| 1974 | 14,334 | 3,032,537 |
| 1975 | 11,606 | 2,684,121 |
| 1976 | 13,455 | 3,250,593 |
| 1977 | 15,350 | 3,819,727 |
| 1978 | 16,959 | 4,223,496 |
| 1979 | 16,764 | 4,245,452 |
| 1980 | 18,143 | 4,798,239 |
| 1981 | 17,423 | 4,854,110 |
| 1982 | 17,365 | 4,759,832 |

Source: *Electronic Market Data Book, 1983* (Washington, D.C.: Electronic Industries Association, 1983), p. 15.

fertilizer for home vegetable gardens were $10, then the total size of this portion of the market would be $10 × 30 million = $300 million.

Another approach toward estimating market size is to survey a representative sample of the population of prospects, asking them how much of the product they had purchased in some past period, say a year. The results could then be projected to the total population to give a total market estimate.

ESTIMATING SIZE OF MARKET SEGMENT. It is desirable not only to estimate the size of the total market but also the size of each of the segments of the market. In Exhibit 9-2 the radio market is divided into four segments, each of which is subdivided again, and there is an estimate of the sales volume in each of these segments. This estimate again came from an indus-

EXHIBIT 9-2      Factory production of radios by product segments, 1982

| Product Segment | Units (000) | Total Units (000) |
|-----------------|-------------|-------------------|
| Table radios |  | 794 |
| AM | 341 |  |
| AM-FM | 453 |  |
| Clock radios |  | 8,433 |
| AM | 144 |  |
| AM-FM | 8,289 |  |
| Portable radios |  | 22,555 |
| AM | 4,847 |  |
| AM-FM | 17,708 |  |
| Auto Radios |  | 12,306 |
| AM | 1,882 |  |
| AM-FM | 10,424 |  |
| TOTAL |  | 36,874 |

Source: *Electronic Market Data Book, 1983,* (Washington, D.C.: Electronic Industries Association, 1983), p. 26.

try trade association. Notice that the segments are based on product types rather than the more desirable groupings of consumers with common needs or problems, but the product segments do represent different benefits. The advertising manager will often find that market segments, as defined in published reports, do not fit the segment definitions that the advertiser might wish.

Exhibit 9-3 shows an advertisement for a new General Electric clock radio that incorporates a telephone. It is interesting to speculate whether this new product is part of the clock-radio product segment or constitutes an entirely new segment.

If the segment size estimates are not applicable, or if they are unavailable, some means should be found to approximate segment size. Sometimes the sales volume of each brand, model, or variety in the market is known and segment size can be estimated by assigning sales of each brand to its approximate segment and building up a segment estimate. The prospect profile contains information from which segment size might be estimated since it reveals the proportion or number of prospects in each segment. If usage rates can be estimated for prospects in each segment, then the usage rate for the segment times the number in the segment gives an estimate of segment size. Segment size can also be projected by research that surveys the purchases of a representative sample in each segment.

ANALYSIS OF MARKET SIZE INFORMATION. Estimates of the size of the total market and the size of the market segments should be examined by the advertising manager to see what direction they indicate for the advertising programs. The size of the market will influence the size of the advertising budget. In addition, the comparative sizes of the market segments will influence the choice of segment to which the product will be directed.

## Forecasting Total Market Growth

In addition to knowing the current size of the total market, it is important to know at what rate the total market can be expected to grow. The advertiser should also forecast, when possible, the future size of each market segment.

FORECASTING TECHNIQUES. Estimation of the future size of the market calls for the use of forecasting techniques. This is a rather technical area and the advertising manager may wish to call on the marketing research group for assistance. However, the advertising manager should at least be familiar with the basic forecasting approaches.

One forecasting approach is to plot graphically past sales over time and fit a trend line. The trend line might be fitted judgmentally or more sophisticated statistical techniques such as a least-squares method might be used. Exhibit 9-4 shows the potential difficulty with extension of historical data. If at the end of 1969 the historical trend in candy sales had been

**EXHIBIT 9-3**    An advertisement for a new G.E. telephone-clock radio. To what product segment does it belong?

# THE BIGGEST INNOVATION IN CLOCK RADIOS SINCE GE INTRODUCED THEM.

Say hello to the only clock radio telephone good enough to be called General Electric.

It combines the reliability of a GE clock radio with the advanced technology of the new GE telephone—in one space-saving unit.

There are two models to choose from—both with a lighted telephone keypad and a special feature that quiets the radio when you pick up the phone.

The model shown here also has a memory for nine frequently called numbers. And three emergency buttons to save you time when you need it most.

**FULL TWO-YEAR WARRANTY.**

The GE Clock Radio Telephones are backed by a full two-year warranty so you can be sure they're built to last. For more information, call the GE Answer Center,™ 800-626-2000, toll-free.

**WE BRING GOOD THINGS TO LIFE.**

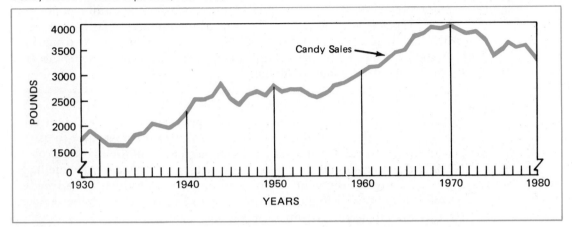

Source:  U.S. Department of Commerce, *Confectionery Manufacturers Sales and Distribution*, 1980.

extended, it would have missed the major downturn of the 1970s. The assumption that the historical trend will continue is a major weakness of this technique. A change in competitive conditions or consumer needs, for example, could cause a major change in the market growth rate. This forecasting approach can be improved if the advertiser estimates changes in market conditions that are likely to occur and then adjusts the trend forecast upward or downward. For example, recent research has indicated sharply increased concern among homemakers about sugar in the diets of family members. This might lead a candy marketer to project the market forecast downward from the historical trend.

Another forecasting approach involves the use of econometric techniques which estimate future market sales based on their relationship to other economic variables. For example, if it could be established that sales of the product category (such as luxury yachts) varied directly with consumer disposable income, a forecast of the market size might begin with a forecast of disposable income. Then product sales could be estimated by their relationship to the forecast of disposable income. Some companies develop sophisticated multiple variable models of this sort to represent their markets and provide forecasts of market growth.

Some products, particularly in industrial markets, are used as components in other products. For example, aircraft engines are components in aircraft, and tires are components in automobiles. Future sales of such products are dependent upon production and sales of the finished product. For these markets, the market growth forecast should begin with a forecast for the finished product and then be translated into the derived demand for the component product. Using automobile tires as an example, if auto manufacturers estimate sales of eight million cars for the coming period and five tires are to be sold per new car, then new car tire demand will be estimated at 40 million tires.

Some forecasts must be "built" from separate components of the market. The automobile tires example mentioned above is a case in point. Automobile tires are sold not only as components on new automobiles, but also as replacement parts. Since the replacement market may have a trend different from that of the original equipment market, the two markets should be projected separately. Both markets can then be combined to give an estimate of total sales potential.

ANALYSIS OF MARKET GROWTH. The market projection should be examined to determine whether or not growth can be expected in the total market. A high projected growth rate encourages the advertiser to use an aggressive advertising program so as to participate in the market growth. The advertiser should also look at growth rates by market segment. In seeking a market segment in which to position a product, the advertiser would clearly prefer to direct advertising efforts to a fast-growing segment rather than to a slow-growing or declining segment.

Product life-cycle theory (see page 14) can sometimes be useful in anticipating growth rates for product categories. The particular life-cycle stage in which a product happens to be can often be estimated by analyzing the competitive environment, past sales and sales growth, and the age of the product category. With this information, changes in future sales-growth rates can be anticipated. Products in the introductory stage tend to experience increasing rates of growth, in the growth stage the rates of growth begin to decline, and in the stage of maturity product growth-rates level out. In the stage of product decline, growth turns negative.

In addition to looking at the projected growth rates, the advertiser should consider how much risk the growth projections contain. Some markets such as the market for staple food products are stable and forecasts can be made with substantial certainty. The candy market projection reveals a highly stable market but without exciting growth prospects. For other forecasts, such as one for a fashion product, projections are highly uncertain. The certainty of growth estimates also varies from segment to segment within a market. The advertising manager should consider the riskiness of the growth projection both in the selection of the target segment and in deciding on the magnitude of the advertising effort.

## Estimating Seasonal Market Sales

For almost any category of product, the level of consumer demand varies by the season or month of the year. As a result, sales in most markets vary in a regular seasonal pattern. Cough syrup sells better in the winter, soft drinks sell better in the summer, and electric razors sell best just before Christmas. Such seasonal sales patterns are important to the advertiser who must decide when to spend advertising dollars.

*seasonal sales index*        A **seasonal sales index** describes the expected seasonal variation in future sales of the advertiser's product category, usually on a month-to-month basis. Construction of a monthly seasonal sales index requires historical sales data for the market, by month, for at least a full year and preferably for several years. The seasonal variation is determined by expressing sales for each month as a percent of total sales for the year. The seasonal variation can be expressed in index form by letting average monthly sales equal 100. Sales for each individual month are then expressed as a percent of average monthly sales. A seasonal sales index of retail sales for tires, batteries, and auto accessories is shown in Exhibit 9-5. Details on construction of a seasonal index will be found in most introductory statistics books under the topic of time-series analysis.

The index itself does not tell why the seasonal variation in sales occurs, but it does provide the advertising manager with a starting point for investigating the cause. Variations in sales by season reflect variations in consumer demand. Cough syrup sales are higher in winter months because cold incidence is greater. Soft-drink sales are greater in summer because higher temperatures increase thirst. Seasonal variations in sales may also reflect the availability of the product as in the case of fresh fruits and vegetables. It is also possible that seasonal sales variations are due to the promotional practices of the individual competitors in the market. The seasonal sales for new automobiles is due, in part, to the timing of new model introductions by car manufacturers.

The seasonal sales index provides important guidance to the advertiser in deciding when advertising funds should be expended during the year. If the sales variation by season reflects variations in the occurrence of consumer needs, then advertising should be timed to coincide with or to precede the occurrence of the need.

## Estimating Geographic Sales Variation

In addition to knowing how sales vary by season, it is important for the advertising manager to know how total market sales can be expected to vary by geographic area. A **geographic index of market sales** expresses this variation.

*geographic index of market sales*

The geographic distribution of sales is determined from historical sales figures. Total market sales in each geographic area are needed for at

Seasonal index of monthly retail sales of tires, batteries, and accessories.

EXHIBIT 9-5

| Month | Index | Month | Index |
|---|---|---|---|
| January | 81.8 | July | 109.4 |
| February | 77.6 | August | 102.9 |
| March | 94.0 | September | 94.2 |
| April | 105.0 | October | 100.6 |
| May | 108.3 | November | 103.7 |
| June | 113.6 | December | 108.9 |

Source: Computed from data in U.S. Bureau of the Census, *Monthly Retail Trade* (Washington).

least one and preferably several years. Sales for each area are then expressed as a percentage of total sales to show how sales are distributed among areas. As an alternative, the data can be put in index form. Average area sales (total sales divided by the number of areas) are set equal to 100 and then sales for each individual geographic area are expressed as a percentage of average area sales.

Historical market sales figures are often not available or the sales figures available may not conform to the geographic territory definitions used by the advertiser. In such a case it may be possible to estimate the geographic distribution of total market sales through use of a correlation approach. If it can be established that sales of the product category are correlated to another known factor, then that factor can be used to predict the geographic distribution of the sales of the product. For example, if a marketer of luxury home furnishings knew from consumer studies that the prime prospects were people with residences of high valuation, published statistics on home valuation by county could be used as a basis for estimating the geographic distribution of total market sales. Readily available figures on retail sales by product categories, income, population, and other broad measures can sometimes also be used as indicators of geographic sales distribution. *Sales Management* magazine publishes annual estimates of retail sales, population, and consumer income by cities, counties, and metropolitan areas. It is important to note, however, that these broad measures cannot validly be used to estimate market sales distribution unless there is positive evidence that sales of the product category and these measures are indeed correlated.

The advertising manager's analysis of the geographic variation in the market should follow the pattern suggested for the seasonal variation. The first step is to try to understand the reason for the geographic variation in sales. If the variation reflects geographic differences in consumer demand for the product, then the geographic sales index will give the advertiser some guidance as to where to allocate advertising effort. On the other hand, analysis may reveal that areas with low sales do not represent a lack of interested prospects, but failure of marketers to reach those areas. In such a case the low sales areas would represent opportunity areas.

## Analyzing Sales of the Advertiser's Product

Thus far the sales analysis has been concerned with the projected sales of the entire product category. The analysis has inquired into (1) the size of the total market, (2) its expected growth, (3) seasonal variations in sales, and (4) the geographic distribution of total sales. In addition to this total market analysis, the advertiser should analyze the sales performance of the company's own product. The availability of the total market analysis makes it possible to compare the performance of the advertiser's product with average market performance.

## Developing Information on Product Sales

The information developed for the advertiser's product should be parallel to the analysis done for the total product category to permit valid comparative analysis. That is, there should be information on (1) the total sales of the product, (2) the growth in product sales, (3) seasonal sales, and (4) sales of the product by geographic area. Each of these analyses begins by arraying historical sales figures for the product and computing the appropriate rates and indexes for the product.

### Analysis of Product Sales Figures

A prime goal in analyzing sales information is to search for problems and opportunities. Since the sales figures for the advertiser's product are placed in the same form as total product category sales, it is possible to compare the two. The sales volume of the advertiser's product can be compared to total market sales to determine brand share (the percentage of total sales enjoyed by the product). Trends in *brand share* indicate whether or not the advertiser's product is keeping pace with the market. The growth rate of the advertiser's brand can be compared to the total market growth. Seasonal sales of the advertiser's product can be compared to the total market seasonal sales to see if the product is taking advantage of seasonal increases in sales. Similarly, the geographic index for the product should be compared with the geographic sales index of the total market to see if there are areas of high potential sales that have been overlooked or that have been underdeveloped. These comparisons contribute substantially to the list of problems and opportunities to which the advertising program for the coming period must respond.

Information contained in the analysis of the product's sales will also be useful in designing the advertising programs. For example, knowledge of the product's market share and projected growth is likely to influence the size of the advertising budget. The seasonal and geographic sales patterns of the product are likely to influence the seasonal and geographic allocations of the advertising budget.

## Analyzing Competitive Sales Performance

The next step in the market analysis is to analyze the sales performance of competitive products. Understanding where competitors are strong and where they are directing their efforts may suggest opportunity segments or areas that have been overlooked by the competition.

### Developing Information on Competitive Sales

Detailed sales data of competitive firms are often difficult to obtain because companies hold these figures in confidence. Consequently it is not realistic to assume that the sales of each competitor can be analyzed in the same detail as the sales of the advertiser's own product. Nonetheless, the advertiser should, insofar as possible, determine who the major competitors are, estimate their market shares, and attempt to understand how each competitor is positioned in the marketplace.

DEFINING COMPETITION. To begin the competitive sales analysis it is necessary to know the major competitors. Care should be taken to see that the list of competitors is consistent with the definition established for the total market. Competitors include only marketers whose products are included in the defined total market and are sold within the defined geographic limits of the market.

*market share*

ESTIMATING MARKET SHARES. The advertising manager should attempt to determine the current market share of each competitive product. **Market share** is the percentage of product category sales realized by a particular product. It is a measure of the sales and competitive strength of a product. Exhibit 9-6 shows how market share in the coffee industry is

**EXHIBIT 9-6**     Coffee market shares, 1982.

| Company/Brand | Regular | Instant |
|---|---|---|
| General Foods | | |
|    Maxwell House | 19.5% | 22.9% |
|    Sanka | 3.7 | 13.0 |
|    Maxim | | 3.2 |
|    Yuban | 1.3 | 1.3 |
|    Max-Pax & Brim | 2.8 | 4.3 |
|    Mellow Roast | 0.6 | 1.0 |
|    Master Blend | 6.9 | |
| Procter and Gamble | | |
|    Folgers | 23.0 | 11.5 |
|    High Point | | 5.5 |
| Hills Brothers | 6.2 | |
| Coca Cola | | |
|    Maryland Club | 1.0 | |
|    Butternut | 2.4 | |
| Nestlé | | |
|    Nescafé Regular | | 7.0 |
|    Nescafé Decaffeinated | | 2.1 |
|    Taster's Choice | | 9.5 |
|    Decaf | | 0.5 |
|    Taster's Choice | | |
|       Decaffeinated | | 7.1 |
|    Sunrise | | 1.0 |
| All Others | 32.6 | 10.5 |

Reprinted with permission from the May 9, 1983 issue of *Advertising Age*. Copyright 1983 by Crain Communications, Inc.

divided among major competitors. In addition to current market share, the advertiser should try to learn which products are gaining in market share and which are declining.

MARKET POSITION. Once competitors have been defined and their success has been appraised by means of market shares, the advertiser should next determine how each competitive product is positioned in the market. This is the most important step in the competitive sales analysis. For each competitive brand, the segment of the market toward which it is directed should be determined.

Competitive strategies, or the segments to which competitive products are directed, can be inferred through examination of the creative and media programs of the competitive products. Advertising copy will reveal the product attribute being offered, and the copy, together with knowledge of the media used, will indicate the market segment toward which the product is directed. Exhibit 9-7 on page 206 shows a summary analysis of candy bar advertising copy developed from a study of competitive advertising, such as the Mr. Goodbar commercial shown in Exhibit 9-8.

## Analysis of Competitive Information

Information on competitive sales will influence decisions at a number of stages in the advertising planning process, but its most important use will be in the selection of the market segment or segments toward which advertising is to be directed. In deciding to what group in the market to direct the advertising, the advertising manager must find a segment of the market with a need that can be satisfied by an attribute of the product. However, positioning of competitors must also be considered. Market segments that are found to be covered by competitive products with strong market positions are less attractive than segments that are lacking strong competition. The analysis of competitive sales performance will help the advertising manager determine which segments of the market are dominated by strong competition and which segments appear to be the less competitive segments.

## Analysis of Environmental Factors

**Environmental factors** are forces that are external to the market, but *environmental factor* that are underlying causes of changes in market size, growth, and distribution. Changes in the market environment operate by changing both the consumer's decision-making process and the constraints the advertiser faces in attempting to satisfy consumer needs. If an advertiser is able to predict a change in consumer requirements, then it might be possible to position a product in a segment that will increase in size. For example, increased concern for physical fitness has generated a sizeable group of joggers. Footwear manufacturers have been quick to seize upon this trend

EXHIBIT 9-7          Candy bar advertising copy analysis.

| Brand | Product Attribute | Campaign Theme | Target Audience |
| --- | --- | --- | --- |
| $100,000 Bar | Chewy & crunchy | If you love chewy caramel. | Kids & teens |
| Butterfinger | Peanut butter & crunch candy | So good you have to earn it. | Teens & adults |
| Marathon | Caramel & chewy | Lasts a good long time. | Kids & teens |
| M & M | Plain or peanut | Melts in your mouth, not in your hand. | Kids |
| Choco-Lite | Smooth & creamy | Smooth & creamy like a glide. | Kids |
| 3 Musketeers | Fluffy nougat | Fluffy taste that gives your spirit a lift. | Kids |
| Starburst | Fruit chews | Burst of fruit flavor. | Kids |
| Snickers | Peanut butter, nougat & caramel | No matter how you slice it, it comes up peanuts. | All family |
| Reese's Peanut Butter Cup | Milk chocolate, peanut butter | Two great tastes in one candy bar. | Kids & adults |
| Mars Bar | Nougat, caramel, & chocolate | At work, rest or play, Mars Bar helps make your day. | Adults |
| Milky Way | Nougat, caramel, & chocolate | At work, rest or play, Milky Way. | Adults |
| Kit Kat | Milk chocolate, crispy wafer | The crispy chocolate bar so good you'll roar. | Adults |
| Hershey Bar | Chocolate | The great American chocolate bar. | Kids & adults |
| Tootsie Roll | Chocolatey chews | Whatever it is I think I see becomes a Tootsie Roll to me. | Kids |
| Baby Ruth | A filling snack | When you gotta have one, you gotta have one. | All family |
| Caravelle | Crisp chocolate & smooth chewy caramel | Discover Caravelle again. It's better than ever. | Kids |
| Mounds | Milk or dark chocolate, coconut | Now there're two kinds of Mounds. Because we don't all like alike. | Teens |
| Almond Joy | Almond Joy has almonds, Mounds don't | Sometimes you feel like a nut. Sometimes you don't. | Adult |
| Nestlé Milk Chocolate Bar | Creamy, smooth milk chocolate | Nestlé madness | Teens & Adults |
| Hershey's Mr. Goodbar | Peanuts in milk chocolate | Good peanuts and good chocolate make a very Goodbar. | Adults |

by positioning a special series of sneakers as ones especially designed for jogging. As a result, footwear manufacturers not only realized increased sales but also improved profit margins that arose from consumer willingness to pay premium prices for products designed especially for this need.

In attempting to identify the effects of environmental factors, the advertising manager should consider three potentially influential factors — economic, regulatory, and cultural.

### Economic Factors

The level of economic activity is one of several economic factors that affect the market for many kinds of products. The sales of capital equipment and consumer durables, for example, are greatly affected by general economic conditions because such purchases are postponable in recession

Storyboard of a Mr. Goodbar commercial used in the copy analysis.                **EXHIBIT 9-8**

BOY: Hey Mr.? Can I have a Mr. Goodbar, Mr.?

ANNCR: (VO) Back in the old days, Mr. Goodbar discovered the magic of peanuts and chocolate.

Ten years later...
MAN: Another Mr. for the Mrs.!

ANNCR: (VO)...people still loved the combination of crunchy peanuts and creamy chocolate.

Even in the forties...

SAILOR: Mr. Goodbar, SIR!

ANNCR: (VO)...even in the sixties...
FLOWER CHILDREN: Peace.

ANNCR: (VO) And even now, one thing's still true:

Good peanuts...

and good chocolate...

make a very good bar.

MAN: Good-Good-Good. Mr. Goodbar!

times and subject to catch-up buying during prosperous times. The advertiser should adjust forecasts of market size and growth to take into account this economy-wide influence.

The advertising manager should also attempt to anticipate changes in other economic factors. These include changes in population composition and in the labor force, emerging technology, changes in availability of raw materials, and changes in the general price level.

POPULATION. Strong population growth and household formation in the Post World War II years stimulated the economy in the fifties and sixties, creating growth markets for housing, automobiles, education, and countless other products and services. In the 1970s, birth rates declined sharply as marriages were deferred and many couples decided on smaller families or no children. This trend has continued into the 80s, causing profound changes in many product markets. Another result has been a shift in the composition of the population. The average age of the population has increased, creating strong demand for medical services and retirement homes. Declining marriage rates have also greatly increased singles households and with it the demand for such products as single-portion meals.

LABOR FORCE. The changing population composition will also affect the makeup of the labor force, which, in turn, determines what group has disposable income. More than half of all adult women now work outside the home, leading to more demand for labor-saving household appliances such as microwave ovens, greater use of household services such as lawn care and cleaning services, and an increase in out-of-home eating. As the number of working women increases, more men are doing the shopping and becoming more influential in brand selection. This phenomenon opens up more new "for men" positioning possibilities.

TECHNOLOGY. Technological change gives rise to new products and can greatly stimulate market growth, especially when the change represents a breakthrough in technology. One analysis of great breakthroughs in industrial technology included these:

1. the transistor
2. the computer
3. thermoplastic materials
4. numerical control
5. digital instrumentation
6. programmable controllers
7. computer graphics
8. integrated circuits
9. lasers
10. industrial robots[2]

---

[2]"Ten Significant Breakthroughs," *Industrial Equipment News*, (July 15, 1983), pp. 11–13.

Each of these breakthroughs has spawned scores of new products. The advertiser who recognizes breakthroughs like these at an early stage has the opportunity to gain competitive advantage through new and improved products.

RAW MATERIALS. Changes in the availability of raw materials shocked a series of markets in the 1970s. Chocolate, sugar, coffee, and lumber each went through severe shortage cycles, sending prices skyrocketing and disrupting market trends. Most far-reaching in its effects was the change in the price and availability of energy. As a result of this change, scores of markets were retarded while dozens of new ones were created, ranging from solar heating systems to energy-efficient appliances, mopeds, and programmable thermostats.

PRICE LEVEL. Changes in the price level can be a disruptive factor affecting the growth rate of markets. Inflation such as that experienced in the seventies hit markets unevenly, restraining the sale of some products while stimulating the sales of others.

In general the advertiser should attempt to direct the company's advertising effort to segments of the market that will grow in response to such basic changes in economic factors.

## Regulatory Factors

Federal, state, and local agencies impose an ever-changing variety of regulations on business that create both problems and opportunities. Regulation tends to constrain the sale of some products and create markets for others. The advertiser's challenge is to anticipate changes in the regulatory environment and to position products in such a way as to take advantage of the opportunities to be presented.

New regulations frequently create an opportunity for new products or new markets for existing products. Federal requirements established in the aftermath of the energy crisis forced auto makers to market more fuel-efficient automobiles. Clean air and water regulations have led to the marketing of emission control devices, waste-water treatment plants, and safer pesticides.

In recent years, the greatest regulatory changes have been deregulation. The move to deregulation began in the 1960s and has been gaining momentum ever since.[3] The intent and the effect have been to introduce intense competition into hitherto protected product categories. Many opportunities for new products and for the repositioning of existing ones have led to new roles for advertising. Industries that are undergoing major transformations because of deregulation include airlines, trucking, financial services, and telecommunications:

---

[3]For a detailed description of the impact of deregulation see "Deregulating America," *Business Week* (November 28, 1983), pp. 80–96.

1. In the airlines industry, both rates and allowable routes have been deregulated. As a result, the major carriers are consolidating and many specialized air services are emerging. New services such as no-frills air service and small aircraft service to minor markets are being introduced. Price competition especially between major markets has been intense. New services, new routes, and price reductions have created many opportunities and many new requirements for advertising.

2. Deregulation of the trucking industry has led to intense price competition with lower rates overall and far more negotiation of rates between shippers and trucking firms. As in the airline industry, there has been a squeeze-out among the large, capital-intensive trucking firms, and an increase among small specialized trucking firms.

3. Deregulation of financial services has dramatically restructured the industry and led to a host of new service offerings. The dividing lines between banks, savings institutions, brokerage houses, and other institutions are disappearing as each attempts to become a financial supermarket. New specialized firms like discount brokerage houses have appeared. New products like money-market accounts, interest-bearing checking accounts, and certificates of deposit also have appeared in great number. Advertisers have tremendous opportunities as they communicate these changes to their customers.

4. The most visible evidence of deregulation of the telecommunications industry has been the forced divestiture by AT&T of its telephone operating companies. At the same time there has been a massive restructuring of telephone rates and the introduction of new competition in both equipment and service. Again, deregulation has created marketing opportunities.

## Social and Cultural Factors

Culture is a set of values, beliefs, and ways of satisfying needs that is accepted by members of a society and transmitted to succeeding generations. Over the course of time, culture undergoes changes, which, although difficult to observe, have a profound effect on consumer behavior. Daniel Yankelovich, an expert in tracking cultural changes, pinpoints the behavioral role of cultural changes saying, "What is different about our culture today is not that Americans have new *desires*. The same desires persist from one generation to the next. But now the culture endorses as morally acceptable many desires that were not acceptable in the past."[4] Advertisers need to anticipate cultural changes and have products positioned to meet the newly sanctioned desires of consumers.

Identification of social trends that will influence an advertiser's product requires gaining perspective on what is happening around the world. Extensive reading and keen observation are needed to successfully predict social changes. Yankelovich sees profound changes taking place in our culture. He notes, "A traditional family life is no longer the prime symbol of respectability; conversely, you no longer lose your respectability if you are

[4]Daniel Yankelovich, *New Rules, Searching for Self-Fulfillment in a World Turned Upside Down* (New York: Random House, 1981), pp. 244–5.

divorced, choose to live alone, refuse to have children, belong to a household in which both spouses work or engage in discreet sexual experimentation. To be the exclusive provider for a family no longer drives the male to endure the frustration of an unsatisfying job, and the housewife-mother role is less often esteemed by society, or by women themselves."[5]

Florence Skelly, well-known expert on social changes, predicted six trends that will influence consumer markets in the year 2000. These predictions, listed below, indicate the kinds of influence to which the advertising manager should be sensitive.

1. A continuing decline in the nuclear family with consequent increases in small and single households.
2. A blurring of sexuality with overlap of men and women in jobs and activities performed.
3. An increase in the numbers and acceptance of the over-50 group as a key consumer group.
4. A decrease in leisure time offset by increased money available for leisure pursuits brought about by an increase of women in the work force and a trend away from compulsory retirement at age 65.
5. An erosion of egalitarianism and reemergence of social classes with a widening gap between the haves and have-nots.
6. A continuing emphasis on the rich, full life that stresses experience and variety.[6]

Each of these trends can have great impact on the market for most products, shrinking some market segments and enlarging others. The astute advertiser will attempt to identify these cultural trends and position products to cater to the natural growth of the market.

## Sources of Market Analysis Information

In order to conduct the market analysis, the advertising manager needs a good estimate of past sales for the total market and for individual products in the market. Future sales can usually be predicted from past sales in order to provide an idea of the market the advertiser will be facing in future years.

### Total Market Data

Every product class has traditional data sources that soon become familiar to the person working in the field. Some of the more important sources are suggested below.

TRADE ASSOCIATIONS. Industry trade associations frequently gather

---

[5]Ibid., p. 147.
[6]"Of the 'Me' Generation and Guerilla Warfare: Skelly Predicts the Year 2000," *Marketing Review* (January-February, 1978), pp. 8–9.

sales or output figures, usually based on reports from individual members. The figures are available to members and frequently to any interested person. For example, the Electronic Industries Association published the estimates of television receiver and radio sales shown in Exhibits 9-1 and 9-2.

TRADE PUBLICATIONS. Trade publications publish sales data gathered from original research or from secondary sources such as those listed here. The information is, of course, available to subscribers to the publication. *Supermarketing,* for example, publishes annual estimates of the sales volume for most food store product categories and *Appliance Manufacturer* estimates sales of major and small appliances.

GOVERNMENT SOURCES. Government census and tax reports provide detailed information on sales or production of a great variety of goods. Two of the most useful reports are the *Census of Business* and the *Census of Manufacturers.* Sales of products subject to tax (such as cigarettes, beer, and wine) are regularly reported by tax authorities. In addition, there is a great variety of other governmental data, some from periodic reports, others from one-time studies of particular industries. The Department of Commerce publishes the *Marketing Information Guide* monthly, listing current sources of marketing data.

*sales audit*      RETAIL AUDITS. **Sales audits** measure actual product sales by analyzing purchase records and inventories from a sample of retail stores. Highly detailed sales data are provided by this approach, but the cost is substantial. The leading commercial supplier of this service is the A. C. Nielsen Company.

A recent innovation is the production of product sales reports generated from data recorded by *optical scanners,* the laser devices at supermarket checkouts that read the universal product codes on packaged foods and other products.

A firm can also establish its own specialized audit system through cooperation of a sample of wholesalers, dealers, and retailers who report sales data to the advertiser.

*diary study*      CONSUMER DIARIES. **Diary studies** also measure actual sales, but do so by collecting purchase information from consumers of the product. A panel of consumers is paid to keep a diary or record of purchases by product category. These purchase figures are then projected to the total population to provide estimates of current sales volume for the product categories being investigated. A leading supplier of this research for consumer goods is Market Research Corporation of America. A marketer can also establish a panel of consumers to obtain sales data. Like the audit approach, the diary or panel approach yields detailed data, but the cost is high.

CONSUMER SURVEYS. Survey studies can be conducted to ask consumers what purchases they made in the product category of interest. Unlike sales audits and diary studies which record product sales as they occur, the survey study asks the consumer to recall all purchases for some past period. Research of this type may be designed and carried out by an advertiser for its own use, but in many major product categories private research companies conduct surveys and sell the resulting data. Mediamark Research, Inc., mentioned in Chapter 7, is one such firm that surveys extensively in consumer products fields.

Sales analysis information is sometimes available from research done for other purposes. Original research conducted to gather information for the consumer profile, described in Chapter 7, can sometimes also be used to provide estimates of market size.

### Advertiser's Product Sales Data

Data on which to base the sales analysis of the advertiser's own product is usually readily available to the advertising manager. Sales results by product are systematically collected by the firm, usually through the accounting or control functions or, in some firms, by a central information system. The advertising manager should review this product sales information on a regular basis.

### Competitors' Sales Data

The advertising manager needs estimates of current sales or share of market (the percentage of total market sales) held by each major competitor. The difficulty in gathering this information is that many firms treat sales by product as confidential information. There are, however, several sources that provide information helpful in making estimates. Many of these sources are the same as those used in estimating total market sales.

ANNUAL REPORTS. Publicly held firms distribute annual reports that include sales figures for the company. Although many multiple-product firms do not show detailed sales by product, there is an increasing tendency, partly because of new regulations, for larger firms to show sales breakdowns by lines of business. Many times sales and market share of major competitive products can be compiled from these annual reports.

GOVERNMENT REPORTS. Firms in many industries, particularly those that are highly regulated, are required to report or publish their sales or production figures. For example, sales figures for each brand in the tobacco and alcoholic beverage industries are readily available from government tax reports. Also, banks and savings-and-loan institutions are required to publish statements of financial condition from which share of deposits or other measures can readily be calculated.

TRADE SOURCES. Trade associations and trade magazines sometimes report or estimate sales figures of individual companies and products. For example, the Automobile Manufacturers Association, a trade association, regularly reports sales of automobiles by make and by model.

RESEARCH STUDIES. Marketing research studies conducted by the firm often yield, as secondary data, information on the market share of competitive products. Several of the research studies discussed as part of the consumer, product, and sales analyses may contain competitive sales or usage information. Retail audits or consumer diary studies, which were mentioned in connection with estimating total market sales, usually contain information on sales by product.

Information gathered for the consumer profile, described in Chapter 7, often includes information on the brand usually purchased in the product category. This information is not the same as sales since usage rates vary among consumers, but it provides a basis for estimating product sales and market share. In a similar way, product use tests and research on perceived product attributes discussed in Chapter 8 may contain some information on the product usually purchased by members of the research sample. If the sample is one that can be projected, some estimate of market share might be possible.

*trade survey*

TRADE SURVEYS. A frequently useful and practical approach to estimating competitive market shares is through informal **trade surveys.** These can sometimes be conducted by the firm's own sales marketing personnel. The survey information is collected from a sample of trade intermediaries who usually handle the type of product under study. The sample wholesalers, retailers, dealers, or jobbers are asked to estimate, based on their experience with the product category, the share of market held by specified leading products. If the sample is reasonably distributed, surprisingly accurate results can be obtained. This technique is applicable to both consumer and industrial products.

*CHAPTER SUMMARY*

The market analysis is designed to identify opportunity markets and market segments and to pinpoint sales problems facing the advertiser's own product. Analysis of total market sales should include an estimate of total market and segment size, a forecast of market growth, and computation of seasonal and geographic sales indexes. The sales analysis of the advertiser's own product should parallel the total market analysis, examining total sales, sales growth, seasonal sales, and geographic sales. This parallel analysis permits comparison of total market performance with the performance of the advertiser's product. Information on competitive sales is difficult to obtain but, if possible, the competitive analysis should estimate competitors' market shares and their market positions.

Environmental forces such as economic, regulatory, and sociocultural influences should also be examined as part of the market analysis. These external factors influence consumer goals and product perceptions and, hence, the size and growth of markets. Knowledge of environmental trends helps to identify potential markets.

Effective market analysis requires that the advertising manager become familiar with sources of sales data for the market, the product, and competitive products.

| | |
|---|---|
| Seasonal sales index | Sales audit |
| Geographic index of market sales | Diary study |
| Market share | Trade survey |
| Environmental factor | |

*KEY TERMS*

1. One of the difficulties in determining the size of the total market lies in deciding what products should be included in the market definition. For the following products, decide what to include in the market definition.

   a. If the advertised product were canned soup, would the market definition include dehydrated soup? Bouillon cubes? Canned beef stew?
   b. If the advertised product were a retail supermarket, would the market definition include convenience stores? Meat markets? Health food stores?
   c. If the advertised product were tea bags, would the market definition include loose tea? Instant tea? Iced-tea mix? Canned iced tea?

2. The size of total market sales can sometimes be approximated from available figures on yearly per capita consumption. From each of the following estimates of per capita consumption, attempt to estimate the retail sales volume of the product market:[7]

   a. Tea per capita consumption, 0.7 lbs.
   b. Margarine per capita consumption, 11.2 lbs.
   c. Wheat breakfast cereal per capita consumption, 2.9 lbs.
   d. Eggs, per capita, 265 (number).
   e. Ice cream per capita, 17.2 lbs.[7]

3. A manufacturer who is considering entering the market for trailers is attempting to determine the size of the major segments of the market. Consumer research has identified two major uses for trailers — as a permanent home and as a temporary home for vacations and recreation. The company has the following figures on trailer production:

*QUESTIONS FOR DISCUSSION*

---

[7]Consumption figures from U.S. Bureau of the Census, *Statistical Abstract of the United States: 1982–83* (103d ed.; Washington, D.C., 1982), p. 127.

Mobile Home Placements and Trailer Unit Shipments (in thousands)

| Type | 1977 | 1978 | 1979 | 1980 | 1981 |
|---|---|---|---|---|---|
| Motorized Homes | 160.2 | 293.6 | 172.6 | 99.9 | 135.2 |
| Travel Trailers | 167.9 | 159.8 | 90.2 | 52.0 | 63.8 |
| Camping Trailers | 53.9 | 48.2 | 31.1 | 24.5 | 35.0 |
| Truck Campers | 31.9 | 24.7 | 13.8 | 5.0 | 5.1 |
| Mobile Homes | 277.0 | 279.9 | 279.9 | 233.7 | 229.2 |

Source: U.S. Bureau of the Census, *Statistical Abstract of the United States:* 1982-83 (103d edition; Washington, D.C.), pp. 619, 749.

   a. Based on the sales trends, which segment appears to offer the most promising market for the manufacturer?

   b. Based on information in the table, what can you say about the relative size of the two segments?

4. One of the most successful new major appliances introduced in recent years has been the microwave oven. Since the introduction in 1970, sales growth, as shown below, has been strong.

| Year | Unit Sales |
|---|---|
| 1970 | 30,000 |
| 1971 | 100,000 |
| 1972 | 325,000 |
| 1973 | 440,000 |
| 1974 | 635,000 |
| 1975 | 1,100,000 |
| 1976 | 1,749,000 |
| 1977 | 2,156,000 |
| 1978 | 2,422,000 |
| 1979 | 2,815,000 |
| 1980 | 3,585,000 |
| 1981 | 4,407,000 |

Source: U.S. Bureau of the Census, *Statistical Abstract of the United States:* 1982-83 (103d. edition; Washington, D.C.), p. 796.

   a. Plot the sales figures for microwave ovens. Do the results conform to product life-cycle theory?

   b. What is your projection of unit sales for 1982? for 1987?

   c. What is your projection of retail dollar sales for 1982? for 1987?

5. The advertising manager for a candy company is engaged in forecasting industry sales. In addition to the chart shown on p. 218, the advertising manager has located the three charts shown on the opposite page.

   a. Based on the four sets of data, what can be said about candy sales? Is the trend up or down?

   b. How can the new information be used in preparing a sales forecast?

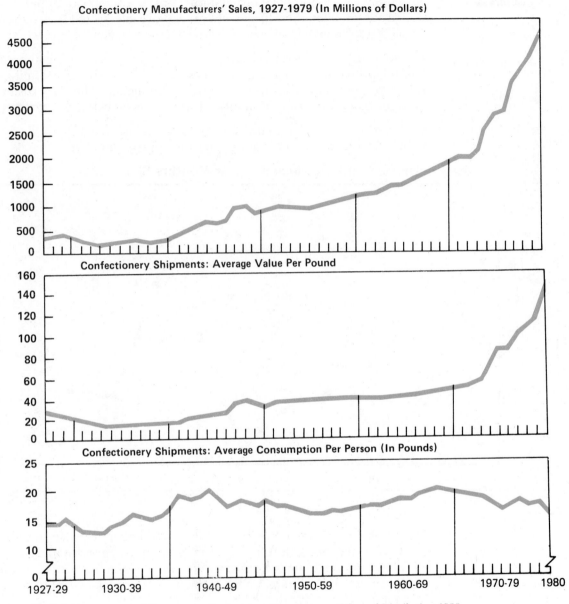

Confectionery Manufacturers' Sales, 1927-1979 (In Millions of Dollars)

Confectionery Shipments: Average Value Per Pound

Confectionery Shipments: Average Consumption Per Person (In Pounds)

Source:  U.S. Department of Commerce, *Confectionery Manufacturers Sales and Distribution*, 1980.

6. An advertising manager for a manufacturer of automobile tires is attempting to construct an index to show the geographic variation in total
market sales. The manager has a reliable estimate of the size of the total
auto tire market, but no estimate of sales by geographic area. However,
figures have been located on the number of cars in use in each state.
The advertising manager feels that these figures can be used to construct the tire sales index because of a belief that tire sales should corre-

late closely with automobile ownership. Thus, if a state had 10 percent of total automobiles, then 10 percent of total tire sales would be assigned to that state. Do you agree with the advertising manager's approach?

7. The advertising manager for a leading candy-bar brand has gathered data for preparation of a seasonal sales index for candy bars. The figures represent manufacturers' monthly shipments. The advertising manager plotted the figures in index form as shown below.

   a. What do you think accounts for the seasonal sales pattern?
   b. Did the advertising manager gather the appropriate data?

## Sales Index for Candy Bar Manufacturer Monthly Shipments

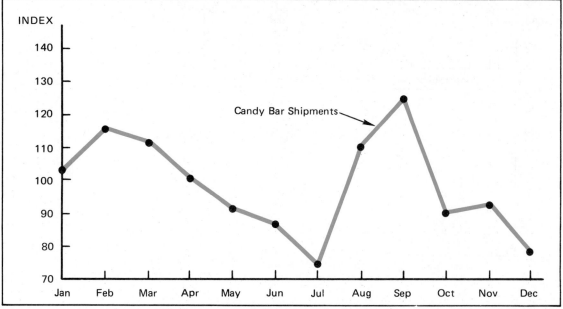

Source: U.S. Department of Commerce, *Confectionery Manufacturers Sales and Distribution*, (June, 1977).

8. One marketing writer notes that there is substantial evidence that the family is weakening as a cohesive social unit and suggests that, as a result, the traditional family dinner with all family members sitting down together to eat is declining.[8] What influence is this social trend likely to have on the market for the following:

   a. Furniture manufacturers?
   b. Food manufacturers?
   c. Appliance manufacturers?
   d. Restaurant services?

---

[8]E. B. Weiss, "Waning Family Unit Alters Concept of Traditional Family Dinner," *Advertising Age*, (April 5, 1971), pp. 51–52.

   The advertising manager for Food Servers, Inc., a food service company, is preparing the advertising plan for a new chain restaurant concept being considered by the firm. The proposed restaurants would have standardized limited menus much like the popular fast-food restaurants, but would be set up within existing retail stores (in a mass merchandiser, for example) rather than as stand-alone outlets. The nationally advertised outlets would be offered either on a franchise basis to the retailer or owned and operated by Food Servers.

   The advertising manager has collected the market information shown below and on page 220 from published sources.

1. How should the advertising manager define the market in which the new restaurants will compete? Which categories listed in the first table should be included in the market?
2. What would you estimate to be the size of the defined market by year for the period 1983 through 1985?
3. What does the data suggest should be the focus of the menu offerings in the new restaurants?
4. What competitive trends can you detect that should be of interest to the new restaurant venture?

Estimated Food and Drink Sales for Selected Eating Places
Sales ($ millions)

| Type | 1970 | 1975 | 1978 | 1979 | 1980 |
|---|---|---|---|---|---|
| Restaurants/ lunchrooms | $13,348 | $22,676 | $30,610 | $33,398 | $36,038 |
| Fast-food restaurants | 6,190 | 13,597 | 22,219 | 24,936 | 27,435 |
| Hotel restaurants | 1,554 | 2,538 | 3,739 | 4,109 | 4,440 |
| Motel restaurants | 643 | 1,007 | 1,226 | 1,301 | 1,368 |
| Grocery-store restaurants | 189 | 343 | 537 | 633 | 705 |
| Department-store restaurants | 424 | 713 | 917 | 987 | 1,040 |
| Drugstore restaurants | 341 | 341 | 338 | 345 | 358 |
| Variety-store restaurants | 389 | 405 | 383 | 419 | 453 |
| Gas-station restaurants | 109 | 202 | 312 | 359 | 383 |
| Bowling-lane restaurants | 190 | 295 | 411 | 458 | 501 |
| Recreation-center restaurants | 211 | 393 | 570 | 632 | 702 |
| Elementary/secondary schools | 1,163 | 1,687 | 1,939 | 2,136 | 2,312 |
| Hospitals | 2,991 | 4,346 | 5,437 | 6,055 | 6,668 |
| Colleges/universities | 496 | 712 | 896 | 1,004 | 1,140 |

Source: *U.S. Bureau of the Census, Statistical Abstract of the United States: 1982–83* (103d edition; Washington, D.C.), 1982.

Fast-Food Sales by Menu Type, 1981–83

| | No. of companies | 1981 | Percent of market | 1982 | Percent of market | 1983E | Percent of market |
|---|---|---|---|---|---|---|---|
| Hamburgers, franks, roast beef, etc. | 107 | $14,327,705 | 47.7% | $15,990,765 | 47.6% | $18,100,598 | 47.2% |
| Steak, full menu | 109 | 6,566,702 | 21.9 | 7,043,017 | 21.0 | 7,849,159 | 20.5 |
| Pizza | 94 | 3,169,601 | 10.6 | 3,605,807 | 10.7 | 4,159,594 | 10.8 |
| Chicken | 30 | 2,833,007 | 9.4 | 3,308,001 | 9.8 | 3,958,399 | 10.3 |
| Mexican (tacos, etc.) | 33 | 1,069,712 | 3.6 | 1,305,277 | 3.9 | 1,576,110 | 4.1 |
| Seafood | 13 | 888,491 | 2.9 | 1,027,226 | 3.1 | 1,211,391 | 3.2 |
| Pancakes, waffles | 15 | 847,650 | 2.8 | 913,320 | 2.7 | 1,009,825 | 2.6 |
| Sandwich and other | 39 | 339,480 | 1.1 | 398,608 | 1.2 | 518,100 | 1.3 |
| Total | 440 | $30,042,348 | 100.0% | $33,592,021 | 100.0% | $38,383,176 | 100.0% |

Reprinted with permission from the November 21, 1983 issue of *Advertising Age.* Copyright 1983 by Crain Communications, Inc.

Top Ten Fast-Food Companies — Sales and Market Share 1980–1982

| | 1980 | | 1981 | | 1982 | |
|---|---|---|---|---|---|---|
| | Domestic sales | Percent of U.S. | Domestic sales | Percent of U.S. | Domestic sales | Percent of U.S. |
| McDonald's | $ 5,049.0 | 18.1% | $ 5,770.0 | 19.2% | $ 6,362.0 | 18.9% |
| Burger King | 1,755.4 | 6.3 | 1,992.6 | 6.6 | 2,191.4 | 6.5 |
| Kentucky Fried Chicken | 1,440.0 | 5.2 | 1,600.0 | 5.3 | 1,700.0 | 5.1 |
| Wendy's International | 1,209.0 | 4.3 | 1,424.0 | 4.7 | 1,632.0 | 4.9 |
| Pizza Hut | 945.0 | 3.4 | 1,126.0 | 3.8 | 1,329.0 | 3.9 |
| American Dairy Queen | 904.0 | 3.2 | 1,022.0 | 3.4 | 1,200.2 | 3.6 |
| Hardee's | 751.5 | 2.7 | 976.9 | 3.3 | 1,167.0 | 3.5 |
| Denny's | 541.0 | 1.9 | 661.0 | 2.2 | 740.0 | 2.2 |
| Red Lobster | 400.0 | 1.4 | 553.0 | 1.8 | 625.0 | 1.9 |
| Arby's | 478.0 | 1.7 | 527.0 | 1.8 | 575.0 | 1.7 |
| Total top 10 | 13,472.9 | 48.2 | 15,652.5 | 52.1 | 17,521.6 | 52.2 |
| Total Industry* | $27,867.0 | 100.0% | $30,042.3 | 100.0% | $33,592.0 | 100.0% |

Reprinted with permission from the November 21, 1983 issue of *Advertising Age.* Copyright 1983 by Crain Communications, Inc.

# CHAPTER 10

*Positioning the Product and Defining Advertising Objectives*

LEARNING OBJECTIVES

In studying this chapter you will learn:

- What positioning is and how it is used.

- How the positioning decision is made.

- The nature and characteristics of advertising objectives.

- The process of defining advertising objectives and their subsequent use.

Positioning the product and defining advertising objectives for the product represent a major turning point in the advertising plan. Up to this point, the advertising plan has concentrated on developing information necessary to the design of the advertising programs. After this point, the advertising plan will utilize the information generated in consumer, product, and market analyses to detail the advertising programs. The positioning and objectives serve as an important transition between analysis of consumer needs and development of an advertising program directed toward satisfying those needs.

The positioning and the advertising objectives both provide direction for the advertising programs, but they provide different kinds of directions and are arrived at through different processes. The process for establishing the positioning, which provides long-term direction, will be outlined first. Following this, we will consider advertising objectives which provide direction for solving short-term problems facing the product.

## Defining a Positioning For the Product

In this book the term *positioning* will be used to refer to the *decision* about the market segment or consumer need toward which the marketing effort will be directed and to the basic *product attribute* that will be offered to that group. It would be difficult to overestimate the importance of the *positioning decision.* It is probably the most important decision in the life of a product and one of the most crucial decisions an advertising manager can expect to make. A faulty positioning decision means that all the advertising efforts which follow upon it in order to promote the product may be wasted. By contrast, creatively defined positioning can set a product apart so that the effectiveness of the advertising it receives is heightened.

## Functions of Positioning

The product positioning serves to direct and coordinate all the marketing efforts for a product. In addition, it defines how a product will compete with other products in the marketplace to gain a competitive advantage.

POSITIONING DIRECTS ALL MARKETING PROGRAMS. Positioning acts as an important intermediate step between the pre-advertising analyses and the advertising programs as such. The positioning decision is based on the consumer, product, and market analyses. The purpose in defining positioning for the product is to provide a single unified direction not only for the advertising programs, but for all other marketing programs on behalf of the product as well. It is intended to unify all marketing programs so that they can effectively move the product toward the same goal.

For many products the positioning is decided upon when the product is first envisioned—before it is even produced and marketed. Although the positioning for a product is not usually changed on a yearly basis, it is not immutable. As the market changes, as consumers' tastes change, and as the product itself changes, the product's positioning must be adjusted. Thus, the positioning of the product should be the subject of scrutiny and review in every advertising plan.

POSITIONING DEFINES HOW A PRODUCT WILL COMPETE. The process for making the positioning decision can be explained by using the consumer decision-process diagram developed in Chapter 5 and shown in Exhibit 10-1. The three elements that must be blended in making a positioning decision are shaded in Exhibit 10-1.

1. Element #1 is the consumer need. The positioning decision begins with the consumer by deciding what consumer need the advertising will attempt to address. If the advertiser has defined consumer segments in terms of needs, then Element #1 can also be stated as the segment (need group) to which advertising will be directed.
2. Element #2 is an attribute or characteristic of the advertiser's product. The advertiser must determine which of the various attributes or need-satisfying qualities of the product will be directed to consumers. The attribute selected depends upon Element #1, the need that the advertiser has chosen to address. The advertiser must find a match between consumer need and an attribute of the product.

The consumer decision-process model showing the three elements of the positioning decision.      **EXHIBIT 10-1**

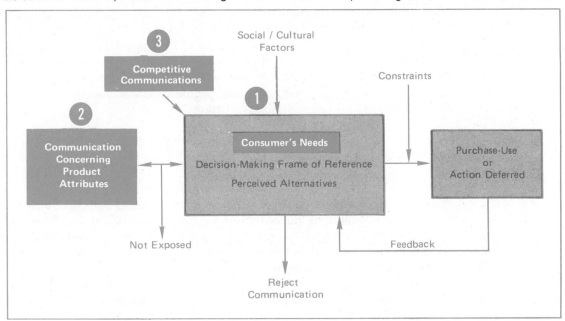

3. Element #3 represents attributes offered by competitive products. The essence of positioning is to select a product attribute to offer to consumers that will give the advertiser's product a competitive advantage. In order to be selected by consumers the product must fulfill the consumer need better than competitive products do.

In summary, **positioning** is the decision that matches a product attribute to a consumer need or consumer segment in such a way as to gain competitive advantage.

*positioning*

## Information Needed for the Positioning Decision

Making the positioning decision requires both creativity and a command of the facts about the product, the consumer, and the market. Those facts must be interpreted and combined in such a way as to define a superior positioning. At this point the factors that go into the positioning decision will be reviewed and their sources pointed out. Each of these factors is derived from one of the analysis sections of the plan which, at this stage of putting the whole advertising plan together, should already have been completed.

CONSUMER NEED OR MARKET SEGMENT. The first information element required in making the positioning decision is an understanding of the needs that consumers are trying to satisfy when they enter the market for a product such as the one to be advertised. For most products there are multiple consumer needs, which require an understanding of the relative importance of each particular need associated with a product. If, in the consumer analysis, prospects have been segmented by need, then the advertiser will be able to position not against individuals but against an entire market segment. The source of consumer-needs information is, of course, the consumer-analysis section of the advertising plan described in Chapter 6. Information on consumer-need segments is also found in the consumer analysis and was described in Chapter 7.

PRODUCT ATTRIBUTES. In the discussion of product analysis in Chapter 8, it was suggested that the product be defined so as to encompass all promotable attributes. This definition makes a full range of product attributes available for consideration in making the positioning decision for the advertiser's product. The advertising manager should consider both the physical attributes and the symbolic characteristics of the product and should evaluate the attributes first in terms of their need-satisfying capabilities and, second, in terms of their superiority over or distinctiveness from the attributes of competitive products.

All of this information and evaluation of the product should be available from the product analysis section of the advertising plan.

SEGMENT POTENTIAL AND COMPETITIVE ADVANTAGE. In matching a product attribute to a consumer need or need segment, the advertiser must also be aware of the different long-term potential offered by alternative positionings. The advertiser should be particularly interested in finding an attribute in the product that represents a competitive advantage. A positioning that utilizes a competitively advantageous attribute is more likely to realize long-term success than is one that relies on a product attribute that offers only competitive parity. By the same token, the advertiser should attempt to position in segments that are expected to grow. Given a choice of market positions, the advertiser should select the one that appears to offer the greatest long-term sales and profit opportunity for the product, one that takes advantage of the strengths of the product and the growth potential present in the market.

This third element in the positioning decision requires information on the characteristics of the market and its segments, particularly those characteristics that permit evaluation of its potential, including the following:

1. Goals or problems for which consumers feel there is no satisfactory solution available represent opportunity segments. This information is developed in the analysis of consumer needs, goals, and problems.
2. Markets or market segments that are served by a large number of competitors or by particularly entrenched competitors offer less potential than uncrowded ones. The competitive sales analysis provides this information.
3. Market segments that contain an above-average proportion of heavy users represent above-average potential. The consumer profile study may indicate the distribution of heavy users.

4. Markets or market segments expected to benefit from environmental trends can be expected to offer growth potential. The impact of economic, regulatory, and cultural trends on market growth can be found in the analysis of environmental factors.

5. The estimates of market and segment sales and the projected growth of sales developed in the market analysis provide quantitative estimates of the current and long-term size of the market.

## The Positioning Decision

Gathering and evaluating facts about the product, consumer, and market represent the analytical phase of determining the positioning for a product. The creative part of the decision involves combining and matching these facts to arrive at a positioning decision. There is no satisfactory way to describe how to be a creative decision-maker, but this section will attempt to give some examples of positioning decisions and discuss some common positioning alternatives.

ELEMENTS OF THE DECISION. The positioning and objectives section of the advertising plan should contain a crisp statement of the positioning of the product that is to be used in the coming planning period. It should be supported by a logical, organized presentation of the facts and evaluations just discussed. The factual basis for the positioning decision should be clearly and succinctly presented.

The statement of the positioning decision should contain three directions to guide the advertising programs:

1. It should specify the market or the segment of the market to which the product is to be offered. The segment should be defined in terms of the need that is common to consumers in that group.

2. It should specify the attribute or need-satisfying quality of the product that is going to be offered to the target consumers.

3. It should describe how this product's position in the market is to relate to the positions held by competitive products.

EXAMPLES OF POSITIONING. The best way to gain an understanding of the positioning decision is to examine some examples. Positioning decisions for three products will be explained and illustrated — Dannon Yogurt, an established consumer product; Canteen Corporation, a service sold to other businesses; and Perma Soft, a new consumer product.

*Dannon Yogurt.* Dannon was the pioneer in expanding yogurt from a food consumed by a narrow base of users in New York City to a truly national product. Dannon, like most yogurts, was originally positioned as a diet food or light snack — nutritional yet low in calories. Dannon marketing research revealed that the barrier to expanding yogurt usage was the unusual sour taste. To overcome this problem Dannon introduced fruit yogurt and advertised this product difference to gain new users. The more attractive taste plus the booming interest in dieting made Dannon Yogurt a nationwide success.

Throughout the years, Dannon was consistent in the need-satisfying quality that it offered to its target customers — Dannon Yogurt is a good-for-you food. However, as the market matured, many other brands entered it and Dannon was challenged to maintain its market leadership. Competition had copied Dannon's good food positioning and its fruit flavors. Moreover, they were consistently underpricing Dannon in order to gain competitive advantage.

The Dannon advertising group was convinced that they had to find a competitively superior product attribute to meet this challenge. Analysis of environmental factors revealed an intense interest at this time in ecology and along with that an interest in more natural foods — foods that were pure and not loaded with chemicals or additives. The Dannon group conducted a product analysis of its own product and discovered that, of all advertised yogurt bands, Dannon was the only one with no artificial ingredients. There was the competitive difference!

The most recent execution of this positioning capitalizes on the rising interest of target consumers in physical fitness. Consumers want good-for-you foods because they contribute to physical fitness. This led to the Dannon promise, "Get a Dannon body," supported by the competitive advantage, "Dannon is the only fruit yogurt that's all natural, low-fat, with no added coloring or flavoring." Exhibit 10-2 shows a television commercial, Exhibit 10-3 a magazine advertisement, and Exhibit 10-4 a radio commercial resulting from the same basic positioning.

*Canteen Corporation.* The need for positioning applies to all sorts of products and services as the next example, an industrial product, demonstrates.

After World War II, Canteen Corporation, which provides food-service vending machines to industry and operates in-plant cafeterias and executive dining rooms, found that price competition dominated the market.[1] Most competitors directed their marketing effort at personnel managers who were assigned responsibility for food service. Canteen wished to set its products apart from the competition and avoid "look-alike" price competition. To do this, Canteen Corporation directed its advertising efforts not to the price-oriented personnel manager but to top-level management. What Canteen offered top management was not a better price, but better food service as a means of getting better employee morale and productivity.

Canteen Corporation's solution to its competitive problem was a distinctive and creative positioning for its product. The need-satisfying attribute that it decided to offer was not price, but the kind of food that makes

---

[1]This example is drawn from Ramon G. Gaulke, *The Parsley-Colored, Synergistic, Coin-Operated Syndrome,* Papers from the 1969 4A Region Convention (New York: American Association of Advertising Agencies, 1970).

A television commercial for Dannon Yogurt.          EXHIBIT 10-2

Singers: Who can get a Dannon Body. You can get a Dannon Body.

Your body can be a Dannon Body.

My body can be a Dannon Body. Who can, you can, get a Dannon Body. WOW!

Anncr: Start an exercise and low calorie eating plan

with Dannon Yogurt part of it.

Of all leading brands, Dannon is the only fruit yogurt

that's all natural, lowfat,

with no added coloring or flavoring.

Singers: Who can, you can, get a Dannon Body. WOW!

# "Get a Dannon Body"

EXHIBIT 10-3        A magazine advertisement for Dannon Yogurt.

Courtesy: The Dannon Co.

employees feel good about their company. The segment of the market to which this solution was offered was not the personnel manager whose problem was economical operation. Instead it was offered to the top management segment that was concerned with maintaining an effective work force. The intended relationship to competition is also clear. Canteen wished to disassociate itself by saying that it offered a solution to a different kind of problem. An advertisement that resulted from this positioning is shown in Exhibit 10-5.

*The Shampoo Market.* The retail sales volume of the shampoo market exceeds $1.2 billion, making it one of the larger and more important of the

A radio commercial for Dannon Yogurt.                                    EXHIBIT 10-4

| CLIENT | Dannon | DATED | 9 March 1981 | **RADIO COPY** |
| PRODUCT | Yogurt | STATION | | |
| COMM'L. NO. | DL 9206<br>Athletes "L" | LENGTH | :60 | **Marsteller Inc.** |

866 THIRD AVE. NEW YORK. N.Y. 10022 • (212) 752-6500

<u>MUSIC UP AND UNDER</u>

<u>ANNCR:</u>

Who's got a fit, trim, great-looking Dannon Body?  Swimmers.
Runners.  Skiers.  Tennis players.  And people who just believe in a program of exercise and eating right.  They also
know Dannon Lowfat Yogurt is lower in fat than the brands
not labeled "low-fat".  Dannon's got plenty of protein and
calcium, and no artificial anything.  Remember, what you get
out of your body depends on what you put into it.  So <u>make</u>
your body a Dannon Body, too.

<u>MUSIC UP AND OUT</u>

Courtesy: The Dannon Co.

personal care markets. Although the shampoo market is large, it has not, in
recent years, shown consistent growth. Its large size makes it an attractive
market for the large personal care product marketers, but also a highly competitive one. It is highly fragmented with only nine brands, led by Procter and
Gamble's Head and Shoulders, holding a market share of three percent or
better. Annual advertising expenditures typically exceed $100 million.[2]

Another factor making competition in this market particularly
difficult has been the similarity of products. Although there have been
some technological changes, it has been difficult for marketers to translate
these into meaningful consumer benefits. As a result, the market has
become increasingly price oriented.[3] To combat this problem, shampoo
marketers have turned to tightly focused positionings, especially for new

[2]"The Lather Wars Have Shampoo Marketers Hunting for Niches," *Business Week* (January 9,
1984), p. 124.
[3]Pat Sloan, "New Shampoos Lather Up after a Draining '84," *Advertising Age* (January 7,
1985), p. 56.

**EXHIBIT 10-5**     A Canteen Corporation advertisement directed to top management.

products that have been introduced in great numbers and with strong advertising support. As can be seen in the examples given below, the more successful marketers have learned to select a relatively narrow segment of the market and deliver to it a product that contains a technological advantage that has been translated through advertising into a superior benefit for the selected segment of consumers.

In a sense, the pioneer in this way of thinking has been the market leader Head and Shoulders, introduced many years ago to the segment of shampoo buyers who were particularly concerned with dandruff. Formulated with a new chemical ingredient that was the first effective dandruff preventive, the product was positioned and continues to be positioned as the shampoo for persons concerned with dandruff that really works.

Recently, many other shampoo marketers have followed Head and Shoulders' lead by introducing new shampoo products with benefits addressed to specialized market segments. Johnson & Johnson, already in the market with Johnson's Baby Shampoo, recently introduced Affinity shampoo. Affinity is positioned as a shampoo for women over 40, offering through a special conditioning formula, to solve the problem of older hair that tends to become brittle as it grays.

Gillette took a different tack with For Oily Hair Only (FOHO), a shampoo whose positioning is revealed by the name. Gillette research determined that the estimated 20 percent of the population suffering from oily hair was dissatisfied with available shampoos. To respond to this need, Gillette undertook development of a special formula shampoo that incorporated a European herbal complex that breaks down oil. The product name and the advertising for the product all focus on establishing FOHO's positioning as a product that meets the needs of people with oily hair because of a superior formula with a herbal complex that breaks down oil.[4]

Another new shampoo product with a tightly focused positioning is La Maur's Perma Soft. As is implied by the product name, Perma Soft is directed to the segment of women who have permanents. The problem that the product addresses is well expressed in the advertising copy shown in Exhibit 10-6: "If you perm your hair you know how nice it looks—at first. But the more you shampoo it—the more your hair frizzes. So you condition it—and your curls droop." The advantage that Perma Soft offers, and the product attribute that sets it apart from competition, is a special shampoo formulation that includes moisturizers and texturizers, permitting shampooing of permed hair "without relaxing the curl."

## Some Positioning Issues

Specifying product attributes, need segment, and competitive position gives the advertiser a good approach toward making the positioning decision. Beyond this, there are two positioning issues that should be considered.

---

[4]Joanne Cleaver, "Awash in a New Wave of Haircare," *Advertising Age* (February 28, 1983), pp. M-22-24.

TOTAL MARKET VS. MARKET SEGMENT. One issue that the advertiser must resolve is whether the advertising for the product should be directed to the total market or to one segment of the market. Sometimes it is desirable to position a product so that it is directed to the total market rather than to a single segment. Such positioning can greatly increase the sales potential available to the product. The total market is simply bigger than a segment of it and consequently the reward for success is greater. On the other hand, the product that attempts to appeal to everyone in the market is usually a compromise and hence is vulnerable to attack by products specifically designed for the particular needs of one segment.

The history of the detergent market illustrates this product vulnerability. The first big detergent brand, Tide, was offered as a general purpose detergent to the total market. It was enormously successful, but it soon attracted competition which attacked Tide's position by offering special products for special segments of the market. There were special detergents for automatic washers, special products for baby diapers, heavy-duty detergents, kind-to-the-hands detergents, and on and on. The result was a serious erosion of Tide's market share.

Similar examples have occurred in many markets, illustrating the strength of market-segment positioning. The product that seeks only a segment of the market is working with smaller sales potential, but by designing the product especially for the needs of people in that segment, the advertiser hopes for a large share of that market subgroup. Furthermore, the close match of product to need usually has the effect of making the product less vulnerable to competitive attack.

In general, the market segmentation approach is favored as a means of entering *mature* markets with established competition and *large* markets that have segments of substantial potential. Total market positioning is most frequently used in new product categories, in markets with few or no competitors, and in small markets that cannot economically be subdivided.

PRIMARY VS. SELECTIVE DEMAND. A second positioning issue that the advertiser faces is whether or not to try to increase purchases of all products in the product category or just purchases of a particular brand. Advertising that attempts to stimulate sales of the total product category is called **primary-demand advertising.** Rather than selecting an attribute of one product, an attribute of the entire product class would be specified in such a primary-demand positioning. Advertising designed to increase sales of a particular brand is called **selective-demand advertising.** Selective-demand positioning would define the attribute of one particular brand for presentation to consumers.

*primary-demand advertising*

*selective-demand advertising*

Most advertising falls in the category of selective or brand demand advertising. The advertiser seeks some competitive advantage in the company's product that will stimulate a consumer to select it over a competing product. Thus Wendy's advertises that its hamburgers are superior because they are made from fresh, not frozen, meat, and Burger King counters that its hamburgers are superior because they are broiled, not fried.

Primary demand advertising, which promotes the use of a class of product rather than a particular brand, is usually less attractive to advertisers because they fear that any increase in product class sales generated by the advertising will be shared with competitors, even those that did not advertise. However, this would not be the case if the advertiser had no competition or if the advertiser had a dominant share of market. Utilities, for example, generally have a monopoly in their service area and may find primary demand advertising to be useful. Electric utilities, before our concern with the cost and availability of fuel, frequently advertised to promote the use of electricity and the building of all-electric homes. While this practice has largely stopped, gas utilities continue to promote the use of gas to heat homes. In both cases, the utilities know that they have a monopoly and will reap all the sales gains generated by product class advertising. AT&T has historically been a heavy user of primary demand advertising. They have encouraged the use of long distance telephone as a way to communicate with friends and family through their " Reach out and touch somebody" campaign. With the breakup of AT&T and the increasing competition for long distance service it would not be surprising to see AT&T drop its primary demand campaign in favor of selective demand advertising.

Companies that enjoy a dominant market share are sometimes users of primary demand advertising. Campbell Soup Company, for example, is a company with a dominant market share, having an estimated 80 percent of the condensed soup market. The current advertising for Campbell's Soup attempts to increase the overall or primary demand for soup. Ads state that soup can play a significant role in a healthful diet because "Soup is good food." Campbell apparently feels that if overall soup consumption increases, they, as market leaders, will capture most of the additional volume for their Campbell's brand.

Marketers of new products (ones that establish an entirely new product category) are sometimes temporarily in a monopoly position and use primary appeals to attract consumers to the new product category. However, the advertiser must be alert so as to be able to switch to selective benefits when competitors enter the market with claims of product differences and superiority.

Manufacturers of a class of products sometimes band together through trade associations in order to sponsor primary-demand advertising programs. Each manufacturer contributes to the campaign, usually in proportion to the expected share in any sales gains realized. The advertisement by the Potato Board shown in Exhibit 10-7 is an example of primary-demand advertising by a trade association. The history of such campaigns has been mixed. Some tend to suffer from a lack of continuity due to the administrative problems of keeping all the members in agreement. More important, the efforts in many cases have attempted to reverse product preferences that are the result of deep-seated social and cultural trends. As discussed earlier, advertising is not a sufficiently powerful tool to accomplish such objectives. Attempts by an association of flour millers in the 1940s to use advertising to reverse the long-term downtrend in the per

# Can you recognize America's favorite diet food?

A potato is one diet food that's hard to disguise.

Because no matter how you dress it up, it's still full of things that are good for you. Without the things that aren't.

A medium-sized potato,* for example, has only about 110 calories — fewer than a cup of yogurt. Or a six-ounce serving of cottage cheese. Or even a green salad with dressing.

And a potato is 99.9% fat free. And 100% cholesterol free.

Plus, potatoes are packed with nutrients your body needs. Like Vitamin C, iron, fiber and hard-to-find Vitamin $B_6$. All at pennies per serving.

So when planning your next menu, remember. The diet food you've been looking for is right under your nose.

## Potatoes. America's Favorite Vegetable.

*150 grams, round type, boiled in skin. Source: "Nutrition Labeling, Tools For Its Use," USDA Bulletin No. 382. 1983–84 National Consumption Study. © 1984 The Potato Board

Advertisement Provided Courtesy of the Potato Board and Ketchum Advertising.

capita consumption of wheat-flour products (such as bread) faced an insurmountable obstacle in the trend to lighter and more expensive diets.[5] These same trends favored the efforts of the citrus-fruit grower and packer associations that had great success in promoting the use of orange juice and other citrus products.

## Setting Advertising Objectives for the Product

Advertising objectives and the positioning decision are different concepts, yet they have much in common. Both the product's positioning and the advertising objectives represent something the advertiser hopes to accomplish through the use of advertising. The positioning defines how a product is intended to compete; i.e., the competitive "niche" that it is to occupy. Objectives are statements of what the advertiser hopes to accomplish in order to solve problems faced by the product. They state what must be accomplished if the positioning is to be realized.

Objectives and product positioning are alike in another sense. The primary use of each of them is to provide direction to the specific advertising programs which will be developed next in the advertising plan. These advertising programs deal with decisions such as (1) how much should be spent on advertising (the budget program), (2) to whom should the advertising be directed (the media program), and (3) what should be the advertising message (the creative program). Decisions such as these are extremely complex and if they are to be coordinated, there must be some form of central direction. Product positioning and the setting-up of advertising objectives serve this central coordinating function.

Despite these similarities, product positioning and advertising objectives are dissimilar in important ways. Objectives are narrower in scope, more specific, and concerned with a shorter time span than is the positioning decision.

### Nature of Advertising Objectives

*advertising objective*

An **advertising objective** is some goal, aim, or end that the advertiser hopes to accomplish in the near term. The meaning of advertising objectives can be stated in terms more reflective of the process by which they are formulated. Advertising objectives are statements of what advertising must accomplish in order to overcome the problems or to realize the opportunities that face the product, including the realization of the desired positioning.

Suppose, for example, that through market analysis the advertiser of an industrial product found that sales were declining in the firm's

---

[5]See "Millers' National Federation" in Neil H. Borden and Martin V. Marshall, *Advertising Management: Text and Cases* (Homewood, Illinois: Richard D. Irwin, Inc., 1959), pp. 51-66.

Northeast sales territory, apparently due to inadequate coverage of prospects in the Northeast by the business magazines used in prior years' advertising schedules. This problem might give rise to an objective stated as follows:

> Advertising exposures per prospect in the company's Northeast sales territory should be increased until they are equal to average exposures for all prospects.

Good advertising objectives are useful tools in the advertising planning process. Some essential characteristics are discussed below.

PROBLEM AND OPPORTUNITY RELATED. Advertising objectives should flow directly from the problems and opportunities facing the product. The objective should be stated so that its achievement would contribute to solving the problem or realizing the opportunity from which it flowed. Note that this is true in the example given above. If advertising were increased in the Northeast area it would directly attack what is believed to be the cause of the sales decline which is the problem to be solved. Objectives should be consistent with and should help to achieve the positioning of the product.

WHAT, NOT HOW. Advertising objectives should specify *what* is to be accomplished, not *how* it is to be accomplished. The advertising programs, taking direction from the objectives, specify how the objectives are to be accomplished. In the example given above, the objective specifies that advertising exposures are to be brought up to parity in the Northeast territory, but it does not specify what new combination of magazines to use. In the media program, detailed consideration would be given to reallocation of funds among magazines or, perhaps, addition of other media to achieve the desired exposures in the Northeast territory.

SPECIFIC GUIDELINES. Advertising objectives should provide specific guidelines to people designing programs that are expected to accomplish the objectives. In the sample objective, it appears that the designer of the media program would have little difficulty in interpreting where additional exposures were required. The direction is specific.

MEASURABLE TERMS. Advertising objectives should be stated in measurable terms so that at the end of the planning period success in meeting objectives can be determined. Thus, advertising objectives not only serve as guidelines for developing advertising programs, but also as guidelines for evaluating the effectiveness of the same programs after they have been implemented. In the earlier example, the objective could serve as one standard for evaluating effective media program performance because it is specific and stated in measurable terms. The geographic distribution of media exposures can be estimated from circulation data provided by each specific medium itself or from audience studies conducted by media research firms. From this information it would be possible to calculate whether or not exposures in the Northeast territory meet the parity objective.

## Process of Defining Advertising Objectives

To be sure that the objectives are closely related to problems and opportunities, it is a good practice to begin by listing the problems and opportunities actually facing the product. These will have been individually defined throughout the consumer, product, and market analyses. With problems and opportunities stated, the advertising manager should next examine each one and decide what must be accomplished in order to solve each problem and what must be accomplished to take advantage of each opportunity. The product positioning should also be examined to determine what specific tasks must be accomplished so as to effect it. The objectives should be stated in the advertising plan together with the evidence or reasoning supporting them.

## Examples of Objectives

A substantial number of problems and opportunities are likely to be uncovered in the preparation of an advertising plan that begins with thorough consumer, product, and market analyses. A list of 20 or more would not be unusual. Some examples of objectives are presented below. For each example the product is named, the problem or opportunity and its source noted, and an objective suggested.

| | |
|---|---|
| **Product:** | Automobile A |
| **Problem:** | (From consumer needs analysis) Consumers fear that model changes will make the product obsolete soon after purchase. |
| **Objective:** | Communicate automobile A's policy of eliminating annual model changes. |
| | |
| **Product:** | Soft drink B |
| **Problem:** | (From analysis of advertising activity) Consumers are aware of our clever advertising but over one half associate it with the brand name of our large competitor. |
| **Objective:** | Achieve greater registration of the brand name and greater association of the brand name with the advertising. |
| | |
| **Product:** | Automatic washer C |
| **Problem:** | (From consumer profile analysis) Company is getting less than its share of sales to laundromat owners, a heavy user group. |
| **Objective:** | Direct greater media and creative attention to the laundromat owners. |
| | |
| **Product:** | Instant coffee D |
| **Problem:** | (From consumer profile study) Average age of purchasers of product D is ten years older than profile of target market. |
| **Objective:** | Direct the advertising effort to younger prospects so as to lower the age profile of product D. |

**Product:**     Menswear store E

**Opportunity:**  (From analysis of perceived product attributes) Store E is perceived as the menswear style leader in the community.

**Objective:**    Utilize style-leadership reputation as a means of reassuring consumers that store provides superior guidance in wardrobe selection.

**Product:**     Machine tool F

**Opportunity:**  (From analysis of physical product-attributes) Unlike its chief competitor, machine tool F is American-made with domestic sources of parts and service.

**Objective:**    Support claims of reliable performance by noting domestic manufacture and nearby sources of parts and service.

**Product:**     Local department store G

**Opportunity:**  (From sales-potential analysis) Fastest growing population area is in the northeast section of city.

**Objective:**    Emphasize availability and location of branch store in northeast-section shopping center.

**Product:**     Condominium apartments H

**Opportunity:**  (From the analysis of cultural trends) There is a growing tendency to avoid the feeling of responsibility that comes with owning material possessions.

**Objective:**    Communicate the provision of total maintenance in the condominium purchase agreement.

## Uses of Advertising Objectives

Advertising objectives serve two distinct roles — as guidelines by which to shape advertising programs and as one of the standards against which advertising effectiveness is measured.

OBJECTIVES AS PROGRAM GUIDES. The advertising objectives specify what is to be accomplished by the advertising program, the next step in the advertising plan (Part 3). They assure that the knowledge gained in the consumer, product, and market analyses is utilized as a guide to the formation of a new advertising program. The objectives, based on problems and opportunities discovered by means of these analyses, provide specific goals that the advertising programs are supposed to accomplish. The objectives, together with the product positioning, give focus and purpose to the advertising programs.

OBJECTIVES AS EVALUATION GUIDES. Advertising objectives are also an important part of the final section of the advertising plan — the evaluation of advertising effectiveness (Part 4). The effectiveness evaluation section, in managerial terms, is concerned with control of the advertising effort. It attempts to measure the success of the advertising program and to give insight into improvements that might be made.

If the effectiveness of advertising is to be evaluated, there must be some standard against which to compare actual performance. One such standard is provided by advertising objectives. One writer notes that this use of objectives is simply an application of the management-by-objective technique to advertising.[6] The advertising objectives are established at the beginning of the planning period as the goals toward which the advertising programs are directed. At the end of the planning period, actual performance is measured and compared to the objectives. To permit this use of advertising objectives, they must be specific and stated in measurable terms. As the advertising programs are developed, additional control standards will be established, but the advertising objectives will continue to be important as effectiveness evaluation devices.

After the evaluation of actual advertising performance is completed, the results provide data for the analysis that takes place in the next planning period. Objectives that were not met become problems in the following period. The objectives thus serve as reminders of past problem and opportunity areas that should be reviewed in the next period.

---

## CHAPTER SUMMARY

The positioning decision defines how a product is to relate to competition. It provides a unified direction to the advertising and other marketing programs for the product. There are three elements that go into the positioning decision. In terms of the consumer decision process, the positioning decision requires selection of an attribute of the product that satisfies a consumer need in a manner superior to competitors' product offerings. Each of the factors in the positioning decision—product attributes, consumer needs, and competitive difference or segment potential—is derived from one of the analysis sections of the advertising plan. The decision may position the product in a single segment, in more than one segment, or in the total market. Total market positioning offers the potential of a larger market, but is competitively vulnerable; single segment positioning is competitively more secure, but operates in an area of less potential. Primary-demand positioning, used chiefly by new product and trade association advertisers, promotes an attribute of the entire product class. Selective-demand positioning, used in most competitive markets, selects a product attribute that will give the product an advantage over competing brands.

Advertising objectives are statements of what must be accomplished by advertising in order to overcome problems or to realize opportunities facing the product and likewise to effect the positioning. To be useful, objectives should be directed to problems and opportunities facing the product. The objectives should specify *what* is to be accomplished, not how.

---

[6]Russell H. Colley, *Defining Advertising Goals for Measured Advertising Results* (New York: Association of National Advertisers, Inc., 1961), p. 4.

They should be specific enough to provide usable guidelines to the development of advertising programs. Objectives should be stated in measurable terms against which actual performance can be measured. If properly written, advertising objectives serve both as guidelines to advertising programs and as one of the sets of standards against which advertising effectiveness is measured.

---

Positioning                              Selective-demand advertising    *KEY TERMS*
Primary-demand advertising               Advertising objective

---

1. One element in the positioning decision requires selection of a product attribute or benefit which will be communicated to target consumers. For the following products, what is the need-satisfying characteristic that is offered by the product's advertising?    *QUESTIONS FOR DISCUSSION*

   a. Diet Pepsi (soft drink).
   b. Bufferin (pain reliever).
   c. Tylenol (pain reliever).
   d. Kellogg's 40% Bran Flakes (cereal).
   e. American Express Travelers Cheques.

2. Another element in the positioning decision is to specify the segment of consumers to which the advertising message will be directed. For the following products, try to identify the segment of consumers (in terms of the problem they are trying to solve) to which the advertising is being directed.

   a. Federal Express (air-freight carrier).
   b. Mazola Corn Oil.
   c. Gatorade (soft drink).
   d. Total (cereal).
   e. Luvs Disposable Diapers.

3. In deciding upon a positioning, the advertiser should try to select a product attribute to be advertised that offers a competitive advantage. What competitive advantage is provided by the attribute featured by these products?

   a. Wagner Power Painter.
   b. Charmin (toilet tissue).
   c. Puritan Cooking Oil.
   d. General Electric Rechargeable Batteries.
   e. Wendy's Restaurants.

4. Advertisers do not usually publicize their positioning, but it can often be inferred from the product's advertising. Referring to advertisements reprinted in this book, attempt to define the positioning for the following products:

    a. Volvo (automobiles; see p. 132).
    b. Lite Beer from Miller (see p. 97).
    c. "Love My Carpet." Rug and Room Deodorizer (see p. 167).

5. Cascade is a detergent for automatic dishwashers. Its primary product claim is: "For virtually spotless dishes nothing can beat Cascade." Cascade is said to have "sheeting" action that fights drops that spot dishes in dishwashers. Is Cascade positioned against the total market or against a market segment?

6. Gerber Products Company, the baby-food marketer, is running a series of magazine advertisements entitled "Gerber Nutrition Report: Answers to Questions Parents Ask Us," in which they discuss various aspects of baby nutrition. Although Gerber baby-food products are illustrated, there is very little emphasis given to Gerber's products or their competitive advantage. Is Gerber following a primary-demand or selective-demand strategy for its products?

7. The concept of positioning has been described as applying to commercially marketed goods and services. Do you think the positioning approach can be applied more widely? For instance, do you think that a political candidate should make a positioning decision? A university? A person seeking a career?

8. The purpose of positioning a product is to give guidance and direction to advertising programs for the product. Using the positioning that was defined for Dannon Yogurt earlier in this chapter, describe the guidance it would provide in making the following advertising decisions:

    a. What advertising medium would be best?
    b. How large should the advertising budget be?
    c. What claims or promises should the advertising copy make?

9. Evaluate the following objective in terms of the criteria for good advertising objectives that were given in the chapter.

    **Product:**     Women's hair conditioner.
    **Problem:**     Research on effectiveness of the advertising indicates

that consumers cannot, without assistance, recall the central claim for the product, which is that is has a secret new ingredient that actually penetrates hair ends, changing their molecular structure in such a way that the hair is more durable.

**Objective:** The product attribute should be explained more clearly by using diagrams and microscopic cross-sectional photographs of hair before and after treatment.

10. Given the following problems, write an advertising objective that would satisfy the criteria for a sound objective.

    a. **Product:** Baby lotion.
       **Problem:** Research indicates that current purchasers of the product are very loyal, but the brand is attracting far less than its proportionate share of first-time users.
    b. **Product:** Men's sneakers.
       **Opportunity:** The brand has just been selected for exclusive use by the men's Olympic track and field team.

---

*PROBLEM*

Wondra Skin Lotion was introduced by Procter and Gamble into test markets in 1977 and rolled out nationally in 1979.[7] Although the product initially gained a 13 percent market share, it subsequently dropped off to a 10 percent share. Marketers responsible for the brand were concerned by its performance and were reviewing its positioning to determine what changes were called for.

The skin lotion market is a $220 million category and has shown about 10 percent annual growth. Wondra was introduced into the market with a heavy advertising and sales-promotion budget—$13 million annually compared to $5 million annually for Vaseline Intensive Care, the market leader. The name chosen for the new P&G product was Wondra and the package chosen was a cosmetic-appearing pink and green plastic bottle with a modern, upside-down shape (the bottle was designed to sit on the cap). Advertising for Wondra stressed its therapeutic value. "Wondra beats the glove. After rough jobs in water, Wondra relieves dry, flaky hands better than if they had been in gloves."

---

[7]This problem was developed in part from Jennifer Alter, "Competition Rubs Skincare Market," *Advertising Age* (September 29, 1980), p. 52.

As indicated above, Chesebrough-Pond's Vaseline Intensive Care, with a 23 percent share, was the market leader in skin lotion. Despite a drop in share from 30 percent, VIC kept a strongly therapeutic positioning, with both the product name and its advertising focusing on relief for problem hands. The most therapeutic of the skin lotion brands was Keri Lotion (8 percent share) that supported its positioning with an intensive sampling program through hospitals. The two leading brands in the cosmetic segment of the market were Rose Milk, a lightly scented pink product, and Jergens Lotion. Jergens cosmetic positioning was supported by copy offering "soft, lovely hands."

In attempting to understand why Wondra had not performed better, the managers responsible for the product solicited the opinions of experts in the field. One observer suggested that Wondra's initial success was due to the fact that people were drawn to sample the new brand, but because brand loyalty in the category is low, they had moved on to try other brands. Another comment was that consumers just shopped for price. Another suggested that aggressive marketing by the numerous smaller brands was adversely affecting all of the majors.

1. What is your evaluation of Wondra's positioning and its implementation?
2. Why do you think Wondra has not been more successful?

---

*PART TWO*

*SELECTED*

*READINGS*

Higgenbotham, James B. and Keith K. Cox. *Focus Group Interviews: A Reader.* Chicago: American Marketing Association, 1979. A collection of readings on conducting and utilizing focus-group interviews, currently the most popular qualitative research approach.

Mitchell, Arnold. *The Nine American Lifestyles.* New York: Macmillan Publishing Co., Inc., 1983. A full and readable report on the SRI research on lifestyles and on the VALS typologies that resulted; provides good understanding of the behavior patterns of these groups.

Day, George S. "A Strategic Perspective on Product Planning," *Journal of Contemporary Business* Vol. 4, No. 2, 1975, pp. 1-34. This article extends the discussion of product analysis in Chapter 8 to a consideration of the interactions between various products and markets of the firm.

Porter, Michael E. *Competitive Strategy.* New York: Macmillan Publishing Co., Inc., 1980. An extensive and intensive presentation of the "how" of market analysis with a desirable focus on analyzing competitors.

Wheelwright, Steven C. and Spyros Makridakis. *Forecasting Methods for Management,* 3d ed. New York: Ronald Press, 1980. An extensive and intensive discussion of the major sales forecasting methods available for the market analysis section of the advertising plan.

Ries, Al and Jack Trout. *Positioning: The Battle for Your Mind.* New York: McGraw-Hill Book Co., 1980. A qualitative and creative description of positioning by advertising practitioners.

Myers, James H. and Edward Tauber. *Market Structure Analysis.* Chicago: American Marketing Association, 1977. A description of the multivariate research techniques available for understanding the structure of markets and for positioning products.

# Part Three

## PROGRAMS FOR REACHING ADVERTISING OBJECTIVES

In describing the advertising planning process, we have considered the analytical groundwork that precedes the creation of advertising. The consumer, market, and product analyses described in Part 2 lead to the product positioning and objectives that give guidance to the advertising. In Part 3 our discussion turns to planning the advertising. At this point the advertising manager has an understanding of the product, consumers, and the market in which the product competes. The advertising manager has a list of the problems and opportunities facing the product, and a set of objectives that it is the job of the advertising to attain.

This next section of the advertising plan is made up of a number of programs, each detailing one part of the total advertising plan to be carried out in the upcoming planning period. We will consider five different programs in Part 3: budget, media, creative, sales promotion, and new products. An advertising plan may not contain all of these programs or it may contain additional ones. The order in which the programs are described is not significant;

usually all the programs, with the exception of the new product program, are prepared simultaneously. The programs are highly interdependent; hence, there must be coordination among them.

By the end of Part 3, you will be able to do the following:

1. Establish the advertising budget at the appropriate level.

2. Select advertising media that will reach target consumers.

3. Direct the creation of advertising that will communicate useful information to target consumers.

4. Design a sales promotion program that will stimulate product sales.

5. Prepare an advertising program to introduce a new product.

# CHAPTER 11

## LEARNING OBJECTIVES

In studying this chapter you will learn:

- Several single-variable approaches used to determine how much should be spent on advertising.

- The advantages and disadvantages of using single-variable budgeting approaches to determine the size of the advertising budget.

- How zero-base budgeting is used in determining the advertising budget.

- A multivariable approach to setting the advertising budget.

- Various approaches to deciding how the total advertising budget is to be divided among competing uses.

- Practices and procedures used to administer the advertising budget.

The advertising budget is concerned with two major decisions about how the advertising effort will be carried out. First, how much is to be spent for advertising in the coming period? Second, how should the total budget be allocated to different geographic areas within the company's total sales territory? These two decisions will be discussed in the first two sections of this chapter. In the third section we will consider the problem of administering the advertising budget.

## Determining the Size of the Advertising Budget

Setting the size of the advertising budget is an important decision for the advertising manager for several reasons. The budget determines the weight of the advertising effort which is an important variable in determining the effectiveness of the entire advertising effort. Spending too little could place the firm at a competitive disadvantage while spending too much would wastefully subtract funds from alternative uses. The advertising budget decision also represents a major commitment of funds by the company. In many firms the advertising budget represents one of the larger, if not the largest, expenditure categories in the total corporate budget. The budget decision, therefore, warrants careful analysis. Finally, the advertising budget decision becomes personally important to the advertising manager because of the frequent need to defend it. The advertising budget is large, conspicuous, and easily cut. If the advertising manager is to support the budget, the budget must be soundly based.

## The Budget-Setting Task

The budget in the advertising plan states the amount to be spent for advertising in the coming period. It also states the principal allocations of the budget. Beyond this, the budget presents the reasoning and the evidence that support the budgetary decisions, including a demonstration that it is adequate to support the advertising objectives.

THE OPTIMUM BUDGET. Is it possible to decide how much to spend on advertising? First of all, spending whatever you can afford is not necessarily a good budget decision because it is just as possible to spend too much on advertising as it is to spend too little. For any product, there is an optimum advertising budget level determined by the change in sales that results from a change in the budget. If an advertising budget that is currently at a rather low level is increased slightly, the result, if other factors remain constant, will be an increase in sales. If the sales increase is enough to pay the increased costs, including the increase in advertising, then the move is desirable. If the advertising budget were increased again, sales would again increase, but not by as much. Eventually, as the advertising budget was increased, the sales increase would not be great enough to cover the increased cost and the advertising increase would reduce profits. At that point the advertising budget would be too large.

Thus for every product, for a particular period, there is an optimum advertising budget. Predicting the optimum budget level is complex because there are so many factors that influence this best-expenditure figure. For example, the optimum budget depends on what competitors spend (and how they spend it); it depends on how many prospects there are and what message must be delivered to them; it depends on what part of the communications job is to be done by other means, such as personal selling; and it depends on how much money the company has available and what alternative uses the management has for the funds. There are more variables involved, but the ones listed above illustrate the complexity of the problem.

SIMPLIFYING THE BUDGET-SETTING PROCESS. It is clear that the advertising manager needs to simplify the budget-setting process so that it is a manageable task. In this section we will develop a manageable budget-setting approach.

One way to solve the budget-setting problem is to assume that, although many factors influence the size of the optimum budget, only one factor is important, and therefore the others can be ignored. One approach, for example, assumes that the important determinant of budget size is competitive spending. A number of these single-variable approaches will be examined. In general, each one is inadequate when used alone. However, there is value in examining these single-variable approaches; each one contains some advantage that should be integrated into a more comprehensive budgeting approach.

## Single-Variable Approaches to Advertising-Budget Size

Three single-variable budgeting approaches will be discussed in this section: the profit maximization model, the percentage of sales approach, and the competitive-parity method. Each of these approaches will be described and then evaluated not only to determine shortcomings, but also to find benefits that might be carried forward to the more comprehensive budgeting approach to be developed later.

PROFIT MAXIMIZATION MODELS. In recent years one frontier area in marketing has been the application of quantitative techniques to the solution of marketing problems. One of the problems that has received attention from these quantitative experts is the problem of determining the size of the advertising budget. The approach of these experts, called management scientists, operations researchers, or quantitative theorists, is to build a *profit maximization model* to represent the problem. They first identify the relevant variables, then form the model by expressing the relationship between the variables in a mathematical equation. The equation relates an independent variable (the factor which the manager will manipulate) to a dependent variable (the factor which will change as a result). The quantitative expert then "solves" the model in order to determine which level of the independent value will result in an optimum value of the dependent variable.

*Description of a Budget Model.* Highly complex advertising budget models have been developed for particular products and companies. Here, however, we need only discuss the general characteristics of budget models.

The independent variable in a budget model is the level of the advertising budget; the dependent variable is profit. The model thus attempts to relate different levels of advertising expenditure to the resulting profit level in each case. The models assume that other factors that might influence profits (such as competitive efforts and other elements in the marketing mix) remain constant and thus do not affect profits.

What is the relation between advertising expenditures and profits? Advertising serves to generate sales and sales, less the costs associated with those sales, equal profit. Thus the model, in word form, says profit equals sales created by some advertising expenditure, less the expenses incurred by those sales.

The model can also be expressed graphically as in Exhibit 11-1. The graphical model shows the same three variables as the word model—sales, expenses, and profit.

The sales volume generated by various levels of advertising expenditure is shown by the **sales-response-to-advertising curve.** Note the shape of the sales-response curve—as the advertising budget increases, sales increase, but at a diminishing rate. Research findings strongly support the diminishing increase in the response curve. Simon, after an extensive review of available evidence concluded: "Both sales and psychological studies suggest that the shape of the advertising response function is invariably concave downward."[1] A decreasing increase in the response curve

*sales-response-to-advertising curve*

Graphical presentation of an advertising budget model.                    **EXHIBIT 11-1**

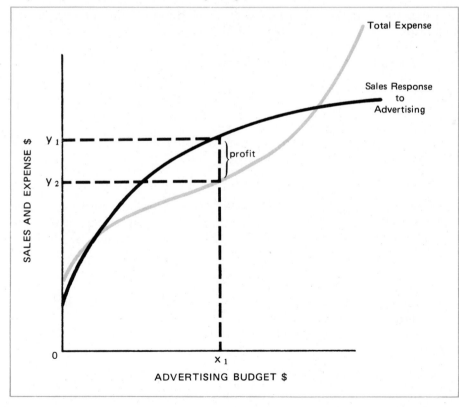

---

[1]Julian L. Simon, *The Management of Advertising* (Englewood Cliffs, New Jersey: Prentice-Hall, Inc., 1971), pp. 55–82.

also conforms to common sense. The first ad a person sees for a product increases that person's knowledge substantially, but each subsequent ad increases knowledge successively less because much is remembered from prior exposure to the ad. Advertising practitioners recognize the declining response rate in the often-quoted media buying rule to the effect that all prospects ought to be reached once before attempting repeat impressions on them. While a second impression has value as a reminder or reinforcement, it increases response less than the first impression.

Total expenses, including advertising, are shown in Exhibit 11-1 as an S-shaped curve. As the advertising budget increases, causing an increase in sales, expenses also increase. Expenses increase at first at a decreasing rate as the company's existing facilities come into full use. After a point, however, the facilities become crowded and overused, causing the increase in expenses to accelerate.

Profit is shown in Exhibit 11-1 as the difference between the sales-response curve and the total-expense curve. The profit for any particular advertising expenditure can be found by measuring the distance between the sales curve and the expense curve, and the optimum advertising budget can be determined by finding the point where the difference between sales and expense is maximized. In Exhibit 11-1 the optimum advertising expenditure is $x_1$, yielding sales of $y_1$, and profits of $y_1 - y_2$.

This simple model can also be expressed as a mathematical equation. Starting with the definition of profit as sales minus expenses

$$P = S - E \quad \text{where } P = \text{profit}$$
$$S = \text{sales}$$
$$E = \text{expenses.}$$

Sales, however, are dependent upon advertising since all other factors are assumed to remain constant. Thus

$$S = f(A) \quad \text{where } f(A) = \text{a function of advertising.}$$

The expression $f(A)$ defines the sales-response-to-advertising curve in Exhibit 11-1. Expenses can be broken into two components, advertising and all other expenses including the cost of labor and materials. Thus

$$E = A + E_0 \quad \text{where } A = \text{advertising expenditure}$$
$$E_0 = \text{all other expenses.}$$

All other expenses ($E_0$) can also be expressed in terms of the advertising expenditure ($A$). As advertising expenditure increases, it causes an increase in sales which, in turn, increases expenses. Thus other expenses rise as the advertising expenditure rises or

$$E_0 = g(A) \quad \text{where } g(A) = \text{a function of advertising.}$$

Total expenses are the sum of the advertising expenditure ($A$) and other expenses ($E_0$). Since $E_0 = g(A)$, then total expenses equal $A + g(A)$.

Returning to the profit equation $P = S - E$, it is now possible to substitute the new expressions for $S$ and $E$. Since $S = f(A)$ and $E = A + g(A)$, then

$$P = f(A) - [A + g(A)].$$

Profit has now been expressed in terms of advertising expenditure.

To find the optimum advertising budget mathematically, it is necessary to know the functional values of $f(A)$ and $g(A)$ that will describe the sales-response and total-expense curves for a particular product. With these values inserted in the model, the optimum advertising level in terms of profit can be determined through the use of calculus. The advertiser might also use simple trial and error methods, inserting various budget-level figures in the model to see what profit level is predicted by the model.

*Data for the Budget Model.* To develop and use a budget model of the type described, the advertiser must develop data on the sales-response and expense functions used in the model. To determine the sales-response-to-advertising curve shown in Exhibit 11-1 [or $f(A)$ in the mathematical model], the advertiser must somehow estimate the level of sales that will be generated by various levels of advertising. These sales results can be plotted and the curve estimated judgmentally or by statistical techniques.

Three approaches might be used to estimate what level of sales will result from various levels of advertising and hence permit definition of the sales-response-to-advertising curve. They are the historical, judgmental, and experimental approaches. In the *historical approach,* past advertising budgets are plotted against whatever sales resulted and then a curve is fitted to the plotted points. The approach relies on the questionable assumption that over the period of the historical data no factor other than the advertising budget has varied in its influence over sales. It assumes, for example, that such influences as price, product quality, consumer goals, and competitive efforts have either stayed the same or that their changes have offset one another.

In the *judgmental approach,* experienced executives are asked a series of hypothetical questions concerning the probable effect on sales if the advertising budget were increased or decreased by a specified amount. The answers provide a series of points to which a judgmental sales-response curve can be fitted.

In the *experimental approach,* a series of small representative areas or cities are set aside and in each one a different level of advertising expenditure is applied, while all other elements in the marketing mix are held constant. The sales results are projected to the total geographic sales area of the product, again forming a series of points to which a sales-response curve can be fitted. The experimental approach is the most sophisticated method of defining the sales-response curve. Although it is expensive and time-consuming to conduct the necessary tests, many advertisers find it a practical and essential approach.

The total-expense curve in Exhibit 11-1 [or $A + g(A)$ in the mathematical model] can usually be estimated from internal accounting records. One approach is to plot historical expenses at various sales levels and fit an expense curve to the points. More advanced accounting systems provide estimates of variable unit-cost from which an estimate of expected costs at various sales levels can be plotted.

*Evaluation of the Budget Model Approach.* The concept of a profit-maximizing budget model has substantial importance to the advertising manager. A budget model is implicit in the reasoning of many advertising managers who, through years of experience, have developed an idea of the shape of the sales-response curve for their product and take it into account when making budget decisions. If, however, these judgments are made explicit by forming a budget model, then not only the advertising manager, but also subordinates will be able to make budget decisions that are more consistent with these judgments.

A second important advantage to using a model in budget setting is that this is the only approach of the ones to be studied that can specify a budget that will optimize profits. Once the model has been formulated, the advertiser can experiment with it to predict the effect on profits of changing the advertising budget. In other words, the model enables the advertising manager to answer the vital budget questions, "What would happen if the advertising budget were increased? What would happen if the advertising budget were decreased?" The model's ability to answer these questions is an advantage that should be carried forward to the more comprehensive budgeting approach to be developed later.

Despite the advantages of the budget model, the user faces major tasks in implementing it. The most important requirement is accurately determining the sales-response-to-advertising curve. The relationship between advertising expenditures and the resulting sales response is a highly complex one. Sales respond to many factors other than advertising. Thus, if the advertising budget were changed, it would not always be clear whether the subsequent change or lack of change in sales was due to the advertising change or to some other factor such as a change in competitive efforts, economic conditions, or other factors in the marketing mix. The experimental approach described earlier is designed to overcome this multiple-causation problem. However, it is only a partial solution since strict control of all factors influencing sales is never possible.

Another problem in relating sales response to advertising budget levels is that sales response typically lags behind advertising expenditure. An advertising expenditure in one period influences sales in that period, but some of the effect also carries over to subsequent periods, diminishing in influence as time passes. Thus, accurate measurement of sales response requires estimation of the carry-over influence so that total sales response over time can be determined. While this has been attempted experimentally, the technique is far from perfect.

The budget model approach is limited in the types of budgets to which it is applicable. In most cases the advertising manager must determine the amount to be budgeted for several end uses, for example, an advertising-research budget, an advertising-production budget, a sales-promotion budget, a consumer mass-media budget, and a trade-advertising budget.

The budget model approach is mainly applicable in determining budgets whose expenditures are directly applied to evoking consumer sales-response. It is a valuable approach in determining the mass-media budget, but it seems less applicable to budgets for other tasks.

ADVERTISING-RELATED-TO-SALES APPROACH. The **advertising-related-to-sales budgeting approach,** according to which a fixed proportion of expected sales is set aside for advertising, is one of the more widely used methods for setting the advertising budget. The popularity of this approach is due in part to the ease with which it can be understood and applied.

*advertising-related-to-sales budgeting approach*

*Description of the Advertising-to-Sales Approach.* The first step in setting an advertising budget under this approach is to state a rule relating advertising expenditures to total sales. A commonly used rule states that the advertising budget will be some fixed percentage of sales. For example, the advertising budget might be set at 3 percent of sales. The budget rule could also be set as a fixed amount per case sold (a case rate) or a fixed amount per unit sold (a unit rate). As examples, the advertising budget rule used by a soft drink marketer might be expressed as 50¢ per case; the budget for an office machine might be $20 per machine.

What is the source of the advertising percentage or unit advertising rate? Generally the answer seems to be "experience" or what has been done in the past, but the amount is frequently adjusted to take into account other variables such as competitive conditions or special advertising tasks. The rule is also undoubtedly influenced by average industry practice, particularly in those industries where figures on average advertising-to-sales ratios or unit advertising costs are widely available. A common practice is to start with last year's advertising rate and then adjust it judgmentally to reflect current problems and opportunities and current industry practice.

The budget amount is determined by applying the advertising rate to some sales figure. Probably the most logical approach is to apply the advertising rate to projected sales for the coming period. The advertising rate, if in percentage form, is multiplied by dollar sales to give the budget figure. For example, if the budget rate is 5 percent of sales and projected sales are $1,000,000, then $.05 \times \$1,000,000 = \$50,000$, the advertising budget. If the advertising rate is expressed in terms of a unit or case rate, then the sales projection must also be converted to units or cases. For example, if the case rate for advertising is 50¢ a case and projected sales are 2,000,000 cases, then the advertising budget is $\$.50 \times 2,000,000 = \$1,000,000$.

*Evaluation of the Advertising-to-Sales Approach.* The advertising-related-to-sales approach, although widely used by practitioners, has been criticized by advertising theorists. A major criticism has been that the approach is not logical. Starting with a sales estimate and then deriving an advertising budget assumes that sales are independent of the level of advertising rather than dependent upon the level of advertising.

It is quite possible, however, that preoccupation with the logic of the advertising-to-sales approach may obscure the way that many advertisers actually apply this method. If the budget figure is accepted and put into effect without question, then this budgeting approach is weak. It has considered budget level only in terms of its relationship to sales, ignoring other important variables.

However, many advertisers recognize the need to adjust their advertising budget to meet changing internal and external problems faced by their product. Advertisers often use the percentage-of-sales budget only as a base to which adjustments can be made. This approach can result in a sounder budget.

What are the other variables that should be considered in adjusting the base budget? Numerous examples might be cited. If major competitors were to substantially increase their advertising budgets, the firm might feel it necessary to adjust its budget upward in order to maintain its market position. Or the firm might face some special advertising problems in the coming year such as introducing a product improvement or expanding the sales area, either of which might require an increased advertising budget. Or perhaps the firm has conducted experiments in the past year to determine what would happen if the advertising budget were slightly reduced. If the tests revealed that the reduced advertising would lower costs more than sales, then the advertising budget might be adjusted downward for the coming year. The statement of problems and opportunities and the advertising objectives would provide good indications of possible adjustments needed.

Using the historical relationship of advertising to sales as the base figure has one important, practical advantage. It gives some assurance, especially to those suspicious of advertising expenditures, that budget deliberations begin with an affordable figure. On the other hand, when using the advertising-to-sales approach there is a temptation to blindly apply last year's figure without rethinking the problems that this year's advertising must solve.

In summary, the desirability of the advertising-to-sales approach depends upon the way in which it is used. If an unchanging rate is applied and the result is used with no adjustment to reflect current problems, then the method is a poor one. If, on the other hand, the percentage-of-sales or case rate is used only to develop a budget base to which adjustments reflecting current problems are applied, then the soundness of the approach depends upon the soundness of the adjustments that are made. Used this way, the method permits the advertiser to adjust the budget to current conditions and it permits adjustments of the budget if evidence indicates that an increase or decrease would improve profits.

*competitive-parity budgeting approach*

COMPETITIVE-PARITY BUDGETING APPROACH. The **competitive-parity budgeting approach,** like the advertising-related-to-sales approach, begins with a rule of thumb that relates the size of the advertising budget to another single variable. In this case the variable is competitive advertising spending.

*Description of the Competitive-Parity Approach.* The rule of thumb used in the competitive-parity budgeting approach is usually expressed in terms of the product's share of advertising. A product's share of advertising is the percentage of its advertising expenditures to advertising expenditures for the total product category. Thus if an advertiser's budget for Product A were $100,000 and all other competitors spent in total $700,000, then the share of advertising for Product A would be

$$\frac{\$100,000}{\$700,000 + \$100,000} = 12.5\%.$$

Rules of thumb concerning what a product's share of advertising should be are based on the product's share of market. One rule says that to maintain its share of market, a product's share of advertising should equal its share of market. The idea is that if a brand is to claim its share of sales, then it must maintain a comparable share of the consumers' attention to product-class advertising. If a product is trying to increase its share of market, then the rule may state that its share of advertising must be greater than its current share of market. Commonly, a new product attempting to grow rapidly and establish itself in the market will apply a competitive advertising share as high as two times its market share.

Computation of an advertising budget using the competitive-parity budgeting method requires estimation of total product-class advertising and the share of market objective for the upcoming planning period. The rule relating share of advertising and share of market is then applied to give a budget figure.

*Evaluation of the Competitive-Parity Budgeting Method.* The competitive-parity budgeting method introduces a new variable into the budgeting process. Competitive advertising should be considered by the advertising manager in setting the budget, but it should not be the sole determinant of budget size.

Like the profit maximizing model discussed first, the competitive-parity budgeting approach seems mainly applicable in determining the mass media budget. Competitive expenditures for other budget categories are unlikely to be known.

The main limitation of this approach, however, lies in considerations other than competitive budgets that are excluded from the budget-setting process. The competitive-parity method does not ask, "What would be the result if we spent at more than or less than the competitive rate?" Suppose, for example, that competitors on the average were spending too little on advertising to maximize their profits. The competitive method would encourage the advertising manager to copy competitors' errors and not realize a prospective increase in profit.

The competitive method also gives little guidance when the advertising program is faced with special problems or has special projects to carry out. Introduction of a new product feature, support of a sales promotion, or expansion of sales territory are examples of advertising problems that require changes in the normal relationship of the budget to competitive spending. With these unique advertising problems there is little experience on which to base a rule of thumb relating the budget to competition.

Another consideration that the competitive method does not take into account is the affordability of the budget to the firm or the product. If, for example, maintaining competitive budget parity calls for spending beyond the firm's cash resources, then more adjustments must obviously be made.

In summary, the competitive-parity budgeting approach suggests an additional relationship that should be considered, but it does not appear by itself to be a complete budgeting method.

## Application of Zero-Base Budgeting to Advertising

The single-variable budgeting approaches reviewed thus far suggest some important considerations in setting the advertising budget, but they have several weaknesses in common. Single-variable approaches tend to be simplistic, since the assumption is that the ideal budget can be determined from a single variable. They also tend to encourage doing in the coming year what was done in the past year whether conditions have changed or not.

Zero-base budgeting has in recent years become a popular budgeting concept in several business areas. It appears to fit the requirements of advertising budgeting rather nicely, and facilitates avoiding some of the problems of single-variable approaches.

*zero-base budgeting approach*

THE ZERO-BASE BUDGETING APPROACH. The essential feature of the **zero-base budgeting approach** is that forming a budget begins with a "zero base," that is, all programs are budgeted each year from the ground up with no references to last year's budget. Thus, each budget has to be fully justified each year with no presumption that whatever was done last year should be repeated.[2]

The zero-base budget process has three steps. First, the program to be budgeted is divided into "decision packages" or discrete activities on which separate decisions can be made. Second, the cost of each decision package is determined and the decision packages ranked in order of importance. Third, the budget is built by approving decision packages one at a time in order of rank until the available funds are exhausted or until the lower-ranked packages cannot be justified in view of the funds required to implement them.[3]

The zero-base approach can be applied to form an advertising budget. Zero-base budgeting ties in closely with the advertising planning process that has been described here. Definition of the decision packages, the first

---

[2]James D. Suver and Ray L. Brown, "Where Does Zero-Base Budgeting Work?" *Harvard Business Review* (November–December, 1977), pp. 76–84.
[3]Peter A. Phyrr, "Zero-Base Budgeting," *Harvard Business Review* (November–December, 1970), pp. 111–121.

step in putting together a zero-base budget, can be drawn directly from the advertising objectives defined in the advertising plan. The advertising manager meets the advertising objectives by building a series of programs. For example, for a consumer product there is likely to be a mass-media program to meet basic objectives of communicating the product's competitive advantage to consumers. There might also be a trade advertising program to persuade retailers to stock and display the product. Other programs will likely be needed—an advertising production program to provide advertising materials needed for the media advertising, consumer promotion programs to provide temporary stimulus to sales, advertising research programs, and new product introduction programs. Each of these objectives and resulting programs represents a "decision package."

The next step is to determine how much it will cost to carry out each of these advertising programs. For each program the advertising manager asks, "How much will this program cost if it is to reach the objectives for which it is designed?" In costing out each program the advertising manager will require assistance from experts in the appropriate field—media cost estimates from media experts, research estimates from researchers, production estimates from producers. The advertiser will need to have someone develop tentative programs for accomplishing each task. These programs will then be costed out so as to provide an estimate of the budget requirement that the task represents. As an example, the task of increasing first-time users of the product might call for a program of price-reduction coupons distributed through magazine or newspaper advertisements. Budget money would have to be allocated for the redemption and handling of the coupons, for the media space, and for the production of the advertisements. This second step in zero-base budgeting is actually one of constructing a series of small budgets, one for each project to be undertaken. For each decision package the advertiser asks, "How am I going to accomplish this task?" and then, "How much will it cost to carry out this solution?"

The final step in forming a zero-base advertising budget is to rank the programs or decision packages in order of importance. The ranking is based on the importance of the objective that the program addresses. At the same time, justification for the amount budgeted to that program is built as part of the budget. The final budget is formed by adding the decision packages one by one until available funds are exhausted or the next program expenditure cannot be justified in terms of the objectives that it serves.

EVALUATION OF THE ZERO-BASE BUDGET APPROACH. One of the strengths of the zero-base budget method is that it recognizes that most advertising budgets are formed by a series of individual budget decisions—one for each program that must be funded. The zero-base approach is applicable to each of these budgeting decisions—not only to the mass-media budget but also the research budget, the production budget, and the sales-promotion budget.

The zero-base budget approach does not directly ask the question, "What would result if the advertising budget were increased or decreased?" However, if the advertising decision packages are listed in order of their importance, what the effect would be of adding or subtracting a program from the budget can be examined. Thus if the budget were decreased, the last program would be dropped from the list; if the budget were increased, then perhaps an additional objective could be accomplished. This approach allows management to see, in terms of objectives to be accomplished, the effect of changes upward or downward in the budget and permits an evaluation of advertising cost as related to prospective accomplishments. By addition or subtraction of programs from the budget, the total budget figure can be adjusted to what management considers an affordable level.

Another strength of the zero-base budget approach is that it does not rest upon blind repetition of the prior year's budget decisions. The zero-base budget approach forces advertisers to define problems and objectives and to define and justify programs to solve those problems. For the advertiser who has followed the analytical planning procedures outlined in earlier chapters, the requirements of the zero-base budgeting process are readily met as a natural part of the planning process.

Despite these strengths, the zero-base approach has a major shortcoming that was glossed over in the description of the budget-setting process. The approach calls for defining advertising objectives, deciding upon a program to accomplish each objective, and then determining the cost of each of these decision packages. But the procedure gives no guidance as to what is a sufficient expenditure to meet a particular objective. The advertiser, in effect, is thrown back upon rules of thumb, experience of experts, or experimentation to determine the right budget level for each program. This means that the zero-base method, like the other approaches that have been reviewed, is not a complete or comprehensive budgeting approach.

## A Sequential Budget-Setting Procedure

Four approaches to the advertising budget-setting process have been described and evaluated—the profit maximizing model approach, the advertising-related-to-sales approach, the competitive-parity approach, and the zero-base budget approach. The purpose in presenting these budget-setting methods was not only to review approaches that are in current use, but also to pave the way to presentation of a more sophisticated advertising budget-setting procedure. A more sophisticated approach should take advantage of the strong points of these simpler methods while avoiding their disadvantages.

VARIABLES IN A COMPLETE BUDGET PROCEDURE. Three of the four approaches that were reviewed based the advertising budget on a relationship between advertising expenditure and some single variable. A major weakness of these budget methods is that they fail to take into account enough variables when determining the budget. The zero-base budgeting approach is weak in that it fails to specify what variable should be taken into account in determining a budget level that is sufficient to reach an objective. The **sequential budget-setting procedure** attempts to overcome this problem by enabling the advertising manager to consider several variables in setting an advertising budget. Five important variables that should be considered in the budget-setting procedure are discussed below.

*sequential budget-setting procedure*

*Affordability.* The most difficult hurdle that the advertising manager faces when presenting a budget recommendation is convincing top management that the budget is affordable. One of the attractions of the advertising-to-sales-rate approach is that it utilizes a budget figure that was affordable in the past and, therefore, is more likely to be viewed as reasonable for the future. Advertising budgets, unfortunately, are too often viewed with the suspicion that they are inflated and adversely affect profits. To be complete, a budget procedure must face this problem squarely, providing the advertising manager and top management with evidence that the proposed budget is affordable, or that it makes sense in relationship to the total funds that the firm has available.

*Consideration of Competitive Activity.* As a practical matter, the advertising budget decisions must consider the level of competitive activity. This does not mean that the advertiser should rigidly follow competition or change the budget each time a competitor changes. But a major change in competitive advertising expenditure that appears to be meeting with success calls for a reevaluation of the level of the advertiser's own expenditure.

*Recognition of Need for Multiple Budgets.* A practical budgeting approach must recognize that the advertising manager must devise budgets for a variety of advertising programs. A decision must be made not only on the mass media expenditure, but also the advertising production budget, the advertising research budget, and perhaps a sales promotion budget. There may be new product budgets and budgets for established products; a budget for geographic expansion or a budget directed to gaining the support of distributors may also be needed. A practical budgeting approach must be applicable to any and all of these budget needs.

*Response to Future Conditions.* Related to the previous requirement, the budgeting approach must permit flexible response in terms of tomorrow's conditions. A budgeting approach that calls for blind repetition of the budget pattern of previous years is not satisfactory. Neither is a budgeting approach relying on quantitative data that were gathered under the assumption that conditions in the future will be the same as those in the past.

*Evaluation of Budget Level.* A practical budgeting approach should help the advertiser answer the question, "If I spend a little less or a little more on advertising, what will be the effect on profits?" The system should make it possible to develop and utilize data so as to be able to forecast the effect of varying the budget level.

A RECOMMENDED MULTIVARIABLE BUDGET PROCEDURE. The budget-setting procedure described next enables the advertising manager to take into account each of the five important variables just discussed. The procedure consists of a series of steps in which the variables are considered in sequence.

*Establishing a Base.* The first step in the budget procedure is to establish a base budget to which successive adjustments will be made, gradually refining the base budget to reflect additional variables. The base budget is best established by taking a zero-base approach. A series of programs or decision packages should be established deriving from the list of problems and opportunities and the statement of objectives given in the advertising plan. The budget figure assigned to each of these programs is based upon the cost necessary to achieve the task. This places heavy reliance on the judgment and experience of the experts designing the programs. The individual program budgets are totaled to give a total base budget.

In establishing the individual program budgets the advertising manager should be alert to the effects of inflation on media prices. As shown in Exhibit 11-2, the costs of all forms of advertising media have escalated sharply. Thus, carrying over a constant media expenditure from one year to the next will actually result in a decrease in media effort.

*Adjustments to the Base Budget.* With a base budget established, each program budget is individually examined to determine if adjustments are needed. Among the adjustments considered should be reaction to changes in competitive advertising pressure. The relationship of the budget to expenditures in previous years should also be examined. If the base budget varies markedly from previous years' expenditures, the reason for the change should be determined and its validity reconsidered.

The affordability of the budget might be checked by comparing the total dollar amount with budgets of previous years or by comparing the current advertising-to-sales-rate or unit rate with the pattern of previous years. Even better would be to incorporate the budget into a projected profit and loss statement for the product. Prospective profitability could then be compared with that of previous years.

The firm may also have established budget constraints—a maximum dollar amount or, perhaps, a maximum percentage of sales. If the sum of the program budgets exceeds these constraints or if the total budget is judged not affordable, then adjustments must be made in the individual program budgets.

The advertising manager will often face the necessity of reducing a budget that is barely adequate to meet the objectives defined. If an across-the-board cut would jeopardize satisfactory achievement of all of the programs, the advertising manager should instead recommend elimination of the lowest priority decision package. This avoids the situation in which the advertising manager is held responsible for accomplishment of programs even though they are underfunded. It also forces those who are evaluating

Index of media costs: 1971–1981

EXHIBIT 11-2

| Unit Cost | 1971 | 1972 | 1973 | 1974 | 1975 | 1976 | 1977 | 1978 | 1979 | 1980 | 1981 |
|---|---|---|---|---|---|---|---|---|---|---|---|
| Night Network Television | 100 | 114 | 130 | 145 | 150 | 175 | 213 | 234 | 283 | 300 | 333 |
| Day Network Television | 100 | 110 | 122 | 136 | 155 | 183 | 230 | 248 | 278 | 311 | 341 |
| Spot Television | 100 | 109 | 123 | 138 | 151 | 178 | 191 | 204 | 213 | 239 | 258 |
| Network Radio | 100 | 111 | 113 | 114 | 120 | 152 | 170 | 190 | 209 | 222 | 242 |
| Spot Radio | 100 | 107 | 114 | 122 | 128 | 135 | 143 | 154 | 167 | 192 | 208 |
| Consumer Magazines | 100 | 97 | 97 | 101 | 107 | 111 | 123 | 130 | 141 | 155 | 170 |
| Sunday Supplements | 100 | 106 | 111 | 124 | 144 | 151 | 164 | 179 | 191 | 212 | 231 |
| Daily Newspapers | 100 | 103 | 110 | 121 | 137 | 153 | 166 | 183 | 197 | 221 | 244 |
| Outdoor | 100 | 108 | 115 | 122 | 132 | 143 | 154 | 166 | 186 | 207 | 226 |
| **Cost-Per-Thousand** | | | | | | | | | | | |
| Night Network Television | 100 | 109 | 121 | 128 | 131 | 147 | 175 | 194 | 223 | 231 | 256 |
| Day Network Television | 100 | 104 | 117 | 126 | 143 | 169 | 219 | 236 | 253 | 285 | 310 |
| Spot Television | 100 | 105 | 114 | 126 | 134 | 154 | 162 | 168 | 171 | 186 | 199 |
| Network Radio | 100 | 109 | 109 | 108 | 113 | 138 | 153 | 168 | 182 | 190 | 207 |
| Spot Radio | 100 | 105 | 110 | 116 | 120 | 124 | 129 | 137 | 145 | 164 | 177 |
| Consumer Magazines | 100 | 99 | 98 | 101 | 109 | 112 | 125 | 134 | 145 | 157 | 171 |
| Sunday Supplements | 100 | 103 | 105 | 114 | 132 | 138 | 146 | 158 | 165 | 181 | 196 |
| Daily Newspapers | 100 | 103 | 108 | 118 | 141 | 156 | 170 | 184 | 198 | 218 | 240 |
| Outdoor | 100 | 108 | 114 | 117 | 122 | 125 | 133 | 142 | 153 | 167 | 181 |

Source: *O & M Pocket Guide to Media* (New York: Ogilvy & Mather), pp. 8–9.

the budget to see what they are giving up (accomplishment of an objective) for what they are getting (a reduction in advertising expense).

*Providing Feedback.* The budget process described thus far has relied heavily on judgment and experience. It would be desirable to supplement the budget-setting process with the optimizing techniques of the advertising budget model described earlier in this chapter. Application of the optimizing approach requires a data-gathering effort. To obtain the necessary information, a testing program should be established as part of the final step in the sequential budget-setting procedure. The testing program would be designed to determine the sales response to varying levels of advertising expenditure. Because of the time and cost involved in such a testing program it would probably be limited to the larger budget packages such as the mass-media or sales-promotion budgets. The testing program would have to be a continuing one since sales response for most products changes over time. Research techniques for gathering the needed information will be described in the section on evaluation of advertising program effectiveness.

As data from the research program become available, they provide important input into the budgeting process, allowing the advertising manager to make budget adjustments supported by facts about the profitability of the change. When the data-gathering program has become well established, current results would be utilized during the preparation of the program budget and its adjustment.

## Allocation of the Advertising Budget

Budget allocation is the process of deciding how the total advertising budget is to be divided among competing uses. The advertising manager has to allocate the budget along several dimensions. One important dimension, *geographic allocation* of advertising funds, will be given particular attention here. Responsibility for recommending geographic allocation of advertising expenditures rests with the advertising manager and should appear in the advertising plan. In most cases, however, the sales manager will be particularly interested in this decision and should be encouraged to participate in it.

### The General Allocation Principle

Microeconomic theory provides an approach for solving the allocation problem. If the objective is to maximize profits, then resources should be allocated between alternatives so that the incremental revenue minus the incremental cost derived from the last unit allocated to each alternative will be equal.

In the case of advertising budget allocation, the alternatives are different geographic or sales areas and the resource being allocated is advertising dollars. For example, assume that there are only two sales territories — A and B — and an advertising budget of $1,000 to divide between them. Begin by arbitrarily dividing the budget equally between the two areas — $500 each. Than take one dollar from Area A and transfer it to Area B. In doing so, assume that the advertiser loses 50¢ in profit (sales minus cost including advertising) in Area A, but gains a profit of 75¢ in Area B. If so, the transfer is worthwhile because the advertiser would have gained a profit of 25¢. Try transferring another dollar of advertising from A to B and continue until the profit gained is equal to profit lost by the transfer. At that point, the allocation of advertising between the two areas is optimal.

### Geographic Allocation of the Advertising Budget

To follow the allocation principle just outlined, a firm would need two classes of information. First, it would be necessary to have a sales-response-to-advertising curve, such as that shown in Exhibit 11-1, for each territory. Second, it would be necessary to have a total expense curve, also shown in Exhibit 11-1, for each territory.

RULES OF THUMB FOR GEOGRAPHIC ALLOCATION. Very few firms have these two classes of information for each of their products. Despite this lack, the allocation principle can provide some guidance for the development of rules of thumb for geographic allocation of advertising funds.

*Spread Expenditures Among Territories.* Based on the general characteristics of response curves, the advertiser should spread advertising expenditures over many territories. Sales-response curves increase at a diminishing rate which means that marginal sales response will decrease as the advertising expenditure in a territory increases. If the advertiser were to concentrate advertising expenditures in one territory, sales results would likely be well along the response curve where marginal response was low. Allocation of some of the money to another territory with no advertising would be likely to yield greater sales response.

The behavior of costs also encourages spreading expenditures among territories. Total costs in each territory should, after a time, begin to increase at an increasing rate due to the law of diminishing returns. This, in turn, reduces profit and encourages spreading the advertising expenditure out to other territories whose costs are increasing at a lesser rate.

*Allocate in Proportion to Market Size.* Sales-response curves all exhibit diminishing returns, which encourages spreading advertising expenditures, but there are differences between territories in the rate at which sales response diminishes. A greater number of advertising dollars should be allocated to those territories in which the rise of the sales-response curve diminishes at a slower rate.

What determines the rate at which the sales-response-to-advertising declines? There are many factors, but one of the most important is the size of the market. In a small market the best prospects can be reached rather quickly with a modest budget; then, as less desirable prospects are reached and repetitive messages are delivered, the rate of response declines. In a very large market, by contrast, it takes a relatively large expenditure just to reach the prime prospects for the first time. In a large market the rate of response declines more slowly with additional advertising expenditures and therefore should receive a proportionately larger share of advertising expenditures.

*Favor Easily Reached Markets.* A second important factor that influences the responsiveness of a market to advertising is the company's ability to reach and appeal to prospects in the various territories. An example will make this clearer. Suppose territory A was a very large one in terms of number of prospects, but the product advertised had only spotty distribution in the area. Adding advertising to area A might initially acquaint prospects with the advertiser's product, but many of them would be frustrated when they attempted to purchase the product. As a result, the increase in sales response would be small. Or to give another example, suppose a firm was directing its product to a segment of the total market that was characterized by high income. If territory B were an average sized territory but had an above average number of high-income families, then the sales-response curve for territory B would diminish at a slower than average rate.[4]

A GEOGRAPHIC ALLOCATION PROCEDURE. There are two dominant ways in which practicing advertisers allocate advertising funds to geographic areas. One practice is to allocate advertising dollars in proportion to actual sales of the advertiser's product. Some sales managers favor this approach because they wish to protect an already established sales volume. The weakness of such an approach is that it may lead the advertising manager to overlook territories with great potential for sales gain. Such an allocation system tends to perpetuate the mistakes of the past and to develop stagnant allocation patterns.

The second common approach is to allocate advertising funds in proportion to forecasted total market sales. This is a practical approach since a geographic sales forecast should be available from the market analysis section of the advertising plan. It is also a theoretically sounder approach than the first, since market size is one of the important factors that determine the rate at which the sales-response curve increases.

The allocation procedure can be improved, however, if the previously discussed adjustments (those concerning cost differentials and those concerning the company's ability to reach different territories) are introduced. Evidence that costs are higher or increase more rapidly in a given territory should cause reduction of the advertising allocation to that territory. Each territory should also be examined to determine whether or not there are impediments to the firm's reaching the potential market. Such findings as lack of distribution, unavailability of effective media, or geographic inappropriateness of the product should all result in a downward adjustment of the advertising allocation for the area.

## Other Allocations of the Advertising Budget

In addition to geographic allocation, the advertiser must divide the budget among available media vehicles, must allocate it seasonally, and must allocate it among the programs to be undertaken by advertising. The

---

[4]Ambar G. Rao, in *Quantitative Theories in Advertising* (New York: John Wiley & Sons, Inc., 1970), pp. 15–37, presents research findings on an actual situation of this type.

proportion to be devoted to each creative approach must be decided, along with how funds will be divided between various ad sizes or commercial time lengths.

The basic allocation principle developed in this chapter is useful in solving these other allocation problems. Two of these problems — media allocation and seasonal allocation — will be considered in more detail in the media selection chapter. The problem of allocation of the budget among competing advertising programs has already been solved if the recommended budget-setting process has been followed.

## Administering the Advertising Budget

The process of setting an advertising budget takes place only once each planning period; in most companies this occurs once a year. After the budget is set, there is the continuing task of administering it.

### The Budget Administration Function

While establishing a budget is part of the advertising manager's planning responsibility, it is through day-to-day administration of the budget that the advertising manager exercises control responsibility. Some of the record keeping and report preparation procedures may be delegated to subordinates, but the results should be funneled back to the advertising manager for decision making. The advertising manager will usually request that advertising agencies establish budgetary control over funds which are expended through the agency and submit budget reports to assist the advertising manager in meeting his or her budgetary responsibility.

### Budgeting Practices

Many firms have standard budgetary practices and report formats to which the advertising manager must conform. If the firm has no such standards, the advertising manager can develop a budget report form.

ESTABLISHING THE STANDARD. The first step in establishing budgetary control is to state the standard — the planned pattern of expenditure. This is usually a statement of monthly expenditures for major budget categories or elements. Monthly planned expenditures permit the advertising manager to control expenditures during the course of the planning period rather than only at the termination of the planning period.

Budgeted expenditures are used as financial guidelines in the preparation of media, creative, and other programs to be discussed in succeeding chapters. The total of all expenditures recommended in these advertising programs will, of course, be equal to the total expenditure determined in this budget section of the plan.

ACTUAL VS. STANDARD. With the budget standard set, some provision must be made for collecting and recording actual expenditures. Collecting and reporting expenditures is, in most firms, the responsibility of the accounting department or controller's office. These figures should be reported directly to the advertising manager. The essence of the control function is the periodic comparison of actual expenditures with planned expenditures. Any differences must be explained by the advertising manager.

EXPLANATION OF DIFFERENCES. When differences between actual and planned expenditures occur, the advertising manager must determine the reasons for the differences. Beyond this, the advertising manager must determine what corrective action is necessary in light of deviations from the budget. No matter how carefully a plan is made and a budget drawn up, there will be changes in conditions that cause actual expenditures to be different from those planned. The advertising manager must be alert to such changes and make revisions in plans if necessary.

---

*CHAPTER*
*SUMMARY*

The advertising budget program is concerned with deciding how much will be spent for advertising and how those expenditures will be allocated. For any product there is an optimum advertising expenditure level, but it is difficult to determine because the best-expenditure level is influenced by many variables. Several approaches to budget setting assume that one of these variables is the dominant factor in the determination of the optimum budget and that the other variables can be ignored.

The profit maximization model applies quantitative techniques to the determination of the optimum budget level. Budget models predict the response of sales and the level of expenses that will be associated with varying levels of advertising expenditure. Subtracting expected expenses from expected sales response gives the relationship between advertising expenditure and profits. The model can be used to determine the level of advertising expenditure that maximizes profits. The budget-model approach is the only profit-maximizing method. It is difficult, however, to determine the needed sales response to advertising information because sales response is influenced by many variables and is subject to lags.

The percentage-of-sales approach to budget setting applies a fixed percentage or amount per unit of expected sales to determine the budget. If the resulting budget figure is used blindly, the approach is weak because it ignores all variables except sales. However, many practitioners use the percentage-of-sales budget figure as a base to which adjustments are made in order to take other variables into consideration. The percentage-of-sales approach has the advantage of assuring that the budget is affordable.

The competitive-parity budget approach determines the advertising budget in relation to competitive spending. This approach is weak because a budget determined solely in terms of what the competition is doing may not result in profit maximization for the advertiser. Although competitive spending should be considered in setting an advertising budget, it should not be the only determinant.

The zero-base budgeting approach is tied closely to the advertising planning process. A list of decision packages or advertising programs is designed that meets advertising objectives. Each program is then costed out and programs are ranked by importance. Justifiable decision packages or program costs are added together to form the total budget. The strength of the zero-base budgeting approach is that it does not permit unjustified repetition of prior years' expenditure levels. Its weakness lies in its lack of guidance as to what is a sufficient expenditure to meet a particular objective.

A sequential budget-setting procedure is suggested that utilizes the single-variable approaches yet permits consideration of several budget-setting variables. These variables are affordability, competitive spending levels, future conditions facing the product, a need for multiple budgets, and the effect on profits of changing budget levels. The sequential procedure begins with the setting of a base budget using a zero-base approach. Next, a series of adjustments are made to the base budget so as to reflect changes in competitive spending, the amount that the company can afford to spend, and other special problems that face the product. As a final step, the budget-setting process should provide for gathering and using information about the effect on profits of varying the level of advertising expenditure.

The general principle in making allocations of the budget is to divide the funds among alternative uses so that the incremental profits derived from the last unit sold in each alternative use are equal. Because calculating incremental profits requires hard-to-obtain data, geographic allocation usually relies on the guidance of rules of thumb. Generally, advertising expenditures should be spread among territories rather than concentrated in one or a few. The allocation should generally be proportional to market size with extra allocations given to easily reached areas.

The advertising manager should exercise control over the advertising budget. Stating the planned pattern of expenditures in the advertising plan establishes a standard. As actual expenditures are recorded, they should be compared to planned expenditures. Differences should be examined and corrective action taken when necessary.

---

Sales-response-to-advertising curve                                 *KEY TERMS*
Advertising-related-to-sales budgeting approach
Competitive-parity budgeting approach
Zero-base budgeting approach
Sequential budget-setting procedure

1. An advertiser established the regular advertising budget for the year at $200,000. The resulting sales were ten times that much, or $2,000,000. In addition, two different budget levels were tested in two representative test markets. In one market, the budget tested was the equivalent of $300,000, and sales rose by 20 percent over the level expected under a $200,000 advertising level. In another market, the advertising budget was cut to half the normal level and sales dropped to 60 percent of previous sales.

   a. Plot the three points on the sales-response-to-advertising curve and estimate from them the shape of the curve.

   b. What do the results indicate about the appropriateness of the current level?

2. An advertising manager for a small company has developed the following model for setting the advertising budget.

$$P = f(A) - A - g(A) \text{ where } P = \text{profit}$$
$$A = \text{advertising \$}$$
$$f(A) = \text{the sales response to advertising}$$
$$g(A) = \text{total costs.}$$

Through analyses of historical records the following values for the sales response and cost curves have been determined:

$$f(A) = \$10,000 + \$1000A^{1/2}$$
$$g(A) = \$\ 5,000 + \$10A$$

   a. Check by trial and error advertising budgets of $1,000, $2,000 and $3,000. Which of these gives the best profit results?

   b. Use calculus or a graphical approach to determine the optimum budget.

3. An advertising manager's mass media budget for a product is currently $1,000,000 with sales of $20,000,000. The manager wishes to establish a sales-response-to-advertising curve and plans to base it on the judgments expressed by three experienced marketers in the firm and the advertising agency. Based on questions asked, the advertising manager gets the following estimates of sales resulting from various budget levels.

| | | Sales Estimates | |
|---|---|---|---|
| Budget Level | President | Sales Manager | Ad Agency Account Executive |
| $   250,000 | $12,000,000 | $10,000,000 | $ 6,000,000 |
| 500,000 | 16,000,000 | 15,000,000 | 12,000,000 |
| 750,000 | 18,000,000 | 17,000,000 | 15,000,000 |
| 1,500,000 | 22,000,000 | 21,000,000 | 24,000,000 |
| 2,000,000 | 23,000,000 | 22,000,000 | 26,000,000 |

   a. Plot the sales-response-to-advertising curve that reflects the combined judgment of the three marketers.
   b. Does the resulting curve appear reasonable?

4. An advertiser has developed an "all you can afford" advertising budgeting method designed to maximize sales growth. Each year the base advertising budget is set at 80 percent of the previous year's profit margin, to which is added 20 percent of the projected sales growth which is estimated at five times the base advertising budget. The formula used looks like this:

Advertising budget = .8 (last year's sales × profit margin)
                     + .2 (5 × .8 × last year's sales × profit margin)

   a. Last year's sales were $1 million with a 10 percent profit margin. What will the advertising budget be?
   b. What is your appraisal of this method of setting the budget?

5. Suppose that a company sets its advertising budget at 2 percent of sales. Sales last year were $600,000 and next year sales are projected to rise to $850,000.

   a. What will the advertising budget be next year?
   b. What other factors should be considered in setting next year's budget?

6. The advertising manager of Food Products Co. sets the advertising budget by the competitive-parity method. The manager's rule of thumb is that the share of advertising should be 20 percent greater than the target share of the market. In the current year competitive expenditures for advertising are estimated to be $32,000,000. They are expected to grow by 10 percent next year. The advertising manager's target share of the market for next year is 20 percent. What will the Food Products Co.'s advertising budget be for next year?

7. The advertising manager for Industrial Products, Inc., has prepared a zero-base budget made up of six decision packages. The packages and the estimated cost to accomplish them are as follows:

| | |
|---|---|
| a. Generate inquiries for salespeople | $100,000 |
| b. Produce three new advertisements to generate inquiries | 11,700 |
| c. Test the effectiveness of direct mail for generating inquiries | 5,000 |
| d. Develop customer awareness of new product X | 30,000 |
| e. Develop new selling kit for salespeople | 3,000 |
| f. Prepare and staff exhibits at four manufacturers' trade shows | 25,000 |
| Total | $174,700 |

The marketing director has not approved the budget, but instead has requested that it be cut by 10 percent. If you were the advertising manager, how would you proceed?

8. An advertising manager is trying to decide what percentage of the advertising budget to allocate to sales area G. In previous years the area had been allocated 10 percent of the advertising budget, but the sales manager argues that the area deserves 15 percent. Currently the company derives about 5 percent of its sales from the area. The company has had difficulty in getting distributors in this territory and the sales manager wants to try to attract distributors by upping the advertising budget. Costs in the area are average. About 10 percent of total industry sales are made in this geographic area. The advertising manager has no information on how competitors allocate their advertising expenditures to this area. Do you think the advertising manager should change the budget allocation to area G?

9. There is a tendency for advertising budgets as a percentage of sales to be greatest in firms whose personal-selling costs as a percentage of sales tend to be low.

   a. Why do you think this happens?
   b. Do you think that it is sound practice?

---

*PROBLEM*

The advertising manager for VoxNet Corporation has been asked to prepare an advertising budget for the company's new line of hand-held, two-way radios. These radios are widely used by municipal police and fire departments as well as in business applications such as at construction sites or by building maintenance crews. VoxNet radios are differentiated from their competition by being smaller (pocket-sized) but just as powerful as the traditional units worn on the belt.

In appraising the tasks to be accomplished by the end of the first year of advertising, the advertising manager has listed the following items in priority order:

1. Recruit fifty communications dealers to carry the product.
2. Prepare sales brochures for use by the dealer salespersons.
3. Develop leads for dealer follow-up from the municipal (fire and police departments) segment of the market.
4. Develop leads for dealer follow-up from the business segment.
5. Develop public-relations releases on the new radios to send to dealer and end-user trade publications.

The advertising manager has estimated the first-year cost for each of the above tasks. She proposes recruiting the fifty new dealers through use of four trade shows. Space-rental fees and other exhibitor expenses will be

$40,000. A new display will have to be built at a cost of $10,000. The sales brochures from task number two can also be used at the shows together with the new radios. The cost of the brochures will be $2,000 for photography and $10,000 for printing costs. Copy and layout can be done internally with no budget impact. Developing sales leads from municipalities is to be done through business periodical advertising that will include inquiry coupons. Space cost will be $50,000 plus $5,000 for production of ads. Adequate coverage of the business segment (which has about ⅓ the potential of the municipal segment) will cost $100,000 in business periodical advertising plus $10,000 in production costs. The proposed public-relations (P.R.) campaign is to be handled by an outside P.R. firm well-known to VoxNet at an estimated annual fee of $10,000.

The company's rule of thumb for advertising is that expenditures should not be greater than 5 percent of projected sales. The company has estimated the market for the new product at $20 million and likewise estimated that it will be possible to achieve a 10 percent share in the first year. The advertising manager has developed an analysis of competitive spending in the market with the following data:

| Competitor | Market Share | Advertising $ Share |
|------------|--------------|---------------------|
| A | 40% | 30% |
| B | 20 | 20 |
| C | 10 | 20 |

Based on her experience with previous new-product introductions, the advertising manager expects that to establish the product during the first year, the advertising-dollar share will have to be 1.5 times the expected market share. Total advertising expenditures by all competitors were difficult to verify, but she has estimated them at $1 million.

A final and practical consideration is of concern to the advertising manager. A consultant hired by the president has suggested to her, in the presence of the president, that the advertising task in introducing the new product should certainly be kept below $125,000 in order to assure acceptable profit margins for the product.

Prepare a budget recommendation with full support and including all allocations by task to be presented to the president for approval.

# CHAPTER 12

## LEARNING OBJECTIVES

In studying this chapter you will learn:

- The various classifications of advertising media.

- The audience measurements commonly used by advertisers.

- The terminology used in media cost measurement.

- A practical, four-step, media-program selection approach.

- The role of the computer in media selection.

The second of the advertising programs to be considered is the selection of media. This program is prepared concurrently with the budget program, especially if a zero-base approach is part of the budget formation process.

The media program is, in essence, an allocation problem. The advertising manager must decide how to distribute the total advertising budget among the many available media. The problem of allocation among media is theoretically the same as the geographic allocation problem considered in the last chapter. The media decision, however, deals with an extremely large number of alternatives (different media and media combinations) and poses acute problems in measuring effects. As a consequence, some practical, simplifying procedures must be developed in devising a media selection process.

The primary objective of this chapter is to describe a practical procedure for media selection. Before this is done, the common classification of media and some media measurement terms and processes will be considered.

## Classes of Media

**Advertising media** are the channels through which a product's advertising is carried to prospective consumers. A medium may contain a

*advertising media*

mixture of editorial or entertainment material and advertising, such as magazines and television, or a medium may contain nothing but advertising, such as a direct mail piece or a "shopper" newspaper.

The media alternatives that are available to the advertiser can be classified in terms of editorial content (and thus the audience of the medium) or classified by the way in which the message is delivered.

## Print or Broadcast Classification

Media can be classified — in terms of the way in which the message is delivered — into a *print class* and a *broadcast class*. The print classifications can be further subdivided into newspapers, magazines, direct mail, and the various forms of outdoor and in-store media. Broadcast media include radio, television, and the new electronic media such as cable television.

The classification of media into print and broadcast is useful because the media in each class have some common characteristics. There are similarities in advertising production processes for the various print media. Likewise, production processes for the broadcast media also tend to be similar. As a result, production personnel tend to specialize in either print or broadcast media. The same specialization is sometimes found among creative personnel because each of the two classes has special creative requirements. Media purchasers also frequently specialize in either print or broadcast because of similarities of purchasing procedures within each classification.

## Media Classified by Audience

The print and broadcast classifications are useful as a basis for personnel specialization, but not as a basis for selection of media. One reason is that the categories are too large. A more important limitation is that the categories do not describe the audience characteristics of each medium. In selecting media, the most important determinant is comprised of the characteristics of the people to whom the medium is directed.

There are several classifications that separate media by audience characteristics. Perhaps the most widely used is the classification developed by *Standard Rate and Data Service*, the publishers of media data services. SRDS first breaks the media into traditional descriptive classes as follows:

| | |
|---|---|
| Business publications | Farm publications |
| Community publications | Newspapers |
| Consumer magazines | Radio |
| Direct mail | Television |

Out-of-home media, not covered by SRDS, must be added to this list. Of more interest, however, are the subclassifications for each of these media types because they represent classification by audience. For example, the category *newspapers* may be subdivided as follows:

| | |
|---|---|
| National newspapers | Weekly newspapers |
| Daily newspapers | College and university newspapers |
| Newspaper comic sections | Black newspapers |
| Newspaper-distributed magazines | Religious weekly newspapers |

Each subclassification is further divided into geographic classes according to the location of its circulation and its readers. Consumer magazines, for another example, are subdivided into 66 groups according to editorial content and, thus, audience. The groups include automotive, computers, boating, photography, senior citizens, and many more.

## Media Classified by Advertising Revenue

Media can be ranked in terms of their advertising revenue dollars. Exhibit 12-1 shows a ranking in terms of 1982 advertising volume. There are several things revealed in Exhibit 12-1 that deserve notice. First, the largest medium in advertising volume, contrary to what most might guess, is newspapers. The tremendous volume in newspaper advertising reflects the heavy use of the medium by local business people and by retailers. Television, the second largest medium, is over $3 billion smaller, although it has grown rapidly.

**EXHIBIT 12-1**    Advertising volume of the major media, 1982.

| Medium | Advertising Volume (in millions of dollars) |
|---|---|
| Newspapers | $17,694 |
| Television | 14,329 |
| Direct mail | 10,319 |
| Radio | 4,670 |
| Magazines | 3,710 |
| Business papers | 1,876 |
| Outdoor | 721 |
| Farm publications | 148 |
| Miscellaneous | 13,113 |
| Total | $66,580 |

Reprinted with permission from the May 30, 1983 issue of *Advertising Age*. Copyright 1983 by Crain Communications, Inc.

The volume of the direct mail medium may be surprising. It is a more privately delivered medium than others, such as television, hence many people do not realize its widespread use. It is, however, the third largest medium, nearly as large as television.

Radio is another medium whose volume may also surprise many. After being threatened by the emergence of television, radio has made a strong comeback and is a major, growing medium today. Magazine volume is, of course, very substantial, especially when it is realized that Exhibit 12-1 divides this category into several subclasses.

## Measurement in Media

Before discussing the media selection process, some background on media measurement is necessary. We will consider two aspects of media which involve measurement problems—audience and cost.

### Media Audience Measurement

For both print and broadcast media, three audience measures commonly used by the advertiser are (1) the size of the audience, (2) the profile of the audience, and (3) the distribution of exposures among the medium's audience.

PRINT AUDIENCE—SIZE. Up to now, the term "audience" has been used without definition in reference to the size of a medium. At this point, more precise terminology must be developed.

*Print Circulation.* The primary measure of size for magazines and newspapers is circulation. **Circulation** is the number of copies distributed in an average issue. For magazines that are sold (there are some that are distributed free) the more useful measure is **average paid circulation,** the number of copies sold of an average issue. This eliminates those copies which are given away for promotional or other purposes.

*circulation*

*average paid circulation*

Circulation figures are reported by newspapers and magazines in publishers' statements, usually issued twice each year. In order to give advertisers assurance that the reported circulation figures are accurate, most major publishers belong to one of the audit services that verify circulation figures through an independent audit.

There are three major magazine and newspaper audit services in the United States, each operating somewhat differently. The Audit Bureau of Circulations is the oldest and largest of the audit services. To qualify as members of this association, newspapers, consumer magazines, and farm publications must have at least 70 percent of their total distribution as paid. Business publications may qualify with a minimum of 50 percent paid and/or non-paid direct-request circulation. Except for some weekly newspapers and small dailies, all members are audited annually, with the resulting Audit Report either verifying or correcting claims made in the preceding two Publisher's Statements. The audit is conducted according to standardized ABC procedures, and standardized definitions are used to insure fair and comparable reporting.

The Audit Reports and Publishers' Statements contain a good deal more information than just the circulation figure. Additional information helps the advertiser to evaluate the quality of that circulation. It includes information on subscription versus single-copy sales, prices, sales incentives, circulation trends, markets served, occupational and business analysis (for business publications), advertising rate base or circulation guarantee (for magazines and farm publications), renewal percentage (for business publications), and a geographic analysis of circulation (by states and counties for periodicals; by counties, towns, and postal ZIP Code areas for daily and weekly newspapers). On an optional basis, members may also report additional demographic data on their circulation audiences.

Along with 2,226 advertiser and advertising agency members, ABC currently audits the circulations of 1,870 daily and weekly newspapers, 519 consumer magazines, 41 farm publications, and 257 business publications, comprising approximately 75 percent of all print-media circulation available to advertisers in North America.

A portion of an ABC daily newspaper Audit Report is shown in Exhibit 12-2.

Business Publications Audit of Circulation, Inc. (BPA) is the leading audit service for business magazines and professional journals. It audits publications with paid circulation, controlled or non-paid circulation, or a combination of controlled and paid circulation. A **controlled or non-paid circulation publication** is one that is distributed free of charge to target audience members in the field served by the publication. For example, the "publisher's statement" in Exhibit 12-3 for *Family Practice News,* is a fully controlled circulation publication directed to general and family practice physicians. The statement demonstrates to potential advertisers that almost all of the publication's circulation is "qualified" because it has been verified as going to physicians in the target audience. About 900 publications are audited by BPA.

*controlled or non-paid circulation publication*

A third audit service is the Verified Audit Circulation (VAC), which also serves controlled-circulation business and farm publications. VAC samples members on the publisher's circulation list to verify receipt of the publication and to determine if the recipients have the characteristics desired by the publisher.

There are, of course, many publications whose circulation is unaudited. Such circulation figures are subject to greater uncertainty.

*audience*

*Print Audience.* A second measure of media size is **audience**, the total number of persons who have read a copy of a particular issue. The audience of a publication is substantially larger than the circulation since the subscriber or purchaser usually shares each issue with members of the family and others. This fact is demonstrated in Exhibit 12-4, which compares circulation and audience figures for several magazines. The difference between the primary measure, circulation, and the audience figure is termed **pass-along circulation or secondary audience.** It is considered less valuable to the advertiser because the reader did not pay for the publication and may therefore be a less serious reader. Pass-along circulation varies substantially from publication to publication. Among the publications in Exhibit 12-4, for example, the average of readers per copy (audience ÷ circulation) varies from a low of 2.9 for *TV Guide* to 7.3 for *Field and Stream.*

*pass-along circulation or secondary audience*

The audience of a magazine cannot be measured through audit of the

Portion of an ABC Audit Report.                                                    **EXHIBIT 12-2**

# ABC Audit Report: Summary Form

**ABC**    THE ORLANDO SENTINEL (All Day, Saturday Morning & Sunday)
See Paragraph 12(b)

Orlando (Orange County), Florida

PRINTED AND RELEASED
BY ABC JULY, 1983

TOTAL AVERAGE PAID CIRCULATION FOR 12 MONTHS ENDED MARCH 31, 1983:

| | AVERAGE PAID CIRCULATION | | |
|---|---|---|---|
| | All Day (Mon. to Fri.) | Saturday Morning | Sunday |
| 1.  TOTAL AVERAGE PAID CIRCULATION | 212,412 | 203,005 | 254,176 |

1A. TOTAL AVERAGE PAID CIRCULATION IN PUBLISHER'S PRIMARY MARKET AREA

CITY ZONE

| | Population | Hslds* |
|---|---|---|
| 1980 Census: | 557,157 | 201,337 |
| 1983 ABC Estimate: | 629,200 | 235,800 |

(See Paragraph 1C for description of area)

| | All Day | Saturday Morning | Sunday |
|---|---|---|---|
| Carriers not filing lists with Publisher See Par. 12(c) | 101,684 | 100,058 | 116,668 |
| Single Copy Sales | 33,017 | 28,999 | 45,840 |
| Mail Subscriptions | 49 | 53 | 202 |
| School - Single Copy/Subscriptions See Par. 12(d) | 847 | 24 | 24 |
| Total City Zone | 135,597 | 129,134 | 162,734 |

BALANCE IN PRIMARY MARKET AREA

| | Population | Hslds* |
|---|---|---|
| 1980 Census: | 298,974 | 113,319 |
| 1983 ABC Estimate: | 345,600 | 135,800 |

| | All Day | Saturday Morning | Sunday |
|---|---|---|---|
| Single Copy Sales and Carriers not filing lists with Publisher See Par 12(c) | 49,485 | 47,880 | 61,080 |
| Mail Subscriptions | 203 | 203 | |
| School - Single Copy/Subscriptions See Par. 12(d) | 508 | 8 | 5 |
| TOTAL BALANCE IN PRIMARY MARKET AREA | 50,196 | 48,091 | 61,085 |
| TOTAL PRIMARY MARKET AREA | 185,793 | 177,225 | 223,819 |

| | Population | Hslds* |
|---|---|---|
| 1980 Census: | 856,131 | 314,656 |
| 1983 ABC Estimate: | 974,800 | 371,600 |

CIRCULATION OUTSIDE PRIMARY MARKET AREA

| | All Day | Saturday Morning | Sunday |
|---|---|---|---|
| Single Copy Sales and Carriers not filing lists with Publisher See Par. 12(c) | 25,781 | 25,187 | 28,727 |
| Mail Subscriptions | 490 | 499 | 1,525 |
| School - Single Copy/Subscriptions See Par. 12(d) | 348 | 94 | 105 |
| TOTAL CIRCULATION OUTSIDE PRIMARY MARKET AREA | 26,619 | 25,780 | 30,357 |
| TOTAL PAID Excluding Bulk (For Bulk Sales, See Par. 5) | 212,412 | 203,005 | 254,176 |

*Households

**EXHIBIT 12-3**    BPA publishers' statement for *Family Practice News*.

| | |
|---|---|
| | BPA Buyer's Guide No.  903 |
| | This Publication Is Reporting On A Comparable Basis |

## PUBLISHER'S STATEMENT
### For 6 Month Period Ending
### JUNE 1983
### ▽BPA
#### BUSINESS PUBLICATIONS AUDIT OF CIRCULATION, INC.
#### 360 Park Avenue South, New York, N.Y. 10010

No attempt has been made to rank the information contained in this report in order of importance, since BPA believes this is a judgment which must be made by the user of the report.

**FAMILY PRACTICE NEWS**

International Medical News Group
Fairchild Division of Capital Cities Media, Inc.
12230 Wilkins Avenue, Rockville, Maryland  20852
(301)  770-6170
OFFICIAL PUBLICATION OF          None

ESTABLISHED    1971        ISSUES PER YEAR    24

### FIELD SERVED

FAMILY PRACTICE NEWS serves General Practice and Family Practice specialists and osteopaths in patient care.  This includes full time office based and hospital based physicians along with residents and interns.

### DEFINITION OF RECIPIENT QUALIFICATION

Qualified recipients are General Practitioners and Family Practitioners in both office based and hospital based patient care as well as osteopaths.  Included are interns and residents in the above specialties, and others as reported in Paragraph 3a.

**AVERAGE NON-QUALIFIED DISTRIBUTION**

| | Copies |
|---|---|
| Advertiser and Agency .. | 1,462 |
| Non-Qualified Paid ..... | - |
| Rotated or Occasional ... | - |
| Samples ............ | - |
| All Other .......... | 391 |
| **TOTAL** | **1,853** |

**1. AVERAGE QUALIFIED CIRCULATION BREAKDOWN FOR PERIOD**

| | Qualified Non-Paid | | Qualified Paid | | Total Qualified | |
|---|---|---|---|---|---|---|
| | Copies | Percent | Copies | Percent | Copies | Percent |
| Single .............. | 70,081 | 100.0% | - | - | 70,081 | 100.0% |
| Group .............. | - | - | - | - | - | - |
| Association .......... | - | - | - | - | - | - |
| Gift ............... | - | - | - | - | - | - |
| Bulk .............. | - | - | - | - | - | - |
| **TOTALS** | **70,081** | **100.0%** | **-** | **-** | **70,081** | **100.0%** |

**U.S. POSTAL MAILING CLASSIFICATION ...... SECOND CLASS**

**2. QUALIFIED CIRCULATION BY ISSUES WITH REMOVALS AND ADDITIONS FOR PERIOD**

| 1983 Issue | Qualified Non-Paid | Qualified Paid | Total Qualified | Number Removed | Number Added | 1983 Issue | Qualified Non-Paid | Qualified Paid | Total Qualified | Number Removed | Number Added |
|---|---|---|---|---|---|---|---|---|---|---|---|
| January    1 15 | | | 69,691 69,649 | SEE | | April    1 15 | | | 70,174 70,150 | SEE | |
| February    1 15 | | | 69,630 69,624 | PARAGRAPH | | May    1 15 | | | 70,100 70,153 | PARAGRAPH | |
| March    1 15 | | | 69,771 70,188 | 11 | | June    1 15 | | | 70,154 71,692 | 11 | |
| | | | | | | **TOTALS** | | | | | |

publisher's records. Instead, large-scale samples of readers must be interviewed to determine what publications they have read. The leading services offering print-audience research results are Simmons Market Research Bureau (SMRB), Mediamark Research, Mendelsohn Media Research, and Scarborough Research. The research methods used in estimating audiences are a subject of considerable controversy. The two leading methods appear to give substantially different results. In the **through-the-book technique** (used by SMRB), respondents are shown skeletonized versions of magazines and asked if they have read that issue. In the **recent-reading technique,** pioneered by Mediamark, respondents are shown a list of magazine titles and asked for which titles they have read the current issue. Audience figures are generally available only for the larger consumer magazines and for major metropolitan newspapers.

*through-the-book technique*

*recent-reading technique*

PRINT AUDIENCE—PROFILE. Besides the total number of people reached by a print medium, the advertiser wants a description of the consumers who read and purchase a particular publication. The value of a medium to an advertiser depends not upon its ability to deliver sheer volume of readers, but on its ability to reach consumers who are prospects for the advertiser's product.

To determine if a publication is effective in reaching prospective buyers, the advertiser needs a description of the medium's circulation or audience. This description usually takes the form of a demographic

Comparison of circulation with audience for selected magazines.

EXHIBIT 12-4

| Publication | Circulation | Adult Audience |
|---|---|---|
| Better Homes and Gardens | 8,088,266 | 35,707,000 |
| Business Week | 849,688 | 5,299,000 |
| Family Circle | 7,400,984 | 29,804,000 |
| Field and Stream | 2,035,211 | 14,608,000 |
| Golf Digest | 1,053,456 | 3,370,000 |
| National Geographic | 10,613,599 | 30,488,000 |
| The New Yorker | 507,861 | 2,586,000 |
| Parents | 1,647,258 | 8,187,000 |
| Playboy | 4,501,324 | 19,394,000 |
| Readers Digest | 17,900,290 | 57,472,000 |
| Time | 4,464,228 | 23,440,000 |
| TV Guide | 17,003,698 | 48,785,000 |

Source: Circulation figures from *Consumer Magazine and Farm Publication Rates and Data* (Skokie, Ill.: Standard Rate and Data Service, July 27, 1983), and audience estimates from *Magazine Audiences* (New York: Mediamark Research, Inc., 1982).

profile. Information on the profile of a publication's circulation is provided, where available, by the publication itself, based on its subscription records and circulation research. Profile characteristics of a publication's audience are available from the audience research service's reports. A page from one of these very voluminous magazine audience reports is shown in Exhibit 12-5.

PRINT AUDIENCE—DISTRIBUTION. A third measurement of print audience used by the advertiser is the distribution of the audience or circulation. Here the concern is with the way the audience builds up or accumulates as successive issues of a print publication are used.

Suppose an advertiser has a media schedule consisting of one ad in one issue of a magazine. The number of readers of that issue would be measured by the average audience figure and the characteristics of that audience would be described by the medium's profile. But suppose then that a second ad is scheduled in the next issue of the same magazine. The readers of the second issue will be made up partly of consumers who have read the first issue, and partly of consumers who have not read the first issue. As more issues or additional magazines are added to the schedule, more new readers are added and many of the old readers are retained. Exhibit 12-6 shows the accumulation of readership over a magazine schedule. As successive issues of the same medium are added, the number of new readers added declines—it is subject to diminishing returns. **Reach** is the total of *reach* the number of people who read one or more of the issues included in a schedule, or who read them during some specified time interval. Reach is an important descriptive measure of media audience.

Using the same example, a second distribution measure can be illustrated. Assume that the schedule of ads included six successive issues of a magazine. Some people will have read all six of these issues; some will have read five; some, four; and so on. The average number of issues read (by those who read at least one) is called **frequency**—a second important *frequency* measure of audience distribution. An even more useful measure would be a full-frequency distribution—usually reported by quintile—showing number of issues read. This would indicate whether the medium tends to spread its exposures evenly or whether it tends to build up heavy frequency with a few readers and deliver exposures with little frequency to the rest.

A third measure of audience distribution is **duplication**, which is the *duplication* overlap in circulation or audience between two media or media vehicles. A **media vehicle** is a particular publication or program in a media class. For *media vehicle* example, *Business Week, Time,* and *Reader's Digest* are each vehicles in the magazine medium. Suppose that after scheduling an ad in magazine A, a second ad was scheduled in magazine B. Some of the people who had read magazine A would also read B. This would be duplication. In this example, the reach for the combined schedule would be the audience of A plus the audience of B minus the duplication. Whether duplication is good or bad depends upon whether the advertiser is trying to build reach or to increase

Magazine audience profile sample page: Education of Head of Household.                    **EXHIBIT 12-5**

| BASE: ADULTS | TOTAL U.S. '000 | GRADUATED COLLEGE | | | | ATTENDED COLLEGE | | | | GRADUATED HIGH SCHOOL | | | | DID NOT GRADUATE HIGH SCHOOL | | | |
|---|---|---|---|---|---|---|---|---|---|---|---|---|---|---|---|---|---|
| | | A '000 | B % DOWN | C % ACROSS | D INDEX | A '000 | B % DOWN | C % ACROSS | D INDEX | A '000 | B % DOWN | C % ACROSS | D INDEX | A '000 | B % DOWN | C % ACROSS | D INDEX |
| ALL ADULTS | 161718 | 30236 | 100.0 | 18.7 | 100 | 27470 | 100.0 | 17.0 | 100 | 57370 | 100.0 | 35.5 | 100 | 46642 | 100.0 | 28.8 | 100 |
| AIR GROUP ONE (GR) | 4501 | 2002 | 6.6 | 44.5 | 238 | 950 | 3.4 | 21.1 | 124 | 1095 | 1.9 | 24.3 | 68 | *457 | .9 | 10.2 | 35 |
| AMERICAN BABY | 3073 | 631 | 2.1 | 20.5 | 110 | 652 | 2.4 | 21.2 | 125 | 1215 | 2.1 | 39.5 | 111 | *576 | 1.2 | 18.7 | 65 |
| ARCHITECTURAL DIGEST | 2698 | 1472 | 4.9 | 54.6 | 292 | 684 | 2.5 | 25.4 | 149 | 449 | .8 | 16.6 | 47 | *93 | .2 | 3.4 | 12 |
| ATLANTIC MONTHLY | 1095 | 663 | 2.2 | 60.5 | 324 | *212 | .8 | 19.4 | 114 | *165 | .3 | 15.1 | 43 | *56 | .1 | 5.1 | 18 |
| BABY TALK | 2402 | 388 | 1.3 | 16.2 | 87 | 510 | 1.9 | 21.2 | 125 | 992 | 1.7 | 41.3 | 116 | *512 | 1.1 | 21.3 | 74 |
| BARRON'S | 981 | 597 | 2.0 | 60.9 | 326 | *154 | .6 | 15.7 | 92 | *130 | .2 | 13.3 | 37 | *101 | .2 | 10.3 | 36 |
| BETTER HOMES & GARDENS | 35707 | 8146 | 26.9 | 22.8 | 122 | 6956 | 25.3 | 19.5 | 115 | 13084 | 22.8 | 36.6 | 103 | 7522 | 16.1 | 21.1 | 73 |
| BON APPETIT | 4358 | 1721 | 5.7 | 39.5 | 211 | 965 | 3.5 | 22.1 | 130 | 1349 | 2.4 | 31.0 | 87 | *324 | .7 | 7.4 | 26 |
| BRIDE'S MAGAZINE | 4194 | 739 | 2.4 | 17.6 | 94 | 702 | 2.6 | 16.7 | 98 | 1863 | 3.2 | 44.4 | 125 | 890 | 1.9 | 21.2 | 74 |
| BUSINESS WEEK | 5299 | 2327 | 7.7 | 43.9 | 235 | 1345 | 4.9 | 25.4 | 149 | 1136 | 2.0 | 21.4 | 60 | 491 | 1.1 | 9.3 | 32 |
| CAR & DRIVER | 3647 | 801 | 2.6 | 22.0 | 118 | 923 | 3.4 | 25.3 | 149 | 1341 | 2.3 | 36.8 | 104 | 583 | 1.2 | 16.0 | 56 |
| CAR CRAFT | 2602 | *314 | 1.0 | 12.1 | 65 | *393 | 1.4 | 15.1 | 89 | 1165 | 2.0 | 44.8 | 126 | 730 | 1.6 | 28.1 | 98 |
| CBS SPEC. INTEREST GRP (GR) | 11341 | 2824 | 9.3 | 24.9 | 133 | 2638 | 9.7 | 23.3 | 137 | 3815 | 6.6 | 33.6 | 95 | 2071 | 4.4 | 18.3 | 64 |
| CHANGING TIMES | 5666 | 1853 | 6.1 | 32.7 | 175 | 1310 | 4.8 | 23.1 | 136 | 1583 | 2.8 | 27.9 | 79 | 918 | 2.0 | 16.2 | 56 |
| CHICAGO | 776 | 342 | 1.1 | 44.1 | 236 | *159 | .6 | 20.5 | 121 | *207 | .4 | 26.7 | 75 | *69 | .1 | 8.9 | 31 |
| COLONIAL HOMES | 2658 | 707 | 2.3 | 26.6 | 142 | 585 | 2.1 | 22.0 | 129 | 907 | 1.6 | 34.1 | 96 | *458 | 1.0 | 17.2 | 60 |
| CONDE NAST PACKAGE (GR) | 40388 | 9927 | 32.8 | 24.6 | 132 | 8879 | 32.3 | 22.0 | 129 | 14523 | 25.3 | 36.0 | 101 | 7060 | 15.2 | 17.5 | 61 |
| COSMOPOLITAN | 14051 | 3233 | 10.7 | 23.0 | 123 | 3471 | 12.6 | 24.7 | 145 | 5004 | 8.7 | 35.6 | 100 | 2342 | 5.0 | 16.7 | 58 |
| COUNTRY LIVING | 3344 | 784 | 2.6 | 23.4 | 125 | 745 | 2.7 | 22.3 | 131 | 1223 | 2.1 | 36.6 | 103 | 592 | 1.3 | 17.7 | 61 |
| CUISINE | 2811 | 1147 | 3.8 | 40.8 | 218 | 709 | 2.6 | 25.2 | 148 | 724 | 1.3 | 25.8 | 73 | *232 | .5 | 8.3 | 29 |
| CYCLE WORLD | 2860 | 338 | 1.1 | 11.8 | 63 | 595 | 2.2 | 20.8 | 122 | 1090 | 1.9 | 38.1 | 107 | 838 | 1.8 | 29.3 | 102 |
| DECORATING & CRAFT IDEAS | 5641 | 956 | 3.2 | 16.9 | 90 | 1064 | 3.9 | 18.9 | 111 | 2326 | 4.1 | 41.2 | 116 | 1296 | 2.8 | 23.0 | 80 |
| DISCOVER | 2460 | 894 | 3.0 | 36.3 | 194 | 708 | 2.6 | 28.8 | 169 | 579 | 1.0 | 23.5 | 66 | *278 | .6 | 11.3 | 39 |
| DUN'S BUSINESS MONTH | 739 | 384 | 1.3 | 52.0 | 278 | *151 | .5 | 20.4 | 120 | *130 | .2 | 17.6 | 50 | *75 | .2 | 10.1 | 35 |
| E/W DOMESTIC INFLIGHT (GR) | 5092 | 2430 | 8.1 | 47.7 | 255 | 1096 | 3.9 | 21.5 | 126 | 1079 | 1.9 | 21.2 | 60 | 486 | 1.1 | 9.5 | 33 |
| EBONY | 7917 | 1047 | 3.5 | 13.2 | 71 | 1183 | 4.3 | 14.9 | 88 | 3115 | 5.4 | 39.3 | 111 | 2571 | 5.5 | 32.5 | 113 |
| ESQUIRE | 4952 | 1245 | 4.1 | 25.1 | 134 | 1015 | 3.7 | 20.5 | 121 | 1624 | 2.8 | 32.8 | 92 | 1067 | 2.3 | 21.5 | 75 |
| ESSENCE | 2874 | 392 | 1.3 | 13.6 | 73 | 614 | 2.2 | 21.4 | 126 | 1019 | 1.8 | 35.5 | 100 | 849 | 1.8 | 29.5 | 102 |
| FAMILY CIRCLE | 29804 | 5934 | 19.6 | 19.9 | 106 | 5762 | 21.0 | 19.3 | 114 | 11618 | 20.3 | 39.0 | 110 | 6489 | 13.9 | 21.8 | 76 |
| FAMILY FOOD GARDEN | 1826 | *233 | .8 | 12.8 | 68 | *277 | 1.0 | 15.2 | 89 | 666 | 1.2 | 36.5 | 103 | 649 | 1.4 | 35.5 | 123 |
| FAMILY HANDYMAN | 5124 | 871 | 2.9 | 17.0 | 91 | 1093 | 4.0 | 21.3 | 125 | 2081 | 3.6 | 40.6 | 114 | 1080 | 2.3 | 21.1 | 73 |
| FAMILY WEEKLY | 23820 | 4233 | 14.0 | 17.8 | 95 | 3995 | 14.5 | 16.8 | 99 | 9602 | 16.7 | 40.3 | 114 | 5992 | 12.8 | 25.2 | 88 |
| FIELD & STREAM | 14608 | 1769 | 5.9 | 12.1 | 65 | 2574 | 9.4 | 17.6 | 104 | 6346 | 11.1 | 43.4 | 122 | 3918 | 8.4 | 26.8 | 93 |
| FOOD & WINE | 1530 | 458 | 1.5 | 29.9 | 160 | 322 | 1.2 | 21.0 | 124 | 500 | .9 | 32.7 | 92 | *250 | .5 | 16.3 | 57 |
| FORBES | 2785 | 1417 | 4.7 | 50.9 | 272 | 660 | 2.4 | 23.7 | 139 | 499 | .9 | 17.9 | 50 | *211 | .5 | 7.6 | 26 |
| FORTUNE | 3662 | 1668 | 5.5 | 45.5 | 243 | 1009 | 3.7 | 27.6 | 162 | 693 | 1.2 | 18.9 | 53 | *292 | .6 | 8.0 | 28 |
| FORUM | 3053 | 618 | 2.0 | 20.2 | 108 | 672 | 2.4 | 22.0 | 129 | 1333 | 2.3 | 43.7 | 123 | *431 | .9 | 14.1 | 49 |
| 4 WHEEL & OFF ROAD | 2716 | *299 | 1.0 | 11.0 | 59 | 443 | 1.6 | 16.3 | 96 | 1345 | 2.3 | 49.5 | 139 | 627 | 1.3 | 23.1 | 80 |
| GALLERY | 1656 | *203 | .7 | 12.3 | 66 | *303 | 1.1 | 18.3 | 108 | 716 | 1.2 | 43.2 | 122 | *434 | .9 | 26.2 | 91 |
| GAMES | 2134 | 516 | 1.7 | 24.2 | 129 | 559 | 2.0 | 26.2 | 154 | 699 | 1.2 | 32.8 | 92 | *359 | .8 | 16.8 | 58 |
| GLAMOUR | 9621 | 2321 | 7.7 | 24.1 | 129 | 2257 | 8.2 | 23.5 | 138 | 3384 | 5.9 | 35.2 | 99 | 1659 | 3.6 | 17.2 | 60 |
| GLOBE | 2540 | *205 | .7 | 8.1 | 43 | *421 | 1.5 | 16.6 | 98 | 849 | 1.5 | 33.4 | 94 | 1064 | 2.3 | 41.9 | 145 |
| GOLF DIGEST | 3370 | 1139 | 3.8 | 33.8 | 181 | 850 | 3.1 | 25.2 | 148 | 1056 | 1.8 | 31.3 | 88 | *324 | .7 | 9.6 | 33 |
| GOLF MAGAZINE | 2769 | 879 | 2.9 | 31.7 | 170 | 823 | 3.0 | 29.7 | 175 | 793 | 1.4 | 28.6 | 81 | *274 | .6 | 9.9 | 34 |
| GOOD HOUSEKEEPING | 31366 | 6766 | 22.4 | 21.6 | 116 | 6147 | 22.4 | 19.6 | 115 | 11830 | 20.6 | 37.7 | 106 | 6625 | 14.2 | 21.1 | 73 |
| GOURMET | 2650 | 1159 | 3.8 | 43.7 | 234 | 607 | 2.2 | 22.9 | 135 | 597 | 1.0 | 22.5 | 63 | *287 | .6 | 10.8 | 38 |
| GQ (GENTLEMEN'S QUARTERLY) | 3037 | 933 | 3.1 | 30.7 | 164 | 789 | 2.9 | 26.0 | 153 | 965 | 1.7 | 31.8 | 90 | *349 | .7 | 11.5 | 40 |
| GRIT | 2253 | *261 | .9 | 11.6 | 62 | *341 | 1.2 | 15.1 | 89 | 825 | 1.4 | 36.6 | 103 | 826 | 1.8 | 36.7 | 127 |
| GUNS & AMMO | 4741 | 653 | 2.2 | 13.8 | 74 | 940 | 3.4 | 19.8 | 116 | 2099 | 3.7 | 44.3 | 125 | 1048 | 2.2 | 22.1 | 77 |
| HARPER'S BAZAAR | 2960 | 941 | 3.1 | 31.8 | 170 | 613 | 2.2 | 20.7 | 122 | 1036 | 1.8 | 35.0 | 99 | *370 | .8 | 12.5 | 43 |
| HARPER'S MAGAZINE | 1421 | 647 | 2.1 | 45.5 | 243 | *246 | .9 | 17.3 | 102 | *317 | .6 | 22.3 | 63 | *211 | .5 | 14.8 | 51 |
| HEALTH | 3896 | 756 | 2.5 | 19.4 | 104 | 700 | 2.5 | 18.0 | 106 | 1449 | 2.5 | 37.2 | 105 | 991 | 2.1 | 25.4 | 88 |
| HEARST MEN'S MAGAZINES (GR) | 22379 | 3779 | 12.5 | 16.9 | 90 | 4497 | 16.3 | 20.1 | 118 | 9107 | 15.9 | 40.7 | 115 | 4999 | 10.7 | 22.3 | 77 |
| HOT ROD | 5838 | 555 | 1.8 | 9.5 | 51 | 1040 | 3.8 | 17.8 | 105 | 2495 | 4.3 | 42.7 | 120 | 1748 | 3.7 | 29.9 | 104 |
| HOUSE & GARDEN | 11470 | 2629 | 8.7 | 22.9 | 122 | 2285 | 8.3 | 19.9 | 117 | 4289 | 7.5 | 37.4 | 105 | 2266 | 4.9 | 19.8 | 69 |
| HOUSE BEAUTIFUL | 8572 | 2216 | 7.3 | 25.9 | 139 | 1801 | 6.6 | 21.0 | 124 | 2951 | 5.1 | 34.4 | 97 | 1604 | 3.4 | 18.7 | 65 |
| HUNTING | 2755 | *313 | 1.0 | 11.4 | 61 | 453 | 1.6 | 16.4 | 96 | 1005 | 1.8 | 36.5 | 103 | 985 | 2.1 | 35.8 | 124 |
| HUSTLER | 6169 | 478 | 1.6 | 7.7 | 41 | 1305 | 4.8 | 21.2 | 125 | 2614 | 4.6 | 42.4 | 119 | 1771 | 3.8 | 28.7 | 100 |
| INDUSTRY WEEK | 1406 | 375 | 1.2 | 26.7 | 143 | 307 | 1.1 | 21.8 | 128 | 445 | .8 | 31.7 | 89 | *279 | .6 | 19.8 | 69 |
| INSIDE SPORTS | 5282 | 1123 | 3.7 | 21.3 | 114 | 1028 | 3.7 | 19.5 | 115 | 2181 | 3.8 | 41.3 | 116 | 950 | 2.0 | 18.0 | 63 |
| JET | 6097 | 737 | 2.4 | 12.1 | 65 | 793 | 2.9 | 13.0 | 76 | 2422 | 4.2 | 39.7 | 112 | 2144 | 4.6 | 35.2 | 122 |
| LADIES' HOME JOURNAL | 22827 | 4965 | 16.4 | 21.8 | 117 | 4665 | 17.0 | 20.4 | 120 | 8451 | 14.7 | 37.0 | 104 | 4745 | 10.2 | 20.8 | 72 |
| LADIES' HOME J./REDBOOK (GR) | 39737 | 8268 | 27.3 | 20.8 | 111 | 8379 | 30.5 | 21.1 | 124 | 15090 | 26.3 | 38.0 | 107 | 7999 | 17.2 | 20.1 | 70 |
| LIFE | 15679 | 3538 | 11.7 | 22.6 | 121 | 3284 | 12.0 | 20.9 | 123 | 5415 | 9.4 | 34.5 | 97 | 3441 | 7.4 | 21.9 | 76 |
| MADEMOISELLE | 4887 | 1365 | 4.5 | 27.9 | 149 | 1158 | 4.2 | 23.7 | 139 | 1654 | 2.9 | 33.8 | 95 | 710 | 1.5 | 14.5 | 50 |
| MCCALLS | 23769 | 4395 | 14.5 | 18.5 | 99 | 4372 | 15.9 | 18.4 | 108 | 9644 | 16.8 | 40.6 | 114 | 5357 | 11.5 | 22.5 | 78 |
| MECHANIX ILLUSTRATED | 7555 | 1133 | 3.7 | 15.0 | 80 | 1788 | 6.5 | 23.7 | 139 | 3272 | 5.7 | 43.3 | 122 | 1361 | 2.9 | 18.0 | 63 |
| METRO SUNDAY COMICS | 28142 | 6668 | 22.1 | 23.7 | 127 | 5690 | 20.7 | 20.2 | 119 | 9815 | 17.1 | 34.9 | 98 | 5970 | 12.8 | 21.2 | 74 |
| MONEY | 6450 | 2391 | 7.9 | 37.1 | 198 | 1516 | 5.5 | 23.5 | 138 | 1793 | 3.1 | 27.8 | 78 | 749 | 1.6 | 11.6 | 40 |
| MOTHER EARTH NEWS | 4536 | 1074 | 3.6 | 23.7 | 127 | 1018 | 3.7 | 22.4 | 132 | 1798 | 3.1 | 39.6 | 112 | 646 | 1.4 | 14.2 | 49 |

Source: *Magazine Audiences 1* (New York: Mediamark Research, Inc., 1982), p. 8.

frequency—duplication builds frequency; adding a medium with low duplication builds reach.

The research firms that conduct audience studies develop data used in the calculation of audience distribution. These studies in print media are limited to major magazines and newspapers.

BROADCAST AUDIENCE—SIZE. Broadcast media, like print media, have two measures of size—a primary measure and an audience measure. The primary measure for a radio or television program is the number of homes whose sets are on and tuned to that program. This primary measure is usually expressed in terms of **rating points,** that is, the percentage of total television-equipped homes (or radio-equipped in the case of a radio rating) with sets tuned to a particular program. For example, if an episode of *The Today Show* scored a 10 rating, it would mean that 10 percent of all television homes had turned their sets to that episode.

*rating points*

The total number of television homes with television sets turned on at a particular time is called **homes using television** or the **HUT** rating. The

*homes using television (HUT)*

**EXHIBIT 12-6**      Increase in total new readers with successive issues.

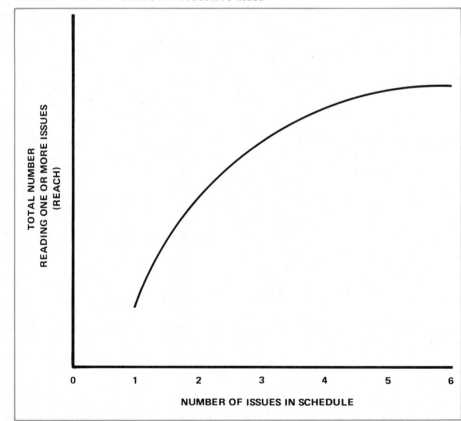

**share of audience** for a program is the percentage of homes using television tuned to that program. Using *The Today Show* example, if that program received a 10 rating and homes using television were 25 percent, then *Today's* share of audience would be 10 divided by 25 or 40 percent. Share of audience figures indicate how a program or a station is faring against its competition for that time period, while ratings indicate the percentage of total television homes delivered.

The audience measure in television and radio, like that in print media, is the total number of people exposed to a program. Total audience for a program is related to program rating in the following way: program rating × total television homes × average viewers per set = total program audience.

Broadcast ratings, audience estimates, and related measurements are purchased by advertisers from commercial rating services. The nature of these services is examined in more detail in Chapter 14.

BROADCAST AUDIENCE — PROFILE. Just as in the case of print media, the advertiser using broadcast media needs a description of those who are viewers or listeners. The broadcast rating services provide demographic information such as age, sex, geographic location, and income of the audience. Such information is available from rating services for network programs and for local programs in major markets.

BROADCAST AUDIENCE — DISTRIBUTION. As in the cast of print, the characteristics of audience accumulation over the course of a broadcast schedule is important. Two measures are commonly used. The first measure is **gross-rating points (GRP)** which is simply the sum of the rating points for individual announcements purchased. For example, if the schedule had three TV spots with ratings of 20, 25, and 18, the GRP would be 63 for the total schedule. It is important to note that the GRP figure includes duplication, although it is not possible from the numbers in the example to determine how much.

The gross rating point measure has, in recent years, been applied to print media audiences. For print media (including out-of-home) the gross rating points delivered by a schedule is the sum of the reach percentages for each advertisement scheduled. The distribution of the audience is extremely important in broadcast because of the tendency for broadcast exposures to build up in certain audience segments.

Media planners estimate reach, frequency, and audience distribution using audience data from rating services in complex models which, today, are usually computerized.

## Media Cost Measurement

As each medium is examined in detail in later chapters, the cost structure for that medium will be considered. There are, however, two cost measurement terms that will be explained here. The first is the unit of purchase for each of the media and the second is the measure of comparison between media vehicles.

MEDIA PURCHASE UNITS. Rates for most media are published and readily available to advertisers, but it is important to understand the units for which rates are quoted because they vary from medium to medium.

Starting first with print media, magazine rates are quoted in terms of pages or fractions of pages. The unit of sale, a page, does not change even though magazine page sizes vary widely, from pocket size to newspaper size.

*line*

The unit of purchase for newspapers is undergoing major change. In years past, newspaper rates were quoted by the agate line or, simply, by the line. A **line** is a standardized measure of space one column wide and 1/14th of an inch deep. Thus a 14-line newspaper ad would be one column wide and one inch deep. This unit of measure has caused substantial problems for large advertisers who use a number of different newspapers because column widths have not been standardized. As a result, an advertisement prepared for one newspaper would frequently not fit in the column width of other newspapers. To overcome this problem, the American Newspaper Publishers Association (ANPA) has established new standardized newspaper-space units called **standard advertising units** or **SAU's**.[1] The SAU program establishes a standard newspaper format of six 2-1/16-inch columns and a page width of 13 inches. The inch has been established as the standard unit of depth. Newspapers have been asked to adopt this format voluntarily on their rate cards and in SRDS listings. Using these new measures, the program defines 56 standard advertising units that each newspaper is asked to accept. Exhibit 12-7 shows these SAU's.

*standard advertising units (SAU)*

*showing*

Outdoor advertising and transit advertising rates are quoted in terms of **showings** or, the more modern term, *gross rating points (GRP)*. A 100 showing or 100 GRP package in an outdoor market includes enough posters to assure that daily circulation of traffic provides gross exposures equivalent to the market's population. Showings of 50 or 25 GRP's would provide proportionately less exposure.

In buying transit advertising, a full or 100 GRP showing means purchasing one advertisement in each vehicle. Half and quarter showings include proportionately less.

The unit of sale in direct mail is more difficult to define. In one sense, the purchase comparable to advertising space is the list of names to which the mail is directed. The cost of direct mail lists is quoted on a cost-per-thousand-names basis.

Radio and television advertisers can purchase either a program within which to air their commercials or they can purchase *spots*, which are simply

---

[1]"Expanded SAU™ Newspaper Advertising Standards," prepared by the ANPA-NAB Working Committee on Advertising Standards; August 5, 1983.

Standard advertising units for newspapers.                                                 **EXHIBIT 12-7**

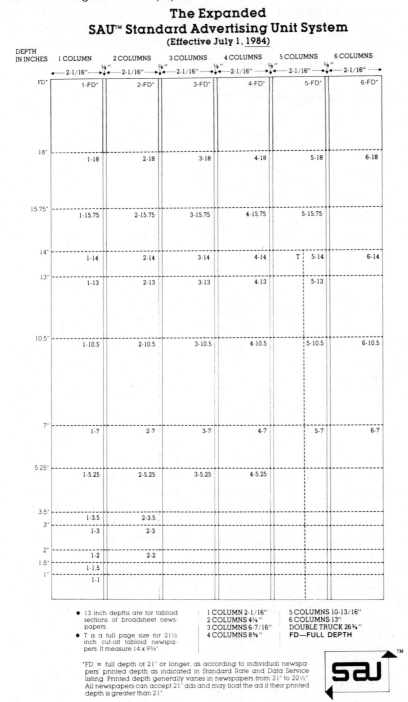

# The Expanded
## SAU™ Standard Advertising Unit System
(Effective July 1, 1984)

- 13 inch depths are for tabloid sections of broadsheet newspapers.
- T is a full page size for 21½ inch cut-off tabloid newspapers. It measure 14 x 9⅜"

'FD = full depth of 21" or longer, as according to individual newspapers' printed depth as indicated in Standard Rate and Data Service listing. Printed depth generally varies in newspapers from 21" to 22½". All newspapers can accept 21" ads and may float the ad if their printed depth is greater than 21"

1 COLUMN 2-1/16"
2 COLUMNS 4¼"
3 COLUMNS 6-7/16"
4 COLUMNS 8¾"

5 COLUMNS 10-13/16"
6 COLUMNS 13"
DOUBLE TRUCK 26¾"
FD—FULL DEPTH

Source:  "Expanded SAU™ Newspaper Advertising Standards," prepared by the ANPA-NAB Working Committee on Advertising Standards; August 5, 1983.

positions between or within programs in which commercials can be aired. Program rates are quoted in terms of hours and fractions of hours. Spots are also sold in varying lengths. The most frequently sold lengths are minutes, 30 seconds, 20 seconds, and 10-second ID's (identifications). As shown in Exhibit 12-8, 30-second spots have become dominant.

EXHIBIT 12-8    Length of television announcements.

| Announcement Length | 1965 | 1970 | Non-Network 1975 | 1980 | 1983 |
|---|---|---|---|---|---|
| 10 seconds | 16% | 12% | 9% | 8% | 6% |
| 20 seconds | 14 | 5 | 1 | — | — |
| 30 seconds | 1 | 48 | 79 | 85 | 88 |
| 45 seconds | — | — | — | — | 1 |
| 60's piggybacked | 5 | 9 | 1 | — | — |
| 60 sec. or more | 64 | 26 | 10 | 7 | 5 |
| | 100% | 100% | 100% | 100% | 100% |

| Announcement Length | 1965 | 1970 | Network 1975 | 1980 | 1983 |
|---|---|---|---|---|---|
| 10 second | —% | —% | —% | 1% | 1% |
| 20 seconds | — | — | — | — | — |
| 30 seconds | — | 25 | 79 | 85 | 87 |
| 60's piggybacked | 23 | 47 | 15 | 11 | 9 |
| 60 sec. or more | 77 | 27 | 6 | 2 | 2 |
| | 100% | 100% | 100% | 100% | 100% |

Source: Broadcast Advertisers Reports, Inc., as compiled in *TV Basics 27* (New York: Television Bureau of Advertising, 1984).

The media costs discussed here do not, of course, represent all of the cost of advertising in a particular medium. In addition, there are advertising production costs and sometimes program charges. Production costs include the cost of preparing the ad or commercial to be used in the medium. Program charges (cost of producing the entertainment or editorial material) are charged to the advertiser in some instances.

MEDIA COST COMPARISONS. In the course of preparing a media program, there will be frequent occasions when the advertiser will wish to make cost comparisons. There are two types of comparisons that will frequently need to be made—those among various media (magazines vs. newspapers) and those among vehicles within a medium (*TV Guide* vs. *Reader's Digest*).

*Vehicle Cost Comparison.* The need for comparison of costs among media vehicles arises after the advertiser has decided which medium to use and wishes to choose the most efficient vehicle in that medium. The problem is to find a fair basis for comparison since each vehicle not only costs a different amount, but also reaches a different number of people. The general approach to achieving comparability is to compare the ratio of cost to number of people reached.

The cost ratio used for most media — broadcast, magazines, outdoor, direct mail — is the **cost per thousand** which is computed as follows:

*cost per thousand*

$$\text{cost per thousand} = \frac{\text{cost of purchase unit} \times 1{,}000}{\text{no. of prospects reached}}$$

The major exception to this approach is the use in newspaper comparison of the **milline rate** which is computed as follows:

*milline rate*

$$\text{milline rate} = \frac{\text{cost of one line} \times 1{,}000{,}000}{\text{no. of prospects reached}}$$

As the new standard advertising units are adopted by newspapers, use of this measure will decline.

The purchase unit used in computing the cost per thousand can either be the standard purchase unit (for example, the page rate in a magazine) or the unit that is actually going to be purchased. For comparative purposes it makes no difference as long as the same unit is used for each vehicle being compared. Note that the denominator in the formula should be neither circulation nor audience, but the number of prospects reached. The value of a medium lies not in how many people see or hear it, but in its ability to deliver messages to those particular people who in terms of their needs have actually been designated as prospects for the product being advertised.

*Comparison Among Media.* The problem of cost comparison among media is much more difficult than that among media vehicles. The cost-per-thousand approach used in vehicle comparisons cannot validly be used in comparing different media because there is no acceptable way to equate the purchase units of different media. For example, to compare the cost per thousand of *McCall's* magazine using the page rate with the cost per thousand of *CBS Evening News* using the one-minute rate would presume that the exposure value of a *McCall's* magazine page was equal to a minute of television. No objective basis exists for such an assumption.

There is no accepted basis for making cost comparisons among the different media, and experts in the field generally avoid the practice. This does not mean that comparisons do not have to be made among media, but only that the process is more complex than a simple cost ratio. This process will be considered further in the next section.

## Framework for Media Selection

With some of the techniques and terminology of media measurement explained, consideration turns now to the central task, the preparation of a media program. The objective of the media selection program is relatively easy to state and understand, although more complex to accomplish. Recall the current status of the advertising plan that is being described. A positioning statement has been prepared that defines, among other things, the group of prospects to whom the advertising is to be directed. In addition a budget has been prepared that sets a limit on the amount that can be spent for media. These, together with any of the other objectives that have media implications are the "givens" with which the media plan begins.

Another important input to the media plan is the creative work being undertaken. It frequently occurs that as creative work proceeds, a need for certain media capabilities arises, such as a need for color, a need for illustration, or a need to demonstrate the product.

Given these requirements—a defined target prospect group, a budget, creative requirements, and perhaps other problem-oriented objectives—what is the task of the media program? It seeks to determine the medium or combination of media that will most efficiently reach the defined prospect target group while still meeting the budget constraint, the creative requirement, and other objectives.

## Quantitative Allocation Approach to Media Selection

In Chapter 11 a general approach to allocating the media budget among competing ends was described. The general approach was to allocate the available resources between the alternatives so that the marginal contribution from each alternative was equal. Media selection appears on the surface to be a suitable application for this principle. The available resources are defined by the advertising budget and the alternatives are the available media and the available media vehicles.

This quantitative approach is helpful as a means of keeping the media selection problem in perspective, but an attempt to use this approach in building a media program runs into some practical difficulties. The most obvious difficulty is that the number of media alternatives is almost beyond calculation. There are not only a substantial number of different media to choose from but within each medium there is an almost infinite variety of vehicles—different television programs, different magazines, different newspapers, plus different page sizes, time units, and the like.

The second obstacle facing a pure application of the quantitative allocation approach is the lack of adequate measurement of the sales effectiveness of each medium. Because it is difficult to evaluate each medium or media combination in terms of sales effectiveness, advertisers usually set a series of other requirements that the media plan must meet. These requirements are ones that are thought to be necessary prerequisites to profitable sales. Media alternatives are then evaluated in terms of their ability to meet these requirements. Thus a practical media selection procedure must permit evaluation of media alternatives in terms of multiple media requirements.

## A Practical Media Selection Approach— The Four-Step Media Program

The suggested practical approach steps back from the quantitative approach, which would select an optimum program, to a more manageable process that expects a satisfactory solution rather than an optimum one. This approach to building the media program is a sequential process that attempts to simplify the problem by breaking it into a series of more manageable steps. The first step is to define the requirements of the media program. With this done, the second step is to select the medium or combination of media that best fit the requirements. The third step is to select the vehicle or vehicles within the chosen medium. The fourth step is to schedule insertions within the vehicle and determine size or time length of the message. Each step in the media-building program will be examined in more detail.

STEP ONE: DEFINE MEDIA REQUIREMENTS. Media requirements are derived from the positioning and advertising objectives. The media requirements define what the media program must contribute if the positioning and objectives are to be realized. Media requirements vary from product to product because each one has a unique positioning and set of objectives. However, there are common classes of requirements that can be suggested.

*Target Audience.* If the positioning is to be realized, the product's advertising must be directed not just to any consumer, but to that segment of consumers that represents the best prospects for the product. The media program, in other words, must selectively direct its messages to prime prospects. The consumers who have been selected as prime prospects are specified in the positioning and a description of their characteristics is available from the consumer profile study. Reaching this group of prospects becomes the first media requirement.

*Distribution of Exposures.* A second important audience requirement defines how messages should be distributed among prospects. This requirement is usually expressed in terms of reach and frequency. The advertiser may choose to distribute the messages widely so that a great many prospects receive at least one message. This would be maximizing reach. Or the advertiser might choose to concentrate on a smaller group of prospects in order to deliver more messages to them. This would mean sacrificing reach in order to gain frequency.

Reach and frequency are competing ends. Generally an increase in reach results in decreased frequency and vice versa. If all prospects were of equal value, most advertisers would strive to reach all of them once (that is, to maximize reach) before building frequency. This reflects the belief that the individual sales response function increases at a decreasing rate. That is, the second exposure increases sales, but not as much as the first. Hence, sales are maximized by first delivering one exposure to each prospect before repeat exposures are begun.

There are, however, some media experts who give higher priority, at least initially, to frequency. Some feel that there is a threshold level of exposures below which no effective communication takes place. If this is the case, reach would be limited to a small group and expanded only after the threshold limit of frequency was delivered to that initial target group. Unfortunately, there is little convincing evidence to either prove or disprove the existence of a communications threshold.

There are other instances that more clearly call for an emphasis on frequency. In many cases all prospects are not regarded as being equal in value. For example, the heavy users within the total prospect group probably represent above-average sales potential. In such a case, a requirement may be set to build frequency of exposure with such groups. Exposure frequency is also considered important for frequently purchased and frequently used-up products and in product categories in which competitive products are frequently advertised.[2] In each case the hope is to have a recent exposure before the product is purchased. In addition, new products, products with complex messages, and products with marginal uniqueness need greater frequency.

*Creative Requirements.* The advertising message not only has an audience target but also a set of creative requirements. Some messages lend themselves to words alone, while others need pictures. Some need color, some don't. Some advertisements need the support of a prestigious medium while others need an interrupting and dominating medium. Airborne Express, in Exhibit 12-9, takes full advantage of television's ability to capture audience attention with a humorously entertaining presentation of a problem solved by its express package service.

As work progresses on the creative materials for the product, the media attributes that would improve creative effectiveness will become apparent and can be expressed as creative requirements of the media program. These creative requirements are no less important than the audience requirements and are particularly influential in step two, selecting the medium.

*Budget Constraints.* The size of the media budget limits the total amount of media that can be purchased. Within this constraint the media program attempts to fulfill its audience requirements with the greatest cost efficiency. This is usually expressed and measured in terms of cost-per-thousand prospects.

The size of the media budget also imposes a limitation on which medium is selected. Media have what might be termed a minimum cost of entry — the minimum expenditure required to enter the medium. This cost of entry covers the minimum space, time, or schedule that can be purchased plus the cost of creative materials for that medium. Many small advertisers will find that the minimum cost of entry rules out some media

---

[2]Joseph W. Ostrow, "What Level Frequency?" *Advertising Age* (November 9, 1981), pp. S–4, S–6, S–8.

A commercial for a low inherent-interest product using the interruptive quality of television.

**EXHIBIT 12-9**

MAN: Hello. Where's my package? My job depends on it.

WOMAN: (SPEAKING QUICKLY) What is the airbill number that it was sent on? When did you send that out? It should be at that particular company that you sent to. I can get that information confirmed if you like.

I'll have a trace agent get the courier delivery . . . (CONTINUES UNDER)

ANNCR: (VO) In the air express business fast talking is funny for commercials, but sad in real life.

At Airborne we don't talk fast. We move fast.

So fast that we make most of our deliveries before 10:30 a.m.

No wonder more people

are switching to Airborne than ever before.

As close as you can come to 100% on time delivery.

So watch out Federal. Here comes Airborne.

Courtesy: Airborne ®

from consideration. The media selection process must work within this constraint.

*Other Requirements.* There will be other media program requirements that will be of greater or lesser importance depending upon the product, its positioning and objectives. Two that might be mentioned are creative materials production requirements and media merchandising requirements. Both the cost and the time required to produce creative materials are of particular importance in the case of some products. For example, a retail food store running different promotional ads each day needs a medium for which ads can be produced quickly and at moderate expense.

Some products require selection of a medium or media vehicle not primarily because of the audience delivered by the medium, but because of its merchandising value, especially with trade intermediaries. Sometimes companies wish to identify with the local community in order to take advantage of preference that some customers feel for a hometown source of products. Advertising in the local newspaper helps to create this local identity. An advertiser wishing a product to appear important might advertise in *Time*. Other advertisers may select *Good Housekeeping,* hoping to reap the benefits of association with the familiar Good Housekeeping Seal.

STEP TWO: SELECT THE MEDIUM. With the requirements of the media program defined, the next step in the sequence is to select the medium or combination of media to be included in the program. The number of alternatives to be considered has been sharply narrowed and made manageable by reserving for later consideration the question of vehicles within the media and size/timing alternatives.

*The Matching Process.* The process of selecting the medium is one of matching the media requirements from step one with the characteristics of the media. In order to carry out this matching process, the characteristics of each eligible medium must be thoroughly understood. Briefly, these characteristics are:

1. What audience does the medium select?
2. How are exposures distributed among its audience?
3. What are the creative characteristics of the medium?
4. What is the minimum cost of entering the medium?
5. What are the production requirements of the medium?
6. What is the merchandising value of the medium?

The next three chapters, 13–15, will be devoted to a study of the characteristics of the major media as an aid to the matching and selecting process.

*Adding Additional Media.* Many media schedules contain more than one medium. One reason sometimes cited is that one medium might theoretically become oversaturated if all the budget were spent in that medium. If only a single medium were used, the total sales response to dollars added to that medium would increase, but at a diminishing rate. Hence at some point it would pay to shift to a second medium even though it was second choice in terms of its characteristics.

However, it seems unlikely in practice that an advertiser would use a medium such as television, for example, to such an extent that saturation would occur. The advertiser can spread advertisements over a variety of programs, stations, times of day, and weeks of the year. As a result, diminishing returns for such a medium would occur only at very high budget levels.

A second and more supportable reason for adding additional media concerns the distribution of exposures. Any medium, as its use is increased, tends to build up exposures with certain groups, while other groups receive infrequent exposure. If the lightly exposed group represents prospective consumers, it may be desirable to add a second medium that directs heavier exposures to this group not well covered by the first medium. The effect is to smooth the distribution of exposures.

Exhibit 12-10 compares audience concentration tendencies by medium. Notice, for example, how the concentration characteristics of television tend to be the opposite of those of magazines. As a result, media buyers will sometimes supplement a television advertising schedule with a magazine advertising schedule. This tends to smooth the distribution of frequency since consumer magazines tend to be most heavily read by light television viewers.

Audience concentration by medium (100 = average)                                    **EXHIBIT 12-10**

| Total Adults | % Population | Total Television Heaviest 20% | Total Television Lightest 20% | Total Radio Heaviest 20% | Total Radio Lightest 20% | Magazines Heaviest 20% | Magazines Lightest 20% | Weekday Newspapers Heaviest 33% | Weekday Newspapers Lightest 33% |
|---|---|---|---|---|---|---|---|---|---|
| **Age** | | | | | | | | | |
| 18-24 | 17.9 | 79 | 116 | 136 | 52 | 136 | 69 | 73 | 129 |
| 25-34 | 23.1 | 71 | 118 | 117 | 69 | 132 | 70 | 79 | 105 |
| 35-54 | 30.3 | 82 | 111 | 102 | 88 | 98 | 92 | 114 | 79 |
| 55+ | 28.7 | 155 | 64 | 62 | 168 | 54 | 152 | 119 | 100 |
| **Education** | | | | | | | | | |
| Any College | 32.2 | 64 | 123 | 100 | 83 | 149 | 47 | 136 | 63 |
| High School Graduate | 38.4 | 96 | 94 | 108 | 81 | 99 | 83 | 98 | 91 |
| Other | 29.4 | 145 | 84 | 89 | 144 | 48 | 180 | 64 | 153 |
| **Household Income** | | | | | | | | | |
| $35,000+ | 17.5 | 56 | 127 | 93 | 85 | 144 | 45 | 157 | 44 |
| $25,000-$34,999 | 19.7 | 66 | 123 | 101 | 85 | 110 | 67 | 116 | 62 |
| $15,000-$24,999 | 25.1 | 93 | 98 | 115 | 78 | 107 | 90 | 98 | 93 |
| $10,000-$14,999 | 19.6 | 131 | 82 | 100 | 110 | 77 | 140 | 77 | 127 |
| Under $10,000 | 18.1 | 154 | 70 | 84 | 151 | 63 | 160 | 56 | 175 |

Source: *O & M Pocket Guide to Media*, 6th ed. (New York: Ogilvy & Mather, 1982), pp. 10–11.

Sometimes the desire is not to smooth the distribution of exposures but rather to supplement exposures to particular consumers. Again, a second medium can achieve this. For example, a department store may achieve general coverage of prospects by use of newspapers and then add direct mail to its charge customers to build frequency with this heavy purchaser group.

STEP THREE: SELECT THE VEHICLE. With a decision made as to what medium is to be used, the next step in the sequence is to select the vehicles to be used.

*The Matching Process.* The selection process for vehicles is much the same as the one followed for the selection of a medium. The list of media requirements again serves as the criterion against which the characteristics of the particular vehicles (particular magazines or particular television programs, for example) must be matched.

*Adding Additional Vehicles.* In all but the smallest media programs, it is likely that more than one vehicle will be used for each medium. Saturation of a single vehicle is reached much sooner than in the case of an entire medium. For example, severely diminished returns would seem to occur if more than one page (or group of pages if the ad requires more than one page) a month were scheduled in a monthly magazine or more than one commercial used in a half-hour television program.

In addition, it is frequently necessary to use combinations of vehicles to achieve coverage of target prospects. In a city with two major morning newspapers, for example, if would be essential to use both papers if the target prospects included most people in the city since most people regularly read one, but not both, of their city's newspapers.

And, finally, multiple vehicles are frequently used because of their effect on the distribution of exposures over the course of a schedule. As in the case of multiple media, the advertiser may select additional vehicles to make the distribution of frequency more even or select additional vehicles that build up frequency in some segment. For example, many television advertisers, rather than buy a fixed commercial position each week in the same program, buy a so-called **scatter plan** that places their commercials in different programs or positions each week. This plan is designed to spread frequency more evenly over the total audience. By contrast, an advertiser desiring to reach all adults but with emphasis on women might supplement evening television positions with daytime television vehicles that deliver a heavy female audience.

STEP FOUR: DETERMINE SIZE/TIMING. With media and media vehicles selected, the size (or time length for broadcast ads) of the advertisements must be determined and the manner of scheduling the ads must be decided.

*scatter plan*

*Size and Time Length.* Some thinking concerning ad size or length may well take place simultaneously with vehicle selection since the number of vehicles required may vary with the size and, hence, number of ads. Assuming the budget imposes a constraint on total expenditure, the advertiser can trade between more, smaller (shorter) ads and fewer, larger (longer) ads. There is consistent research evidence indicating that, in general, larger ads and longer ads are more effective than smaller or shorter ones, but the increase in effectiveness is not proportional to the increase in size or time length. For example, studies of print ad readership by Starch INRA Hooper, Inc., consistently show that increases in ad size result in proportionately smaller increases in readership. And, in spite of the discount given for larger space units and longer time units, it still appears that, on the average, the increase in effectiveness is not proportional to the increase in cost. In other words, ad size/length response appears to be subject to diminishing returns. A full-page ad, for example, is more effective than a half-page ad, but not twice as effective.

If the advertiser had data on the change in sales response to different sized ads for a particular product and its particular creative approach, a decision could be made on ad size using the marginal allocation approach. Since most advertisers lack this data, the decision must be made judgmentally. Perhaps the best approach to this decision is to prepare a number of alternative schedules, each one meeting the budget constraint and showing the effect of different ad sizes or time lengths. Judgments of experienced advertisers can then be gathered on each alternative.

One consideration that will influence the size/length decision is the impact that different sizes and lengths have on the creative product. Some advertisements have a long message to communicate, others require complex forms of presentation. The effectiveness of such ads might be greatly diminished if very short time lengths or small sizes were utilized.

The decision of whether to use color or black-and-white ads can be similarly made. Color ads are generally more effective than black-and-white ads, but of course they cost more. Creative requirements are particularly important in the color decision. Some products—such as foods, clothing, cosmetics—virtually require color ads if the product is to be adequately presented. For other product advertisements, color serves primarily as an attention-getting device. An example would be a red headline for a department store sale advertisement.

*Schedule Timing.* There are two media timing decisions that the advertiser must make—the schedule duration (start and stop dates) and the distribution of messages over the duration of the schedule.

Some products are advertised continuously and thus the schedule duration is the same as the planning period. Such products are ones that are sold continuously over the entire year. There are, however, some products that are sold only seasonally. Cold remedies, suntan lotions, and football tickets are examples. Advertising for such products should be concentrated in the period when consumers feel the need for the product. This is usually adequately defined by the index of seasonal sales potential. The advertising schedule, however, should usually lead the sales period since there is a lag between the appearance of an advertisement and its sales effect.

With the start and stop dates of the advertising determined, the scheduling of messages between those dates must be decided. Ads may be spread smoothly over the time schedule or in waves — with heavy advertising followed by light or no advertising. Advertisers frequently schedule their advertising in waves when they feel that regular scheduling would *flighting or pulsing*  spread messages too thinly to be effective. The practice of **flighting** or **pulsing** is frequently used when advertisers feel that the advertising budget level is so low that messages would be "lost" if spread evenly. One media expert states: "Of all the reasons we use flighting, the most important is that it helps crack through the general noise level — not just the competitive ad level, but the din from all advertising."[3]

Pulsing may be desirable even if the idea of the threshold level of effectiveness discussed earlier is not accepted. It must be remembered that the term "frequency" that is being discussed here is frequency of exposure to a media vehicle, not exposure to an advertisement.[4] It may require several exposures to a media vehicle before all or most of the target audience sees a particular advertisement, especially in the case of vehicles that are cluttered with many ads. Anheuser-Busch reported that pulsing patterns were found to yield "slightly better" results than normal patterns in test markets.[5]

## Incorporating the Media Program into the Advertising Plan

The suggested approach to building a media program serves as an outline for the media program section of the advertising plan. The media requirements, as well as the reasoning that led to the selection of the final media schedule, should be stated in full.

The plan should contain detailed media schedules in tabular form showing the purchase to be made in each medium and media vehicle, time lengths or page sizes, insertion dates and times, and anticipated costs. These become working guides to media specialists who place media orders and also provide guides to financial officers for cash planning. When media goals such as projected reach, frequency, and cost efficiency have been established, they should be stated in the advertising plan so

---

[3]"Admen See Pulsing as Way to Beat Soaring TV Time Costs," *Advertising Age* (July 4, 1977), p. 27.
[4]See Jack Z. Sissors and Jim Surmanek, *Advertising Media Planning*, 2d ed. (Chicago: Crain Books, 1982), pp. 154 ff.
[5]Russell L. Ackoff and James R. Emhoff, "Advertising Research at Anheuser-Busch, Inc.," *Sloan Management Review* (Winter, 1975), pp. 10–11.

as to provide benchmarks against which actual performance can be compared. Exhibit 12-11 suggests an outline for the media section of the advertising plan.

## The Role of the Computer in Media Selection

During the late 1960s many people predicted that computer models would come to dominate media selection. Having reviewed the media selection process, it should be clear why advertisers were interested in substituting computer models for individual media planners' judgments. Media selection is an extraordinarily complex problem with thousands of alternatives that might be evaluated. Data available for evaluating alternatives is very extensive, but it is largely quantifiable. Utilizing such quantitative data to choose from among many complex alternatives appears to call for the computational power of the modern computer.

In response to this problem, a number of media selection models were developed that reduced the advertiser's media requirements and the characteristics of alternative media to mathematical terms. Computational routines were carried out by the computer to match advertiser requirements with media alternatives, producing a suggested media program.

Large advertising agencies seized upon the apparent opportunities in

Outline of a typical media plan.                                                    **EXHIBIT 12-11**

---

I. **Media Requirements**

    A. Target audience (demographic description)
    B. Audience distribution (reach and frequency)
    C. Creative requirements
    D. Budget limits and allocations
    E. Other

II. **Selection of Media**

    A. Definition of media alternatives
    B. Matching media alternatives with media requirements
    C. Selection of primary, additional media

III. **Selection of Media Vehicles**

    A. Definition of media vehicle alternatives
    B. Matching of media vehicles with media requirements
    C. Selection of media vehicles

IV. **Definition of Media Schedules**

    A. Specification of time and size/length schedule
    B. Definition of media targets—rating/audience levels; reach and frequency
    C. Dollar budget summary of media plan

computerized media selection by developing their own media models and investing in computer installations. The results were disappointing and by the late 1970s, media selection models were not in widespread use and agencies were giving up their in-house computers.[6]

A study by Evelyn Conrad Associates revealed several reasons for agency disaffection:

1. Most important, agencies found that running the exhaustively detailed optimization models was highly expensive with little savings to offset the expense.
2. Neither agency planners nor advertisers were convinced that the computer model results were of higher quality than those produced through the efforts of agency media planners.
3. Data needed to run the models was not available or was not of adequate quality.[7]

Despite the disappointment with media selection models, computer usage for media planning and implementation is making a comeback, but usage has changed. Fewer agencies own a computer. Instead, more are using computer service bureaus that sell computer time and programs, thus spreading the investment cost over more uses.[8] In place of intricate models that generate media plans, computers are now used more often as information services to help evaluate and implement media programs developed by media planners. Among the functions provided by current computerized media systems are these:

1. Reach and frequency estimates are generated by simulating the exposure of the proposed media program to a model of computer viewing, reading, or listening patterns stored in the computer.
2. Media estimates are prepared for approved media programs together with purchase and insertion orders to be sent to the media.
3. Client billing is prepared and accounts receivable accounting maintained.
4. Analyses of media effectiveness are prepared by comparing media buying objectives with actual ratings or audience figures that have been stored in the computer's memory.

It can be seen from this list that the current use of the computer in media selection focuses on providing information to aid the media planner and on taking over many of the previously labor-intensive media accounting functions.

---

[6]The history of media model development is reviewed in Roger J. Calantone and Ulrike de Brentani-Todorovic, "The Maturation of the Science of Media Selection," *Journal of the Academy of Marketing Science* (Fall, 1981), pp. 490–524.

[7]Evelyn Conrad's study is reported in "Should an Agency Own One?" *Media Decisions* (November, 1978), pp. 66–67, 168–170.

[8]*Ibid.*, pp. 66–67.

Media can be classified in several ways, but the most important classification is in terms of the characteristics of the audience of the medium. Selection of media requires that the advertiser be able to measure both media audiences and media costs. Media audiences are measured in terms of their size, in terms of their profile or demographic characteristics, and in terms of the distribution of exposures among their members. The cost or rate for a medium is expressed in terms of a standard purchase unit such as line rates for newspapers, page rates for magazines, and spot rates for broadcast media. Cost comparisons between media vehicles utilize a ratio of cost to audience—the milline rate for newspaper comparisons and cost per thousand for most other media.

Media selection is a form of allocation problem, but so complex that it requires a step-by-step approach that yields a satisfactory rather than optimum result. A recommended four-step media program begins with a definition of media requirements specifying the segment to be reached, the desired distribution of exposures, creative requirements of the media, and the budget constraint. The second step is to select the medium to be used by matching available media with the media requirement. The third step is to select vehicles within the selected medium by again using the media requirements as selection criteria. The final step is to specify the size or time length of the advertisements and the timing of their appearance. Currently, computers are used in media selection to provide information to the media planner and to provide accounting assistance.

| | |
|---|---|
| Advertising media | Media vehicle |
| Circulation | Rating points |
| Average paid circulation | Homes using television (HUT) |
| Controlled or non-paid circulation publication | Share of audience |
| Audience | Gross-rating points (GRP) |
| Pass-along circulation or secondary audience | Line |
| Through-the-book technique | Standard advertising units (SAU) |
| Recent-reading technique | Showing |
| Reach | Cost per thousand |
| Frequency | Milline rate |
| Duplication | Scatter plan |
| | Flighting or pulsing |

1. The audience shown in Exhibit 12-4 for *Field and Stream* is seven times its circulation while the audience for *TV Guide* is less than three times its circulation. Why is the "pass along" rate so much lower for *TV Guide*?

2. An advertiser has prepared a media schedule utilizing two monthly magazines, with one insertion per month in each magazine over the four-month period of the advertising effort. The first magazine has a circulation of 100,000 and the second magazine has a circulation of 50,000. Half of the circulation of the second magazine duplicates readers of the first magazine. Assume for the four-month period that there is no turnover in subscribers.

   a. What would be the reach of the schedule over the four-month period?
   b. What would be the average frequency with which readers would be exposed to an advertisement for the product?

3. Suppose that the advertiser in question 2 had the alternative of substituting a third magazine for the second one described above. Magazine three has a circulation of 35,000 and 20 percent duplication with the first magazine.

   a. If the advertiser wishes to maximize frequency, should magazine three be substituted for magazine two?
   b. If the advertiser wishes to maximize reach, should magazine three be substituted for magazine two?

4. City T has 200,000 homes, 95 percent of which are equipped with television sets. During one particular time period, half of the television-equipped homes had their sets turned on. Of these, 40 percent were tuned to station A and the remainder to station B, the only other station received in the market.

   a. What was the HUT rating for this time period?
   b. What was station B's rating?
   c. What was station B's share of audience?

5. During a recent period the adult audience CPM for a four-color magazine page in four magazines was as follows:

   | | |
   |---|---|
   | *Readers Digest* | $2.44 |
   | *Prevention* | 4.69 |
   | *BusinessWeek* | 6.67 |
   | *Yachting* | 8.82 |

   a. What accounts for the difference in CPM's?
   b. Which magazine is the most efficient?

6. An advertiser who is selling a product whose purchase is specified by architects is attempting to decide which of two magazines to include in the media schedule. Magazine S has circulation of 100,000 of which two thirds are architects and one third are builders and contractors. Magazine T has circulation of 200,000, half of which goes to architects and the other half to builders and contractors. Magazine S costs $1,000 for an advertising page while magazine T charges $1,800 per page. Which magazine represents that most efficient purchase for this advertiser?

7. Listed below are a number of media requirements that might be found in media plans. For each one, suggest a medium that might be chosen to fulfill the requirement.

   a. Provide an opportunity to demonstrate how the product works.
   b. Provide an opportunity to use high quality, full color reproduction.
   c. Make it possible to time advertisements to coincide with relevant news stories.
   d. Direct advertising to mothers of school-aged children.
   e. Provide national coverage at a low total cost.

8. What media vehicles might be selected to satisfy each of the following media requirements?

   a. Direct advertising messages to top managers of large companies.
   b. Provide heavy frequency among teenagers.
   c. Provide coverage among upper-income New Yorkers.
   d. Utilize a medium that will enhance the product's standing among parents.

9. Using the audience data presented in Exhibit 12-5, answer the following questions:

   a. Which magazine has the largest total audience?
   b. Which magazine has the largest number of readers that are college graduates?
   c. Which magazine has the highest proportion of its readers that are college graduates?

10. Using the audience data shown in Exhibit 12-10, indicate what second medium you would select under the following circumstances:

| Target Audience | First Medium | Second Medium |
|---|---|---|
| 18–24 year olds | magazines | |
| non-high-school graduates | television | |
| high-income households | magazines | |

*PROBLEM*

In January, the advertising manager for Scripto was preparing plans for a new advertising campaign for the Scripto Erasable, a ball-point pen that wrote in ink which could be erased.[9] The Scripto Erasable was first introduced in 1980 and in subsequent years achieved the number two position in the market of about $130 million. Gillette's Erasermate was the market leader and the Bic Erasable was third.

To combat Bic's price-promoted entry, Scripto was introducing a second-generation, 69-cent erasable. The advertising plan was largely completed except for the media program. The budget for the year had been set at $3 million. Initial creative exploration had come up with the copyline "The Scripto erasable pen beats the blotchies, stops the smudgies, and grabs the globbies. Its smooth writing ink won't skip or glob like other erasable pens." Beyond this, it was anticipated that copy requirements would be short.

Scripto believed that the major users of the erasable pen were teenagers who favored the pens for school work. The heaviest retail sales occurred during the back-to-school period.

Based on the available information:

1. Prepare a list of media requirements for the Scripto Erasable pen.
2. What medium or media would best meet the media requirements?

---

[9]This problem was based on Gay Jervey, "Scripto Rewrites Erasable Pitch," *Advertising Age* (January 30, 1984), p. 38.

# CHAPTER 13

The media selection approach developed in the last chapter relies heavily upon the advertiser's knowledge of the characteristics of alternative media and media vehicles. In the next three chapters we will consider the characteristics of each of the major media. This chapter details newspapers, magazines and newspaper supplements, while Chapter 14 describes television and radio. Direct advertising and out-of-home media are examined in Chapter 15.

## Newspapers

Newspapers, the largest of the advertising media, are particularly important to local advertisers and retailers, but they also have characteristics that make them valuable to some national advertisers.

### Classes of Newspapers

Although daily city newspapers are by far the dominant type in number and in advertising volume, the advertiser should be aware of the other types of newspapers available and their characteristics.

NATIONAL NEWSPAPERS. There are some newspapers available that offer national circulation, such as *The Wall Street Journal, The Christian Science Monitor,* and *USA Today.* Their editorial content does not focus on particular geographic areas, hence their audience appeal is not limited to a particular city. There are also publications frequently classed as national newspapers such as *Women's Wear Daily,* and *The Sporting News.* Although some of these publications are issued daily and have the physical appearance of newspapers, their editorial content (and consequently their audience) has specialized characteristics much like that of some magazines.

DAILY NEWSPAPERS. Dailies, the dominant class of newspapers, can be distinguished not just by frequency but by their distinctly limited geographic circulation. A daily newspaper originates in a particular city—it is usually printed there, its news coverage focuses on the locality, and its circulation is concentrated in the residential and business zones of the city. Daily newspapers can be further classified as morning, evening, or Sunday. In 1982 there were 1,710 daily newspapers of which 1,277 were evening papers and 399 morning papers. In addition, there were 768 Sunday newspapers.[1]

WEEKLY NEWSPAPERS. Probably the fastest growing class of newspapers is the weekly. Many weekly newspapers originate in small cities unable to support a daily newspaper. In 1983, by one count, there was a total of 6,855 weekly newspapers in the nation.[2] A fast-growing class of weekly newspapers are those distributed in a suburban area of a larger city. By one estimate, there are today 3,300 of these community weekly newspapers.[3] The editorial content of the weekly newspaper focuses almost entirely on news and activities in the local community.

SHOPPING GUIDES. Another distinctive class of newspapers is the shopping guide. Shopping guides, often called *shoppers,* are usually published weekly. Containing little or no editorial material, they consist of advertisements, usually retailer advertisements, from stores in the shopper's limited circulation area. The number of shoppers in existence is a matter of conjecture, but a recent survey estimates that about half of all homes receive a shopper, with distribution highest among single-family dwelling units.[4]

SPECIAL AUDIENCE NEWSPAPERS. The daily and weekly newspapers considered thus far offer editorial material of general interest, specialized only in a geographic sense. There is, however, a variety of newspapers that offers specialized editorial content aimed at particular groups of consumers.

[1]*Key Facts About Newspapers and Advertising 1982* (New York: Newspaper Advertising Bureau, Inc., 1982), p. 24.
[2]*The IMS '83 Ayer Directory of Publications* (Ft. Washington, Pennsylvania, 1983), p. VIII.
[3]Estimate provided by American Newspaper Representatives, Inc., New York.
[4]Gerald C. Stone, "How the Public Views Shoppers," *Advertising Age* (July 28, 1980), p. S–2.

There are an estimated 325 black newspapers in the nation, circulated mainly in urban areas with heavy black population.[5] Religious newspapers make up another special audience newspaper class. The largest denominational group of religious newspapers consists of about 140 Catholic newspapers. Other special-audience newspapers include over 1,000 college newspapers plus numerous foreign language and fraternal newspapers.

## Characteristics of Newspapers as an Advertising Medium

Following the four-step media selection procedure discussed in Chapter 12, the advertiser prepares a list of requirements that the media program must meet. Available media are then reviewed to see which one best meets these requirements. Each of the six media characteristics suggested is designed to evaluate the medium's match to one of the requirements. Again, these media characteristics are:

1. Audience selected.
2. Exposure distribution.
3. Creative characteristics.
4. Minimum cost of entry.
5. Production requirements.
6. Merchandising value.

We will examine newspapers with these characteristics as a guide. Although our discussion will center on daily newspapers, many of the characteristics of the dailies apply to the other newspaper classes.

AUDIENCE SELECTIVITY. **Selectivity** is the ability of a medium to deliver an audience that is limited to people with certain common characteristics. Two types of selectivity will be considered—demographic selectivity and geographic selectivity. A **demographically selective medium** is one whose audience is limited to people with certain common demographic characteristics such as a certain age group (teenagers), a certain educational group (holders of MBA degrees), or a certain occupational class (purchasing agents). A **geographically selective medium** is one whose audience is limited to a particular geographic area such as region, a city, or a neighborhood.

*media selectivity*

*demographically selective medium*

*geographically selective medium*

*Demographic Selectivity.* Daily newspapers are not a demographically selective medium; their audience is not restricted to a particular class of consumers. In fact, of the major media, newspapers are the least selective on a demographic basis. This lack of selectivity results from the widespread readership of newspapers. On an average weekday 67 percent of all adults read a daily newspaper.[6]

---

[5]Bob Donath, "Target for Black Newspapers: Black Middle Class Affluence," *Advertising Age* (November 17, 1975), p. 130.
[6]*Key Facts About Newspapers and Advertising 1982* (New York: Newspaper Advertising Bureau, Inc., 1982), p. 26.

Although newspapers are read by nearly all adults, there are some small variations in readership. As shown in Exhibit 13-1, readership tends to increase by age, income, and education. The advertiser can, of course, through the construction and placement of an advertisement within the newspaper select out certain readers. An advertisement headed "Attention Cigar Smokers" and placed on the sports page would undoubtedly get higher male readership than female. However, such a practice does not mean that the medium itself is selective since the full circulation must be paid for even though only a portion of the readers are attracted to the advertisements.

The nonselective characteristic applies not only to daily newspapers, but also to Sunday and weekly newspapers and to shopping guides. By contrast, specialized newspapers are selective, with audience characteristics similar to those of specialized magazines which will be discussed later in this chapter.

*Geographic Selectivity.* In contrast to their lack of demographic selectivity, newspapers offer great geographic selectivity. About 6,600 towns publish a newspaper, of which about 1,500 are served by dailies.[7] The advertiser can purchase one or a combination of these newspapers to deliver advertising to areas where the product is distributed. The advertiser can also vary the advertising weight from area to area to reflect differences in sales potential. The circulation pattern of any particular newspaper closely follows population patterns and, hence, consumer purchasing power. Local retailers frequently favor newspaper as a medium because they find its circulation pattern closely matches the area from which they draw their customers.

*audience distribution*     AUDIENCE DISTRIBUTION. **Audience distribution** is concerned with the total number of readers and the frequency of their readership over a series of issues. It is usually measured in terms of reach and frequency.

*Audience Reach.* The audience reach for a single issue of a newspaper is very high compared to most media. As shown in Exhibit 13-2, in the case of an average daily newspaper, total audience reach for a single issue starts at the very high level of 68 percent of the adult population. This high initial reach offers the advertiser the opportunity to cover nearly all of the market very quickly. This is a particularly important characteristic for the advertiser, such as the one shown in Exhibit 13-3, who has a news announcement (new product, product warning) or who wishes quick action (a limited-time offer, an upcoming event).

Also shown in Exhibit 13-2 is the effect of additional advertisements on reach. With additional advertisements, reach tends to increase only slowly because of its high starting level and because of the way that newspapers are purchased. More than three-fourths of all daily newspapers are

---

[7]*The IMS '83 Ayer Directory of Publications, op. cit.,* p. VIII.

Daily newspaper audience by demographic characteristics.    **EXHIBIT 13-1**

| Characteristic | Number (in 000's) | Percent of Total Adults |
|---|---|---|
| Total Adult Readers | 108,366 | 67% |
| **By Sex:** | | |
| Men | 52,399 | 69% |
| Women | 55,967 | 66 |
| **By Age:** | | |
| 18–24 years | 16,675 | 59% |
| 25–34 years | 23,158 | 61 |
| 35–44 years | 18,064 | 69 |
| 45–54 years | 17,201 | 76 |
| 55–64 years | 16,349 | 75 |
| 65 years or older | 16,919 | 69 |
| **By Education:** | | |
| Grammar school or less | 11,537 | 51% |
| Some high school | 14,273 | 61 |
| High school graduate | 44,024 | 69 |
| Some college | 19,190 | 71 |
| College graduate | 19,342 | 78 |
| **By Household Income:** | | |
| $40,000 or more | 18,301 | 78% |
| $30,000 or more | 35,679 | 77 |
| $25,000 or more | 47,965 | 75 |
| $20,000–$24,999 | 14,251 | 70 |
| $15,000–$19,999 | 12,275 | 67 |
| $10,000–$14,999 | 16,840 | 64 |
| Under $10,000 | 17,035 | 52 |
| **By Occupation:** | | |
| Professional, technical | 13,679 | 76% |
| Manager, administrator | 9,220 | 77 |
| Clerical, sales | 16,655 | 69 |
| Craftsman, foreman | 8,238 | 65 |
| Other employed | 19,244 | 62 |
| Not employed | 41,330 | 65 |

Source: *Key Facts About Newspapers and Advertising 1982* (New York: Newspaper Advertising Bureau, Inc., 1982), p. 26.

home delivered to regular subscribers; thus the population that receives a newspaper changes little from day to day.[8] Note in Exhibit 13-2 that reach varies only slightly by demographic group.

*Audience Frequency.* Exhibit 13-2 also shows how newspaper frequency builds. Both newspaper delivery and readership tend to be highly routinized activities. As a consequence, frequency tends to nearly equal the number of issues. Because readership is so widespread, frequency tends not to be highly concentrated among particular groups.

[8]*Key Facts About Newspapers and Advertising 1982, op.cit.,* p. 24.

EXHIBIT 13-2     Daily newspaper reach and frequency by demographic group.

| | One Day | Two Days | Three Days | Four Days | Five Days |
|---|---|---|---|---|---|
| **Total Adults:** | | | | | |
| Reach | 68% | 79% | 84% | 87% | 89% |
| Avg. Frequency | 1.0 | 1.7 | 2.4 | 3.1 | 3.8 |
| GRP's* | 80 | 160 | 240 | 320 | 400 |
| **Total Men:** | | | | | |
| Reach | 69% | 80% | 85% | 87% | 89% |
| Avg. Frequency | 1.0 | 1.7 | 2.4 | 3.2 | 3.9 |
| GRP's | 83 | 166 | 249 | 332 | 415 |
| **Total Women:** | | | | | |
| Reach | 67% | 78% | 83% | 86% | 88% |
| Avg. Frequency | 1.0 | 1.7 | 2.4 | 3.1 | 3.8 |
| GRP's | 78 | 156 | 234 | 312 | 390 |
| **Adults, Age 35–44:** | | | | | |
| Reach | 71% | 82% | 87% | 90% | 91% |
| Avg. Frequency | 1.0 | 1.7 | 2.4 | 3.2 | 3.9 |
| GRP's | 84 | 168 | 252 | 336 | 420 |
| **Adults, College Graduates:** | | | | | |
| Reach | 79% | 90% | 93% | 95% | 97% |
| Avg. Frequency | 1.0 | 1.8 | 2.5 | 3.3 | 4.1 |
| GRP's | 98 | 196 | 294 | 392 | 490 |
| **Adults, HH Income $35,000 and over:** | | | | | |
| Reach | 79% | 90% | 94% | 96% | 97% |
| Avg. Frequency | 1.0 | 1.8 | 2.5 | 3.3 | 4.1 |
| GRP's | 99 | 198 | 297 | 396 | 495 |
| **Adults, Professional & Technical Workers:** | | | | | |
| Reach | 78% | 88% | 92% | 94% | 95% |
| Avg. Frequency | 1.0 | 1.8 | 2.5 | 3.3 | 4.1 |
| GRP's | 95 | 190 | 285 | 380 | 475 |

*Gross rating  points

Source: *Key Facts About Newspapers and Advertising 1982* (New York: Newspaper Advertising Bureau, Inc., 1982), p. 29.

CREATIVE CHARACTERISTICS. Every medium has a unique set of creative attributes and shortcomings that define dimensions within which the creator of advertisements must work and which either enhance or detract from the final product. Creative characteristics will be reviewed in five categories for newspapers and for each of the other media reviewed later. These characteristics are *media form, color, environment, life,* and *clutter.*

*Media Form.* The physical form of a medium determines the form of advertising in that medium. Some media offer a visual message, others an oral message; some media are static, while others can show motion.

Use of newspaper advertising for a news announcement.

EXHIBIT 13-3

# FREE SEMINAR:

# HOW TO FEEL A LOT BETTER ABOUT INCOME TAXES NEXT APRIL 15TH.

If you filed a federal income tax return this year with taxable income of $18,000 to $24,000 or more as an individual, or a joint return on $24,000 to $28,000 or more, we'd like to invite you to attend an exclusive seminar that could save you a lot of money. It's a thorough, comprehensive review of tax-exempt municipal bonds, and what they might mean to you. For example, you'll learn:

● What are municipal bonds? Who issues them? What is the money used for?
● Who should own municipal bonds? How much can you save in your tax bracket?
● Why do some bonds pay higher rates than others?
● How safe are they? Are they suitable for conservative investing? For capital gains? How are they rated?

● Can you buy them to mature at dates convenient to you, long term or short term?
● Are they easy to sell before maturity? How would you go about it? How big is the market?
● Should you buy individual bonds or invest in a bond fund or trust?
● What are the eight different kinds of municipal bonds? How do they differ?
● How can Merrill Lynch, as one of the largest underwriters and distributors of municipal bonds and bond trusts help you?

Find out how you may increase your spendable income by thousands of dollars a year for many years to come.

For free reservations—without obligation on your part—simply call the number below.

**DATE:** Wednesday, July 18th    **TIME:** 7:30 p.m.
**PLACE:** Merrill Lynch Office - 4th Floor Conference Room,
Corner of Mill & Garden Streets, Poughkeepsie

## MAIL TODAY—OR CALL—FOR FREE RESERVATIONS

Mail to: Merrill Lynch, Mill & Garden Streets - P.O. Box 629, Poughkeepsie, NY 12602
For reservations call: Cindy at (914) 431-2213

☐ YES, I would like to attend your Seminar on Tax Exempt Municipal Bonds.
Please reserve_____seat(s) for me at the Seminar.
☐ I cannot attend, but please send me a free copy of the 36-page booklet.
"Investing in Municipal Bonds for Tax-Free Income.

Name _____

Address _____

City_____State_____Zip_____

Business Phone_____ Home Phone_____

Merrill Lynch customers, please give name and office address of Account Executive:

_____

**Merrill Lynch**
Merrill Lynch Pierce Fenner & Smith Inc
**A breed apart.**

Courtesy:  Merrill Lynch, Pierce, Fenner & Smith Inc.

The newspaper medium is, of course, strictly visual. Persuasive, personal selling approaches from owners or well-known personalities are difficult to present in newspaper because they depend upon the warmth of the individual's voice. Newspaper does, however, lend itself to illustration. Food, clothing, automobiles, appliances, and other products can be shown and their features detailed.

Newspaper as a static medium can depict motion or sequences only crudely. Thus, it is not a good medium, creatively speaking, for the advertiser who wishes to demonstrate how a product works. A lawn-mower manufacturer, for example, can state in a newspaper that its mower is easy to start. However, the mower's ease of starting could be more effectively demonstrated in a television commercial.

*Color.* Color, though actually an aspect of media form, is important enough to be considered separately. Color reproduction is available to advertisers in newspapers, but with a number of limitations to its use. Because of these limitations, color advertising represents a very small part of total newspaper advertising linage.

*ROP color*

Three types of color are offered by newspapers — run-of-press (ROP) color, color preprints, and free-standing inserts. **ROP color** is color printing carried out by the newspaper on its own presses using the normal paper stock on which the entire newspaper is printed. Some newspapers can print only one or two colors (called "spot" color) while others offer three colors plus black that can be superimposed for a variety of shades.

*color preprints*

**Color preprints** are ads prepared in a continuous roll and supplied by the advertiser for insertion into scheduled newspapers. The newspaper cuts off individual ads and inserts them as a page in the newspaper. One form of preprint is called "Hi-Fi." In this form the ad is designed with a repeating pattern like wallpaper so that it makes sense to the reader regardless of where it is cut off. A more recent development, Spectacolor, has fixed cut-off points at top and bottom, thus avoiding the necessity for a repeating, wallpaper-type design.

*free-standing inserts*

Another option with newspapers that offers high-quality, controlled-color reproduction as well as great format flexibility is the free-standing insert. A **free-standing insert** is a pre-printed, multi-paged newspaper section containing the advertising of one advertiser that can fit into and be distributed with a daily newspaper. Inserts can vary widely in size and format and can include coupons, reply cards, and even product samples. The use of inserts has increased rapidly in recent years while the use of Hi-Fi and Spectacolor has declined. An example of a free-standing insert is shown in Exhibit 13-4.

Most newspapers in major markets offer full color for full-page and less than full-page advertisements. As shown in Exhibit 13-5, the largest gap in color availability is in the very largest markets with some markets, like New York City, not offering color. In addition, very small markets frequently lack color capability. Overall, however, about 90 percent of the

A free-standing insert.

EXHIBIT 13-4

Source: Lowe's Companies, Inc., 1984.

EXHIBIT 13-5        Percent of daily newspaper circulation offering ROP color.

| Market Rank: | Accept Less Than Full-Page Ad | | | Accept Full-Page Ad | | |
|---|---|---|---|---|---|---|
| | One Color | Two Colors | Full Color | One Color | Two Colors | Full Color |
| Top 25 | 84.5% | 73.7% | 71.4% | 88.8% | 81.9% | 79.7% |
| 26–50 | 100.0 | 97.2 | 92.8 | 100.0 | 97.2 | 92.8 |
| 51–75 | 95.8 | 99.6 | 97.2 | 99.6 | 99.6 | 97.2 |
| 76–100 | 100.0 | 98.1 | 97.0 | 100.0 | 98.1 | 97.0 |
| 101–200 | 99.1 | 97.6 | 97.2 | 100.0 | 99.8 | 99.4 |
| 201–300 | 100.0 | 98.9 | 97.5 | 100.0 | 98.9 | 97.5 |

Source: *Key Facts About Newspapers and Advertising 1982* (New York: Newspaper Advertising Bureau, Inc., 1982), p. 18.

circulation in the top 300 markets offers color advertising. Most newspapers can handle Hi-Fi color inserts, but because of machinery requirements, fewer are able to handle Spectacolor. Almost all newspapers accept free-standing inserts.

ROP newspaper color is not of high quality when compared to the quality available in the major magazines. Because newspaper stock is of lower quality, there is a tendency for material on the back side of the page to show through. Also, the registration of color is sometimes poor, giving an impression of blurring. Preprinted ads and free-standing inserts offer substantially higher quality due to the better paper and a controlled printing process. The repeating pattern of Hi-Fi is a creative limitation, however.

Newspapers charge a higher rate for color advertising. The premium varies from newspaper to newspaper, but tends to increase with the number of colors required and to decrease with larger ad sizes. One analysis showed that the average premium charge for a full-page, three-color ad was 31 percent.[9] The color preprint and insert premium is even greater.

*Environment.* The meaning and the acceptance of an individual advertisement is affected by the medium in which it appears. The medium itself has a meaning to consumers, some of which carries over to products using that medium. The marketer of men's products will advertise on football telecasts because that vehicle has high male viewership. However, it is probably also hoped that some of the masculinity and popularity of football will be absorbed by the product.

To understand the environment of a medium it is helpful to ask: What does this medium mean to consumers? In the case of newspapers, the answer is that it means several things. First, to its readers the newpaper means news. They buy it and read it because it brings them up to date on current events and new things. Thus, the advertiser who has news to tell — such as a new product introduction, the addition of trading stamps, a

[9]*Basic Facts About Newspapers* (New York: Newspaper Advertising Bureau, Inc., 1978), p. 5.

switch to discount pricing, or a change of store hours — will find that the newspaper environment heightens the news value of the announcement.

The daily newspaper means news to its readers, but in particular, newspapers mean local news. Of all the media, newspapers are closest and most in tune with events and people in their local community. Consumers can turn to television and weekly news magazines for national and international news, but newspapers are their most important local news source. If the advertiser wishes to fit into or identify with the local community, newspapers' localized environment will help to achieve that aim.

Newspaper advertising also ranks as the most believable. In a study of six media, newspaper advertising believability was ranked first, far ahead of other major media. Test results are shown in Exhibit 13-6.

Newspapers are valued by consumers because they carry shopping ads. Newspapers, unlike many other media, are purchased in part because of the advertising, not in spite of it. In a recent study, 44 percent of those questioned said that they looked forward to newspaper ads. By contrast, the positive response to magazines was 29 percent, to radio 10 percent, and to television 9 percent.[10]

Consumers pre-shop by reviewing newspaper retail advertising before shopping. One study showed that four out of five supermarket shoppers felt that newspaper ads were the most helpful to them in doing their weekly shopping.[11] As was shown in the consumer behavior model in Chapter 5, placing advertising for a product in a medium to which the consumer looks for information helps solve the problem of selective exposure. Thus, to the advertiser with shopping news (food stores, discount stores, department stores, for example) the newspaper is a natural medium.

Responses to "Which of these five media would you say has the most believable advertising?"

**EXHIBIT 13-6**

| | Percent Selecting Medium | Rank of Medium |
|---|---|---|
| Newspapers | 42% | 1 |
| Television | 26 | 2 |
| Magazines | 11 | 3.5 |
| Radio | 11 | 3.5 |
| Direct mail | 5 | 5 |
| All about equal | 2 | NA |
| No opinion | 3 | NA |

Source: Opinion Research Corporation, Caravan Express, August, 1981, as reported in *Key Facts About Newspapers and Advertising 1982* (New York: Newspaper Advertising Bureau, Inc., 1982). p. 1.

[10]From a study by Audits and Surveys, 1977, as reported in *Key Facts About Newspapers and Advertising 1982* (New York: Newspaper Advertising Bureau, Inc., 1982), p. 1.
[11]"Mom still Reads Dailies for Food Ads: Burgoyne," *Advertising Age*, Vol. 40, No. 49 (December 8, 1969), p. 32.

*media life*

*Life.* **Media life** refers to how long a particular media vehicle is actively used and considered by a consumer. Some media, such as the telephone directory Yellow Pages, have life of a year or more, while the life of a radio message is only as long as the message itself.

The daily newspaper is not a medium with a long-life. In most homes the newspaper is read when received and discarded the same day. Despite this relatively short life, the newspaper can be saved, studied, and clipped. Because a newspaper ad can be studied, it is a useful medium when copy must be long or when the story is complex. For example, a grocery store can give a much more detailed list of prices in a newspaper ad than could be absorbed from a radio commercial.

A newspaper also enables the advertiser to deliver a message that can be saved by the reader. A newspaper advertisement can deliver a coupon, a map, or an address that the reader can clip out and save for later use. Newspapers are far and away the favorite means of delivering coupons to consumers. In 1981, 78.5 percent of all coupons were distributed through newspapers, free-standing inserts, and supplements.[12]

*clutter*

*Clutter.* In any medium, the advertiser's message must compete with other advertisements for the consumer's attention. The presence of a great many competitive messages in a medium is termed **clutter**.

Most newspapers are highly competitive, cluttered media vehicles. Not only are there a great many advertisements in most major newspapers, but also a great many of them are very large. Large food, discount, and department stores frequently purchase multiple full pages or, at least, an ad size that dominates the page. This competition for attention places a considerable burden on the creator of the advertisement to develop an approach that somehow stands apart from the clutter. The problem is particularly acute for the advertiser who cannot afford to purchase large space units, but somehow must avoid being buried by the advertisements of the large retailers.

MINIMUM COST. The minimum cost of entering a medium is a function of a number of cost factors such as the cost of a single insertion, the minimum ad size accepted, the requirement for a series of purchases, and the cost of producing advertising materials for the medium.

Newspaper, in terms of most of these cost factors, is decidedly a low minimum cost medium. The advertiser can limit an advertising purchase to a single insertion. Newspapers do not generally have a minimum linage requirement so that ads as small as one line can be scheduled. Examples of minimum cost newspaper advertising are readily found by looking in the classified advertising section of most newspapers where both business and individual advertisements of as few as two or three lines are common. However, some advertisers feel that in order to avoid being overlooked in the

---

[12]Nielsen Clearing House, 1982, as reported in *Key Facts About Newspapers and Advertising 1982* (New York: Newspaper Advertising Bureau, Inc., 1982), p. 2.

clutter, their advertisements must be large enough to dominate the page on which they appear. The cost of producing newspaper advertisements (preparing the materials from which the ad is printed) must also be paid by the advertiser. This cost is generally low compared to those of other media and is not a barrier to small advertisers.

PRODUCTION REQUIREMENTS. The preparation of advertising materials has two dimensions which influence media selection—time and cost.

The advertising production process for some media is very extended, requiring a long interval between the decision to advertise and the appearance of the advertisement. On the other hand, the production process for a newspaper can be very rapid. The time required varies with the nature of the advertisement, but quality materials can frequently be prepared in as little as 24 hours. Color ads and ads for which original artwork must be made up take longer, but even in these cases the process is relatively fast. Because of the short production lead time, newspaper advertising can be used for timely news announcements and for presenting updated information to consumers.

The second dimension of advertising production is cost and it is another instance in which newspaper enjoys distinct advantages. The cost of producing a newspaper ad varies with its complexity, but overall the cost is modest. All-print ads are the least expensive, with cost rising as illustrations and color are added. The low cost of production permits the newspaper advertiser to change ads frequently, making the copy timely and tailored to geographic or seasonal requirements. This flexibility is a great advantage to retailers, with whom newspaper is a favorite medium.

MERCHANDISING VALUE. An advertising medium is chosen primarily because of its ability to reach the ultimate consumer. In addition, however, media selection also has an effect on salespeople and trade intermediaries who handle the product. This trade influence is termed the **merchandising value of the medium.** If trade intermediaries and salespeople are aware of and have confidence in the medium to be used, they are more likely to stock the advertiser's product, to display it prominently, and to sell it actively.

*merchandising value of the medium*

Newspaper is a medium that can offer substantial merchandising advantages to the advertiser, particularly to one selling a product through local retailers. The retailer knows and values newspaper because it is the medium that retailers themselves use. Newspaper is seen as a medium that builds store traffic.

The merchandising value of newspaper advertising is heightened in many cases by merchandising programs conducted by the newspaper for individual advertisers. In most cases the newspapers' efforts focus on making trade intermediaries aware of the newspaper advertising for the product and encouraging them to stock and display the product. These efforts, however, are only made when the advertiser requests the assistance. In addition, newspaper merchandising departments are often very knowledgeable about local market conditions and can be very helpful in solving problems that affect the advertiser in their local markets.

## Users of Newspapers

It is useful to look at the pattern of actual users of the various media. An advertiser may not wish to follow the media pattern of a particular industry, but the patterns reveal opinions concerning the appropriateness of certain media for certain classes of products.

The users of newspaper advertising can initially be divided into three broad groups—local advertisers, national advertisers, and an in-between class, cooperative advertisers.

LOCAL ADVERTISERS. The dominant users of newspaper as an advertising medium are local businesses. This should not be surprising considering the audience and creative characteristics of newspapers. Another reason is the nature of newspaper rate structures. Generally, local businesses enjoy a more favorable rate than national advertisers. Currently, just under 85 percent of all advertising expenditures in newspapers are by local advertisers.[13] Of this, about one third is in classified advertising.

Who are the local advertisers who utilize newspaper advertising so heavily? In the typical city the large retailers head the list—food stores, department stores, drugstores, appliance retailers, furniture stores, discount houses, clothing stores. Automobile dealers and tire dealers are also typically heavy advertisers. Amusements, restaurants, and local service companies also rely on newspaper advertising.

NATIONAL ADVERTISERS. National advertisers who are heavy users of newspaper are predominantly large firms and are remarkably concentrated by industry. This can be seen in Exhibit 13-7 which lists the top 25 national newspaper advertisers in 1982. Note the concentration by industry—automobile, tobacco, and airline campaigns make up 16 of the top 25.

A tabulation of the product categories most heavily advertised on a national basis in newspapers reveals a similar pattern. Currently, the most heavily advertised categories are tobacco products, transportation (largely airlines), and automotive.[14] Why do these industries use newspapers so heavily? Auto manufacturers sell through local dealers. The local identity and geographic flexibility of newspapers is ideal for them. Newspapers also heighten the news value of automobile price promotions and new-car introductions. Tobacco marketers, prohibited from broadcast media, find a mass audience in newspaper. Transportation companies, primarily airlines,

---

[13]*Key Facts About Newspapers and Advertising 1982, op. cit.,* p. 14.
[14]*Ibid.,* p. 12.

Top 25 newspaper advertisers, 1982.                                    **EXHIBIT 13-7**

| Rank | Advertiser | Expenditures (Add 000) |
|------|-----------|------------------------|
| 1 | R. J. Reynolds Industries | $123,174.8 |
| 2 | General Motors Corp. | 86,965.2 |
| 3 | Philip Morris Inc. | 83,793.8 |
| 4 | Ford Motor Co. | 45,582.6 |
| 5 | Batus Inc. | 42,893.6 |
| 6 | AT&T Co. | 34,467.2 |
| 7 | Chrysler Corp. | 29,597.5 |
| 8 | RCA Corp. | 28,273.3 |
| 9 | Delta Air Lines | 24,664.6 |
| 10 | Pan American | 24,077.7 |
| 11 | Loews Corp. | 22,645.4 |
| 12 | Eastern Air Lines | 21,625.4 |
| 13 | Time Inc. | 20,186.7 |
| 14 | Trans World Corp. | 19,857.3 |
| 15 | Warner Communications | 18,875.6 |
| 16 | AMR Corp. | 18,813.0 |
| 17 | Volkswagen of America | 16,025.3 |
| 18 | CBS Inc. | 15,917.7 |
| 19 | Toyota Motor Corp. | 15,611.1 |
| 20 | American Express Co. | 11,840.3 |
| 21 | Texas Air Corp. | 10,574.9 |
| 22 | American Broadcasting Cos. | 10,299.3 |
| 23 | Seagram Co. Ltd. | 9,851.3 |
| 24 | Nissan Motor Corp. | 9,742.8 |
| 25 | U.S. Government | 9,633.6 |

Reprinted with permission from the September 8, 1983 issue of *Advertising Age.* Copyright 1983 by Crain Communications, Inc.

use the geographic flexibility of newspaper to present localized information on flight schedules. Airlines call this destination advertising. An example from a Florida newspaper is shown in Exhibit 13-8.

COOPERATIVE ADVERTISERS. **Cooperative advertising** is an arrangement by which manufacturers pay part of the local dealer's advertising expenditure. This practice is common, for example, in the automobile, tire, clothing, and beverage industries. Manufacturers who offer cooperative advertising funds to their dealers or retailers usually do so subject to an agreement as to how funds are to be spent. The agreement usually specifies the content and timing of the advertising and the amount to be spent. The percentage to be paid by the manufacturer (most commonly 50 percent) is also specified. Cooperative advertising is not limited to the newspaper field, but it is here that it started and where it continues to be utilized most frequently.

*cooperative
advertising*

Cooperative advertising in newspapers offers several advantages. Because the advertising is placed through a local dealer or retailer, the advertisement can be purchased at the lower local rate. Local placement

**EXHIBIT 13-8**         An example of destination advertising.

Courtesy:  Northeastern Airlines.

also permits the dealer to localize the copy and, out of self-interest, the dealer is more likely to check to see that the ad runs where and when requested. Dealers, of course, are happy to receive the advertising support and the manufacturers, with the dealer paying part of the cost and by gaining the local rate, stretch their advertising budgets.

The cooperative arrangement, however, is subject to serious abuses if not carefully controlled by the marketer. Both creative quality and media selection can deteriorate if not controlled. Marketers can attempt to control creative quality by supplying retailers with finished ads which leave space for the retailer's identification. Media rates actually paid by the dealer must also be carefully monitored. In some industries where cooperative allowances have been granted, but performance not monitored, dealers and retailers have come to claim the allowance even though no advertising is run. The cooperative allowance in time becomes part of the expected trade discount and is difficult to discontinue.

## Purchasing Newspaper Space

The purchase of media space is, by itself, a highly specialized field. Advertising agencies have specialists who devote their efforts solely to this field, but often the smaller advertiser without an advertising agency must undertake this task alone.

NATIONAL VS. LOCAL PURCHASE. National and local advertisers usually purchase newspaper space through somewhat different channels. The national advertiser, usually represented by an advertising agency, most often purchases space through a sales agent who represents the newspaper. These sales agents, called newspaper representatives or "reps," usually represent several newspapers. They supply the media buyer with information on the newspaper they represent and transmit purchases and instructions from the buyer to the newspaper.

The local newspaper advertiser, by contrast, usually deals directly with the advertising department of each newspaper in which advertising will be placed. Newspapers generally have well-developed sales departments with salespeople who call on local accounts. The head of this department, curiously, is traditionally called the advertising manager.

NEWSPAPER RATES. The existence of a two-rate structure in newspaper advertising has already been mentioned. Generally, national advertisers are charged about 50 percent more than a local advertiser for comparable space. Originally designed to encourage regular advertising by local businesses, many feel that the two rates form a discouraging barrier to the national advertiser. There are a few newspapers offering a single rate to both local and national advertisers, but the practice is not widespread.

Newspaper rates are quoted by the column inch (or line) as either flat rates or open rates. A **flat rate** offers no discount for quantity purchases: an **open rate** means that discounts are available. Discounts, where offered, are usually based on the number of column inches purchased in a year. When a flat rate is quoted, the cost is simply the number of column inches

*flat rate*
*open rate*

*short-rate bill*

purchased times the rate. When discounts are offered, the advertiser can predict the number of column inches expected to be purchased over the year and pay at the appropriate discounted inch rate. At the end of the year the advertiser receives a rebate if too much has been paid or a **short-rate bill** if too little has been paid.

Some newspapers levy additional charges if preferred positions are requested, such as next to the comics or on the front page. However, many position requests, although not guaranteed, are granted without charge.

*combination rate*

Publishers owning more than one newspaper often quote a **combination rate** that provides space in both newspapers at a single rate. The combination is usually a morning paper and an evening paper in the same market.

INFORMATION SOURCES. There are three important sources of information about the characteristics of individual newspapers with which the buyer of media should be familiar. The prime source of circulation data

*publisher's statement*

for a newspaper is its publisher's statement. The **publisher's statement** contains total circulation figures, data on geographic distribution of circulation, and information on pricing and promotional practices that affect circulation. For a newspaper holding membership in one of the audit

*audit report*

services, the audited form of the publisher's statement is called an **audit report.** Publisher's statements and audit reports are available upon request directly from the newspaper.

Newspaper advertising rates may be obtained directly from the newspaper and those advertisers qualified for the retail rate should obtain rate schedules in this way. Other advertisers, particularly those using a number of newspapers, find Standard Rate and Data Service (SRDS) a more convenient source. SRDS's *Newspaper Rates and Data* provides information on dailies, while their *Community Publication Rates and Data* covers weeklies and shoppers. These SRDS volumes contain current rate information as well as information on personnel, production requirements, summary circulation figures, and special facilities available. A sample of an SRDS listing is shown in Exhibit 13-9.

Data on newspaper audience size and audience characteristics are available for the larger newspapers for commercial research studies and from studies conducted by the newspapers themselves. The two leading suppliers of syndicated newspaper audience studies are Scarborough Research Corp. and Simmons Market Research Bureau (SMRB). These audience studies provide — in either on-line or in printed form — reach and frequency estimates arranged according to demographic characteristics for newspapers in about 100 major markets. Recently, standardized demographic classifications were adopted for both of these studies so that results pertaining to newspapers can be compared with those that are valid for other media.[15] Exhibit 13-10 shows a sample page form a Scarborough National Newspaper Audience Ratings Study.

---

[15]"Data on Newspaper Ad Reach Studies Are On-Time from 4 Computer Services," *Marketing News* (December 9, 1983), p. 18.

Excerpt from a sample page of Standard Rate and Data Service's *Newspaper Rates and Data*.          **EXHIBIT 13-9**

Established 1872, per copy daily .25, Sunday .50.
**Net Paid—Sworn 9-30-83 (P.O. Stat. Att.)***

| | Total | CZ | TrZ | Other |
|---|---|---|---|---|
| Morn | 14,235 | 8,465 | 5,770 | ... |
| Sun | 14,235 | 8,465 | 5,770 | ... |

(*) V.A.C. Membership applied for June 1, 1983.
For county-by-county and/or metropolitan area breakdowns, see SRDS Newspaper Circulation Analysis.

## Bakersfield

Kern County—Map Location E-9
See SRDS Consumer market map and data at beginning of the state.

### The Bakersfield Californian

Box 440, Bakersfield, CA 93302.
Phone 805-395-7259, Telecopier, 805-324-8002.

(ABC)

**Media Code 1 105 0900 7.00**                    Mid 016137-000
MORNING AND SUNDAY.
(Published all holidays.)
Member: INAME; NAB, Inc.

**1. PERSONNEL**
Director of Marketing & Sales—Lynn Bryan.
Nat'l. Adv. Mgr.—Jan Hefner.

**2. REPRESENTATIVES and/or BRANCH OFFICES**
Story & Kelly-Smith, Inc.

**3. COMMISSION AND CASH DISCOUNT**
15% to agencies; No cash discount. Transients, cash with order.

**4. POLICY-ALL CLASSIFICATIONS**
Alcoholic beverage advertising accepted.
60-day notice given of any rate revision.
        **ADVERTISING RATES**
        Effective July 1, 1984.
        Received February 6, 1984.

**5. BLACK/WHITE RATES**

| | | | Morn. | Sun. |
|---|---|---|---|---|
| Open, per inch | | | 24.78 | 25.83 |

Inches charge full depth: col. 21; pg. 126; dbl. truck 262.5.
NEWSPLAN—Inch Equivalent.

| Pages | % Disc. | Morn. | Sun. | Inches |
|---|---|---|---|---|
| 6 | 6 | 23.2932 | 24.2802 | 756 |
| 13 | 8 | 22.7976 | 23.7636 | 1,638 |
| 26 | 10 | 22.3020 | 23.2470 | 3,276 |
| 52 | 12 | 21.8064 | 22.7304 | 6,552 |
| 65 | 14 | 21.3108 | 22.2138 | 8,190 |
| 78 | 15 | 21.0630 | 21.9555 | 9,828 |
| 91 | 16 | 20.8152 | 21.6972 | 11,466 |
| 104 | 23 | 19.0806 | 19.8891 | 13,104 |

See Newsplan Contract and Copy Regulations—items 1, 2, 3, 5, 10, 14, 21, 24.

**7. COLOR RATES AND DATA**
Available daily, by reservation. Leeway required for 2 or 3 colors. Minimum 600 lines.
Use b/w rate plus the following applicable costs:

| | b/w 1 c | b/w 2 c | b/w 3 c |
|---|---|---|---|
| Extra | 370.00 | 482.00 | 582.00 |

Closing Time: 11:00 a.m. 3 days in advance.

**9. SPLIT RUN**
2 sets of copy same size run in alternate copies of newspaper, 600 line minimum, use general rate plus 100.00 service charge. Complete camera-ready copy preferred Monday and Tuesday only at publisher's option..

**11. SPECIAL DAYS/PAGES/FEATURES**
Best Food Day: Thursday.
Personal Finances, Monday; Fashion, Tuesday; Automotive, Wednesday; Home, Wine column, Thursday; Weekend, Friday; Gardening, Saturday; Travel, Real Estate, Agriculture, Sunday.

**12. R.O.P. DEPTH REQUIREMENTS**
Ads over 19 inches deep charged full col.

**13. CONTRACT AND COPY REGULATIONS**
See Contents page for location of regulations—items 1, 2, 3, 5, 7, 9 thru 13, 19, 21, 22, 23, 24, 26, 27, 30 thru 35.

**14. CLOSING TIMES**
Wednesday & Friday, 11:00 a.m. 2 days in advance; Saturday, 1:00 p.m. Wednesday; Sunday, 11:00 a.m. Thursday; Monday, 11:00 a.m. Thursday; Tuesday, 11:00 a.m. Friday; Thursday Food Section, 11:00 a.m. previous Friday.

**15. MECHANICAL MEASUREMENTS**
**For complete, detailed production information, see SRDS Print Media Production Data.**
PRINTING PROCESS: Offset.
**6/12-4/9—6 cols/ea 12 picas-4 pts/9 pts betw col.**
Inches charge full depth: col. 21; pg. 126; dbl. truck 262.5.

**16. SPECIAL CLASSIFICATIONS/RATES**
POSITION CHARGES
Position neither sold nor guaranteed. Requests filled when possible.

**17. CLASSIFIED RATES**
For complete data refer to classified rate section.

**18. COMICS**
**POLICY—ALL CLASSIFICATIONS**
When orders are placed through Puck-The Comic Weekly—see that listing.
        Effective January 1, 1984.
        Received November 4, 1983.
**COLOR RATES AND DATA**
Four colors:

| | | | |
|---|---|---|---|
| 1 page | 1,441.00 | 1/3 page | 603.00 |
| 2/3 page | 1,048.00 | 1/6 page | 347.00 |
| 1/2 page | 819.00 | | |

**CLOSING TIMES**
4 weeks before publication.
**MECHANICAL MEASUREMENTS**
Standard page size: 13" wide x 19-3/4" deep.
For ad sizes see Puck—The Comic Weekly listing.

**19. MAGAZINES**
        **TV Weekly**
SUNDAY.
        Effective July 1, 1984.
        Received February 6, 1984.
**BLACK/WHITE RATES**
Per inch ..................................................... 24.70
**COLOR RATES AND DATA**
Use b/w rate plus the following applicable costs:

| | b/w 1 c | b/w 2 c | b/w 3 c |
|---|---|---|---|
| Extra | 176.00 | 310.00 | 381.00 |

**CLOSING TIMES**
12 days before publication date (camera ready).
**MECHANICAL MEASUREMENTS**
PRINTING PROCESS: Offset.
**4/9-3/6—4 cols/ea 9 picas-3 pts/6 pts betw col.**
Page size 6-5/8" x 9-5/8".

**20. CIRCULATION**
Established 1866. Per copy daily .15; Sunday .35.
**Net Paid—A.B.C. 9-30-83 (Newspaper Form)**

| | Total | CZ | TrZ | Other |
|---|---|---|---|---|
| Morn | 76,100 | 58,613 | 16,995 | 492 |
| Sun | 84,162 | 63,763 | 19,811 | 588 |

—METRO CIRCULATION—Optional Compilation—
Morn 76,608; Sun 83,574.
For county-by-county and/or metropolitan area breakdowns, see SRDS Newspaper Circulation Analysis.

## Banning-Beaumont

Riverside County—Map Location G-10
See SRDS Consumer market map and data at beginning of the state.

### RECORD-GAZETTE
**A Scripps League Newspapers, Inc., Newspaper**
218 N. Murray, Banning, CA 92220.
Phone 714-849-4586.

**Media Code 1 105 0975 9.00**                    Mid 016138-000
EVENING (except Saturday and Sunday).
(Not published January 1, Memorial Day, July 4; Labor Day, Thanksgiving or Christmas.)

**1. PERSONNEL**
Publisher—Neil C. Harrand.

**2. REPRESENTATIVES and/or BRANCH OFFICES**
Scripps League Newspaper, Inc.

**July 12, 1984**                    **Newspaper Rates and Data**

**EXHIBIT 13-10**    Scarborough National Newspaper Audience Ratings Study, 1983. Sample page.

SCARBOROUGH'S NATIONAL NEWSPAPER AUDIENCE RATINGS STUDY, 1983

BUFFALO ADI   PAGE   1

PROJECTED NUMBERS IN HUNDREDS (00)

BASIC DEMOGRAPHIC CHARACTERISTICS AND SELECTED NATIONAL PRODUCT USAGE AMONG NEWSPAPER AUDIENCES

BASE: BUFFALO ADI

NEWSPAPER AUDIENCES

| | | TOTAL ADULTS | DAILY NEWS (E) AVG. ISSUE | 2 ISSUE CUME | 5 ISSUE CUME | SUNDAY NEWS AVG. ISSUE | 2 ISSUE CUME | 4 ISSUE CUME | SATURDAY NEWS AVG. ISSUE | 2 ISSUE CUME | 4 ISSUE CUME |
|---|---|---|---|---|---|---|---|---|---|---|---|
| TOTAL ADULTS | | 12963 | 6958 | 8240 | 9547 | 8404 | 9575 | 10449 | 6070 | 7003 | 7782 |
| | COVERAGE | 100% | 53.7 | 63.6 | 73.6 | 64.8 | 73.9 | 80.6 | 46.8 | 54.0 | 60.0 |
| | COMPOSTN | 100.0 | 100.0 | 100.0 | 100.0 | 100.0 | 100.0 | 100.0 | 100.0 | 100.0 | 100.0 |
| **SEX** ADULT MEN | | 6119 | 3503 | 4180 | 4843 | 3919 | 4437 | 4829 | 3013 | 3416 | 3750 |
| | COVERAGE | 100% | 57.2 | 68.3 | 79.1 | 64.0 | 72.5 | 78.9 | 49.2 | 55.8 | 61.3 |
| | COMPOSTN | 47.2 | 50.3 | 50.7 | 50.7 | 46.6 | 46.3 | 46.2 | 49.6 | 48.8 | 48.2 |
| | INDEX | 100 | 107 | 107 | 107 | 99 | 98 | 98 | 105 | 103 | 102 |
| ADULT WOMEN | | 6844 | 3455 | 4060 | 4694 | 4485 | 5138 | 5618 | 3057 | 3587 | 4033 |
| | COVERAGE | 100% | 50.5 | 59.3 | 68.6 | 65.5 | 75.1 | 82.1 | 44.7 | 52.4 | 58.9 |
| | COMPOSTN | 52.8 | 49.7 | 49.3 | 49.2 | 53.4 | 53.7 | 53.8 | 50.4 | 51.2 | 51.8 |
| | INDEX | 100 | 94 | 93 | 93 | 101 | 102 | 102 | 95 | 97 | 98 |
| **AGE** 18 - 24 | | 2579 | 1030 | 1370 | 1756 | 1532 | 1852 | 2092 | 958 | 1164 | 1344 |
| | COVERAGE | 100% | 39.9 | 53.1 | 68.1 | 59.4 | 71.8 | 81.1 | 37.1 | 45.1 | 52.1 |
| | COMPOSTN | 19.9 | 14.8 | 16.6 | 18.4 | 18.2 | 19.3 | 20.0 | 15.8 | 16.6 | 17.3 |
| | INDEX | 100 | 74 | 84 | 92 | 92 | 97 | 101 | 79 | 84 | 87 |
| 25 - 34 | | 2615 | 1472 | 1719 | 1968 | 1780 | 1993 | 2150 | 1202 | 1371 | 1512 |
| | COVERAGE | 100% | 56.3 | 65.7 | 75.3 | 68.1 | 76.2 | 82.2 | 46.0 | 52.4 | 57.8 |
| | COMPOSTN | 20.2 | 21.1 | 20.9 | 20.6 | 21.2 | 20.8 | 20.6 | 19.8 | 19.6 | 19.4 |
| | INDEX | 100 | 105 | 103 | 102 | 105 | 103 | 102 | 98 | 97 | 96 |
| 35 - 44 | | 1783 | 1033 | 1184 | 1336 | 1316 | 1469 | 1574 | 891 | 1032 | 1148 |
| | COVERAGE | 100% | 57.9 | 66.4 | 74.9 | 73.8 | 82.4 | 88.3 | 50.0 | 57.9 | 64.4 |
| | COMPOSTN | 13.8 | 14.8 | 14.4 | 14.0 | 15.7 | 15.3 | 15.1 | 14.7 | 14.7 | 14.8 |
| | INDEX | 100 | 108 | 104 | 102 | 114 | 112 | 109 | 107 | 107 | 107 |
| 45 - 54 | | 1999 | 1154 | 1334 | 1514 | 1320 | 1501 | 1635 | 1115 | 1243 | 1346 |
| | COVERAGE | 100% | 57.7 | 66.7 | 75.7 | 66.0 | 75.1 | 81.8 | 55.8 | 62.2 | 67.3 |
| | COMPOSTN | 15.4 | 16.6 | 16.2 | 15.9 | 15.7 | 15.7 | 15.6 | 18.4 | 17.7 | 17.3 |
| | INDEX | 100 | 108 | 105 | 103 | 102 | 102 | 101 | 119 | 115 | 112 |
| 55 - 64 | | 2072 | 1208 | 1401 | 1593 | 1228 | 1397 | 1530 | 1024 | 1163 | 1278 |
| | COVERAGE | 100% | 58.3 | 67.6 | 76.9 | 59.3 | 67.4 | 73.8 | 49.4 | 56.1 | 61.7 |
| | COMPOSTN | 16.0 | 17.4 | 17.0 | 16.7 | 14.6 | 14.6 | 14.6 | 16.9 | 16.6 | 16.4 |
| | INDEX | 100 | 109 | 106 | 104 | 91 | 91 | 92 | 106 | 104 | 103 |
| 65 AND OVER | | 1915 | 1062 | 1232 | 1405 | 1229 | 1363 | 1467 | 880 | 1030 | 1156 |
| | COVERAGE | 100% | 55.5 | 64.3 | 73.4 | 64.2 | 71.2 | 76.6 | 46.0 | 53.8 | 60.4 |
| | COMPOSTN | 14.8 | 15.3 | 15.0 | 14.7 | 14.6 | 14.2 | 14.0 | 14.5 | 14.7 | 14.9 |
| | INDEX | 100 | 103 | 101 | 100 | 99 | 96 | 95 | 98 | 100 | 101 |
| (25 - 49) | | 5176 | 2955 | 3448 | 3940 | 3622 | 4049 | 4358 | 2522 | 2882 | 3181 |
| | COVERAGE | 100% | 57.1 | 66.6 | 76.1 | 70.0 | 78.2 | 84.2 | 48.7 | 55.7 | 61.5 |
| | COMPOSTN | 39.9 | 42.5 | 41.8 | 41.3 | 43.1 | 42.3 | 41.7 | 41.5 | 41.2 | 40.9 |
| | INDEX | 100 | 106 | 105 | 103 | 108 | 106 | 104 | 104 | 103 | 102 |
| (35 - 49) | | 2561 | 1483 | 1729 | 1973 | 1842 | 2056 | 2207 | 1320 | 1511 | 1668 |
| | COVERAGE | 100% | 57.9 | 67.5 | 77.0 | 71.9 | 80.3 | 86.2 | 51.5 | 59.0 | 65.1 |
| | COMPOSTN | 19.8 | 21.3 | 21.0 | 20.7 | 21.8 | 21.5 | 21.1 | 21.7 | 21.6 | 21.4 |
| | INDEX | 100 | 108 | 106 | 105 | 109 | 107 | 107 | 110 | 109 | 108 |
| **EMPLOYMENT STATUS** EMPLOYED | | 7150 | 3988 | 4660 | 5338 | 4729 | 5426 | 5934 | 3480 | 3986 | 4405 |
| | COVERAGE | 100% | 55.8 | 65.2 | 74.7 | 66.1 | 75.9 | 83.0 | 48.7 | 55.7 | 61.6 |
| | COMPOSTN | 55.2 | 57.3 | 56.6 | 55.9 | 56.3 | 56.7 | 56.8 | 57.3 | 56.9 | 56.6 |
| | INDEX | 100 | 104 | 103 | 101 | 102 | 103 | 103 | 104 | 103 | 103 |
| EMPLOYED FULL-TIME | | 5645 | 3266 | 3821 | 4370 | 3749 | 4285 | 4676 | 2809 | 3286 | 3679 |
| | COVERAGE | 100% | 57.9 | 67.7 | 77.4 | 66.4 | 75.9 | 82.8 | 49.8 | 58.2 | 65.2 |
| | COMPOSTN | 43.5 | 46.9 | 46.4 | 45.8 | 44.6 | 44.8 | 44.8 | 46.3 | 46.9 | 47.3 |
| | INDEX | 100 | 108 | 106 | 105 | 102 | 103 | 103 | 106 | 108 | 109 |
| EMPLOYED PART-TIME | | 1505 | 722 | 839 | 964 | 980 | 1141 | 1258 | 672 | 700 | 724 |
| | COVERAGE | 100% | 48.0 | 55.7 | 64.1 | 65.1 | 75.8 | 83.6 | 44.7 | 46.5 | 48.1 |
| | COMPOSTN | 11.6 | 10.4 | 10.2 | 10.1 | 11.7 | 11.9 | 12.0 | 11.1 | 10.0 | 9.3 |
| | INDEX | 100 | 89 | 88 | 87 | 100 | 103 | 104 | 95 | 86 | 80 |
| NOT EMPLOYED | | 5813 | 2970 | 3580 | 4212 | 3676 | 4149 | 4511 | 2590 | 3017 | 3377 |
| | COVERAGE | 100% | 51.1 | 61.6 | 72.5 | 63.2 | 71.4 | 77.6 | 44.6 | 51.9 | 58.1 |
| | COMPOSTN | 44.8 | 42.7 | 43.4 | 44.1 | 43.7 | 43.3 | 43.2 | 42.7 | 43.1 | 43.4 |
| | INDEX | 100 | 95 | 97 | 98 | 97 | 97 | 96 | 95 | 96 | 97 |
| RETIRED | | 2101 | 1200 | 1375 | 1552 | 1308 | 1428 | 1523 | 1031 | 1180 | 1304 |
| | COVERAGE | 100% | 57.1 | 65.4 | 73.9 | 62.3 | 68.0 | 72.5 | 49.1 | 56.2 | 62.1 |
| | COMPOSTN | 16.2 | 17.2 | 16.7 | 16.3 | 15.6 | 14.9 | 14.6 | 17.0 | 16.8 | 16.8 |
| | INDEX | 100 | 106 | 103 | 100 | 96 | 92 | 90 | 105 | 104 | 103 |
| HOMEMAKER | | 2045 | 976 | 1176 | 1389 | 1321 | 1489 | 1617 | 846 | 991 | 1115 |
| | COVERAGE | 100% | 47.7 | 57.5 | 67.9 | 54.6 | 72.8 | 79.1 | 41.4 | 48.5 | 54.5 |
| | COMPOSTN | 15.8 | 14.0 | 14.3 | 14.5 | 15.7 | 15.6 | 15.5 | 13.9 | 14.2 | 14.3 |
| | INDEX | 100 | 89 | 90 | 92 | 100 | 99 | 98 | 88 | 90 | 91 |
| (TOTAL LABOR FORCE) | | 8132 | 4454 | 5257 | 6069 | 5356 | 6172 | 6765 | 3862 | 4435 | 4912 |
| | COVERAGE | 100% | 54.8 | 64.6 | 74.6 | 65.9 | 75.9 | 83.2 | 47.5 | 54.5 | 60.4 |
| | COMPOSTN | 62.7 | 64.0 | 63.8 | 63.6 | 63.7 | 64.5 | 64.7 | 63.6 | 63.3 | 63.1 |
| | INDEX | 100 | 102 | 102 | 101 | 102 | 103 | 103 | 101 | 101 | 101 |

Source: Scarborough Research Corporation.

## Magazines

Magazines are, like newspapers, a major print medium, but magazines have characteristics that are in marked contrast to newspapers. Magazines, for the most part, are a more specialized medium in terms both of readers and advertisers.

### Classes of Magazines

Standard Rate and Data Service divides magazines into three broad classes — consumer, farm, and business publications. Each of these broad classes is then subclassified into groups according to the editorial content and audience appeal of the magazine. There are over 50 consumer magazine groups (from airline in-flight to youth), 11 farm groups (dairy to poultry), and over 150 business publication groups (advertising to woodworking).

Another way to classify magazines, and one which gives perspective on the true nature of the medium, is in terms of the degree of audience specialization. Rather than dividing magazines into distinct classes, they can be thought of as running from general mass appeal to special-purpose, limited-appeal magazines. This concept is diagrammed in Exhibit 13-11. At one extreme are the very large mass-circulation magazines such as *Reader's Digest.* Moving along the spectrum, the audience appeal of the magazines progressively narrows until at the far right are found magazines such as *The Physics Teacher,* that is published for teachers of introductory physics courses.

When the term "magazine" is mentioned, most people, especially those not in advertising, think of the general mass-appeal publications. Their

Classification of magazines in terms of specialization.   **EXHIBIT 13-11**

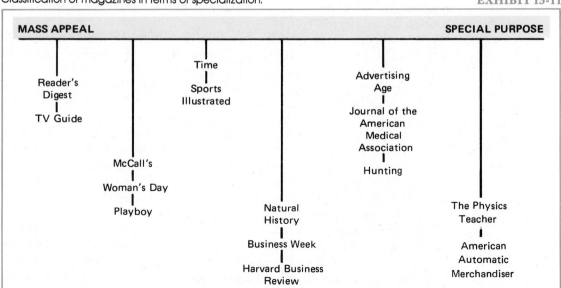

names and content are very familiar while special-purpose magazines are not widely familiar. Yet the specialized magazines outnumber the mass-appeal magazines and provide a nearly indispensable medium for many types of products.

This wide range of magazines makes it difficult to generalize about the characteristics of the medium. *Sports Illustrated* as an advertising medium probably has less in common with *The Physics Teacher* than it does with Monday-night football on television. In considering magazines as a medium, then, it is important to specify the class of magazine.

## Characteristics of Magazines as an Advertising Medium

The characteristics of magazines to be considered are the same as those discussed for newspapers to facilitate a comparison between the two media.

Audience selectivity. Magazine selectivity will be considered in terms of demographic selectivity first and then in terms of geographic selectivity.

*Demographic Selectivity.* Magazines vary greatly in their ability to pick out certain socioeconomic groups. Magazines whose appeal positions them on the left side of the scale in Exhibit 13-11 are read by members of all classes and groups. Mass-appeal magazines such as *Reader's Digest,* for example, have audiences with slightly above-average income and education, but still, every socioeconomic class is represented in their reader profiles.

Moving to the right on the scale, magazines become more selective. *McCall's* is read predominantly by women and *Sports Illustrated* has mainly male readers. Both tend to have above-average income and education profiles, yet both are mass circulation magazines with readership in all socioeconomic classes.

The majority of magazines, however, lie well to the right on the scale with highly specialized audiences. *Business Week,* for example, claims to deliver 88 percent of its circulation to people in management. Like some other special-purpose magazines, *Business Week* maintains its highly specialized audience by refusing to sell the magazine to people who do not hold a position related to the magazine's special field. The controlled-circulation magazines, which do not charge for their publications, are distributed only to people influential in the magazine's specialized field. *American Automatic Merchandiser,* for example, is a controlled-circulation magazine distributed free to vending-machine operators. Magazines on the right side of the scale of Exhibit 13-11 provide some of the most selective media vehicles available to the advertiser.

Some large-circulation magazines offer special demographic editions which permit advertisers to place ads in only those copies of the magazine that go to a pre-specified group. *Time,* for example, has demographic editions for urban subscribers, business executives, top management, high-income people, and college students.

*Geographic Selectivity.* While some magazines make it possible to select certain geographic areas for advertising coverage, they do not have the city-by-city flexibility offered by newspapers.

There are several ways in which geographic selectivity can be achieved in magazines. There are some magazines that are edited for particular regions or cities and are distributed only in those areas. *Yankee* (New England), *Southern Living* (South), and *Sunset* (West), for example, are magazines devoted to regional interests and are largely distributed in those regions. City and suburban magazines are a newer and growing media phenomenon that offer high geographic selectivity in a "glossy" editorial environment. Examples include *Chicago, Connecticut* (Hartford, New Haven, Fairfield County), and *Houston City*. There are also regional farm and business magazines. *Southern Farm Equipment* is edited for farm equipment dealers in 18 southern states and nearly all of its circulation is in this area. *Florida Trend* is a magazine that focuses on Florida business.

A second way in which geographic selectivity can be achieved is through the use of geographic editions of magazines. A growing number of magazines divide their circulation into geographic groupings and permit the advertiser to limit an advertisement to specified geographic areas. *Reader's Digest,* for example, offers advertisers the choice of any combination of ten regional editions plus ten editions directed to major markets such as Detroit and Philadelphia. Standard Rate and Data Service lists 218 consumer magazines offering geographic and/or demographic editions.[16] A substantial number of business and farm publications also offer this service. Usually it is the larger circulation publications that offer geographic editions.

AUDIENCE DISTRIBUTION. Magazine audience research services provide cumulative audience data and audience duplication data that can be used in audience distribution models to estimate reach, frequency, and distribution of audience.

Magazine reach for a single magazine insertion is low even for the larger magazines. As additional insertions in the same magazine are added, reach increases slowly since a magazine adds new readers to its audience gradually. The reach of a magazine schedule can be increased by adding different magazines to the schedule. If the added magazines selected are ones that have little audience duplication, then reach will be substantially increased.

Magazine schedules do not tend to deliver frequency of impressions as do some other media. Newspaper ads can be scheduled every day and radio commercials every fifteen minutes, but magazines are published only once a week or less so that ads can be scheduled only infrequently. Frequency can be increased by scheduling simultaneous ads in different magazines with overlapping audiences. However, frequency is probably better

---

[16]*Consumer Magazine and Farm Publication Rates and Data* (Skokie, Ill.: Standard Rate and Data Service, August 27, 1978).

obtained through use of other media in combination with magazines. Industrial advertisers, for example, often use magazines for basic coverage, supplemented by direct mail to build frequency with key prospects.

CREATIVE CHARACTERISTICS. Creatively, magazines are a very different medium from newspapers, offering a number of quality advantages, but perhaps less flexibility.

*Media Form.* Magazines are, of course, a visual medium taking physical form. As with newspapers, magazine ads are restricted to printed words and static illustrations. Magazines are an excellent medium with which to deliver coupons, schedules, addresses, or detailed instructions.

Most magazines offer reproduction quality that far surpasses that available from newspapers. Magazines are generally printed on higher quality paper and use printing processes that result in excellent reproduction. This is a particular advantage for advertisements in which illustrations are a dominant part of the ad.

Some magazines, particularly the larger ones, offer at an extra charge a variety of special advertising units that can enhance the creative value of the medium. **Bleed pages** are ones that permit the illustration to extend without a border to the very edge of the paper, giving an impression of greater size. A **gatefold** is an oversized page which the reader can fold out to full size. Bleed pages and gatefolds are attention-getting devices that also provide an extra-large advertising space. Other unusual page sizes and shapes are also available in some magazines. Inserts of various forms are possible in many magazines. An advertiser can have coupons, reply cards, recipe booklets, and many other items separately inserted into the magazine together with the advertisement. Some marketers have had product samples attached to the advertisement.

*bleed pages*

*gatefold*

*Color.* One of the most highly valued attributes of magazine advertising is the availability of high quality reproduction in full color. Of course, not all magazines offer full color, but most of the larger ones do and generally the color quality is better than that available in any other mass print medium. The availability of good quality color makes magazines a favorite medium when color is an important attribute of the product. Fashion goods such as clothing and cosmetics need color ads to show available shades. Food products use color magazine ads because the color makes the product appear appetizing.

An advertiser using color in a magazine, as in newspapers, is charged a substantially higher rate, often amounting to a 50 percent premium for full color. Use of black plus one or two other colors is often available at extra cost, but at a lower rate than full color.

*Environment.* Because of their less frequent publication and broader circulation than newspapers, magazines offer neither the news environment nor the localized atmosphere of the newspaper. Magazines have a different meaning to consumers, one that can create a highly desirable environment for advertisements.

Magazines, first of all, are a self-interest medium. People purchase and read particular magazines because the content is relevant to them. Particularly in the more specialized magazines the advertiser can expect that the reader is a voluntary one and is involved in the topic treated by the medium. Thus, an advertiser of furniture in *Better Homes and Gardens* would expect the magazine audience to be made up of people interested in home improvement. Beyond this, the advertiser would expect the reader to be in a "home-improvement mood" while reading the magazine and the advertisements.

Another environmental value of magazines, like newspapers, is that readers appear to welcome rather than resent the advertisements in magazines. In one survey of business publication readers, 69 percent reported that they welcomed advertisements in business magazines while only 10 percent rated them unfavorably.[17] In other surveys, television, by contrast, has received an almost opposite rating. It should be noted, however, that one reason why readers appreciate magazine ads is that they can quite easily be skipped. Magazine ads, unlike television ads, do not force themselves on the reader.

Finally, many magazines have an aura of prestige, expertise, and credibility that rubs off on their advertisers. To many people, the prestige of a product is enhanced if it is advertised in a well-known national publication such as *Time*. A product advertised in *Parents* benefits from the presumed concern and expertise of the magazine in the field of child care. Readers, in other words, tend to transfer some of the reputation of the magazine to the products appearing in its advertisements.

*Life.* Another distinctive attribute of magazines is their long life. While newspapers are usually read upon receipt and then discarded, magazines are usually retained in the home for several days and read intermittently over this period. Readership data in a recent magazine audience study suggests that magazine readers typically spend an hour or more over a period of 2 to 3 days reading an average magazine issue.[18]

The life of particular magazines varies considerably from the average. In general, the longer the time between issues, the longer the life. There are some magazines that are permanently retained by readers for continuing reference. Professional journals typically fall into this class as do directory or special topic issues of other magazines. People retain some magazines, such as *National Geographic* and *Gourmet,* in their libraries.

The creative value of the longer life of magazines is twofold. First, longer life means that the reading of the magazine (and hopefully, of the advertisements) is less hurried, more considered. This permits the copywriter to use longer, more detailed information and explanation. Second,

---

[17]"Executives Rate Magazine Tops in Information: McGraw-Hill," *Advertising Age,* (October 20, 1969), p. 140.
[18]*Magazine Audiences 2* (New York: Mediamark Research, Inc., Spring, 1982).

the prolonged and intermittent reading period means that readers have multiple opportunities to be exposed to the ads.

*Clutter.* The problem of media clutter is so widespread that it is difficult to point to any medium that has escaped the problem. Magazines are no exception. The better magazines, in terms of their value as advertising media, attract a great many advertisers. Magazine publishers attempt to control the clutter problem by maintaining a reasonable proportion of editorial material to advertising. The editorial material serves to separate advertisements from one another and slow the reader's progress through the publication. Yet magazines today are on the average more than half advertisements. Frequently there will be several consecutive pages of advertising unseparated by editorial material. To stop, hold, and inform a reader under such circumstances is a formidable task.

MINIMUM COST. The minimum cost of entering the magazine medium varies substantially with the selectivity of the vehicle. The large, mass-circulation magazines require a considerable investment. The space cost itself is very high in these magazines. For example, a full-page, four-color ad in *Reader's Digest* costs over $100,000; a full-page, four-color ad in *Time* costs over $50,000. In addition to the space cost, there are production costs. To take advantage of the fine reproduction available in magazines, careful and expensive production methods must be used, especially for color advertisements. The minimum magazine cost will be high if the advertiser feels, as many do, that some schedule continuity—such as one ad per month—must be maintained.

By contrast, the more specialized magazines with much smaller circulations have much lower minimum costs of entry. The space cost is much less, and the production requirements are often less stringent. For example, a full-page ad in *Advertising Age,* a leading magazine of the advertising industry, costs about $5,000 and space sizes as small as one column inch can be purchased for $74.

PRODUCTION REQUIREMENTS. The preparation of advertising materials is more demanding for magazines than it is for newspapers, both in time and money. There are a number of factors that tend to make magazine production more demanding. It has already been noted that magazines offer higher quality reproduction of advertisements, but to take advantage of this the advertising materials must be prepared with greater care. There is a tendency also to make heavy use of illustrations in magazines because they can be reproduced so well. Illustrations increase production time and cost—both in obtaining the original illustration and in preparing it for reproduction. The use of color, particularly in full-color illustrations, is another factor substantially increasing production time and cost.

The total production process for a magazine ad tends to be lengthy. For a four-color ad the total time for the initiation of production to final appearance in a magazine is often six months or more, not including the time spent in initially designing the ad. Magazine **closing dates** (the date when advertising materials must be delivered to the publication) usually fall eight weeks or more before the appearance of the ad and production of the ad often makes necessary an additional three months' lead time. Thus, the decision to use magazines must be made well in advance. Because magazines do not offer time flexibility in the way that newspapers do, they are more suitable for advertisers with advertising programs that can be planned well in advance.

MERCHANDISING VALUE. A magazine advertising schedule is usually purchased primarily because of its effectiveness in reaching the ultimate consumer of the product. However, magazine advertising can also influence the way that trade intermediaries perceive the product and can influence the sales effort that the intermediary places behind the product.

For example, if a retailer learns that a product is to be advertised in an impressively large magazine such as *McCall's* or *Reader's Digest,* it may encourage the retailer to take on extra stock of the product or display it prominently. An advertising schedule in a technical or professional journal may enhance the opinion that salespeople have of the competence and expertness of the firm.

Some magazines increase their merchandising value by promoting customers' schedules to salespeople and trade intermediaries. Although the magazines' merchandising staffs are usually quite limited, they might, if requested, mail ad reprints and schedules to retailers, appear at sales meetings to explain the importance of their magazine, or assist in other ways to help stimulate the trade.

## Users of Magazines

The leading users of magazine advertising listed in Exhibit 13-12 are predominantly large consumer products firms. Tobacco and liquor marketers, prohibited from broadcast advertising, are prominent on the list. Large food and household products companies are also heavy magazine users. These and other frequent magazine advertisers often find that magazine schedules complement their television schedules by reaching light television viewers. Automotive firms, for instance, make use of magazines to illustrate car models and as a complement to heavy television schedules. The ability to use long copy also attracts some advertisers such as book and record firms (Time, CBS, RCA), and food companies anxious to present recipes in their ads. Magazines are also widely used by some of these same advertisers to deliver coupons, reply cards, and contest entry blanks.

## Purchasing Magazine Space

Magazine space can be purchased either directly from the magazine or through its sales representative if it retains one. Magazines do not offer

EXHIBIT 13-12    Top 25 magazine advertisers, 1982.

| Rank | Advertiser | Expenditures ($000) |
|------|-----------|---------------------|
| 1 | Philip Morris Inc. | $130,094.3 |
| 2 | R. J. Reynolds Industries | 111,102.6 |
| 3 | General Motors Corp. | 86,079.7 |
| 4 | Batus Inc. | 73,461.5 |
| 5 | Seagram Co. Ltd. | 62,024.0 |
| 6 | Ford Motor Co. | 58,735.2 |
| 7 | Sears, Roebuck & Co. | 51,179.4 |
| 8 | AT&T Co. | 40,858.3 |
| 9 | American Brands | 32,279.5 |
| 10 | Time Inc. | 30,206.7 |
| 11 | Procter & Gamble | 29,969.4 |
| 12 | General Foods Corp. | 29,746.5 |
| 13 | Loews Corp. | 28,955.4 |
| 14 | Volkswagen of America | 28,599.5 |
| 15 | Johnson & Johnson | 28,535.4 |
| 16 | CBS Inc. | 28,248.0 |
| 17 | Norton Simon Inc. | 26,742.3 |
| 18 | Dart & Kraft | 26,110.3 |
| 19 | U.S. Government | 25,631.1 |
| 20 | Chrysler Corp. | 25,582.2 |
| 21 | Bristol-Myers Co. | 25,244.0 |
| 22 | GrandMet USA | 25,205.7 |
| 23 | Warner Communications | 24,929.6 |
| 24 | Hiram Walker Resources | 23,652.4 |
| 25 | RCA Corp. | 23,362.1 |

Reprinted with permission from the September 8, 1983, issue of *Advertising Age*. Copyright 1983 by Crain Communications, Inc.

special lower rates for local or retail advertisers; consequently, all advertisers purchase through the same channels.

MAGAZINE RATES. Magazine space rates are usually quoted in units of pages and fractions of pages. There are usually separate rates quoted for color and for some special positions in the magazine such as covers, with separate rates or additional charges for special services such as bleed pages, inserts, and regional or demographic editions.

Almost all magazines offer discounts for quantity purchases in some time period, usually a year. The discount may be based on the dollar volume purchased, on the number of insertions, or on some other basis. These volume discounts are a substantial incentive to the advertiser to maintain continuity in a magazine. As an example, *McCall's* offers a 5 percent discount for three to five pages in a year, 7 percent for six to eleven pages, 10 percent for twelve to seventeen pages, and so on.[19]

---

[19]*Consumer Magazine and Farm Publication Rates and Data* (Skokie, Ill.: Standard Rate and Data Service, Inc., July 27, 1983), p. 554.

INFORMATION SOURCES. Each magazine publishes a rate card containing space rates, discounts, closing dates, and other information. Exhibit 13-13 shows a section of a rate card for *McCall's*. However, most frequent magazine advertisers subscribe to Standard Rate and Data Service's *Consumer Magazine and Farm Publication Rates and Data* and to their *Business Publications Rates and Data*. These services summarize rates, production requirements, personnel, special services, and circulation figures for all major publications.

SRDS does not contain audience data nor does it have detailed breakdowns of circulation. There are several independent research firms that regularly survey the audience of the larger magazines and, in turn, sell the results to advertisers. These services were described and illustrated in Chapter 12.

Magazine circulation figures can be obtained directly from publishers' statements. In addition, many magazines provide extensive audience data based upon research that they themselves have sponsored. Most of these studies concentrate on describing the characteristics of their readers. Occasionally a group of magazines will join together to sponsor audience studies for all participating publications.

## Newspaper Supplements

Newspaper supplements are a smaller medium than either magazines or newspapers, but they are unusual in that they combine some attributes of both. Supplements can best be understood by comparing their characteristics to newspapers and magazines.

### Classes of Supplements

Newspaper supplements are special sections of a newspaper, prepared

A section of a rate card for *McCall's*.                                        **EXHIBIT 13-13**

| SPACE UNITS | FOUR COLOR | | BLACK & 1 COLOR | | BLACK & WHITE | |
|---|---|---|---|---|---|---|
| | RATE | CPM* | RATE | CPM | RATE | CPM |
| Page | $64,620 | $10.42 | $60,950 | $9.83 | $52,560 | $8.48 |
| 2/3 Page Ver./Hor. | 49,100 | 7.92 | 42,970 | 6.93 | 37,200 | 6.00 |
| 1/2 Page Ver./Hor. | 38,560 | 6.22 | 34,100 | 5.50 | 29,700 | 4.79 |
| Digest Size | 38,560 | 6.22 | 34,100 | 5.50 | 29,700 | 4.79 |
| 1/3 Page Ver./ Sq. | 27,280 | 4.40 | 23,190 | 3.74 | 20,150 | 3.25 |
| 2nd Cover | 79,670 | 12.85 | — | — | — | — |
| 3rd Cover | 76,320 | 12.31 | — | — | — | — |
| Back Cover | 91,390 | 14.74 | — | — | — | — |
| Agate Line | — | — | — | — | 167.90 | |

*Cost per thousand readers

Source: *McCall's*, Rate Card No. 91 (McCall Publishing Co., 1984).

in magazine format and distributed as part of a newspaper at no extra charge. Usually distributed with the Sunday newspaper, they are frequently called Sunday supplements. The content of the supplements is similar to that of a general circulation magazine, containing feature articles, columns, and fiction. There are some supplements, however, whose content consists primarily of television schedules and program descriptions.

A media form closely related to newspaper supplements is the Sunday comic section. These sections have a different editorial environment than magazine-styled supplements, but many of their other characteristics are the same.

Supplements and comic sections can be further classified as group publications or independent publications. A group supplement or comic section is one that is distributed in a number of markets and purchased in multiple market combinations by advertisers. *Family Weekly, Parade,* and *Sunday* are the three group or national supplements. Each has a very large circulation. *Parade,* the largest, has a circulation in excess of 20 million and an audience in excess of 40 million, making it an equivalent of the largest consumer magazines. The two nationally distributed Sunday comics sections are *Metro Comics* and *Puck. Metro,* the largest, is distributed with 95 newspapers and offers circulation in excess of 20 million.

Independent supplements and comic sections are ones published individually by a newspaper and purchased individually by advertisers. The largest and probably best known independent newspaper supplement is the *New York Times Magazine Section.*

## Characteristics of Supplements as a Medium

Newspaper supplements are published in the format of a magazine, but are distributed like a newspaper. Consequently this medium tends to have audience characteristics like those of a newspaper and some of the creative characteristics of a magazine.

AUDIENCE SELECTIVITY. The newspaper supplement audience, like that of the newspaper that distributes the supplement, is intensive rather than demographically selective. Accompanying the Sunday newspaper, the supplement is delivered to a majority of families regardless of social or economic standing.

On the other hand, supplements, like newspapers, can be highly selective geographically. If independent supplements or comic sections are used, the advertising area can be built up on a city-by-city basis to match the advertiser's distribution area or the pattern of advertising weight desired. If the entire edition of a large supplement group is purchased, coverage is very extensive. Circulation tends to focus in urban areas with "holes" in the coverage from cities that do not distribute that supplement. Most supplement groups offer regional editions similar to those available from the larger magazines. This increases the geographic flexibility of the group supplements.

AUDIENCE DISTRIBUTION. The distribution of the audience for a schedule of advertisements in a supplement would be like that realized in a newspaper advertising schedule, since the supplement is distributed automatically with the newspaper. Initial reach would include a large proportion of the market and then rise only slowly with additional insertions unless supplements in additional markets were added to the schedule.

As with the newspaper, there would be a tendency for frequency to rise with the number of insertions in a particular supplement. If an additional supplement were added to the schedule, the frequency increase would be negligible as there tends to be little duplication between supplements. Because supplements appear only weekly, it takes longer to build up frequency with successive insertions than it does in daily newspapers.

CREATIVE CHARACTERISTICS. Supplements and comic sections are physical-form media, lending themselves to illustration, longer, more detailed copy, and delivery of items such as coupons, entry blanks, and addresses.

The quality of reproduction in supplements is generally better than in newspapers because of the printing process used and the higher grade of paper. Most supplements offer full-color reproduction. The color quality is better than that found in newspapers, though not as good as in major magazines. Comic sections generally offer color reproduction, but the quality is not equal to that offered by supplements.

The environment in which a supplement ad appears is less distinctive than the environment in the case of either newspapers or magazines. The supplement, because of its more generalized editorial content, does not fully share the environment of urgency or news value found in the regular newspaper sections. Neither does it have, particularly for the supplement groups and comic sections, a local community orientation. Supplements also lack the special-interest environment of magazines; editorial material is designed to be acceptable to everyone rather than being directed to special interests. The supplement, because it is seen as free, may not be treated as seriously as a magazine which is purchased separately. Supplements probably do not have the prestige of the better magazines.

The life of a supplement in the home tends to be short. In most cases, an exception being those supplements containing television schedules, the supplement or comic section is disposed of with the newspaper, usually after one day. Supplements are a cluttered medium. Not only is there a large proportion of advertising to editorial material, but also the ads themselves tend to be what advertisers term "busy," containing many visual elements and a great deal of copy.

MINIMUM COST AND PRODUCTION REQUIREMENTS. Since independent supplements can be purchased singly and minimum space units are usually small, supplements can be a low minimum-cost medium like newspapers and the specialized magazines. However, the purchase of a supplement group requires a substantial minimum investment much like a major consumer magazine. A single, full four-color page in *Parade* or *Sunday,* for example, would cost in excess of $200,000. The decision to use color also increases minimum cost because production charges are higher, minimum ad size is larger, and space cost is greater.

If the advertiser plans to use color advertisements in a supplement group, the production requirements are similar to those for magazines. Although supplements are frequently printed by a different process than are magazines, it still takes a substantial period of time to produce quality materials. The supplement groups also require materials well in advance of the issue date—eight weeks is not unusual.

Conversely, the local advertiser using black-and-white ads in independent supplements has production requirements more like those of a newspaper. The advertising materials can be prepared more quickly and the supplement often requires materials less than a week in advance.

## Users of Supplements

Newspaper supplements appear to have attracted a few distinctive classes of advertisers who dominate most supplement issues. Food products and women's fashion products are frequently featured in supplements. Supplements deliver very large female audiences and they offer the opportunity to use good quality color reproduction that is important to these products. Supplements are also used frequently to announce special sales promotions such as contests, reduced price sales, or other purchase incentives since they enable the advertiser to physically deliver the promotion details or coupons to the reader.

Perhaps most obvious in reading an issue of a supplement is the very heavy use of the medium by mail-order advertisers. Record and book clubs, seed and flower companies, correspondence schools, and gadget vendors are very heavy supplement advertisers. Supplements offer mass audiences, the opportunity for long copy and illustration of the product, and enable the mail-order advertiser to provide coupons and mailing instructions. Exhibit 13-14 shows a typical supplement ad by a mail-order advertiser.

## Purchasing Supplement Space

Advertising space in independent supplements is purchased directly from the distributing newspaper or its sales representative. Supplement or comic-section groups are purchased from the supplement publisher rather than from each individual newspaper. The larger publishers usually have branch offices or sales representatives in major cities.

SUPPLEMENT RATES. Supplement and comic-section rates are generally quoted in terms of pages and fractions of pages and, occasionally, for very small-sized ads, in terms of column inches or lines. These publications normally offer discounts for quantity purchases and for continuity of purchases that compare favorably with the discounts offered by magazines and newspapers.

A typical supplement ad by a mail-order advertiser.

EXHIBIT 13-14

INFORMATION SOURCES. Information on rates, discounts, production requirements, and circulation can be obtained from supplement publishers' rate cards and publishers' statements. The *Newspaper Rates and Data* edition of Standard Rate and Data Service contains summary information for all supplements and comic sections.

The major national supplement and comic groups are included in the syndicated-magazine audience-studies and hence good audience data are available. Independent supplements, except for a few very large ones, are not included. However, since the audience of the independent supplement is virtually the same as that of the newspaper which distributes it, newspaper audience studies, which are available for many newspapers, give good evidence concerning the expected characteristics of supplement audiences.

*CHAPTER SUMMARY*

Although city dailies are the dominant class of newspapers, there are also national newspapers, weekly newspapers, shopping guides, and special audience newspapers. Daily newspapers are demographically nonselective, but offer geographic selectivity by city. Newspapers offer very large initial reach and evenly distributed exposure. Creatively, newspapers offer the opportunity to use illustration, but printing quality and color are only fair. Newspapers offer a news environment and a local community orientation which provide a valuable association for some products. They are also used by consumers as a source of shopping information. Newspapers are a short-lived, cluttered medium, but low cost of entry and flexible production requirements make them a favorite of small advertisers. Local advertisers, also drawn by favorable local rates, localized environment, and geographic flexibility, are the heaviest users of newspapers.

Magazines vary from general interest, mass-circulation magazines to specialized, limited-appeal magazines. The specialized magazines are selective in their audiences while the general interest magazines have a broad audience. Magazines generally do not have the city-by-city geographic flexibility that newspapers have. Magazine-schedule audience-distribution is one of low frequency and initially low and slowly growing reach. Creatively, magazines offer high quality reproduction and good color, but most important, they are a self-interest medium for readers. Magazines offer longer life than most media. Production requirements are lengthy and costly, especially for color advertising. Magazines are used by a wide variety of consumer and industrial products marketers, but not usually by local advertisers.

Newspaper supplements, since they are distributed by newspapers, have audience characteristics similar to newspapers. Creatively, however, newspaper supplements are more like general-circulation magazines, offering quality color reproduction and a general-interest editorial environment.

Media selectivity
Demographically selective medium
Geographically selective medium
Audience distribution
ROP color
Color preprints
Free-standing insert
Media life
Clutter
Merchandising value of the medium

Cooperative advertising
Flat rate
Open rate
Short-rate bill
Combination rate
Publisher's statement
Audit report
Bleed pages
Gatefold
Closing dates

1. The Wall Street Journal claims that it is a national newspaper. It has daily circulation of nearly 2 million and is clearly a successful medium.

   a. Would you classify the *WSJ* as a newspaper?
   b. What special media characteristics does it have?

2. One of the distinctive characteristics of "shoppers" is that they are given away free, relying entirely on the sale of advertising for revenue. What are the advantages and disadvantages to the advertiser of this free distribution?

3. A recent study of computerized scanner data from a sample of stores revealed that when products were featured in newspaper ads at regular prices, their sales doubled as compared to the non-advertised period.[20] When the product was advertised and featured at a price cut, sales of the product were three times as great as sales during the non-advertised period. What do these results suggest about the characteristics of newspapers as an advertising medium?

4. One of the most important advantages of advertising in newspapers is the medium's ability to quickly reach a large proportion of the adult population of a city. For each of the following problems, evaluate the importance of fast, extensive reach as a media requirement.

   a. Recall of a defective product.
   b. Introduction of a new automobile model.
   c. Reminder advertising for a soft drink.
   d. Announcement of a department store menswear sale.
   e. Stimulation of leads for industrial sewing machine salespeople.

---

[20]*Key Facts About Newspapers and Advertising 1982, op. cit.,* p. 11.

5. Some newspaper advertisers feel that to be effective, their advertisement must be large enough to "get over the fold" (i.e., be larger than one-half page). What problems do advertisers try to overcome with this approach?

6. Each of the advertiser categories listed below is a frequent user of newspaper advertising. Indicate for each the *creative* attribute of the newspaper medium that would tend to attract these advertisers.

   a. Food advertising by a supermarket.
   b. Loan advertising by a local bank.
   c. Advertising of flight schedules by an airline.
   d. Distribution of a coupon by a soap advertiser.
   e. Introduction of a new food product.

7. The three business magazines with the greatest number of advertising pages in a recent year were *Travel Agent, Electronic News,* and *The Blood Horse.*[21]

   a. By consulting the appropriate volume of Standard Rate and Data Service, determine the audience characteristics of these three publications.
   b. Based on the above, what advertisers do you think would advertise in each?

8. One of the most important attributes of a magazine is the readers' self-interest in the contents of the magazine. Advertisers try to take advantage of this interest by placing advertising for their products in magazines whose editorial content concerns subjects related to the products. Following this approach, suggest an appropriate magazine for each of the following products.

   a. Ceiling tile for self-installation in homes.
   b. An investment advisory service.
   c. A cosmetic for teenage girls.
   d. An educational toy for preschool children.
   e. Advertising space in a new magazine.

9. Some consumer magazines are sold primarily by subscription with only limited sales on newsstands. Other magazines, such as *Women's Day* and *TV Guide* are sold primarily on a single issue rather than subscription basis. From an advertiser's standpoint, what is the advantage offered by each of these two types of sales approaches?

---

[21]"Top 50 Business Magazines by Advertising Pages," *Advertising Age* (May 10, 1982), p. M-8.

10. Newspaper supplements have had a very uneven record of success through the years, but recently several major newspapers have discontinued their locally produced supplements, reporting that retailers, their most important advertisers, have turned to alternate media. What media do you expect retailers might substitute for supplements?

---

*PROBLEM*

An old, established manufacturer of marine hardware is attempting to expand its distribution by adding to the number of dealers carrying the line. The company has established a special budget of $12,500 for this effort in addition to the company's regular advertising which is generally directed to end consumers.

The company's product line contains over 800 items, including products such as blocks, cleats, ventilators, and turnbuckles. The products have application on pleasure craft and on small commercial vessels such as fishing boats. The products are sold directly to boatbuilders and to consumers through marine supply stores, marinas, and boat yards. It was among these consumer outlets that the company wished to recruit new dealers. Dealers were desired throughout the United States although, of course, most of them would be concentrated in coastal boating areas.

The media requirements for this effort specified that the prospects to be reached were marine supply retailers, marina operators, and boat yards. The creative requirements for the media were modest — small space print ads were anticipated in black and white with a small reply coupon included for those wishing further information. Inquiring dealers would be visited personally by a company salesperson. Production costs of $1,000 were anticipated. This expense would come out of the $12,500 budget. A final media requirement was to stress reach rather than frequency to attempt to cover as many different prospective dealers as possible.

1. Using a copy of Standard Rate and Data Service's *Business Publications Rates and Data,* make a list of possible publications which might be used for this media program.
2. Refine the list by examing circulation information for each publication, eliminating those whose audience does not fit the prospect definition.
3. Compute a cost estimate per thousand prospects for each of the publications on the list in question 2.
4. Prepare a recommended publication list and schedule of insertions for the company's dealer recruitment objective.

# CHAPTER 14

*The Media Program — Television, Radio, and the New Electronic Media*

LEARNING OBJECTIVES

In studying this chapter you will learn:

- The types of time purchases available for radio, television, and the new electronic media.

- The respective characteristics of radio, television, and the new electronic media as advertising media.

- Who the heavy users are of the advertising time in radio, television, and the new electronic media.

- The information sources used and the media specialists relied upon when purchasing time in the broadcast media.

Television and radio, the two broadcast media, are among the largest and most important media available to the advertiser. While television and radio have numerous technical similarities, from the standpoint of the advertiser, they have major differences both in the characteristics of their audiences and in their creative characteristics. A third class of broadcast media, the new electronic media, are an outgrowth of television, but will be considered separately.

## Television

Television did not become important as an advertising medium until the 1950s, but since that time, it has been the fastest growing medium. It now ranks second only to newspapers in advertising revenue.

Television's ranking in total revenue may not completely explain the relative importance of the medium. There are some types of manufacturers for whom television has become a highly dominant and indispensable medium much as newspapers have historically been the indispensable medium of the retailer. The large-scale marketers of consumer packaged goods (foods, drugs, toiletries, household cleaners) are a leading example of a group that devotes a dominant portion of its advertising to television. These heavy users of television are among the nation's largest corporations. In 1982 television was the most important medium for 85 of the top 100 national advertisers. (The notable exceptions are tobacco and liquor marketers that are prohibited from broadcast advertising.) The heavy users of television advertising spent an average of 67 percent of their total media budgets in this one medium, compared to only 16 percent for magazines, the next most important medium.[1]

## Types of Television Purchases

There are a number of different types of television time purchases available to the advertiser. These different types permit the television advertiser to vary the location and characteristics of the audience.

NETWORK VS. LOCAL PURCHASES. One way to purchase television is to buy time on a local television station. The advertiser's commercial is then telecast by the local station and seen only in the viewing area of that station. Combinations of several stations in different areas might be used to form larger geographic patterns.

An alternative type of purchase is a network buy. Each of the three dominant television networks—National Broadcasting Company (NBC), Columbia Broadcasting System (CBS), and American Broadcasting Company (ABC)—has a series of affiliated local television stations to which it supplies programs and services. The networks each try to have enough affiliates distributed nationally to cover all homes with television sets. NBC, CBS, and ABC each have more than 200 affiliates, giving each network almost complete national coverage. When an advertiser purchases advertising time from one of the networks, the commercial is transmitted as part of the network's program to the local affiliated stations across the nation and broadcast through each local station to its audience. The result is nearly complete national advertising coverage.

PROGRAM VS. SPOT. The television advertiser can purchase a program or part of a program and then schedule the commercial within that program or the advertiser can puchase a **spot** which is a position between programs when the commercial will be broadcast. Local stations sell their own programs (such as local news and weather shows) to advertisers, but programs originated by the networks (such as *Cheers* or *Hill Street Blues*) are sold only by the networks, typically on a national basis. Local stations can sell spots before and after (and sometimes partway through) network programs during station breaks.

*spot*

The difference between the audience reached by a program and the audience reached by a spot is a qualitative difference. Spots do not consistently reach a different type of person than do programs, but the program

---

[1]*Advertising Age* (September 8, 1983), p. 24.

audience is probably more attentive than the spot audience. During station breaks, viewers are less attentive and tend to leave the viewing area. Purchasers of program time, moreover, may benefit from association with a program that they sponsor.

TIME PERIOD AND DAY OF WEEK. The television buyer can vary the audience for advertising through selection of time and day. During daytime hours on weekdays, the television audience is heavily weighted with homemakers and preschool children. Late hours in the evening have mainly adult viewers, Saturday mornings have heavy viewership by young children, and weekend afternoons have above-average adult male viewership. Exhibit 14-1 illustrates the change in television audience by "daypart."

EXHIBIT 14-1    Indexes of television viewing by daypart

| | Daytime Mon.–Fri. 10AM– 4:30PM | Early Evening Mon.–Fri. 4:30– 7:30PM | Prime Mon.–Sun. 8–11PM | Late Evening Mon.–Sun. 11:30PM– 1AM | Weekend Mornings Sat.–Sun. 7AM–1PM |
|---|---|---|---|---|---|
| **Total Persons** | | | | | |
| Average Weekly Viewing Hours | 4.42 | 4.27 | 6.65 | 1.64 | .68 |
| Index | 100 | 100 | 100 | 100 | 100 |
| **Men** | | | | | |
| Total | 58 | 89 | 102 | 120 | 75 |
| 18–24 | 55 | 66 | 77 | 127 | 75 |
| 25–34 | 40 | 70 | 99 | 129 | 72 |
| 35–54 | 41 | 80 | 101 | 116 | 74 |
| 18–49 | 44 | 71 | 93 | 123 | 74 |
| 55+ | 95 | 132 | 124 | 112 | 76 |
| **Women** | | | | | |
| Total | 145 | 109 | 113 | 116 | 74 |
| 18–24 | 135 | 91 | 97 | 112 | 90 |
| 25–34 | 137 | 89 | 108 | 120 | 74 |
| 35–54 | 138 | 102 | 115 | 132 | 68 |
| 18–49 | 134 | 91 | 106 | 119 | 75 |
| 55+ | 164 | 141 | 124 | 101 | 72 |
| **Teens** | | | | | |
| Total | 79 | 85 | 86 | 88 | 99 |
| Male | 53 | 80 | 86 | 100 | 109 |
| Female | 106 | 90 | 86 | 77 | 88 |
| **Children** | | | | | |
| Total | 96 | 113 | 71 | 21 | 225 |
| 2–5 | 135 | 119 | 56 | 12 | 250 |
| 6–11 | 72 | 110 | 81 | 26 | 210 |

Source: *O & M Pocket Guide to Media*, 8th ed. (New York: Ogilvy and Mather, 1983), pp. 22–23.

PROGRAM TYPE. In addition to deciding the time of day and day of week, the television advertiser can influence the characteristics of the audience by the type of program bought or by the type of program next to which a spot is purchased. *NFL Football, Magnum PI,* and *Hill Street Blues* have heavy male viewership while *Dallas* and *Dynasty* have heavy female viewership and *Facts of Life* attracts children and teenagers. Exhibit 14-2 shows how audience composition varies for popular program types.

## Characteristics of Television as an Advertising Medium

Television can have different advertising characteristics depending upon the type of purchase made. In the section that follows, attention will be given to ways in which the television purchase can be tailored to an advertiser's particular objectives.

Audience composition by selected program type: regularly scheduled network programs 6–11 p.m. (average minute audiences).

EXHIBIT 14-2

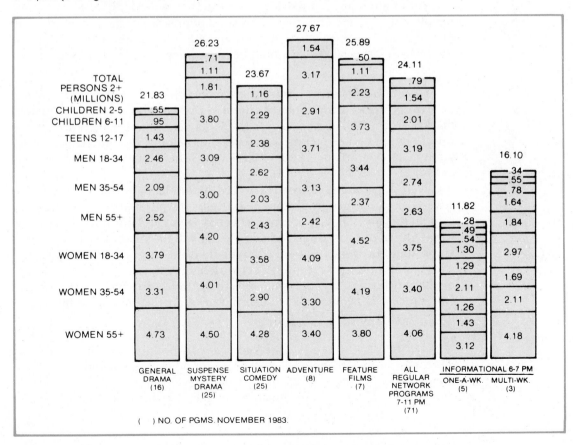

Source: *'84 Nielsen Report on Television* (Chicago: A. C. Nielsen Co., 1984), p. 11.

AUDIENCE SELECTIVITY. Television is not a highly selective medium. It offers neither the geographic selectivity of newspapers nor the demographic selectivity of the specialized magazines.

*Demographic Selectivity.* Although television can be purchased to give emphasis to certain audience groups, it offers weak demographic selectivity. Television's great strength lies in its ability to reach a mass audience. Today, nearly every home has a television set—98 percent of all homes are equipped with sets and more than half of all households have multiple sets.[2] Moreover, the amount of time spent viewing television far exceeds the time spent with any other medium. In 1982, the members of television households are estimated to have spent 6¾ hours a day viewing television. As shown in Exhibit 14-3, the time spent in viewing varies substantially by age group. Older adults, women, and preschool children are very heavy viewers, a fact which reflects the greater amount of time they spend in the home. There is some decline in viewing by the upper economic class, but there is still considerable television usage by all economically important demographic groups.

Although television reaches a mass audience made up of all classes of people, it is possible to emphasize certain demographic groups by the type of program and the time of day purchased. The audience, however, will not be highly specialized, as would be, for example, the audience of a medical journal.

*area of dominant influence (ADI)*

*designated market area (DMA)*

*Geographic Selectivity.* Television geographic coverage is designated in term of **areas of dominant influence (ADIs),** also termed **designated market areas (DMAs).** An *ADI* or *DMA* is a geographic market area made up of counties whose television viewership belongs predominantly to the same metropolitan area. Exhibit 14-4 shows the Designated Market Areas as assigned by A. C. Nielsen, Inc.

Note how large an area is covered by a television station. While the advertiser can be geographically selective by buying spots in only one or in combinations of DMAs, the area covered is large. The smaller marketer whose distribution is limited to a single city will find that even a single television station covers an area far larger than the business's customer area. This results in wasted coverage. Network television is, of course, a national medium offering no geographic selectivity under ordinary circumstances. Occasionally networks will sell a program on a regional basis, but this is increasingly rare.

AUDIENCE DISTRIBUTION. Audience distribution is concerned with the total number of people exposed to an advertiser's schedule and the number of times they see one of the advertiser's commercials. The distribution of the audience is determined by people's viewing habits. Nearly every-

---

[2] *Nielsen Report on Television, 1983* (Chicago: A. C. Nielsen Co., 1983), p. 3.

Weekly hours of viewing by age group.    EXHIBIT 14-3

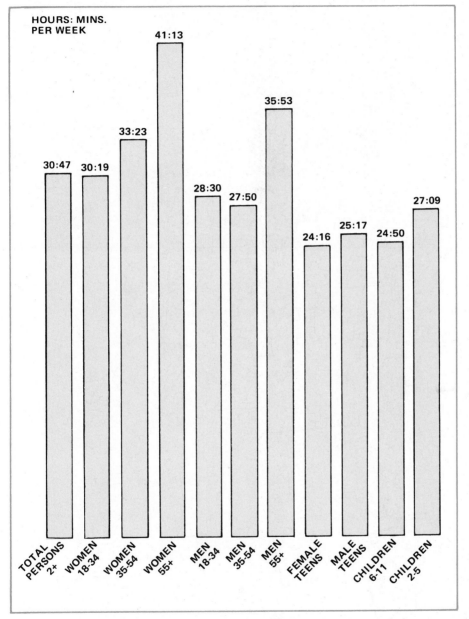

Source: '84 Nielsen Report on Television (Chicago: A. C. Nielsen Co., 1984), pp. 8–9.

one views television and average viewing time is great, but viewing is spread over a variety of stations (three or more in major markets) and over many hours of telecasting each day.

*Television Reach.* Because viewing is widely spread, the number of persons seeing any one program episode or any one spot announcement is

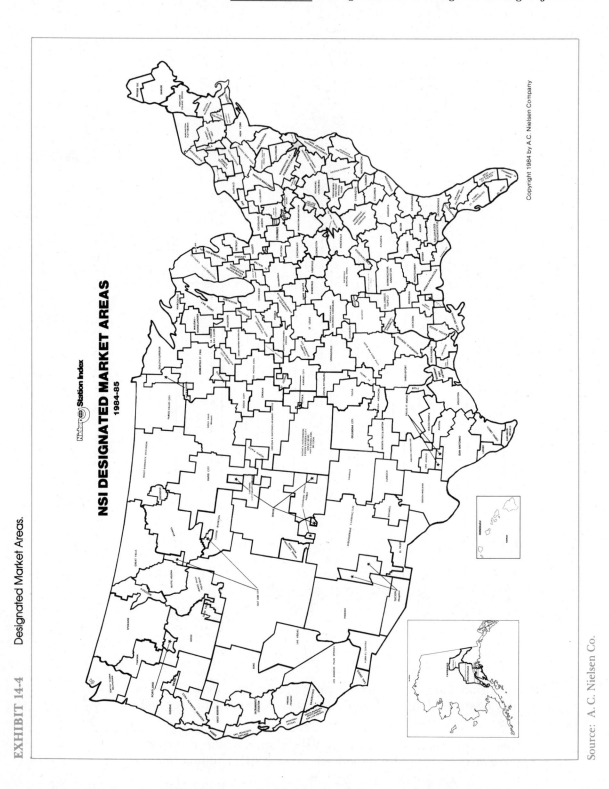

**EXHIBIT 14-4**    Designated Market Areas.

Source:  A. C. Nielsen Co.

likely to be low. For example, only the most popular evening programs and a few special-event telecasts are seen by as many as 20 percent of all television households and the majority of telecasts are seen by considerably fewer. As additional announcements are added to the schedule, however, reach grows rapidly, reflecting the heavy viewing in the average home. If schedules are extended over several weeks, total reach grows to include nearly all television homes. It is estimated that a schedule of 5 spot announcements in a week in the top 100 markets in prime evening time will reach 45 percent of all television homes in just one week and over a four-week period will reach 71 percent of all television homes in those markets.[3]

*Television Frequency.* The frequency also increases as successive announcements are added to the television schedule. The increase in frequency is, however, rather slow since exposures are spread over such a large total audience and each successive announcement tends to reach a large proportion of different viewers. Thus, successive announcements increase reach more than frequency. If three prime-time evening announcements were used in the top 100 markets, the result would be an average frequency of 1.5. If the schedule were extended from three exposures in one week to twelve exposures over four weeks, the average viewer's exposure would rise to only 3.8 times over the four weeks.[4]

*Manipulating Reach and Frequency.* The advertiser can influence reach and frequency results by the type of schedule purchased. Recall that frequency is increased when media vehicles with high duplication of audience are chosen. If an advertiser wishes to emphasize frequency, the commercial could be placed in the same program on consecutive days or weeks, because most programs have substantial numbers of loyal viewers. If, however, the advertiser wishes to emphasize reach, the commercials should be in different time periods and programs, thus minimizing duplication.

*Distribution of Television Viewing.* Figures on reach and frequency and average viewing behavior obscure an important characteristic of the television audience. Viewing of television is very unevenly distributed. There is a relatively small number of heavy television viewers who account for a disproportionate percentage of total viewing time. It also follows that there is a substantial number who are counted as viewers who really do very little viewing. Therefore, as a television schedule is extended, frequency tends to build up with this relatively small group of heavy viewers. As a result, the advertiser finds that a great many messages have been delivered to the heavy-viewer group, but relatively few to the light viewer. If the heavy viewer and the light viewer are of equal value as prospects, this result would be undesirable. The advertiser can attempt to alleviate this problem in two ways. Every effort could be made to scatter the television buy to

---

[3]*TV Basics, 21* (New York: Television Bureau of Advertising, 1978).
[4]*TV Basics, 13* (New York: Television Bureau of Advertising, 1970).

obtain maximum exposure to different audience segments — that is, to strive for reach.

Another alternative is to supplement the television schedule with other media that tend to have an audience made up of light television viewers. Which medium this will be varies with the particular nonviewer segment desired. Male teenagers, for example, are light television viewers, but form a heavy radio listener group.

CREATIVE CHARACTERISTICS. Television offers a unique combination of creative attributes that probably affords greater creative latitude than any other medium.

*Media Form.* Television alone of the major media combines sight, sound, and motion. This combination makes television a highly powerful medium when product demonstration is needed. On television the advertiser can show the product, demonstrate how it works, and give a verbal explanation. The television commercial in Exhibit 14-5 is a good example of the use of television to demonstrate a product. Television advertisers can also have persuasive personalities or experts explain the product with heightened effectiveness since they are both seen and heard.

Television is not, of course, delivered in a physical form like a magazine, making it impossible to deliver items such as coupons and making delivery of directions, mailing instructions and addresses difficult.

The quality of reproduction offered by television is in most cases good, although it is rather difficult to find a standard for comparison. Better antennas, use of relay stations, and wiring of individual homes for television have reduced problems of poor reception.

*Color.* For many years television lacked the critical creative dimension of color. The technical problems of color television were overcome some 25 years ago, but its availability to advertisers was limited by the lack of color broadcasting facilities at television stations and the low ownership level of private color television sets. Both of these problems have been substantially overcome. Today nearly all television stations are able to telecast color film or videotape supplied by the advertiser. Color television set ownership had very slow initial growth, but is now increasing rapidly. By 1983, 89 percent of all television households had color sets as compared to only 3 percent in 1964.[5]

Along with increased availability of color facilities there has also been an improvement in the quality of color telecasting. Although television color-casting does not have the color fidelity of a good magazine page, it is adequate to represent most products.

*Environment.* Like almost everything else about the medium, the advertising environment in television is unique. Television is the dominant entertainment medium in our society and people turn to it first for relaxation

---

[5]*Nielsen Report on Television, 1983, op. cit.,* p. 3.

Example of the use of television to demonstrate a product.   **EXHIBIT 14-5**

Seventeen hours...

That's how long it took us to paint this house with a brush.
SUPER: "EXCLUDING TRIM"

Then we painted it in just six and a half hours with a Wagner Power Painter.

This wicker chair took over an hour.

But less than five minutes

with a Wagner Power Painter.

A shutter that ...

took twenty minutes.

A power painter finished in only three.

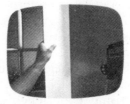

It's a tool so versatile

It has a flexible spray tip

and a way to draw paint right from a can.

A Wagner Power Painter.

It's the right tool for painting.

and amusement. However, television has also made strides as a source of news and through its news and documentary programming has enhanced its believability. Generally, though, viewers do not watch television in order to see the commercials; they suffer commercials as the price for the entertainment and their attentiveness to commercials is likely to be low. Commercials, particularly during station breaks, provide viewers with time to leave the room or carry on a conversation. However, this low interest in the commercials is offset by the intrusive nature of television. Television viewers are, in part, a captive audience and commercials intrude or force their way into the viewers' minds.

What can be said about the carryover effect of television programs themselves on the advertisers' products? Some television programs are educational, uplifting, and prestigious, but this does not characterize the great mass of television programming. Television programming has been accused of being too bland, too escapist, and aimed too low intellectually. Most television advertisers today make little effort to relate their products directly to the programming vehicle. Instead they scatter their commercials among many different vehicles. While there are exceptions, sports programs being a notable one, most advertisers apparently see little value in program association.

*Life.* As far as the advertiser is concerned, television is a very short-lived medium. The advertiser's message lasts a minute or fraction of a minute and then disappears. Nothing tangible is left for the viewer to examine or consider at leisure; therefore, the advertiser's message must be simple and easily understood in the short viewing time. Complicated directions, involved arguments, or long lists cannot be presented effectively on television. Good television commercials focus on presenting a single, simple, memorable selling proposition.

The use of television by some retailers illustrates how some advertisers have misunderstood this characteristic of television. These retailers, whose advertising experience has been mainly in newspapers, tend to use newspaper-styled ads for television. Long lists of products and prices are presented at breathtaking speed. The viewer has no time to pause and consider the offerings, as is possible with newspapers. Other retailers, better appreciating the characteristics of television, concentrate each commercial on a single product or perhaps on a single attribute of their stores.

*Clutter.* Because commercials on television have become so numerous, many advertisers feel that television's value to them has seriously diminished. A number of factors have contributed to the clutter problem on television. First, with increasing demand for television time, television stations and networks have turned over a greater amount of time to commercials as contrasted to programming. Under current standards, television networks schedule 10 minutes of non-program materials (commercials and program promotions) per hour during prime time (7:30 P.M.–11:00 P.M.) and

16 minutes during non prime time.[6] Secondly, as was shown earlier in Exhibit 12-8, advertisers have shifted to greater use of the shorter-length commercials so that a greater number of commercials now appear in a given time period. Recently, all three television networks, under pressure from advertisers, have begun accepting split 30's on an experimental basis. Split 30's are two 15-second commercials for unrelated products of the same advertiser presented piggyback fashion in the same 30-second time period. If split 30's become generally accepted, television clutter will increase dramatically.

It is difficult to assess quantitatively the impact of increased clutter on television, but most observers believe that it lowers overall attentiveness to commercials and increases confusion in identifying products. The television advertiser must use clear, simple messages, presented in a way that will make them stand apart from the clutter. This is a difficult creative task.

MINIMUM COST. The minimum cost of entering the television medium presents some barriers to use by smaller advertisers. Network television, in particular, has such high costs even for a minimum schedule that only the large advertisers can consider it. A single 30-second participation in a prime-time network program will frequently cost in excess of $50,000 and for highly popular programs or special events its cost can exceed $100,000. A minimum schedule for an advertiser would include a number of such spots, so that the total budget requirement becomes very large. To this minimum budget requirement must be added the cost of producing television commercials. It is rare that an advertiser with an annual budget of less than a million dollars finds it feasible to use network television.

The minimum cost of spot television, while substantially less than network, is usually higher than the cost of newspaper advertising. There are two reasons why this is so. First, television stations, even a single station, usually cover considerably more geographic area and more people than does a city newspaper. As an example, the Detroit Free Press has circulation for its morning paper of about 635,000, whereas television originating in Detroit covers nearly 1,692,000 households, over 2½ times more.[7] Television spot costs are generally proportional to the audience reached, even though some of this audience may be superfluous to the small marketer.

The minimum cost of spot television is further increased by the cost of producing television commercials. Production costs vary widely but tend to be substantially higher than for newspapers. This is particularly burdensome to the smaller advertiser if copy must be changed frequently.

PRODUCTION REQUIREMENTS. Under normal circumstances the television advertiser must provide either film or videotape commercials for

---

[6]"Television-Network Time Standard Guidelines," *B & B Media Guidelines* (New York: Benton & Bowles, 1983), p. 16.

[7]*Newspaper Rates and Data* (Skokie, Ill.: Standard Rate and Data Service, August 12, 1983), p. 458, and *Spot Television Rates and Data* (August 15, 1983), pp. 9–13.

broadcast. There are only a few instances in which commercials are delivered live by an announcer or by the star of the program, and in those cases only a script is required.

It is difficult to generalize about the time and cost requirements of television production because there is such great variation. It is possible, for example, to produce commercials on videotape (an electronic method of recording sound and picture simultaneously) that are ready for instant use at a cost of under $1,500. On the other hand, a film commercial involving location shooting or elaborate sets, a number of actors, and complex opticals or editing problems can take several months to complete and cost well over $30,000.

Whether an advertiser's television production requirements will be of the quick, inexpensive kind or the more time-consuming, expensive variety will depend upon the nature of the product story and the creative execution of that story. Heavy and continuous users of television will most likely find that their average commercial lies between the extremes of cost and time. It should be emphasized that the size of the advertiser does not influence the production requirements for a product. The small advertiser should not assume that because of the small size of the firm it is possible to get by with lower quality commercials. The commercials must compete for consumer attention and consideration alongside those of the biggest national advertisers.

MERCHANDISING VALUE. Trade intermediaries such as wholesalers and retailers are generally well aware of the power of television in building brand preference and store traffic. If a manufacturer shows a wholesaler or retailer that the product will be backed by a substantial television schedule, the wholesaler or retailer will be motivated to stock and display the product.

There is probably also some prestige value to being on television. Trade intermediaries recognize the high minimum cost of television and, consequently, the medium, especially network, may connote bigness and importance.

Television stations and the networks have not been as active as some media in promoting their advertiser's schedules to trade intermediaries. It may be that because of the great natural growth in demand for television time that the television sellers have not felt that this added service was necessary. Despite this, there are some merchandising services made available, mainly by the local stations for their spot television users. The predominant form of assistance is periodic mailings of advertising schedules to retailers and wholesalers.

## Users of Television

In order to get a clear picture of what companies and products are heavy users of television it is necessary to look both at total national usage and at patterns of usage within local markets.

LEADING NATIONAL TELEVISION USERS. The companies listed in Exhibit 14-6 as the heaviest users of television are very similar to one another in terms of the products that they market. This list shows mostly consumer packaged-goods marketers—soaps, food, cosmetics, drugs, toiletries, and beverages. One notable exception is automobile manufacturers.

Why is it that these advertisers use television so extensively? All of the heavy television users sell high sales-volume products and are able to afford the high minimum cost of television. Additionally, many of the producers of consumer packaged-goods have low production costs relative to sales prices and are thus able to allocate a large portion of each sales dollar to advertising. The products of heavy television advertisers are not only sold in volume, but they are very widely used. This means that a medium with very broad coverage is appropriate and television certainly meets that requirement. The ability to show these products in use and demonstrate

Top 25 television advertisers, 1983 (Add 000)                              **EXHIBIT 14-6**

| Rank | Advertiser | Spot TV | Network TV | Total TV |
|------|-----------|---------|-----------|----------|
| 1. | The Procter & Gamble Co. | $229,251.8 | $366,663.1 | $595,914.9 |
| 2. | General Foods Corp. | 73,018.4 | 170,064.5 | 243,082.9 |
| 3. | General Motors Corp. | 25,672.2 | 201,350.4 | 227,022.6 |
| 4. | General Mills Corp. | 112,981.7 | 100,250.3 | 213,232.0 |
| 5. | Ford Motor Co. | 38,130.3 | 172,308.1 | 210,438.4 |
| 6. | PepsiCo, Inc. | 121,862.7 | 73,955.2 | 195,817.9 |
| 7. | American Home Pdts. Corp. | 31,896.8 | 161,442.2 | 193,339.0 |
| 8. | American Tel. & Tel. Co. | 40,497.9 | 146,603.8 | 187,101.7 |
| 9. | McDonald's Corp. | 105,024.4 | 80,930.9 | 185,955.3 |
| 10. | Philip Morris, Inc. | 50,368.9 | 128,266.1 | 178,635.0 |
| 11. | Anheuser-Busch Co's. Inc. | 60,196.8 | 116,661.3 | 176,858.1 |
| 12. | Sears Roebuck & Co. | 29,315.1 | 145,006.8 | 174,321.9 |
| 13. | Coca Cola Co. | 72,036.4 | 95,888.7 | 167,925.1 |
| 14. | Lever Brothers Co. | 55,791.5 | 110,302.6 | 166,094.1 |
| 15. | Johnson & Johnson | 9,194.8 | 131,265.9 | 140,460.7 |
| 16. | Pillsbury Co. | 60,825.0 | 74,336.9 | 135,161.9 |
| 17. | Bristol-Myers Co. | 10,066.5 | 120,974.3 | 131,040.8 |
| 18. | Ralston Purina Co. | 35,863.7 | 94,438.5 | 130,302.2 |
| 19. | Dart & Kraft, Inc. | 42,572.6 | 87,414.8 | 129,987.4 |
| 20. | Warner-Lambert Phar. Co. | 39,229.8 | 74,655.1 | 113,884.9 |
| 21. | Warner Communications Inc. | 27,438.5 | 84,259.8 | 111,698.3 |
| 22. | R. J. Reynolds Industries | 39,640.5 | 69,939.6 | 109,580.1 |
| 23. | Esmark, Inc. | 20,434.2 | 88,153.0 | 108,587.2 |
| 24. | Kellogg Co. | 34,130.8 | 72,970.3 | 107,101.1 |
| 25. | Sterling Drug, Inc. | 23,930.9 | 82,682.3 | 106,613.2 |

Source: Broadcast Advertisers Reports, Inc., as compiled in *TV Basics 27* (New York: Television Bureau of Advertising, 1984).

their attributes on television is another reason to use the medium. And finally, many of these products are of low inherent interest to consumers. Whereas many consumers may not voluntarily take the time to read a print ad about some of these products (mouthwash, headache remedies, or cola drinks, for example), television thrusts the message on the viewer so that it takes less effort to view it than to avoid it.

LEADING LOCAL TELEVISION USERS. Use of television by local advertisers is increasing as they learn how to use the medium and how powerful it can be. The leading categories of local television advertisers are shown in Exhibit 14-7. Local advertisers have learned that television can be highly effective in building store traffic. Notice how many of the categories are dependent on store traffic to build sales.

## Purchasing Television Time

The purchase of television time, particularly large-scale purchases, is a highly specialized phase of the advertising business. Heavy users of television tend to utilize broadcast media specialists in advertising agencies or in specialized media buying services. Many smaller advertisers, however, perform the purchasing function themselves.

TIME-BUYING PROCESS. The procedure for buying television time is different from the space-buying procedure. In buying space in magazines, for example, the media program would specify the magazine, the space unit, the insertion date, and the position desired. With these specifications, buying becomes almost mechanical. By contrast, the time buyer does not have a television schedule specified in advance in the media program because the programs and spot positions that will be available are not known until the actual time of purchase. Instead the media program will specify the overall television schedule targets in such terms as reach and frequency, cost per thousand, total budget available, audience composition desired,

**EXHIBIT 14-7**    Leading categories of local television advertisers, 1983 (Add 000)

| Rank | Category | Expenditures |
|------|----------|--------------|
| 1. | Restaurants & Drive-Ins | $498,133.1 |
| 2. | Food Stores & Supermarkets | 229,020.5 |
| 3. | Auto Dealers* | 172,875.3 |
| 4. | Banks, Savings & Loans | 165,639.7 |
| 5. | Department Stores | 163,585.0 |
| 6. | Furniture Stores | 144,035.1 |
| 7. | Radio Stations & Cable TV | 126,504.3 |
| 8. | Amusements & Entertainment | 99,351.9 |
| 9. | Movies | 97,865.1 |
| 10. | Leisure Time Activities & Services | 81,691.7 |

Source: Broadcast Advertisers Reports, Inc., as compiled in *TV Basics 27* (New York: Television Bureau of Advertising, 1984).

proportion of each time length desired, and program environment desired.

Given these targets for the total schedule, the time buyer must select from available programs and spot-positions the combinations that will best meet the targets. The first step in this process is to call for **availabilities**, the programs or spots that are available for sale. Spot availabilities are provided by television stations in the local markets or through their sales representatives. Network program availabilities are requested from the networks themselves.

*availabilities*

With the availabilities in hand, the time buyer must then match available times with the targets established by the media program, building the schedule spot by spot. The buying job becomes enormously complex for large multi-market schedules. Consider, for example, the number of variables involved in a 100-market spot schedule, which would involve 200-300 different stations, each of which might offer 100 or more spot availabilities.

TELEVISION RATES. Spot television and local program rates can be obtained from the individual station's rate card or from the **SRDS** *Spot Television Rates and Data.*

Local station rates are rather complex because of the variety of time periods available. Rates vary with the length of the spot or program. Stations usually offer 60-second, 30-second, 20-second, and 10-second (identification or ID) spot time lengths plus various program lengths. Rates vary substantially by time of day. During time periods when viewership is typically high, rates are correspondingly high, with rates lowered when expected viewership is low.

Different rates are also quoted depending on the preemptibility of the spot. A **preemptible spot** is one that is sold to an advertiser on the condition that it can be resold to another advertiser who is willing to pay a higher nonpreemptible rate. The preempted advertiser is given advance notice when the commercial is "bumped." Spot and program rates are also subject to a variety of frequency discount plans that substantially reduce per spot or per program costs for regular advertisers. In addition to these rate variations, individual stations are likely to have various other special rates that apply to specialized "package" buys. These are sometimes detailed on rate cards and sometimes are the subject of individual negotiations with the station.

*preemptible spot*

Network television rates are quoted directly by the television networks with costs depending upon the popularity of the program in which the commercial will appear and the level of demand for network programs by major advertisers. Advertisers commonly purchase "packages" or combinations of program position, sometimes months in advance. Rates for these purchases are the subject of considerable bargaining between the networks and the advertiser or agency.

TELEVISION RATING SERVICES. The measurement of the size and characteristics of television audiences is taken by television rating services.

*Audience Measurement Techniques.* The rating services gather viewership information from a sample of television homes and then project the data to the total population of the viewing area. The most widely used means of gathering viewership information from the sample are diaries, meters, and personal interviews.

With the diary approach the rating service recruits a panel of households whose members agree to record in a diary their actual viewing behavior — who viewed, times of viewing, and programs viewed. This method provides rich data on the characteristics of individual viewers, though it does rely on the accuracy of the panel members' record keeping. With the meter approach, the panel of television homes recruited is made up of members who agree to the installation of an electronic meter on their television set. This meter records the time the set is on and the channel or program to which it is tuned. Because this measurement is an electronic one not relying on human memory or attentiveness, it provides accurate results. However, it does not reveal who in the family, if anyone, was actually viewing the program that was tuned in. A third approach is to interview people about their actual viewing. One interviewing method used that is designed to reduce reporting errors by viewers is the telephone coincidental method. Viewers are called and asked if at that moment they are viewing television and, if so, to what program they are tuned.

*Network Television Audience.* The primary source of network television audience data is the A. C. Nielsen Company's Nielsen Television Index (NTI). Data for these reports is gathered through a combination of the meter method and the diary method. The national area-probability sample is made up of 1,700 households with meters and about 3,200 households with diaries. NTI rating reports are issued twice a month to subscribers and are supplemented by several longer, analytical reports each year. Information provided by the reports includes program ratings, total homes viewing, plus standard demographic and geographic composition of the audience from the diary portion of the sample. The information provided by these reports is on a national basis, not for individual markets. The usefulness of these reports is limited, therefore, to buyers of network television. Exhibit 14-8 shows an audience estimate page from a recent NTI rating report.

*Local television audience.* Buyers of local television, both spot and program, need information on local television audiences to enable them to match their requirements with available television vehicles. The two major services providing local television audience information are the Arbitron Co. and, again, the A. C. Nielsen Company.

Both Arbitron and Nielsen utilize the diary method for gathering local television audience data and each provides separate reports for over 200 TV markets. All markets are measured at least 4 times yearly during

A sample page from a *Nielsen Television Index Report.*     EXHIBIT 14-8

*Nielsen* **NATIONAL TV AUDIENCE ESTIMATES**                     EVE.THU.   MAY 12, 1983

A-8

| TIME | 7:00 | 7:15 | 7:30 | 7:45 | 8:00 | 8:15 | 8:30 | 8:45 | 9:00 | 9:15 | 9:30 | 9:45 | 10:00 | 10:15 | 10:30 | 10:45 |
|---|---|---|---|---|---|---|---|---|---|---|---|---|---|---|---|---|

**ABC TV**

TOTAL AUDIENCE (Households (000) & %) { 14,830 / 17.8 — J.DENVER&MUPPETS HOLIDAY — ; 11,410 / 13.7 TOO CLOSE FOR COMFORT (R) ; 9,660 / 11.6 AMANDA'S (OP) ; 10,080 / 12.1 — 20/20 —

AVERAGE AUDIENCE (Households (000) & %) { 10,500 / 12.6 ; 12.6* ; 12.5* ; 9,580 / 11.5 ; 8,080 / 9.7 ; 7,410 / 8.9 ; 8.8* ; 8.9*
SHARE OF AUDIENCE % : 23 ; 24* ; 22* ; 19 ; 15 ; 14 ; 14* ; 15*
AVG. AUD. BY ¼ HR. % : 13.0 ; 12.3 ; 12.2 ; 12.8 ; 11.2 ; 11.8 ; 9.7 ; 9.8 ; 8.6 ; 8.9 ; 9.0 ; 8.9

**W E E K 1**

**CBS TV**

TOTAL AUDIENCE (Households (000) & %) { 21,410 / 25.7 — MAGNUM, P.I. (R)(OP) — ; 30,740 / 36.9 ; MISS USA BEAUTY PAGEANT

AVERAGE AUDIENCE (Households (000) & %) { 15,580 / 18.7 ; 17.0* ; 20.3* ; 20,330 / 24.4 ; 20.8* ; 24.3* ; 25.9* ; 26.6*
SHARE OF AUDIENCE % : 34 ; 32* ; 35* ; 39 ; 34* ; 39* ; 42* ; 44*
AVG. AUD. BY ¼ HR. % : 16.0 ; 18.1 ; 19.6 ; 20.9 ; 20.1 ; 21.5 ; 23.9 ; 24.7 ; 26.0 ; 25.8 ; 26.8 ; 26.4

**NBC TV**

TOTAL AUDIENCE (Households (000) & %) { 12,080 / 14.5 — FAME (R)(OP) — ; 12,990 / 15.6 GIMME A BREAK (R) ; 13,580 / 16.3 CHEERS (R)(OP) ; 17,240 / 20.7 — HILL STREET BLUES —

AVERAGE AUDIENCE (Households (000) & %) { 8,250 / 9.9 ; 9.2* ; 10.5* ; 11,250 / 13.5 ; 11,830 / 14.2 ; 14,410 / 17.3 ; 16.9* ; 17.7*
SHARE OF AUDIENCE % : 18 ; 17* ; 18* ; 22 ; 23 ; 28 ; 27* ; 29*
AVG. AUD. BY ¼ HR. % : 8.8 ; 9.6 ; 10.2 ; 10.8 ; 13.1 ; 13.9 ; 13.9 ; 14.5 ; 16.2 ; 17.6 ; 18.0 ; 17.4

**ABC TV**

TOTAL AUDIENCE (Households (000) & %) { 16,410 / 19.7 — I LOVE TV TEST — ; 12,830 / 15.4 TOO CLOSE FOR COMFORT (R) ; 10,160 / 12.2 AMANDA'S (OP) ; 16,910 / 20.3 — 20/20 —

AVERAGE AUDIENCE (Households (000) & %) { 11,330 / 13.6 ; 13.4* ; 13.9* ; 11,080 / 13.3 ; 8,750 / 10.5 ; 12,830 / 15.4 ; 15.6* ; 15.3*
SHARE OF AUDIENCE % : 24 ; 24* ; 24* ; 21 ; 17 ; 27 ; 26* ; 28*
AVG. AUD. BY ¼ HR. % : 13.3 ; 13.4 ; 13.8 ; 14.0 ; 13.2 ; 13.3 ; 10.8 ; 10.1 ; 15.1 ; 16.0 ; 15.7 ; 14.8

**W E E K 2**

**CBS TV**

TOTAL AUDIENCE (Households (000) & %) { 25,320 / 30.4 — MAGNUM, P.I. (R)(OP) — ; 15,990 / 19.2 — SIMON & SIMON (R) —

AVERAGE AUDIENCE (Households (000) & %) { 15,990 / 19.2 ; 17.3* ; 18.4* ; 19.9* ; 21.3* ; 12,250 / 14.7 ; 15.2* ; 14.2*
SHARE OF AUDIENCE % : 32 ; 31* ; 31* ; 32* ; 34* ; 26 ; 26* ; 26*
AVG. AUD. BY ¼ HR. % : 16.5 ; 18.1 ; 18.2 ; 18.7 ; 19.6 ; 20.1 ; 21.3 ; 21.2 ; 15.8 ; 14.7 ; 14.0 ; 14.3

**NBC TV**

TOTAL AUDIENCE (Households (000) & %) { 14,580 / 17.5 — FAME (R)(OP) — ; 11,660 / 14.0 GIMME A BREAK (R) ; 14,160 / 17.0 CHEERS (R) ; 18,160 / 21.8 — HILL STREET BLUES —

AVERAGE AUDIENCE (Households (000) & %) { 9,500 / 11.4 ; 11.2* ; 11.7* ; 9,910 / 11.9 ; 12,410 / 14.9 ; 13,580 / 16.3 ; 16.0* ; 16.6*
SHARE OF AUDIENCE % : 20 ; 20* ; 20* ; 19 ; 24 ; 28 ; 27* ; 30*
AVG. AUD. BY ¼ HR. % : 11.4 ; 10.9 ; 11.4 ; 12.0 ; 11.1 ; 12.7 ; 14.4 ; 15.3 ; 15.6 ; 16.3 ; 16.8 ; 16.5

| | 7:00 | 7:15 | 7:30 | 7:45 | 8:00 | 8:15 | 8:30 | 8:45 | 9:00 | 9:15 | 9:30 | 9:45 | 10:00 | 10:15 | 10:30 | 10:45 |
|---|---|---|---|---|---|---|---|---|---|---|---|---|---|---|---|---|
| TV HOUSEHOLDS USING TV WK. 1 (See Def. 1) | 48.8 | 49.5 | 48.9 | 51.0 | 52.2 | 54.2 | 55.8 | 58.7 | 60.8 | 62.9 | 62.8 | 63.3 | 62.6 | 62.2 | 61.5 | 60.2 |
| WK. 2 | 53.2 | 54.7 | 55.7 | 56.3 | 56.2 | 57.1 | 57.7 | 59.3 | 60.8 | 62.9 | 62.9 | 62.5 | 59.4 | 58.7 | 56.8 | 54.4 |

U.S. TV Households: 83,300,000                    For explanation of symbols, See page A.

A-9                                          EVE.THU.   MAY 19, 1983

Source: *Nielsen Television Index,* New York, May 9–22, 1983, p. A-9, A. C. Nielsen Company.

the "sweep" months of February, May, July, and November. (A "sweep" is the simultaneous measurement of all local markets.) For the smaller markets these are the only reports, while for larger markets there may be as many as eight reports yearly. Reports can be purchased for individual markets from any measurement period.

The local television rating reports contain program ratings, estimates of total households viewing, and demographic characteristics of individual viewers. Exhibit 14-9 shows one page from the Nielsen Station Index (NSI) rating report for Chicago.

**EXHIBIT 14-9**   A sample page from the *Nielsen Station Index Report* for Chicago.

CHICAGO, IL

WK1 2/03–2/09 WK2 2/10–2/16 WK3 2/17–2/23 WK4 2/24–3/02

THURSDAY
8.30PM–10.45PM

| | STATION / PROGRAM | DMA HH RATINGS (WEEKS) 1 2 3 4 | MULTI-WEEK AVG RTG SHR | SHARE TREND NOV'82 MAY'82 FEB'82 | DMA RATINGS — PERSONS 2+ 18+ | WOMEN 18-49 18-34 18-49 25-49 25-54 | FEM WG | PER 12-24 | MEN 18+ 18-34 18-49 25-49 25-54 | TNS 12-17 | CHILD 2-11 6-11 |
|---|---|---|---|---|---|---|---|---|---|---|---|

DMA HH — RATINGS / MULTI-WEEK AVG / SHARE TREND

R.S.E. THRESHOLDS 25+‡ (1 S.E.) 4 WK AVG 50+‡

| 8.30PM | WBBM SIMON & SIMON | 18 12 18 19 | 17 24 | 26 | 23 23 | 10 12 10 8 | 12 9 10 12 12 12 | 6 | 7 | 11 8 9 10 11 | 7 | 4 5 |
| | WCIU AVG. ALL WKS | | 1 1 | | | | 1 1 1 | | | | | |
| | CHARYTIN | 1 1 | << 1 1 | | | | | | | | | 1 1 |
| | QUE OPINA | | 1 2 | | | 1 1 1 1 | 1 3 2 2 2 | | | | | 3 |
| | WFBN SUBSCRIPTION | << 1 1 1 | 1 1 | X NR NR | | | | | 1 1 1 1 1 | |
| | WFLD AVG. ALL WKS | | 5 7 | 6 | 7 7 | 4 3 4 4 | 3 3 4 4 2 | 3 | 4 | 3 3 4 4 4 | 5 | 5 5 |
| | 7 OCLOCK MOV | 5 6 7 4 | 5 7 | | | 4 3 4 4 | 3 3 4 4 2 | 3 | 4 | 3 3 4 4 4 | 5 | 5 5 |
| | FILM FILL | 4 | 4 6 | | | 3 2 3 4 | 2 3 2 1 1 | | 4 | 5 3 4 4 4 3 | 5 | 8 |
| | WGN AVG. ALL WKS | | 7 10 | 18 | 14 17 | 4 5 5 4 | 4 4 4 4 4 | 3 | 3 | 5 4 5 6 6 | 2 | 3 3 |
| | WGN PRIME MOV | 8 8 | 10 | 9 12 | | 5 6 5 5 | 5 5 5 4 5 4 | 4 | | 5 5 6 7 7 | 3 | 4 4 |
| | VIRGINIA SLIMS | 3 | 3 5 | | | 2 2 2 1 | 2 1 2 3 2 2 | | | 2 1 1 2 2 | |
| | WLS AVG. ALL WKS | | 20 28 | 22 | 22 24 | 12 13 12 11 | 13 12 11 11 10 | 13 | 11 | 11 9 9 10 10 | 11 | 8 12 |
| | IT TAKES TWO | 17 14 13 | 15 21 | | | 10 9 9 9 | 12 11 11 11 10 | 13 | 10 | 7 7 6 9 6 | 11 | 9 13 |
| | WINDS OF WAR 5 | 34 | 34 46 | | | 21 26 20 15 | 26 21 24 25 22 | 11 | 13 | 24 18 20 22 16 | |
| | WMAQ AVG. ALL WKS | | 20 28 | 24 | 30 26 | 14 14 16 16 | 15 19 18 17 17 16 | 18 | 15 | 12 14 13 14 13 | 14 | 12 14 |
| | SHOGUN–PT 4 | 22 | 22 30 | | | 16 18 19 18 | 20 25 24 23 21 21 | 21 | 18 | 15 12 15 17 16 | 17 | |
| | CHEERS | 18 21 19 | 19 27 | | | 13 13 14 15 | 14 17 16 16 15 14 | 16 | 14 | 11 14 13 15 14 | 12 | 13 15 |
| | WSNS SUBSCRIPTION | << << << 1 | << | 1X 1 1 | | | | | | |
| | WTTW THIS OLD HOUSE | 7 3 7 6 | 6 8 | 8X 6 6 | 3 4 3 2 | 3 3 4 4 | 5 | 1 2 | 4 3 4 5 5 | 1 | 2 2 |
| | HUT/PUT/TOTALS * | 74 74 68 68 | 71 | 65 63 70 | 51 55 52 49 | 57 55 55 58 57 51 | 47 | 44 | 52 45 48 52 53 | 45 | 38 44 |

| 9.00PM | WBBM KNOTS LANDING | 17 14 17 20 | 17 23 | 28 | 26 22 | 10 12 11 10 | 15 14 16 16 16 14 | 14 | 10 | 7 6 6 6 6 | 11 | 4 4 |
| | WCIU VANESSA | 1 1 1 1 | 1 2 | 1 1 1 | | 1 1 1 1 | 1 1 1 1 1 | | | 1 1 1 1 | |
| | WFBN SUBSCRIPTION | 1 1 1 << | 1 1 | 1X NR NR | | 1 1 1 | | | 1 1 1 1 | |
| | WFLD CNN HEADLN NWS | 2 2 1 2 | 2 2 | 5 8 6 | 1 1 1 | 1 1 1 1 | | | 2 1 1 1 | 2 |
| | WGN AVG. ALL WKS | | 8 10 | 14 | 12 14 | 5 5 3 3 | 5 3 3 4 4 4 | 2 | 2 | 6 3 4 4 4 | 2 | 2 3 |
| | 9 OCLOCK NWS | 8 7 6 | 7 9 | | | 4 5 3 2 | 5 2 3 4 3 3 | | 1 | 5 3 3 4 4 | | 1 1 |
| | WGN PRIME MOV | 11 | 11 16 | | | 7 7 5 6 | 6 5 5 5 6 9 | 6 | 7 | 8 4 6 6 7 | 9 | 8 |
| | PRIME )LT NWS | 8 | 8 12 | | | 5 5 4 4 | 4 4 3 4 7 | 5 | 5 | 5 3 4 4 6 | 5 | |
| | WLS AVG. ALL WKS | | 18 25 | 17 | 22 22 | 11 13 10 8 | 14 10 11 11 11 11 | 9 | 8 | 13 8 10 10 11 | 6 | 3 4 |
| | 20–20 | 17 13 10 | 13 19 | | | 8 9 7 6 | 10 7 8 7 7 7 | 8 | 7 | 9 7 7 7 7 | 4 | 3 4 |
| | WINDS OF WAR 5 | 34 | 34 44 | | | 20 25 20 14 | 26 18 21 24 25 23 | 11 | 11 | 24 13 18 20 23 | 8 | 3 |
| | WMAQ HILL ST BLUES | 32 22 32 29 | 29 39 | 37 | 30 32 | 18 20 23 22 | 19 24 23 25 24 23 | 17 | 19 | 21 23 23 24 23 | 18 | 7 9 |
| | WSNS SUBSCRIPTION | << << << 1 | << | 1X 1 1 | | | | | | |
| | WTTW MYSTERY | 4 2 4 4 | 3 5 | 4 3 4 | 2 2 1 | 3 1 1 2 2 | | | 2 1 1 2 | |
| | HUT/PUT/TOTALS * | 77 76 70 69 | 73 | 67 67 71 | 50 58 54 50 | 61 57 59 63 63 58 | 45 | 43 | 54 47 49 53 53 | 41 | 18 22 |

| 9.30PM | WBBM KNOTS LANDING | 16 15 18 21 | 17 24 | 28 | 26 23 | 10 12 11 11 | 16 14 16 16 16 15 | 14 | 10 | 7 6 6 6 6 | 11 | 4 4 |
| | WCIU VANESSA | 2 1 1 1 | 1 2 | 1 1 1 | | 1 1 1 1 | 1 1 1 1 | | | 1 1 1 1 | |
| | WFBN SUBSCRIPTION | 1 1 1 1 | 1 1 | X NR NR | | 1 | | | 1 1 1 1 | 1 |
| | WFLD CNN HEADLN NWS | 2 1 1 2 | 2 2 | 3X 7 6 | 1 1 1 | 1 1 1 | 1 | 1 | 1 1 1 1 | 1 |
| | WGN AVG. ALL WKS | | 6 8 | 10 | 13 13 | 3 4 3 2 | 4 2 3 3 3 | 1 | 1 | 4 2 3 3 3 | 1 | |
| | 9 OCLOCK NWS | 7 6 5 | 6 8 | | | 3 4 3 2 | 4 2 3 2 3 | | | 4 2 3 3 3 | | 1 |
| | LATE NWS | 7 | 7 9 | | | 3 4 3 2 | 4 3 2 3 6 3 | 2 | 2 | 4 1 3 4 4 | 3 | 1 |
| | WLS AVG. ALL WKS | | 17 24 | 16 | 22 22 | 10 13 10 8 | 13 9 10 11 11 11 | 8 | 7 | 12 8 9 10 11 | 5 | 3 3 |
| | 20–20 | 15 11 9 | 12 17 | | | 7 8 6 6 | 9 6 6 6 7 6 | 7 | 5 | 8 6 6 6 7 | 4 | 3 3 |
| | WINDS OF WAR 5 | 33 | 33 43 | | | 20 25 20 14 | 27 18 21 24 25 23 | 11 | 11 | 24 13 18 20 23 | 8 | 3 |
| | WMAQ HILL ST BLUES | 32 22 33 31 | 30 41 | 41X | 30 33 | 19 21 24 23 | 20 25 24 26 25 24 | 17 | 19 | 22 25 24 25 25 | 18 | 7 9 |
| | WSNS SUBSCRIPTION | << << << << | | 1X 2 1 | | | | | | |
| | WTTW MYSTERY | 3 2 4 5 | 3 5 | 4 3 3 | 2 2 1 | 3 1 1 2 2 2 | | | 2 1 1 1 2 | |
| | HUT/PUT/TOTALS * | 74 77 70 71 | 73 | 67 67 71 | 49 57 54 49 | 61 58 59 63 63 57 | 44 | 41 | 53 47 49 53 54 | 39 | 15 19 |

| 10.00PM | WBBM THE 10PM NWS | 19 16 20 24 | 20 28 | 30 | 29 31 | 12 15 12 8 | 16 11 14 17 17 15 | 3 | 4 | 13 8 10 12 12 | 3 | 1 1 |
| | WCIU INFORMACION 26 | 1 << << 1 | 1 1 | X | 1 | | | | 1 1 1 | |
| | WFBN SUBSCRIPTION | 1 << << 1 | << | X NR NR | 1 | | | | 1 1 1 | |
| | WFLD MASH 2 | 11 11 11 13 | 11 17 | 11X 13 16 | 7 8 9 10 | 8 10 9 9 9 9 | 8 | 9 | 8 11 9 9 8 | 7 | 2 3 |
| | WGN AVG. ALL WKS | | 13 13 | 13 9 | 6 6 7 8 | 6 9 7 6 5 4 | 11 | 10 | 6 8 7 6 6 | 9 | 2 2 |
| | SOAP | 9 12 10 | 10 14 | | | 6 7 9 11 | 7 11 9 7 6 5 | 14 | 12 | 7 10 9 8 7 | 10 | 2 1 |
| | LATE NWS | 6 | 6 9 | | | 3 3 2 4 | 4 5 4 4 4 3 | 2 | 2 | 2 2 2 2 3 | 3 | 2 |
| | WLS EYEWIT NWS-10 | 12 20 10 12 | 13 19 | 18 | 19 20 | 8 10 9 7 | 10 8 10 11 12 10 | 7 | 5 | 9 8 9 10 10 | 4 | 2 3 |
| | WMAQ CH5 NWS-10 | 18 12 17 16 | 16 23 | 29 | 26 23 | 9 11 9 6 | 12 7 9 11 11 10 | 3 | 3 | 10 6 8 10 10 | 3 | 1 |
| | WSNS SUBSCRIPTION | << << << 1 | << | 1X 1 1 | | | | | | |
| | WTTW NITE BSNSS RPT | 2 1 2 1 | 1 2 | 2X 3 2 | 1 1 1 | 1 1 1 1 | | | 1 1 1 | |
| | HUT/PUT/TOTALS * | 70 70 67 68 | 69 | 65 67 68 | 44 54 50 42 | 56 50 53 59 59 51 | 33 | 33 | 51 44 48 52 52 | 27 | 8 9 |

| 10.15PM | WBBM THE 10PM NWS | 19 17 19 23 | 19 29 | 30 | 29 31 | 11 15 12 8 | 16 11 13 16 16 14 | 3 | 4 | 13 8 10 12 12 | 2 | 1 1 |
| | WCIU INFORMACION 26 | 1 << << 1 | 1 1 | X | 1 | 1 1 | 1 | | | 1 1 1 | |
| | WFBN SUBSCRIPTION | 1 << 1 1 | 1 1 | X NR NR | 1 | 1 1 | | | 1 1 1 | |
| | WFLD MASH 2 | 12 12 13 14 | 13 19 | 13X 16 17 | 8 9 10 10 | 8 11 10 9 9 10 | 9 | 10 | 9 12 11 9 9 | 8 | 2 3 |
| | WGN AVG. ALL WKS | | 14 14 | 13 10 | 6 6 8 9 | 6 10 8 6 6 4 | 12 | 10 | 6 9 8 7 7 | 9 | 2 2 |
| | SOAP | 9 13 10 | 11 16 | | | 7 7 10 12 | 7 13 10 8 7 6 | 15 | 13 | 8 11 10 8 9 | 11 | 2 2 |
| | LATE NWS | 5 | 5 8 | | | 2 2 2 3 | 2 3 2 3 4 1 | 4 | 3 | 2 2 3 3 3 | 4 | 1 |
| | WLS EYEWIT NWS-10 | 12 17 8 10 | 12 17 | 16X 18 18 | 7 8 8 6 | 9 7 9 10 10 9 | 5 | 4 | 8 7 8 9 9 | 3 | 2 3 |
| | WMAQ CH5 NWS-10 | 14 11 14 15 | 14 20 | 27 | 24 20 | 8 10 7 5 | 11 6 8 9 9 8 | 3 | 3 | 9 5 7 8 8 | 2 | 1 |
| | WSNS SUBSCRIPTION | << << << 1 | << | 2X 1 1 | | | | | | |
| | WTTW NITE BSNSS RPT | 2 1 2 1 | 1 2 | 2X 2 2 | 1 1 1 | 1 1 1 1 | | | 1 1 1 1 | |
| | HUT/PUT/TOTALS * | 68 68 65 65 | 66 | 63 65 66 | 43 52 49 42 | 53 48 51 56 55 48 | 32 | 33 | 50 45 47 50 50 | 27 | 8 9 |

| 10.30PM | WBBM CBS LATE MOV | 11 14 13 13 | 13 23 | 28 | 33 30 | 7 9 8 6 | 10 8 9 10 10 9 | 4 | 4 | 8 6 6 7 7 | 2 | 1 1 |
| | WCIU LUISANA | 2 << 1 1 | 1 2 | 1 1 | 1 1 | 1 1 1 | | | 1 1 1 1 | |
| | WFBN SUBSCRIPTION | 1 << 1 << | 1 1 | X NR NR | 1 1 | 1 1 1 | | | 1 1 | |
| | WFLD BENNY HILL | 8 7 6 7 | 7 12 | 9X 10 11 | 4 5 5 4 | 4 5 5 5 3 2 | 9 | 3 | 6 5 6 6 5 | 3 | 1 1 |
| | WGN CHARLIES ANGEL | 8 11 10 9 | 9 17 | 16X 15 12 | 6 6 7 7 | 9 9 8 8 5 5 | 8 | 10 | 6 5 5 5 5 | 9 | 1 1 |
| | WLS AVG. ALL WKS | | 10 17 | 17 16 | 5 7 6 3 | 6 4 6 7 8 7 | 7 | 2 | 8 6 6 8 8 | 3 | 4 1 |
| | ABC-NITELINE | 10 12 8 | 10 17 | | | 6 7 6 3 | 7 5 6 7 8 7 | 7 | 2 | 8 6 6 8 8 | 3 | 4 1 |
| | VIEWPOINT | | 5 6 | | | 5 6 5 3 | 5 3 4 6 6 6 | | 1 | 8 6 7 7 7 | | 1 |
| | WMAQ TONITE SHW | 12 11 14 13 | 12 22 | 26 | 23 24 | 7 9 8 6 | 9 7 8 9 8 7 | 5 | 4 | 8 7 7 8 7 | 7 | 1 |
| | WSNS SUBSCRIPTION | 1 << << 1 | 1 1 | 2X 1 1 | 1 1 1 | 1 1 1 1 | | | 2 1 1 | |
| | WTTW MOVIE 11 | 6 5 4 4 | 5 8 | 6 2 2 | 3 3 3 3 | 3 2 2 3 4 | | | 3 4 4 4 4 | 2 | 1 |
| | HUT/PUT/TOTALS * | 56 59 55 55 | 56 | 55 56 56 | 35 42 41 34 | 43 39 43 46 46 37 | 29 | 29 | 42 36 38 41 42 | 23 | 7 8 |

THURSDAY
8.30PM–10.45PM

FEBRUARY 1983

Source: *Nielsen Station Index*, "Viewers in Profile," Chicago, 1983, p. 110, A.C. Nielsen Co.

New Electronic Media

The new electronic media, which include cable television, pay TV, and videotex, began as an outgrowth of television. However, as these new media emerge, it is clear that they are different from television and need to be evaluated as a separate media class. Much remains to be learned about these new and rapidly changing media. This brief section will highlight differences between these new electronic media and traditional television.

## Types of New Electronic Media

Cable television is currently the dominant member of the new electronic media group and will be the focus of this section. At the same time, there are other new electronic media that the advertiser needs to understand and follow because of the rapid changes taking place.

BASIC CABLE TELEVISION. The most widespread and most mature of the new electronic media is cable television or basic cable. Cable television is a medium that delivers television signals through wire rather than through air. Originally developed to give better quality reception especially in remote areas, it has expanded rapidly in major markets as well because it offers subscribers a wider range of stations. In order to receive basic cable, homes must subscribe to the service by paying a hookup fee and a monthly charge. It is estimated that in 1983 there were 5,000 operating cable systems with 30.2 million subscribers representing 36 percent of television-equipped homes.[8]

When a home becomes a basic cable subscriber, the channels that it has available for viewing expand from the standard 12 to 36 or 52, or more. Cable homes continue to receive the TV channels previously received through the antenna, but in addition the cable service offers a variety of other programming from cable networks, superstations, and (for an additional charge) pay TV.

ADVERTISING ON CABLE — CABLE NETWORKS. Advertisers can purchase cable spots locally from cable system operators or they can purchase cable network or superstation time. One recent study indicated that about half of cable-system operators were offering locally purchased advertising time, but most of this remained unsold.[9] Local system operators are more interested in selling their service to households and they have not concentrated on attracting local advertisers to this new advertising form.

Most cable advertising is placed through the cable networks which are fed by satellite to the cable operators and then through cable to subscribers. The number and variety of cable networks is changing very rapidly as the

---

[8]*TV Basics, 26, op. cit.*
[9]Ronald B. Kaatz, *Cable, An Advertiser's Guide to the New Electronic Media* (Chicago: Crain Books, 1982), pp. 146–7.

industry grows. There are both cable networks that accept advertising and those that do not but instead are simply offered as a service by the cable-system operator. Among the larger advertiser-supported networks are ESPN (sports), USA (sports), CBN (religious), CNN (news), and MTV (music).

Advertising purchases available on cable networks are more varied than those available on regular television. Spots of varying time lengths and program sponsorship are available.

SUPERSTATION ADVERTISING. Another cable advertising alternative is the superstation. Superstations are independent network stations that feed their signal via satellite to cable system operators for their subscribers. There are currently three superstations — WGN Chicago, WOR New York, and WTBS Atlanta. Programming on the superstations is made up largely of sports, movies, and reruns of network program series. Both spots and program sponsorship are available to advertisers.

PAY TELEVISION. For an additional monthly charge, cable subscribers can receive one or more of the pay television networks. Most pay television systems focus on presenting recent movies plus, in some cases, sports and entertainment specials. Leaders in this service are Home Box Office (HBO), Showtime, and The Movie Channel (TMC). Although advertising time is not sold on pay television, some consideration is being given to adding advertising to help alleviate financial pressure. A related service is pay-per-view TV for which subscribers pay a fee for particular programs or events such as a heavyweight championship bout.

CABLE-SYSTEM COMPETITORS.. Although cable TV is itself a new medium, advancing technology and deregulation are already encouraging alternative program delivery systems.[10] Some of these systems represent competitive means to deliver the same programming (and advertising) as do cable systems, while others offer alternative programming. Among the systems currently available are:

1. Direct Broadcast Satellite (DBS) send signals directly from a satellite to rooftop earth stations in homes.
2. Multipoint Distribution Service (MDS) offers an over-the-air (microwave) pay TV service.
3. Subscription Television (STV) uses a standard television channel to send a scrambled signal to households that can be decoded by devices installed in the subscribing homes.
4. Satellite Master Antenna Television (SMATV) is a minicable system for large apartments and condominiums.
5. Home Earth Stations are now available for $5,000 to $10,000 and permit households to pick up programming direct from satellites.

---

[10]"The Pack of Competitors Cable Must Keep at Bay," *Business Week* (November 1, 1982), pp. 108–9.

6. Low-Power Television (LPTV) are newly proposed low-power television stations with range limited to from 10 to 20 miles and designed to meet the needs of specialized audiences.

INTERACTIVE SYSTEMS. Interactive video systems permit viewers, in addition to receiving messages, to respond to questions and to request specific information which is then supplied.

The first interactive system was Warner Communications' Qube, initially offered in Columbus, Ohio, and which has later spread to six markets. Subscribers to Qube, a special cable service, receive special programming to which they can send a return signal to vote on an issue, to request more information, and, eventually, to purchase a product. Qube has potential both as a research tool and as a direct sales medium.

A second class of interactive system is videotex which is undergoing tests in several markets. Videotex allows a subscriber to call up on the television screen "pages" of text and graphics on a subject of choice. Information available might include news or weather. More important, it would allow such activities as banking and shopping to be conducted from the home. Opinions on the future of videotex are divided, but if it proves attractive to consumers, it could have enormous impact on advertising and shopping patterns. Recently IBM, Sears, and CBS announced a joint venture to develop a national videotex service that would utilize a household's already existing micro-computer as a terminal.[11]

## Advertising Characteristics of the New Electronic Media

The new electronic media are so recent and evolving so fast that characteristics are not yet well defined. We will focus here on the advertising characteristics of basic cable, the oldest of this new media class.

AUDIENCE SELECTIVITY. The term **narrowcasting** (to contrast with broadcasting) has been invented to describe the audience delivery capability of the new electronic media. One of the strengths of these new media is that they attract, through specialized programming, specific narrow viewer-groups. ESPN and USA, for example, program sports that attract predominantly adult male viewers while MTV programs music-video that attracts teenagers. The selectivity of cable stands in sharp contrast to the mass, homogeneous character of television audiences.

*narrowcasting*

The geographic coverage of cable and the other new electronic media is very spotty. Cable coverage is available in those markets that have been wired for cable. As noted earlier, this included 36 percent of all TV homes in 1983. Cable network purchases offer little geographic selectivity to the advertiser.

[11]"Three Big Backers Give Videotex a Shot at Success," *Business Week* (February 27, 1984), pp. 36–37.

AUDIENCE DISTRIBUTION. Cable homes have the choice of many alternative programs with the result that cable network programming in particular has low average ratings. Because of these low ratings and the spotty geographic coverage, cable does not offer strong reach. However, because cost per spot is low, cable offers the opportunity to supplement frequency with key prospect groups. For this reason, most cable advertisers do not use this medium alone, but as a supplement to a more general audience medium.

CREATIVE CHARACTERISTICS. Creatively, cable and the other new electronic media are much like television, offering sight, sound, motion, color, intrusiveness and demonstration power. Some cable advertisers use the same 30-second commercials on cable that they do on regular television. However, cable offers creative flexibility well beyond this. In addition to standard television length commercials, many cable networks will accept longer length **informercials**, in-depth informational commercials up to 10 minutes in length. Cable will also sometimes accept advertiser-produced films and programs with integrated commercials. Dealer tags (identification of the local dealer at the end of the commercial) or direct sales offers with toll-free telephone numbers are frequently accepted. Overall, cable is more flexible than standard television, but taking advantage of this flexibility requires producing special materials for use on cable. This, in turn, drives up the minimum-cost and the production-time requirements.

*informercials*

## Who is Using Cable Advertising and Why

Advertising on cable has grown from $34 million in 1980 to $190 million in 1982 and is forecasted by one source to reach $2 billion by 1990.[12] Despite the rapid growth, cable and the other new electronic media make up only a small proportion of total advertising.

Cable advertising expenditures are not yet tracked with the same detail or frequency as are more mature media. However, a recent study did report on cable-advertising distribution by industry group. The leading industry groups using cable were packaged foods, drugs and cosmetics, automobiles, appliances, entertainment, beverages, and airlines.[13] This list is very much like the list of leading television advertisers. For the most part, cable advertisers are large national firms with large advertising budgets who use cable to supplement their primary advertising efforts.

The above-mentioned study and the experience of media directors

[12]*Cable Update* (New York: Vitt Media International, July, 1983), p. 2, and Howard Polskin, "Casting for Cable Numbers," *Advertising Age* (May 24, 1982), p. M-29.
[13]Sarah Stiansen, "With Data, If You've Got Them, Flaunt Them," *Advertising Age* (November 15, 1982), p. M-22.

give some clues to the motives of advertisers in using cable as well as the other new electronic media. The leading reason why current advertisers are using cable is that it allows them to experiment and gain experience in the new medium. One advertising agency executive, when asked why advertisers purchased cable, stated, "You are buying to establish beach-heads. It is research and development money at this point. It is not a media buy, but a learning experience."[14] To very large advertisers, the expenditure is a minor one. A second motive is to take advantage of the narrowcast ability of the medium, the ability to reach narrowly defined prospect groups. Another motive is provided by the ability to gain program sponsorship and program identification. And finally, advertisers are attracted to cable because of the cost efficiencies. Cable offers costs-per-thousands well below those of standard television.

In time, experimental purchases in the new media will decline in importance and the distinctive audience and creative characteristics will become paramount.

### Purchasing the New Electronic Media

As noted in the earlier section, cable television can be purchased locally from some cable-system operators, but most purchases are made on a network basis from the cable networks that accept advertising.

Time-buying processes are much like those in regular television except that availabilities are more numerous and offer more flexibility with regard to time periods and programs that can be purchased. Rate cards are available direct from the networks and summary rate information is included in SRDS — *Spot Television Rates and Data.*

One troublesome major difference between cable and standard television is the amount of audience-measurement data available. Measurement of the audience for the new electronic media is still experimental with much of the current effort being devoted to finding which data-collection method is most accurate. A number of special, one-time audience studies have been conducted, but currently the only on-going audience-measurement service for the new electronic media is Nielsen's *Home Video Index.* Data for these reports is collected by telephone from a national sample four times a year. The reports provide audience size and age/sex breakdowns for cable, pay cable, subscription television, multi-point distribution systems, and interactive systems plus usage of video-cassette and video-disc players and video games.

## Radio

Although radio was a forerunner of television, it stands today as a very different medium from television, serving very different advertiser needs.

---

[14]"Why Advertisers Are Rushing to Cable TV," *Business Week* (November 2, 1981), p. 96.

## The Changing Nature of Radio

The value of radio as an advertising medium today can perhaps be appreciated better if the advertiser is aware of the dramatic changes that have taken place in the medium, particularly over the past 25 years.

CONSUMER ROLE OF RADIO. Commercial radio became a reality on a widespread basis in the 1920s. It was regarded as a technical marvel in much the way that television was in the early 1950s. As the number of radios and radio stations increased, people began to view it less as a technical novelty and more as a form of entertainment. In the late 1920s a number of radio networks were formed to provide centrally produced programs to local stations. During morning and afternoon hours the networks provided dramatic serials usually called soap operas because they were traditionally sponsored by soap companies. During evening hours the networks supplied dramatic and comedy programs featuring such performers as Jack Benny and Bob Hope. In addition, the networks supplied newscasts featuring newscasters who later became well-known personalities.

As a result of these and other program features, radio became a family entertainment medium. Families listened to radio in much the same way that they view television today. During this period, which lasted until about 1950, the networks were very strong and most advertising time was purchased on the networks, reaching a national audience.

A dramatic change in the role of radio began in the 1950s with the growth of television. Because it added a visual dimension, television was easily able to supplant radio as the dominant family entertainment medium. Radio stations were faced with the problem of finding a new role to play for consumers and advertisers. The result was the transformation of radio into what amounts to a different medium. First of all, it became a highly localized medium featuring locally originated programs — especially music and local news. The role of the networks diminished greatly, although they still provided news and program features. Secondly, individual radio stations specialized their programming so that they appealed not to all consumers, but instead to rather narrow segments of the total listener group. The third major change in radio was the shift from full-time, attention-absorbing programs to a programming that serves as a background to other activities. Radio became a medium to be listened to while reading, while driving, and during work or social events.

CURRENT DIMENSION OF RADIO. Today radio appears to be approaching still another revolution, driven by new technology and deregulation.[15] Technology has expanded out-of-home radio listening to about 40 percent of the total, first by making possible small, efficient portable radios and

---

[15]J. Fred MacDonald, "Radio: New Tools, New Tunes," *Advertising Age* (July 11, 1983), pp. M-9–12.

now by making possible the walkabout radio. Computer technology has enhanced radio news reporting by tying together reporters and stations through computer terminals and telephone lines. Communications satellites have taken over transmissions of radio networks. Because satellites offer a greater number of separate communications options, the networks can deliver simultaneously a variety of specialized programming, allowing stations to select that which is best suited to their audience. New technology has also made stereocasting possible; some 200 stations now offer stereo broadcasts.

Deregulation is also changing the nature of radio. Many FCC rules governing radio programming have been dropped. Licensing requirements for new stations have been eased with the result that the number of stations in operation is expected to grow.

Radio today is a dynamic medium—it is growing, becoming more specialized in its programming and in its audience, becoming a more portable medium, and becoming more personality-oriented. Today there are over 470 million radios in use, an average of 5.5 per household, and 123 million automobiles have radios.[16] Eight million walkabout radios were in use in 1983 and 57 percent of all adults had a radio at work. The average person over 12 years of age listens to radio nearly 3.5 hours a day, second only to television. As radio usage has grown, so have radio advertising revenues, reaching $4.7 billion in 1982.[17]

## Types of Radio Purchases

The classifications of radio purchases are much the same as those found in television, but their importance and use in selecting desired audiences is somewhat different.

NETWORK VS. LOCAL. Radio can be purchased nationally on a network basis or on a local, station-by-station basis. Unlike television, network radio is only a minor part of total radio advertising, although it has shown recent growth as satellite feeds have made a greater variety of programming available. News, sports, and information programming dominate network program offerings. Also available are music and concert programs and radio personalities like Paul Harvey and Larry King. In addition to buying entire programs, the advertiser can also purchase national spot schedules through the radio networks. In 1982 only about 7 percent of all radio advertising expenditures were placed through a network.[18]

Most radio advertising time is purchased locally from individual stations. Combinations of stations in different cities can be purchased to provide coverage that conforms to the advertiser's distribution area.

---

[16]*Radio Facts, 1983* (New York: Radio Advertising Bureau, 1982).
[17]"U.S. Advertising Volume," *Advertising Age* (May 30, 1983), p. 42.
[18]*Advertising Age* (May 30, 1983), p. 24.

PROGRAM VS. SPOT. As in television, the radio advertiser has the choice of buying spots or sponsoring programs. There are programs offered both by the networks and by local stations. Program sponsorship is less widely used in radio than it is in television. One reason is that there are fewer programs on radio than on television. Another reason is that there appears to be less of a qualitative difference between spots and program announcements on radio. Radio formats are rather fluid and both spots and programs are frequently placed at random rather than in fixed positions. As a consequence, radio listeners perceive spots and program announcements as much the same thing. The end result is that program sponsors tend to benefit less from program association and probably do not get a much more attentive audience than do spots.

TIME PERIOD AND DAY OF WEEK. Radio audiences vary with the time of day and the day of the week. By and large, radio listenership is highest during daytime hours, but the advertiser who is seeking a particular prospect group must be aware of that group's most frequent listening period.

There are two time periods that typically have very high listenership — the early morning from 6 A.M. to 10 A.M. and the late afternoon from 4 P.M. to 7 P.M. on weekdays. These two time periods are called *drive times*. Listenership is heavy because people use radio as a medium to wake up to, as background during breakfast and dinner, and as entertainment while driving to work. The audience during drive time has a much heavier component of working people than other times of day.

The weekday time period between drive times tends to be dominated by the homemaker audience. Evening radio tends to have a nontelevision, reading audience, including a large group of students. Late night radio has a small, but unique audience of travelers, students, and night workers. The sharp differences in audience by time period tend to be less distinct on weekends when radio serves as background to social and hobby activities for a wide variety of people. Out-of-home listenership tends to be heavy on these days.

STATION FORMAT. Even more important than time of day in audience selection is the program format of the station. Radio stations have become highly selective by presenting program materials that appeal to certain groups or segments of the market.

The program format of a radio station is made up of a number of components. The most important of these is usually music, which is programmed to appeal to particular groups. In addition, the format includes news, sports, and talk or commentary which also serve to attract certain audience segments. Radio formats are usually categorized in terms of their dominant element. Some currently popular formats are:

1. *Contemporary* formats feature current music favorites from popular music polls; most play the "top 40" from the polls. Contemporary formats appeal to youths, but also to a broad range of adults.
2. *Rock* formats feature the various forms of rock music, appealing mainly to youths and young adults.
3. *Middle-of-the-road* music formats feature show tunes, old standards and currently popular nonrock tunes, popular vocalists, and news/information programs. Its primary appeal is to a broader, older audience than rock 'n' roll.
4. *Good music* stations play old standards, show tunes, and semiclassical music, mostly instrumental. The appeal of good music stations is to adult audiences, usually with higher income and better education.
5. *Country and Western* formats feature music originating in southern and western regions, frequently supplemented by farm and country news and information in rural areas. Appeal is primarily to nonurban, middle to lower income, adult age groups.
6. *Classical* stations feature semiclassical, symphonic, and operatic music with few interruptions aside from occasional news reports. Appeal is to higher-income, better-educated adults.
7. *Talk* and *All News* formats have no music. Programming may feature long interviews with personalities, telephone chats with listeners, or continuous news programs. Primary appeal seems to be among older adults.
8. *Ethnic/Minority* formats feature programming for a particular ethnic or minority group. Black and Spanish stations are probably the two leading representatives of this format. The stations, located in areas of ethnic or minority group concentration, have strong listenership among members of the target group.

Exhibit 14-10 shows the audience for a range of radio formats as measured by one research firm.

AM VS. FM. Advertisers can purchase broadcast time on either AM radio or FM radio. In its early years, FM radio programming was primarily classical music directed to upper socio-economic, adult listeners while AM radio offered popular music formats to other segments. In recent years there has been a nearly complete turnaround in AM and FM programming and audiences. Today, over 60 percent of all listening is on FM and, among the 18–34 age group, 80 percent of all listening is on FM since many FM stations have adopted rock formats.[19] As a result, FM radio now leads AM radio in advertising revenue.

## Characteristics of Radio as an Advertising Medium

The basic strength of television as an advertising medium lies in its mass audience and in its creative power. Radio offers less of a mass audience, but it does permit the advertiser to aim the message more precisely

---

[19]Mark Liff, "Rock FM: Branching Out," *Advertising Age* (July 11, 1983), p. M-26.

EXHIBIT 14-10          Radio format popularity in terms of audience.

| Format | Average One Day Audience (000) |
|---|---|
| Adult contemporary | 38,452 |
| AOR/progressive rock | 14,067 |
| Beautiful music | 14,807 |
| Black | 8,058 |
| Classical | 2,127 |
| Contemporary/top 40/rock | 31,437 |
| Country | 27,231 |
| Disco | 5,044 |
| Jazz | 1,868 |
| News | 12,961 |
| Oldies | 4,412 |
| Religious & gospel | 2,940 |
| Talk | 11,102 |

Source: *Multimedia Audiences*, Spring 1982 (New York: Mediamark Research, Inc., 1982).

and deliver it more frequently. While radio does not have the creative impact of television, it does offer creative flexibility and the opportunity to personalize the message.

AUDIENCE SELECTIVITY. Radio is more selective than television, both demographically and geographically.

*Demographic Selectivity.* It has already been noted that, as part of its response to the competitive pressure of television, radio has become an increasingly selective medium. By careful selection of station format and time period, the advertiser can use radio to select certain rather narrow consumer groups.

There are some groups that radio is particularly able to select. Foremost is radio's ability to reach youth. Young people because of their mobility, their social interests, and their school or work requirements are a particularly difficult group to reach with advertising. However, radio is their medium — it fits their work and social life pattern, and much of the programming is directed to them. This fact is illustrated in Exhibit 14-11 that shows how much more time high school students spend with radio than with any other medium.

Radio also has the ability to reach working men and women, traditionally another difficult group to reach. Radio advertising reaches these workers during driving times and meals, and while they are at work. Radio also has considerable ability to reach light television viewers and thus can serve as a supplement to television with the effect of extending reach.

Average daily time high school students spend with major media.    **EXHIBIT 14-11**

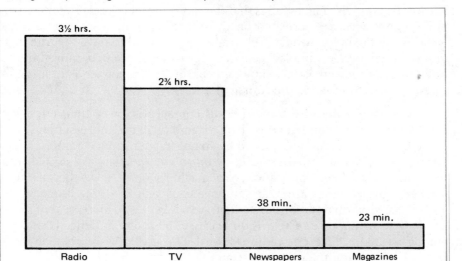

Source: *Radio Facts* (New York: Radio Advertising Bureau, 1978), p. 25.

*Geographic Selectivity.* If the radio advertiser places advertising on a spot rather than network basis, it is possible to be geographically selective. Radio tends to offer greater geographic selectivity than television because the radio marketing area (RMA) over which its signal is received is of smaller diameter than the television ADI/DMA. (There are exceptions; the high-powered, clear-channel radio stations, for example, have nighttime audiences spread over many hundreds of miles.) A television station usually covers several cities, whereas a radio station's audience is usually limited to a single city. This means that radio has less waste coverage for the small advertiser with limited distribution. It also means that the advertiser has greater flexibility in combining stations in several cities to fit the advertising coverage to the desired distribution pattern.

AUDIENCE DISTRIBUTION. The strength of radio lies in its ability to deliver frequency rather than reach. This is in direct contrast to television. The reason for the difference in radio's audience distribution pattern lies in the listening habits of the radio audience.

On the average, the time spent listening to radio is about 35 percent less than the time spent viewing television.[20] Listenership to radio is very unevenly distributed (as is television viewership). While it is probably true that most people listen to radio sometime during the week, there is a small group of heavy listeners who greatly influence the average listening figure. Radio audience distribution is also influenced by the fact that there are

[20]*TV Basics, 26, op. cit.*

many radio stations available to listen to, typically more radio stations than television channels. The result is that the radio audience is fragmented, i.e., more highly selective. A related factor that affects radio listening patterns is the listener's station loyalty. Television viewers tend to have favorite programs and change channels freely in order to see those programs, but the radio listener's loyalty is to a station. Typically, a listener tends to listen to three or fewer stations in the course of a week.

*Radio Reach.* Because total radio listenership is lower than television viewership and the audience is divided among many more stations, the percentage of radio homes reached by any particular radio commercial will usually be very low. Furthermore, as more commercials are added to a schedule on a particular station, reach climbs only slowly because the listener's loyalty to a particular station means that few new listeners are added. As additional stations are added, reach begins to increase, but more slowly than in the case of television because the radio audience is split up among so many different radio stations. The ability to reach many different homes is not the primary strength of radio.

*Radio Frequency.* Where does radio's strength lie? Certainly one of its major attributes is the ability to inexpensively deliver repetitive messages to relatively narrow segments of the market. Because listeners are loyal to particular stations, a radio station advertising schedule tends to build up frequent exposure to those listeners, especially among those who are heavy listeners.

*Distribution of Radio Exposures.* The results of the large number of radio stations available, of audience loyalty, and of the very uneven listenership time can also be looked at in terms of the distribution of exposures that is likely to result from a radio advertising schedule. If several radio stations are used, the total number of people exposed will eventually be substantial, but the vast majority of these exposures will be concentrated among the heavy listeners who are loyal to the stations on the schedule. The distribution of exposures, in other words, will be highly uneven.

Whether this distribution is good or bad depends upon the advertiser's objectives and the care with which the stations on the schedule are selected. If the advertiser wishes to build up frequency and can find radio stations that consistently reach good prospects for the product, then the audience distribution is a positive attribute.

CREATIVE CHARACTERISTICS. Radio does not offer the creative latitude of television, but, properly understood, it does have important creative attributes for the advertiser.

*Media Form.* Radio is a much more restricted media form than is television, since radio is limited to sound alone. The advertiser on radio cannot show the product or its color, demonstrate how it works, or deliver coupons, entry blanks, or lists of dealers.

On the other hand, radio advertisers can use persuasive salespeople or well-known personalities. The warmth and persuasiveness of the human voice is an important selling tool that can be used in radio advertising. Another important attribute of radio's form is the ability to use music. The dominant attraction of radio to its listeners is music, so music as a part of a commercial fits in well with the format of most radio stations.

*Environment.* Radio is not a dominating, intrusive, national medium like television, but it has developed its own distinctive place in the consumer's way of life. The environment or surroundings that radio offers can be used to advantage by the advertiser if the advertising is designed to fit the medium.

One important consideration is that radio is a background medium. The radio audience tends to listen while engaged in other activities. As a result, the attention paid to radio programming and to commercials is low. To overcome this problem, radio advertisers utilize several devices. Simplicity and repetition are used to make the message more easily understood. Various audio devices are used to attract listener attention to the commercial message. These include unusual sounds, provocative statements, music, and well-known or unusual voices.

Another environmental characteristic of radio is that it has become a very personal medium. Listeners use radio for companionship while they are working, especially when they are alone. The disc jockeys on radio stations develop strong rapport with their audiences. They become local celebrities with strong personal followings. In their conversation, their music, and their programs they attempt to speak the language of their listener group. The advertiser who wishes, in the same way, to speak personally with a radio station's audience must make the commercial fit into this same format. One way to do this is to allow the disc jockeys or announcers to present the commercial in their own style, using language that communicates with their listener groups.

Another environmental characteristic, related to this last one, is that radio has become increasingly localized. Stations now feature local news, local sports, and local personalities. In this sense radio has drawn closer to the position in the community held by the local newspaper. Advertisers who wish to identify with the local community will find that radio advertising can help to build that identity.

*Life.* Like television, radio is a short-lived, almost instantaneous medium. This short life, when combined with the absence of visual presentation, suggests that radio is not an appropriate medium for complex messages, multiple product messages, long lists or detailed instructions. Radio advertisers usually strive to state their message simply and clearly, and they usually make use of repetition to be sure that the message is understood.

*Clutter.* The clutter problem in radio ranges from very severe to very mild. The primary variables determining the degree of clutter are station popularity and time of day. Stations which have higher listenership tend to attract more advertisers, even though their rates are generally higher. Clutter also tends to be greater at the times of day when listenership is heavy. The drive times in particular tend to be very crowded with commercials.

Radio stations attempt to control clutter by placing programming between commercials. On most stations this means that commercials are alternated with musical selections. In crowded time periods, however, two or more commercials are often placed back to back between musical numbers. The distraction caused by this babble of advertising again calls for clarity, simplicity, and repetition of message.

MINIMUM COST. Radio is a low cost-of-entry medium. This attribute, together with radio's restricted geographic coverage, makes it a popular medium with smaller, local businesses. There are two factors that account for the low entry cost of radio. First, radio commercials are inexpensive to produce relative to other media. It is quite feasible to produce a variety of recorded radio messages for a small investment. Live commercials (commercials delivered by the announcer in person during the program) are widely used in radio and generally cost little to produce. The use of music increases costs if composers and musicians must be hired.

The minimum cost for radio is also low because schedules can be purchased on a single-station basis and since the coverage of individual stations is small, cost per spot is low.

PRODUCTION REQUIREMENTS. Flexibility and low cost of production are important advantages of advertising over the radio. The radio advertiser must provide to the radio station either a script of the commercial to be read by the radio announcer or a recording of the message that can be broadcast by the station.

Radio commercials can be produced on very short notice. For commercials delivered live, the production process involves only preparation and delivery of a script. Even if the commercial is to be recorded, the process can be very rapid. Radio commercials today are generally recorded on tape in a recording studio and then converted to audio cassettes which are mailed to individual stations. This entire process can sometimes be completed in as little as one or two days.

Radio commercials are also inexpensive to produce. Live commercials, of course, have no production cost. For recorded commercials there would normally be charges for recording studios, talent used in the commercial, and the preparation of the transcriptions. Some radio stations will record commercials to be used on their own station at no charge. Once talent has been assembled and studio time rented, it is possible to produce several commercials for little additional cost.

MERCHANDISING VALUE. The favorable attitude of the trade to radio is heightened by its local characteristics. Retailers are very likely to consider radio a hometown medium and to know some of the local radio personalities. Use of radio by an advertiser can help a product fit into the local scene.

The merchandising assistance offered by radio stations is usually rather limited due to the limited personnel available. However, because radio personalities are locally known, they can sometimes be a very beneficial influence with local trade factors. Through trade calls, mailings, meetings, contests, and similar activities the radio station personalities try to make the trade aware of advertisers' schedules and encourage them to stock and display the advertisers' products.

## Users of Radio

Tabulations of the heaviest investors in radio advertising do not give an accurate picture of the use of radio as an advertising medium because it gives undue weight to national rather than local advertisers. The same point was made with regard to television users, but in the case of radio the point is more important. In 1982 about one dollar out of four spent in television advertising represented local advertising, but in radio about three out of four advertising dollars were local.[21]

LOCAL RADIO USERS. Knowing the characteristics of radio, it should not be surprising that radio is a favorite medium of local advertisers. The medium is geographically flexible and its coverage can be confined to local areas; it has low cost-of-entry even when frequent copy changes are needed; and its local orientation helps an advertiser to fit in with the community. Heaviest local users of radio are shown in Exhibit 14-12.

NATIONAL RADIO USERS. Heavy national radio user categories, such as those shown in Exhibit 14-12, are attracted to radio by the characteristics of its audience. Auto and oil companies use radio to reach automobile drivers, many of whom listen on car radios while driving. Travel companies value radio because its flexibility permits copy tailored to the travel market; e.g., airlines advertise flights available in each city. Soft drink and cosmetics advertisers value radio because of its effectiveness in reaching their prime youth prospects. Other advertisers, such as food and drug marketers, often use radio in combination with other media such as television. Television provides great reach, while radio augments the frequency and reaches additional light TV viewers.

## Purchasing Radio Time

The process of purchasing radio time and the information sources used are very similar to those discussed for television. Media specialists who purchase television in most cases purchase radio time as well.

TIME-BUYING PROCESS. As in television, the radio-time buyer works from a media program that specifies budget, target audience, and time

---

[21]*Advertising Age* (May 30, 1983), p. 24.

**EXHIBIT 14-12**     Top 10 local and top 10 national radio advertiser categories, 1981.

| Rank | Category |
|---|---|
| Local | |
| 1 | Auto dealers |
| 2 | Department stores |
| 3 | Banks |
| 4 | Clothing stores |
| 5 | Restaurants |
| 6 | Supermarkets |
| 7 | Furniture stores |
| 8 | Bottlers |
| 9 | Appliance stores |
| 10 | Savings & loans |
| National | |
| 1 | Automotive |
| 2 | Food products |
| 3 | Travel & shipping |
| 4 | Beer, ale, wine |
| 5 | Consumer services |
| 6 | Cosmetics |
| 7 | Gasoline & oil |
| 8 | Drug products |
| 9 | Soft drinks |
| 10 | Apparel |

Source: *Radio Facts, 1983* (New York: Radio Advertising Bureau, 1982), pp. 30–31.

schedules. The time buyer calls for availabilities from the stations and selects from the availabilities those that best fit the requirements of the plan.

The decision as to which station or stations to use in a particular market is far more important in radio than it is in television. Most television stations appeal to a generalized audience, so audience selectivity is achieved by time period and program. Radio stations, by their format, appeal to particular audiences; the radio buyer must understand the program format of each station in the market and pick the station(s) that reach the target audience.

The same decision must be made with regard to time period. Listener characteristics vary greatly throughout the day, thus time periods chosen must be determined in the light of the target audience to be reached.

RADIO RATES. The structure of rates in radio is similar to that found in television. Rates vary with the length of the spot and with the time of day (highest cost time periods are the drive times). Frequency and continuity discounts are also offered by most stations, and radio stations, even more than television stations, are likely to offer a number of special package or combination plans.

Radio rates are more likely to be negotiable or subject to bargaining than are television rates. This presumably reflects competition among the large number of radio stations in a given area. The principle beneficiary of this competition tends to be the local advertiser who can negotiate person-ally with local stations. Some radio rate cards offer a lower rate to local advertisers much as is offered by most newspapers.

Radio station rates, formats, and other necessary information for time buying is available directly from the stations on their rate cards and is sum-marized in Standard Rate and Data Service's *Spot Radio Rates and Data*. Net-work radio information is also summarized in the same SRDS volume.

RADIO RATING SERVICES. Arbitron is the major radio rating service available for local radio. Arbitron collects its rating information through panels of consumers who are enlisted to keep radio listening diaries.

Arbitron covers 250 local radio markets with one to four rating re-ports per year. Rating reports contain the number of listeners and the rating by station with breakdowns by time period, by age group, and by sex, plus a variety of other data. Given the large number of stations in each market area, radio ratings can become very complex.

Network radio is measured by Statistical Research Inc.'s (SRI) RADAR service. RADAR's listenership figures are collected through a telephone in-terview technique.

---

*CHAPTER*
*SUMMARY*

Television, the second largest medium, can be purchased through na-tional networks or through individual stations. The advertiser can choose between program sponsorship and purchase of spot announcements be-tween programs. Television is a nonselective medium reaching a mass audi-ence. It is geographically selective if individual stations are used, although the coverage area of even a single station is extensive. Television reach cumulates quickly over a television advertising schedule while frequency increases slowly. In addition, frequency is unevenly distributed because of heavy viewing by a small proportion of the total audience. Creatively tele-vision offers sight, sound, motion, and color. Viewer attentiveness to commercials is likely to be low, but television has intrusive power to force itself on viewers. Clutter is an increasingly serious problem in television. Television's minimum cost of entry is higher than for most media, tending to limit its use to larger advertisers. The leading users of television tend to be marketers of high volume, widely used consumer goods and services. Purchase of television schedules is a specialized function requiring famil-iarity with rates, alternative units of purchase, and audience characteristics. Television rating services provide indispensable audience information to buyers.

The new electronic media, including cable TV, superstations, and videotex, offer opportunities to "narrowcast" advertising to viewer groups that are narrower than those of regular television. Although the new elec-tronic media are growing rapidly, they still offer limited reach and uneven geographic coverage with the result that they are most often used as a supplementary rather than a primary medium. Creatively the new electronic media are much like television, but offer greater flexibility. Most advertiser use of the new electronic media focuses on cable TV which is largely purchased through cable networks rather than locally. Audience measurement research is still very limited.

Radio met the challenge of television by becoming a more localized and specialized medium offering background listening. Technological advances and deregulation have encouraged further specialization and greater out-of-home use of radio. Most radio advertising is purchased as spots on a station-by-station basis. Time of day and station format are important determinants of radio audience. Radio is demographically more selective than television. Young people and working people are two groups that radio is particularly adept at reaching. Unlike television, radio's strength is in building frequency rather than reach. Distribution of radio exposures is highly uneven due to concentration of listenership among heavy listeners and the listeners' station loyalty. Creatively, radio is limited to sound, but this permits use of persuasive personalities and music. Radio is local in orientation and a personal medium; minimum cost is low due to low production cost and its localized coverage. Heaviest users of radio are local retail and service organizations. The process of purchasing advertising schedules is very similar to the television purchase process except that knowledge of individual markets and stations is even more important.

## KEY TERMS

| | |
|---|---|
| Spot | Preemptible spot |
| Area of dominant influence (ADI) | Narrowcasting |
| Designated market area (DMA) | Informercials |
| Availabilities | |

## QUESTIONS FOR DISCUSSION

1. Television networks and television stations sometimes offer advertisers *scatter plans* that contain a group of rotating commercial positions so that the advertiser's commercial appears in a different position each time. How would the reach and frequency of a scatter plan compare with a fixed commercial position schedule?

2. Through choice of time and program, the television advertiser can emphasize certain groups in an audience. By using Exhibits 14-1 and 14-2, suggest for each of the groups listed below the time period, day of the week, and program type that would most likely reach the desired audience.

   a. Women with preschool children.
   b. Women with school-aged children.

   c. Working women.

   d. Working men.

   e. Preschool children.

3. By 1982, Nielsen reported that 55 percent of all homes had more than one television set. As this figure continues to increase, what changes does it make in the characteristics of television as an advertising medium?

4. Using the sample *Nielsen Television Index Report* in Exhibit 14-8, answer the following questions:

   a. At what hour is the HUT rating the highest?

   b. At that time what is the total household audience?

   c. What program receives the highest rating?

   d. What is the difference between the average audience figure and the total audience?

5. If split 30s come into widespread use in television, what advantages will they offer to advertisers? In what ways will television be weakened as a medium?

6. In newspapers, some advertisers attempt to solve the problem of clutter by using an ad size that dominates the page. In television the clutter problem is also severe. What can the television advertiser do to solve the clutter problem?

7. The *Nielsen Station Index* shown in Exhibit 14-9 provides the media buyer with the ratings of programs, but it must be used in the purchase of spots that occur not during programs, but at the station breaks between programs. How can the rating report be used to evaluate these spot positions?

8. One of the attributes of cable television is said to be its ability to direct its message selectively to narrow consumer groups. For each of the cable services listed below, indicate the segment to which they "narrowcast."

   a. Entertainment and Sports Programming Network (ESPN)

   b. Music Television (MTV)

   c. Nashville Network

   d. Nickelodeon

   e. Arts

9. One concern of advertisers has been that the advent of multiple viewing options on cable television would result in a diminished audience for network television. This, in turn, would force advertisers to supplement their network schedules with cable network schedules. Based on the data shown at the top of p. 380, do you believe that this fear is well-founded?

| Viewing | Viewing by Type of TV Household[22] (avg. hours per week) | | |
|---|---|---|---|
| | Non-Cable Homes | Basic Cable Homes | Pay Cable Homes |
| Over-the-air | 46.4 | 44.9 | 46.9 |
| Cable originated | — | 3.0 | 4.6 |
| Pay-cable | — | — | 9.8 |

10. Radio listeners frequently use radio as background for other activities such as driving, studying, reading, or talking. What creative limitation does this practice impose on radio advertising?

11. Correctly purchased, radio has the ability to select certain listener groups for the advertiser. Indicate the station format, weekday or weekend, and the time of day for which advertising should be purchased in order to reach each of the following groups:

   a. Middle income, suburban homemakers.
   b. Urban high school students.
   c. Urban blue-collar workers.
   d. Farmers.

12. One of the standard time classifications in which the advertiser can purchase radio advertising time is "late night," a time period usually extending from midnight to 6 a.m.

   a. What characteristics would you expect the late-night audience to have?
   b. For what kinds of products do you think this time period would be appropriate?

---

PROBLEM          Assume that you are a media buyer for a southeastern advertising agency. One of your clients is a regional soft-drink bottler whose product line includes a tropical fruit flavored drink called Tropic. You have been asked to recommend for the coming year a Tropic media schedule for Atlanta, Georgia, the most important market area for the product.

You have been supplied with the advertising plan for Tropic which has the following media requirements:

   1. The target prospect for Tropic is teenagers and under-35 adults from lower- to middle-income families. Consumption is higher among blacks.

---

[22]*TV Basics*, 26, *op. cit.*

2. The media program should emphasize frequency to the key consumer groups since this is a frequently purchased impulse item.
3. The media schedule should permit use of live commercials delivered by local on-air personalities. Commercial length should be 60 seconds.
4. Consumption of the product is somewhat seasonal, with purchases higher during the warm weather months.
5. The budget allocated to Atlanta for Tropic is $100,000 for 12 months, including production costs.

While it has been decided that radio is to be the only medium used in Atlanta for Tropic, stations, time periods, and schedule have not yet been specified.

1. Using a copy of Standard Rate and Data Service's *Spot Radio Rates and Data,* list the stations available in Atlanta. Based on the descriptive information available in SRDS, evaluate how well each station would reach the Tropic target-prospect group.
2. Decide which station or stations you would recommend for the schedule.
3. What time period and days of the week would you recommend?
4. Construct a schedule showing recommended stations, time periods, and costs.

# CHAPTER 15

LEARNING OBJECTIVES

In studying this chapter you will learn:

- The various classes of direct-mail advertising and types of outdoor advertising and transit advertising.

- The media characteristics of direct-mail, outdoor, and transit advertising.

- The preparation problems involved in direct-mail advertising.

- The characteristics of other advertising media including store-display materials, advertising specialties, packaging materials, trade shows, and advertising directories.

The two final classes of media to be considered are direct mail and out-of-home media. Direct mail includes those forms of advertising delivered directly to consumers without being included in a media vehicle such as a newspaper or television program. Out-of-home advertising includes out-door posters, transit advertising, and point-of-purchase materials. Direct mail and out-of-home advertising have some quite different characteristics that require separate and special attention. At the end of this chapter, several miscellaneous media types will be discussed.

## Direct Mail Advertising

Before considering direct advertising, an important distinction needs to be drawn between *direct advertising* and *direct marketing* or *direct response marketing.*

## Direct Advertising vs. Direct Marketing

**Direct marketing** is a system, fully controlled by the marketer, that distributes products directly to the consumer. The direct marketer develops products, promotes them directly to the end consumer, accepts orders direct from consumers, and distributes the products directly to the purchaser without the use of retailers, wholesalers or other intermediaries. The key to success in direct marketing lies in defining and reaching narrow market segments with relevant advertising and products tailored to segment needs.

*direct marketing*

Direct marketing is one of the most dynamic, fastest growing areas in all of marketing. Sales volume from direct marketing was estimated at $138 billion in 1982 and by the year 2000 is forecast to account for one of every four consumer dollars.[1] Leading direct marketing firms include such well-known names as Sears, Roebuck and Co., Franklin Mint, L. L. Bean, and Book-of-the-Month Club.

**Direct advertising** is but one part of a direct marketing system and includes the medium and the communication directed to direct-marketing prospects. In this chapter, we will focus on the characteristics of direct mail, one of the leading media used in direct marketing. It should be noted that direct mail is not the only medium used in direct marketing, although it is a large one. Exhibit 15-1 shows the different media used in direct marketing and their relative importance. At the same time, the distinctive characteristics of direct mail, the ability to select and address prospects one at a time, make it a valuable medium in uses other than direct marketing.

*direct advertising*

### Classes of direct mail advertising

One of the distinctive characteristics of the direct mail medium is that there are no ready-made media vehicles as there are for other media. The advertiser, in effect, has to put together a media vehicle each time this medium is used. The media vehicle is made up of two elements—the means of delivery and the list of names or addresses that determine to whom the advertisement is to be sent. The choice of delivery system (for example, mail vs. messenger) determines the physical form of the medium and its creative attributes. The choice of the list from which the individual direct advertisements are addressed determines the characteristics of the audience. Both decisions will be considered in discussing the characteristics of direct mail advertising.

The two basic elements which make up the direct mail medium—the delivery system and the distribution list—provide a convenient means of classifying the basic types of direct mail advertising.

---

[1]Lori Kesler, "Marketing's Stepchild Comes Into Its Own," *Advertising Age* (November 28, 1983), p. M–9.

EXHIBIT 15-1          Direct marketing media expenditures, 1982.

| Medium | Expenditure ($ millions) |
|---|---|
| Coupons | 127.1 |
| Direct mail | 11,359.4 |
| Consumer magazines | 167.0 |
| Business magazines | 66.0 |
| Newspapers | 70.6 |
| Newspaper preprints | 2,500.0 |
| Telephone | 12,935.6 |
| Television | 339.0 |
| Radio | 33.0 |
| Total | 27,597.7 |

Reprinted with permission from the November 28, 1983 issue of *Advertising Age.* Copyright 1983 by Crain Communications, Inc.

CLASSIFICATION BY MEANS OF DELIVERY. The means of delivery suggests a four-way classification of direct-mail advertising. The classes are solo direct mail, mail-order catalogs, unmailed direct mail, and take-ones.

*solo direct mail*

*Solo Direct Mail.* Individual advertisements sent to prospects through the mail are termed **solo direct mail.** This form of direct mail is heavily used as a medium in direct marketing. In addition, it is frequently used as a door-opener that paves the way for salespeople. Solo direct mail is also used, particularly in industrial marketing, as a supplement to other media such as business publications in order to increase frequency with key prospects.

*mail-order catalog advertising*

*Mail-Order Catalogs.* Sending catalogs through the mail in an attempt to get consumers to purchase products by return mail is termed **mail-order catalog advertising.** Catalogs may focus on a single class of products ("Harry and David's gift-food catalog") or may present a wide variety of items as does the Sears, Roebuck catalog.

*unmailed direct advertising*

*Unmailed Direct Advertising.* Advertising delivered directly to consumers is classified as **unmailed direct advertising.** It might be delivered door to door, distributed in stores, placed on automobiles, or included in shopping bags.

*take-ones*

*Take-Ones.* Display cards holding reply cards, pads of order forms, or information pamphlets are another form of direct mail. Prospects are invited by the display card to "take-one" of the items. **Take-ones** are frequently seen on university campuses, for example, advertising magazine subscriptions, travel opportunities, and part-time jobs.

CLASSIFICATION BY NATURE OF LIST. The characteristics of the audience of direct mail advertising are most strongly influenced by the nature of the distribution list used. Direct mail lists are best understood if they are viewed, as were magazines, as ranging along a scale of specialization. At the nonspecialized end of the scale would be door-to-door delivery to all homes in a community or "occupant" mailings (addresses, but no names) to an entire community. Slightly more specialized would be an advertisement that was handed to all people walking past a particular counter in a store.

Direct mail that would be at the specialized end of the scale would use a distribution list limited to people with specific characteristics. The advertisement, for example, might be distributed only to licensed optometrists, only to people owning late-model sports cars, or only to mothers with children under the age of one.

The choice between nonspecialized and specialized direct mail depends upon the nature of the consumers who are prospects for the product. If the target prospects are a restricted group with distinct characteristics, then a specialized list would be used to reach them even though such a list would be more expensive to obtain. Many specialized industrial products — machinery, chemicals, tools — would require a special mailing list. Conversely, there are products, such as books, magazines, and insurance, that have broad consumer usage and consequently require less specialized distribution lists.

## Media Characteristics of Direct Mail

Because of its importance as a general-use medium, our discussion of direct mail will tend to focus on solo direct mail, but many of these characteristics apply to the other direct-mail forms as well.

AUDIENCE SELECTIVITY. The flexibility of direct mail is nowhere more apparent than in its selectivity characteristics. Direct mail can be randomly distributed and be totally nonselective, yet it can also be the most selective medium available to the advertiser.

*Demographic Selectivity.* The ability of direct mail to select certain demographic groups is dependent upon the mailing list used. At one extreme are the "occupant" lists which result in audience characteristics similar to those of a newspaper covering the same area. While direct mail does provide broad, nonselective coverage in this case, other media can frequently do so more efficiently.

The greatest strength and the more frequent use of direct mail is as a highly selective medium. Direct mail lists can be developed that only include those who are prime prospects for the advertiser's product. For example, a manufacturer of a specialized skin cream might use a list containing only dermatologists; a retail store selling industrial safety shoes might develop a list of all people working in factories in their locality; or a printer of checkbooks might use a list of purchasing agents for banks.

Perhaps even more important than its demographic selectivity is the behavioral selectivity of direct mail. By building mailing lists of people who have exhibited certain behavior, the direct-mail advertiser is able to define and communicate with need-based segments. For example, mailing lists can be prepared that include only people just graduated from college or who have just moved or those who have flown first class on TWA between New York and Los Angeles or who rent cars more than six times a year.

*Geographic Selectivity.* The geographic selectivity of direct mail is much like its demographic selectivity. By acquiring or developing the appropriate mailing list, the direct-mail advertiser can deliver advertising to any area desired. The advertiser has great flexibility in adapting the area of advertising coverage to match the area in which the product is available. As a result, direct mail is frequently used by retailers and other local businesses that wish to restrict their advertising to a particular city or neighborhood.

Direct-mail distribution is often controlled geographically by mailing to selected zip codes. Several services are available that offer zip-code mailing lists. The more advanced of these computerized data bases (Claritas Corporation's PRIZM, for example) allow the advertiser to select zip codes made up of residents that exhibit specified life styles, predetermined demographics, or life-cycle stages.

AUDIENCE DISTRIBUTION. If an advertiser schedules a series of direct mailings, the distribution of exposures to those advertisements depends upon the way in which the mailing list is used. If six direct mailings are scheduled, each a month apart, and each mailing sent to the same list of names, the result will be a frequency of six times to each name on the list. If the six mailings are each sent to a different set of names, then the mailings will reach six times as many people as if one list were used, with a frequency of one.

Direct mail is often used as a medium to supplement the frequency obtained through other media. For example, a television station might use a trade magazine such as *Advertising Age* to inform advertising people of the coverage or audience of the station. However, of all the people in advertising, one particular group — television time buyers — would be particularly important in the buying decision. Direct mail might be sent to this group to supplement the *Advertising Age* exposure, thus increasing frequency with this key prospect group.

CREATIVE CHARACTERISTICS. Direct mail is probably the most flexible print medium because it does not have to conform to rigid requirements of a separate media vehicle.

*Media Form.* Direct mail is in physical print form and thus shares many of the form characteristics of newspapers and magazines. It is a static, visual medium. It lends itself to use of illustrations, but cannot depict motion well. It is not a good medium for demonstrating product use.

Direct mail is a more flexible form than newspapers or magazines. The quality and shape of the paper on which the advertisement is printed can be varied to suit the needs and intent of the message. There can be single pages, multiple pages, cutouts, popups, and special foldings. Direct mail has the special advantage of being able to include such items as coupons, samples, gifts, or reply cards.

The only limits on the form of direct mail are the costs of production and the limits on dimensions imposed by the Postal Service. Variety in paper, shape, and color is used to create intriguing, attention-getting mailing pieces to counteract the tendency of some consumers to discard direct mail without seriously considering its message. The ability to enclose items with a direct-mail piece, together with the ability to direct it to certain people without duplication, makes it a favorite medium for distributing coupons, samples, and free offers.

*Environment.* Unlike a magazine ad, a direct mail advertisement is not contained in a separate media vehicle that provides it with an environment. The direct mail advertiser can, to some extent, create an environment. At one extreme the direct mail advertiser can prepare personally addressed letters to prospects to give a feeling of importance and personal attention. On the other extreme, many nonpersonalized, mass-mailed pieces lack prestige, look cheap, and deserve the frequently used description "junk mail."

Direct mail is a medium that consumers neither request nor pay for. It is not a medium that consumers look forward to receiving and reading as they might a magazine to which they subscribe. The advertiser must offset this low level of interest by creating direct mail that contains useful information and by sending it to those prospects who have a need for the information.

*Life.* There is little question that a great deal of direct mail, particularly that which is not selectively distributed, has a very short life. Much of it is discarded unopened before it ever reaches its intended recipient. However, because of its physical form, the recipient can retain direct mail for reference.

Direct mail can be used effectively to provide complex information, specifications, price and item lists, or directions because the recipient can study the message and save it for reference. This is one reason why industrial advertisers with technical product messages and complex product lines find direct mail an advantageous medium.

*Clutter.* One of the advantages of direct advertising is its isolation from other advertising. A direct mailing, for example, generally contains only a single advertisement as compared to a newspaper in which many ads appear; yet people may receive several different direct mail advertisements at one time. This competition for attention is a form of clutter. One study indicated that the average U.S. home receives 6.5 pieces of direct mail per week or slightly less than one piece per day.[2] Clutter is a more serious problem with such people as doctors or industrial purchasing

---

[2]"What People Think About Direct Mail," (New York: Direct Mail Advertising Association).

agents who receive heavy amounts of direct advertising because they are particularly influential in purchase decisions.

MINIMUM COST. Direct advertising is a low minimum cost medium, making it a popular medium for small manufacturers and retailers. This is true despite the fact that direct mail's cost per unit is higher than for any other medium. The low minimum cost stems from the ability to restrict circulation to small numbers and the low cost of preparing materials. A direct-mail program, for example, could consist of one hand-typed letter sent to one sales prospect. Even for larger campaigns, cost can be minimized by restricting circulation to key prospects, preparing one's own mailing list, and using inexpensive reproduction methods to produce the mailing piece. There is no business too small to utilize this medium.

*merchandising the advertising*

MERCHANDISING VALUE. Use of direct mail as a primary medium ordinarily has little direct merchandising value with trade factors. However, direct mail is frequently used as a secondary medium directed to distributors of a product to inform them of the company's consumer advertising program. This activity is commonly termed **merchandising the advertising.** These mailings may be sent by the advertiser or, in some cases, the publications or stations used by the advertiser will use direct mail to merchandise their advertisers' schedules.

## Preparation of Direct Mail

The user of direct advertising has unique preparation problems, for the advertising manager not only has to produce the advertisements, but also must obtain the list and location of the persons to whom the advertising is to be directed.

PRODUCTION REQUIREMENTS. The direct advertiser has more responsibility for preparing the direct-advertising materials than those of other media because the advertiser takes over the responsibilities assumed in other cases by the medium itself. Thus direct advertisers must have copy, layout, and artwork prepared as they would for newspapers or magazines. In addition, direct advertisers must purchase the paper, have the printing done, provide envelopes or some method of enclosing the ads, and provide a means for addressing them. Finally, the mailing pieces must be wrapped or inserted in envelopes, stamped or metered if they are to be mailed, and delivered either to homes or to post offices.

Users of direct mail must decide upon the extent to which they will direct the preparation of the advertising materials themselves. Some heavy users of direct advertising have personnel and equipment to prepare copy and layout, print the advertisements, and insert them into envelopes. Other advertisers subcontract these jobs or contract with an outside firm to do the entire job. There are firms that specialize in handling direct advertising and some specialized advertising agencies or advertising departments will handle this task.

DIRECT ADVERTISING LISTS. In addition to preparing the advertisement that is to be distributed to consumers, the direct-mail advertiser must obtain a list of persons to whom the advertising will be sent. The advertiser can either compile or purchase a list.

*Compiling a List.* Compiling a distribution list is a demanding, time-consuming process, and maintaining the list (adding the names of new prospects and discarding useless names) is equally demanding. The source for compiling one's own list depends upon the characteristics of the prospects that the advertiser seeks to reach. Commonly used sources are trade directories, customer lists, membership lists, tax rolls, city directories, and telephone directories.

Some direct-mail advertisers use a two-step approach to building a direct-mail list. A first mailing or perhaps an ad in another medium is directed to a broad list of prospects with an offer of a sample, free information, or some other way to indicate interest in the marketer's product. Those who respond are then placed on the prospect list and receive subsequent more specific direct mailings.

*Purchasing a List.* Because of the specialized nature of the job of compiling and maintaining distribution lists, many companies purchase their lists from outside firms. The direct advertiser can either purchase a list directly from the owner of the list or through a list broker. A list broker locates the type of list needed by the advertiser and advises the advertiser on distribution-list problems. These broker services are generally free to the list purchaser.

The advertiser can also purchase lists directly from the compiler. Standard Rate and Data Service in their *Direct Mail List Rates and Data* offers an extensive description of mailing lists that are available. These lists are indexed by the markets that they serve. The SRDS listings also provide other information that the list purchaser should consider in the selection of a list. The SRDS volume shows the source of the names which should help the purchaser to estimate the quality of the list. For some lists, it indicates what efforts are being made to maintain the list. If the list owner will permit the prospective purchaser to test the list by mailing to a sample of names from the list, this information is also included.

Finally, SRDS also specifies the other services offered by the list owner. Many list owners perform the printing, inserting, and addressing function for the advertiser.

DIRECT ADVERTISING COSTS. The two basic cost elements in a direct advertising program are production of the advertising materials and cost of delivery.

The cost of producing a direct advertising piece can vary widely because of the differences in design and size that are possible. A single mimeographed letter might be produced for less than ten cents, but a four-color gift catalog could well cost more than a dollar. In estimating cost the advertiser must estimate the cost of copy, layout, and artwork; the paper and the envelope or wrapper; the cost of printing; and the cost of inserting and addressing.

The cost of delivery in the case of direct mail comprises two elements — the cost of the list and the postage cost. List costs vary widely, tending to increase with the selectivity of the list. Costs are quoted per thousand names and can be found in *Direct Mail List Rates and Data*. Costs of $40–$75 per thousand names are not unusual. Most direct mail qualifies for the third class postal rate, although some personalized direct-mail pieces are sent first class. In recent years postal rates have risen rapidly, adding substantially to the cost of direct mail. Mailings that qualify for the lowest third class rate (the bulk rate) cost about eleven cents per piece.

Total cost for direct mailings varies widely. For a simple solo direct-mail piece produced in volume, total cost may range from 30 to 70 cents per unit. This gives a CPM of $300 to $700. This is higher than most other media, but this cost is offset by the selectivity of the medium which reduces waste circulation.

## Outdoor Advertising

Outdoor advertising is not delivered to people, but is stationary — people come to it. As a result, an important determinant of the value of the medium is how well it has been located.

### Types of Outdoor Advertisements

Outdoor advertising has almost infinite variety, ranging from handpainted signs gracing a roadside vegetable stand to the elaborate displays in Times Square in New York City. Although any categorization of outdoor advertising is likely to be overlapping, four general classes are posters, painted bulletins, spectaculars, and signs on roadsides, on stores, and in malls.

*poster panels*

POSTER PANELS. Standardized **poster panels** (called billboards by those outside the advertising business) are large metal frames to which paper advertisements are pasted. The standardized poster panel measures 12′3″ high by 24′6″ long. Three different sizes of printed posters can be attached to the standardized poster panel. They are illustrated in Exhibit 15-2. The smallest of these is the 24-sheet poster measuring 19′6″ by 8′8″. (The term 24-sheet derives from the number of sheets of paper that were formerly used to form the poster. Today, with larger printing presses, fewer sheets are required.) A second poster size, and the most popular one, is the 30-sheet, measuring 21′7″ by 9′7″ or about 25 percent larger than the 24-sheet. It leaves a smaller white border around the panel. The third size is the bleed poster. Bleed posters measure 22′8″ by 10′5″ and extend to the metal poster frame, leaving no paper border.

Two other frequently used poster sizes are the 8-sheet measuring

Three standard printed-poster sizes.

EXHIBIT 15-2

**24-Sheet Posters**
The printed copy area measures 19'6" by 8'8". The area between the design and the frame is covered with white blanking paper.

**30-Sheet Posters**
The printed copy area measures 21'7" by 9'7". It provides about 25% more design space than the 24-Sheet Poster.

**Bleed Posters**
The printed copy area measures 22'8" by 10'5". It provides 40% more design space than the 24-Sheet Poster.

Courtesy: The Stroh Brewery Company.

6 × 12 feet and the 3-sheet, 82″ tall × 41″ wide. The eight sheet in particular has been growing rapidly because its smaller dimensions make it easier to place in urban and suburban locations.

Outdoor advertisers use a variety of devices to stimulate passersby to notice and read their posters. Most important for posters is the ability to change the advertising copy by changing the poster. Posters are generally changed every 30 days. Many posters are lighted to facilitate night viewing.

*painted bulletins*

PAINTED BULLETINS. **Painted bulletins** are nearly three times larger than poster panels, measuring 48 feet long by 14 feet high. Painted bulletins are painted one at a time from the advertiser's design either in the outdoor advertising company's studio in sections to be erected on location or are painted directly on location. Bulletins may be permanent, remaining in one location, or rotary: those that are moved every 60–90 days to a new location.

Some bulletin advertisers use embellishments, extensions to the standard bulletin to give a three dimensional effect. Exhibit 15-3 shows an embellished bulletin. Other special effects used on bulletins include backlighting, high-intensity "holophane" lighting, reflective discs, and inflatable attachments.

SIGNS. The most widely used form of outdoor advertising is the sign. This category includes signs on the outside of buildings which advertise the name of a store and the products sold. It also includes roadside signs that advertise the location of motels, restaurants, service stations, and tourist attractions. Two fast-growing new categories of signs are mall signs placed in shopping malls and signs placed in bus shelters, usually in urban areas.

Signs come in every conceivable shape, size, and method of printing and many are illuminated by neon, fluorescent, or incandescent lights.

*spectaculars*

SPECTACULARS. Large illuminated, often animated, displays such as those found in Times Square, are called **spectaculars**. They are custom-built, one-of-a-kind advertising signs, usually placed in very high traffic areas. Because of the construction expense, spectaculars usually represent long-term commitments by the advertiser.

## Characteristics of Outdoor as an Advertising Medium

In our discussion of the characteristics of the outdoor medium, we will focus on outdoor posters because they constitute the most standardized class of outdoor. The other outdoor classes, because they are custom-built, must be evaluated in terms of their individual merits. However, many of the characteristics of posters apply equally to these other forms.

AUDIENCE CHARACTERISTICS. Outdoor posters are a mass audience medium rather than a selective medium. A group of posters, located in

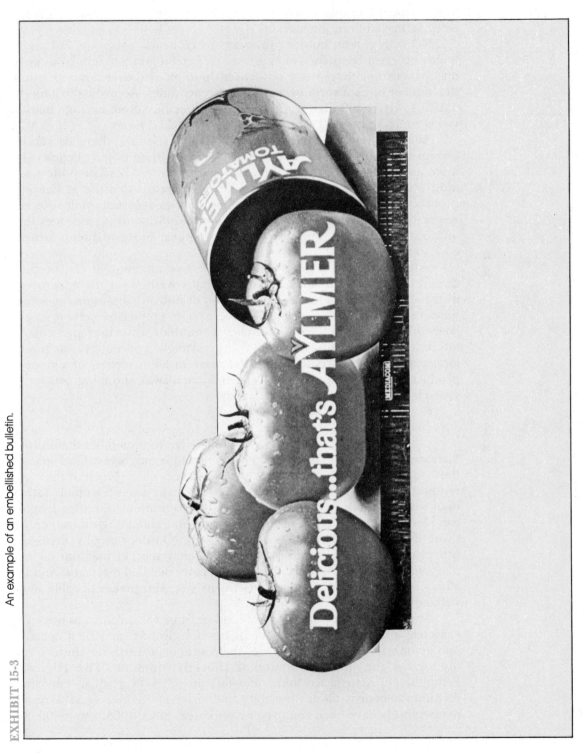

An example of an embellished bulletin.

EXHIBIT 15-3

high-traffic areas and distributed throughout the market area, will reach nearly every adult in the market.

Not only can an outdoor program reach nearly everyone, but it also builds up great frequency of exposure. A person going to and from work may pass two or three of an advertiser's posters, and over a month's time the number of exposures may increase twenty times. According to a recent SMRB study, a 100 gross-rating-point outdoor buy in an average market yields an 82.5 percent reach with frequency of 23.3 times.

Although outdoor advertising is not highly selective, there are certain groups who are more likely to be exposed to it than others. People who drive automobiles are more often exposed to posters because posters are most often placed along roadsides. This also means that the audience is probably more heavily weighted with working people and adults. Recent research reported by the Institute of Outdoor Advertising indicates that outdoor coverage is greatest among younger, more affluent, better-educated adults.

Outdoor can be a geographically selective medium. It can be purchased on a market-by-market basis so that coverage fits the advertiser's distribution area. In addition, the location of individual posters can sometimes be specified, permitting the advertiser to emphasize certain neighborhoods in a market. For example, an outdoor advertiser particularly interested in reaching blue-collar workers might concentrate on poster locations near access roads to local factories, or an advertiser of a grocery product might attempt to rent posters located near shopping centers to give a last-minute reminder to shoppers.

CREATIVE CHARACTERISTICS. It is important to remember that the audience is exposed to an outdoor advertisement for only a very brief span of time, so the message must be very short and very clear. Much of the communication in outdoor advertising is through the use of symbols rather than words; outdoor is definitely not an appropriate medium for long or complex messages. Notice the Sunkist poster in Exhibit 15-4; it uses only a short nine word headline and a simple graphic. Outdoor usually serves as a reminder and is frequently used to supplement another medium such as magazines or television that can provide a more detailed message. Outdoor allows the use of color and, because of its size, also makes possible some striking effects.

The outdoor medium does not lend prestige to a product as does, for example, a quality magazine. The association, in fact, may be a negative one among those people who feel that outdoor advertising clutters and obliterates the natural beauty of the environment. The Highway Beautification Act enacted in the mid-'60's provided for gradual elimination of outdoor boards along interstate and primary highways. As a result, many posters have been removed or relocated. Since 1965, about 100,000

Outdoor poster using a short headline and simple graphic.                    **EXHIBIT 15-4**

Courtesy: SUNKIST GROWERS, INC.

nonconforming signs have been removed from along interstate and primary highways.[3]

The advertiser should also recognize that outdoor advertising is a nonintrusive medium. Despite the great frequency with which people pass by an outdoor bulletin, they may not perceive it. Unless the outdoor message is provocative and changed regularly, it has a tendency to become a part of the background. This is a particular problem for the more permanent forms of outdoor such as painted bulletins and signs. Rotating bulletins, embellishments, and other special effects are designed to alleviate the problem.

MINIMUM COST. Outdoor bulletins are used primarily by larger national advertisers — the minimum cost discourages the small advertiser.

There are two minimum cost problems in using outdoor bulletins — the cost of preparing the paper to be posted and the need for long-term commitment to the medium. The major cost in preparing the outdoor poster paper is the fixed cost of design, artwork, and of setting up the presses. Once this expenditure is committed, the cost of printing is relatively small and additional copies cost little extra. The national user of outdoor spreads the fixed production cost over many units and enjoys low cost per unit. The local user, however, has about the same fixed cost, but spread over only a few units. This high initial cost of preparation discourages local

---

[3]Richard L. Gordon, "Outdoor Sees Tranquility in Highway Beautification Act," *Advertising Age* (March 10, 1980), p. S–4.

use. The problem is only intensified by the need to post a new design (hence new preparation costs) each month.

The second minimum cost problem concerns the need for a long-term commitment to outdoor. Outdoor bulletin advertising is sold on a monthly basis. However, in many markets there is an undersupply of poster locations. Currently there are about 250,000 standard poster panels, 20,000 fewer than in 1970, a result of restrictive regulation.[4] Continuous advertisers are usually allowed to retain their locations and they constantly work to add more desirable locations to their showing. Intermittent advertisers must select from the locations that are left.

Despite these considerations, outdoor is not impossible for the smaller advertiser. There are some printing methods, such as silk-screening, that have lower preparation costs for short runs, although the technique has some creative limitations. Another alternative for the smaller advertiser is the use of signs and painted bulletins. The commitment is likely to be long-term and the preparation cost per unit high, but purchase can be limited to a few units.

PRODUCTION REQUIREMENTS. The user of outdoor bulletins is responsible for providing the posters. Preparation of outdoor advertising materials requires substantial lead time. Even after layout and artwork are available, the advertiser should allow 4–6 weeks for printing, particularly for large quantity color runs. Shipping time to the outdoor plants plus the lead time required by the plant operators must also be added to the schedule. Because of this rather long preparation time, outdoor advertising lends itself more to advertising programs that are planned well in advance.

The production of painted bulletins and spectaculars is usually handled by the owners of the properties that will serve as locations in cooperation with the advertiser. Sign production is usually carried out by specialized sign companies who assist with design, produce the sign, erect it, and maintain it. The production lead time for each of these operations is substantial.

## Users of Outdoor

There is a sharp distinction between firms using outdoor posters and those using signs. Outdoor posters tend to be used by national advertisers, while painted bulletins and signs are more heavily used by local advertisers.

NATIONAL ADVERTISERS. The top 25 users of outdoor posters in 1982 are listed in Exhibit 15-5. The list is heavily dominated by a few industries. Most prominent of these are tobacco and liquor marketers that account for nine of the top ten. Outdoor delivers the male audience that both of these advertisers seek. Both are also excluded from broadcast advertising; outdoor is thus one of their few alternatives. The short copy requirements of

---

[4]*Ibid.*

EXHIBIT 15-5

Top 25 outdoor advertisers, 1982.

| Rank | Company | Expenditure (Add 000) |
|------|---------|------------------------|
| 1 | R. J. Reynolds Industries | $77,233.2 |
| 2 | Philip Morris Inc. | 50,538.0 |
| 3 | Batus Inc. | 42,537.1 |
| 4 | Loews Corp. | 23,661.8 |
| 5 | Seagram Co. Ltd. | 16,064.2 |
| 6 | American Brands | 12,314.4 |
| 7 | Hiram Walker Resources Ltd. | 8,931.8 |
| 8 | Brown-Forman Distillers Corp. | 7,680.1 |
| 9 | National Distillers & Chemical Corp. | 6,459.1 |
| 10 | General Motors Corp. | 5,009.0 |
| 11 | Anheuser-Busch Cos. | 4,820.1 |
| 12 | Rapid-American Corp. | 4,719.9 |
| 13 | GrandMet USA | 4,652.0 |
| 14 | McDonald's Corp. | 4,142.9 |
| 15 | Coca-Cola Co. | 3,189.4 |
| 16 | Norton Simon Inc. | 3,006.3 |
| 17 | Beatrice Foods Co. | 2,652.9 |
| 18 | American Honda Motor Co. | 2,631.1 |
| 19 | Holiday Inns | 2,570.4 |
| 20 | Eastern Air Lines | 2,499.4 |
| 21 | Toyota Motor Corp. | 2,111.8 |
| 22 | Bacardi Corp. | 2,105.7 |
| 23 | G. Heileman Brewing Co. | 2,083.7 |
| 24 | Hughes Tool Co. | 2,026.8 |
| 25 | Schering-Plough Corp. | 1,907.3 |

Reprinted with permission from the September 8, 1983 issue of *Advertising Age.* Copyright 1983 by Crain Communications, Inc.

outdoor pose few problems to either tobacco or liquor marketers since product similarity and legal restrictions reduce them to largely symbolic advertising in any medium. These advertisers rely heavily on frequency, one of the strengths of outdoor advertising.

Other heavy outdoor advertisers include makers of automobiles and auto-related products and highway-dependent advertisers such as motel and restaurant chains. To these advertisers outdoor offers a way to select automobile drivers through a relevant message.

LOCAL ADVERTISERS. Local advertisers are heavy users of outdoor advertising, especially signs and painted bulletins. Because these forms of outdoor do not require new designs or new printed material each month, they are financially feasible for the small advertiser.

Probably the widest use made of outdoor by the local advertiser is to indicate the location of the business and the service available. Thus hotels and motels, gas stations, restaurants, and amusements are heavy users of signs.

### Purchasing Outdoor

The purchase of outdoor advertising is another of the many specialized areas of advertising with unique terminology and procedures. Advertisers that use outdoor on a heavy, continuous basis often rely upon outdoor specialists either on their staff or in their advertising agency. A major task of these specialists is continual evaluation and upgrading of the locations included in the outdoor purchase.

*gross-rating points (GRP)*

UNIT OF PURCHASE. Outdoor space is purchased by the month on a market-by-market basis, with purchase ranging from a single market to combinations of markets to cover a particular region or even to provide national coverage.

In most markets today posters are sold in packages of **gross-rating points (GRP).** (In some markets the less precise term "showing" is still used.) A 100 GRP package would deliver daily exposure opportunities equal to the population of the market. A 50 GRP package offers half as many exposure opportunities and a 25 GRP package, one quarter as many.

Rates for outdoor advertising space are quoted on a monthly basis for the various GRP packages offered. The rates generally increase with the size of the market and the number of people covered. Discounts for continuous use are sometimes offered.

Space for painted bulletins and spectaculars is usually purchased on an individual location basis. Rates vary depending on the expected audience for the location; the term of the purchase usually runs for a year or longer.

PURCHASE PROCEDURE. The outdoor advertiser does not purchase the outdoor bulletins or other outdoor units but merely rents space on these units for a month or some other time period. The bulletins themselves are generally owned and serviced by local and regional companies called outdoor plants. Outdoor signs present a somewhat different case—often the advertiser owns the sign, but sometimes they are rented from a local sign plant that places and services them. Outdoor bulletin space can be purchased either directly from the outdoor plant or through an advertising agency.

The advertiser's prime source of information on outdoor rates and data is *The Buyers Guide to Outdoor Advertising*. Issued twice a year, the Guide lists rates and showing sizes by market and identifies the outdoor company servicing the market. Both poster and rotary bulletins are listed. Exhibit 15-6 shows a rate page from the Guide.

AUDIENCE MEASUREMENT. The Traffic Audit Bureau audits outdoor advertising plants to validate the number of panels available, the quality of their location, and the number of potential viewers passing each location.

Several research services provide audience size, reach and frequency, and audience demographics for standard GRP levels. Simmons Market Research Bureau (SMRB) includes this information in its periodic audience

Sample rate page from *The Buyers Guide to Outdoor Advertising,* March, 1983                    EXHIBIT 15-6

# OUTDOOR RATES AND MARKETS

CALIFORNIA          04                                                                                     CALIFORNIA          04

| PLANT NO. | MARKET NO. | MARKET NAME | COUNTY NAME | POP. | EFF. DATE | GRP/ SHOW | POSTERS NON ILL. | POSTERS ILL. | COST PER MONTH | DIS. |
|---|---|---|---|---|---|---|---|---|---|---|
| 4105.0 HEYWOD | 27450 | PALM SPRINGS METRO LOS | RIVERSIDE-SAN BERNARDINO | 562.0 | 01/01/3 | 100 50 25 | 18 12 6 | 18 12 6 | 10008.00 6672.00 3564.00 | 49 49 49 |
| | | | SINGLE PANEL RATE-ILL 380.00 REG 300.00 | | | | | | | |
| 7227.0 3MNAT | 28050 | PASO ROBLES MARKET SBA          SEE MARKET NO. 04-05120** | SAN LUIS OBISPO | 41.3 | 07/01/3 | 100 75 50 | 4 3 2 | | 756.00 567.00 378.00 | 68 68 68 |
| 7231.0 3MNAT | 28400 | PETALUMA MKT SFO          SEE MARKET NO. 04-05140** | SONOMA | 52.5 | 07/01/3 | 100 75 50 | 5 4 3 | | 945.00 756.00 567.00 | 68 68 68 |
| 7227.0 3MNAT | 28900 | PISMO BEACH MKT. SBA          SEE MARKET NO. 04-05120** | SAN LUIS OBISPO | 48.1 | 07/01/3 | 75 50 | 3 2 | | 567.00 378.00 | 68 68 |
| 7227.0 3MNAT | 30050 | PORTERVILLE MKT FRE          SEE MARKET NO. 04-05210** | TULARE | 50.0 | 07/01/3 | 75 50 25 | 8 4 2 | | 1040.00 520.00 260.00 | 68 68 68 |
| 7231.0 3MNAT | 30800 | REDDING-RED BLUFF MKT CIC          SEE MARKET NO. 04-05130** | SHASTA-TEHAMA | 135.2 | 07/01/3 | 75 50 25 | 7 5 1 | 4 2 2 | 2060.00 1282.00 610.00 | 68 68 68 |
| 7227.0 3MNAT | 30810 | REEDLEY/SANGER FRE          SEE MARKET NO. 04-14650** | FRESNO | 61.0 | 07/01/3 | 50 25 | 6 3 | | 1008.00 504.00 | 68 68 |
| 4930.0 MAROAA | 30820 | RIDGECREST LOS | KERN | 26.0 | 09/01/2 | 100 50 | 2 1 | 2 1 | 880.00 440.00 | 37 37 |
| 4915.0 MAROAA | 31750 | RIVERSIDE EAST COUNTY MKT PHX | RIVERSIDE-IMPERIAL-YUMA, AZ | 15.5 | 09/01/2 | 100 50 | 2 1 | 2 1 | 880.00 440.00 | 37 37 |
| 3595.0 GANNET | 32400 | SACRAMENTO METRO MKT SAC          SEE MARKET NO. 04-25500** | SACRAMENTO-PLACER-YOLO | 1031.2 | 09/30/2 | 100 75 50 25 | 18 14 9 5 | 36 27 18 9 | 18216.00 13802.00 9108.00 4694.00 | 32 32 32 32 |
| 3325.0 F-K | 32650 | SACRAMENTO METRO MKT. SAC          SEE MARKET NO. 04-25620** | SACRAMENTO-PLACER-YOLO | 776.5 | 10/01/2 | 100 75 50 25 | 10 8 5 3 | 50 38 25 13 | 21100.00 16148.00 10550.00 5598.00 | 57 57 57 57 |
| 7227.0 3MNAT | 32850 | SALINAS-MONTEREY MKT SLN          SEE MARKET NO. 04-05120** | MONTEREY | 286.7 | 07/01/3 | 75 50 25 | 8 5 3 | 7 5 2 | 3381.00 2280.00 1101.00 | 68 68 68 |
| 4915.0 MAROAA | 33300 | SAN DIEGO EAST COUNTY MKT. SAN | SAN DIEGO | 1.0 | 09/01/2 | 100 50 | 2 1 | | 360.00 180.00 | 37 37 |
| 3745.0 GANNET | 33380 | SAN DIEGO METRO MKT SAN          SEE MARKET NO. 04-38200** | SAN DIEGO | 1500.0 | 09/30/2 | 100 75 50 25 | 20 15 10 5 | 60 45 30 15 | 27560.00 20670.00 13780.00 6890.00 | 28 28 28 28 |
| 3310.0 F-K | 33400 | SAN DIEGO METRO MKT SAN          SEE MARKET NO. 04-38220** | SAN DIEGO | 1500.0 | 10/01/2 | 100 75 50 25 | 20 15 10 5 | 60 45 30 15 | 27560.00 20670.00 13780.00 6890.00 | 57 57 57 57 |
| 3595.0 GANNET | 33770 | SAN FRANCISCO METRO MKT SFO          SEE MARKET NO. 04-33950** | SAN FRANCISCO-SAN MATEO | 1314.1 | 09/30/2 | 100 75 50 25 | | 70 53 35 18 | 25620.00 19398.00 12810.00 6588.00 | 32 32 32 32 |
| 3325.0 F-K | 33800 | SAN FRANCISCO METRO-ZONE 1 SFO          SEE MARKET NO. 04-33960** | SAN FRANCISO-SAN MATEO | 1234.3 | 10/01/2 | 100 75 50 25 | | 68 51 34 17 | 24888.00 18666.00 12444.00 6222.00 | 57 57 57 57 |
| 3595.0 GANNET | 33950 | SAN FRANCISCO-OAKLAND METRO MKT SFO          SEE MARKET NO. 04-33970** | ALAMEDA-CONTRA COSTA SAN FRANCISCO-SAN MATEO | 3089.7 | 09/30/2 | 100 75 50 25 | 28 21 14 7 | 150 113 75 38 | 62740.00 47238.00 31370.00 15868.00 | 32 32 32 32 |
| | | --SUB MKTS. (ALSO SOLD SEPARATELY) OAKLAND METRO MKT, CA SAN FRANCISCO METRO MKT, CA | | | | | | | | |
| 3325.0 F-K | 33960 | SAN FRANCISCO-OAKLAND METRO MKT. SFO          SEE MARKET NO. 04-34030** | ALAMEDA-CONTRA COSTA SAN FRANCISCO-SAN MATEO-SOLAND | 2945.1 | 10/01/2 | 100 75 50 25 | 20 15 10 5 | 162 122 81 41 | 64892.00 48852.00 32446.00 16406.00 | 57 57 57 57 |
| | | --SUB MKTS. (ALSO SOLD SEPARATELY) OAKLAND METRO-ZONE 2, CA SAN FRANCISCO METRO-ZONE 1, CA | | | | | | | | |
| 3595.0 GANNET | 33970 | SAN FRANCISCO-OAKLAND-SAN JOSE (BAY SFO          SEE MARKET NO. 04-25500** | AREA) METRO MKT. SANTA CLARA-ALAMEDA CONTRA COSTA-SAN FRANCISCO SAN MATEO-SOLAND | 4745.3 | 09/30/2 | 100 75 50 25 | 44 33 22 11 | 200 151 100 51 | 85520.00 64506.00 42760.00 21746.00 | 32 32 32 32 |
| | | --SUB MKTS. (ALSO SOLD SEPARATELY) SAN FRANCISCO-OAKLAND METRO MKT, CA SAN JOSE METRO MKT, CA VALLEJO-NAPA METRO MKT, CA | | | | | | | | |

ADI CODE SEE NOTE TO BUYER
**FIRST 2 DIGITS INDICATE STATE

GRP GROSS RATING POINTS

ISSUED MARCH 1983

Courtesy: F. R. Cawl & Associates, Inc.

studies with data generated through large interview samples. Audience Market by Market for Outdoor (AMMO) provides computer generated reach and frequency figures for markets included in the *Buyers Guide to Outdoor Advertising*. Several other services are available as well.

## Transit Advertising

There is another group of out-of-home media that are connected with transportation systems. The most important of these is transit advertising which will be the focus of this section. Other similar advertising opportunities are presented by airport advertising, in-flight advertising, taxicab ads, and bus-stop shelter or bench advertising.

### Types of Transit Advertising

*transit advertising*     **Transit advertising** consists of paper posters placed on transit vehicles and in transit stations.

INSIDE CARDS. Most metropolitan buses or subway cars have special racks over the windows on the inside of the vehicle designed to accept advertising. In addition, some vehicles have special poster spaces, usually at the ends of the car or bus. The standard size for an inside card is 11 inches high by 28 inches wide. Longer sizes are frequently available usually in multiples of 14 inches (11 × 42, 11 × 56). The transit cards are printed on cardboard or vinyl and can generally be changed every 30 days. The inside car end posters vary in size, but are usually larger, 22 by 21 inches being a common size.

OUTSIDE POSTERS. Most metropolitan-area buses offer outside advertising space of varying sizes depending upon the location on the bus. There are five sizes and locations that are commonly offered. King-size posters, 30 × 144 inches, are located on the street side of the bus. Queen-size posters, 30 × 88 inches, and traveling displays, 21 × 44 inches, are located on the sidewalk side of the bus. Front-end displays, 11 × 42 inches, are located between the headlights, and taillight displays, 21 × 72 inches, on the rear.

STATION POSTERS. Metropolitan transit and commuter railroad systems in big cities often have poster advertising space in passenger stations and terminals. Poster sizes vary, but are usually consistent within a particular transit system. Some station posters are posted much like outdoor bulletins with the paper being renewed each month; others use cardboard or vinyl posters.

## Characteristics of Transit as an Advertising Medium

Transit advertising is similar to outdoor advertising in many of its creative characteristics. The audience of transit advertising is its most distinctive feature and depends on the medium's location.

AUDIENCE CHARACTERISTICS. Like outdoor, transit advertising is exposed to a mass audience. However, the transit medium selects a different audience than does outdoor. The greatest exposure of transit is among those who ride public transportation regularly. This, in turn, means that the audience is slanted toward lower-income adults, blue-collar workers, and shoppers.

Another characteristic of the transit advertising audience is its distinctly urban makeup. This is a natural result of the presence of mass transit systems only in cities, particularly in large cities. Transit does offer the advertiser considerable geographic flexibility in terms of the cities that can be selected. About 380 cities have transit advertising available. It can be purchased on a city-by-city basis and combined to create the city coverage pattern required by the advertiser. The coverage of transit advertising is usually the entire metropolitan area of a city, so that a business drawing only neighborhood customers might find the medium wasteful in coverage.

The reach delivered by transit advertising is lower than for outdoor because fewer people in most cities use transit systems as opposed to cars. Transit, however, delivers very high frequency to its audience because of the regularity with which transit riders use the system.

CREATIVE CHARACTERISTICS. Creatively, the transit medium is much like the outdoor medium, particularly with regard to the outside posters and station posters. These posters have the advantage of size, high quality reproduction, and color. Inside cards are smaller in size, but have comparable high quality reproduction. Inside cards also have the advantage of being able to deliver information physically by means of "take-one" cards which have pads of coupons, mailers, or other messages fastened to the advertisement.

Like outdoor, transit advertisements, particularly outside posters, are seen for only a few seconds. Consequently, the advertising message must be short and easily understood. Symbolic communication can be used effectively. Messages tend to be reminders, supplementing other media. Inside cards can be viewed for longer periods, although both physical conditions for reading and the audience's frame of mind are frequently unfavorable. Hence the message should be crisp and effective.

Transit advertising of all types is a nonintrusive medium. To a regular transit rider, the cards and posters tend to fade into the background. The outdoor advertiser must include attention-getting devices in the ads to make the message stand out.

The environment in which transit advertising appears rarely lends prestige to the product. Transit vehicles are frequently dirty, they operate in crowded and unattractive surroundings, and the advertisements themselves are often defaced. On the other hand, the transit advertiser is definitely identifying with the life of a city when an advertising message appears on local buses or subway cars.

MINIMUM COST. The minimum investment to enter the transit medium is not so large that small or local advertisers are prohibited from using it. Production costs for transit are less than for outdoor because of the substantially smaller size, especially for inside cards.

Transit advertising space can be purchased on a monthly basis, although most advertisers use it on a continuous basis. However, the intermittent advertiser does not suffer by getting poorer positions than the regular advertisers since both appear in the same vehicles.

PRODUCTION REQUIREMENTS. Transit advertisers have production requirements much like those faced by outdoor advertisers. The transit advertiser supplies the cards or posters to be used. Transit cards are printed on heavy stock and the outside signs are weatherproofed. Vinyl cards are being increasingly used because they resist both weather and defacement. The advertising almost always is printed in color. As was true for outdoor posters, the cost per card decreases with the number printed since fixed costs are a large proportion of total cost. However, transit advertising materials are much smaller than 24-sheet posters and consequently the set-up costs are lower, making the medium more feasible for local and regional advertisers.

Transit advertisers usually change their advertisements monthly in order to provide both clean, undefaced materials and variety in appearance. For monthly changes, the advertiser must have a series of ads available. The time required to produce transit cards tends to be shorter than for the large, outdoor posters, but a lead time of several weeks is common.

## Users of Transit Advertising

Transit advertising is used by both national and local advertisers with dollar volume about evenly divided between them.

Among the national advertisers, products making heavy use of transit include beer, wine, liquor, cigarettes, proprietary medicines, and chewing gum. Most of these products are heavily used by middle- to lower-income, urban consumers. Consequently transit provides a desirable medium to supplement coverage with these important consumers.

Local advertisers seek the same audience through transit advertising. In addition, transit, serving as a last-minute reminder, is an attractive medium for restaurants, theaters, financial institutions, and retailers.

## Purchasing Transit Advertising

Transit advertising is sold by transit advertising companies who contract with local transit systems to sell and service their advertising space. Local advertisers, therefore, purchase space not from the transit system or bus line, but from a transit advertising company. A national advertiser may purchase directly from local transit advertising companies or through national sales representatives who represent many individual transit advertising companies.

Transit advertising is purchased market by market, the unit of purchase being the gross-rating point package. Purchase of a 100 GRP package means that one advertisement will appear in each vehicle in the system. Fifty GRP or 25 GRP packages providing ads in a half or a quarter of the system's vehicles are also commonly offered. Outside displays can be purchased on a unit basis.

Transit advertising rates are usually quoted on a monthly basis, although transit advertisers usually contract for longer periods such as three, six or twelve months. Continuity discounts are frequently offered to encourage long-term use of the medium. Cost for a GRP package varies with the size of the market covered, but, in general, transit advertising cost per thousand riders is very low.

Details on transit advertising rates, production requirements, and other information for each transit advertising company are contained in Standard Rate and Data Service's *Transit Advertising Rates and Data*. In addition, studies have been done to measure the size of the transit advertising audience in particular cities or combinations of cities. The Transit Advertising Association sponsors some of these studies on behalf of its member transit advertising companies. Some of these companies, particularly the larger ones, also conduct periodic audience studies for their markets. These studies provide estimates of reach and frequency and compile the demographic characteristics of the transit audience.

## Other Media

The media that have been discussed thus far by no means exhaust the possibilities available to advertisers. Although the other media to be discussed briefly here do not account for a large part of total advertising volume, to some advertisers they represent a large part of their total advertising expenditure.

There are several other media that have sufficiently broad application to warrant discussion here. They are point-of-purchase or store display materials, advertising specialties, packaging materials, trade shows, and directories.

It should be noted that not all advertisers would consider these items to be advertising media and, indeed, in many companies these items would not be charged to the advertising budget. Point-of-purchase and packaging materials, for example, are frequently under control of a merchandising manager. Specialties and directories are frequently under the control of the sales manager. However, regardless of who controls these expenditures, it is helpful to evaluate them as media so that their contribution to the total effort directed to consumers can be coordinated.

### Point-of-Purchase Advertising

*point-of-purchase advertising*

**Point-of-purchase advertising** includes signs and display materials placed inside retail stores where the advertiser's product is available. There is an infinite variety of point-of-purchase material because the medium is flexible, but the common types can be classified by their location in the store. Among the most common types are window streamers, floor displays, counter displays and racks, over-the-wire banners, shelf talkers, and permanent functional signs, such as clocks and thermometers.

New and less traditional forms of in-store advertising include shopping cart and shopping bag advertising, in-store broadcasting, and in-store television.

MEDIA CHARACTERISTICS OF POINT-OF-PURCHASE. The value of the point-of-purchase medium stems from its placement in the store close to the advertiser's product. This location makes point-of-purchase advertising highly selective, reaching people while they are in the process of shopping.

A study of consumer shopping behavior summarized in Exhibit 15-7 revealed that half of all supermarket purchases are unplanned, while other purchases are planned as to product but not as to brand.[5] Point-of-purchase advertising is particularly influential in these unplanned purchases.

Creatively, the point-of-purchase medium is flexible in color, shape, and dimensions, but the advertising message must be like that of outdoor—short and simple. Consumer attention can be held by display signs for only a few seconds. Attention-getting devices are highly important in this medium.

---

**EXHIBIT 15-7**    Supermarket purchase decisions.

| | |
|---|---|
| Specifically planned | 35.3% |
| Generally planned | 14.8 |
| Substitute | 3.0 |
| Unplanned | 46.9 |
| Total | 100.0% |

Reprinted with permission from the June 27, 1977 issue of *Advertising Age*. Copyright 1977 by Crain Communications, Inc.

---

[5]Louis J. Haugh, "Buying Habits Study Update: Average Purchase up 121%," *Advertising Age* (June 27, 1977), pp. 56, 58.

The ability of point-of-purchase advertising to locate prospects just before their decision to purchase and the limitations on copy length both influence the use of this medium. The dominant use of point-of-purchase advertising is to provide consumers with a reminder of the advertiser's brand just before they buy. Frequently the advertiser tries to remind the consumer of advertising done in another medium by repeating illustrations, copy lines, or other devices used in the main media effort. Another use of point-of-purchase materials is to enhance the display of the product, making it more easily seen. Gum and cigarette racks, for example, often contain minimal advertising, but they display the product to advantage. Point-of-purchase displays are also used frequently to point out to consumers a special value in a particular product. Food and drug stores, for instance, frequently use large floor displays containing marked-down merchandise.

CONTROLLING POINT-OF-PURCHASE USE. One of the most difficult problems with point-of-purchase material is getting it used in stores. A great deal of display material produced never gets used. If an advertiser decides to use point-of-purchase, a program to insure that the materials are used in the store should be established.

What are some of the steps that can be taken to insure usage? First, a decision must be made concerning who is to install the materials. If the display material is simply packed in the shipping cases which are sent to the retailer or is mailed to the retailer separately, very little of it will be used because the retailer will seldom take the time to install it. Usage of display materials can be considerably increased if the company's sales force or a special display crew installs it. However, this is an expensive approach and its cost should be considered as part of the media cost.

A second factor that influences the use of point-of-purchase materials is the design of the materials themselves. Retail outlets today, particularly large supermarkets, discount stores, and self-service drugstores, severely limit the point-of-purchase materials that may be erected. The managers of these stores attempt to maintain a clean, uncluttered appearance in their stores and display materials that clutter will not be used. The advertiser should prepare display materials that suit the decor of the store and do not give a cluttered appearance. Retailers are perhaps most receptive to displays that are functional. Racks to hold merchandise, for example, contribute to the neatness of product display and signs with clocks, thermometers, or other information contribute to customer convenience.

The advertiser who uses the point-of-purchase medium should establish a method of checking the utilization of the display materials. This can be accomplished by periodic sampling of stores to determine usage of the materials and to check retailer reaction to materials supplied. For more expensive, permanent display (such as lighted signs, clocks, thermometers), advertisers sometimes use display agreements with retailers guaranteeing long-term use of the material.

PURCHASE OF DISPLAY MATERIALS. Point-of-purchase materials may be prepared by the advertiser or purchased from firms specializing in design and production of these materials.

Many retail stores and some manufacturers that utilize display materials extensively have facilities for production of their own signs, banners, and similar simple, printed material, permitting flexibility in design and speed of production.

Most manufacturers rely upon outside specialists for both design and production of display material. Smaller advertisers can sometimes get cost advantages by using stock display pieces to which the individual advertiser's name and message can be attached.

The cost of individual point-of-purchase items varies widely, from a few cents each for simple paper signs to over ten dollars apiece for permanent lighted or functional displays.

## Advertising Specialties

*advertising specialties*      **Advertising specialties** are utilitarian items containing a brief advertising message that are given to prospects, usually at no charge, by the advertiser. There is a great variety in types of specialties, including calendars, key chains, matchbooks, pencils and pens, and T-shirts.

MEDIA CHARACTERISTICS OF SPECIALTIES. The unique form of specialty advertising makes it difficult to compare it with other classes of media. Specialties have three different characteristics that influence the way they are used.

First, most specialties have room for only a short message. Second, specialties are designed to have value to the recipient. If the recipient finds the specialty useful, it will be retained and become a long-life medium. Finally, specialties can be a highly selective medium if distributed carefully to prospective customers.

USERS OF SPECIALTY ADVERTISING. Expenditures for advertising specialties are difficult to trace, but probably amount to $2–$3 billion a year. The heaviest users of specialty advertising tend to be smaller manufacturers and retailers, especially those firms that have salespeople contacting their customers.

For these firms, specialty advertising serves two related purposes. First, specialty items are distributed by salespeople to their customers and prospects with the hope that customers will appreciate receiving them. Second, specialty items are also designed to serve as a reminder to the recipient of the product or company advertised. If the item is used over a period of time, it serves its reminder function again and again.

Advertising specialties that tie in to the product provide timely reminders. For example, paint manufacturers give away paint hats and paddles which provide reminders while the customer is painting.

CONTROL OF SPECIALTY ADVERTISING. In many firms advertising specialties are considered selling aids and come out of the sales budget rather than the advertising budget. This may be a desirable approach if the specialties are distributed by the company's salespeople. In such cases it is difficult for the advertising manager to control the materials to assure that they are selectively distributed.

Regardless of the budgetary treatment, it is important to establish that specialty items are an expensive advertising medium (the cost per thousand is clearly high) that is worthwhile only if the specialties are distributed to real prospects. Distribution policies should be established and communicated to those who distribute the specialties.

PURCHASE OF SPECIALTIES. Advertising specialties are usually purchased through specialty supply houses that act as sales agents for a variety of manufacturers. These supply houses usually have catalogs showing stock items available and they can also arrange for custom manufacture of special design items. Smaller users of specialties can realize major savings by using stock specialty items that can be imprinted with the buyer's advertising message.

Users of large quantities of a specialty item—such as a large calendar order—frequently deal directly with the manufacturer. Purchase of specialties, like point-of-purchase materials, is seldom done through an advertising agency since these media grant no commission to an agency.

## Package Advertising

Product packaging is best considered as part of the product itself rather than as an advertising medium, but the package can have some media-like characteristics that can be tied in to the media program.

First, for many products the package serves as a display device much like point-of-purchase material. It represents the advertiser's last chance to communicate with the consumer before a product is selected. The package or label provides an opportunity for the advertiser to deliver a brief message—sometimes only the brand name, but often a reminder of the central promise or feature as communicated by other media.

A second advertising use of the package is to provide reassurance to the consumer after purchase. When purchasing a product, particularly if it is an important, infrequent, or new product purchase, the consumer seeks some reassurance that the purchase decision was a sound one. The package provides an opportunity to supply the purchaser with reassuring information. A message may be printed on the package or on a package insert, a printed message placed inside the package. The same purpose is served by owner's manuals supplied with new automobiles and new appliances. These manuals not only provide instructions, they can also reassure the consumer and build product loyalty.

## Directory Advertising

Directories are books that list the name and location of dealers or manufacturers who have particular products or services available. There are industrial directories and consumer directories, both of which usually accept advertising.

The best-known consumer directories are the Yellow Pages or classified sections of telephone books. Businesses with telephones are listed automatically in these directories, but larger-sized listings or advertisements can be purchased. The advertiser can purchase space locally through the local telephone office, but if a number of directories are to be used, the National Yellow Pages Service serves as a single sales agent for any or all of the roughly 4,500 directories available.

There are many industrial directories which offer advertising space. They range from general industrial directories like the *Thomas Register of American Manufacturers* to directories specializing in listings of firms in particular industries or functions.

Directory advertising offers two rather obvious advantages as a medium. A directory has very long life and is usually consulted over and over; an advertisement in a directory has an opportunity for repeated exposure. The Yellow Pages, for example, are estimated to be used 40 times a year by the average adult. The second, more important advantage is that a directory advertisement reaches prospects when they are actively searching for information about products like the advertiser's. Consumers use directories to locate sources of products and services. Directory ads give the prospect an opportunity to pre-shop through the study of advertisements located in the product or service section of interest.

## Trade Shows

Trade shows are an advertising medium that is invisible to the ordinary consumer. Yet over 8,000 trade shows are held each year and annual expenditures on trade shows rank them just after television and newspapers as a viable medium.

*trade shows*

**Trade shows** are events held in major cities, often in conjunction with industry conventions, where business firms can display, demonstrate, and sell their products. One reason for the low consumer visibility of trade shows is that the audience is usually restricted to business persons. For that reason trade shows can be a highly selective medium.

Several purposes are served by trade shows. Frequently manufacturers use trade shows as an opportunity to display their lines to dealers and retailers (for example, the annual Toy Show or the Housewares Show). In these cases, the manufacturers hope to write major orders for their products right at the show. In other cases, the displaying firm may be attempting to enlist dealers who are willing to carry the product. Sometimes rather than sell products at the show, the marketer attempts to get leads that can be followed up later by salespeople. Part of the trade-show effect in this case is to "qualify" the leads, which means to verify that the inquiring firm is a valid prospect for the product.

Participants in a trade show rent display space directly from the sponsors of the show. The participant is responsible for construction, erection, and manning of a display booth at the show. The design and construction of trade-show displays has become a very sophisticated project usually purchased from specialized trade-show display-service firms. Company salespersons are usually assigned to staff the booth but should first be given special training for this different type of selling job. Advertising managers must, of course, closely coordinate their specific trade show activities with those of the sales department.

---

*CHAPTER SUMMARY*

Direct advertising has two components — a delivery system which determines its creative characteristics and a list of recipients which determines its audience characteristics. Direct advertising is usually used as a highly selective medium by using lists containing names of prime prospects. Creatively, direct mail is highly flexible in form, but it may suffer from a bad reputation among its audience. Because of its form, direct mail is a useful medium for supplying complex information and items such as coupons or samples that consumers may wish to save. Direct mail is also widely used as a supplementary medium and to merchandise advertising programs to the trade.

Outdoor advertising includes painted bulletins, signs, spectaculars, and posters — the most widely used form. Outdoor is a demographically nonselective mass medium that delivers great frequency. Creatively, it is limited to short reminder-type advertising. High fixed production costs and shortages of prime locations encourage large scale and continuous use of this medium.

Transit advertising has many of the characteristics of outdoor advertising. It delivers a large audience and high frequency, but it is an urban audience, heavily weighted with low-income adults. Creatively, transit is limited to short, easily understood messages. Low fixed production costs make this a practical medium for local advertisers.

Other advertising media include point-of-purchase or display materials, specialties, packaging, directories, and trade shows. The value of point-of-purchase advertising stems from its ability to act as a reminder to consumers while they are in the process of shopping. If an advertiser uses point-of-purchase materials, a program must be established to insure their actual use in the store. Advertising specialties are a selective, reminder medium used largely as giveaways by salespeople. It is a difficult medium to control. Product packaging can serve a media function by means of a reminder message on the container or reassurance information in the form of package inserts or instruction manuals. Directories provide a long-life medium that reaches prospects while they are actively seeking product information. Trade shows provide the opportunity to expose products to other manufacturers, to dealers, and to retailers.

KEY TERMS

| | |
|---|---|
| Direct marketing | Painted bulletins |
| Direct advertising | Spectaculars |
| Solo direct mail | Gross-rating points (GRP) |
| Mail-order catalog advertising | Transit advertising |
| Take-ones | Point-of-purchase advertising |
| Merchandising the advertising | Advertising specialties |
| Poster panels | Trade shows |

QUESTIONS FOR DISCUSSION

1. A common practice followed by advertisers in business magazines is to obtain reprints of their advertisements and use them as direct-mail pieces. The mailing list used is a subscriber list obtained from the magazines used in the media program. What would be accomplished by such a use of direct mail?

2. Sellers of direct-mail lists often offer prospective purchasers the opportunity to use a sample of names on the list for test purposes. Suppose you were the advertising manager for an insurance company using direct mail to generate leads for salespeople. How would you set up a test to evaluate a possible new direct-mail list?

3. What source might you use if you wished to compile your own direct-mail list for each of the following groups of prospects:

   a. New home owners?
   b. Executives in leading corporations?
   c. Advertising agency media directors?
   d. Directors of trade associations?
   e. Publishers of daily newspapers?

4. Direct mail is the favorite medium of direct-response marketers, but many also use magazines. How do direct mail and magazines compare as direct-response media relative to each of the following criteria:

   a. CPM?
   b. selectivity?
   c. response time?

5. The cost per thousand for a direct-mail piece is commonly $300–$700 per thousand, the cost per thousand for television $2 for a 30-second network spot, and the cost per thousand for outdoor averages about $0.35.

   a. What accounts for the vast disparity in cost efficiency between these media?

   b. How can an advertising manager justify using a high-cost medium such as direct mail?

6. Users of outdoor attempt to have their posters placed in locations where their prime prospects are likely to pass by and close to the point of sale to act as a last minute reminder. For each of the following products, suggest the locations that the outdoor advertiser should attempt to obtain.

   a. Suntan lotion.

   b. Beer.

   c. Airlines.

   d. Gasoline.

7. The 1965 Federal Highway Beautification Act forced the removal of some outdoor signs and posters from major highways. The purpose of this requirement was to beautify the highways and permit an unrestricted view. Have consumers suffered any loss as a result of this removal? Have advertisers?

8. Some outdoor industry executives fear that the rise of cable television will divert advertising from outdoor. Other outdoor executives suggest that cable companies may become one of outdoor's best customers. Why would a cable company use outdoor advertising?

9. The size of the audience for transit advertising is measured by counting the number of people who ride the transit vehicles containing the advertisement. Do you think that this is a valid method of measurement? Explain.

10. Point-of-purchase advertising is seldom used as an advertiser's sole medium, but is usually used in conjunction with other media.

   a. Why is point-of-purchase advertising not usually appropriate as an advertiser's only medium?

   b. What role does point-of-purchase advertising play when it is used in conjunction with other media?

---

*PROBLEM*

   The advertising manager for Personal Computer Software, Inc., is preparing a direct-mail advertising program for its line of software packages. PCS, Inc., has developed a series of programs for use on popular personal computers such as the Apple II and IBM-PC. PCS's programs specialize in home finance and personal income-tax applications rather than applications for businesses. The program packages are well documented and have undergone full use-testing.

The advertising manager believes that the prime prospects for the software line are households that have already purchased a personal computer and use it in the home. The market for the product is national. The software is available at retail from computer stores and from mail-order computer outlets.

The direct-mail campaign will be a supplement to a schedule of advertisements in *Popular Computing* and *Personal Computing*. The direct mailing will include reprints of the magazine ads plus a special refund offer to purchasers of one of the software packages. A budget of $10,000 has been set aside for purchasing mailing lists for the first year.

1. Using a copy of Standard Rate and Data Service's *Direct Mail List Rates and Data,* locate a classification of lists appropriate to the software product and select five lists in the classification that appear most promising for the product.
2. Evaluate each of the five direct-mail lists in terms of (a) the appropriateness of the names on the list, (b) the cost efficiency of the list, and (c) the quality of the list.
3. Select the list or combination of lists that you would recommend if you were the advertising manager.

# CHAPTER 16

*The Creative Program—
Determining Content*

LEARNING OBJECTIVES

In studying this chapter you will learn:

- The elements of the creative program.

- The advertising manager's role in the creative program.

- How to determine the content of the advertising message.

- About problems in determining copy content.

Advertising programs are the end product of the advertising planning process. The budget program specifies how much money is to be spent on advertising; the media program specifies to whom the advertising is to be directed; the creative program specifies what message is to be communicated to the audience. Thus far, the budget program and the media program have been considered. In this and the next two chapters, we will discuss the creative program.

## Elements of the Creative Program

The creative program is an integral part of the advertising plan. Its purpose is to provide direction for the creation of advertising during the planning period.

### Inputs to the Creative Program

The creative program is based on decisions and information generated in the earlier sections of the advertising plan. The basic direction for the creative program is provided by the positioning decision. If the positioning is properly defined, it specifies the market segment to be addressed and indicates the product attribute to be presented as a consumer benefit and competitive advantage.

413

Advertising objectives are the second vital input to the creative program. These objectives specify the steps to be taken in order to solve immediate problems facing the product. They influence both what the advertising says and the manner in which it is presented.

The third input to the creative program is information developed from the consumer, product, and market analyses. In particular, the creative program should be based upon a clear description of the characteristics of the target consumers and the needs that the consumers are trying to fulfill. Development of the creative program also relies on detailed information about the product to be advertised as well as detailed information about competitive products.

All of these inputs can be derived from the sections of the advertising plan that precede development of the creative program.

## Steps in Developing the Creative Program

There are three essential steps in building a creative program for a product or service: (1) the content of the advertising message must be determined; (2) how the message will be presented must be decided; and (3) how the advertisement will be produced must be spelled out.

SPECIFYING CONTENT. The creative program defines the information that is to be communicated to consumers. *The most important content decision consists in selecting the key benefit that will be delivered to consumers if they use the advertiser's product.* In specifying the key benefit, evidence that explains and supports it should also be detailed. In addition, the content decision must specify what other necessary information (such as price, where the product is or will be available, and how it is used) has to be presented. Some content may be directed specifically at overcoming problems or realizing opportunities that are faced by the product. The purpose in specifying the content is to standardize the information being delivered to consumers so that each advertising impression is consistent and reinforcing even when advertisements appear in different media.

DETERMINING THE CREATIVE APPROACH. In addition to deciding *what* is to be said, the creative program must consider *how* it is to be said. Good advertising is more than a stark listing of relevant product facts. Creative advertising is built around a central idea that helps to illustrate, highlight, and explain the central attribute of the product. *This central idea and the way in which it is expressed* is the heart of the second step in the creative program — creating the advertisements.

PROVIDING PRODUCTION SPECIFICATIONS. After decisions have been made concerning the content of the advertising and the way it is to be executed, the creative program must determine how the advertising will be produced. Production of advertising refers to the process of converting creative ideas into the finished materials to be used by the media. Much of this production is of a technical nature, carried out by production specialists. However, both production time schedules and production cost estimates need to be made generally available because they influence other programs, including the budget and media programs.

### The Creative Program and the Advertising Plan

Each of the three steps in building a creative program should be represented in the advertising plan as a set of directions to those who are to implement the program.

The manner in which the advertising is to be presented is sometimes difficult to express in words and as a consequence it is a usual practice to provide in the advertising plan some prototype advertisements that illustrate the creative approach to be used. In addition to these prototypes, the creative program should contain necessary implementation instructions such as the order in which different versions should be scheduled to appear and details on programs for informing the trade and sales force of the advertising program.

Technical details on production of the advertising are sometimes omitted from the advertising plan because they are not of general interest. However, estimates of production costs and production time schedules should be included in the plan.

## The Advertising Manager's Role in the Creative Process

Advertising managers and their agency counterparts, the account representatives, usually do not create advertisements themselves. Instead, they rely on creative specialists for preparation and implementation of the creative program. Because of the great importance of the creative program to the success of the advertising effort, the advertising manager must develop a productive relationship with the creative team. To do this, it is necessary to understand the characteristics of these creative specialists and the process by which they create advertisements.

### Utilizing Creative Specialists

In a managerial capacity, the advertising manager and the agency account representative have several responsibilities toward the creative program, but writing copy, designing layouts, and filming commercials are not among them. The creation of advertising requires different skills than does management of the advertising function, and, hence, the creative area tends to attract different kinds of talent than does management. Creative specialists typically have an education in the arts. Their interests tend to lie in music, art, literature, theater, and current events. Their approach to work is intuitive rather than analytical. They are experts at observing other people and understanding other points of view. In general, their background tends to produce the qualifications needed by creators of advertisements, namely communications skills, design ability, consumer empathy, and knowledge of technical processes in advertising production. To take advantage of the best creative skills, the advertising manager will need to rely on these creative specialists. The functions of the various creative specialists were described in Chapter 2.

## Understanding the Creative Process

Establishing an effective working relationship with creative specialists is made difficult by the likelihood that these specialists have backgrounds, interests, and points of view that are substantially different from those of a person whose background and training are in management. A further difficulty in establishing the relationship stems from misunderstanding that managers frequently have of the creative process.

MANAGER'S VIEW OF THE CREATIVE PROCESS. There is an enormous variety in background and insight among managers, so that the manager's view of the creative process presented here cannot be seen as universally true, but, rather, as a tendency. Managers tend to attack problems and projects in a logical, orderly, analytical fashion. Their education, job experience, and the reward system within the organization strongly encourage this approach.

The manager, asked to create an advertisement, would be most likely to take this same logical and orderly approach to the problem. The management-trained person would first break the job of writing the advertisement into a series of smaller tasks, arrange these tasks in a logical sequence, and then, step-by-step, build the ad. The first step might be to write a headline; the second step, to write body copy which would have three sections—an opening, an elaboration, and a closing summary; a third step might be to select an illustration. The steps continue—selection of a logotype or signature, addition of a package illustration, statement of product price—until finally the manager is ready to assemble all the pieces to make the advertisement. The manager has now created the advertisement in a logical, orderly, step-by-step way in much the same way that, brick-by-brick, a mason builds a wall.

Even though managers are not often called upon to create advertisements, their perception of what an advertisement is will be colored by their view of how they or others should approach the job of creating an advertisement. They tend to view an advertisement as a series of individual pieces (or bricks) that have been assembled to build an advertisement.

CREATIVE SPECIALIST'S VIEW OF THE CREATIVE PROCESS. The view that the creative specialist has of the creative process and of the way in which advertisements are created differs greatly from the manager's view. Again, this description should be viewed as a tendency rather than an invariable approach since creative specialists also vary greatly in their work patterns.

Typically, creative specialists begin by immersing themselves in information about the product, the consumer, the competition, the market, the positioning and objectives, and any other data that appear relevant. This step is not much different from the approach that a manager would be expected to take in doing the job. The next step, however, is different in that the creative person searches for a big idea that will be the centerpiece or focal point of the advertisement. The purpose of this central idea is dramatically to bring home to consumers the central attribute or key benefit of the product to be advertised. The creative person seeks this key selling idea not in a logical step-by-step fashion, but by ranging freely over a large number of associations, combinations, and notions.

Only when the key, central idea has been decided upon does the creative person begin to construct the advertisement. With the key idea as the centerpiece, the individual parts of the advertisement—headline, copy, illustration—are designed so that they supplement and add to the central idea.

To the creative person, then, an advertisement is not a series of individual pieces assembled to build an advertisement, but instead a central selling idea that is supported and enhanced by the separate components of the advertisement.

## Creative Responsibility of the Advertising Manager

Because creative specialists are often utilized, does this mean that advertising managers never create advertising? Certainly not. There are many instances, particularly among smaller advertisers, where advertising managers also prepare creative materials. In effect, such people hold two jobs—a manager's job and a creative specialist's job. This is an effective approach if the advertising manager has adequate managerial skills plus creative skills equal to those available from creative specialists.

Furthermore, if the advertising manager does decide to delegate the job of creating advertisements to specialists, it does not mean that responsibility for the creative product is avoided. The manager is responsible for providing adequate direction to the creative specialist, establishing productive working relationships, and controlling the final creative product. Exhibit 16-1 is a good summing-up by a leading advertising agency of the creative responsibilities that are part of the job of any manager of an advertising program, and, in this case, of those duties that concern the agency's own account representatives.

SETTING CREATIVE DIRECTION. By far the most important creative responsibility of the advertising manager is to provide the creative specialists with clear direction that assures that the creative program carries out the positioning, meets objectives, and is coordinated with other programs such as the media program. To give this direction, the advertising manager must provide to the creative specialists the product positioning and the advertising objectives.

EXHIBIT 16-1          Creative responsibilities of advertising account managers.

1. The account manager represents the agency to the client, and the client to the agency.
2. The account group should create a climate that breeds outstanding creative work.
3. The account manager must provide information. Facts about the product, the market, the target audience.
4. The first requirement for great advertising is a great strategy—one that is simple and persuasive. One the creative group can embrace.
5. Creative thinking requires time. The account manager must provide the time in which big ideas can be conceived and grow.
6. The account manager should show faith by leaving the creative team alone to do its work.
7. An essential skill is developing and evaluating copy. The account manager should be a student of advertising, able to comment knowledgeably (rather than nitpick).
8. Creative work and creative people must be protected from too many meetings that waste time and erode advertising ideas.
9. Once the agency recommendation is settled, the account manager is responsible for organizing the most persuasive way of presenting the agency's work.
10. One mark of a good account partner is the courage to support original ideas.

Source: *What Ogilvy and Mather Believes About Creating Advertising*. Reprinted with permission.

The advertising manager should also provide the information that the creative team needs in order to become thoroughly familiar with the product, the target consumers, and the efforts of competitive products. Much of this material is available from the analysis sections of the advertising plan, but the advertising manager should also accept responsibility for supplying additional information or answers to questions when called upon to do so by the creative group.

ESTABLISHING THE CREATIVE RELATIONSHIP. The creation of advertising is a project that is more likely to be successful if the creator has a confident, enthusiastic attitude toward the product and the advertising manager. Differences between managers and creative people can lead to friction and conflict with a resulting loss in the quality of the creative output.

Given this situation of potential conflict, what can the advertising manager do to establish a productive relationship? Here are several guidelines. First, the best creative talent available should be selected, people in whom the advertising manager has confidence. Second, the advertising manager should be prepared to delegate the creative job to these specialists. If they represent the best talent available, the manager should have little hesitancy in giving them responsibility. The advertising manager demonstrates confidence in the creative team by delegating to them. The advertising manager should not write advertisements in competition with them nor presume to rewrite their efforts, for this destroys their enthusiasm. This does not mean, however, that everything the specialist creates must be accepted.

A third guideline is this—the advertising manager should protect the integrity of the advertisement. It has been pointed out that an advertisement is not formed by arranging a series of little building blocks. Rather, it begins with a key, central idea to which each element must contribute. Recognizing this, the advertising manager should act as protector of the totality of the advertisement. There will be many people, not creatively trained, who will be tempted to add, subtract, and rearrange the "pieces" of an advertisement without recognizing how they contribute to the central selling idea of the advertisement. By protecting against these incursions, the advertising manager may not only save the advertisement, but will also earn the gratitude and enthusiasm of the creative specialists.

EVALUATING CREATIVE OUTPUT. If the creative work has been delegated to creative specialists, the advertising manager should not interfere with the creative process except to provide needed information. However, when the creative team has formulated its creative approaches, they should be brought to the advertising manager for evaluation. The advertising manager has the responsibility for deciding whether or not these ideas should be produced and used as finished advertisements.

To carry out this evaluation, the advertising manager should utilize specific evaluation criteria that have been clearly stated in advance to the creative team. The criteria should be managerial, not creative. If the advertising manager has confidence in the creative team and has delegated to them because of their superior creative skills, then it is destructive to second-guess the creativity of their advertisements by applying personal judgments to them.

What criteria, then, should be used? Five are suggested below:

1. Does the advertisement carry out the agreed upon positioning? The purpose of advertising is not to be brilliant, witty, or beautiful, but to communicate a specific message to a particular audience. Advertising that does not execute the product's positioning is irrelevant and should be rejected by the advertising manager.
2. Does the advertising meet the advertising objectives? Not every advertisement can work simultaneously on every problem facing a product, but the total effect of all advertisements *must* do so. Thus every advertisement should contribute in some way to meeting the advertising objectives.
3. Is the advertising truthful and tasteful? The advertising manager should accept responsibility for seeing that no advertisement is accepted that is not truthful and tasteful. Since both truthfulness and good taste are difficult and subjective concepts, the advertising manager should attempt to establish truth and taste standards in advance and then evaluate advertisements by these standards.
4. Should the advertisement be researched? The advertising manager should not make personal judgments about the creative value or ultimate effectiveness of particular advertisements, but should always reserve the right to conduct research on the effectiveness of advertisements. Copy research techniques are expensive and the results imperfect. Therefore, not every advertisement should be tested. Usually research is reserved for evaluating

new approaches and major creative departures. Armed with research findings, even though they are imperfect, the advertising manager is in a better position to make decisions about the potential effectiveness of the advertisements.

5. Does the advertisement represent the best efforts of the creative team? To accept the creative judgment of specialists, the advertising manager must be convinced that they are the best available, that they have given the task their best efforts, and that they really have confidence in their own creative product. If advertising is rejected for any of these reasons, the advertising manager should probe more deeply to find the underlying cause. Was the creative team poorly selected? Have they been given inadequate direction? Have they been provided an environment conducive to work?

It should be emphasized that the evaluation criteria do not include the question, "Do I like the ad?" Although it is difficult to accomplish, the advertising manager must suppress his or her personal likes and dislikes so that the advertising is prepared to meet the requirements of the product rather than the advertising manager's personal preferences.

LEGAL EVALUATION OF CREATIVE OUTPUT. Although the legal problems confronting the advertiser will be covered in more detail later, it is important to note here the increasing role of legal counsel in the creative process. Especially for large firms whose advertising is highly visible to the public, legal counsel has become a partner in the creation of advertising. In past years it was sufficient in these firms to obtain legal review of advertising after the advertising was prepared. Today's legal environment is so complex and perilous for the large advertiser that legal counsel must be engaged every step of the way, starting with selection of the positioning to conceptualization of the central idea to final production of the advertisement. It is the advertising manager's responsibility to see that this legal counseling is integrated into the creative process.

## Determining Advertising Content

While much of the creation of advertising is delegated to specialists in the field, the advertising manager must have a good understanding of how the creative program will be developed. As noted earlier, determining the content of the advertising message is the first step in building the creative program and will be discussed in the remainder of this chapter. Creating the advertisements is the second step and will be detailed in Chapter 17. Producing the advertisements, the final step, will be the subject of Chapter 18.

### Functions of the Advertising Content

Advertising copy serves to communicate product information to consumers. The advertising content serves both the advertiser's objectives and the consumer's objectives.

HOW CONTENT SERVES THE ADVERTISER. From the advertiser's point of view, the function of advertising content is to carry out the advertising objectives of the product, particularly the positioning. The advertising serves to translate the product benefit designated in the positioning into a benefit for the target market segment also designated in the positioning.

In Chapter 10 we suggested that Dannon Yogurt was positioned as a good-for-you food that contributes to physical fitness with the competitive advantage of being low fat and all natural.

Exhibit 10-3 on page 228 shows a print advertisement for Dannon Yogurt. Note how clearly the ad focuses on communicating the benefit of physical fitness. The benefit is communicated in the headline "Get a Dannon Body," is clearly the focus of the illustration, and is supported in the body copy that suggests light, nutritious Dannon Lowfat Yogurt as part of a physical fitness program.

Note how clearly both the illustration and the copy in the Betty Crocker ad in Exhibit 16-2 focus on the competitive advantage of Creamy Deluxe. There are many prepared frostings available to the home baker, but Betty Crocker has attempted to set itself apart by positioning Creamy Deluxe as the only prepared frosting with real butter added. The ad content has translated this product difference into a consumer benefit — taste.

In addition to communicating the product's differentiating benefits to the target market segment, the advertising copy may be asked to contribute to achieving the advertising objectives. If one of the objectives for a product is to inform consumers where the product can be purchased, the copy can help to meet this objective with content that reads "available in all food stores." If an objective is to reduce confusion of the advertiser's product with competitive products, the copy content might contribute by frequent mention of the brand name in connection with its benefits.

CONTENT FROM THE CONSUMER'S POINT OF VIEW. From what has been stated, it perhaps sounds as though advertising content is no more than a restatement of the product positioning and objectives. This is not so, for there is a major and important difference between positioning and objectives statements and effective advertising copy. Positioning and objectives statements represent goals that an advertiser hopes to achieve. They are written for the advertiser and from the advertiser's point of view. Advertising content or advertising copy is not a statement of what the advertiser wants to achieve, but rather information concerning what is offered to the consumer. Advertising copy is written from the *consumer's* point of view, not the advertiser's. The essential skill of the copywriter is the ability to look through the consumer's eyes and translate the positioning and objectives into information that is understandable, useful, and persuasive to the consumer.

*The Product Benefit.* The overall guide for determining what should be included in the copy content is the information usefulness proposition. A consumer is more likely to read and act on an advertisement if it satisfies a

EXHIBIT 16-2        Advertisement for Betty Crocker Creamy Deluxe frosting.

consumer need. In determining the content of the advertising, the creative specialist must first understand the need the consumer is trying to satisfy and then state in the copy how the advertiser's product can help to satisfy that need. Considered from the consumer's standpoint, the copywriter's task is to translate the key product attribute into a consumer benefit. This consumer benefit is frequently also referred to as "the appeal."

*Flagging Prospects.* In addition to communicating the key benefit, consumers need additional information that the advertising must transmit. As a first consideration, the ad must attract those consumers who are the target prospects specified in the positioning. The advertisement for the Tall Collection in Exhibit 16-3 uses a headline supported by an illustration designed to attract readership of women 5′6″ or taller. This approach not only attracts readership of the best prospects, but also communicates that the product offering is designed especially for them.

*Supporting Evidence.* If consumers' attention is directed to the ad and if they find that the key benefit meets their needs, they will next seek evidence that supports the claimed benefit. The Betty Crocker better taste claim is supported by showing that real butter has been added. The Tall Collection ad explains seven ways in which the advertised fashions fit taller women better.

*Shopping Information.* If the supporting evidence is persuasive, consumers will still need information on how and where to purchase the product. The Tall Collection ad specifies that purchasing is by mail order, and offers a free catalog. Ads for expensive products frequently explain payment terms, guarantees, or return policies.

*Reassurance.* Even after consumers purchase the advertiser's product, there remains a further function that the content can serve—reassurance. After purchase of a product, particularly a new or expensive product, consumers are likely to read advertising for the product as reassurance that their choice is a wise one.

### The Copy Platform

The message that is to be delivered to consumers by the advertiser should be stated in the copy platform, which is a fundamental element in the direction of the creative program. A **copy platform** is a statement, in consumer language, of the claims, evidence, and information that advertising is to present to the consumer. There should be a single copy platform for each campaign or set of advertisements on a single topic. From this single copy platform many different individual advertisements may be created, but they all spring from common content stated in the copy platform. This assures that all the advertisements in the campaign are coordinated, delivering the same messages to consumers.

*copy platform*

PREPARATION OF THE COPY PLATFORM. The copy platform is ordinarily prepared by advertising agency personnel if the advertiser retains an

EXHIBIT 16-3          An advertisement that flags key prospects.

agency, but both the advertising manager and the account representative play an active role along with the creative team. Regardless of who prepares it, the advertising manager and all other advertising personnel should be involved in reviewing the final version since all efforts must be guided by it.

What should be included in the copy platform? Since the copy platform must serve both to carry out the advertiser's objectives and to satisfy the consumer's need for information, these functions serve as guides in deciding what information should be included in the copy platform. Usually the platform should include some or all of the following:

1. Copy indicating for whom the message is intended. This positioning statement should indicate who the target market segment is, and should attempt to attract the attention of this group.
2. Copy offering the product as a solution to the need or problem facing the consumer. This element of the copy is known as the benefit or appeal. It presents the advertiser's product not as a physical object, but as a need-satisfying alternative.
3. Copy providing evidence to support the promised benefits. Consumers have some natural skepticism concerning an advertiser's product. In order to evaluate the product as an alternative, the consumer needs information that describes how this alternative is different from others that are available.
4. Copy providing information that consumers will need in order to evaluate the product and enable them to obtain it. This information includes the name of the product, where it can be found, its price, size, colors, and styles.
5. Copy providing information to overcome constraints to purchase action. If the advertiser is seeking immediate consumer response (rather than a gradual modification of attitudes toward the product), the copy may contain special purchase incentives, payment terms, return privileges, or offers of purchase assistance.
6. Copy providing, for those who have already purchased the product, reassurance that the product selection was a wise one.

Not every advertisement will contain all this information. Clearly some advertisements can contain only a fraction of this information (an outdoor advertisement, for example), while other ads will contain nearly all the elements (a long-copy newspaper ad, for example). The purpose of the copy platform is to provide a standardized source of the information that is to be communicated by the total creative effort.

A SAMPLE COPY PLATFORM. Exhibit 16-4 shows a copy platform prepared for Hershey's Cocoa. Hershey's Cocoa is a pure cocoa product that can be used to make hot or cold cocoa drinks or as a baking ingredient. It is this latter use on which Hershey focuses this campaign. The Hershey's Cocoa positioning directs the product to "scratch bakers" as a substitute for baker's chocolate; the product is easier to use, is more economical, and gives a better quality end product. Note that the copy platform, although phrased in consumer terms, carries out this positioning with the key benefit and its support.

**EXHIBIT 16-4**          Copy platform for a Hershey's Cocoa campaign.

| | |
|---|---|
| **Target Audience:** | People who bake from scratch. |
| **Key Benefit:** | Hershey's Cocoa gives richer, moister, more chocolatey baked goods than baking chocolate. |
| **Support:** | In a test of 108 women, seven out of ten preferred cakes baked with Hershey's Cocoa over cakes baked with baking chocolate. |
| **Other Information:** | Hershey's Cocoa doesn't require messy melting; there's no danger of scorching. |
| | Hershey's Cocoa is easy to substitute for baking chocolate using this handy formula: three tablespoons of cocoa plus one tablespoon of shortening or oil equal one square of baking chocolate. |
| | Hershey's Cocoa can also be used in cookies, frosting, and fudge. |
| | Hershey's Cocoa is more economical than baking chocolate. |
| **Reassurance:** | The Hershey name is your guarantee of top quality and good taste. |

In addition, the copy platform provides information on how to use the product by stating how to convert a recipe from baker's chocolate to cocoa. Considerable attention is also given to reassuring the user that results will not be disappointing. This reassurance is important because scratch bakers prize the ego rewards that they gain from pleasing family and friends.

In later chapters we will see advertising that developed from this copy platform.

## Problems in Determining Copy Content

In preparing the copy platform and copy for the individual advertisements that follow, the creative specialist will face many difficult decisions. The choice of the key benefit or appeal is the most critical of these decisions. In this section several frequently occurring copy content problems will be considered.

### Rational vs. Emotional Benefits

The choice between promising rational benefits and appealing to emotion is one that has long been of concern to advertisers. The earliest books on advertising spend considerable time discussing this issue.[1] Their authors suggested various rules of thumb for deciding between emotional and rational approaches. One rule, for example, suggested that certain types of products (such as jewelry, insurance, and smoking items) should promise emotional benefits while others (such as building materials) should use rational benefits.[2]

The choice between rational and emotional benefits is also the subject of comment by today's social critics of advertising who see emotional appeals as socially undesirable because they appeal to people's weaknesses and to unnecessary needs.

DEFINITION OF TERMS. One of the difficulties in considering the choice between "emotional benefits" and "rational benefits" is the wide variety of meanings given these terms. The choice becomes clearer if the terms are defined as follows: **rational benefits** are promises to satisfy utilitarian needs; **emotional benefits** are promises to satisfy social or psychological needs. When the benefits are defined in this way, the choice should be made by determining the type of need the target consumer is trying to satisfy with the product. If the consumer is trying to satisfy a utilitarian need, then the benefit should be rational. If the consumer is trying to satisfy social or psychological needs, then the benefit should be emotional.

*rational benefits*
*emotional benefits*

CHOICE BETWEEN EMOTIONAL AND RATIONAL. It is quite possible that the market for a product will contain both consumers with emotional needs and consumers with rational needs. These two groups represent different segments of the market and the advertiser must decide in which segment the product should be positioned. Note the contrast between the approaches taken by the two skin lotion advertisements in Exhibits 16-5 and 16-6. The approach for Vaseline Dermatology Formula is highly medicinal with the almost painful illustration and fact-oriented copy. Keri Lotion's ad, by contrast, is far more emotional in its appeal. Although the copy makes some effectiveness claims, the copy and especially the illustration offer far more emotional benefits.

Then too it is likely in many cases that a consumer may have both emotional and rational motives for the purchase of a product so that a mix of emotional and rational benefits may be called for. Increasingly advertisers appear to be introducing emotional appeals into advertising that was once purely utilitarian, particularly in products with only slight differentiation. Ogilvy and Raphaelson, two noted copywriters note that "Few purchases of any kind are made for entirely rational reasons. Even a purely functional

---

[1]See, for example, Daniel Starch, *Principles of Advertising* (New York: McGraw-Hill, 1923), pp. 369–372; and Melvin Thomas Copeland, *Principles of Merchandising* (Chicago and New York: A. W. Shaw, 1926), pp. 158–162.
[2]Harry Tipper and others, *The Principles of Advertising* (New York: The Ronald Press, 1920), pp. 75–81.

**EXHIBIT 16-5** An advertisement for a skin lotion offering rational, utilitarian, medicinal benefits.

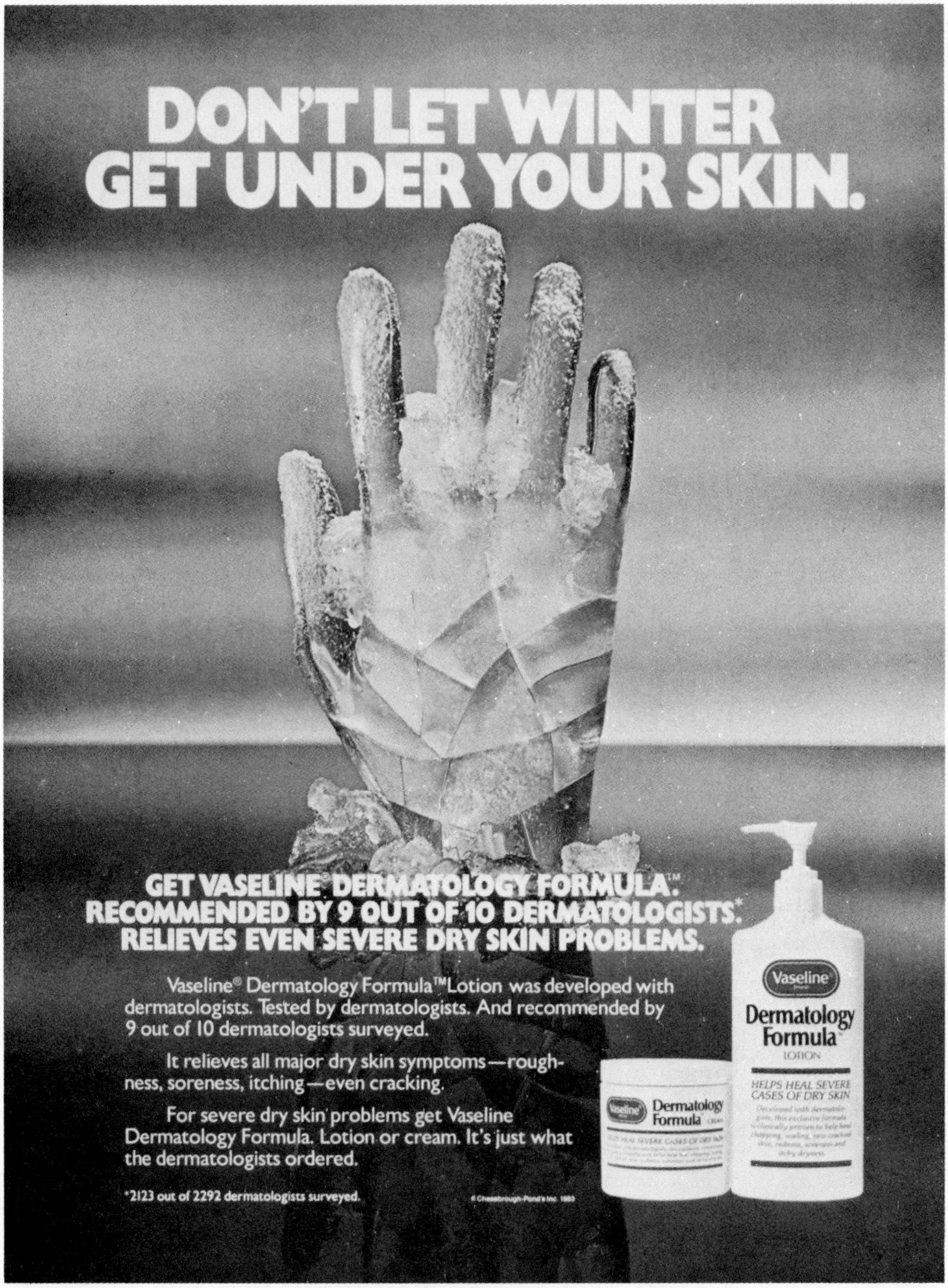


Reprinted with the permission of Chesebrough-Pond's Inc., the owner of the registered trademarks VASELINE and DERMATOLOGY FORMULA.

An advertisement for a skin lotion offering emotional, psychological, cosmetic benefits. EXHIBIT 16-6

**Keri is so very different**—it doesn't feel like ordinary lotion. It's concentrated. It was specially made for dry, rough skin. **Keri is so very rich**—in emollients. It can even make rough elbows and heels feel soft again. It can turn problem skin into the very skin you've been wanting. **Keri is so very recommended**—by dermatologists. It may cost a little more, but after all, it's the only skin you've got.

THERAPEUTIC
**Keri lotion**

FOR DRY SKIN CARE

WESTWOOD

c 1984 Westwood Pharmaceuticals

Courtesy: Westwood Pharmaceuticals, Inc.

product such as laundry detergent may offer what is now called an 'emotional end benefit' — say, the satisfaction of seeing one's children in bright, clean clothes. In some product categories the rational element is small. These include soft drinks, beer, cosmetics, certain personal-care products, and most fashion products. And who hasn't experienced the surge of joy that accompanies the purchase of a new car?"[3]

Under the suggested definition of emotional and rational benefits, it is also difficult to accept the social critic's notion that advertisers have a responsibility to avoid emotional approaches. This places the advertiser in the position not just of determining what need the consumer wishes to fulfill, but also of evaluating the inherent worth of that need. This would place the advertiser (or some governmental agency, on the consumer's behalf) in the position of imposing values on the consumer rather than accepting the consumer's values and responding to them.

### Need-Arousing vs. Need-Satisfying Benefits

Another issue to be faced in deciding upon the creative content is whether the advertising should attempt to arouse consumers needs or simply promise benefits that satisfy already salient needs.

AROUSING DORMANT NEEDS. Recalling the model in Chapter 5, consumer needs are presumed established in individuals by forces more basic and more powerful than advertising. However, some needs may remain dormant unless activated by some outside stimulus, or consumers may be unaware of a problem unless it is brought to their attention. The Colgate toothpaste ad in Exhibit 16-7, as an example, attempts to bring to people's attention the need to stop childhood tooth decay before it really gets started.

Behavioral scientists have conducted various studies to evaluate the need-arousing vs. the need-satisfying approaches. Many of these gave equivocal results. However, a study by Janis and Feshback did indicate that fear-arousing approaches could have negative results if the people receiving the scare message were not also relieved of their anxiety by showing them how the aroused problem could be solved.[4]

COMBINING AROUSING AND SATISFYING APPROACHES. These findings led several observers to suggest that need-arousing and need-satisfying benefits are not alternative, but rather complementary approaches to

---

[3]David Ogilvy and Joel Raphaelson, "Research on Advertising Techniques that Work and Don't Work," *Harvard Business Review* (July-August, 1982), p. 18.

[4]I. L. Janis and S. Feshback, "Effects of Fear-Arousing Communication," *Journal of Abnormal and Social Psychology*, Vol. 48 (January, 1953), pp. 78–92.

An advertisement that brings a problem to the reader's attention.                    EXHIBIT 16-7

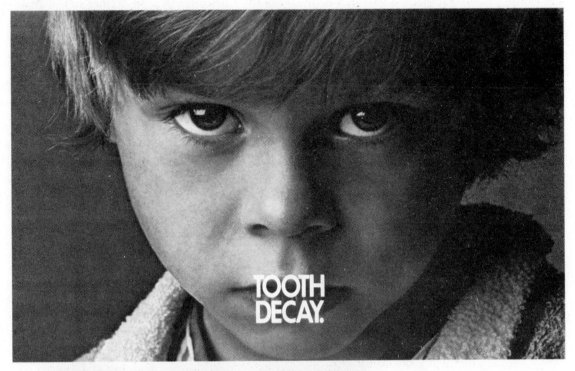

# CAUGHT SOON ENOUGH, EARLY TOOTH DECAY CAN ACTUALLY BE REPAIRED BY COLGATE!

Now Colgate, and only Colgate, offers exclusive X-ray proof. Colgate helps prevent early tooth decay from becoming a cavity. These special X-ray photos represent a tooth magnified many times! They show that early tooth decay, when caught soon enough, can be repaired by Colgate—with the most clinically proven fluoride in any toothpaste.

### NEW PROOF: EXCLUSIVE X-RAY EVIDENCE!

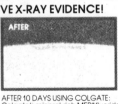

**BEFORE**

**AFTER**

EARLY TOOTH DECAY: Teeth are made of minerals. But decay acids can cause mineral loss—unless these minerals are replaced, the early tooth decay seen here can turn into cavities.

AFTER 10 DAYS USING COLGATE: Colgate's mineral-rich MFP* fluoride formula helps replace lost minerals to actually help repair early tooth decay.

**COLGATE.**
**THE MAXIMUM FLUORIDE PROTECTION IN ANY TOOTHPASTE.**

Courtesy: Colgate-Palmolive Company.

creating copy.[5] The need-arousing approach alerts the consumer to a potential problem, encouraging the consumer to read further in the advertisement. To be effective, the copy should continue with need-satisfying content that explains to the consumer how the advertiser's product will solve the problem. The resulting advertisement presents a familiar format, especially in television advertising — establish a problem, then present the product as a solution.

One expert, George Gallup, reports that television commercials that set up a problem, offer the product as a solution, and then demonstrate the product, sell four times as much of the product as commercials that merely present product claims.[6] Note how the Hostess Donuts advertisement in Exhibit 16-8 has used this approach. The problem: "How do I keep my family home for breakfast?" The solution: To serve them something they will enjoy — Hostess Donuts.

The combined approach can be used in print advertising as well. Note in the Aim advertisement that after posing the problem of plaque build-up, a solution is suggested — a program of regular dental care, checkups, and, of course, the use of Aim can prevent the problem.

### Fear Appeals

*fear appeal*

Fear appeals are a special case of the emotion-arousing approach that is of sufficient importance to warrant separate attention. **Fear appeals** are designed to raise anxiety concerning a dangerous or harmful problem facing the consumer.

USE OF FEAR APPEALS. Examples of fear appeals in advertising that come most immediately to mind are public service campaigns promoting early cancer detection, highway safety, and prevention of smoking, drug, and alcohol abuse. Insurance advertisements also frequently use this approach.

If the use of the fear approach were limited to these few cases the subject would not deserve special attention. However, more subtle fear appeals, expressed in terms of one's social and psychological security, as well as one's physical security, are widely used in advertisements for proprietary remedies, toiletries, and personal care items.

EVIDENCE CONCERNING FEAR APPEALS. Behavioral scientists and marketing theorists have worked extensively to determine the conditions under

---

[5]Carl I. Hovland, "Effects of Mass Media of Communication," *Handbook of Social Psychology,* edited by Gardner W. Lindzey (Cambridge, Mass.: Addison-Wesley, 1954), p. 1976, and Raymond A. Bauer with Donald F. Cox, "Rational vs. Emotional Communication: A New Approach," *Risk Taking and Information Handling in Consumer Behavior,* edited by Donald F. Cox (Boston: Division of Research, Graduate School of Business Administration, Harvard University, 1967), pp. 469–486.

[6]Quoted by David Ogilvy, *Confessions of an Advertising Man* (New York: Atheneum, 1963), p. 132.

A problem-solution television commercial.

EXHIBIT 16-8

(SFX: SCHOOL BUS HORN)
SON: Breakfast? Who's got time for breakfast?

FATHER: No time, hon, I'll eat with the guys.

MOTHER: Now I keep 'em home for breakfast and Hostess helps.

SON: Hey, Hostess Donuts.

I'll take cinnamon.

Mmmmm.

FATHER: Powdered donut for me.
SON: Tastes great, huh Dad.

MOTHER: And you know, breakfast at home costs about half the price of eating out.

FATHER: That's important.

MOTHER: So...
ALL: Keep 'em home for breakfast.

MOTHER: With Hostess...

and save.

which fear appeals are effective. One of the earliest and most influential studies was the Janis and Feshback study mentioned above. In their study, groups of students were first warned of the danger of failure to take proper care of their teeth. The students were then exposed to instruction on proper dental care. To their surprise, the researchers found that groups exposed to the strongest warnings were less motivated to adopt the recommended dental procedures than were those receiving a mild fear appeal. They concluded that too strong a fear appeal triggered a defense mechanism in the subject that blotted out both the anxiety and the problem solution information that followed.

Later investigators found that a similar defense mechanism was aroused when the fear appeal concerned something very important or unavoidable to the subject.[7] Anti-smoking campaigns, for example, have been generally ineffective with smokers, and safe-driving campaigns have had no measurable effect in reducing accidents among car drivers. On the other hand, advertisers have had notable success in using fear appeals to sell deodorants and other personal care products. One observer of this reaction notes that "fear might be highly effective as a motivator if the person subjected to it had a weak tie to the behavior being propagandized against, *or* if the person could extinguish the source of danger in a single act so that it would not upset entrenched or treasured habits."[8]

### Positive vs. Negative Approach

Product benefits can be expressed in either a positive or a negative way. The Del Monte advertisement in Exhibit 16-9 is a negative appeal stating that low quality peas are not accepted according to Del Monte Brand standards. The benefits might have been stated positively — "Only high quality peas are used for Del Monte Brand" — but the appeal would have been less distinctive.

If the advertiser has a choice between a positive approach and a negative approach, which should be used? There appears to be some prejudice on the part of advertisers against the use of a negative approach, stemming from a feeling that it is better to have positive, optimistic, and cheerful ideas associated with the advertiser's product. However, available research evidence does not support this intuitive feeling. Although it is now quite old, considerable experimental research has been conducted with the purpose of comparing the effects of positive and negative approaches.[9] Lucas and Benson, for example, compared the sales effectiveness of matched pairs of advertisements for correspondence courses.[10] The two ads in each

---

[7]Bauer, *op. cit.*, pp. 471–473.

[8]John R. Stuteville, "Psychic Defenses Against High Fear Appeals: A Key Marketing Variable," *Journal of Marketing*, Vol. 34 (April, 1970), p. 41.

[9]An extensive summary is found in Darrell Blain Lucas and Stuart Henderson Britt, *Advertising Psychology and Research* (New York: McGraw-Hill, 1950), pp. 166–172.

[10]D. B. Lucas and C. E. Benson, "Some Sales Results for Positive and Negative Advertisements," *Journal of Applied Psychology*, Vol. 14 (August, 1930), pp. 363–370.

An advertisement using a negative approach in stating the product benefit.   EXHIBIT 16-9

Source: The Del Monte Corporation.

pair were alike in all respects except for the benefit—one was stated positively, the other negatively. Twenty-eight pairs of advertisements were tested, but no consistent pattern developed favoring either positive or negative approaches. Other tests have failed to show either approach as better than the other.

With this evidence it appears that the choice between a positive and a negative approach should depend on the product, the situation, and the competition. Evidence indicates, for example, that there are far more positive approaches used than negative.[11] An advertiser might find that the promised benefit would stand apart from competitive appeals if expressed in negative form.

## Sex in Advertising

In recent years there has been an increasing public openness about sex and nudity that has spread into the popular media, especially the movies, television, and magazines. Despite the apparent public acceptance of sexual topics in the media, there has been comparatively less use of sex and nudity in advertising. The reason seems to be that the use of sex in advertising has so far been of uncertain effectiveness.

Yovovich has summarized some of what is known from research about the effectiveness of sex in advertising.[12] In research on a pair of sexy jeans commercials, Gallup & Robinson, Inc., an advertising and marketing research company, found that the commercials had good stopping power, but were below average in changing buying attitudes. Another study of a series of ads which included sexy elements concluded, "Ads that used sexual themes and sexual elements simply as attention-getting devices proved to have the lowest brand recall scores."[13] Focus-group studies by Needham, Harper & Steers, Inc., an advertising agency, confirmed this finding, but also found that when the sex in the advertisement focused attention on the primary benefit, then it was acceptable and effective.

David Ogilvy, agency founder and gifted copywriter, perhaps summarized it best with an example from his own experience:

> The first advertisement I ever produced showed a naked woman. It was a mistake, not because it was sexy, but because it was irrelevant to the product—a cooking stove. The test is *relevance*.[14]

Recent research by Judd and Alexander tends to confirm this.[15] Their research on ads using suggestive illustrations confirmed the decline in recall scores found in other research. In diagnosing the reason for the decline in

---

[11]Lucas and Britt, *op. cit.*, p. 171.
[12]B. G. Yovovich, "Sex in Advertising—the Power and the Peril," *Advertising Age* (May 2, 1983), pp. M-4, 5.
[13]*Ibid.*, p. M-4.
[14]David Ogilvy, *Ogilvy on Advertising* (New York: Crown Publishers, Inc., 1983), p. 25.
[15]Ben B. Judd and M. Wayne Alexander, "On the Reduced Effectiveness of Some Sexually Suggestive Ads," *Journal of the Academy of Marketing Science* (Spring, 1983), pp. 156–168.

recall, they found that the suggestive illustrations succeeded in attracting attention, but distracted readers from the copy in the ads. The researchers conclude, like Ogilvy, that to be effective, sexual themes must be integrated into the overall creative approach.

---

The advertising manager delegates much of the creative program planning and implementation because it requires specialized skills. However, the advertising manager retains responsibility for forming a productive relationship with the creative team, for providing information and direction to the creative team, and for evaluating the creative output in terms of specific, pre-established criteria.

The first step in building a creative program is to determine the content of the message. The advertising content serves the advertiser by accomplishing the positioning and objectives set for the product. The content serves the consumer by providing useful information about satisfying needs. Advertising content is defined in a copy platform which is a statement in consumer language of the claims and information to be communicated by the advertising. The copy platform should attract prospects for the product, present the product benefit or appeal, give evidence supporting the promised benefit, and contain other information to facilitate purchase.

The advertiser faces numerous difficult choices in deciding how to approach the key benefit or appeal. In choosing between emotional and rational benefits, the advertiser should offer rational benefits when prospects face utilitarian needs and emotional benefits when needs are social or psychological. In considering whether need-arousing or need-satisfying approaches should be used, the advertiser should consider the possibility of using both, thus forming a problem-posing/solution-offering advertisement. Research evidence indicates that fear appeals raise consumer defenses if the problem is a vital or unavoidable one, but may be effective with less important problems. The choice between stating benefits positively or negatively appears to be largely a matter of creative judgment. The use of sex in advertising must meet the test of relevance.

*CHAPTER SUMMARY*

---

Copy platform
Rational benefits

Emotional benefits    *KEY TERMS*
Fear appeal

1. Direct marketing or mail-order firms frequently do not retain an advertising agency, but instead maintain their own staff of advertising specialists, including copywriters and artists. The advertisement in Exhibit 16-3 for Tall Collection typifies advertising used by these marketers. Why would these direct-marketing firms tend to use their own advertising specialists rather than an advertising agency?

2. The advertising manager is responsible both for providing direction to the creative team and for controlling its creative output.

   a. Explain how the advertising plan can be used by the advertising manager to direct and control creative efforts.
   b. Does use of the advertising plan in this way mean that the creative team should not participate in the preparation of the plan?

3. Research done on commercials thought most annoying by consumers has found that the Mr. Whipple commercials for Charmin are high on the list. In spite of this fact the product has been a highly successful one in a product category where advertising is a dominant element in the marketing mix. What is the relationship of annoyance to advertising effectiveness? Should the advertising manager for Charmin permit the use of such techniques or is it a matter of creative judgment best left to the creative team?

4. In many firms, particularly larger ones, advertising executions prepared by the advertising agency must be successively approved by a hierarchy of marketing executives. For example, a recommended layout may be submitted for approval first to an assistant brand manager who would forward it to a brand manager who, in turn, may send it to the advertising manager who may review it with the marketing manager.

   a. What creative problems might such a multi-level approval process create?
   b. Suggest an alternative approval process to avoid these creative problems.

5. The text suggests several elements that should be included in a copy platform. See if you can write a copy platform for the Tall Collection ad shown in Exhibit 16-3 by answering the following questions:

   a. For whom is the advertisement intended?
   b. What solution is promised to the target audience?
   c. What evidence supports the promise?
   d. What information is offered to aid in purchasing?

6. The discussion of the copy platform in this chapter lists six different kinds of information frequently included in a copy platform. For each of the following copy statements, indicate the kind of information being conveyed.

   a. It makes sense to buy this month at these reduced prices. See your dealer today!
   b. Here's a message for every person who ever wished to own a sports car.
   c. Order today and your first payment won't be due for three months, easy payments spread over 36 months.
   d. A nationwide survey of 1,000 repairers confirmed that this brand had a lower repair rate than any other washer.
   e. At last, a product that gives all-day and all-night relief from cold's miseries in just a single dose.

7. The following advertising appeals are currently being made for automobiles. Classify each of them as emotional or rational:

   a. "Colt, it's fine to have fun while you save money."
   b. "A five-year or 50,000-mile Protection Plan."
   c. "It's amazing what fits inside a Volkswagen wagon."
   d. "The new 190 class: the quickest reflexes Mercedes-Benz has ever built into a sedan."
   e. "Pontiac 6000, engineered for total response."

8. One widely used and apparently effective television commercial approach shows a homemaker, usually young, going to an older woman for advice on some difficulty. The older woman recommends the advertiser's product and shows how the product works. What do you think accounts for the apparent effectiveness of this type of commercial?

9. Based on the evidence presented on the effectiveness of fear appeals, do you think that it would be desirable to use fear appeals in advertisements designed to accomplish the following:

   a. Discourage young people from experimenting with drugs.
   b. Discourage driving while intoxicated.
   c. Discourage dropping out of school.
   d. Encourage use of room deodorizers.

10. Many advertising appeals can be written in either positive or negative form. For each of the following slogans, identify whether it is in positive or negative form. Then rewrite it to place it in the opposite form. Finally, compare the positive and negative forms of each slogan and decide which one sounds more appropriate.

   a. "If you buy universal life from Metropolitan, you won't have to worry whether you've done the right thing."

   b. "Nothing unimportant ever happens at the Plaza."
   c. "If you can point, you can use a Macintosh."
   d. "When spreadsheets don't give you the picture get Energraphics."
   e. "Your PC can't manage without the new Context MBA."

*PROBLEM*

Peters, one of three large Australian ice cream marketers, was facing an increasingly competitive situation from lower quality, cut-priced, private-label ice creams and ice milks.[16] To combat the resulting sales decline, Peters decided to introduce a new product—a natural ice cream to coincide with Australians' increasing interest in natural foods. The product would contain only natural ingredients such as real eggs, fresh milk and cream, raw sugar, and natural flavorings and colorings.

The new ice cream, which had not been named, was to be marketed initially in two flavors—vanilla bean and honey-nut. The product was to be premium priced at nearly twice the price of regular ice cream. The new product would be packaged in traditional cardboard packages rather than in more modern plastic containers.

From research conducted on the new product, Peters' marketing executives believed that prime prospects were woman in higher socio-economic classes and those with awareness and interest in health foods. Women in their 20s and those over 40 with grown children appeared to be above-average prospects. It also appeared that the best prospects tended to be people not currently buying regular ice cream.

1. Prepare a positioning statement for Peters' new natural ice cream.
2. Write a copy platform for the new product.
3. What would you name the new product?

---

[16]Based on Ramona Bechtos, "Peters Joins Health Food Craze with Natural Ice Cream," *Advertising Age* (May 19, 1975), pp. 50ff.

An ad for Bisquick using a recipe as a central idea. **EXHIBIT 17-3**

## And you thought Bisquick® only made pancakes.

### Impossible Cherry Pie

*The pie that's impossibly easy because it makes its own crust. And it's filled with the harvest-fresh goodness of Thank You Brand® cherry pie filling.*

1 cup milk
2 tablespoons margarine or butter, softened
¼ teaspoon almond extract
2 eggs
½ cup Bisquick® baking mix

¼ cup sugar
1 can (21 ounces) Thank You® cherry pie filling (or Thank You® Lite cherry pie filling)
Streusel (below)

Heat oven to 400°. Grease pie plate, 10 x 1½ inches. Beat all ingredients except pie filling and Streusel until smooth, 15 seconds in blender on high or 1 minute with hand beater. Pour into plate. Spoon pie filling evenly over top. Bake 25 minutes. Top with Streusel. Bake until Streusel is brown, about 10 minutes longer. Cool; refrigerate any remaining pie.

**Streusel:** Cut 2 tablespoons firm margarine or butter into ½ cup Bisquick baking mix, ½ cup packed brown sugar and ½ teaspoon ground cinnamon until crumbly.

**High Altitude:** Increase second bake time to 15 to 20 minutes.

*Bisquick is a registered trademark of General Mills, Inc.              © General Mills, Inc. 1983
*Thank You is a registered trademark of Curtice-Burns, Inc.

Published courtesy of General Mills, Inc.

**EXHIBIT 17-4**     An analogy used as a central idea.

Courtesy: Lowe's, Inc. and J. Walter Thompson.

Use of exaggerated visuals as a central idea for IBM's Displaywriter.

**EXHIBIT 17-5**

**INFORMATION SYSTEMS GROUP**

## "DEMO REV. 2"

COMM'L NO.: IMDO 3053

LENGTH: 30 SECONDS

ANNCR: (VO) We'd like to give you a quick demonstration of the IBM Displaywriter Office System. It let's you type . . .

edit . . .

and file, electronically.

It points out misspelled words--and the correct alternatives.

It can be used as a computer

and it can send information to whoever needs it.

The IBM Displaywriter . . . helps you get your job done so quickly,

it helps you look good.

Courtesy: IBM

Produced by Doyle Dane Bernbach, Inc.

# "dBASE II® helps keep us on our toes."

*Robert Hubert*
*Marketing Director*
*The Boston Ballet*

"The Boston Ballet was a company in search of a computer when I joined the organization earlier this year. And, after discovering that a large computer system was being considered, I urged a smaller, more sensible first step.

"Since almost no one at The Boston Ballet had any previous computer experience, I strongly recommended the purchase of a microcomputer and dBASE II.

"dBASE II, the relational database management system from Ashton-Tate, would give the people in the Company the time and the opportunity to get used to computing before bringing in a larger, more expensive system later on.

"dBASE II is a command-driven, highly flexible system that can be used for a great variety of applications ranging from very simple to highly complex."

## A premier performer from Day One.

"dBASE II manages our extensive season subscriber mailings; keeps track of all our advertising insertions, costs and efficiency; and makes project time management a snap. We are now making plans to use dBASE II in handling the special promotions and manpower analyses critical to our day-to-day management.

"dBASE II made an immediate and sizeable impact on the efficiency of our operation."

## The real kicker.

"Recently, we hired a custom systems house to develop a long-range computer program for The Boston Ballet. Without prejudice, they came back and said the new system should be based on dBASE II."

dBASE II can provide you with virtuoso performance, regardless of your application.

For more about dBASE II, contact Ashton-Tate today. 10150 West Jefferson Boulevard, Culver City, CA 90230. (800) 437-4329, ext. 217 . In Colorado (303) 799-4900. In the U.K. (0908) 568866.

## ASHTON·TATE ▪

# CHAPTER 17

The first step in building the creative program, determining the advertising content, has been described. The copy platform resulting from this first step provides a common message base for the many individual advertisements that must be created for the product. In this chapter we will consider the second step in the creative process — creating the ads that will carry the advertiser's message to the consumer.

## Finding a Central Idea

In Chapter 16 we described the process of creating an advertisement. The creative specialist first absorbs factual information about the consumer, the product, and the market, and notes the direction indicated by the positioning, the objectives, and the copy platform. With this background the specialist searches for a central idea that will provide the focal point around which the individual advertisement will be built.

### Relationship of the Central Idea to the Content

The measure of a good central idea is its effectiveness in expressing the copy content to the consumer.

WHAT IS A CENTRAL IDEA? The **central idea** in an advertisement is the verbal or visual device used to present the copy content to the reader, listener, or viewer of the advertisement. Copy platforms, even though they are expressed in consumer language, usually make dull reading. A copy platform by itself would make a poor advertisement.

The central idea provides a context or situation within which the copy content can be expressed or illustrated. The central idea may be a visual element (an illustration), a verbal element (a statement), or a combination of the two.

After finding a central idea, illustrations must be selected, the various elements of the copy content integrated into the advertisement, the product name or package illustration added, and the layout of these various elements decided.

FUNCTIONS OF THE CENTRAL IDEA. The purpose of the central idea is to help communicate the copy content. The central idea contributes to this communication goal in several ways, which can perhaps best be illustrated by referring to the advertisement for the Ford Escort Diesel shown in Exhibit 17-1. This model is positioned as a subcompact car that gives competitively superior fuel economy because of its diesel engine.

To clearly and convincingly communicate this key benefit, the creators of the ad seized upon a simple and easily understood central idea—comparison of the mileage of the Ford Escort Diesel with that of a motorcycle.

*Attracts Prospects.* The central idea must attract prospects to the ad and quickly communicate the key benefit of the product. Usually the central idea is communicated through the illustration and the headline. According to an often-quoted advertiser's rule of thumb, 80 percent of all consumers who look at an ad notice only the illustration and the headline. These two elements must communicate the product benefit and its relevance to the consumer's need or the reader will be lost. The headline and the associated illustration in the Ford Escort ad quickly communicate that the ad has information for people considering an automobile purchase and particularly those who are interested in fuel economy.

*Clarifies Key Benefit.* Perhaps the most important contribution that the central idea must make is to clarify the benefit offered by the advertiser's product. The central idea must make the product attribute understandable and should help to establish the credibility of the promised benefits. In the Escort ad the most important function of the central idea is to draw reader attention to the mileage benefit and to make its competitive superiority both memorable and believable. One of the problems is that there is such a welter of competitive fuel economy claims that consumers both forget and confuse the advertisements. Escort attempts to overcome this with a distinctive comparison of their car's economy with a consumer standard of economical transportation—the motorcycle.

An advertisement with a distinctive central idea.

EXHIBIT 17-1

# Ford Escort Diesel: Better mileage than this leading import.

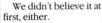

We didn't believe it at first, either.

But EPA testing figures established it. Our new Escort Diesel is rated approximately four miles per gallon higher than a Honda 750.*

Just take a look at our numbers:

**46** EPA EST. MPG.

**68** EST. HWY.

And because this diesel is an Escort, there's a lot more to talk about than great economy.

Like the fact that Escort's the best-selling car in the world.**

Or that it comes with more total passenger room and more total cargo room than a Honda Accord.†

More standard features than a Toyota Tercel.††

There's even a fully independent suspension system for a smoother ride than a Nissan Sentra.

All of which means Ford Escort not only gives you a big advantage over that motorcycle pictured above.

It also beats more than its share of cars.

*THE BEST-BUILT AMERICAN CARS.*

When we say "Quality is Job 1," we are talking about more than a commitment. We are talking about results. A recent survey concluded Ford makes the best-built American cars. The survey measured owner-reported problems during the first three months of ownership of 1983 cars designed and built in the U.S.

And that commitment continues in 1984.

* For comparison, Honda 750 mileage is obtained from EPA emissions testing and is *not* an official rating. FS Diesel mileage applicable to sedans without power steering and A/C. Available for order. Your mileage may vary depending on speed, trip length, weather. Actual highway mileage lower. All Escort Diesel models except the FS available in California.

** Sales estimates based on worldwide production figures.

† Based on EPA Interior Volume Index.

††Escort GL (shown) compared to Toyota Tercel 3-door deluxe liftback.

Get it together — Buckle up.

**Have You Driven A Ford... Lately?**

*Sets Product Apart.* If the central idea in an advertisement is unique or distinctive, it will serve to set the advertiser's product apart from competition. Advertising ideas that are too much like competitor's advertisements run the serious risk of being misidentified by consumers as the competitor's advertising or simply not remembered at all.

Most studies of the misidentification problem have been done with television although the problem undoubtedly occurs as well in other media. In one famous early study using a sample of television viewers only 26 percent were able, when asked, to recall a particular commercial. Of this 26 percent, only 9.4 percent could identify the name of the product advertised, 10.1 percent did not know, and 6.5 percent named the wrong product.[1] A more recent study conducted over a five-year period revealed that while 65 percent of a target TV audience recalled a brand name, only 38 percent were able to link the brand name to a communications point in the brand's commercial. The clutter of too many advertisements is a prime cause of lack of identification and misidentification. Creatively this problem can be attacked by finding distinctive central ideas that make the advertiser's approach very different from that of other advertisers.

*Does Not Obscure Product.* The function of the central idea is to make the product the "hero" of the advertisement. A danger that must be guarded against is the central idea that overshadows or is irrelevant to the product itself. William Bernbach, chairman of the board of Doyle Dane Bernbach, Inc., stated:

> Our job is to sell our client's merchandise, not ourselves. Our job is to kill the cleverness that makes us shine instead of the product. Dullness may not sell a product, but neither will irrelevant brilliance. Our job is to simplify, to tear away the unrelated, to pluck out the weeds that are smothering the product message. Be provocative. But be sure your provocativeness stems from the product.[2]

Robert Levenson, creative director of the same agency, had a similar warning concerning television commercials:

> If you fall in love with the brilliance of a commercial take the product out. If it's still brilliant, it's no good. The commercial should crumple when its reason for existence is taken away.[3]

Judge for yourself if the Ford Escort ad meets this test. Is the product and its promised benefits the "hero" of the ad?

---

[1]"Only 38% of TV Audience Links Brands with Ads," *Marketing News* (January 6, 1984), p. 10.

[2]William Bernbach, "Bill Bernbach Defines the Four Disciplines of Creativity," *Advertising Age* (July 5, 1971), p. 22.

[3]"Just Hard Work Is Key to Creative Success, Four Tell AA Workshop," *Advertising Age* (August 2, 1971), p. 2.

## Examples of Central Ideas

The nature and importance of the central idea can perhaps be illustrated with some of the more widely used types of central ideas.

TESTIMONIALS, CELEBRITIES, AND CONTINUING CHARACTERS. According to a recent study, one out of three television commercials features a celebrity,[4] and the use of a celebrity as a central idea is not limited to television. This central idea can take a wide variety of forms. Some are testimonials in which celebrities (like Arnold Palmer for Pennzoil) testify why they use the advertiser's product. In other cases the executive of a company may serve as the spokesperson for that company. Lee Iacocca, the chief executive officer of Chrysler Corporation, served in this way for Chrysler cars. Exhibit 17-2 shows a commercial featuring Gloria Vanderbilt promoting jeans that carry her name. Sometimes advertisers use continuing characters, like Titus Moody for Pepperidge Farm, who are not celebrities and sometimes these characters are imaginary like the Jolly Green Giant of the Green Giant Co. (a division of Pillsbury Co.), or Elsie the Cow and Family used in many of Borden's commercials.

What is it that the advertiser accomplishes by using these personalities? Most obvious, perhaps, a celebrity attracts attention to an advertisement. They are celebrities because people are interested in them and listen to them. Continued use of personalities in advertisements also sets an advertiser apart from its competition. Hertz's long-term use of O. J. Simpson has certainly separated it in people's minds from Avis.

More important, perhaps, personalities can enhance and support the central message that they are delivering if they are selected because they are somehow identified with the product field. Gloria Vanderbilt is a relevant spokesperson for jeans not because her name is on the product, but because she is known as a fashion designer. Titus Moody is an appropriate personality for Pepperidge Farms because he represents an era of old-fashioned, wholesome foods and cooking.

Some advertisers feel that celebrities are overused and a distraction. Ogilvy suggests: "Viewers have a way of remembering the celebrity but forgetting the product."[5]

PRODUCT USES AND RECIPES. A central idea frequently used for products that have a variety of uses or applications is to illustrate one or more specific ways in which the product can be used. Food ingredient products frequently take this approach by featuring recipes using the advertised product. Exhibit 17-3 at the beginning of the chapter illustrates the recipe as central idea as it is used for Bisquick Baking Mix. The year-in, year-out popularity of the recipe approach indicates that practitioners find it a powerful central idea. Its effectiveness probably lies in the specific problem solution that the recipe and the product provide to the reader.

---

[4]"The Big New Celebrity Boom," *Business Week* (May 22, 1978), pp. 77–80.
[5]David Ogilvy, *Ogilvy on Advertising, op. cit.*, p. 109.

**EXHIBIT 17-2**    A celebrity testimonial commercial for Gloria Vanderbilt jeans.

(MUSIC UNDER THROUGHOUT)
GLORIA VO: When a woman wears black

she expects something to happen.

When a woman wears my new Gloria Vanderbilt Black Denim jeans it usually does.

(LIGHTS START GOING OFF MAGICALLY)
They've got the fit the jeans are famous for...

(HALL LIGHTS GO OFF AS WOMAN WALKS PAST THEM)
The tailoring, the details and more.

Gloria Vanderbilt Black Denims...

have all the mystery and magic...

(CANDLES GO OUT)
of black.

Gloria Vanderbilt Black Denim...jeans? It's a shame to call them jeans.

ANALOGY AND ASSOCIATION. Product attributes, particularly social and psychological benefits, are often communicated symbolically. Rather than directly claiming that the product contains the attribute, the claim is established by association of the product with objects symbolizing the desired attribute.

The Kitty Litter Brand advertisement in Exhibit 17-4 at the beginning of the chapter utilizes an amusing yet graphic analogy as its central idea. The skunk-like cat is not only an arresting illustration, but the analogy of the cat with the skunk's reputation as a foul-smelling animal is very clear.

EXAGGERATED SITUATIONS. A central idea frequently involves fantasy, exaggerated situations, or photographic tricks. To be effective, the exaggerated situation or graphic device must focus on clarifying the product promise. By its unusualness, the exaggerated situation can also attract readers or viewers to the advertisement, make the message memorable, and set the advertiser apart from competitive products.

While exaggerated situations are frequently used in television where trick photographic effects are possible, they can also be used in print advertising. The commercial for IBM's Displaywriter in Exhibit 17-5 at the beginning of the chapter uses this sort of exaggerated situation. By means of photographic tricks, filing cabinet drawers, dictionaries, and mail slots are made to spring out of the computer screen to illustrate the capabilities of the Displaywriter.

CASE HISTORIES AND SLICE OF LIFE. Another widely used central idea employs a case history to show the benefit that one user obtained from the advertiser's product. This approach is widely used for business products and services such as in the Ashton-Tate advertisement for *dBASEII*® shown in Exhibit 17-6 at the beginning of the chapter. The case history relates how one organization, the Boston Ballet, used the *dBASEII*® software package with a microcomputer as a way of introducing themselves to computing before investing in a large and expensive system. This central idea serves all the functions of attracting prospects, clarifying the promise, and setting the product or service apart, but, in particular, the story adds believability to the promise by presenting the benefits actually received by one user.

The case history approach can be used in any medium that provides an opportunity to present a rather long story. One central idea form similar to the case history has developed in television and is called "slice of life." Slice-of-life commercials are short playlets in which a problem is set forth and the actors use the advertiser's product to solve the problem. Since these slice-of-life situations are not usually true-to-life portrayals, their purpose is less to establish believability than to explain the benefit of the product. The Hostess Donut television commercial shown in Chapter 16, page 433, to illustrate problem-solution content uses a slice-of-life approach to presenting the product benefits.

DEMONSTRATIONS. A demonstration illustrates the benefit of the advertiser's product by showing how the product works, usually in a contrived situation. Demonstration is a widely used type of central idea in television because television can show a sequence of events, usually necessary in a demonstration. However, as illustrated by the demonstration approach in the Wagner Power Painter ad in Exhibit 17-7, demonstration can also be effective as the central idea in print media. The relative effectiveness can be judged by comparing this print ad with the television commercial for the same product shown in Exhibit 14-5. The strength of the demonstration approach lies in its ability to clarify how the product works and how it can benefit the consumer. The demonstration can, if it is not overly artificial, lend believability to the advertiser's promise.

### Techniques for Expressing the Central Idea

Once the central idea has been devised, many questions will remain concerning the most effective way of expressing it to consumers. Presentation styles and devices available are considered in the sections which follow.

THE USE OF HUMOR. The advertiser frequently has the choice between a humorous and a serious style of presentation. When the humorous approach is well executed, it encourages the consumer to read or view the advertisement because it promises entertainment. A humorous advertisement tends to stand out from the clutter of competitive advertising and be memorable. On the other hand, truly humorous advertising is probably the most difficult form of presentation to write; advertising that attempts to be humorous but is not may create unfavorable consumer reaction. Humorous advertising may also lose much of its attractiveness to its audience if the advertisement is used repeatedly. Perhaps the most common problem with humor is the danger that the product benefit will be obscured by the cleverness of the presentation.

There are guidelines regarding humor that are often suggested in advertising practice. The first is that the humor in an advertisement should be relevant to the product; the humor must revolve around the product and the consumer benefit. The second guideline is that serious products (products perceived by the consumer as solving serious problems) should not be presented humorously. One study showed that humorous ads for banks, insurance, and investment services performed poorly. "Evidently money, property, life, and death are not laughing matters."[6] On the other hand, as so often happens in advertising, there have been notable exceptions to the rule. E. F. Hutton's commercials ("When E. F. Hutton talks, people listen.") and Prudential's life insurance series are both humorous spoofs of serious topics.

---

[6]"Humor is Best Utilized with Established Products," *Marketing News* (October 1, 1982), p. 6.

EXHIBIT 17-7 Use of a demonstration as the central idea in a print ad.

WHO SHOULD PRESENT? The central idea, particularly in broadcast commercials, frequently requires that someone act in the role of the presenter. Use of a celebrity or known personality attracts attention to the message and provides a form of implied endorsement; use of an unknown presenter may create less distraction from the central promise.

In recent years some advertisements have used ordinary consumers as presenters. Because they are not perceived as professional salespeople, these presenters can be highly believable. Radio advertisers sometimes have their radio commercials presented by each program's disc jockey to take advantage of the announcer's rapport with local listeners.

ANIMATIONS VS. LIVE ACTION. In television commercials either animated (cartoon-style) presentation, live action (filmed live actors), or a combination of the two can be used. Animation is attention-getting, and it can be adapted to humor, fantasy, and exaggerated situations. It is particularly well suited to children's commercials such as the Hostess Fruit Pies commercial shown in Exhibit 17-8. There is always a danger in animation that the cleverness of the technique will overwhelm the message. Live action is better suited to presenting more serious, more realistic situations.

In print advertising a choice must be made between photographic illustration and original artwork (including cartoons). Photographic illustrations are most often used to project reality, immediacy, and believability; artwork is better adapted to romantic, abstract, and, if desired, exaggerated situations.

COMPARATIVE ADVERTISING. A decision that the advertiser faces, and one that has aroused considerable controversy, is whether or not to directly compare one's products with competitors' products. Even more controversial, should competitors be referred to by name?

Prior to 1971, there was little comparative advertising that identified competitors and both regulatory authorities and trade associations discouraged its use. A major change came about in 1972 when the Federal Trade Commission persuaded television networks to relax their bans on comparative advertising. After that, many trade associations also relaxed their previous opposition and the use of comparative advertising increased markedly.[7]

The FTC's encouragement of comparative advertising is based on the belief that it results in better-informed consumers who are alerted to the brands available and the questions that they should be asking about them.[8] However, if the competitive comparisons are inaccurate or unfair, comparative advertising is a disservice to consumers and is illegal. Comparative advertising has been the source of a great many complaints to

---

[7]*Identifying Competitors in Advertising,* (New York: The National Advertising Review Board, July, 1977), pp. 3–7.
[8]"Westen: Comparative Ads Spur Flow of Facts," *Advertising Age* (November 14, 1977), p. 6.

An animated commercial designed especially for children.

EXHIBIT 17-8

(MUSIC UNDER)
(SFX: THUNDER, LIGHTNING)

GIRL: This house isn't haunted, is it?
(SFX: CRASH)

BOY: Do something, Fruit Pie the Magician.

FRUIT PIE: My wand...
BOY: We're falling!

FRUIT PIE: Oh, drat! So are the Hostess Fruit Pies and...Twinkies Cakes.

GIRL: I wanna go home.

TWINKIE: That's easy! Yahoooo!
BOY: Twinkie the Kid.

BOY & GIRL: Saved!

FRUIT PIE: Now for Hostess Fruit Pies. Apple and Cherry.
TWINKIE: And Twinkies.

GIRL: Creamed filling.

BOY: Real fruit filling.

EERIE VOICE: You get a big delight in every bite of Hostess Fruit Pies and Twinkies Cakes.

regulatory authorities since 1972. The National Advertising Review Board has provided guidelines for comparative advertising which say that such ads should be accurate, should not be used solely to upgrade a product by comparison, should make comparisons in terms of significant (to the consumers) benefits, should provide claim substantiation, and should not disparage competitors.[9]

When should the advertiser consider using comparative claims and naming competitors? According to two studies done by Ogilvy & Mather advertising agency, the answer is "never." Their research showed comparative ads to be more confusing, less memorable, and more likely to be misidentified as to sponsor than noncomparative ads. Other studies have shown no significant difference in persuasiveness between comparative and noncomparative ads.[10]

On the other hand, the widespread use of comparative ads suggests that they may be useful in some cases. If, for example, a brand has a clearcut, demonstrable product advantage of which consumers are unaware, then comparative advertising may be desirable, especially if the product advantage is potentially important to the purchaser. Small, lesser-known brands also find comparative advertising an effective approach in challenging better-known brands. However, the better-known brand should generally refrain from counterattacking the comparative ads of a lesser-known competitor with its own comparative ads.

COLOR VS. BLACK AND WHITE. The decision to use color should be based upon the requirements of the central idea. For some products, such as foods, clothing, and fashion items, color illustration is essential to the product portrayal. In such cases color is a valuable supplement to the central idea of the advertisement. The Bisquick advertisement shown in Exhibit 17-3 at the beginning of the chapter appropriately uses color to heighten the appetite appeal of the recommended recipe. Sometimes color is used more as an embellishment to call attention to the advertisement or to emphasize one element in the advertisement. As an example, see the Ashton-Tate ad in Exhibit 17-6 at the beginning of the chapter where color is limited to the illustration, calling the reader's attention to it and lending it a special artistic quality.

In a medium where color is the exception rather than the usual practice, the use of color may increase the number noting the advertisement. However, the audience may note the color rather than the product benefit if the two are not integrated. The better practice is to attract consumer attention with a compelling product idea rather than with an irrelevant element.

---

[9]*Identifying Competitors, op. cit.,* pp. 12–14.

[10]Nancy Giges, "Comparative Ads: Better Than...?" *Advertising Age* (September 22, 1980), p. 60.

MUSIC AND SOUND EFFECTS. Music and sound effects used in broadcast advertising are sometimes the principal element of a central idea (such as a jingle in a radio commercial), but more often music is used to integrate the various visual and verbal elements in a commercial to give a sense of flow and continuity.

The decision to use music or sound effects should be made using the same criterion applied to the use of color. Music and sound effects should be used if they contribute to expression of the central idea and the product benefit.

SIGNATURE OR SIGN-OFF LINES. Many ads and commercials are closed with a standardized **signature line** that is designed to provide integration and continuity among different advertisements of the same product. Examples include Ford's "Have you driven a Ford...lately?" and Maxwell House's "Good to the last drop." Signature lines are often used in conjunction with a trademark or with a logotype. A **logotype** is a company or product name having a distinctive type treatment or a distinctive art treatment or both. The Ford Escort ad in Exhibit 17-1 is an exemplification of the use of both a signature line and a logotype.

*signature line*

*logotype*

Signature or sign-off lines are usually used to tie together various ads in a series and to relate them to a more general reputation of the advertiser. Care should be taken that signature items do not clutter an advertisement and detract from communicating the product benefit and other useful consumer information.

PRODUCT NAME AND PACKAGE. In addition to using a product symbol, advertisements must clearly name and identify the product being advertised to combat the acute problem of consumers misidentifying the product. Ogilvy & Raphaelson report that television commercials that do not show the product package or do not end with a visual of the brand name score below average in changing brand preference.[11] Using a picture of the product also helps consumers identify the product inside the store.

## Creating the Print Advertisement

Determining the central idea is the vital step in the creation of any advertisement, whether intended for a print or a broadcast medium. However, once the central idea has been decided upon, the process of completing the creation of an advertisement is different for print than for broadcast advertising. Consequently further steps in creating advertisements will be considered separately for print and broadcast.

---

[11]Ogilvy and Raphaelson, *op. cit.*, p. 15.

## Elements of the Print Advertisement

A print advertisement has four basic physical elements—headline, illustration, body copy, and signature. Each of these elements should support the central idea of the advertisement and, in so doing, help present the promised benefit from the product. Each of the four print elements plays a special part in this process of communicating with the consumer. The function of each element will be illustrated by means of the KitchenAid dishwasher advertisement shown in Exhibit 17-9. It appears from the advertisement that KitchenAid has positioned its new dishwasher as one that is competitively superior because it has a filtration system and hard food grinder that permits dishes to be washed without prerinsing. The central idea in the ad is a demonstration of the messy prerinsing job that is avoided through use of the KitchenAid dishwasher.

FUNCTION OF THE HEADLINE. The headline in a print advertisement is normally the first part of the advertisement read. It is important that it quickly present the problem that the ad is directed to or the benefit offered. This permits the reader to judge the relevance of the information and to judge whether or not to read further. (Remember the rule of thumb that 80 percent of all readers do not go beyond the headline.) The headline thus serves to select those readers to whom the ad is relevant. This is best done by posing the problem to be solved or by presenting the product benefit being offered. This can often be accomplished by stating the central idea in words. In the KitchenAid ad, the headline clearly states the no-more-rinsing benefit offered by the new dishwasher. The headline in this case is, as it should be, closely related to the illustration with the headline serving to explain or amplify the central idea pictured in the illustration. The headline statement "you've just rinsed your last dish" is closely related to the illustration that demonstrates a messy dish-rinsing chore.

Finally, the headline, in the course of presenting the product benefit, will frequently identify the brand name of the product being advertised. Practice varies in this respect, depending on the strength of product identification in the illustration and signature elements. Somewhere in the advertisement there should be strong product identification to prevent consumer confusion concerning which brand is being advertised. The headline, as in the case of the KitchenAid advertisement, offers one opportunity for product identification.

FUNCTION OF THE ILLUSTRATION. The illustration plays a major role in communicating the central idea and through it the product benefit. This is how the illustration is used in the KitchenAid dishwasher ad. The illustration is a vivid demonstration of the disagreeable job of rinsing that can be avoided by using a KitchenAid dishwasher.

In selecting the illustration, primary consideration should be given to its ability to clearly and quickly communicate the central idea and product benefit. Illustrations need to be relevant to the product and the benefit

An ad illustrating the four elements of a print ad.

EXHIBIT 17-9

The new KitchenAid® KD-21 dishwasher will revolutionize the way you do dishes—actually let you go right from the table to the dishwasher.

So now you can skip the rinsing. And your dishes will *still* come out cleaner than ever.

This is no ordinary dishwasher. It has a unique triple filtration system, with a hard-food disposer, that grinds up and washes away bits of food.

# THE NEW KITCHENAID® DISHWASHER. YOU'VE JUST RINSED YOUR LAST DISH.

Even an occasional olive pit is no problem. (Naturally, you'll want to drop bones or large food pieces in the trash can.)

We're convinced this is the best dishwasher money can buy. But don't take our word for it. An independent testing lab proved the new KitchenAid dishwasher cleans better than GE, Maytag, Whirlpool and Sears.

If you'd like to see the results, write us. Better yet, stop in and talk to your local KitchenAid dealer.

After all, haven't you done enough rinsing?

**KitchenAid®**
For the way it's made.™

Courtesy:  HOBART CORPORATION

being offered. If the illustration is of dominant size, it is an important element in attracting reader attention because readers usually see the illustration first and judge from it the relevance and usefulness of the entire ad. If the illustration is relevant to a problem that your prospects have, they will be attracted to the ad. Pictures of children and animals tend to be eye-catching, but if such an illustration is not germane to the benefit being offered, it will attract the wrong prospects and deliver the wrong message to them. The KitchenAid illustration, although perhaps not as eye-pleasing as a picture of a child or an animal, deliver a strongly relevant message to readers.

Advertisers in selecting illustrations often include the product. This, again, is an opportunity to reinforce product identification. In the case of products sold in self-service outlets this is particularly important since it helps consumers to identify the product in the store. In the KitchenAid ad, although the product is not shown in the main illustration, it is shown in a secondary illustration that is a part of the signature.

FUNCTION OF THE BODY COPY. The primary function of the body copy is to provide explanation and support for the product benefit being promised by the advertisement. The body copy uses the central idea as a springboard for amplifying or clarifying the benefits offered by the product, thus maintaining close integration of illustration, headline, and the body copy. The body copy provides evidence that supports the validity of the benefits being promised in an attempt to make them believable. Other necessary purchase information is also included in the body copy.

The length of the body copy and the amount of detail provided depend on both the product and the needs of the audience. The KitchenAid dishwasher advertisement has rather long copy for a consumer ad because there is a considerable amount of supporting information available that explains why the dishwasher does not require prerinsing of dishes. One of the problems that KitchenAid would have with an advertisement offering this benefit would be to gain reader believability. Since the purchase is a high cost, high risk one, consumers would probably find the long copy useful.

FUNCTION OF THE SIGNATURE ELEMENTS. The signature elements include product name or logotype, product illustrations, and signature lines. These elements serve two functions. They name the product and provide a visual symbol by which the consumer can identify the product. A picture of the product provides an important service to consumers by helping them to identify it, as was mentioned above. In today's self-service outlets the consumer does not ask for the product, but looks for it.

In addition, the signature elements tie together or integrate different advertisements for the same product. Standardized signature elements help a consumer to relate one advertisement for a product to another for the same product so that the effect of the messages is cumulative.

KitchenAid effectively uses a product picture, their logotype, and the signature line "For the way it's made" as integrative elements.

## Layout of the Print Advertisement

The arrangement of the elements of a print advertisement is formed in a layout. A **layout** is a design showing the size and spatial arrangement of the elements of the advertisement. Preliminary layouts are termed "roughs" or "rough layouts." They are progressively refined to form "finished" or "comprehensive" layouts. Exhibit 17-10 shows a rough layout prepared for Hershey's Cocoa whose positioning and copy platform were presented in Chapter 16. The finished advertisement that resulted from this layout is shown in Exhibit 17-11.

*layout*

Preparation of advertising layouts requires design skills and is usually entrusted to an art director or designer who works in conjunction with the copywriter. To be effective, the design of the advertisement must accomplish four objectives, each of which is discussed in the sections which follow.

UNIFYING THE ELEMENTS. The most important function of the layout is to unify the four elements of the print advertisement — illustration, headline, body copy, and signature elements. The designer of the layout must arrange the elements so that they each contribute to the central idea rather than allowing them to function as independent elements.

Note how the Wolverine Waterproof Boot advertisement in Exhibit 17-12 has achieved this unity of design. The headline and the illustration establish the central idea (a negative one in this case) that wearing the wrong boots results in wet feet. The illustration pictures the central idea while the headline expresses it in words. The headline has been placed around the illustration so that both are viewed and considered as a single unit.

The solution to the problem is contained in the body copy and signature elements. The body copy picks up the problem statement of the central idea and then offers Wolverine Waterproof Boots as the solution. The picture of the boots and the Wolverine logotype illustrate the solution being proposed in the body copy. Note how the designer has integrated the signature elements into the body copy so that the reader views the copy and the illustration of the boots at the same time.

GUIDING THE READING SEQUENCE. By the arrangement of the elements and the weight given to them, the design of the advertisement can encourage the consumer to read the advertisement in the desired sequence.

Readers have a natural tendency to enter an advertisement somewhere on the upper portion and to the left of center, then to proceed down the page as they are attracted by the elements of the advertisement. Designers tend to take advantage of this natural tendency by placing the element that should be viewed first in the upper half of the page, often to the left. Note how the placement of the illustration in the Wolverine advertisement encourages immediate viewing of this particular element.

EXHIBIT 17-10 A rough layout for a Hershey's Cocoa advertisement.

If you think this cake is moist, rich and chocolatey...

you should have tried this one!

Hershey's Cocoa made it better.

EXHIBIT 17-12        An advertisement for Wolverine Waterproof Boots.

# Stop messing around with the wrong boots.

You don't have to put up with wet socks and soggy feet when you're messing around in mud or snow or just plain wet.

What you need is waterproof boots. Not just water-repellent boots, but boots that really don't leak. Wolverine Waterproof Boots.

Made with a unique polyurethane sole, it's oil proof and wears many times longer than any other sole yet is astonishingly light and has a strong non-slip grip.

The uppers are top-grade, genuine English cowhide, especially tanned to be waterproof and acid resistant. A boot in breathable leather that won't leak. We're so sure we guarantee it.

The whole boot is insulated and cushioned for the most comfort you've ever felt.

They have all the style you'd expect from Wolverine. The makers of the finest in work and sport boots.

So when you mess around, do it in new Wolverine Waterproof Boots. So you won't get off on the wrong foot.

# Get the new Wolverine Waterproof boot.

A product of
**WOLVERINE**
WWW WORLD WIDE

For the Wolverine dealer nearest you, call this toll free number: 800-243-6100. In Connecticut: 853-3600.

©1971 WOLVERINE WORLD WIDE, INC., ROCKFORD, MICHIGAN 49341 – Hush Puppies® shoes, hats; Wolverine® shoes, boots, gloves, caps; Rossignol™ Skis; Trappeur™ ski boots; Wolverine/Killy après ski boots, gloves, helmets; Bates Floaters.® Phi Bates shoes; Sioux Mox® moccasins, slippers; Trendsetter sandals, boots; Verde® shoes; Clarino® poromeric upper material; Pigskin by Wolverine.®

Courtesy: Wolverine World Wide, Inc.

The readers' sequence after the initial contact is influenced by their interest in the subject and their desire to get more information, but the design can also influence the sequence. Because the natural tendency is to read from top to bottom of the page, the elements of layouts are usually arranged in logical sequence from top to bottom. Readers tend to move from illustrations to captions or explanation. In the Wolverine advertisement the headline serves as a caption and is a natural second element to view. The readers' sequence will tend to follow visual directions such as arrows, lines, and "gaze motion," the direction in which people or animals in illustrations are looking.

Readers' sequence is also influenced by the weight given to the elements in the advertisement. The larger the element, the more important it appears and the sooner it is likely to be read. Usually the illustration and the headline are given dominant weight in an advertisement because the advertiser wants the reader to start with those two elements. This was evidently the desire behind the Wolverine advertisement that has a dominant illustration-headline unit.

CREATING AN APPEARANCE. The design of an advertisement creates an impression of the product and the advertiser. The designer can control this impression by the way the individual elements are presented and arranged.

The layout of an advertisement should have some form of symmetry. The Ford Escort ad that was reviewed is an example of formal symmetry, connoting the strength, the solidity and the reliability that are appropriate to this kind of product. The Wolverine ad in Exhibit 17-12 presents a relaxed, less formal layout with less symmetry.

The appearance of an advertisement is also influenced by the number of elements in the advertisement and the orderliness with which they are arranged. Simple, orderly layouts appear easy to read and give the impression that the product is clean, controlled, and perhaps, expensive. Jumbled, disorderly layouts are somewhat like a crowded, disorderly store. The shopper has to work harder, but is drawn on by the suspicion that a bargain lurks somewhere within the jumble. Retailers and mail-order advertisers, in particular, sometimes use crowded, jumbled layouts to give this "bargain-basement" impression.

The selection of type style can substantially alter the appearance of an advertisement. There are hundreds of different typefaces available to select from in trying to convey an impression suitable to the product and the central idea of the advertisement. Notice how the selection of typeface (the design of the print characters) in the Wolverine advertisement contributes an impression of masculinity, authority, and strength. A quite different impression could be conveyed by type selection for a women's fashion product, for example. In that case script or a delicate form of type (having the appearance of handwriting) might convey the proper impression of femininity. Note how the selection of the typeface in the Keri Lotion ad (Exhibit 16-6, p. 429) conveys femininity.

SEPARATING THE ADVERTISEMENT FROM THE ENVIRONMENT. A final objective of the design of the advertisement is to make it stand out from the other advertisements and the editorial matter on the printed page with which the advertisement must compete for reader attention. In using design techniques that call reader attention to the advertisement, care must be taken that these devices do not detract from the central idea of the advertisement. The use of a boldly colored headline in a predominantly black and white medium is an example of an attention-getting design device that may prove distracting to the central message of the advertisement.

A satisfactory way of separating an advertisement from the environment is by using white space. Leaving areas of the advertising space blank by using wide borders and space between elements makes the advertisement stand out from the normally crowded editorial areas and invites attention by making the advertisement appear orderly and easy to read. The Wolverine advertisement is an example of judicious use of white space.

## Creating the
## Broadcast Advertisement

A television or a radio commercial draws its content from the copy platform and relies, for its interest and its focus, on a creative central idea just as does an effective print advertisement. However, the structure of a broadcast commercial is much different from that of a print advertisement. Broadcast advertising is not instantaneous as is a print advertisement. It takes place over a span of time and thus the design of the commercial must assure continuity or a compelling flow of action.

### Elements of the Broadcast
### Advertisement

Broadcast commercials are most frequently analyzed by time sequence, dividing the commercial into opening, middle, and close. The function of each of these elements is described below using the S.O.S. television commercial in Exhibit 17-13 as an example.

FUNCTION OF THE OPENING. The beginning seconds of a broadcast commercial constitute the opening. The length of the opening varies from commercial to commercial, but it can usually be recognized by its attention-getting, introductory nature.

The opening attracts the prospect viewership or listenership in the audience and introduces the central idea of the commercial. Audience members learn to anticipate when commercials are coming and, unless their attention is attracted quickly, they may physically or mentally wander away until the program resumes. The opening attempts to overcome this with a quick, provocative introduction. David Ogilvy, dean of the copywriters, suggests, "When you advertise fire extinguishers, open with the

A commercial illustrating the elements of a broadcast advertisement.

EXHIBIT 17-13

MAN'S VOICE: Honey, should rice be black?

YOUNG MAN'S VOICE: Mama, I'm bringing the whole team home for your chicken!

(SFX)

WOMAN'S VOICE: Was the meal a little greasy?

2ND MAN: Nooooooooo.

VO: You can always count on S.O.S,

because no matter how dirty, greasy...

baked or burnt your pots and pans get...

nothing cleans them faster or easier than a super grease-cutting S.O.S soap pad.

2ND WOMAN'S VOICE: Has anyone seen the roast?

VO: S.O.S. It's crazy to cook without it.

Courtesy: Miles Laboratories, Inc.

fire."[12] A usual approach is to arouse the self-interest of the prospect by stating the problem that is to be considered by the commercial. This approach attempts to focus attention-getting efforts on prospects only rather than on the total audience.

The opening also serves to introduce the central idea that will be elaborated upon in the middle of the commercial. The expression of the central idea often serves as the interest-awakening device. In the Miles Laboratories S.O.S. commercial in Exhibit 17-13, the curiosity and interest of the prospect audience is aroused by a dimly lit view through the back of a kitchen storage cabinet — a view dominated by the outline of what appears to be a box of some kind. The problem is posed by a naive query: ". . . should rice be black?" The second frame quickly reveals that the square outline is really a box of S.O.S. cleaning pads about to be snatched from the cabinet. The central idea of the commercial is thus made clear: S.O.S. pads are the solution to difficult and unusual cleaning problems that arise during the preparation of food. This idea is further developed during the next four frames of the storyboard.

FUNCTION OF THE MIDDLE. The middle of the commercial usually takes up half or more of the commercial time. The middle carries the principal burden of telling the advertiser's story.

In the middle of the commercial the central idea is unfolded. The purpose of this central idea is to provide a situation that dramatizes the product benefit. Finally, the central idea provides, in this middle section, a means to present support or documentation for the product benefit. All during this long middle part of the commercial, the central idea must serve to hold viewers' attention and provide ample opportunity for product identification. It should be clear in examining the structure and time constraints that a television commercial (like most other ad forms) must concentrate on only a single benefit and a single central idea.

The middle of the S.O.S. commercial is a demonstration that makes the transition from the package shots in the opening to individual soap pads being used to clean dirty, greasy pots and pans. In this commercial the middle serves primarily to reinforce and document through demonstration that S.O.S. provides a superior solution to the problem raised in the opening.

FUNCTION OF THE CLOSE. The final seconds of a commercial, after the central idea has been presented, are devoted to the close. The close is most often used to repeat the key elements of the message as a memory aid. Usually the product promise is repeated and considerable emphasis is placed on the product name and package. This is done both to overcome misidentification and to aid the consumer's recollection when shopping.

The close often includes information to facilitate action or a suggestion

---

[12]David Ogilvy, *Ogilvy on Advertising, op. cit.*, p. 111.

that the consumer take action ("Buy some today!"). Such information might include names and addresses of dealers carrying the product, information on price or payment terms, or styles, sizes, and varieties available.

The close of the S.O.S. commercial provides a brief reprise of the problem ("Has anyone seen the roast?") and the solution ("S.O.S. It's crazy to cook without it.") The closing frames show a close-up of the product to reinforce recognition of the package and brand name and hopefully to reduce confusion concerning the product being advertised.

## Design of the Broadcast Advertisement

The design of a print advertisement is concerned with the spatial arrangement of the elements of the advertisement. In a broadcast commercial the design is concerned primarily with creating a desirable time relationship among the elements.

The design of a television commercial is prepared in the form of a storyboard. The storyboard has renderings of frames to suggest the video action. Video directions in words are printed separately, usually below the frames. The spoken words and audio directions are also included below each frame showing how the spoken words coincide with the video action. Radio commercials are presented in script form such as that shown in Exhibit 17-14. The script contains both the words to be spoken and the audio direction describing the manner in which the message is to be delivered and any sound effects or music that are to be added.

The objectives that should be met in designing the broadcast advertisement are discussed below.

CREATING UNITY OF ACTION. The elements of a broadcast commercial must be unified into a smooth and continuous flow of action. This is much the same objective as in print advertising. In print, the objective of design is to unify the layout so that the reader perceives a single central idea rather than a number of independent elements. In broadcast commercials, the elements must be unified in the dimension of time. Rather than seeing an opening, a middle, and a close, the design of the commercial should assure that the viewer perceives continuous action focused on the central idea. When action is choppy or broken into sections, it interrupts viewer attention and encourages directing attention elsewhere.

Some copywriters feel that a good commercial (in television, particularly) should be designed like a very short play. The central idea is the plot and the action must be designed to maintain continuous viewer attention to the central idea from the opening when the problem is posed to the close when it is resolved. Notice in the S.O.S. commercial how smoothly the transition between opening, middle, and close is made. The opening ends in the kitchen scene which provides the location for the demonstration in the middle and for the close.

**EXHIBIT 17-14**      Radio script for a commercial.

# NH&S COPY

Needham, Harper & Steers Advertising, Inc.
909 Third Avenue, New York, N.Y. 10022
Telephone 212-758-7600

CLIENT:    ITT-CORPORATE          ET#62 - Band #2
PRODUCT:   "Flygt"
MEDIA:     Radio 60 sec.          (NB-2661)
W. O. NO.
DATE:      8/30/77               <u>AS RECORDED</u>

ANNCR:    Around parched Sunnyside, Utah, it's hard to believe there could
          ever be -- too much water.

(SFX:     WHISTLE, RUSH OF MANTRAIN UNDERGROUND)

ANNCR:    But at Kaiser Steel Corporation's Sunnyside Coal Mines,
          underground water can make mining all but impossible.

(SFX:     WATER CASCADING INTO MINE)

MINER:    We have to pump out approximately three million gallons a day...

(SFX:     ACCENT <u>PUMPING EFX</u> AND CONTINUE UNDER)

ANNCR:    The pumping's done by rugged, hardworking pumps...developed by
          Flygt, the pump people of ITT.

MINER:    We have some of these pumps that have been here...for years and
          years.

ANNCR:    These Flygt pumps by ITT haul the water through a thousand miles
          of underground pipes.

(SFX:     GRINDING AT COAL FACE)

ANNCR:    Some is used to keep down coal dust...some to wash the coal...
          and some of the water is pumped up 1200 feet to storage tanks
          and used by local farmers around Sunnyside, Utah, when their
          own water supply runs low.

MINER:    What it does, it helps keep the town green.

(SFX:     WHISTLE, MANTRAIN EFX, MINERS' VOICES)

ANNCR:    At ITT, we think the best ideas are the ideas that help people.

Courtesy: ITT Corporation and Needham, Harper & Steers Advertising, Inc.

COORDINATING AUDIO AND VIDEO. In addition to creating a smooth flow of action, there must be coordination between the audio or sound elements and the video or visual action. Radio, of course, has only audio elements, but they must be coordinated so that, for example, sound effects emphasize rather than obscure the spoken words of an announcer.

As a general rule, in television the audio and video should be coordinated so that they tell a single story at a particular moment. If, for example, the video portion is demonstrating one particular attribute of a product, the voice portion should be discussing the same attribute. All too often this rule is violated with the result that the viewer becomes confused and disinterested.

Broadcast commercials also use special audio and video effects. Sound effects and musical effects should be used to enhance the central idea, not overwhelm it. Music can be used effectively to tie together the visual elements of a commercial and give a sense of continuity or flow. Both music and sound effects can be used to accentuate or intensify certain portions of a commercial.

Many different video effects are available in television. Some, such as animation and trick photographic devices, are so intriguing that they can distract from the product message. In television, the product benefit, product name, and other information are sometimes superimposed over the picture to lend emphasis. These **supers** should appear at the time that the statement or name is spoken in the audio. In this way the audio and video messages reinforce each other. *supers*

The S.O.S. commercial does not use a super to emphasize the product benefit or name, but the package shot at the close serves the same purpose. Note how the audio and video are coordinated in the last frame.

ADJUSTING TO AVAILABLE TIME. The broadcast commercial must be designed so that it fits within the allotted time and so that the pace of the action is satisfactory. Both the proposed video action and the audio dialogue must be carefully timed to assure that they do not require more commercial time than is available. Failure to do this (and it is a common problem) makes necessary expensive revisions during production of the commercial.

The designer of the commercial must also take into account the desired pace of the audio and video action. A commercial for a prestigious perfume brand would probably require a slow pace—the action would emphasize grace rather than speed. The pace of the audio would also be slow and, perhaps, romantic. For such a commercial, there can be far less audio and video action than in the case, for example, of a commercial for a cold remedy. The pace of a commercial depends upon the product and the central idea, and it must be designed into the commercial with appropriate time allowances.

Integration of
the Creative Program

The preparation of a creative program usually involves not just a single advertisement, but a series of advertisements. The program may include advertisements for different media and advertisements directed to different audiences. Despite this diversity, each advertisement in a program should reinforce the other advertisements in the program.

### Reason for Integrating the Creative Program

*creative integration*

The process of tying together the various creative elements of an advertising program is termed **creative integration** of the campaign. The guiding principle is that all the creative elements should be unified both visually and verbally. The purpose of this unity in appearance is to reinforce one message by a later one. Suppose that a consumer sees a television commercial for a product and then, in shopping, sees a point-of-purchase display for the same product. It would be desirable if the display triggered recollection of the television commerecial.

In the same way, other elements of the program can be mutually reinforcing. For example, if two different media are used, such as television for reach and radio to build frequency, it would be desirable to have the radio commercial recall and reinforce the television message. Many times advertising is directed to the distribution channels as well as to the consumer. These trade advertisements should be tied-in to the consumer advertisements to serve as a reminder that the product is an advertised one.

### Techniques for Integrating the Creative Program

Integration of the program is achieved by using common or shared visual or verbal elements in each advertisement. Exhibit 17-15 shows some of the creative elements used in the campaign introducing an improved package for SPAM® luncheon meat made by Hormel. The central idea in this effort was a demonstration of the ease of opening the new can. The picture of the can being opened (which included a picture of the product and the SPAM® luncheon meat logotype) provided a memorable integrative device that was used in each advertisement.

INTEGRATING DIFFERENT ADVERTISEMENTS IN THE SAME MEDIUM. Tying together advertisements in the same medium is relatively easy. Since each advertisement is guided by the same positioning and the same copy platform, the product benefit will be the same and will be stated in the same way. With advertisements in the same medium, the central idea is sometimes the same or related in each advertisement. The risk in this form of

Integrated creative element in an advertising program for SPAM® luncheon meat.          **EXHIBIT 17-15**

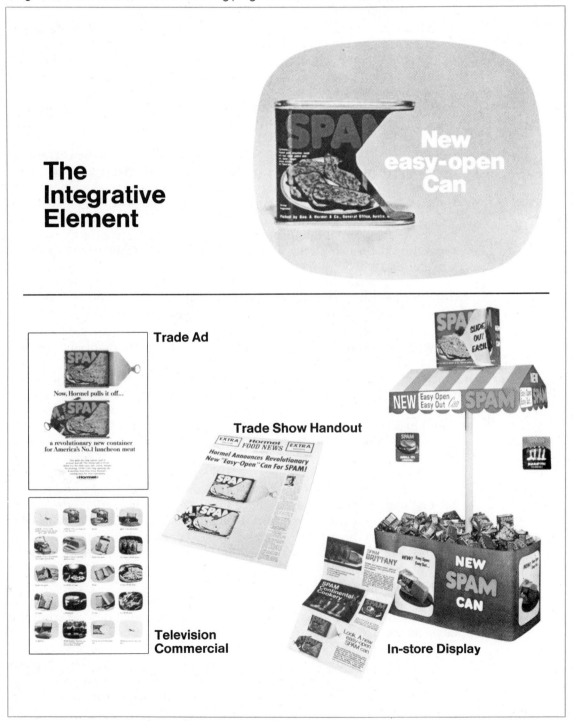

Courtesy:  Geo. A. Hormel & Co. and Batten, Barton, Durstine & Osborne, Inc.

integration is that the advertisements will look too much alike and not arouse new interest.

Other tie-in elements that can frequently be used within the same medium are common layout styles and common use of distinctive type styles, illustration techniques, logotypes, and package illustrations. In broadcast commercials it is possible to tie together different advertisements by consistent use of the same spokesperson, personality, or announcer, and by using the same music or sound effects. Signature lines are included in many advertisements as integrative devices.

INTEGRATING ADVERTISEMENTS IN DIFFERENT MEDIA. When an advertising campaign utilizes more than one medium, the advertisements in the different media should be integrated so that they reinforce one another. Integration between media is more difficult, however, because creative elements that work well in one medium may not be effective when transferred to another medium. A demonstration, for example, that is effective on television would probably not be used in radio commercials which offer no visual effects.

What creative elements can be used to tie together advertisements in different media? The positioning and the copy platform will, of course, be common to all advertisements giving each advertisement the same direction and message structure. Frequently there is a central visual device related to the central idea that can be applied to advertisements in different media. The illustration of the side pull-tab opening can in the SPAM® luncheon meat advertisement in Exhibit 17-15 provides a strong integrative device that ties together advertisements in several different media. Other creative elements that can sometimes be used to unite advertisements in different media include common use of a signature line, a personality or spokesperson, or, for broadcast commercials, music or sound effects.

INTEGRATING SUPPORTING PROMOTIONAL ELEMENTS. In addition to relating media advertisements, there should be a tie-in between the advertising and supporting promotional elements such as point-of-sale displays, store signs, and the product package. These creative elements serve as last-minute reminders to the consumer. If they contain a creative tie-in with the mass media effort, they will then serve to remind consumers of the central message just prior to purchase.

Point-of-sale displays can be integrated with the mass media effort, as was done for SPAM® luncheon meat, by utilizing visual devices from the advertisements in the displays. Frequently the illustration from a print advertisement or a central visual device from a television commercial can form the principle illustration in the point-of-sale materials. Displays often effectively state the basic product benefit, show a product or logotype, and utilize color or design elements that provide unity with other advertising.

Another approach that can be effective in uniting point-of-sale materials and mass media efforts is to show an illustration of the point-of-sale display in the advertisement. This will also provide the consumer with a visual clue to help in locating the product in the store.

Store signs and product packages have reminder value if integrative elements are included. Signs usually have only very brief messages, but the product logotype and product benefit statement can often be used to provide a tie-in with the campaign. The product package, like the point-of-sale materials, can often have two-way integration. The package can often be shown in the advertisement to show the consumer what to look for in the store. In some cases it is also possible to include on the package or label a brief reminder of the media advertising.

## Merchandising the Advertising

In most cases the primary reason for advertising is to influence consumers. However, in many instances consumer advertising also has a beneficial effect on the sales force and the distribution channels of the advertiser's product. Salespeople and distributors are more likely to stock, display, and sell products that are advertised. As a consequence, the creative program should include provision for acquainting the sales force and the trade with details of the forthcoming advertising program. This part of the creative program—frequently termed *merchandising the advertising*—may be carried out by the advertiser and may also involve assistance from the advertising media. See Chapter 15, page 408.

MERCHANDISING TO THE SALES FORCE. In the program to merchandise the advertising, the advertiser has two targets—the company's own sales force and the distributors (wholesalers, retailers, dealers) of the product.

An excellent approach to salespeople is through a sales meeting presentation of the upcoming advertising program. The presentation should be dramatic and exciting, because one of its principal objectives is to build enthusiasm. The meeting should also be informative so that the salespeople, in turn, can merchandise the program to their customers. Salespeople should be provided with printed materials that they can use in explaining the advertising program. Reprints of advertisements, copies of TV storyboards, and flyers containing media schedules can all be useful.

If a full-scale sales meeting is not possible, the advertising manager should transmit information about the advertising and printed materials to the sales force either by means of regional meetings, video conferences, or, if necessary, by mail.

MERCHANDISING TO THE TRADE. In addition to coordinating the efforts of the sales force in presenting the advertising program to trade members, the advertiser may utilize advertising aimed directly at the trade in order to merchandise the program. The two media most frequently used in this effort are trade magazines and direct mail. The advertising message should focus on describing the creative programs and the media program and should encourage stocking and display of the product. These advertisements should have a strong visual tie-in to the consumer effort.

MEDIA MERCHANDISING. In the discussion of the characteristics of the various media, it was pointed out that some of the media offer merchandising assistance to purchasers of media time or space. The most beneficial use of this merchandising assistance is in the presentation of the advertiser's plans to the trade.

Merchandising assistance by the media consists mainly of personal calls and mailings to the trade. Advertisers can effectively utilize media assistance if they follow two guidelines. First, there must be a specific request for assistance, specifying what kind of help would be most useful. Second, the media must be provided with advertising materials so that the media merchandising materials can be integrated with the mass media campaign.

---

*CHAPTER SUMMARY*

The process of creating an advertisement begins with a search for a central idea that will provide a context for communicating the copy content. The central idea attracts prospects to the ad, makes the content clear, and distinguishes the product, but it should never obscure the product. Among the more widely used central idea forms are endorsements, case histories, recipes, demonstrations, analogies, and fantasy situations. A great many techniques, such as humor, famous personalities, color, music, and sound effects, are available to help in expressing the central idea. Care should be taken that these techniques will support, rather than overshadow, the copy content.

A print ad has four physical elements—illustration, headline, body copy, and signature—each of which support the central idea and the product benefit. The illustration serves to attract readership and present the central idea. The headline states the central idea, relating it to the product benefit and the product name. Body copy serves to amplify the benefits of the product and provide supporting evidence. The signature names the product and provides a visual symbol for product identification. The most important step in laying out a print ad is to unify the elements of the ad so that each contributes to the central idea. The elements should be arranged in such a way as to encourage reading of the ad in the desired sequence. The design should convey the desired impression of the product, and should help the ad stand apart from its environment.

A broadcast advertisement can be viewed as having three elements— opening, middle and close. The opening serves to attract viewers and introduce the central idea. In the middle the central idea unfolds, dramatizing the product benefit and providing support for it. The close usually repeats the benefit and emphasizes product identification and availability. The most important job in laying out a broadcast advertisement is to create a continuous flow of action. Audio and video elements should be synchronized and the pace of the commercial should be adjusted to fit within the allotted time.

The various advertisements in a creative program should be integrated by using common visual and verbal elements. As a result of unity in appearance, the advertisements will complement and reinforce each other. The creative program should provide for acquainting the sales force and the trade with details of the advertising programs. This merchandising of the advertising program encourages sales, stocking, and display efforts on behalf of the product.

| | | |
|---|---|---|
| Central idea | Layout | *KEY TERMS* |
| Signature line | Supers | |
| Logotype | Creative integration | |

*QUESTIONS FOR DISCUSSION*

1. Referring to the advertisement for Vaseline Dermatology Formula Lotion in Exhibit 16-5, determine what the central idea is in this ad. Of the three functions of the central idea that have been suggested in this chapter, which ones do the central idea in this ad perform? Does this central idea overshadow the product?

2. Listed below are headlines from several advertising programs. Classify the central idea suggested by each headline:

   a. "Our IBM small computer steered us to greater profitability." (IBM computers)
   b. "Stop feeding your computer junk food." (Microsoft software)
   c. "Join our team to help beat MS." (Steve Garvey, National MS Sports Committee)
   d. "Protect the way hospitals do—with Baby Magic." (Mennen Baby Magic baby lotion)

3. An advertisement for the Okidata computer printer features an illustration of a violinist standing on top of an Okidata printer playing his violin. The headline reads, "The printer built like a Sherman tank performs like a Stradivarius."

   a. How would you classify this central idea?
   b. Do you think the central idea is relevant to the product and the product benefit?

4. One of the most widely used techniques in radio commercials is the jingle. Is a jingle a form of central idea? What do you think accounts for the popularity of this commercial form?

5. A central idea widely used by automobile dealers in their advertising is to have the owner of the dealership, rather than a professional announcer, present the advertising message. What do you think the dealer is trying to accomplish by this approach? Do you see any disadvantage to this approach?

6. Using the Kitty Litter Brand advertisement in Exhibit 17-4, identify the basic physical elements in that print ad. Explain how each element contributes to the message being directed to the consumer.

7. At a stockholders' meeting of a large automobile manufacturer, a stockholder rose to criticize the company's advertising because of its extensive use of white space. The stockholder suggested that the company economize either by shrinking the space to fit the copy or enlarging the message to fit the space purchased. How would you respond to this stockholder's suggestion?

8. In some commercials the transition between sections is so smooth that they are difficult to identify. Can you identify the open, middle, and close in the Gloria Vanderbilt jeans commercial in Exhibit 17-2? How does each of these elements contribute to the commercial?

9. Exhibit 17-7 is a print ad for the Wagner Power Painter and Exhibit 14-5 shows a television commercial for the same product. What are the elements, if any, that provide integration between these two advertisements?

10. In introducing a new product, marketers sometimes use the demand created by mass consumer advertising to force retailers to stock the product. It is, however, wasteful to schedule consumer advertising to run before distribution has been achieved because consumers, after seeing the ads, will be frustrated in their attempts to find the product. How can a new product marketer overcome this dilemma?

## PROBLEM

Quaker State Oil Refining Corporation has about 20 percent of the $2.5 billion motor oil market with its Quaker State brand. Recently the company decided to repackage its entire product line by moving from aluminum cans to plastic containers.[13] Quaker State was the first major motor oil brand to switch to plastic packaging. For most motor oil companies, the cost of plastic containers was prohibitive, but because of Quaker State's

[13]Based on Robert Raissman, "Quaker Converts to Plastic Bottles," *Advertising Age* (March 12, 1984), p. 6.

large sales volume plus some advances in plastic packaging technology, the company felt that plastic packaging was affordable. Quaker State marketing executives felt that the new plastic packages would give them a distinctive competitive advantage because they were easier and less messy to use.

Quaker State planned a major introductory campaign for the new packages and had set aside a $14 million budget for the effort. The introductory program was to utilize both magazine and television advertising.

A copy platform for the introductory advertising had developed as follows:

**Product name:**  Quaker State Motor Oil.

**Benefit:**  Now Quaker State comes in clean, easy-to-pour, plastic bottles.

**Support:**  Say good-by to spouts, oily rags, dirty hands, and leaky cans. Now Quaker State comes in the most convenient container you can buy. They're a cinch to open, close, and reseal. If your oil is less than a quart low, you can top it off and save the rest until later. Best of all, this unique plastic bottle is made to cost you nothing extra.

**Other information:**  If the new bottle isn't in your store now, it will be there soon. Quaker State is made from 100% Pennsylvania crude oil.

**Signature:**  Today you need an oil this good in a package this good.

1. Think of two or three central ideas that might be used for the Quaker State new package introduction. Briefly describe or sketch out the major elements of each central idea.
2. Select the best of the central ideas and prepare copy and a rough layout for a 500-line newspaper advertisement to introduce the new packages.
3. Using the same central idea, try to prepare a rough storyboard for a 30-second television commercial for the new package introduction.

# CHAPTER 18

**LEARNING OBJECTIVES**

In studying this chapter you will learn:

- The print production process.
- The broadcast production process.
- The advertising manager's role in production.

After determining content and creating the advertisements, the next step in the development of a creative program is producing the advertisements—converting layouts and storyboards into the form required for reproduction by publishers and broadcasters.

Advertising production is an area where the advertising manager must rely heavily on specialists. Not only is the knowledge and talent of these specialists required, but, in addition, production of advertising requires specialized facilities that few advertisers can afford to own themselves. The advertiser using an agency will usually have agency production specialists subcontract for and supervise the production of the advertising. The advertiser who does without an agency must double as production supervisor. In either case, the advertising manager should be conversant with the production process so that adequate control over the results can be maintained.

In the sections that follow, we will consider the print advertising production sequence separately from broadcast production because the processes are very different. We will also discuss methods by which the advertising manager controls the production process.

## The Print Production Process

The purpose of the print production process is to reproduce the creative product in a form that can be distributed to each publication scheduled to print the advertisement.

## Approval of the Print Layout

The print production process begins with the approval of the final layout by the advertising manager. In approving the layout, the advertising manager should have a realistic understanding of the relationship between the layout and the appearance of the finished advertisement.

A layout, first of all, can only imperfectly represent the finished advertisement. The illustration is usually only a sketch, the headline is hand lettered, and the body copy is shown as a blocked-off space. As the advertising manager looks at this layout, sometimes without color and not in the context of the medium, difficulties will often arise in attempting to visualize the appearance of the finished advertisement.

The advertising manager should not rigidly insist that the finished advertisement follow the layout without deviations. Much can be gained by letting the advertisement evolve during the production process. The advertising manager should, in fact, insist on the involvement of the creator of the advertisement in the production process. In this way, the advertising manager is assured that the essential creative ideas will be correctly translated in the finished advertisement and the opportunities for improvement occurring during the production process will be realized. Typically a good many improvements in the advertisement result from the interaction between the creative specialist and the production specialist.

## Setting Type for the Print Advertisement

The physical process of setting type is done by typography shops, with direction given to them by creative and production specialists, although in recent years, with the advent of phototypesetting, many large advertising agencies have established in-house typesetting facilities.

SPECIFYING TYPE. The first step in having type set is to specify for the typesetter the type or typeface desired. This is usually done by the art director who prepared the layout. Type is usually specified by writing directions or specifications to the typesetter on the typed copy that is to be set. Exhibit 18-1 shows the "spec'd" copy for the Hershey's Cocoa ad shown in Exhibit 17-11. The directions to the typesetter include typeface and size, line width, and various spacing indications. Note also that the copy was apparently still changing right up to the time of setting the type.

*Typeface.* The typeface is the *design* of the letters and numerals used. There are over a thousand standard typefaces available, with more being created every year. Typefaces are classified in groups and the groups subdivided into families. The principal type groups—roman, block, cursive, and ornamental—are illustrated in Exhibit 18-2, page 483.

*Roman typefaces* are characterized by a chiseled look derived from combinations of thick and thin strokes terminated by serifs (short cross-lines at the ends of strokes).

**EXHIBIT 18-1**      Hershey's Cocoa ad copy specified for type.

**OGILVY & MATHER INC.** *Advertising*          2 EAST 48 STREET, NEW YORK 10017—MU 8-6100

*Date:*  May 9, 1978                                    *Copy*

*Client:*   HERSHEY'S          *P. O.*

*Product:*  COCOA          *Specifications:*   4/C junior spread

*(handwritten: Goudy Extra Bold centered longest line to: 4¼" WIDE)*

HEADLINE: 1   If you think this cake is moist, rich and chocolatey...
2   you should have tried this one.  Hershey's Cocoa made
3   it better.
4

BODY COPY: 5   The "cake that got away" was made with Hershey's Cocoa
6   instead of baking chocolate.  It was richer, moister, *(handwritten: italic)* ®
7   more chocolatey.
8
9   In ~~nationwide tests~~, 7 out of 10 ~~women~~ preferred ~~cocoa~~ *(handwritten: a test of 108 Women ... every)*
10  ~~to baking chocolate.~~ *(handwritten: cakes baked with Hershey's Cocoa over)*
11  *(handwritten: cakes baked with baking chocolate.)*
12  So, ~~to see~~ how much more chocolatey a Hershey's Cocoa *(handwritten: see for yourself)*
13  cake really is ~~you'll just have to~~ bake one ~~yourself~~. *(handwritten: today)*
14  There's no messy melting, no scorched chocolate.
15  Use the handy formula below.
16
17
18  But look fast, before they gobble it all up.
19
20
21
22
23   *(handwritten: V.I.P. GOUDY OLDSTYLE F/L  10pt. 11½   2 even cols.  12½ picas max. width ea. col.  1pica 9 indent.)*
24
25
26
27

| Typeface Groups | Extended and Condensed Type |
|---|---|
| This is a roman typeface. | This is an extended typeface. |
| This is a block typeface (sans serif). | This is a condensed typeface. |
| This is a block typeface (square serif). | |
| **This is an ornamental typeface.** | |
| *This is a cursive typeface.* | **Type Depth** |

| Bold and Lightface Type | Type Depth |
|---|---|
| | This is 6 point type. |
| **This is boldface type.** | This is 10 point type. |
| This is lightface type. | This is 14 point type. |

| Italic Type | |
|---|---|
| *This line is set in italics.* | This is 24 point type. |
| This line is not set in italics. | This is 30 point type. |

*Block faces* (also called gothic or contemporary), in contrast to roman faces, have strokes of uniform thickness and are either without serifs (termed sans serif) or with short, squared serifs. *Cursive* or *script faces* have the appearance of handwriting. The letters are slanted and appear to be connected in a continuous flow. The *ornamental group* of faces is made up of embellished or decorative forms. Usually these convey the feeling of a particular era, location, or event.

Each type group is divided into families and each family is available in a variety of styles. When type is specified for the typesetter, it is done by indicating the name of the type family to be used—for example, Bodoni, Futura, Garamond, or Caslon. In addition, the weight must be specified, and it must be designated as condensed or extended. Typeface weight is designated as *bold* (thick or heavy strokes) or as *light* (thin strokes). Many typefaces are also available in *italic* type, a slanted version of the typeface. Italics are harder to read than ordinary type. Their use should be reserved (and not overused) for words needing emphasis. Type families also have extended and condensed faces. *Extended* faces have wider letters whereas the characters in *condensed* faces are narrower.

The selection of typeface and variety should rest on two considerations. First, the type selection should be legible to encourage readership. Second, as discussed in Chapter 17, the typeface should contribute to the overall appearance the layout is attempting to express.

*Type Depth.* The depth or height of the type to be set must also be specified. Type depth is measured in *points*. There are 72 points to the inch, so that six lines of 12 point type, set without spacing between the lines, would take up one inch.

Textbooks are commonly set in 10 to 12 point type and body copy in advertisements is commonly 12 to 14 point and seldom less than 10 point type. Typefaces in common use are usually available in sizes from 6 points to 120 points, with the larger sizes used for headlines.

*Line Width.* The width of the typeface is not specified because this depends upon the design of the typeface and the particular letters used. However, the width of each line that the typesetter is to set must be specified. Line width is usually measured in picas. A *pica* is equal to 12 points or one-sixth of an inch.

*Line Spacing.* If type is set "solid," that is, with no added spacing between lines, there will be only a slight amount of white space between lines making the copy difficult to read. Readability is improved by adding space, called *leading* (pronounced like "led" plus "-ing"), between lines. The smaller the type size and the larger the line, the more space (leading) should be left between lines. Leading depth is specified in points.

*Uppercase and Lowercase.* Type can be set in all capital letters (*uppercase*), in small letters (*lowercase*), or in a combination of uppercase and lowercase. Copy set in lowercase or a combination of upper- and lower-case is easier to read than an all uppercase text. For this reason, all uppercase type should usually be reserved for headlines or special emphasis situations.

FITTING COPY. At the same time that type is being specified, the copy must be fitted to the space allocated in the layout. The process of fitting copy involves counting the number of characters in the copy and then determining from a specimen book of type the space that will be required for the desired copy. If the copy does not fit — being either too long or too short — there are two possible solutions. One is to cut or expand the copy to fit the space available. The other solution is to change the size or spacing of the type selected.

SETTING TYPE. After copy has been specified for type and fitted to the available space it is sent to the typesetter, who will use one of several different typesetting methods available. Hand typesetting, the most flexible method, is used primarily for setting headlines, where special effects are needed, or when a small amount of an unusual typeface is needed. Metal typesetting (called *hot type* because the typesetting machines cast entire lines of copy from molten lead as the typesetter types the copy) is used for longer, reasonably standardized typesetting jobs including most body copy. There are a variety of metal typesetting machines in use, but typesetters are rapidly phasing out their metal typesetters in favor of photocomposition equipment. Photocomposition (called *cold type*) sets type by a photographic method and offers the advantage of greater clarity or sharpness, in addition to a wider variety of typefaces and sizes than are sometimes available from metal typesetters.

TYPE PROOF. After type has been set the typographer returns a type proof, a printed sheet which shows the copy as it has been set. Exhibit 18-3 shows the type proof returned for the Hershey's Cocoa ad shown earlier in Exhibit 17-11. The proof must be carefully read and corrections indicated. Typographical errors and mis-set type should be noted on the proof using standard proofreaders' marks. Errors in estimating the space required must be corrected. *Widows,* one- or two-word lines at the ends of paragraphs, should be eliminated by cutting or filling in copy to make the line even. Problems of this sort must, of course, be corrected, but the advertiser should resist the impulse at this stage to rewrite copy since it necessitates resetting the copy at the advertiser's expense.

When all corrections have been completed, a final proof — called a "repro" (for reproduction) proof — is returned by the typesetter for use in a later step in the production process.

## Obtaining Illustrations for the Print Advertisement

At the same time that the copy is being set in type, the illustrations to be used must be obtained. It is from the type proofs and the finished artwork that the materials required by the media are prepared.

SELECTING PHOTOGRAPHERS AND ILLUSTRATORS. Taking photographs and preparing drawings for advertisements is another instance of the advertiser's need to use specialists. If the advertiser uses an advertising agency, the agency usually suggests an appropriate photographer or illustrator. Photographers and illustrators are almost all free-lance people in business on a small scale. Agencies maintain extensive files on these artists with samples of their work, and art directors within the agency develop familiarity with the artists' work.

In selecting an artist or photographer, professional competence and the ability to contribute positively to the finished advertisement are important. Most artists and photographers have a distinctive style and many have subject matter in which they are particularly competent.

The cost of photographs and illustrations depends upon the reputation of the artist, the nature of the job, and the use that the illustrations will have. Top name artists and photographers are not affordable for minor illustrations or low budget advertisements unless the advertisement will

EXHIBIT 18-3          Type proof for the Hershey's Cocoa ad.

# If you think this cake is moist, rich and chocolatey... you should have tried this one. Hershey's Cocoa made it better.

## Hershey's Disappearing Cake

¼ cup butter
¼ cup shortening
2 cups sugar
1 teaspoon vanilla
2 eggs
¾ cup Hershey's Cocoa

1 ¾ cups unsifted all-purpose flour
¾ teaspoon baking powder
¾ teaspoon baking soda
⅛ teaspoon salt
1 ¾ cups milk

Generously grease and flour two 9-inch round cake pans. Cream butter, shortening, sugar and vanilla until fluffy; blend in eggs.

Combine cocoa, flour, baking powder, baking soda and salt in bowl; add alternately with milk to batter. Blend well. Pour into pans; bake at 350° for 30 to 35 minutes or until cake tester inserted in center comes out clean. Cool 10 minutes; remove from pans.

And use cocoa in your favorite frosting recipe, too!

The "cake that got away" was made with Hershey®s Cocoa instead of baking chocolate. It *was* richer, moister, more chocolatey. In a test of 108 women, 7 out of 10 preferred cakes baked with cocoa over cakes baked with baking chocolate.

So, see for yourself how much more chocolatey a Hershey's Cocoa cake really is—bake one today. There's no messy melting, no scorched chocolate. Use the handy formula below.

But look fast, before they gobble it all up.

3 tablespoons of cocoa

$+$          $=$

1 tablespoon of shortening or oil

1 square (1 oz.) of baking chocolate

Ad No. 78-BC-05
Hershey—Baking Cocoa
This Advertisement Prepared By:
Ogilvy & Mather Inc.
To Appear In:
Magazines—Sept.—Nov., 1978
Size: Digest bleed Spread, 4/c
Each page: 5⅝ x 7 11/16 Safety: 4½ x 6¾
Job No.: 38499
TGC 73192
ªR
**REPRO TYPE DEPT.**

11/11½ Goudy Oldstyle 12½ max minus one half
10/11 Goudy oldstyle 21½ minus one half
14 Goudy Boild

Z   5-24-78

get repeated use. The use of stock photographs provides a lower cost means of obtaining illustrations. There are firms that specialize in selling stock photographs and will provide prints of the type of situation to be illustrated. Prices for these photographs range from a few dollars to several hundred dollars depending on the photograph and the intended use. This is usually less expensive than having original photographs taken.

SHOOTING SESSIONS. Artists usually work alone in a studio, following the directions provided by the designer or other person designated as supervisor. Photographers, however, set up shooting sessions in a studio or on location. Models must be selected, props gathered, and wardrobes prepared. Usually advertising agency specialists and the photographer cooperate in these selections. The advertiser should encourage the creative representative to attend and become involved in these shooting sessions to solve any problems and to act on any ideas for improvements that arise.

OBTAINING FINISHED ARTWORK. When the artist completes an illustration and delivers it to the advertiser or agency, it is, presuming approval, in finished form. Photographers, by contrast, usually submit a number of unfinished prints for considerations, sometimes as many as fifty. The photographer and creative personnel successively narrow the choice until the desired photograph is selected.

A print of the selected photograph is, when necessary, sent to a retoucher to remove minor blemishes and imperfections. Care must be taken that excess retouching is not used, for it can rob a photograph of its naturalness and vitality. Retouching is also expensive. It is often less expensive to take the time to get the detail and quality needed in the original photograph, thus minimizing retouching. At any rate the retouched photograph constitutes the finished artwork which must be prepared for publication.

## Preparing Materials for the Print Medium

With type proofs on hand and the finished art available, the advertiser must next have the materials put into the form required by the publications in which the advertisement is to be printed.

DETERMINING PRODUCTION SPECIFICATIONS. The critical pieces of information in preparing the advertisement for the publication are the printing method to be used by the publication and the dimensions of the page (termed the *mechanical measurements*). Both of these pieces of information can be obtained from the medium itself or, particularly if there are a number of publications on the schedule, from the Standard Rate and Data Service catalog for the medium. More detailed production specifications for most print publications are contained in Standard Rate and Data Service's *Print Media Production Data* catalog.

There are four basic printing processes in widespread use in producing advertising — letterpress, offset lithography, gravure, and silkscreen. *Letterpress* printing, employed by many newspapers and some magazines, uses a raised printing surface to carry the ink, much like a rubber stamp or a typewriter. The advertiser must supply letterpress publications with engravings of the complete advertisement from which to effect reproduction. Letterpress, once the dominant method for newspapers and widely used by magazines, is rapidly being displaced by offset lithography. The remaining foothold for letterpress is among the very large newspapers for whose operators conversion to offset would be very expensive. *Offset lithography,* or simply offset, is a printing process that uses smooth printing plates that are chemically treated so that the ink adheres only in desired places. The design of the advertisement is transferred to the printing plate photographically. The publication does not need an engraving from the advertiser, but only a copy of the advertisement which can be projected photographically on the printing plate. Offset, used by most major magazines, by many newspapers, and for printing outdoor posters and display materials, provides excellent reproduction quality and especially fine color reproduction.

*Gravure* is a printing process in which the design to be printed is engraved into the printing plate with the ink being carried in the depressions in the plate. The primary use of gravure is the newspaper supplements. Gravure provides high quality reproduction of illustrations and good color reproduction. Gravure plates are usually prepared by the publication from a copy of the advertisement.

*Silkscreen* is a quite different printing process that operates on the principle of a stencil. Silkscreen printing is not used for publications, but is useful for outdoor or transit posters or display materials. It is an economical process for relatively short runs and thus useful for the smaller advertiser. More advanced silkscreen techniques are available for longer runs. Colors can be produced well by silkscreening, but illustrations requiring gradations of tone (*halftones*) are not reproducible by this method.

PREPARING THE MECHANICAL. After the printing method and dimensions of the advertisement have been determined, the next step is to prepare a *mechanical*. A mechanical, sometimes termed a "paste-up," is begun by transferring the dimensions of the finished advertisement to a sheet of white paper. (For very large advertisements, such as an outdoor bulletin, the mechanical is scaled down to a convenient working size.) The type from the reproduction proof received from the typesetter is then pasted on the sheet in exactly the position in which it is to appear in the finished advertisement. Any line art (illustrations made up of solid black lines with no gradations of tone) is also pasted into position. Finished artwork to be reproduced in halftone (such as a photograph which requires gradations of tone) is not pasted into the mechanical, but its exact position is indicated by lines or by pasting a duplicate print into position. Exhibit 18-4 shows the mechanical for the Hershey's Cocoa ad shown earlier in Exhibit 17-10.

The purpose of the mechanical is to provide a precise form from which the printing plate is made. A separate mechanical (or a copy) must be supplied to each publication that uses offset, gravure, or silkscreen printing. Letterpress printing can actually be done from the metal type set by typesetters, but, except for small printing jobs or small publications, this is rarely done. Instead, a mechanical is prepared and the type, line art, and halftone are engraved to form a single printing plate.

SCREENING OF HALFTONE ART.   The finished mechanical contains only two tones—solid black and complete white. Printing plates can be prepared to print black (an ink area) or white (a non-ink area), but they cannot (at least for non-color work) print gray. However, most illustrations

The mechanical for the Hershey's Cocoa ad.                                                 **EXHIBIT 18-4**

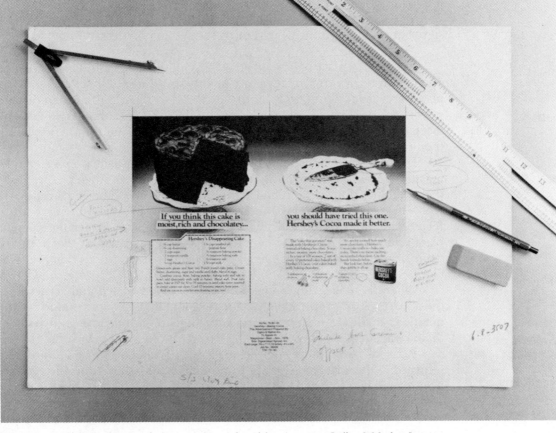

Courtesy:  © 1979 Hershey Foods Corporation. Advertising Agency:  Ogilvy & Mather Inc.

require gradations of tone (various shades of gray) in order to be reproduced, and these are the illustrations that we call halftones. To reproduce the tonal values, the finished artwork must be rephotographed through a screen, a glass or plastic plate crisscrossed with fine black lines. The resulting screened photograph is made up of a series of black dots; in the dark areas of the photograph the dots will be large, in the gray areas they will be small, and in the white areas they will almost disappear. The illusion created is one of gradations of tone, but in fact the screened illustration is made up of only two tones, black and white.

The quality of the illusion of gradations of tone depends upon the fineness of the screen used. A fine screen has more lines and hence more dots per square inch. Screens usually available range from 50 lines to 150 lines per linear inch. Coarse screens create dots that are visible to the naked eye so that the quality of the illustration is lowered. However, coarse screens are required when the printing paper is of low quality (such as in most newspapers) because ink is absorbed and fine dots tend to run together. Fine coated papers, such as those used in many magazines, permit use of much finer screens and, hence, provide higher quality reproduction of illustrations. Selection of the proper screen is a technical matter requiring the judgment of a print production specialist.

The screening of the finished art is sometimes performed as a separate step, but often it is done as part of the engraving process.

PREPARATION OF PRINTING PLATES. With the mechanical and screened art prepared, printing plates must next be produced. Offset and gravure plates are usually prepared by the publication from the mechanical and screened art. The plates are prepared by photographing the art and mechanical using a photosensitive printing plate as the film. The plate is then treated chemically to form the finished plate.

For letterpress publications, the advertiser must usually prepare engravings to be used in the printing process. Usually an engraving is prepared that combines the type and line art with the halftones. The engraver works from the mechanical and the screened or original artwork which are transferred photographically to a photosensitive metal plate. The exposed metal plate is immersed in an acid bath that eats away the portions that are to be white, leaving as raised ink-carrying projections the portions that are to be black.

When the engraving is completed, proofs are pulled and returned to the advertiser or a representative for review. These proofs are studied and notations made directly on the face of the proof concerning corrections that are needed.

With all corrections completed, a set of final proofs is pulled and returned to the advertiser for approval. Exhibit 18-5 shows one of a series of proofs returned for the Hershey's Cocoa ad shown earlier in Exhibit 17-10. The agency's instructions to the engraver for corrections are shown written on the proof. An ad such as this one would normally go through a half dozen or more proofs.

**EXHIBIT 18-5** One of a series of proofs returned for the Hershey's Cocoa ad marked with corrections for the engraver.

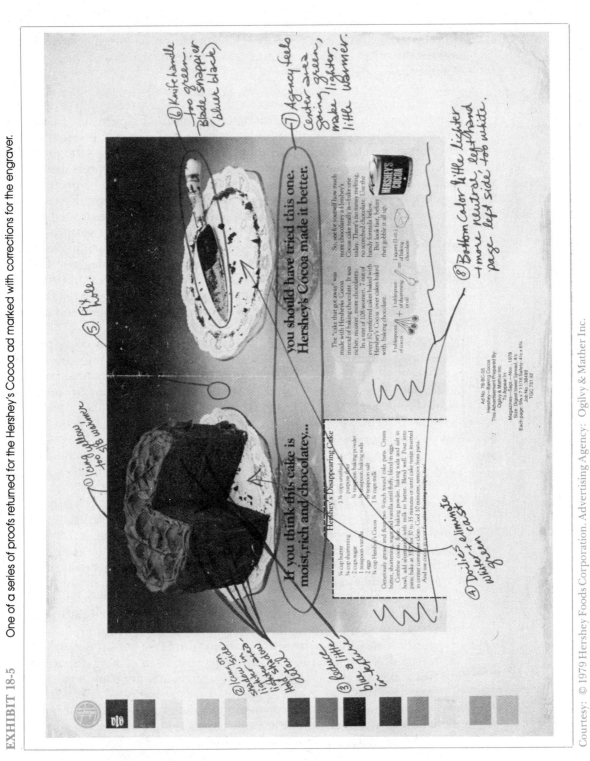

If an advertiser has both letterpress and offset publications to supply with materials, final repro proofs can be used in place of art and mechanical for the offset publications as long as the size is correct and the screen is appropriate.

MATERIALS FOR COLOR ADVERTISEMENTS. The process for preparing plates for printing color advertisements is more complex, but follows a process parallel to production for black and white. Printing presses generally obtain the effect of full color by using only four colors—the primary colors (red, yellow, and blue) plus black. Since a printing press can print only one color at a time, four different printing plates must be prepared.

Each color plate is produced separately by photographing the color artwork through color filters that screen out all except the desired color. The resulting image is transferred to a printing plate which is processed in a way similar to the process used for black and white. Obtaining faithful reproduction of the original colors requires a substantial degree of technical skill and painstaking correction of the individual plates. In printing, the four color plates are printed one at a time, with special care taken to assure that each color printing is in register (correctly aligned) so that the final impression is not blurred.

When a color engraving is completed, a set of seven color proofs (called progressive proofs or "progs") is returned. There is one proof for each color plus three proofs showing the results obtained by progressively adding one more of the four colors. (For a visual explanation of the four-color production process, see the first four pages of this book.)

For letterpress publications, the advertiser must usually provide the color plates. For offset or gravure, as in black and white, the publisher usually makes the plates. The advertiser must supply a mechanical plus color separated negatives (photographic negatives for each of the four colors) of the artwork.

PROVIDING DUPLICATE PLATES. Media schedules frequently contain numerous publications which run the same advertisement at about the same time. This requires that the advertiser provide duplicate materials to each publication. For offset or gravure publications, duplicate materials are easily obtained by sending photostatic copies of the mechanical and copies of the screened art. Repro proofs, if available, can be sent as an alternative. Care must be taken, in either case, that the material provided fits the page measurement of the publication.

In the case of letterpress publications, duplicate printing plates must be provided. There are two basic approaches used in making duplicates—electrotyping and stereotyping. *Electrotypes* are duplicate plates made when fine quality reproduction and long press runs are indicated. They are prepared by making a mold, usually plastic, of the original plate. This mold is then electrolytically coated with copper or nickel to form a durable, duplicate printing plate.

A *stereotype* is a negative mold of the original plate made by pressing a damp paper pulp over the original. When dried, the stereotype is light-weight and easily shipped to the publication. The publication does not print from the stereotype, but uses it as a mold into which molten lead is poured to form a printing plate. Stereotypes are most often used for news-papers where runs are short and reproduction quality is lower.

For somewhat greater quality and durability, *plastic plates* can be pre-pared by pouring a plastic into a stereotype mold. The result is a plastic duplicate plate that the advertiser can ship to publications.

## The Broadcast Production Process

The production of broadcast commercials (radio and television) begins with approval of the script and storyboard by the advertising manager.

It was pointed out that for print advertising the layout is only a guide to the appearance of the finished advertisement. In radio and television, it is even more difficult to visualize from the scripts and storyboards the nature of the finished commercial. There are two reasons for this. First, scripts and boards can convey only a portion of the creative ideas of the writer of the commercial. It cannot, for example, convey action, or music, or the personality of an actor, and these elements alter the character of a commercial from the way that it appears in the script or on the board.

Secondly, broadcast commercials, even more than print advertise-ments, evolve or change in character during the production process. New ideas emerge during production sessions and good ideas should be incor-porated into the finished product.

As in the case of print, the advertising manager should not insist on slavish adherence to static scripts and storyboards, but rather should encourage writers, directors, and producers to be alert to opportunities to improve the commercial during production. To encourage this form of experimentation, the advertising manager must provide for it with suffi-cient shooting time and an ample production budget.

### Selecting the Production Method

In broadcast, the advertiser must provide the medium with finished materials ready for broadcast. The method of production can be selected by the advertiser, which is not true in the case of print advertising.

FILM VS. TAPE PRODUCTION. Television commercials can be produced on film or shot on videotape. Film is the older, more established medium for commercials and probably still accounts for a majority of all commer-cials produced, particularly among large national advertisers. Videotape is a newer way to produce commercials and, as equipment has advanced tech-nically, has become correspondingly more widely used.

Film is more familiar to and more comfortable for many experienced directors and producers who grew up in the era of film. Newer, younger producers, by contrast, may be more experienced with tape. However, the choice between film and tape should really be dictated by the type of commercial desired. Hooper White, an expert in television production, suggests that film be used:

1. Where subtle, complex lighting and close-ups are used.
2. For on-location shots where film equipment is still more portable than tape units despite rapid advances in portable tape units.
3. For stop-motion and traditional animated commercials that are shot one frame at a time.
4. For commercials requiring extensive and time-consuming editing.[1]

Suggesting the use of film for heavily edited commercials does not mean that tape cannot be edited. Although this was a problem in its early years, computerized editing equipment is now available for tape, making it a highly flexible medium. There are some situations in which tape should be favored for use:[2]

1. For commercials that are attempting to project a "live" feel or a "real time" look.
2. For tight budget, live action commercials with minimal editing.
3. For situations where immediate playback of results is needed.
4. For commercials requiring special tape capabilities such as freeze frame, slow motion, or reverse action.
5. For computer-animated commercials.

*live action commercial*

*animated commercial*

LIVE ACTION VS. ANIMATION. **Live action commercials** utilize actors and actresses filmed or taped in a studio or on location. An **animated commercial** uses hand-drawn cartoon or stylized figures and settings. It is also possible to use combinations of live action and animation.

The choice between live action and animation is usually designed into the commercial at the time it is created. Live action contributes to the realism of the situation, permits the use of interesting, persuasive, or well-known personalities, and permits the use of interesting locales. Animated commercials, on the other hand, attract viewers because of their entertainment value. They can be made to stand apart from competitive commercials because of the wide variety of animation and art styles possible. While live action is better able to convey realism, animation's strength is the ability to create fantasy.

There are many animation techniques available, with more being developed every year. In addition to the familiar cartoon figures, puppet

---

[1]Hooper White, *How to Produce an Effective TV Commercial* (Chicago: Crain Books, 1981), pp. 156–158.
[2]*Ibid.*, pp. 159–164.

figures can be animated or inanimate objects such as packages can be animated through stop-motion technique. A recent innovative technique, called *rotoscope,* converts filmed live action into animation by painting and stylizing the filmed figures and backgroud. A Levi's commercial using this technique is shown in Exhibit 18-6.

New and rapidly changing forms of animation are emerging through the use of computer-assisted cameras.[3] One approach is to use computers to control the movement of the camera and the camera shutter as it moves among a series of models or items of artwork. Complex effects are achieved through multiple exposures on the same frame of the film. Other computerized devices can create animation effects that give the appearance of motion from a single model or piece of artwork. Other electronic devices permit visual images to be duplicated, flipped, turned, moved in patterns, and allow many more optical effects to be created. Computer graphics technology has also been applied to commercials. Specialized computer software allows the producer to draw and color pictures on a television screen and then to manipulate the drawings as they are recorded on videotape.

RADIO PRODUCTION METHODS. Most radio commercials today are tape recorded. The alternative is to have the commercials delivered live by local stations. Tape recording is the preferred method when the advertiser desires uniformity from station to station. In a taped commercial, music, sound effects, personalities, and special styles of delivery can be used and will be uniform throughout all uses of the commercial.

Live commercials are used when the advertiser wishes to use local announcers and wants to fit into the format of local programs. In such situations the advertiser sends the station a script to be used by the local announcers plus a recording of any music or special effects which are to be included. An alternative approach is to send the station a fact sheet about the product rather than a script. The local announcers are expected to create, usually extemporaneously, their own commercial messages expressed in their own language. Although this approach is difficult to control, the resulting commercial may be more attention-getting and more believable coming from announcers using their own personal styles.

## Preparing for Production

The importance of the preparations made before filming and taping sessions begin cannot be overemphasized. Film or tape studios and the shooting crews are paid according to the time they spend on the set or on location. A cost of $40,000 for a day's shooting would not be unusual. At these prices it is clearly desirable to preplan in detail so that time is not wasted on the set in working out minor details.

---

[3]*Ibid.,* pp. 223–233.

**EXHIBIT 18-6**          A commercial where live action has been converted into animation.

(Music) Yessir, this drive started over a hundred years ago, back in California.

Just a few head of Levi's Blue Jeans, and a lot of hard miles.

Across country that would've killed ordinary pants.

But Levi's? They thrived on it! If anything, the herd got stronger —and bigger.

First there was kid's Levi's. Ornery little critters…seems like nothing stops 'em.

Then there was gal's pants, and tops, and skirts. Purtiest things you ever set eyes on.

And just to prove they could make it in the big city, the herd bred a new strain called Levi's Sportswear.

Jackets, shirts, slacks… a bit fancy for this job, I reckon, but I do admire the way they're made.

Fact is, pride is why we put our name on everything in this herd.

Tells folks, "This here's ours!" If you like what you got, then c'mon back!

We'll be here. You see, fashions may change…

…but quality never goes out of style!

SELECTION OF THE PRODUCTION HOUSE. For film or tape commercials, production studios, equipment, and personnel are usually rented from film or tape production houses that specialize in the production of commercials. It is important that final selection of the production house be made early in the preparation stage because personnel from the production house play an important role in preproduction planning. Advertisers using an advertising agency usually have the agency lead in the selection of the production house.

There are two dominant considerations in the selection of a television commercial production house—the specialty of the film house and its directors and the cost. Production houses tend to specialize in certain kinds of production. They may specialize in film or in videotape, in live action or in animation. Some houses are particularly adept at location shooting while others have particularly elaborate studio facilities. Production houses also develop production styles which reflect the special abilities of their directors. Advertisers often select directors rather than production houses. In selecting a production house, an effort should be made to select from among those whose special abilities enable them to contribute creatively to the ultimate development of the commercial.

The second consideration is cost. Because of the magnitude of production costs, it is normal procedure to ask a number of qualified production houses to bid competitively on the job. Bids are based on a review of the storyboard plus other specifications provided by the advertiser or a representative. The bidding procedure not only provides comparative cost estimates, but includes discussions with the bidding production houses that often reveal opportunities to reduce cost by making slight changes in the commercial.

Selection of a recording studio for radio commercials and television sound tracks follows the same criteria as those indicated for filming or taping. However, these studios are less specialized and overall costs are lower with the result that the selection is less critical and often handled less formally.

PREPRODUCTION SESSIONS. When the production house has been selected, one or more preproduction sessions are scheduled for the planning of the actual shooting or recording sessions. These preproduction sessions should include the director from the film house, the producer (usually an agency specialist), the writer and art director who created the commercial, the advertising manager or the agency account representative, and prop and casting directors.

At these sessions the concept of the commercial is explained. Detailed responsibility is assigned for obtaining props, wardrobe, actors, equipment, and any other personnel or materials needed for the shooting. Finally, the storyboard is analyzed in detail. Each shot and each piece of action is studied, timed, and agreement must be reached on how it is to be performed.

CASTING. Actors and actresses for commercials are usually selected by the advertising agencies. Advertisers without agencies select the actors themselves or with assistance from the production house. Larger agencies have casting directors who maintain files on available talent, and they invite likely candidates to audition. Professional models and actors are unionized so that payment is standardized except for the most famous models, actors, and actresses who command more than the minimum scale rates.

SETS, LOCATIONS, AND PROPS. Prior to shooting, a set (the room, furnishings, and surroundings in which the action takes place) must be constructed. Production houses usually build the sets from specifications provided by the creator of the commercial. For elaborate sets, a design is submitted for approval.

If a commercial is to be shot "on location," that is, outside a studio, a site is located and, where necessary, permission is obtained to use the area. Provision must be made for weather problems, transportation, and the handling of onlookers.

The gathering of props is a tedious chore in which many people may have to participate. If the product appears in the commercial, the advertising manager must see that it is made available. Package labels or cartons sometimes have to be "color corrected" so that they will exhibit the proper contrast and tones when viewed on television.

MUSICAL SCORES. If the commercial is to have background music, a score must be provided in advance. Commercial music writers and arrangers or "jingle" writers can be commissioned to write original music. The right to use existing music can be purchased and arranged to suit the commercial. Advertisers should note that it is not permissible to use copyrighted music without permission (which means payment) in a commercial. For current popular tunes the cost of usage rights is high. A lower cost alternative is to review previously recorded music available from "needle-drop" libraries. These prerecorded music libraries are available through recording studios. If an appropriate music track is located, it can be used for a licensing fee ranging from $50 to $200. Public domain, or PD, music (music on which the copyright has expired), can be used without permission or charge.

The music arranger must see to it that the muscial score fits the action in the commercial. In some cases the music is adapted to the action after the commercial has been shot. In other cases the music is arranged first and the action is timed to the music.

## Shooting the Commercial

The preproduction planning we have discussed applies in large degree to both radio and television commercials of a wide variety. However, the process of actually filming or recording the commercials has greater variation and will be considered by type of commercial.

LIVE ACTION. Each sequence in a filmed, live-action commercial is shot separately, to be joined with other sequences during the editing process. Sequences are often shot out of order to minimize set changes and actors' time use. Each sequence is rehearsed and usually filmed several times — while changing camera angles, acting style, or the flow of action — to assure that a good "take" is obtained.

ANIMATION. Most people know that motion pictures are, in reality, a series of closely spaced, still pictures which, when projected in rapid sequence, produce the effect of motion. In live-action commercials the series of pictures is taken of actors in scenes to form the "moving picture." In animation, motion is created by taking a series of pictures of pieces of artwork. The positions of the figures or objects in the artwork are gradually changed as each photograph is taken, thereby creating motion in the finished film. The process of shooting an animated commercial is much more extended than that of a live-action commercial. Exhibit 18-7 details the animation process.

RECORDING SESSIONS. If actors have on-camera speaking parts during a television commercial, the commercial will be produced **sound-on-film,** that is, the audio portion will be recorded simultaneously with the filming

*sound-on-film commercial*

Process for producing an animated commercial.                    **EXHIBIT 18-7**

1. Five or six key drawings are made to set the style of the commercial (done by an outside illustrator or from within the animation studio staff). This will determine characters, background, colors to be used, etc.

2. Layouts are made, done in pencil on tracing paper, laying out the entire action (about 30 drawings for a 30-second spot). These pencil layouts will follow the illustrator's style and suggest movement.

3. The track is recorded. If lip-sync (synchronization) is needed, the timing will be derived from "reading" the track. An exposure sheet with timings will be given to the animator, a frame-by-frame guide of what should be happening, beat by beat. The editor does this so the animator can start.

4. Three hundred to 400 drawings are made on tissue sheets from the layouts. These are done in rough pencil form, and will show overall movement. Done in pencil and held for two frames each, these roughs become the "pencil test" to be shown to agency and client for approval (or change) before final animation.

5. Upon approval, inking starts. The inkers trace the animation drawings on the celluloids. Then the opaquer turns over the inked cells and paints in the colors. Since we now have a series of transparent layers, each camera shot is done with top light.

6. After several weeks of intensive work (allow at least 10 weeks for animation), the job is done and ready for approval.

to ensure audio and video synchronization. However, for **voice-over com-mercials** (the announcer is heard, but not seen), for animated commercials, and, of course, for all radio commercials, the sound track must be sepa-rately recorded.

The sound track, recorded on magnetic tape, may be recorded in a number of sections and spliced together or it may be recorded without interruption. Several trials are usually required to get the desired reading with the correct timing; scripts often have to be adjusted in length to meet timing requirements. If the announcer is to synchronize the time to prerecorded music or to a film sequence, the music is played or the film is projected for timing as the announcer speaks the lines.

## Editing the Commercial

Editing is the process of selecting, joining together, and refining the filmed and recorded sequences to form the finished commercial.

THE ROUGH CUT. After the shooting session, film is sent to the labora-tory to be developed. (If tape is used, this step is omitted.) A copy of the original film, called a *work print,* is used in the editing process to prevent damaging the original. The person editing the film reviews all the footage, splicing together the best takes to form a rough cut of the commercial. At this point the sound and the picture have not been joined together on the film, but the editor can synchronize the separate sound reel and the picture reel on a special editor's projector (a Moviola, Kem, or Steenback) that per-mits cutting the film to the sound track.

When the rough cut is completed, a screening session called an *interlock* is sometimes held. A special projector synchronizes film and sound track, projecting the picture on a movie-sized screen to give a feeling for its finished appearance.

Editing can also be done on videotape. This will, of course, be the approach if the commercial was shot on videotape, but it is also possible to transfer film to videotape and do the editing of the film on tape. Videotape editing is highly automated, using computers that bring up on a screen the requested footage, join it together with other sections, even add opticals and titles, which are explained in the next section. The editing instructions are all captured by the computer in memory and when completed can be applied to the original tape to make the final version of the commercial.

OPTICALS. The next step in processing the commercial is to add the optical effects. In the rough cut version of the commercial, the transition from one scene to the next is abrupt. In some cases this quick cut from scene to scene is desirable. A smoother, more gradual change of scene can be achieved by having one scene dissolve into another (a *dissolve*), by having one scene fade away after which another gradually appears (a *fade*), or having the new scene "push" the old one away (a *wipe*).

Another optical effect is the addition of lettering superimposed on the picture. These printed words are termed *supers.* Other trick optical effects can be achieved at this stage such as creating split screen pictures or having one product dissolve into another product.

MIXING. The results of the recording session must be edited to the time allowed for the commercial. For a television commercial, this part of the sound track editing is often done before the film is edited so that the film editor can cut the film in time to the voice.

After the voice track is edited, and usually after the film editing is completed, the additional audio elements must be combined with the voice track in a **mixing session.** Sound effects are added to the sound track, music is "dubbed in," and any additional voices or sound effects added.

*mixing session*

ANSWER PRINTS. The commercial is now ready for final assembly. The film has been cut together, the optical effects made, and the sound track assembled. In the final assembly the original film rather than the work print is used. The film, opticals, and sound track when combined and printed provide an **answer print,** which gives an answer as to the quality of the finished product.

*answer print*

The answer print is usually screened for the advertising manager's approval before films are prepared for stations. It should be noted that although some minor adjustments are possible at this stage, any major change this late in the process would involve major expense.

For radio commercials the finished product is the mixed tape containing all music and effects. This too is reviewed by the advertising manager before materials are prepared for the individual stations.

## Preparing Materials for the Stations

Just as in the case of print advertising, duplicates of the original broadcast commercial must be prepared for distribution to the stations on the media list. This provides materials for multiple stations and protects the original from damage.

DUPLICATING TELEVISION COMMERCIALS. Distribution copies of television commercials can be prepared either on film or on tape. This choice is available whether the original was shot on film or on tape. In earlier years, tape commercials were converted to 16mm films or "kinescopes" for distribution to stations. Today, however, most television stations are programmed to use tape rather than film. Even if films are sent to stations most of them will convert the film to tape. As a result, almost all commercials, whether shot on tape or on film, are duplicated on tape for distribution to stations.

DUPLICATING RADIO COMMERCIALS. The original of a radio commercial will be on tape. Duplicates of the tape can be prepared or, more commonly, duplicates are made in the form of audio cassettes. These cassettes have good reproduction quality and are inexpensive to ship.

## The Advertising Manager's Role in Production

It should now be clear that the advertising production process is a highly specialized one in which the advertising manager will delegate a considerable portion of the work. The advertising manager does, however, set standards as to what is expected and then monitors progress during the course of production.

### Preproduction Control

The advertising manager's control of the production process starts before production begins—when layouts and storyboards are presented for approval.

EVALUATION OF LAYOUTS AND STORYBOARDS. The criteria an advertising manager should use to evaluate creative materials were suggested in Chapter 16. It is important that this form of control take place before production begins since changes at the preproduction stage may involve only a slight rephrasing of a script or modifying a sketch. Once production has begun, the cost of making changes multiplies enormously. A one-word change in a script could involve a whole new recording session. A one-word change in print copy could require resetting type, a new mechanical— even a new engraving. Changes in illustration or in filmed sequences are extremely costly if new shooting sessions are required.

PRODUCTION ESTIMATES. Prior to awarding the production job to an outside specialist, the advertising manager should obtain an estimate of the production cost. If the advertiser uses an advertising agency, the agency should be required to submit a production estimate for approval along with the layout or storyboard. The production estimate specifies the anticipated expenses for each production cost element. These estimates are obtained from the specialists and suppliers who will do the actual production work. For major production jobs, such as the production of a television commercial, competitive bids should be required.

In recent years, costs of production, led by television production, have been soaring. Costs of $100,000 for a television commercial, once thought absurd, have now become commonplace. In the face of this, advertising managers have come under considerable pressure to control production costs. An insistence upon an approved production estimate and the use of competitive bidding is essential to production cost control. Because of the particular problems in television, the Association of Independent Commercial Producers (AICP), has developed a standard six-page television production estimate form. The summary page from this form is shown in Exhibit 18-8.

Having received a set of production estimates for a job, the advertising manager needs to evaluate the reasonableness of the estimates. One measure is to compare the estimated cost to the amount that was allocated to the

Summary page of the AICP television production estimate form.                    EXHIBIT 18-8

## VIDEOTAPE PRODUCTION COST SUMMARY

|  |  |  | Bid Date |  | Actualization Date |  |
|---|---|---|---|---|---|---|
| Production Co.: |  |  | Agency: |  | Agency job # |  |
| Address: |  |  | Client: |  | Product: |  |
| Telephone No.: |  | Job # |  |  |  |  |
| Production Contact: |  |  | Agency prod: |  | Tel: |  |
| Director: |  |  | Agency art dir: |  | Tel: |  |
| Cameraman: |  |  | Agency writer: |  | Tel: |  |
| Set Designer: |  |  | Agency Bus. Mgr.: |  | Tel: |  |
| Editor: |  |  | Commercial title: | No.: | Length: |  |
| No. pre-prod. days | pre-light/rehearse |  | 1. |  |  |  |
| No. build/strike days | Hours: |  | 2. |  |  |  |
| No. Studio shoot days | Hours: |  | 3. |  |  |  |
| No. Location days | Hours: |  | 4. |  |  |  |
| Location sites: |  |  | 5. |  |  |  |
|  |  |  | 6. |  |  |  |

| SUMMARY OF ESTIMATED PRODUCTION COSTS |  | ESTIMATED | ACTUAL |  |  |
|---|---|---|---|---|---|
| 21.  Pre-production and wrap costs | Totals A & C |  |  |  |  |
| 22.  Shooting crew labor | Total B |  |  |  |  |
| 23.  Location and travel expenses | Total D |  |  |  |  |
| 24.  Props, wardrobe, animals | Total E |  |  |  |  |
| 25.  Studio & Set Construction Costs | Totals F, G, and H |  |  |  |  |
| 26.  Equipment costs | Total I |  |  |  |  |
| 27.  Videotape Stock | Total J |  |  |  |  |
| 28.  Miscellaneous | Total K |  |  |  |  |
| 29. | Sub-Total:  A to K |  |  |  |  |
| 30.  Director/creative fees (Not Included In Direct Cost) | Total L |  |  |  |  |
| 31.  Insurance |  |  |  |  |  |
| 32. | Sub-Total: Direct Costs |  |  |  |  |
| 33.  Production Fee |  |  |  |  |  |
| 34.  Talent costs and expenses | Totals M and N |  |  |  |  |
| 35.  Editorial and finishing per: |  |  |  |  |  |
| 36. |  |  |  |  |  |
| 37. | Grand Total (Including Director's Fee) |  |  |  |  |
| 38.  Contingency |  |  |  |  |  |

Comments:

Source:  Association of Independent Commercial Producers, Inc.

job in the plan budget. Overspending against this budget, of course, jeopardizes the ability to achieve all the production planned for the year and should thus be guarded against.

Most items of production involve a one-time cost—that incurred at the time of production. There is one important exception—the cost of talent in broadcast commercials (actors, models, announcers, some musicians, and dancers). Talent is paid not only for performance during the filming or recording session, but also receives reuse payment for each time the commercial is broadcast. The rates paid are governed by rather complex union contract rates. In general, however, the charge increases with the number of times the commercial is used and with the geographic coverage of the media schedule. These **reuse payments** (payments after the first period of use, usually 13 weeks) frequently are not fully shown on production estimates and, as a result, can lead the advertising manager to misestimate the status of the production budget. For a commercial using a number of actors, reuse payment can quickly amount to more than the original production cost of the commercial.

*reuse payments*

ESTABLISHING QUALITY STANDARDS. The advertising manager should establish quality standards for the advertising production. High quality production can be purchased, at a high price. Obtaining a top-name actor, a famous photographer, or top-quality engraving can result in a better advertisement, but it will almost certainly increase its cost. When quality appearance is important and when an advertisement will receive long and wide exposure, the extra cost of top quality may be worthwhile and the advertising manager should specify that this level of quality is the one wanted. The advertising manager should also be alert to the possibility of realizing important economies by pressing the production specialists to suggest alternative, money-saving approaches that will not greatly decrease the quality of the finished product.

## Control During Production

Control during production is difficult because much of the process is carried on by specialists who are far removed both physically and technically from the advertising manager.

The advertising manager should realize that during production, there will be problems and opportunities that require changes in the advertisement. While the manager should encourage the practice, making changes during production complicates control.

There are two techniques that the advertising manager can use to maintain control while still encouraging improvements. First, the advertising manager should insist upon the involvement of creative specialists (those who wrote and designed the advertisement) in the production process. As creators of the advertisement they should be on hand to solve creative problems and evaluate potential creative changes during the course of the production. They should also be available to help interpret to the producers the layout, storyboard, or script which may only imperfectly express their ideas.

Second, the advertising manager should keep abreast of the evolution of the advertisement during the production process. There are numerous check points in the production where the advertising manager can view progress to date. For example, in production of the television commercial, the manager might view the rough cut, listen to the voice track, attend the interlock, and view the answer print. At each of these stages, the advertising manager's responsibility is to review any changes that have been made to be certain that the resulting advertisement is still consistent with the product's positioning and objectives.

---

## CHAPTER SUMMARY

The advertising manager must be conversant with the production process in order to maintain control over the results. The print production process begins with approval of the final layout. Creative specialists must provide typesetters with directions as to typeface, size, and spacing. The typeface and arrangement should promote readability and the desired appearance of the ad. If original photographs or drawings are to be used, the artist or photographer is chosen on the basis of professional competence and skills required by the ad. The advertiser must determine the physical dimensions of advertisements and the printing process to be used by the publication. A mechanical is prepared to the precise dimensions of the desired advertisement and all halftone art is screened. Printing plates are prepared from the screened art and mechanical, the process varying for different printing processes. Color advertisements require a separate printing plate for each color used in the advertisement. When printing plates are completed, the advertiser receives a proof for final approval. Duplicate plates are prepared if several publications are to run the same advertisement simultaneously.

Broadcast production is guided by the approved storyboard, but commercials often evolve during the production process. The advertiser must choose film or tape production. Film offers maximum production flexibility, but it is slow. Commercials are more often shot on film than tape although differences in the capability are no longer great. Film is perhaps more versatile, but tape gives faster results and a "live" look. Preproduction sessions, to include personnel from the selected production house, must preplan shooting and recording sessions so that expensive studio time is not wasted. Actors must also be selected, sets built (or locations chosen), props obtained, and musical scores arranged. After the shooting and recording sessions, the sequences must be edited together. Optical effects and the sound track are added to the film and an answer print prepared for advertiser approval. Duplicate films, tapes, and recordings must be prepared for distribution to stations on the advertiser's schedule.

The advertising manager relies on specialists in producing advertisements, but retains responsibility for controlling the production process. Preproduction control requires careful production planning and advance estimation of cost. During production the advertising manager should encourage the involvement of the creative team in improving the commercial, but should insist that changes be consistent with the product's positioning and objectives.

*KEY TERMS*

Live action commercial
Animated commercial
Sound-on-film commercial
Voice-over commercial

Mixing session
Answer print
Reuse payments

*QUESTIONS FOR DISCUSSION*

1. If a company wishes to advertise a product in both newspapers and magazines, they will almost certainly have to produce different advertising materials for the newspapers than for the magazines. What are the differences between these two media that make it necessary to produce different advertising materials?

2. A frequently seen type of television commercial uses unrehearsed testimonials from ordinary consumers, often filmed in supermarkets, at work, or at other "live" locations. Given the unpredictability of what consumers may say in such situations, what steps can be taken to assure that the actions and speech of the consumers will conform to the storyboard?

3. In choosing a typeface for an advertisement, it is important that the type selected both aid readability and contribute to the overall impression that the ad is trying to create. For the following situations, describe the typeface and spacing that would be appropriate.

   a. Newspaper ad for an expensive restaurant featuring Oriental food.
   b. Newspaper ad for a going-out-of-business sale for a low-priced clothing store.
   c. Newspaper ad for new women's spring fashions in a high-fashion boutique.
   d. Television commercial super for a floor wax.

4. The type used for the chapter narrative in this book is 10 point Baskerville (ITC). What leading is used? What is the line width? How

many inches of space would be required to set copy containing 3,800 characters?

5. In deciding on the illustration for a print advertisement, the advertiser must decide whether to use a photograph and must also determine what special skills the photographer or illustrator should have. For each of the following situations, indicate whether you would use a photograph or a drawing and what special skills you would look for in the photographer or illustrator.

   a. Small space newspaper ad for lawn service.
   b. Endorsement of sky-diving equipment by a famous sky diver (magazine ad).
   c. Direct mail advertisement for a fresh-fruit, mail order firm.
   d. Full page newspaper ad for high-fashion women's wear.

6. Suppose that a large, downtown department store decided to switch a major portion of its promotional newspaper advertising to television. Which would be the most appropriate production method for such an advertiser — film or videotape? Explain why.

7. The choice between live action and animation is influenced by the central idea of the commercial. For each of the following central ideas, indicate whether you would recommend live action or animation. Explain why.

   a. Endorsement.
   b. Exaggerated situation.
   c. Case history.
   d. Association.

8. In broadcast commercials, under what circumstances would casting *precede* the writing of the script? What determines whether the musical score precedes or follows the filming of a television commercial?

9. If an advertising manager is frequently disappointed with answer prints for television commercials and is forced to request expensive revisions, it may indicate that something is wrong with the way in which the manager is controlling the television production process. What kinds of control would you suggest that the advertising manager consider?

10. A rule of thumb in television production is that costs charged by the production house make up only about 60 percent of the total cost of the finished commercial. What categories of cost can the advertiser expect above and beyond those charged by the production house? (A review of the AICP production estimate form may help.)

**PROBLEM**                The advertising manager for XYZ Boats has approved the rough layout shown on the opposite page for the company's Action class sailboat.
The advertisement will appear in the May issue of *Yachting,* a magazine
directed to serious boating hobbyists. The Action class is an advanced
design sailboat intended for skilled sailboat racers rather than for begin-
ners. The boat hull is constructed of fiberglass and incorporates numerous
design features to make it a more efficient racing machine. It commands a
premium price.

1. It has been decided that the advertisement shown will take up a full
   page, but the question of color is still unsettled. Would you recommend the use of color? If so, make a tracing of the layout and indicate on it how you would use color.
2. Consult a specimen type book and select a typeface for the headline
   ("Action"), the company name ("XYZ Boats"), and the body copy.
3. Decide whether or not the illustrations should be drawings or
   photographs. Write a brief set of instructions to the photographer
   or illustrator explaining the effect you hope to create with the
   illustrations.
4. Consult the appropriate Standard Rate and Data Service catalog for
   production specifications for *Yachting.* What are the mechanical
   measurements for the advertisement? By what method will the
   ad be printed? What materials will be required by the magazine?
   What is the date by which this material must be received by the
   publication?

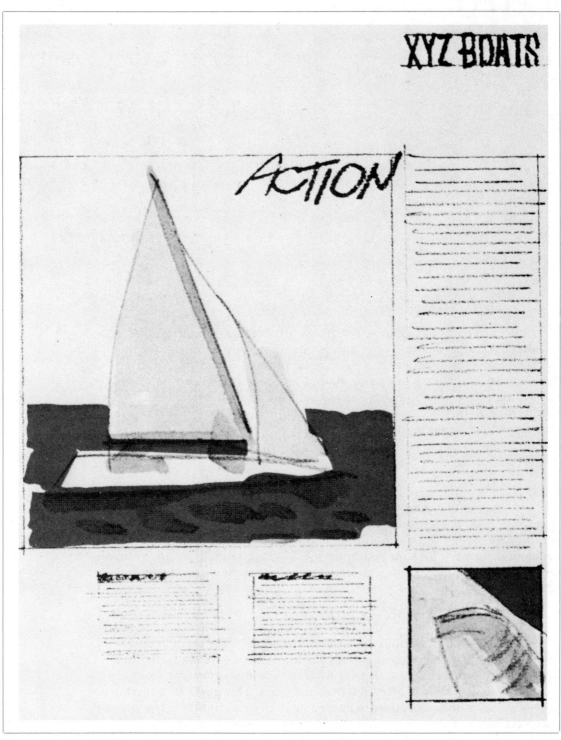

# CHAPTER 19 _____

*The Sales*
*Promotion Program*

LEARNING OBJECTIVES

In studying this chapter you will learn:

- What a sales promotion is.
- How to plan a sales promotion program.
- The problem areas in sales promotion.

Budget, media, and creative programs are necessary in the planning of any advertising effort. For many products, however, there are also specialized advertising efforts that need to be planned separately, Although these special advertising programs should be coordinated with the main advertising effort, they may have specialized media, budget, and creative requirements. In such cases they should be presented as separate yet coordinated programs in the advertising plan.

## What is Sales Promotion?

One specialized program that should be treated separately in the advertising plan is sales promotion. The term sales promotion is one that is widely and rather loosely used in marketing. We will use the term **sales promotion** to refer to a limited-time, special-offer advertising program directed to consumers, to the trade, or to both, designed to achieve fast response.

*sales promotion*

### Characteristics of Sales Promotions

Sales promotions are fully integrated programs. They include advertising (often to both consumers and the trade), point-of-sale materials, and aids for sales representatives. A sales promotion centers on some form of special purchase incentive offered to the consumer. This might be a special price reduction, an opportunity to enter a contest, or a gift offer. The special offer in the Curity sales promotion advertisement in Exhibit 19-1

A sales promotion advertisement with a mail in, free goods offer. **EXHIBIT 19-1**

# Oh boy, free Curity® undershirts.

## The best reasons for Curity are little ones.

### Buy 3, get 1 free.

When you buy three CURITY undershirts or training pants, you get one pure white CURITY undershirt **free**. Just send in your store receipt and plastic bags or paper labels totaling three CURITY undershirts and/or training pants, for each free garment ordered.

Please check size:

☐ Birth to 13 lb.  ☐ 14-18 lb.  ☐ 19-26 lb.  ☐ 27-32 lb.

Name_____

Address_____

City_____ State_____

Zip_____ Phone_____

MAIL TO: Free CURITY Undershirt Offer, P.O. Box 9737, St. Paul, MN 55197.

IMPORTANT: Returned coupon must be received no later than July 31, 1984. Offer good in U.S.A. Void where prohibited or restricted by law. Please allow 6 to 8 weeks for delivery. Limit 2 per family, group or organization.

Courtesy: COLGATE-PALMOLIVE CO.

consists of the opportunity to mail in to the company and receive one free baby undershirt for each three purchased through a normal retail outlet.

A sales promotion is short term. The special offer itself may be good only for a short period such as 60 or 90 days. Note in the Curity ad that the offer, which ran in April magazines, expires in July. The advertising campaign that accompanies the sales promotion is likely to run for an even shorter duration than the offer. Sales promotions are designed to get immediate response from consumers. Immediate response is encouraged by making it clear that the special offer is a temporary one.

### Who Uses Sales Promotions?

The use of sales promotions is not limited to one particular industry or class of goods. Grocery and drugstore product advertisers are very heavy users of sales promotions as are marketers of consumer durables. For example, marketers of automobiles frequently use contests and special temporary price reductions on accessories as consumer incentives. Marketers of products to industry often use sales promotions. The offer, for example, of a free gift in return for listening to a salesperson's presentation of a product is not an uncommon practice.

Retailers are the heaviest users of sales promotion. When retailers run a clearance sale, a white sale, or a Washington's Birthday sale, they are using sales promotion. For many retailers their entire advertising effort revolves around a series of limited time, special offer campaigns. Other retailers maintain a mixture of advertising that promotes the continuing attributes of the store together with sales promotion advertising.

Both the magnitude and the growth of sales promotion expenditures are surprising, particularly to those outside the advertising business. Estimated expenditures on sales promotion in 1983 were $71.7 billion compared to $42.1 billion for advertising in the same year. (The advertising figures do not include direct mail and miscellaneous expenditures, many of which were transferred to the sales promotion figure.) Not only is there a larger dollar amount of sales promotion expenditure than advertising expenditure, but the sales promotion figure is growing considerably faster — 12 percent for sales promotion compared to 9 percent for advertising over the past nine years. Among the factors accounting for the growth in sales promotion expenditures, according to one expert, are increased short-term competitive pressures and the increasing parity of products.[1]

### Objectives of Sales Promotions

Sales promotions can be directed either to consumers of a product or to retailers or distributors of the product. The objective in each case tends to be different.

---

[1]Don E. Schultz, "Why Marketers Like the Sales Promotion Gambit," *Advertising Age* (November 7, 1983), p. M-52.

CONSUMER PROMOTIONS. A usual objective of a consumer sales promotion is to get non-users to try or "sample" the advertiser's product. In established product categories, many consumers become habitual purchasers of particular brands. A sales promotion offers a special incentive designed to break brand loyalty and encourage trial of the advertiser's product. In other cases, such as may be the case in the Curity sales promotion, the objective can be to get the consumer to stock up or buy a larger than normal supply. This is termed "taking the consumer out of the market."

Sometimes sales promotions are not designed to generate sales directly, but simply to build traffic in the retail outlet, thus giving the salespeople an opportunity to present the product. Automobile dealers frequently use sales promotion in this way. Ford's "Pass, Punt, and Kick" contest is probably not, by itself, expected to sell automobiles, but the requirement that consumers pick up an entry blank at a Ford showroom gives salespeople an opportunity to use personal selling.

TRADE PROMOTIONS. Some sales promotions are directed to wholesalers or retailers who distribute the advertiser's product. Trade promotions are usually designed to improve distribution, encourage a build-up of stock, or encourage special selling effort.

New products, for example, try to establish initial distribution by making a special offer to the trade. Seasonal products often offer special incentives to the trade to encourage them to stock up prior to the season. For example, retailers are usually offered a special price for large stock-up orders for cold remedies at the end of summer, and for suntan products in the spring. The marketer's objective is to be certain that the retailer does not run out of stock at the peak of the season. Another purpose of trade sales promotions is to encourage display of the advertiser's product. The marketer of suntan products would not only like to have retailers stock up on the product for the summer months, but also prominently display them during the summer. Trade promotions can offer a special incentive to retailers to build product displays. Trade promotions can also encourage extra selling effort by offering some form of special incentive to wholesale or retail salespeople.

## Elements of the Sales Promotion Program

The planning of a sales promotion requires preparation of a program just as in media planning or creative planning. Preparation of a formal program is particularly important in sales promotion planning because of the necessity of coordinating efforts of marketing departments other than advertising. Successful sales promotions rely heavily upon the contributions of merchandising specialists and sales managers in addition to the usual advertising agency support.

## Defining the Objective of the Sales Promotion

The sales promotion program should begin by stating the specific objective that the advertiser hopes to achieve. The objective serves as a coordinating guideline for the various elements of the promotion. If stated in specific, measurable terms, the objective also becomes a standard against which the actual accomplishment of the promotion can later be evaluated.

A sales promotion can, and frequently does, have both a consumer objective and a trade objective. For example, the Curity sales promotion presented in Exhibit 19-1 is directed primarily at consumers to stimulate their purchase of Curity infants' undershirts. In addition, however, the promotion offers an incentive to the retailer to stock and display the product. In order to qualify for the free goods offer, the consumer must first purchase three Curity shirts in a retail store and obtain a retail store receipt. Thus the retailer can expect increased store traffic and sales if he supports the promotion.

A trade promotion frequently serves both trade and consumers objectives. A trade promotion to increase display of a product provides an incentive to the retailer, since the resulting displays can significantly influence purchases by consumers.

## The Basic Offer

*basic offer*

With the objective or objectives of the sales promotion determined, the next step is to find a **basic offer** to the consumer or trade. The basic offer is the incentive offered to the consumer or trade to encourage purchase or display or some other response. The basic offer selected depends, of course, on the desired response specified by the promotion's objective. The basic offer also serves as a promise or appeal in the creative materials that support the promotion.

CONSUMER OFFERS. Designing a compelling consumer offer requires ingenuity and creativity. There are some common types of offers that have been widely used. The challenge, however, is to find a variation sufficiently different to set the promotion apart from competitive efforts, yet directed to the promotional objective. Some of the more widely used consumer offers are considered below.

*price-off*

*Price-offs.* A temporary price reduction, termed **price-off,** is a widely used special consumer offer. A food product such as coffee may have a special label that promotes the price as 10¢ off the regular price. The price reduction can also be in the form of a two-for-the-price-of-one offer, a 1¢ sale, or other variations. A clearance sale in a department store is, in effect, a consumer sales promotion using reduced price as an incentive. When price-offs are used it is important to make clear that the price reduction is a temporary measure so that it acts as an incentive to immediate action. In order to be an effective incentive, price reductions need to be at least 15 to 20 percent.[2]

Price-offs can be used effectively to sell excess merchandise, encourage in-store display, or blunt competitors' efforts by loading up regular buyers. The disadvantages of price-offs are that they tend to attract a nonloyal consumer group, and they can degrade the brand if used too often. Price-offs are not generally considered effective in generating trial by new users.

*Coupons.* Price-off coupons are the most widely used form of sales promotion offer and also one of the fastest growing. Currently, it appears that over 60 percent of all packaged goods sales promotions are based on a price-off coupon.[3] In 1982, an estimated 120 billion coupons were issued.[4] It is estimated that three out of four households use coupons. Coupons, of course, are a form of price reduction. Coupons can be distributed to consumers through direct mail, through newspaper or magazine advertisements, or by placing them in product packages.

Coupon offers are used to encourage non-users to try a product, to encourage heavier use by regular users, to encourage repurchase by initial users, or to encourage regular users to trade up to larger or more expensive products. Price reduction coupons, once used almost exclusively for products sold in food stores, are now used for products sold through a wide variety of retail stores and even for products sold to business, like airline tickets, for example. Exhibit 19-2 shows a coupon offer for a new food product, presumably designed to assist the new product in gaining consumer trial.

The advantage of couponing rather than on-label price reduction is the added control offered. Coupons can be distributed selectively and purchase limited to one per customer.

Couponing has some disadvantages. Coupons tend to appeal more to loyal users rather than attracting new users. The combination of the face value of the coupon plus the cost of handling makes coupons expensive. Another important cost, and a serious problem is **coupon misredemption,** that is, the cashing of a coupon without product purchase. There are three sources of coupon misredemption: (1) gathering and redemption of coupons in bulk by criminal organizations; (2) gathering and redemption of coupons by store employees; and (3) coupon redemption by consumers who do not purchase the product.[5] Estimates of the level of misredemption vary, but a recent study estimated that 33 percent of all coupons redeemed were misredeemed.

*coupon
misredemption*

---

[2]William A. Robinson, "What Are Promos' Weak, Strong Points?" *Advertising Age* (April 7, 1980), p. 54.

[3]Ed Myer, "It's On the Package," *Advertising Age* (May 17, 1982), p. M-26.

[4]Mary McCabe English, "Like 'em or not, Coupons Surely Here to Stay," *Advertising Age* (August 22, 1983), p. M-26.

[5]Louis J. Haugh, "More Talks Slated as USPS, Industry Battle 'Coupongate'," *Advertising Age* (February 27, 1978), pp. 2, 89.

EXHIBIT 19-2        A coupon sales promotion offer for a new food product.

Courtesy: Nabisco Brands, Inc.

In electing to use coupons as the basic offer in a sales promotion, the advertiser must also select the method by which the coupons will be distributed. Available alternatives include newspapers, Sunday supplements, magazines, and direct mail. In choosing the distribution method, the primary consideration should be the nature of the audience that the promotion is designed to reach. In addition, the advertiser should be aware of the different redemption rates achieved by alternative media. Exhibit 19-3 shows an estimate of coupon redemption rates by A. C. Nielsen, a clearing agent for coupons.

The cost of a couponing promotion should be closely tracked by the advertiser. The choice of the coupon distribution method and the resulting redemption rate are important determinants of cost as are the face value of the coupon, printing costs, and coupon handling costs. Exhibit 19-4 shows a formula used by one company to calculate couponing costs.

*Samples.* Providing a free sample assures that consumers will try a product. Sampling is used primarily with new products or improved products, especially when it is felt that the product differences can only be appreciated if the product is tried. The objective, of course, is to convert the tryer to a regular user as the result of a satisfactory experience with the sample.

Sample distribution can be selective and controlled. It is, however, an expensive promotional offer because both the cost of the product and the cost of distribution must be borne entirely by the marketer.

*Premiums.* Consumers can be offered an incentive in the form of a gift if they purchase the product. The gift may be in the form of an item such

Estimated coupon redemption rates by distribution medium.                    **EXHIBIT 19-3**

| Distribution Type | Nielsen Average |
|---|---|
| Newspaper | |
| r.o.p. solo | 3.1% |
| Co-op (all) | 3.4% |
| Sunday | |
| magazine/supplement | 2.1% |
| FSI | 5.1% |
| comic section | 1.5% |
| comics co-op | nr |
| r.o.p. | nr |
| Magazine | |
| on-page/r.o.p. | 2.6% |
| pop-up | 5.6% |
| co-op | nr |
| Direct mail | 11.6% |
| co-op | nr |
| solo | nr |

Reprinted with permission from the June 8, 1981 issue of *Advertising Age.* Copyright 1981 by Crain Communications, Inc.

EXHIBIT 19-4     Calculation of couponing costs

|   |   |
|---|---|
| 1. Distribution cost<br>   10,000,000 circulation × $4/M | $ 40,000 |
| 2. Redemptions @ 3.1% | 310,000 |
| 3. Redemption Cost<br>   310,000 redemptions × $.15 face value | $ 46,500 |
| 4. Handling Cost<br>   310,000 redemptions × $.07 | $ 21,700 |
| 5. Total program cost 1 + 3 + 4 | $108,200 |
| 6. Cost-per-coupon redeemed<br>   cost divided by redemptions | 34.9¢ |
| 7. Actual product sold on redemption (misredemption<br>   estimated at 20%) 310,000 × 80% | $248,000 |
| 8. Cost-per-product moved —<br>   program cost divided by product sold | 43.6¢ |

Reprinted with permission from the June 8, 1981 issue of *Advertising Age.* Copyright 1981 by Crain Communications, Inc.

*in-pack premium*

*self-liquidating premium*

as a glass or a dishtowel included in the product package (termed an **in-pack premium**) or it may be an offer that the consumer can order by mail after saving labels or coupons. Some premiums are offered free for purchasing the product while there are others, termed **self-liquidating premiums,** for which the consumer must pay. The advantage of the self-liquidating premium is, of course, that the consumer helps to defray the cost.

Premiums serve a much different purpose than coupons and price-offs. Premiums are ineffective in building trial or moving excess merchandise because consumer participation in these offers is typically low. However, if the premium is relevant to the product, it can make highly interesting advertising and build awareness of the product with both consumers and the trade.[6]

*Contests.* Contests and sweepstakes have long been popular as consumer promotion offers. The contests provide a consumer purchase incentive by requiring that a label or facsimile be mailed in with each entry or that the contestant visit a dealer to pick up an entry blank. It is, of course, beneficial if the central idea of the contest is attractive to key prospects for the product. Baking contests conducted by flour companies undoubtedly attract heavy flour users. Less selective contests tend to attract habitual contest enterers. Overall, contests are best used to lend occasional excitement

---

[6]William A. Robinson, "Twelve Basic Promotion Techniques: Their Advantages and Pitfalls," *Advertising Age* (January 10, 1977), p. 55.

to an established brand. They are not particularly good at generating mass trial because only a very small portion of prospects ever enter a contest. There is also a disappointment factor in contests, since there are only a few prizes compared to the number of entries. Efforts should be made to spread the prizes around and give the feeling that winning something is a possibility.

There are highly complex legal problems that plague contests and sweepstakes. Sweepstakes are regulated not only by the federal government, but also by all 50 states, each of which has its own laws. As a result, most advertisers using this form of promotion on a national scale use a sweepstakes consultant.[7] There are two legal problems that the advertiser should avoid. First, federal regulations require that, in a contest, the prizes advertised must actually be awarded. Second, if a contest is judged to be a lottery, it will become illegal in many states. A contest becomes a lottery when it includes a prize, the element of chance, and a consideration (a purchase requirement).[8] What is deemed "a consideration" varies from state to state.

*Refund Offers.* A refund paid by the manufacturer directly to the purchaser of a product is a long-established and heavily used special offer. Consumers are usually required to submit labels or package certificates to qualify for the refund. In recent years refund offers have been a favorite device of marketers of big ticket items such as appliances and automobiles.

For more expensive items, refunds serve to create point-of-sale activity and switch buyers from competitive products. For packaged goods products, where buyers have to save labels from a series of packages, refund offers serve to reinforce brand loyalty and load current users.

TRADE OFFERS. Some offers made to consumers, such as contests and reduced prices, can be used in sales promotions directed to the trade; other offers are unique to the trade field. The trade incentives to be described next can be used in a sales promotion directed solely to the trade or they can be used in conjunction with a consumer incentive to provide response from both trade and consumers.

*Trade Allowances.* The incentive most widely used in trade promotions is a temporary reduction in the price of the product to the retailer. This price reduction can be accomplished in several ways. Sometimes the manufacturer simply offers an extra percentage off the regular price of purchase during the specified promotion period (for example, an extra 10 percent discount on all purchases during June). In other instances the extra discount is offered only on purchases above some minimum (for example, an extra 10 percent off on all orders over 10 cases). Exhibit 19-5 shows a selling sheet for a sales promotion directed to the trade. Special

---

[7]Rose Thomas, "The Quirks of the Law," *Advertising Age* (May 3, 1982), p. M-11.
[8]*Ibid.*

**EXHIBIT 19-5**          A sales promotion offer directed to the trade.

performance allowances are offered to wholesalers on five products in American Chicle's "Star" campaign.

Allowances are also given in the form of "free goods." In the drug trade, for example, a frequently offered allowance is "one free with eleven," meaning one case is given free if eleven are purchased. This, of course, is simply a price reduction. Special price allowances to the trade are used primarily to "load" the trade—i.e., to encourage building up of inventory prior to an important selling season and increasing displays during the selling season. Also, new products are almost always introduced with trade allowances.

*Display Allowances.* In order to encourage retailers to give special display to a product during an important selling period, a special display allowance is sometimes used. The allowance may be an extra discount to the retailer for giving special display to the product. Frequently the manufacturer will specify in a display agreement exactly what type, size, and duration of display is required to qualify for the discount. Proof of performance in the form of a photograph of the display or inspection by a salesperson is also required by some marketers. Without these controls, there is substantial danger that the display allowance incentive will be abused.

*Push Money.* Retail sales clerks are sometimes given temporary incentive to push a product as part of a sales promotion. To encourage this special effort, the salespeople are offered a cash payment (called PM or "spiff") for each unit sold. **Push money** is usually used as a supplementary incentive in conjunction with other promotional offers. Some retailers will not permit push money because they prefer to decide which products are to be pushed by their salespeople.

*push money*

*Trade Contests.* Sales promotions directed to the trade frequently use contests as a form of incentive for wholesalers, retailers, and sales personnel at both the wholesale and retail level. Automobile manufacturers, for example, frequently run contests for dealers and their salespeople with prizes such as an all-expense-paid trip to Hawaii for the person selling the most cars during the promotion. Contests can focus on other elements as well, such as most new accounts opened or most displays placed in stores.

*Special Displays.* Retailers and dealers often provide extra display and sales effort when they are offered a special display unit. For example, a retailer might be offered a special display that shows movies or a display that has an animated figure. Sometimes displays include an item of value which the dealer can keep after use. A wheelbarrow might be used to hold the display of products. Sometimes dealers can be enticed by a display that permits related items to be shown. For instance, a marketer of suntan oil might offer a beach accessories center with space for sunglasses, hats, transistor radios, and beach towels as well as the suntan oil.

*Cooperative Advertising Allowance.* Advertisers frequently offer to pay for the part of a dealer's or retailer's advertising that supports a sales promotion. The most common practice is for the manufacturer to pay half of the retailer's cost if the advertising conforms to the media and creative requirements specified by the manufacturer. Advertising participation is usually used in combination with other incentives such as a special display and a special price reduction. **Cooperative advertising allowances** must be controlled to insure that the money is actually spent, that it is accurately invoiced, and that it is spent for support of the manufacturer's promotion.

*cooperative advertising allowance*

## Providing Media Support

A sales promotion program is like an advertising plan within the advertising plan. It contains the same programs as does the full advertising plan. After determining the basic offer, the next step in the sales promotion program is to select media which will carry messages about the sales promotion to consumers.

SHOULD THERE BE MEDIA ADVERTISING? The first question is whether or not media advertising support is needed in a sales promotion. The answer is an emphatic "Yes." Experience indicates that sales promotions that lack media support rarely generate enough consumer or trade participation to meet their objectives.

The central purpose of the media advertising is, of course, to provide a channel by which consumers and the trade can be informed that the special offer is available. In addition the media provide means to deliver the physical elements of the promotion such as coupons, samples, and contest entry blanks. Finally, media advertising is necessary to communicate urgency — to let consumers and the trade know that they must act at once in order to take advantage of the special offer. Without advertising — without meeting these three needs — a sales promotion cannot succeed.

SALES PROMOTION MEDIA REQUIREMENTS. The procedure for selecting the advertising media for a sales promotion should follow the steps for media selection suggested in Chapter 12. There are, however, several special requirements that sales promotion media have that should be considered. First, in defining the audience to be reached by the media, consideration should be given both to the consumer audience and to the trade (dealer, retailer, wholesaler) audience. Even if the sales promotion offer is directed to the consumer, the trade should be informed of the offer through advertising to encourage them to stock and display the product early in preparation for the promotion.

Media selected for sales promotion support should have high impact. That is, the media should be able to inform a majority of the selected audience quickly and urgently. Newspapers are a favorite sales promotion medium because a single issue can reach a great portion of the advertiser's market. The news environment also connotes the idea that immediate action is necessary.

The media selection depends upon the physical delivery requirements of the sales promotion. Contests, coupons, and samples, for example, require media that permit physical delivery, such as that provided by newspapers, magazines, and direct mail.

## Creative Requirements of the Sales Promotion

A sales promotion requires a complete and separate creative program able to communicate information about the promotion to consumers and the trade. A separate copy platform should be written for the sales promotion advertising and, based on this, separate advertisements created.

One difference between sales promotion advertising and advertising in the continuing campaign is that during the sales promotion an important new product attribute, the sales promotion offer, has been added. The offer plays an important part as an added product benefit or appeal in the sales promotion advertisements.

Usually one central creative idea is used throughout all advertisements for a sales promotion that serves to integrate all the separate advertisements and is used to tie together merchandising elements used in the sales promotion. The central idea may spring directly from the basic sales promotion offer or it may be an idea that attempts to tie together the sales promotion and the regular or continuing advertising campaign.

## Sales Force and Trade Participation in the Sales Promotion

The active support of the manufacturer's sales force is vital to the success of a sales promotion. Although media advertising to the trade can be helpful, the sales force carries the main burden of informing the trade of an upcoming sales promotion. To salespeople, a sales promotion represents an extra incentive that can be used to convince retailers or wholesalers to stock, display, and push the product.

INFORMING THE SALES FORCE. A sales meeting is usually arranged to provide salespeople with the information that will make it possible for them to present the sales promotion to their customers. In addition, the salespeople should be supplied with selling kits, including selling sheets or presentation charts, information sheets to be given to customers, order forms for displays, cooperative advertising contracts, and details on special allowances or other trade offers.

INFORMING THE TRADE. In many cases the efforts of the sales force are supplemented by advertising in trade magazines. The trade ads attempt to arouse dealer interest in the sales promotion so that retailers or wholesalers will be, at least in part, presold by the time the salesperson reaches them.

## Merchandising Support for the Sales Promotion

If the sales promotion is designed to build traffic or to encourage product trial, it is important that the consumer's attention be drawn to the product inside the store itself. To accomplish this, most sales promotions make use of a variety of in-store displays. For food store and drugstore products, the central merchandising piece is frequently a shelf, aisle-end, or floor display which actually holds a supply of the featured product. Banners, window streamers, shelf displays, and handout literature can be used to supplement the central product display.

It is important that display materials be closely integrated with the sales promotion media advertising so that they trigger recollection of the advertising message and remind consumers of the need to take immediate action.

## An Example of a Sales Promotion

ITT Continental Baking markets a wide variety of baked goods nationally through food and convenience stores. Among the better known Continental brands are Home Pride Bread, Wonder Bread, Hostess Cakes and Snacks, and the Hostess Breakfast Bake Shop. Hostess became an official sponsor of the 1984 Olympics and as such was entitled to use Olympic themes and symbols in its advertising. Continental took advantage of its sponsorship rights by using the Olympic theme as an integral part of the basic offer in a variety of sales promotions for its brands. These Olympic sales promotions took place over a two-year period and involved all of the Continental brands. One of these sales promotions, conducted for Hostess Cakes, will be used as an example in the sections which follow.

OBJECTIVE OF THE SALES PROMOTION. The Hostess Cake line includes Twinkies Cakes, Suzy Q's Cakes, and Hostess Cupcakes, each packaged in individual snack packs as well as in multiple-unit family packs. Hostess Cakes had been experiencing a sales decline caused, the marketing manager believed, by a downturn in the economy. The primary objective of the sales promotion was to help slow that sales decline. Secondary and supporting objectives for the sales promotion were (1) to improve consumer attitudes toward the quality of Hostess products, (2) to motivate the sales force by providing exciting selling materials, and (3) to attract the attention and enthusiasm of the retail trade. It was hoped that an outcome of greater trade attention would be a more favorable future display of Hostess products.

THE BASIC OFFER. The basic offer in the Hostess sales promotion consisted of providing, in the Hostess family packs, instant winner game cards, shown in Exhibit 19-6, good for cash and merchandise as prizes, plus entry blanks for a $60,000 grand prize drawing. As a tie-in to the Olympic theme, the game cards featured Olympic sports events and, in addition,

Game cards from the Hostess Winner Games sales promotion.                          **EXHIBIT 19-6**

Courtesy: ITT Continental Baking Co., Inc.

Hostess pledged to contribute $10,000 to the U.S. Olympic Committee in the name of the grand prize winner. By including game cards and grand prize entry forms in Hostess packages, the basic offer provided a direct and immediate stimulus to sales, the primary objective of the promotion. The Olympic tie-in was designed to provide a quality association that would have a favorable effect on consumer attitudes toward the brand. How the basic offer served to generate sales force and trade enthusiasm will be clearer as the sales and display materials are described.

MEDIA SUPPORT. Primary support for the Hostess promotion came from in-store displays, special packaging, and public relations and sales force efforts. In addition, during the period of the promotion, Hostess focused its national television advertising campaign on the brand's sponsorship of the U.S. Olympic Team. One of the television commercials that was run during the Hostess sales promotion period is shown in Exhibit 19-7.

CREATIVE APPROACH. The creative problem in the Hostess cakes sales promotion was to tie together Hostess' sponsorship of the U.S. Olympic Team, which is presented in the television advertising, to the Hostess sales promotion. Since the sales promotion was run at the time of the Olympic Winter Games, a play on words, "Hostess Winner Games," was used as the central idea to integrate the Olympics and the instant winner game card consumer offer.

An execution of the central idea is shown in Exhibit 19-8, the cover of the selling sheet that salespeople used in presenting the promotion to retailers.

SALES AND MERCHANDISING SUPPORT. In the Hostess promotion, in-store merchandising materials and personal selling efforts by the Hostess salesforce played a major role in promoting the Winner Games promotion. A wide variety of promotional materials was prepared to support these efforts, each integrated by U.S. Olympic team symbols and the Winner Games theme. Sales and merchandising elements available for the promotion included those discussed below.

*In-store Merchandising.* Several in-store point-of-purchase display pieces were prepared, including a large pole display, a shelf display, a shelf dangler, and a shelf talker. A sample of these items is shown in Exhibit 19-9. Note how each of these items is integrated around the Olympic symbols and the Winner Games theme. In addition to these items, Hostess had available for retailers a wide variety of wire display racks for Hostess cakes.

*Sales Aids.* A special four-page, full color sales brochure was prepared explaining to retailers all the features of the Winner Games promotion. The cover of the brochure was shown in Exhibit 19-9 and the inside pages are shown in Exhibit 19-10. The sales promotion was announced to the sales force at a special sales meeting and a coordinated sales contest was announced.

*Packaging.* Special packaging was designed for all Hostess cakes for use during the promotion. The special packages, in addition to enclosing the game cards and entry blanks for the grand prize, had the Winner Games announcement printed on the outside and the contest rules detailed on the bottom. Exhibit 19-11 shows the special Winner Games package produced for Twinkies.

*Public Relations.* A special public-relations program was implemented which on the local level was to focus on publicizing prizewinners. The

An Olympic sponsorship commercial for Hostess Cakes.

**EXHIBIT 19-7**

(MUSIC UP AND UNDER)
ANNCR: (VO) The Olympic Ideal.

American through and through.

A heritage of striving,

of greatness.

Here's a salute to our Olympians from another American tradition . . .

Hostess Twinkies Cakes.

Fresh golden sponge cakes with their creamed filling . . .

American through and through for over half a century.

Hostess, the makers of Twinkies Cakes,

is a proud supplier and official sponsor of the 1984 U.S. Olympic Team.

Hostess Twinkies Cakes and the Olympics . . .

American through and through.

Courtesy:  ITT Continental Baking Co., Inc.

**EXHIBIT 19-8**        Hostess Winner Games selling sheet front cover.

Courtesy:  ITT Continental Baking Co., Inc.

public-relations program also included—for this and other promotions—
a goodwill tour by Olympic gold-medal winner Bob Mathias in order to
promote the sponsorship of the United States Olympic team by Hostess
and other brands.

   It should now be clear from a review of this example, which was only
one of a series implemented by Continental for its products, just how
detailed a modern sales promotion is. Effective sales promotion requires
that a detailed written plan be prepared for each promotion. It is equally

**EXHIBIT 19-9**

In-store display materials for the Hostess Winner Games promotion.

Courtesy: ITT Continental Baking Co., Inc.

important that attention be paid, as was done in the Hostess example, to tying together the many elements of the sales promotion. The basic offer and the central creative idea are the most useful tools in achieving this integration.

## Problem Areas in Sales Promotions

Sales promotions are an important competitive weapon used by the advertiser. They provide a means for disrupting consumers' purchase habits and encouraging trial of a different brand. Sales promotions also provide a means for invigorating sales force and dealer enthusiasm and effort on behalf of a product. Sales promotion, however, is not without its

EXHIBIT 19-10     Inside of the Hostess Winner Games sales brochure.

Courtesy: ITT Continental Baking Co., Inc.

disadvantages. It can be used too often and it can be used incorrectly. Several problems connected with sales promotion are discussed below.

### Effect of Sales Promotions on Product Reputation

Both the frequency and the form of the sales promotion conducted for a product influence the reputation of the product.

Inside of the Hostess Winner Games sales brochure.                         EXHIBIT 19-10

Courtesy: ITT Continental Baking Co., Inc.

FREQUENCY OF PROMOTIONS. It is possible, through frequent use of sales promotions, to cheapen the product in the eyes of consumers. Brands that are perpetually offering "specials" become known to the trade and consumers alike as "price brands." This frequently reflects unfavorably on consumers' perceptions of the quality of the product. Wholesalers and retailers may come to regard a product as unstable and basically weak if it is sustained by a series of sales promotions.

**EXHIBIT 19-11**        Special Winner Games package for Hostess Twinkies.

Courtesy: ITT Continental Baking Co., Inc.

In some cases advertisers use the frequency of sales promotions to help position the product. Some retailers, for example, are heavy users of sales promotions and this activity communicates to consumers a great deal about what kind of store it is. A women's wear store, for example, that moves from inventory clearance to fire sale to lost-our-lease sale in successive months gives the impression that it is a cut-rate or bargain store. This is not necessarily bad. The strategy of the store may, indeed, be to position itself as the low-price store serving economy-minded clothing shoppers. By contrast, another women's wear store attempting to position itself as a high-fashion boutique would most likely hold few, if any, sales promotions for its products.

TYPE OF OFFER. The degree to which a sales promotion marks a product as a price brand depends in part on the type of offer that is used as the incentive. Direct monetary incentives such as price-offs, one-cent sales, and two-for-the-price-of-one promotions give a cut-rate appearance, particularly when the offer is made directly on the package. By contrast, a product-related contest or premium offer, or a promotion based on a free sample can focus attention on the product rather than on the price. The advertiser should consider carefully what sales promotion offers imply about the product and suit the offers to the position that the product is supposed to occupy.

## The "Borrowing" Problem in Sales Promotions

A familiar result of a sales promotion is a temporary bulge in sales volume during the term of the promotion, followed by a temporary decline in sales to below normal volume. Often, the decrease in sales volume after the promotion offsets the increase in sales volume during the promotion.

THE EFFECT ON SALES. This pattern of sales bulge followed by sales decline occurs because sales promotions tend, in effect, to borrow future sales. For example, a regular buyer of a brand of mouthwash might purchase a reduced-price package even if the current supply would last for another month, or the regular user might buy two packages instead of the normal one. In both of these cases, the sales promotions have had the effect of borrowing future sales rather than creating new sales.

THE EFFECT ON PROFITS. The borrowing problem affects profits as well as sales. Most sales promotion offers involve either a lower price (such as a cents-off offer) or a higher product cost (the cost of a premium or contest prizes). This means that the sales borrowed from the future are made at a lower than normal margin, thus reducing profits.

OVERCOMING THE BORROWING EFFECT. The borrowing effect sometimes works to the advertiser's advantage. If an advertiser is attempting to blunt a competitive sales promotion or combat a competitive new product, the advertiser may direct a sales promotion to the brand's regular users. They will tend to stock up on their regular brand at the bargain prices and thus not be responsive to competitive offers. This is termed taking customers "out of the market" and is an important defensive tactic.

In most other instances, however, the objective of the sales promotion is not to load current users, but to attract new users. In most cases it is difficult to focus a sales promotion only on potential new users. Magazine publishers seem to succeed in doing it by offering cut-rate subscriptions only to those who are not current subscribers. Most sales promotion offers, however, are less selective than this. Coupons and samples can sometimes be directed selectively to low-user groups. Some offers can also be limited to one to a customer so as to discourage stocking up by current users.

## The Danger of Competitive Retaliation

If a sales promotion is conducted by an advertiser, the increase in sales realized may come in part from new customers drawn into the market, but probably most will be customers drawn away from competitors. If the sales promotion is a successful one, it will probably cause competitors to lose market share. Their response is likely to be a counter sales promotion to win back their lost customers. If this counter effort is successful, the net result can be an increase in cost to both advertisers with little increase in sales.

DEFENDING AGAINST RETALIATION. This outcome serves to point out an important truth about sales promotions. If, after trying the product, consumers do not find it preferable to other products, it will be easy for competitors to attract them away to try yet another product. Thus a sales promotion can serve to get consumers to try a product, but it cannot create loyal customers. The attributes of the product must do that. Therefore, the best defense against competitive retaliation is a product that offers superiority in terms of the way its attributes are matched to consumer needs.

RETALIATION IN TRADE OFFERS. Competitive response to sales promotion offers occurs at both the wholesale and retail levels. If one marketer offers a special 10 percent trade allowance just before a big selling season, there is pressure for marketers of similar products to do likewise. In fact, in many product categories trade offers become standardized in both amount and timing. Retailers and wholesalers come to expect these special allowances and plan their buying around them. Manufacturers find that they are forced by competitive action to offer these reductions. As a result the sales promotion is not a special incentive to purchase, but simply part of the normal and expected discount structure of the product.

## Distraction from the Regular Advertising Program

Most advertisers use promotions as a temporary supplement to the regular advertising campaign. Frequently the regular advertising effort is suspended or reduced during the period of the promotion in order to concentrate media weight on the sales promotion. There is a danger that a sales promotion will interrupt the continuity of the regular advertising campaign and distract consumers from its central message. It is desirable to avoid this distraction and, if possible, to design the sales promotion so that it supplements the regular advertising campaign.

FREQUENCY OF PROMOTIONS. One way to avoid having sales promotions distract from the regular advertising campaign is to limit the frequency with which sales promotions are conducted. It is difficult to state the point at which sales promotions become so frequent that they overshadow the regular campaign. One four-week sales promotion in a year would seem to run minimal risk of serious distraction, but three or four sales promotions in the same period would create a substantial distraction danger.

RELEVANCE OF THE OFFER. The problem of distraction from the regular campaign is also lessened if the basic offer is relevant to the product or to the appeal made in the regular campaign. The Olympics sales promotion staged for Hostess cakes may not at first glance appear to be highly relevant to the product. However, at the time, the Olympics was a newsworthy subject that attracted consumer attention to its sponsors. More important, recall that one of Hostess' objectives was "to improve consumer attitudes toward the quality of Hostess products." Hostess undoubtedly felt that association with athletics and with the Olympics in particular would enhance consumer attitudes toward Hostess cakes' quality.

CREATIVE TIE-INS. In addition to making the offer relevant to the regular campaign, many times it is possible to relate the creative materials used in the sales promotion to the regular advertising campaign. If this can be done, then the sales promotion advertising supplements rather than distracts from the regular advertising. This suggestion is, of course, simply an extension of the campaign integration procedure suggested in Chapter 17.

---

*CHAPTER SUMMARY*

Sales promotions are short, special-offer advertising programs directed to consumers, the trade, or both, and designed to achieve fast response. They are used by both consumer and industrial advertisers and by retailers.

The development of the sales promotion program is guided by its objective. The objective of most consumer promotions is to get the consumer to try the product or to build traffic in retail outlets. Trade promotions are usually designed to build distribution, stocking, or sales effort. Sales promotions are built around a basic offer which serves as a special incentive to the consumer or the trade to take immediate action. Widely used consumer offers include price reductions, coupons, samples, premiums, contests, and refunds. Trade offers include special discounts, display allowances, push money, contests, displays, and cooperative advertising allowances. Media advertising should be used to communicate the offer to consumers and the trade. The sales promotion medium should have high impact and permit physical delivery if required by the basic offer. A separate creative program should be developed to communicate information about the promotion. There should be a separate copy platform and separate advertisements that focus on the special incentive offer. The sales force must be provided with selling tools that will aid them in presenting the sales promotion to customers. Trade advertising may also be used in this effort. For sales promotion designed to build traffic and encourage trial, a variety of in-store displays can be useful. All displays, ads, and selling tools should be integrated creatively around a single central idea which expresses the basic offer.

Although useful in stimulating product trial and in invigorating the sales force, sales promotions can also create problems if not carefully used. The reputation of a product can be cheapened if sales promotions are used too frequently, particularly if the promotions focus on price reductions. Sales promotions may also gain sales increases at the expense of future sales or they may invite competitive retaliation that results in simply trading sales at lower prices. Sales promotions also distract from the regular advertising program which is normally reduced or suspended during the term of the sales promotion.

---

*KEY TERMS*

| | |
|---|---|
| Sales promotion | In-pack premium |
| Basic offer | Self-liquidating premium |
| Price-off | Push money |
| Coupon misredemption | Cooperative advertising allowance |

---

*QUESTIONS FOR DISCUSSION*

1. The selection of a basic offer for a sales promotion depends upon the objective that the marketer is trying to achieve. What objective would be served by the following offers? How do they differ from each other?

   a. Two bars of face soap banded together and sold at a reduced price.
   b. Reduced price on an extra large bag of charcoal briquettes.
   c. 10¢ off on a trial-size tube of toothpaste.

2. Would it be possible for a manufacturer of air conditioners to moderate the seasonal factor in air conditioner factory sales through the use of sales promotion? What kind of consumer offer might accomplish this goal? What kind of trade offer might accomplish it?

3. The marketer of a brand-based, adult breakfast cereal has found through home use testing that initial reaction to the product taste is negative, but that if consumers can be convinced to try a second or third package of the product they acquire a taste for it and become extremely loyal customers. Upon introducing the product, the company finds that the introductory advertising is successfully getting trial of the product, but repurchase is very low. What kind of basic offer in a sales promotion might overcome this problem?

4. In one form of consumer offer, known as a "cross ruff," a marketer of two products might offer purchasers of one product a special incentive to buy the second product. A marketer of shampoo, for example, might wish to encourage purchasers of the shampoo to also try the company's hair spray.

   a. What kind of basic offer would accomplish this objective?
   b. What advantage is there in capturing this group of prospects?

5. Different forms of basic offers work at different speeds. Compare the speed with which the following basic offers could be implemented and results realized.

   a. Magazine-distributed coupon.
   b. Newspaper-distributed coupon.
   c. Home-delivered free sample.
   d. Label price-off.

6. If marketers use a premium as the basic offer, they should attempt to select a premium that is relevant to the product that they are selling. Consider the premium offers listed below and decide whether or not the premium offer fits well with the product.

   a. Mainstay brand dog food — unbreakable drinking mug or four "Thank You" notes with envelopes.
   b. Chex Cereals — family full color portrait from Sears Portrait Studios.
   c. Nature's Organics Plus shampoo and conditioner — digital quartz watch.
   d. Contac cold medicines — Feverscan thermometer.

7. If a manufacturer of aerosol shaving cream offers retailers one case free with each eleven purchased, what is the effective percentage reduction in price? Is there any advantage in offering the free goods rather than an equivalent reduction in price?

8. As shown in Exhibit 19-3, the rate at which coupons are redeemed varies considerably depending on the medium through which they are distributed. Review that exhibit and answer the following questions:

   a. What do you think accounts for the difference in redemption rates between the media?
   b. Direct mail has the highest redemption rate. Does this mean that it is the most efficient for coupon distribution?

9. Recently Johnson & Johnson conducted an Adorable Babies Photo Contest for which contestants submitted a photo of their baby along with a humorous caption plus two proofs of purchase from any of several Johnson's baby products. Prizes included college scholarships for each "Baby of the Month" plus appearance in the Johnson & Johnson Adorable Babies Calendar.

   a. Does the contest idea selected by Johnson & Johnson seem relevant to the products?
   b. What objectives do you think this sales promotion will fulfill?

10. One method of coupon distribution is the use of cooperative mailings in which marketers of several different products include their coupons in a common direct mail piece. What advantages do you see in this coupon distribution method? Do you see any limitations?

11. Suppose you were the marketer of a men's after-shave lotion sold in small, regular, and economy size and you have received advance word that your principal competitor plans a 10¢-off-label promotion on the regular size package.

a. What kind of sales promotion would you run to counteract your competitor's offer? What would be your basic offer? On what product size?

b. Assuming you were able, when would you like to make your offer — before your competitor's offer, at the same time, or afterwards?

---

*PROBLEM*

Diane Huberson, general manager of the Home Style Cafeteria, is interested in building a greater share of clientele from nearby Central States University. The cafeteria, which was established three years ago, has a large modern location only one block off the Central States campus. Central States is a private, primarily residential university with about 5,000 students and constitutes the largest source of economic activity in the small town in which it is located.

The Home Style Cafeteria is the only cafeteria-style restaurant in the town. It is open from 7:00 a.m. to 9:00 p.m., seven days a week, serving breakfast, lunch, and dinner. The menu offers a wide variety — typically five or six meats, various vegetables, salads, breads, beverages, and desserts. No alcoholic beverages are served. Because food is served cafeteria-style, it is possible to keep prices relatively low. Typically a breakfast with eggs costs $1.25, lunch $2.00, and dinner about $3.50. Since patrons serve themselves, there is no tipping required. In the three years that it has been open, the cafeteria has drawn its clientele from the middle-income group, including young couples with children as well as older couples. Students occasionally patronize the cafeteria, particularly on weekends, but their number is not great.

From inquiries among students, Huberson has determined that most students eat regularly at the University's cafeteria. Although students can buy single meals at the University's cafeteria, most purchase a meal ticket at the beginning of each semester that entitles them to three meals a day, seven days a week. There seem to be two reasons why students purchase the meal tickets. By "signing on" the students realize a considerable saving in cost per meal over the single meal price. More important, perhaps, there is pressure from parents who fear that their children will not get well-balanced, regular meals if allowed to select their own eating time and place. Students, however, complain vehemently about the university food. They feel that it is bland, tasteless, and lacking in variety and they also feel the urge to get away from the campus for meals. Students, in fact, sometimes skip already-paid-for university meals and eat in town simply to get away from the campus.

Huberson is interested in getting a larger share of the student meal market. Her cafeteria has substantial excess capacity and the incremental cost for serving additional meals is modest. Her idea for attracting students is to offer a student meal ticket plan that would satisfy parents' desire for regular, well-balanced meals and students' interest in greater variety and an off-campus eating site. The plan is to offer semester-long meal tickets in a choice of three types: a three-meal-a-day ticket, a lunch and dinner ticket, and a dinner-only ticket. The three-meal ticket, which is most comparable to the University's system, will cost about 10 percent more than a University meal ticket. There is no University plan comparable to the two- and one-meal tickets, but the ticket prices have been scaled downward to reflect the smaller number of meals received. Each ticket plan specifies what food the student will be entitled to, but generally they will be free to select from the full menu. Huberson is willing to bill the cost of the ticket to parents of students who have proper identification.

Huberson realizes that if the plan is to be successful, she will have to get students to purchase the meal tickets during or just before the three-day University registration period when they have to make the decision whether or not to sign on at the University cafeteria. Generally once the student signs on with the University the decision is irreversible for the semester. Huberson feels that once the meal ticket plan gets established, she will get repeat business from word of mouth. She feels, however, that some kind of special effort will be necessary to establish initial ticket purchases. She is willing to spend up to 10 percent of initial ticket sales on some form of promotion, although this could only be temporary since it would reduce the contribution on those sales to near zero.

Design a sales promotion that would aid in the introduction of the Home Style Cafeteria student ticket plan.

1. Define the objective of the promotion.
2. What would be the basic offer in the promotion? To whom would it be directed?
3. What kind of media support would you recommend for the promotion? To whom would it be directed?
4. Write a copy platform for the sales promotion advertisements.
5. Explain what other elements would be used in the sales promotion.

# CHAPTER 20

*The New Product Program*

LEARNING OBJECTIVES

In studying this chapter you will learn:

- How new product ideas can be created.

- How to develop a new product introduction program.

- The process for testing the new product program.

The development and introduction of new products is, at one and the same time, the most exciting and the most difficult assignment that an advertising manager can receive. The general process that has been described for developing an advertising plan applies to new products as well as to existing products. There are, however, special problems involved in the advertising of new products that will have to be discussed in this chapter.

The first problem has to do with the development of the new products themselves. Where do new products come from, what characteristics should they have, and how can successful new product ideas be distinguished from unpromising ones? A second problem is that new products, especially during the introductory stage, usually have special objectives arising from the newness of the product. These special objectives require that the advertising programs—budget, media, creative, and sales promotion—for the introductory period be specially designed. A final problem area is the pretesting of introductory programs for new products. New product introductions are extremely expensive undertakings and the risk of failure is high. Testing of the new product program is designed to reduce this risk by suggesting improvements to the program before the introduction is made. In this chapter each of these special problems in new product advertising will be considered.

540

Developing
The New Product

Working on the development of new products may seem to be a job that is rather far afield from advertising management. However, modern marketing thinking is quite likely to place the advertising manager in the very center of the product-development process. The reason is that new products, if they are to be successful, must represent a superior need satisfaction from the consumer's point of view and it must be possible to communicate this superiority to consumers. Advertising managers have an important role to play in developing new products because their specialties are knowledge of consumers and knowing how to communicate with them.

## Planning for New Product Ideas

New product ideas do not just happen. They are the end result of a careful planning process. There is, to be sure, a good deal of creativity involved in dreaming up a new product idea. However, like the creation of an advertisement, the search for new products has a much greater chance to be successful if it is preceded by careful fact-finding and analysis.

WHAT IS A NEW PRODUCT? It is difficult to define what constitutes a new product. New products vary considerably in their innovativeness. Certainly the first television sets and the first computers were new products. These products, in fact, established entirely new product categories. Other new products represent improvements of existing products. Color television was an improvement over black-and-white television and personal computers certainly represented an advance over huge mainframes. These products represent such an improvement over existing products that they are usually classified as new products. However, as improvements become progressively more minor, it is less clear whether or not the resulting product is new. Did, for example, the portable personal computer qualify upon introduction as a new product? Would the gel form of a toothpaste qualify as a new product? How about a new flavor?

A **new product** can be more usefully defined by using the positioning     *new product*
concept. When a product is sufficiently changed so that a new positioning results, the product can be considered new. This means that a new central product attribute is offered to consumers for the satisfaction of their needs. Following this thinking, the portable personal computer would certainly qualify as a new product, the gel form of a toothpaste might qualify, and a new toothpaste flavor probably would not.

This definition of a new product also suggests a direction for a program of new product search. What the advertiser seeks in a new product development program are new positions in a market. The advertising planning process provides an excellent approach to a planned, new product program.

DEFINING OPPORTUNITY MARKETS. A planned approach to new product development begins with the selection of the market or product category that the company wishes to enter. This concentration then permits focused market analysis and the search for a new product.

The company's corporate strategy may guide the selection of new product markets to be investigated by defining the endeavors to which the company can best devote its resources. Lacking these guidelines, a firm should seek product categories in which there are unmet or poorly met consumer needs and product categories where the firm has some special capability in meeting consumer needs. Finding an unmet consumer need that is matched by some special competence that the firm has indicates an opportunity market to be investigated.

Black and Decker, for example, recently introduced the Scrub Brusher, a cordless, rechargeable power scrubber shown in the advertisement in Exhibit 20-1. The Scrub Brusher is designed to solve the problem of difficult and dirty household cleaning chores. The appliance relies upon Black and Decker's special competence in cordless, rechargeable technology which they developed for their power tool line as well as for household products.

ANALYZING THE NEW PRODUCT MARKETS. With the target market specified, the advertiser is next able to gather and analyze information on the market selected. The analysis of problems and opportunities that was suggested as the basis for a sound advertising plan also provides an outline for analyzing a new product target market. The consumer, market, and product analyses should all be carried out for the target product class much as was described in Chapters 6 through 9.

In conducting these analyses for new product markets, there are certain areas that need special emphasis. The consumer analysis should, in particular, attempt to discover needs and goals that are incompletely satisfied by existing products. The market analysis should assist in the search for opportunities by attempting to define high potential and fast growth market segments. In addition, the market analysis should help to pinpoint market segments where competition is weak.

The product analysis will also have a different focus. Emphasis will not be placed on analyzing the advertiser's product, since no product will have been developed. Instead the analysis should focus on the characteristics that consumers would most readily want such a product to have and an exploration of available technology able to supply those characteristics. For example, suppose that a marketer of baked goods found through consumer research that a substantial number of consumers desired a lower calorie bread. A major task of the product analysis in such an instance would be to determine whether or not it was technically possible to develop a product that met this need, yet did not suffer in taste appeal.

An introductory advertisement for Black and Decker's cordless, rechargeable household appliance.

EXHIBIT 20-1

# SCRUB EVERY IDEA YOU'VE EVER HAD ABOUT SCRUBBING.

## SCRUB BRUSHER™ FROM BLACK & DECKER

Now you can scrub away dirt and grime with a lot less elbow grease.

Black & Decker's Scrub Brusher™ is the cordless rechargeable scrubber with the power to take even your worst scrubbing jobs to task. And Scrub Brusher™ is U.L. listed, so you can use it safely around water.

The Scrub Brusher™ wet/dry scrubber from Black & Decker. It's a clean break from the drudgery of the past.

Scrub Brusher™ also comes with a smaller brush for hard-to-reach places like faucets.

Scrub away the grime on barbecues.

Take Scrub Brusher™ into the shower and scrub away rust and mildew from tiles.

Smoke stains and soot come clean-a lot easier with Scrub Brusher.™

On carpeting, Scrub Brusher™ has the power to do those tough spot-cleaning jobs.

Scrub Brusher™ stores neatly on the wall in its own recharging unit. So it's always ready when you need it.

**B·D Black & Decker**

© 1983

## Creating New Product Ideas

With the new product market defined and with opportunity areas in that market identified, the advertiser is next ready to begin the process of creating new product ideas.

THE SEARCH FOR NEW PRODUCT IDEAS. Many creative minds should be involved in the search for new product ideas. The director of the new product search should provide each participant with a definition of the new product market under consideration and the results of the consumer, market, and product technology analyses. Providing this information gives each participant sufficient background to make meaningful new product suggestions. It is important, however, that the information be presented as a stimulus to new ideas rather than as a constraint to suggestions. It is important that participants in the search process let their minds roam freely in devising new product approaches.

Participation in the new product idea search should be as broad as possible. Sales managers and salespeople should be involved because of their close contact with the market. Marketing researchers, because of their research experience, often have unique insights into the market and consumers. Advertising agency personnel, because of their creative and marketing skills, should certainly participate. Product research and engineering personnel, because of their technical knowledge, are often good sources.

What the director of this new product effort desires, as was noted earlier, is suggested new product positions. In most cases, however, new product suggestions will not be received in the form of a positioning statement. It is the responsibility of the director of the search to transform the suggestions into potential new positionings by identifying the new central attribute of the product, matching it to the appropriate consumer need segment, and relating it to competitive products.

RESEARCH SOURCES OF NEW PRODUCTS. Two questions arise concerning the role of research in developing new product ideas. First, can consumers be approached directly by marketing researchers to determine what new products they would like? This approach has been tried many times and results are generally disappointing. The average consumer is simply not very creative when it comes to thinking up new product ideas. The better role of research is to determine what consumer needs and goals are unfulfilled. Once new product ideas have been suggested to meet these needs, then researchers will help refine them by seeking consumer suggestions for improvement of the product idea. While consumers are not good at creating new product ideas, they do provide rich insights that are useful in refining product concepts so that they better meet consumer needs.

The second question concerns the role of product-development researchers in defining new products. Should new product ideas come from the laboratory or from marketing? The answer, of course, is that both must participate. Technical advances from the laboratory that meet no consumer need will not make successful new products; new product ideas with great consumer appeal that cannot be economically produced have no value either. It is important that both marketers and product researchers be involved in new product development at both the idea generation stage and the idea evaluation stage.

## Evaluating New Product Ideas

If the recommended process for creating new product ideas is followed, it is likely that numerous new product ideas will be suggested. The usual problem, if participation in the program is wide, is too many new product ideas rather than too few.

The new product ideas must be screened or evaluated to determine which ones warrant further development. The process of developing the physical product in marketable form and preparing a marketing plan for the product is expensive and time-consuming. Consequently, inferior ideas must be eliminated and the remaining ideas ranked in terms of their potential, permitting development work to start with the most promising new product idea.

New product screening involves a series of tests, each somewhat more demanding than the previous one. At each test stage the list of new product candidates will be narrowed. Four tests that are frequently used are discussed below.

CHECKING TECHNICAL FEASIBILITY. Many new product ideas rely upon a new ingredient, a new design, or a new manufacturing process. The new low-calorie bread idea envisioned earlier might, for example, rely upon a new recipe, or a new ingredient, or even a new baking process. Automated supermarket checkout stations were made possible by the development of highly miniaturized lasers to scan and record package codes and electronic watches became feasible with the development of quartz-crystal timing devices.

A good place to start in evaluating new product ideas is to check the availability of the necessary technology. There are several questions to be answered in this area. First, are the ingredients, components, or processes necessary to the product available? Second, if they are not available, could they be developed? If so, what is the likely range of investment that would be required? Only rough estimates are needed at this point, but some estimate is needed in order to know if the investment would be prohibitive. Third, it would be useful to estimate per-unit product costs. What is sought here is a product cost low enough to permit competitive pricing and still realize a profit. A final technical question to be answered concerns product performance. If the product is developed, is it likely to be reliable, will there be safety problems, will it provide a difference noticeable to the user? Each of these questions will rely upon judgments by product development experts or on existing research if the product itself is not, at this stage, available for physical testing.

EVALUATING THE MARKET POSITION. New product ideas that appear technically feasible should next be evaluated in terms of their marketing feasibility. The most successful new products are the ones that have a really distinctive product attribute that better meets consumer needs. It should be possible to write a positioning for the new product that separates it from competitive brands. Another test that can be revealing is to have some rough advertisements prepared for the new product idea. If the creative group cannot create clear and distinctive advertisements for the product, it may indicate that the product does not really have distinctive attributes or that the attributes cannot be easily communicated. In either case, it indicates a product with a poor chance of success.

Another marketing consideration is the size of the market to which the new product will appeal. The positioning statement for the product should identify the segment or segments toward which the new product would be directed. The size of the segment and the new product's probable share of market should be estimated to give an approximate forecast of sales of the product. New products will vary considerably in their potential sales, giving another basis for ranking the new product ideas.

The competitive situation will be a consideration in evaluating the market. If the new product must gain market share from strong, entrenched competition, then sales will be more difficult to gain and a larger promotional investment will be required. If the new product enters a new market segment or one with little competition, a share of that segment will be easier to achieve, although the segment itself is likely to be smaller.

CONCEPT TESTING. Product feasibility and market position evaluations substantially narrow the list of new product ideas. Ideas that still seem promising can next be exposed to consumers to get their evaluation of the products. This step is commonly called **concept testing.**[1] Testing new product ideas at this stage presents a difficult research problem because in most cases the product itself is not available so that the consumer can use it.

*concept testing*

In one research approach to concept testing, written descriptions of new product ideas called **concept statements** are presented to a representative group of consumers usually in focus-group sessions. Testing at this stage tends to be qualitative. Consumers are asked if they understand the idea, how well it would meet their needs, what improvements they would suggest, and whether or not they would be interested in purchasing the product. This approach helps both to evaluate the product idea and to refine it in order to make it more acceptable to consumers.

*concept statement*

A more polished approach to concept testing is to prepare an advertisement for each of the new product ideas. Then consumers are shown advertisements of the new products. The consumers are questioned to determine whether or not the benefits of the new product were communi-

---

[1]See Neil Holbert, *Research in the Twilight Zone*, Monograph Series #7 (Chicago: American Marketing Association, 1977).

cated clearly. The thinking here is that a new product whose major benefit cannot be communicated clearly to consumers by advertising is not likely to be successful.

PRODUCT TESTING. Another stage in testing new product ideas occurs after sample quantities of the new product are available for use by consumers. Product testing is necessarily a late step in new product development since it requires the expensive process of final formulation or design of the product and the setting up of at least pilot production facilities. Clearly, by this stage the number of new product ideas will have been narrowed down to a very few.

The most popular approach to product testing is the use test which was explained in Chapter 8. Essentially this test consists of providing a sample of consumers with a supply of the new product with instructions that they use it in a normal way. After use, sample members are questioned concerning their reactions to the test product. A variety of questions are asked, but it is particularly important to determine whether or not consumers perceive the differences that were built into the product. In addition, of course, it is important to know if target consumers find that the product aids in satisfying a need.

## New Product Introduction Programs

The result of the screening tests will be selection of a new product idea for market introduction. At this point the advertising manager resumes the normal role of building advertising programs to communicate the benefits of the product to consumers. This means that an advertising plan must be prepared. However, the problems and opportunities facing the new product marketer are different and hence different objectives and advertising programs are required.

### Introductory Advertising Objectives

The approach to building budget, media, creative, and other programs for new products is the same as it is for established products. Problems and opportunities facing the product must be determined, advertising objectives defined, and advertising programs constructed that will help to achieve the objectives.

NEW PRODUCT PROBLEMS AND OPPORTUNITIES. The advertising plan for the new product should begin, as for established products, with analyses of consumers, the market, and the product. If the recommended new product development process has been followed, much of the analysis will already have been completed. Market analysis and consumer analysis would have been conducted as preparation for the search for new product ideas. Some product analysis would also have been done but with the new product now developed, this analysis will have to be enlarged to include the strengths and weaknesses of the product that were uncovered in development.

There are several problem areas facing a new product that are different from those facing established products and these deserve special attention. One problem is the need to establish distribution; advertising must help to convince wholesalers, dealers, and retailers to stock the new product.

Another new product problem is consumers' lack of awareness of the product, its name, appearance, and the benefit it provides. There are no carryover effects from prior promotion upon which the new product advertising can build, unless it is just an improvement of an earlier brand.

A related problem is that the product has no base of loyal users upon which to build. Not only has no one sampled the product, they may also view trying the unknown as a risky venture. Advertising, in other words, has substantial inertia to overcome.

NEW PRODUCT OBJECTIVES. Product objectives must be established in order to provide overall guidance to the advertising programs which follow. The positioning statement which provides direction for the marketing of the product should already have been written as the description of the new product idea.

Advertising objectives for the new product should next be defined. Many of these objectives will be similar to those normally associated with established products, but it is also likely that there will be special introductory advertising objectives that attempt to deal with the problems of a new product. For example, the problem of lack of distribution can lead to a variety of objectives. Impressing the trade with heavy initial advertising might aid distribution. An introductory promotion to encourage stocking and to build traffic might also attack the distribution problem. Informing the trade of advertising and sales promotion plans might also encourage stocking of the product.

Lack of initial product awareness might be attacked by both creative and media objectives. A creative objective might be to concentrate on name and package recognition in introductory advertising. A media objective might be to concentrate on blanketing the market with initial coverage in order to establish name registration.

The problem of reluctance to try a new brand is often solved with a sales promotion objective. An introductory offer designed to give consumers an incentive to sample the new product might help overcome the frequently encountered reluctance to try a new product.

### Introductory Budget and Media Programs

The product positioning and advertising objectives will guide the preparation of the new product's advertising programs. The budget and media programs will be prepared, followed by the creative and sales promotion programs for the new product.

NEW PRODUCT BUDGET LEVEL. In setting the advertising budget for a new product, there are two budget decisions to be made. Usually there is a special introductory budget, set at a higher-than-normal level to give the new product initial momentum, and to establish consumer awareness of it. This introductory budget, which in some cases consumes much of the initial sales revenue, should be considered an investment in the product to be repaid from longer term profits. The second budget decision sets the usually lower, sustaining advertising budget level, which is designed to give the product long-term support after the introduction. A heavy introductory budget is also needed to gain initial distribution for the product by stimulating consumer demand, thus encouraging retailers and wholesalers to stock the product. Finally, the introductory budget may be heavier than usual because of the need to support an introductory sales promotion.

The three-step budgeting approach suggested in Chapter 11 (establish a base, make adjustments, provide for feedback) assures a sound basis for setting both the introductory and sustaining budget levels for a new product. There are, however, some special budget considerations for new products, especially with regard to setting the introductory level.

MEDIA SELECTION FOR NEW PRODUCTS. The media program, both introductory and sustaining, should be developed from a set of media requirements such as were suggested in Chapter 12. The media requirements should specify creative requirements, the target segment to be reached, and the desired distribution of the advertising.

During the early introductory period new products tend to have several special media requirements. It is usually desirable that introductory media programs have what advertising people refer to as **high impact.** This means that the introductory advertising should quickly reach the total target audience, making the advertising effort appear impressive and the product appear important. Newspapers, television, and dominant space units in print media meet this high impact requirement for consumer products. The use of a high-impact introductory campaign draws quick attention to the new product, building awareness and trial purchases.

A high impact introduction can also have a favorable effect on decisions made by retailers and wholesalers to stock the product. Thus the trade reputation and merchandising value of the media selected should be carefully considered. It is important to convince potential distributors that the product will be given strong advertising support and thus will be a volume seller. In addition to selecting media that will be impressive in the eyes of the trade, there should be a thorough effort made to merchandise the media program to the trade. This may require a separate media effort directed to the trade and including, perhaps, direct mail, trade magazines, and presentation materials for use by the sales force.

*high impact*

### Introductory Creative Program

The creative program for a new product is of critical importance. The advertiser begins with a clean slate—consumers have no awareness, no knowledge, and no predispositions toward the product. The creative program fills this void with useful information. There are several questions to be considered next that are likely to arise during the preparation of creative programs for new products.

CREATIVE CONTENT FOR THE NEW PRODUCT. The creative content communicates the product benefit and other useful product information to the consumer. When the product is a new one, particular care must be taken to be sure that the product story is clear and complete. The product benefit should be presented simply and clearly because the story will be unfamiliar to consumers. Full information on where and how to purchase should be included, particularly for products not widely available or easily obtained. Guarantees, warranties, return privileges, and other risk-reducing features are particularly important during the introductory stage.

Extra attention should be given to attaining recognition of the brand name and package appearance. There is always considerable danger that advertising for a new product will be confused with existing advertising for better-known, established products.

STRESSING NEWNESS. Another question that is likely to arise concerning new product creative content is whether or not the copy should stress the newness of the product. The advantage of telling consumers that a product is new is that it encourages them to reconsider their existing purchase pattern by suggesting that a different means of satisfying a need is available.

However, if a product has to be advertised as "a remarkable new discovery," it probably isn't. If a product is really new, consumers will recognize its newness without being told. In fact, the description "new, new, new!" may lead consumers to suspect that the product is not really new at all. A valid use of the word "new" is in connection with the product benefit. To the consumer, the fact that a product is new is not important. However, the consumer does consider it useful to know that a new solution to a problem is now available.

CREATIVE PROGRAM CONTINUITY. If new products have high impact media introductions followed by sustaining media programs, should there also be two creative programs—an introductory creative program and a sustaining creative program?

Many times it is desirable to use special introductory advertisements in order to stress the newness of the solution, the product name, the product guarantee, and the other new product content items discussed earlier. However, if there is a special introductory creative program, it is important that there be strong continuity between the introductory advertisements and the sustaining program that follows. Although the sustaining program may give less emphasis to newness, the basic copy platform and the central idea used should be the same as in the introductory program. A new product struggles to establish awareness, identity, and consumer knowledge of itself. Any break in the continuity of the creative approach forces the advertiser to start over in establishing the product in the consumer's mind.

## Introductory Sales Promotion Program

One of the most valuable uses of sales promotions is in the introduction of new products. Special care must be taken in linking the sales promotion to the continuing advertising program.

INTRODUCTORY SALES PROMOTION OBJECTIVES. A sales promotion during the introductory period fulfills both consumer and trade objectives. For new products, the consumer objective of a sales promotion is to encourage the consumer to try the product for the first time. To consumers who already have a favorite brand of a product, trying a new brand presents the risk that the new product will not meet their needs as well as the usually purchased product. To offset this risk, advertisers offer a special introductory incentive to try the new product.

Introductory sales promotions can also help to fulfill the objective of gaining distribution through wholesalers and retailers. The most desirable wholesalers and retailers are generally offered many more products than they can actually distribute and thus select only those which they feel will be volume items and will return a good profit. The trade objective of an introductory sales promotion should be to help overcome wholesaler and retailer reluctance to carry the new product. A successful sales promotion that establishes good sales volume will also encourage them to retain the product.

INTRODUCTORY OFFER. The special incentive used to encourage consumer trial of the new product is usually a monetary incentive — some form of reduced price. Price-off coupons are probably the most frequently used introductory incentive for consumer products. They are direct, easily understood, and geographically controllable. The introductory offer on behalf of a new product should be a simple one that does not distract attention from the primary-product story. Contests and premiums, for example, would not usually be desirable introductory incentives. They require too much explanation that would be better devoted, in the case of a new product, to the product itself.

In addition to the consumer offer, a special incentive is frequently offered directly to the trade. The trade offer, usually directed to the retailer, is designed to give added incentive to purchase an introductory quantity of the new product. The introductory trade incentive is usually an extra discount or a case allowance.

MEDIA AND CREATIVE SUPPORT. The consumer introductory sales promotion is usually timed to coincide with initial distribution of the product. The product must be available so that consumers are not frustrated in their search for it. On the other hand, the consumer offer should not be delayed long after availability of the product since good product movement may be needed to retain distribution. The trade offer should precede the consumer offer, being made at the time that the sales force attempts to establish initial distribution.

Media selection for an introductory sales promotion does not differ greatly from normal sales promotion needs. High reach media are favored and physical form media must be selected if a coupon or other promotional element must be delivered to consumers. Trade advertising, usually business magazines or direct mail, is often used to support the trade offer in addition to a personal selling effort.

In designing creative materials for introductory sales promotions, it should be kept in mind that the primary advertising objective during the introductory period is to present a clear product promise and register the brand name. The introductory sales promotion advertising should present details of the consumer offer and link the special offer, the product story, and the product name together so that they are mutually supportive.

## Testing the New Product Program

Only a small portion of the new product ideas conceived by a company are developed into finished products with complete marketing and advertising plans, and only a small portion of those which are introduced into the marketplace become commercial successes. The investment in product development and marketing before introduction can be very heavy, but, in addition, because of the uncertain outcome in new product introduction, a marketer accepts a substantial additional financial risk when introducing the new product. The company's additional investment during market introduction includes heavy initial advertising expense, introductory sales promotion expense, direct or indirect selling costs to achieve distribution, and research costs for monitoring the introduction.

To reduce the risks of new product introduction to more acceptable levels, it is normal and prudent to test the new product program before the product is introduced. These tests of the total new product program are in addition to the concept tests, product use tests, and other research done on individual elements of the plan.

Three types or levels of new product program tests are in widespread use and will be described in the sections which follow. They are market tests, controlled store tests (or minimarket tests), and simulated test markets or test market laboratories. Exhibit 20-2 shows a recent estimate of the use of these and related testing approaches by consumer goods marketers.

Usage of new product introduction testing technique                    EXHIBIT 20-2

| Testing technique | Percent using in past year: |
|---|---|
| Own test markets, with outside auditing | 33 |
| Controlled store testing | 36 |
| Test market laboratories | 37 |
| Test market purchase diaries | 18 |
| Test market telephone tracking studies | 54 |
| UPC consumer diary panel split cable | 23 |
| UPC consumer diary panel no split cable | 11 |

Reprinted with permission from the February 20, 1984 issue of *Advertising Age*. Copyright 1984 by Crain Communications, Inc.

## Market Tests

Of the three new product introduction testing methods, market testing is the oldest and still probably the most frequently used. We will use the market test as our standard, explaining it fully and will then compare the other two test methods to it. It should be noted that marketers do not always limit themselves to just one of these tests per product. Frequently, for example, a simulated test market is used to refine and verify the introductory plan which is then retested in a market test.

WHAT IS TESTED? **Market tests,** and the other two methods to be examined, evaluate the total introductory program for a new product. Rather than testing individual items in the program, the market test focuses on the interaction of all the introductory elements to estimate the overall success of the introductory program.

*market test*

There are three things that marketers hope to find out from the market test. First, they hope to determine sales response to the total marketing effort for the new product. This information will be used in deciding whether or not sales response to the new product, using the set of introductory programs tested, is sufficient to warrant expansion from the test area to the full marketing area.

Second, the market test seeks to determine, under actual market conditions, which elements of the introductory program need to be improved. There are literally hundreds of unforeseen problems that might arise when the comprehensive introductory program is first exposed to the market. The market test is not only used to predict the degree of success of the new product, but also to discover the strengths and weaknesses of the elements of the introductory program.

Finally market tests can be used to evaluate alternative introductory marketing programs. Suppose, for example, that a marketer is unable to decide judgmentally between two different positionings of a new product. It would be possible to create complete but separate introductory approaches for each alternative and then test each one in a separate set of markets.

Sales results could then be compared to determine which positioning was the better.

*test market*

DESIGN OF MARKET TESTS. Market tests are experiments that are performed in an actual marketplace in order to experience realistic conditions. Rather than introducing the new product nationwide, the introductory program is tested by introducing the product in a controlled and limited area, usually consisting of only a few markets. These areas are called **test markets** and they must be representative of the total area into which the product will later be introduced. The new product program must be faithfully reproduced in a scaled-down version and introduced into the test cities. Results of the test introduction are carefully measured in the test markets and projected in order to estimate how the program would fare if it were used nationally.

SELECTION OF TEST MARKETS. The markets selected for a market test must collectively be representative of the total marketing area and be large enough in terms of the number of prospective customers to allow the marketer to have confidence that the results attained do in fact represent what would occur in a full-scale introduction. The usual rule of thumb is that the combined test markets should equal about three percent of the total market into which the product will finally be introduced. The markets selected should be neither very large (like New York City, for example) nor small rural areas. Usually the criterion of three percent is achieved by selecting several middle-sized markets. Exhibit 20-3 lists 25 cities recommended as test markets by one advertising agency.

The test markets selected should not only contain an adequate number of consumers, but should also be as nearly representative of the total population as possible. The demographic makeup of the markets should be like that of the total area. Important demographic factors to check out for consumer product tests include age, income, education levels, and ethnic composition. Usage of products of the type being tested should be normal in percent of population using, level of use, and distribution of use. Another important factor to check on is competition. The competitors expected in the total market should be present in the test markets as well and ideally should have normal market shares in each test market. The channels of distribution through which the product would subsequently flow should be present in the test market cities.

Finally, it is important that the test cities have a full complement of advertising media, particularly the ones ultimately to be used for the test product, and that the media not be abnormal with regard to their coverage of the markets. For example, if television is to be used in the test, there should be three to five stations available, including all three major networks, and station share in the markets should be normally distributed.

*media spill-in*

**Media spill-in** (the percentage of media coverage originating from outside the test market) should be minimal.

EXHIBIT 20-3

Dancer Fitzgerald sample recommended test markets

| | Market | Percent of U.S. Households |
|---|---|---|
| 1. | Albany-Schenectady-Troy, N.Y. | .63 |
| 2. | Albuquerque | .36 |
| 3. | Amarillo, Tex. | .22 |
| 4. | Austin, Tex. | .25 |
| 5. | Cedar Rapids-Waterloo, Ia. | .38 |
| 6. | Chattanooga, Tenn. | .33 |
| 7. | Cleveland | 1.75 |
| 8. | Colorado Springs-Pueblo | .25 |
| 9. | Columbia-Jefferson City, Mo. | .18 |
| 10. | Davenport-Rock Island-Moline, Ia.-Ill. | .41 |
| 11. | Des Moines | .45 |
| 12. | Duluth-Superior, Minn.-Wis. | .22 |
| 13. | Fargo, N.D. | .26 |
| 14. | Grand Rapids-Kalamazoo-Battle Creek, Mich. | .66 |
| 15. | Greenville-New Bern-Washington, N.C. | .30 |
| 16. | Greenville-Spartanburg-Asheville, S.C.-N.C. | .68 |
| 17. | Indianapolis | 1.03 |
| 18. | Jackson, Miss. | .34 |
| 19. | Jacksonville, Fla. | .45 |
| 20. | Kansas City, Mo. | .86 |
| 21. | Knoxville | .49 |
| 22. | Lexington, Ky. | .29 |
| 23. | Louisville | .58 |
| 24. | Memphis | .72 |
| 25. | Milwaukee | .92 |

Reprinted with permission from the February 4, 1980 issue of *Advertising Age.* Copyright 1980 by Crain Communications, Inc.

*Translation of the Introductory Program.* The introductory marketing program placed in the test areas must be an accurately scaled-down version of the effort to be used nationally or in the full marketing introduction area. Therefore, it is essential that the product introduction program first be prepared for the total marketing area, and then be scaled down to the test area. If this scaling-down is not accurately done, the test area results will be distorted and thus not be projectable.

Of the four advertising programs—budget, media, creative, and sales promotion—the easiest to translate to the test area is the creative program. It simply requires that the advertisements that are to be used in the full area or national introduction also be used in the test markets.

Scaling down the budget is a more complex problem. One approach is to make the test market budget proportional to the percentage of prospects in the test markets. Thus if 2 percent of the total prospects live in the test markets, the test area budget will be 2 percent of the total plan budget. This is termed the **as-it-falls approach** and is usually acceptable if large test

*as-it-falls approach*

markets are used. Unfortunately, this approach causes distortions, particularly in small markets if test market media costs are above or below average. This problem can be overcome by placing equivalent media weight rather than proportional dollars in the test areas. For example, if the introductory plan calls for use of television spots and it is predicted that on the average each market buy will produce 100 gross rating points a week, then enough money will be allocated to the test markets to purchase 100 gross rating points a week. This is termed the **little-U.S. approach** and is a preferred method, especially for mini-test markets.[2]

*little-U.S. approach*

Translation of the media program requires purchasing the same or equivalent media in the test markets as would be purchased during the full introduction. This is not usually difficult if locally originating media such as spot television, spot radio, or newspapers are planned. However, if national media such as magazines or network television are indicated in the national plan, then some substitute media must be found for the market test. The usual practice is to substitute newspaper supplements for magazines and spot television for network. These substitutions are, however, compromises.

If an introductory sales promotion is part of the introductory program, it should be accurately scaled down to the test markets by using the approaches already described. The planned creative materials should be used, the budget should permit proportional media weight or, perhaps, proportional delivery of coupons, and comparable media should be found.

*Monitoring of Test Results.* In order to read the outcome of a market test, it is necessary to utilize research measurement procedures. In most test markets several measurement techniques are used, each one focusing on a different test outcome.

The most important monitoring activity is the measurement of test market sales. If the company sells the test product direct to end users, as industrial firms often do, sales results can be captured as part of the company's internal accounting procedure. However, if the new product is sold through trade intermediaries (manufacturer to wholesaler to retailer to consumer, for example), then the problem is more complicated. In that case, the company's accounting system records sales to the wholesaler, but the measure of test market success is sales to consumers. There are three techniques in general use for capturing these consumer sales or, as it is termed in the trade, **consumer take-away.** The first of these is the retail audit in which a research firm monitors retail sales for selected products in a sample of stores by conducting periodic physical inventory counts. A second approach, available for products sold through supermarkets, is to tabulate warehouse withdrawals or the movement of product from the supermarket warehouse onto the retail shelf. While this is not the same as consumer take-away, it is a close approximation since little stock is held

*consumer take-away*

---

[2]"Plan Two Test Markets," *Marketing News* (January 1, 1974), p. 8.

on the supermarket shelf and turnover is very rapid. A third and newer technique is to measure consumer sales in a sample of stores using data generated by scanners at checkout stations. Scanner data, available mostly from food stores, is collected by store computers and is, in turn, compiled by research services.

Usually other tests and measurements are made in the test market to evaluate other elements of the introductory program. Measures of creative effectiveness are often used as well as measures of media audience and sales promotion results. These and other measurement techniques are explained in greater detail in Chapter 22.

EVALUATION OF MARKET TEST RESULTS. The market test must be allowed to continue long enough to gather meaningful results. Unfortunately, companies often feel an urgent need to get an early prediction of results, often before valid data are available. According to one expert, research suggests that "the ratio of forecasting accuracy in test markets is one out of seven after two months.... The odds of accurately forecasting national results steadily increase to five out of six after 10 months."[3]

One reason that market tests are lengthy is that the results measured should be trends rather than single period data. This is especially important in the measurement of sales results. Particularly for consumable goods, the important measure is not initial purchase, but repurchase, because repurchase indicates basic product satisfaction upon which long-term success depends. It is also important to allow trends to develop in distribution, awareness of advertising, and competitive reactions.

The results of the market test might indicate that the product and its introductory plan are ready for full introduction or they might indicate a need for a revised product or plan. If the revisions required are substantial, a new market test should be conducted. The marketer should not give up on a new product if the problem of lack of acceptance is identifiable and potentially correctable. Many new products have gone through several market tests before eventual success.

When a successful market test has been completed, the product is ready for more general introduction. The introductory program, from which the test market was drawn, provides the basis for the general introduction of the product. The general introduction of the new product may extend distribution to the company's total marketing area all at one time or the introduction may be a gradual one. An introduction that spreads out gradually from one area to another is termed a **roll-out.** The advantage of the roll-out approach is that it allows concentration of introductory resources (money and human resources) in one area at a time. It also permits further refinement of the program as the introduction proceeds.

*roll-out*

---

[3]"How to Improve Your Chances for Test-Market Success," *Marketing News* (January 6, 1984), p. 12.

STRENGTHS AND WEAKNESSES OF MARKET TESTS. Market tests are the most valid, most reliable method for predicting new product success. The sample size, compared to other techniques, is large and because the test is conducted in the field, it is a representative experience.

The strengths of the market test also lead to its disadvantages. Because of the size of the test, it is very expensive compared to other smaller scale techniques. Market tests are also slow to show valid results. In most cases, twelve months of data are needed before accurate conclusions can be drawn. Another serious shortcoming of market tests stems from the fact that they are conducted in the field in full view of competition. Usually competitors will become aware of market tests in progress through reports from their sales force or distributors. They may choose to disrupt the test by injecting an unusual marketing effort of their own into the test markets, spoiling the representativeness of the test and making it difficult to inter- pret results. Worse yet, competitors may anticipate the success of the mar- ket test and rush a copy-cat product into the market. There have been cases in which competitors have copied a product being market tested and put it into national distribution, without a market test, thereby preempting the originator of the product.

Exhibit 20-4 compares on a summary basis the attributes of the three testing methods to be discussed in this section.

## Controlled Store Testing

*controlled store testing (minimarket testing)*

**Controlled store testing,** sometimes also referred to as **minimarket testing,** is a second way in which new product introduction programs can be tested. Controlled store testing is an evolutionary development of the traditional market test that was designed to provide lower cost, and faster, more confidential results.

DESIGN OF CONTROLLED STORE TESTING. Controlled store testing was first used in the 1950s and continues today as an important new product program test method. It is sometimes used as a prelude to a full-scale market test and sometimes as a stand-alone test before full introduction.

Controlled store tests are usually conducted through research firms that offer this testing service in limited sets of markets. Burgoyne, Inc., originator of controlled store testing is one of the leaders in this field.[4] The markets chosen for controlled store testing are generally smaller than those used for traditional market tests. The larger difference, however, is that the research firm arranges contractually for complete distribution of the test product in a panel of retail outlets in the minimarket area. As a result, the marketer does not have to conduct a personal selling effort to retailers

---

[4]Cynthia Hardie, "Profile of a Consultant: Delivering the Goods," *Advertising Age* (February 4, 1980), pp. S-16–17.

| Attribute | Introductory Test Method | | |
|---|---|---|---|
| | Full-Scale Test Market | Minimarket Test | Laboratory Test Market |
| **Predictor of volume and share** | Poor | Fair | Good |
| **Timing** | Very slow, 9–12 mos. minimum | Slow, 2–3 mos.— faster than full-scale test | Very fast— 12–14 weeks |
| **Can be influenced by competition (i.e., heavyups, etc.)** | Yes | Yes | No |
| **Confidentiality** | Completely open to competition | Not confidential, but not monitored by Nielsen, etc. | Confidential |
| **Can predict trade response** | Yes | No | No |
| **Can test alternative marketing mixes easily and cheaply** | No | Yes, but to a lesser extent than laboratory test marketing | Yes, although accuracy is not precise |
| **Cost** | High — over $500M | Medium — about $175M | Low — $60M |

Reprinted with permission from the February 4, 1980 issue of *Advertising Age*. Copyright 1980 by Crain Communications, Inc.

as a part of the test. This eliminates retailer acceptance as one of the variables of the test.

Except for distribution, an effort is made to duplicate normal introductory conditions in the controlled markets. The introductory advertising creative, media, and budget programs are translated into the controlled markets as is done in the traditional market test. Likewise the introductory sales promotion program is proportionally implemented.

SELECTION OF MARKETS. The selection of markets in a controlled store test differs substantially from those used in a traditional market test. The markets used are generally smaller and the total population in all the markets used is usually under 1 percent of the total population. An attempt is made to select representative markets, but selection is in large measure determined by the ability of the research firm to establish a contractual arrangement with a panel of retail stores having the characteristics necessary for the test.

There is one recently introduced form of controlled store testing that has even more stringent market selection criteria. BehaviorScan, a Chicago-based research firm, offers a controlled store testing program that, in addition to using controlled store distribution, utilizes scanner systems to audit consumer purchases and cable television as a means of translating and controlling the advertising effort.[5] This research firm actually equips supermarkets in the test cities with scanner equipment so that the test results can be collected. Cities selected are relatively small — population of 100,000 to 150,000 — and must be isolated from other major shopping cities, must have at least ten supermarkets willing to cooperate, 75 percent of the population must receive cable television, and other media, especially newspapers, must be available. Markets currently used include Visalia, California; Grand Junction, Colorado; and Williamsport, Pennsylvania.

STRENGTHS AND WEAKNESSES OF CONTROLLED STORE TESTING. The controlled store test represents a halfway point between the realistic conditions of the market test and the artificial and highly controlled conditions of the test market laboratory to be described next. The controlled store test trades off the large sample of the test market for a substantially smaller set of markets with better control. Results from a controlled store test are probably a poorer predictor of success than are traditional test market results if the market test is not interrupted by competition or other uncontrollable factors. Controlled store tests are somewhat more confidential than market tests because they are run in small areas and may be overlooked by competition.

Because of their smaller scale, controlled store tests are less expensive to run than market tests, and since the sell-in period is eliminated by contracting for distribution, test results are available earlier from the controlled store test. On the other hand, the contractually arranged distribution provides no test of the trade's response to the new product. The ability to gain distribution for the new product is simply eliminated as a variable in the test.

As is probably obvious from the description, controlled store testing services are at present available only for products sold through food stores. However, the description of the method might suggest — to marketers of other products — controlled test designs that the marketer could carry out with the company's own staff.

## Test Market Laboratories

*test market laboratory (simulated test market — STM)*

The third and most recently developed new product introduction testing technique is the **test market laboratory** or, as it is sometimes termed, the **simulated test market (STM).** Of the three approaches, the test market laboratory is the most controlled, most removed from normal market conditions, and most confidential.

DESIGN OF TEST MARKET LABORATORIES. Test market laboratories are offered as services by a number of marketing research firms. Among the

---

[5]Ellen Norris, "Product Hopes Tied to Cities with the Right Stuff," *Advertising Age* (February 20, 1984), pp. M-10ff.

services available are BASES by Burke Marketing Services, ASSESSOR by Management Decision Systems, and Laboratory Test Market by Yankelovich, Skelly, and White.

The design of most test market laboratories is made up of a number of phases.[6] In the first phase, consumers are intercepted in shopping centers and brought to a test location in the center for interviewing. Demographic, product use, and product attitude information is recorded. The test consumers are next shown a test commercial or advertisement for the test product. The advertisement may be in finished form or it may be a rough or unfinished concept board. The test members are then reinterviewed to determine any changes in attitude toward the test product and to determine their interest in purchasing it. A first set of projections of introduction success may be made from these results. Typically about 300 consumers in each of three or four cities are included in these tests.

In the next phase, after viewing the test advertisement and being reinterviewed, the consumers are given price-off coupons or purchase credits toward products in the test category. They are then taken to a simulated store shelf that has a variety of brands in the test category and are allowed to select a product using their coupons. The choice of product is recorded and, based on the results, new market introduction results are calculated using complex computer models. In some tests, the simulated purchase phase is skipped and a supply of the test product is given to those test participants who expressed an interest in trying the product. They, like the ones in the simulated purchase experiment, are asked to take the product home for use.

Typically, the third phase in a test market laboratory involves a reinterview, usually by telephone, of the test participants who purchased or were given the test product. The participants are asked if they used the test product, their opinion of it is compared to competitive products, and they are asked to rate it along a number of dimensions. The participants' stated intention to purchase the test product if it becomes generally available becomes an important measure used in the projection of product success.

MEASURING TEST RESULTS. The results of the interview that are gathered at each phase of the test market laboratory are used to project the outcome of the introduction of the test product. The projections are made by manipulating the interview response data in complex computer models that are proprietary to each research firm offering the service. These firms validate and revise their models based on the actual results achieved by products introduced after going through test market laboratories. Published validation results are complex, but, in general, suggest a high degree of accuracy for test market laboratories.

----

[6]"How It's Done," *Advertising Age* (February 20, 1984), p. M-11.

STRENGTHS AND WEAKNESSES OF TEST MARKET LABORATORIES. The characteristics of test market laboratories are a result of their abstract yet controlled design. Because these tests are conducted on a much reduced scale, they are far less expensive than the two alternative testing techniques described earlier. Results are also available much more quickly than in the case with the alternative tests.

Because the test is conducted in the controlled, laboratory setting, confidentiality can more easily be achieved and competitive interference is ruled out. On the other hand, the laboratory setting has its disadvantages. It does not test the ability of the product to gain and hold distribution nor the reactions and responses of the competition. Consumer reactions to the product are more artificial than those gained in a field test and, although test market laboratory results have been validated by experience, many feel that the only truly valid test is one that takes place in the marketplace. It should be noted again that test market laboratories are frequently used as a first test to determine which new product candidates should go into a test market. Test market laboratory services are generally available only for consumer packaged goods.

---

*CHAPTER SUMMARY*

The search for new products begins by defining the market to be explored based on the firm's special competence and the presence of unmet consumer needs. The selected market should be analyzed so that consumer problems may be understood, so that high-potential market segments may be identified and available production technology explored. With the analysis as a guide, a wide variety of persons are asked to contribute new product suggestions. Each suggestion should be transformed into a positioning statement. New product ideas are then screened to determine those that are worth product development work. Screening involves checking technical feasibility, evaluating the marketing potential, testing the concept by means of consumer research, and by consumer testing of product samples.

When a new product idea has been selected, an advertising plan should be developed. Consumer, market, and product analyses should define problems and opportunities facing the product. These analyses lead to the definition of objectives, including special objectives to solve the problems of lack of distribution and lack of consumer awareness faced by new products. The budget program often calls for heavier introductory expenditures to help establish initial distribution and product awareness. The introductory media program stresses high-impact media to stimulate quick consumer attention, product trial, and trade stocking. The creative program should stress full information and clear presentation, product name and package, and risk-reducing features. A sales promotion is frequently part of the introductory plan to stimulate both consumer sampling and trade stocking. The basic offer both to consumers and to the trade is usually some form of reduced price. The promotion should receive separate creative and media support.

Because of the high risk involved in introducing a new product, the program for such an introduction should normally be tested. The purpose of the testing is to improve upon the introductory plan before it is fully implemented and to predict the likelihood of success of the new product upon introduction. Three techniques for testing new product introduction programs are in general use. They are the market test, the controlled store test, and the test market laboratory. Selection of the test method to be used depends upon a variety of factors including time and money available, the need for confidentiality, the need for accuracy, and the availability of the method required by the product type to be tested.

---

| | | |
|---|---|---|
| New product | Little-U.S. approach | *KEY TERMS* |
| Concept testing | Consumer take-away | |
| Concept statement | Roll-out | |
| High impact | Controlled store testing | |
| Market test | (minimarket testing) | |
| Test market | Test-market laboratory | |
| Media spill-in | (simulated test market | |
| As-it-falls approach | — STM) | |

---

1. Consider each of the following recently introduced products and decide whether you would classify each as a new product or as a minor product improvement.      *QUESTIONS FOR DISCUSSION*

   a. "Light" jams and jellies.
   b. Disposable razors.
   c. Diesel-powered small cars.
   d. Disc cameras.
   e. Gourmet popping corn.

2. One organizational approach to new product development that has become popular is the use of venture teams. Each team is made up of people with different specialties representing different functional areas in the company. The team is assigned responsibility for a new product all the way from the idea stage to successful test marketing.

   a. What areas or specialties do you think should be represented by members of the venture team?
   b. What advantages do you see in this organizational approach to new products?

3. Some companies, rather than develop new product ideas on their own, wait for other companies to pioneer a new market. If the product is successful, they then enter the market with a copy of the new product. What advantages and disadvantages do you see in this approach?

4. In recent years it has become a become a common practice for a company to attempt to disrupt the market test of a competitor. Techniques used have included buying up the test product, injecting a special consumer or trade promotion into the test area, saturating the test market with advertising, or reshelving the test product to undesirable locations. What limitations do you think a marketing manager should place on such disruptive tactics by his or her own firm?

5. Concept testing consists of explaining one or more new product ideas to consumers by means of descriptions or prototype advertisements. Why is this approach used rather than giving consumers actual samples of the proposed new products to try and compare?

6. Supermarket chains, faced every year with hundreds of requests to stock new products, frequently establish buying committees to evaluate new products. These committees often permit a brief presentation by a company representative on behalf of its new product. If you were making such a presentation, what information would you provide to the committee to convince them that they should stock your product?

7. When The Stouffer Corporation market tested its Lean Cuisine product line its initial test markets were Dayton, Cincinnati, Cleveland, Columbus (Ohio), Omaha, Denver, and Philadelphia.[7] Using the test market selection criteria suggested earlier in the chapter:

   a. Do you think Stouffer used the right number of test markets?
   b. Did they select cities in appropriate geographic areas?
   c. Do the cities appear to be representative?

8. It is difficult to decide how much to spend on advertising for new products because there is little historical data to use for guidance. There are no past advertising budgets, no actual sales results, and sometimes no competitive spending. In the absence of these historical guidelines, how would an advertiser go about setting a new product advertising budget?

9. In selecting media for the introduction of a new product, it was suggested that a high impact medium like newspapers or television be used initially. These media, of course, are appropriate for introducing consumer products. What media would produce high impact in the introduction of a new industrial product?

---

[7]"Tested Product #8," *Adverting Age* (February 20, 1984), p. M-40.

10. Exhibit 20-4 that lists new product introduction test technique usage contains four test techniques that were not described in the text. They represent variations of the first three listed. Based on the descriptive name, how do you think the following test techniques work?

   a. Test market purchase diaries.
   b. Test market telephone tracking studies.
   c. UPC consumer diary panel split cable.
   d. UPC consumer diary panel no-split cable.

11. Many times marketers who have developed a new product are reluctant to take it into a test market because of fear that competitors will steal the product idea.

   a. List the advantages and the disadvantages of test marketing before a general introduction.
   b. What conditions might make you willing to skip the test market?
   c. Would it make a difference if the product were a major hard good like a refrigerator rather than a consumer packaged good like a frozen vegetable? Suppose it were an industrial product?

---

*PROBLEM*

Pillsbury, one of the nation's leading consumer food products marketers, was about to begin national marketing of Milk Break Milk Bars, an entry into the cereal-meal-bar category.[8] This category had retail sales of $350 million and had experienced growth of over 100 percent in the previous four years.

Despite the potential of this market, Pillsbury had not had a product in the market and was concerned about its late entry. Both General Mills and Quaker Oats, two of Pillsbury's largest competitors, had marketed chewy granola bars which were part of the product category. Moreover, General Mills and Sunkist had recently introduced dried fruit rolls into the category. Even more recently, Quaker had introduced — with a very heavy $24 million advertising and promotion budget — Granola Dipps, a chewy granola bar. Retail shelf space in this snack section was becoming crowded with the introduction of new products and already some of the older products were losing some of their shelf space or being dropped entirely.

Pillsbury's Milk Break Milk Bars was a four flavor line of chocolate covered wafers with cream filling, packed six bars to a box and designed to retail at $1.79 a box. Pillsbury hoped to have the new product shelved in food stores' "good-for-you" snack section. Although children were the primary consumers of these products, mothers were thought to be the key

---

[8]This problem was drawn from Janet Neiman, "Pillsbury's Milk Break Hits Cereal Bar Market," *Advertising Age* (March 26, 1984), pp. 3, 77.

purchasers. Milk Break's product difference, as reflected in the product name, was that each bar contained a half glass of milk. Pillsbury had tentatively set aside a budget of $16 million for the introductory advertising. It was generally considered in the trade that if the Milk Break introduction was successful, additional products would be added to the line. The Milk Break products were to be introduced nationally without a test market.

1. Prepare a positioning statement for Milk Break Milk Bars.
2. Prepare a list of the problems that you feel Pillsbury would face in introducing Milk Break Milk Bars.
3. In the light of those problems, outline an introduction program for Milk Break Milk Bars, including selection of media, creative approach, and sales promotion approach.

*PART THREE*

*SELECTED
READINGS*

*The Advertising Budget — Preparation, Administration and Control.* New York: Association of National Advertisers, 1967. A review of advertising budgeting practices as they are actually carried out by leading advertisers.

Sissors, Jack Z. and Jim Surmanek. *Advertising Media Planning,* 2nd ed. Chicago: Crain Books, 1982. A complete and authoritative treatment of modern day media evaluation and selection.

Calentone, Roger J. and Ulrike de Brentani-Todorovic. "The Maturation of the Science of Media Selection," *Journal of the Academy of Marketing Science,* Fall, 1981, pp. 490–524. A thorough review of the literature and history of the use of computer models in media selection.

Nash, Edward L. *Direct Marketing: Strategy, Planning, Execution.* New York: McGraw-Hill Book Company, 1982. A comprehensive and up-to-date description of the process for developing and implementing a direct marketing program, written by a leading practitioner in the field.

Young, Robert F. and Stephen A. Greyser. *Cooperative Advertising: Practices and Problems.* Cambridge, Mass.: Marketing Science Institute, 1982. A new analysis of a widely used yet problem plagued form of advertising.

Ogilvy, David. *Ogilvy on Advertising.* New York: Crown Books, 1983. Ogilvy, a copywriter, agency founder, and dean of advertising creative talents, tells what works and what does not work in creating advertising. His observations are strongly based on advertising effectiveness research.

Nelson, Roy Paul. *The Design of Advertising,* 4th ed. Dubuque, Iowa: William C. Brown Company, 1982. A textbook on copywriting, layout, and production of print advertising.

Bockus, H. William Jr. *Advertising Graphics,* 3rd ed. New York: MacMillan Publishing Company, 1979. A book that focuses on the functions of the print art director, including advertising design, layout, and production.

White, Hooper. *How to Produce an Effective TV Commercial.* Chicago: Crain Books, 1982. Detailed yet easily understood explanation of modern television commercial production techniques. Written to meet the needs of the advertising manager who controls and oversees television production.

Schultz, Don E. and William A. Robinson. *Sales Promotion Essentials.* Chicago: Crain Books, 1982. A detailed description of sales promotion techniques and their application as practiced by marketers today.

Cafarelli, Eugene J. *Developing New Products and Repositioning Mature Brands.* New York: John Wiley and Sons, Inc., 1980. A thorough, state-of-the-art review of current new product development processes from conceptualization through introduction.

## Part Four
## CONTROL AND EVALUATION OF THE ADVERTISING PROGRAMS

We noted earlier in the book that the responsibilities of the advertising manager were to plan advertising programs, to implement them, and to control the results of the advertising effort. Thus far, our focus has been on the first two responsibilities. In Part 4 our attention turns to the third function of the advertising manager—control. What does it mean to say that the advertising manager has control responsibilities? The control process involves measuring actual results, comparing them with target results, and then taking corrective action to remedy deficiencies revealed by the comparison. In the case of advertising, the manager measures the actual accomplishment of the advertising effort, compares it with the accomplishment standards developed in the advertising plan, and then revises future advertising programs accordingly.

There are several areas in which the advertiser should exert control. It is essential that the effectiveness of the advertising programs in meeting advertising-plan objectives be evaluated. This topic will be considered in Chapters 21 and 22. It is equally essential in today's business environment that the advertiser evaluate whether or not the advertising meets consumer responsibility standards and legal standards. These control programs will be considered in Chapters 23 and 24.

By the time you have completed Part 4, you will know for each of the above control programs:

1. How to set standards for desired performance.

2. How to measure actual or projected performance.

3. When to take corrective action and who should have responsibility for taking it.

# CHAPTER 21

*Evaluating
Advertising Effectiveness*

LEARNING OBJECTIVES

In studying this chapter you will learn:

● How advertising effectiveness is measured.

● What an advertising effectiveness evaluation program should include.

● The design of effectiveness evaluation procedures for each element of the advertising program.

The advertising manager must have an objective program of advertising evaluation. The size of advertising budgets makes it mandatory to be able to back up continued requests for advertising funds by pointing to specific results. More important, improvement of future advertising programs requires a constant flow of feedback concerning results of current programs. This effectiveness feedback permits improvements to be made in future advertising programs. The advertising manager who relies on intuition, rather than scientifically gathered data, to provide effectiveness feedback will probably find it difficult to convince superiors and will tend to be blind to problems in the advertising program.

The issue, then, that concerns us regarding advertising effectiveness evaluation is not whether it should be done, but how it should be done. This chapter covers the approach to building a program for advertising effectiveness evaluation. Before the specific steps to building the program are presented, we need an understanding of what constitutes effectiveness. In the first section of this chapter, therefore, we will consider how consumers respond to advertising and what response indicates an effective advertisement or advertising program.

## The Measurement of Advertising Effectiveness

The purpose of advertising is to provide information that will change consumers' mental and behavioral responses in a manner favored by the advertiser. The difficulty is that there is more than one response typically resulting from an advertisement. Thus the advertiser must decide what response best describes the effectiveness of the advertisement to be evaluated, and then must devise a test to measure that response.

There are two competing proposals concerning which response or responses should be measured in order to determine advertising effectiveness. One proposal states that the ultimate purpose of advertising is to get people to purchase the advertised product. Therefore the only response of real interest is sales. This proposal, to be called the **sales effect of advertising,** will be examined first. The second proposal is termed the **hierarchy of effects.** This proposal acknowledges that the ultimate objective of advertising is sales, but suggests that before the sale an advertisement takes consumers through a series of intermediate steps. Any one of these intermediate steps, according to this proposal, can be useful as a measure of advertising effectiveness.

*sales effect of advertising*

*hierarchy of effects*

### The Sales Effect of Advertising

If you ask business people, "What is the purpose of advertising?" their immediate response is likely to be, "To generate profitable sales." If this is the purpose of advertising, then it seems reasonable that the most valid measure of advertising effectiveness is the sales (or profits) generated by the advertising to be evaluated.

THE SALES-EFFECT MODEL. The sales effect measurement can be illustrated by using the SIR diagram presented in Chapter 5. The stimulus is the element of the advertising effort to be evaluated and is represented by the first box in Exhibit 21-1. The stimulus might be a single advertisement, the media program, or the total advertising plan.

The SIR model form applied to advertising effects.                     **EXHIBIT 21-1**

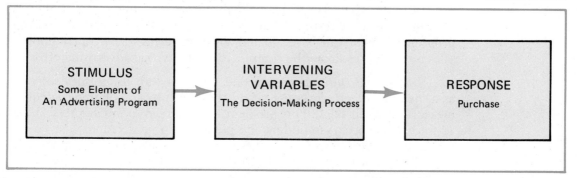

| STIMULUS | INTERVENING VARIABLES | RESPONSE |
|---|---|---|
| Some Element of An Advertising Program | The Decision-Making Process | Purchase |

If the stimulus is perceived by consumers, they use it in their decision-making process, which is represented by the middle box. In the view of advocates of the sales-effect approach, the nature of this decision-making process is only dimly understood and is difficult to measure. However, they contend that any response that is beneficial to the advertiser must result eventually in increased sales of the advertiser's product. Thus sales become, according to this model, the ultimate and preferred measure of effectiveness. The third or response box is purchase, the variable to be measured in evaluating effectiveness.

Interpretation of the response measurement requires some base for comparison. If, for example, an advertiser were evaluating a media program which consisted of radio announcements, the sales resulting from the radio campaign might be measured. However, in order to decide whether the results were good or bad, it would be necessary to compare those sales results to some standard. One kind of standard often used is established by testing an alternative such as, in this case, TV advertising. In this way the two sales results can be compared and the better alternative selected.

EVALUATION OF THE SALES-EFFECT MODEL. The strengths of the sales-effect model are that it is conceptually simple and it evaluates advertising in terms of its ultimate objective — sales. The sales-effect model is not, however, without its weaknesses, three of which are discussed below.

*Other Objectives of Advertising.* While it is perhaps true that the ultimate, long-term, objective of advertising is to produce profitable sales, it also seems to be true that advertising frequently has other very important short-term objectives. For example, a company may use advertising to enhance its reputation in the community, or to get leads for its salespeople, or to advise consumers of a change in service policy. These short-term objectives of the advertising are developed as an essential step in the advertising planning process. They are derived from the analysis of problems and opportunities facing the product and, in turn, provide guidance to the advertising programs.

It is true that ultimately all of these objectives, if achieved, should lead to an increase in sales. However, it is of practical importance to know whether or not these intermediate advertising objectives have been fulfilled. The sales-effect measurement approach does not provide this information. To presume that the effectiveness of each advertising-program element can be evaluated solely in terms of its contribution to sales is to underestimate the complexity of the typical advertising effort.

*Measurement Difficulties.* A second problem with using sales response as a measure of effectiveness lies in the difficulty in obtaining adequate measurements of sales. This problem was referred to in Chapters 11 and 12 since it also occurs in budget and media program decisions.

There are two major difficulties in obtaining valid measures of the sales response to advertising. The first difficulty is that sales are influenced by so many different factors that it is difficult to isolate the sales generated by one particular element in the advertising program from those generated by another factor. Furthermore, it is difficult to isolate the sales effect of the total advertising program from the effects of other elements of the marketing mix.

The usual approach of researchers to the problem of measuring the sales effect of a single advertising-program element is through experimentation. The use of experimentation as a testing technique was considered in some detail in Chapter 20. Briefly, a market test, the most basic form of market experimentation, is a test in a limited geographic area in which one advertising element is changed while all other elements are kept unchanged. Then any increase or decrease in sales in the test area, as compared to another control area in which nothing is changed, can be attributed to the test element that was varied. For example, suppose an advertiser who sold a product in several different cities wished to know whether or not to shift the media effort from radio to television. One city could be designated as a test city and in that market a change made from radio to television. The marketing effort in the test city would have to remain the same in all other respects. Sales in the test city would be compared to sales in other cities where use of radio would be continued, to serve as a control. If sales in the test city increased while sales in the control cities stayed the same, the increase in sales could be attributed to the use of television. The validity of the test depends upon all other influences on sales in the test market and in the control markets staying in an unchanged relationship to each other, a condition difficult to attain. Test results, therefore, contain considerable uncertainty and offer only a partial solution to the problem of measuring sales effectiveness.

A second difficulty in measuring sales response is the lag between stimulus (the advertising) and response (the resulting sales). If, for example, an advertisement that is to be evaluated was used in January, it would partially affect sales in January, but some of its effect would carry over to influence sales in February, March, and perhaps later. An advertiser, therefore, cannot be certain which sales should be attributed to which stimulus. Again, it is possible to estimate carry-over effects through experimentation, but this is costly and inexact.

*Measurement vs. Description.* Another shortcoming of the sales-effect model is the nature of the measurements provided. The sales measure, if obtained, tells whether or not a particular program element meets the objectives. It will also tell, when two alternative advertising elements are compared, which one is more effective. What it does not reveal is why the results occurred and, therefore, does not tell the advertiser what corrective action is needed.

For example, suppose that a new creative program is prepared and then tested against the current program. If the new program were to score lower in a sales effectiveness test than the current campaign, how much would really have been learned? The test results reveal little about what changes might improve the new program.

## The Hierarchy-of-Effects Model

The hierarchy-of-effects model differs from the sales-effect model in that it examines the intervening variables or the decision-making process itself rather than just the sales response.

ASSUMPTIONS OF THE HIERARCHY-OF-EFFECTS MODEL. The hierarchy-of-effects model employs two assumptions. The first is that the process by which a consumer decides to purchase a product is made up of a number of steps or stages. The consumer begins the process with a low level of conviction and then, step by step, becomes increasingly knowledgeable about and motivated toward a particular product. The final step is purchase of the product.

The second assumption of the model is that the purpose of advertising is to move people along the steps in the decision-making process. The ultimate purpose of moving people through these stages is, of course, to produce sales.

*AIDA formula*

STEPS LEADING TO PURCHASE. There have been numerous formulations of the stages that a consumer must pass through in making a purchase decision. One of the earliest was the **AIDA formula** that has for many years been presented as the basis for successful personal selling.[1] The initials stand for Attention, Interest, Desire, and Action and represent the steps through which the salesperson must take the prospect to achieve a sale.

Advertising experts have also proposed descriptions of the steps in a purchase decision, relating them in particular to the response to advertisements. There are many of these descriptions, but probably the most widely quoted is:

| | |
|---|---|
| 1. awareness<br>2. knowledge | cognitive component |
| 3. liking<br>4. preference | affective component |
| 5. conviction<br>6. purchase | conative component |

The authors of this list point out that it contains three components which correspond to the three basic dimensions of behavior. The cognitive component is concerned with information gathering; the affective component is concerned with the formation of feelings or attitudes; and the conative component, with motivation or action.[2]

THE HIERARCHY AND THE CONSUMER DECISION-PROCESS MODEL. The assumption that consumers pass through a series of stages in making a pur-

---

[1]An early presentation of the AIDA formula is to be found in E. K. Strong, *The Psychology of Selling* (1st ed.; New York: McGraw-Hill, 1925), p. 9.
[2]Robert J. Lavidge and Gary A. Steiner, "A Model for Predictive Measurements of Advertising Effectiveness," *Journal of Marketing* (October, 1961), pp. 59–62.

chase decision is consistent with the consumer decision-process model presented in Chapter 5. In Exhibit 21-2 a simplified version of the consumer decision-process model is shown and the steps of the hierarchy of effects appear underneath to indicate where the two models correspond.

Awareness occurs in the consumer model only if the consumer is exposed to the advertisement. Knowledge occurs if the consumer goes one step further and acknowledges the usefulness of the information and considers the product as a potential solution. Liking and preference, which are closely related steps, refer to the decision-making process itself. Liking and preference mean that the consumer evaluates the product and finds it, first, a satisfactory solution and second, the preferred solution. Conviction represents the outcome of the decision. After the decision, the consumer has conviction with regard to purchasing the product or, as was stated in Chapter 5, the consumer is motivated to buy the product. The final step, purchase, corresponds directly to the response variable in the consumer decision-process model.

ADVANTAGES OF THE HIERARCHY-OF-EFFECTS MODEL. If, as the hierarchy-of-effects model suggests, consumers move through a series of steps in arriving at a purchase decision, how does this aid in measuring the effectiveness of advertising?

*Measurement Advantages.* The hierarchy model suggests that advertising's effectiveness can be measured in terms of its ability to move people along the steps. If, for example, an advertisement is successful in increasing people's knowledge about a product, then it is effective. If two advertisements are tested and the first increases knowledge more than the second, the first is the more effective advertisement.

The use of changes in knowledge as a measure of advertising effectiveness presumes that increases in knowledge about a product ultimately lead

The hierarchy of effects related to the consumer-decision process.                    **EXHIBIT 21-2**

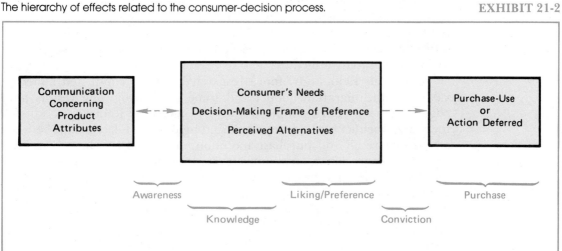

to increases in sales of the product. The advantage of measuring an intermediate step such as knowledge rather than sales is that more precise, less expensive measurement is possible because the two measurement difficulties associated with the sales-effect model are ameliorated. While it is very difficult to separate the effect on sales of a single advertisement, it is more feasible to relate a particular advertisement to changes in intermediate steps such as awareness or knowledge. The intermediate steps are also less affected by the lags that make sales effects difficult to trace.

*Descriptive Results.* In addition to avoiding some of the measurement problems inherent in the sales-effect model, the hierarchy model provides more descriptive results. Measuring in terms of the intermediate steps, especially if several steps are measured, often provides information indicating why a particular advertisement or other test element was effective or not effective. Suppose, for example, that measurement of the response to a particular advertisement indicated that consumers were aware of the advertisement, that their knowledge of the product had increased, but that their liking of the product had declined. This would suggest that the consumers had gotten the message, but that the appeal did not offer an appropriate solution to their problem. Such information gives a good basis for taking corrective action.

CRITICISM OF THE HIERARCHY-OF-EFFECTS MODEL. Two important criticisms of the model should also be considered — whether such a hierarchy exists and what the direction of its effects is.

*Existence of a Hierarchy.* One criticism of the model argues that there is little scientific evidence to support the idea that movement from one intermediate step to another increases the ultimate probability of purchase. One very influential study, published in 1966, critically examined previously published studies plus some new data to see if support for the hypothesis emerged.[3] The researcher, Palda, found little support for the hierarchy hypothesis in either previously published research or in his new data. He felt that the lack of support reflected, in part, the extreme methodological difficulties in researching this subject and, in part, the possible lack of validity of the hierarchy effect.

Since the 1966 study, more research has been conducted aimed at validating the hierarchy model and some more promising results have begun to emerge. For example, a study by Gallup and Robinson conducted for Sears, Roebuck and Co. reported finding positive relationships between advertising recall and purchase intention and actual purchase.[4] Another study using correlation techniques studied relationships reported in food-purchase diaries kept by a large sample of homemakers.[5] The study found

[3]Kristian S. Palda, "The Hypothesis of a Hierarchy of Effects, A Partial Evaluation," *Journal of Marketing Research* (February, 1966), pp. 13–24.
[4]"G & R Research Links Recall, Buying Intent," *Advertising Age* (August 16, 1971), p. 3.
[5]Terrence O'Brien, "Stages of Consumer Decision Making," *Journal of Marketing Research* (August, 1971), pp. 283–289.

awareness of a product to be a causative factor prior to attitude change, intention to purchase, and purchase, and also that attitude change and intention to purchase were causative factors prior to actual purchase. Still another study conducted by the Strategic Planning Institute (SPI) and reported in 1980 provided empirical evidence of a link between brand awareness and market share.[6] The SPI study, conducted with 73 businesses, revealed that increases in advertising resulted in increases in brand awareness and that increases in awareness, in turn, resulted in increases in market share for those brands. The study also suggested that products that were differentiated from competitive products were most successful in converting increases in awareness into increases in market share.

*Direction of Effect.* Another criticism leveled at the hierarchy model is the suggestion that movement through the steps of the hierarchy can go in either direction. For example, while an increase in awareness may ultimately lead to a purchase, it has also been suggested that one result of a purchase is an increase in awareness. Why might this happen? One theory holds that after purchase, consumers are quite likely to seek out and read advertisements for products that they purchased in order to reassure themselves that they had made a wise purchase. Research has shown that this reverse hierarchy effect does occur.[7] This phenomenon has also been noted by practicing advertisers who point out that advertisements for top-selling products tend to gain higher advertising awareness than do advertisements for less popular products.

If progress along the hierarchy can take place in either direction, it means that care must be taken when using the hierarchy model in measuring advertising effectiveness. If, for example, knowledge about a product increases after a particular advertising campaign has been in effect, it may mean that the advertising was effective in increasing consumer knowledge. It might also mean, however, that some other factor (such as personal selling or good publicity) led to better attitudes toward the product which, in turn, made people more interested in reading advertisements for the product. Measurements of advertising effectiveness using the hierarchy model must be carefully controlled so that the correct direction of the effect is measured.

*Order of the Hierarchy.* Another question that has been raised about the hierarchy of effects concerns the order in which the steps occur. The traditional order of the hierarchy is cognition, affect, conation or, in more familiar advertising terms, advertising for a brand creates an awareness that leads to a preference for the brand which in turn leads to purchase. A counterproposal is that the sequence is cognition, conation, affect; in other

---

[6]"Brand Awareness Increases Market Share, Profits: Study," *Marketing News* (November 28, 1980), p. 5.

[7]A pioneering study in this field is Danuta Ehrlich and others, "Post-Decision Exposure to Relevant Information," *Journal of Abnormal and Social Psychology* (January, 1957), pp. 98–102.

words, advertising creates awareness that leads to purchase that, in turn, leads to preference.

Why might this occur? The argument is as follows:[8] Consumers disbelieve much of advertising because they perceive it to be a biased source of information and defend themselves against it with information screening processes as discussed in Chapter 5. Thus consumers, when exposed to advertising for a brand, may indeed become aware of the brand. However, if they disbelieve the information because of its source, the result is likely to be increased uncertainty rather than preference. The consumer is then motivated to overcome the uncertainty. How is that done? By going to a more believable source of information which almost certainly will include sampling the product, perhaps through purchase of a trial amount. If the product trial is satisfactory, the consumer's attitude changes in the direction of a preference for the brand. Thus we have advertising creating awareness that creates uncertainty that leads to trial purchase that results in preference, i.e., cognition to conation to affect.

Research on this question, as well as common sense, suggests that this reordered hierarchy is most likely to occur when consumers perceive high risk in the purchase of the product. In these cases they will probably want more information before committing themselves and will be more mistrustful of information perceived as biased. In such cases, advertising might well limit its objectives and focus on trying to pursuade the consumer to sample the product before making the ultimate purchase decision.[9] Automobile advertising, as an example, appears often to take this approach, urging prospective customers to visit a dealer and to take a test drive. Introductory sales promotions for new products take a similar approach, trying to induce trial of the new brand and at the same time offering incentives that reduce the risk of purchase.

USE OF THE HIERARCHY MODEL. Despite the cautions noted, the hierarchy-of-effects model has wide acceptance among advertising practitioners and is the basis for most of the advertising effectiveness measurement techniques in common use in the field. The use of the hierarchy model does not preclude measuring the sales effect of advertising since sales or purchase is also part of the hierarchy. However, when measuring the sales effect of an advertising program element turn out not to be practical, the hierarchy model does suggest use of intermediate measurements such as awareness or preference.

## Designing an Advertising-Effectiveness Evaluation Program

The program for evaluating advertising effectiveness requires detailed advance planning. The procedures to be followed in evaluating the advertising should be included in the advertising plan. It is as essential a part of

---

[8]Robert E. Smith and William R. Swinyard, "Information Response Models: An Integrated Approach," *Journal of Marketing* (Winter, 1982), pp. 81–93.
[9]*Ibid.*, p. 89.

the advertising plan as the other programs, such as the media program or the creative program. Steps to follow in preparing the evaluation of effectiveness program are considered in the sections which follow.

## What Should Be Evaluated?

An advertising-effectiveness evaluation program begins by specifying what is to be evaluated. The advertising plan presents a series of decisions in the form of programs—a budget program, a media program, and a creative program—each of which must be evaluated. No single measurement technique can evaluate the decisions in all of these programs. Thus the advertising evaluation program is made up of a series of tests, each designed to provide information that will help to evaluate one or more advertising decisions.

BUDGET EVALUATION. There are two ways in which the advertising budget program might be evaluated. The first question is, was the budget expended according to the plan? The budget program in the advertising plan represents the control standard to which actual expenditures are compared. This type of control should be used during as well as after budget expenditure so that corrections can be made during the budget period.

A second evaluation of the budget is to ask whether or not a more effective budget could be formulated. The procedure for formulating a budget program described in Chapter 11 was designed to aid in selecting the best budget level and the best allocation of that budget. However, these budget decisions were subject to substantial uncertainty. As was stressed in that chapter, the advertising manager must strive to gather information so as to be able to answer the "what if" questions—what if the budget were larger or smaller, or allocated differently. To determine this, the advertising manager might conduct a market test to determine the effect of a larger or smaller budget. A larger budget, for example, might be tested in a small market area and the sales results measured and compared with those from a similar market in which a normal budget level was applied. Results of the test could be used in determining the appropriate budget level for the next year.

MEDIA EVALUATION. The media program, because of the large expenditure involved, also calls for substantial control and evaluation. Again, there are two aspects of the program that have to be evaluated. First, did the program perform as planned, and second, are there alternative media approaches that would yield better results?

The media program ought to have specified, expected performance levels that can serve as evaluation standards. If print media are designated for use, the circulation or audience to be reached by the schedule should be estimated. If broadcast media are to be used, there should be estimates of total audience, gross rating points, or reach, and frequency estimates. One phase of media program control is to gather estimates of the actual audience or ratings achieved from the rating services or audience studies described in the media program chapters.

The other consideration in media program control is the evaluation of the media alternatives selected. The media selection procedure outlined in Chapter 12 relies in many instances on subjective judgments. The effectiveness of the media program could be improved if more information were available on the results that alternative media selections could achieve. The media evaluation program, therefore, might test alternative media, different media vehicles, or variations in geographic or seasonal allocation.

CREATIVE EVALUATION. The evaluation of the creative program is concerned with questions similar to those asked about the budget and media programs. Was the creative program that was carried out effective? Are there creative program alternatives that might be more effective? The copy content, the creative execution of the content, and the overall effectiveness of the finished advertisements might be evaluated. The evaluation might focus on particular advertisements or be concerned with the results from the total campaign. It has become standard procedure for large advertisers to pre-test advertisements before utilizing them in their multi-million dollar media programs. A study by the Advertising Research Foundation, for example, showed that nine out of ten large advertisers subject their television commercials to consumer testing before letting them be broadcast.[10]

TOTAL PLAN EVALUATION. Each of the individual programs in the advertising plan contributes to the overall success of the advertiser's product and, as such, each can be individually evaluated. In addition, however, it is frequently desirable to evaluate the interactive effect of all the programs to determine whether the total advertising program, rather than one particular element, is moving the product toward meeting the objectives. This form of total plan evaluation requires different forms of testing than those needed for testing individual plan elements, but such test techniques are available and will be considered in the next chapter.

## Elements of Effectiveness Evaluation

After deciding what elements of the advertising program are to be evaluated, an effectiveness evaluation procedure is designed for each element. This procedure must specify a standard, suggest a means of measurement, and make provision for corrective action.

SPECIFYING STANDARDS. It is essential in advertising evaluation that a standard, a target level of performance, be specified in advance in order to provide a basis for comparison. When actual performance is measured, it will be compared to the standard to determine whether or not it is satisfactory.

---

[10]"Marketing," *The Wall Street Journal*, (October 21, 1982), p. 31.

*Characteristics of Standards.* The standards set in the evaluation plan should be both specific and measurable. If, for example, a particular network television purchase is to be evaluated, it is not adequate to say that the standard is a "good" rating or an above-average cost efficiency. The standard should state, instead, that the goal is an 18.0 rating and a cost per thousand of $4.50. The standard should also be stated in measurable terms. A media standard set in terms of target ratings is not useful if the advertiser does not subscribe to rating services that provide such measurements. Likewise, a creative standard that calls for a particular campaign to increase sales by 5 percent would not be a useful standard unless someone could devise a way to isolate and measure the change in sales caused by that advertising campaign.

*Types and Source of Standards.* If the performance evaluation seeks to determine whether or not planned advertising programs have been carried out, then the standard should be found in the program itself. The advertising budget, broadcast rating targets, and coupon redemption targets are all examples of such standards. Creative programs standards are sometimes stated in terms of target scores on specified measurement techniques.

If the evaluation measure seeks to determine whether or not some alternative program would be more effective than the one in use, then the standard is usually the current program. If, for example, radio is being considered as a substitute medium for the currently used medium of television, then the standard with which radio would be compared would be the performance of television.

SPECIFYING MEANS OF MEASUREMENT. For each program element to be evaluated, the evaluation program should specify the measurement technique to be used. In many cases the measurement chosen will be a standardized measurement available from outside suppliers. Television ratings are an example of this type of measurement. In other cases the measurement will be custom-designed. The selection of a measurement device should consider its technical attributes, its validity, its acceptability to those being controlled, and the depth of information provided by the results.

*Technical Attributes and Validity.* A technically sound measure is one that measures accurately and gives consistent results if repeated. A valid measure is one that actually measures what it purports to measure. Television commercial measurement techniques, for example, typically evaluate commercials on the basis of a single exposure to consumers, yet commercials are typically designed to be used repeatedly over substantial periods of time. This raises a question of validity. A considerable amount of research has been done by comparing television-commercial test results based on a single exposure to the commercial with results derived from multiple exposures. The research has consistently shown the importance of multiple exposures in arriving at valid test results. Responses to commercials tend to be superficial after one exposure, but after two or more exposures they result in considerably more awareness, understanding, and motivation. Look, for example, at the results in Exhibit 21-3 from a single- versus a double-exposure test of a commercial for a food product whose product benefit was supported by "reason-why" copy. After two exposures, the reason-why was far better understood, with the result that conviction increased along with motivation.[11]

*Ideal Measurement Procedure (IMP)*

One investigation of advertising-effectiveness measurement techniques gave rise to a set of ideal characteristics which the technically perfect measurement technique would have. This list of seven attributes, termed the **Ideal Measurement Procedure (IMP),** provides a basis for evaluating the technical quality and the validity of measurement techniques. The seven attributes of the IMP are:

1. *Scope.* Ideally a measurement technique should permit evaluation of multiple insertions or exposures since most campaigns depend upon repetition. It should also be possible to evaluate exposures in multiple media rather than just a single medium.
2. *Response.* The response measured should ideally be purchase and, if possible, purchase under natural rather than artificial conditions.
3. *Exposure.* The consumers being measured should be exposed to the stimulus under natural conditions. That is, the advertisement should appear in its natural medium and the consumer should review, read, or hear the medium in a natural rather than a forced context.
4. *Measurement.* Responses of consumers should be measured in such a way that the measurement process does not distort their behavior. This, ideally, means that the subject should be unaware of the measurement.
5. *Sample.* Ideally the consumers selected for the measurement (the sample) should be selected randomly and should be adequate in number so that errors are controlled. The consumers should be drawn from the full population.
6. *Comparison.* The measurement should make it possible to compare the results with those of other alternatives. There should, in other words, be some sort of standard built into the technique.
7. *Result.* Ideally it should be possible to determine from the test results the profitability of each alternative used.[12]

*Acceptability.* In addition to technical soundness and validity, the test technique must be accepted by those people who develop advertising programs. These people are naturally sensitive about the means used to evaluate their work. If they do not accept the measurement techniques, they will not be inclined to accept the results, making corrective action difficult. As one noted advertising agency creative person put it, "Creative people don't want report cards and imperfect rulers measuring their work."[13]

---

[11]"Multiple Exposure Test Needed to Evaluate Commercials," *Marketing News* (September 21, 1979), p. 13.

[12]Based on Homer M. Dalbey, Irwin Gross, and Yoram Wind, *Advertising Measurement and Decision Making* (Boston: Allyn and Bacon, Inc., 1968), pp. 38–45.

[13]Jack J. Honomichl, "TV Copy Testing Flap: What to Do About It," *Advertising Age* (January 19, 1981), p. 59.

**EXHIBIT 21-3**

Single- versus double-exposure test results for a television commercial featuring "reason-why" copy.

|  | Single exposure | Double exposure |
|---|---|---|
| **Recall:**  Claim (slogan) | 32% | 35% |
| "Reason Why" | 10 | 22 |
| **Conviction:**  Claim (slogan) | 14 | 29 |
| **Motivation:**  (indexed to norm) | 75 | 144 |

Source: "Multiple Exposure Test Needed to Evaluate Commercials," *Marketing News,* (September 21, 1979), p. 13.

If the people whose work is to be evaluated help choose the measurement technique, they will accept the results more readily. If, for example, media program results are to be evaluated by television ratings, it would increase the acceptability of the results if the person who prepared the media program also helped select the rating-evaluation service.

*Information for Improvement.* In selecting a measurement technique, it is of foremost importance that the measure accurately reflect the effectiveness of the element being tested. In addition, it would be useful if the measurement technique provided information leading to improvement. This is particularly true in the case of evaluation of the creative program. As one expert noted, "Most users and practitioners believe that copy testing is more diagnostic than predictive. Its major function is to red-flag failures of communication and to suggest remedial action."[14]

For example, a measurement technique might be devised to measure the change in consumers' knowledge about a product after exposure to a test advertisement. It would be additionally helpful if the measurement technique provided responses from the test consumers indicating what part of the advertisement was difficult to understand, what part was interesting, and what information was not relevant to them. This would enable the copywriter to improve the advertisements and would provide ideas for future advertisements.

PROVIDING FOR CORRECTIVE ACTION. The value of a program of effectiveness evaluation is lost if it does not result in corrective action. The evaluation program in the advertising plan should specify who is responsible for initiating corrective action. It should also indicate the schedule on which performance results should be reviewed and corrective action taken.

*Responsibility for Corrective Action.* Responsibility for determining what corrective action is necessary should begin with the person implementing the program that has been evaluated. This will be the advertising manager, the advertising department staff, or advertising agency members to

[14]Donald L. Kanter, "Researchers Gear Down to Realistic Expectations," *Advertising Age* (July 15, 1974), p. 43.

whom the advertising manager has delegated responsibility for implementation. For example, if the advertising manager delegates responsibility for implementing the media program (buying and scheduling the media vehicles) to the agency's media department, the assigned media buyer should have the responsibility for initiating corrective action. In some cases the buyer would have authority to take the corrective action and in other cases would initiate a recommendation for change.

Responsibility for taking corrective action should lie with the person planning and implementing the program because that person has greatest direct knowledge of the program. This also encourages the feeling that the evaluation program is designed to create improvement. If corrective action began with the advertising manager, there would inevitably be the feeling that the evaluation program was being used to check on subordinates or the advertising agency. This tends to lead to rejection of the measurement technique and results.

*Timing of Corrective Action.* Since the value of an evaluation program lies in the corrective action taken, it is desirable that measurement results be available as soon as possible so that corrections can be made before problems become serious and opportunities escape.

Corrective action can occur during three different phases of implementation of the advertising plan. An advertising program can be corrected before it is implemented. This requires pre-testing — testing of an advertising element with a limited group before it is committed to general use. The advantage of pre-testing is that it may permit correction before a costly mistake is made. The pre-test results can be incorporated into the advertising plan itself.

Some corrective action can be taken during the process of implementation. This requires effectiveness measures that feed back early warning of problems so that corrections can be made before the problems become serious. This type of mid-course program correction can be implemented by providing periodic (perhaps every three months) progress reviews.

Finally, there should also be evaluation at the termination of the implemented advertising plan. This evaluation questions the effectiveness of the advertising plan in reaching the objectives and overall standards set in the plan. Termination evaluation represents the beginning of a new planning cycle — the results of the current advertising plan are analyzed in the analysis section of the next year's plan and the findings are stated as problems and opportunities to be resolved in the upcoming period.

---

*CHAPTER*
*SUMMARY*

An advertising effectiveness evaluation program is needed to support requests for funds and to improve future advertising. There are two competing ideas of the best way to evaluate advertising effectiveness. The sales effect approach attempts to measure the sales generated by the advertising being evaluated. This approach faces measurement difficulties, does not recognize advertising's objectives other than sales, and does not give descriptive results. The hierarchy-of-effects approach measures how well advertising has moved consumers through the series of steps that leads to sales. These steps are defined as awareness, knowledge, liking, preference, conviction, and purchase. Although the hierarchy-of-effects model is a widely used measurement approach, some are skeptical of the validity of the step-by-step approach and the order or direction in which consumers progress through the steps.

The evaluation program begins by defining the elements and decisions to be evaluated, including elements from the budget program, the media program, and the creative program. Next, an effectiveness evaluation procedure is designed for each element. This must include specification of a standard as a base for comparison. This standard should be both specific and measurable. The procedure must also specify the means by which actual performance will be measured. The measurement selected should be technically sound and valid and should be accepted by those people whose work is being evaluated. It is also desirable that the measurement technique provide information that suggests improvement in the program being evaluated. The final step in forming an effectiveness evaluation program is to provide for corrective action. Both the person responsible and the timing of corrective action should be specified. Normally responsibility for corrective action should lie with the person who planned and implemented the program. Corrective action should be planned to occur as early as possible, before problems become serious.

---

| | | |
|---|---|---|
| sales effect of advertising | AIDA formula | *KEY TERMS* |
| hierarchy of effects | Ideal Measurement Procedure (IMP) | |

---

1. This chapter notes that the purpose of advertising is not always to generate immediate sales. In each of the following instances, suggest the probable purpose of the advertising.

    a. An advertisement in the *Wall Street Journal* featuring the year-end earnings report of the company.
    b. A consumer ad featuring a 50-cents-off coupon.
    c. An ad to wholesalers promoting the test-market results for a new product.
    d. A newspaper ad by a savings and loan institution opposing changes in the tax deductibility of home-mortgage interest.
    e. A magazine publisher's ad in *Advertising Age* announcing circulation gains.

*QUESTIONS FOR DISCUSSION*

2. A resort-condominium marketer uses advertisements containing keyed coupons by which interested prospects can request further information. Each inquiring prospect is mailed further information and a salesperson calls on the prospect to attempt a sale. The sales results of each coupon inquiry are recorded and attributed to the ad from which the coupon was taken. In this way total sales resulting from the ad can be calculated. Does this approach provide a valid measure of the sales effectiveness of each advertisement?

3. The advertising manager for an automobile leasing firm has decided to test alternative copy benefits that might be used in advertising about the firm's service. One approach promotes the convenience of leasing while the other promotes tax savings. For the test, three ads per week are scheduled for three months using the convenience appeal and, following this, three ads per week are scheduled using the tax-savings appeal. At the end of the six-month test period, sales realized during the first three-month period will be compared to sales achieved during the second three-month period in order to determine which benefit approach was the more effective.

   a. Will the results help to determine which copy approach is more effective?
   b. In what ways might the test approach be improved?

4. Smith and Swinyard's communications model (p. 578) suggests that consumers gain awareness of products from advertising, but because they distrust advertising they are likely to seek more reliable sources of product information (by asking a friend, for example) before becoming committed to the product.

   a. If this model is accurate, what do you see as the role of advertising?
   b. Does this view of advertising support the hierarchy-of-effects approach or the sales-effect approach to measuring advertising effectiveness?

5. In conducting tests of the effectiveness of a creative program for candy bars an advertising agency asks the questions listed below. For each one, identify the stage in the hierarchy of effects that is being measured.

   a. What is your favorite brand of candy bar?
   b. Can you remember seeing any candy-bar advertising this week?
   c. Have you purchased a candy bar in the last week? If so, what brand?
   d. What can you tell me about Brand "X" candy bar?
   e. If you were to buy a candy bar today, what brand would you buy?

6. If an advertiser sets up a plan to test the effectiveness of the total advertising plan, is it also necessary to set up tests of individual elements of the advertising plan? Why?

7. Suppose that an advertiser wishes to have the effectiveness-evaluation program examine the questions listed below. What should be used in each instance as the standard against which actual performance is compared?

   a. Did the people notice the money-back guarantee that was added to all advertisements last year?
   b. Did the advertising increase the level of brand-name awareness in the past year?
   c. Should the advertising budget be doubled?
   d. Did the advertising increase the number of leads generated for sales representatives?
   e. Should the print advertising be changed from black and white to full color?

8. Most major television advertisers make it a practice to test their television commercials before they are used in order to evaluate their effectiveness. At the same time, most of these advertisers test competitive commercials as well as their own. Why do you think they do this? Do you think that the expense is justified?

9. An advertising agency has developed a scrapbook test for evaluating alternative advertisements. In the test a number of consumers in a nearby neighborhood are called on by an interviewer and asked to look through a scrapbook containing a copy of the ad to be tested, several other "control" ads, and some editorial material (basically anecdotes, short articles, and cartoons). Then with the scrapbook closed, the interviewer asks the consumer what ads are remembered in the scrapbook, thus generating an advertising-recall score. Then for each ad remembered the consumer is asked what information is recalled in the ad to give a content-recall score. Evaluate this measurement technique in terms of the IMP (Ideal Measurement Procedure).

10. Advertising effectiveness measurements can be pre-tests, progress tests, or post-tests. For controlling each of the program elements listed below, determine which approach or approaches you would use.

   a. Control of amount of advertising spending.
   b. Evaluation of a change in copy content.
   c. Evaluation of a sales promotion premium.
   d. Control of geographic allocation of the budget.
   e. Evaluation of the reach of a television schedule.

*PROBLEM*        The New England Office Machines Company is a long-established distributor of office machines in a major New England city. It carries a line of nationally known and marketed office machines including electronic typewriters and business computers. In addition to selling these machines, the company provides repair and maintenance service on either a call- or service-contract basis. Both in order to get service business and to get future new and replacement machine business, NEOMC attempts to develop a permanent relationship with its customers, maintaining it with periodic calls by a company sales representative.

Several months ago, the company initiated an advertising program for the first time in its 46-year history. Mr. David Alexander, the owner of the firm, was concerned that the company was not effective in generating new customers even though it did appear able to hold the loyalty of established customers. An advertising program was developed in an attempt to get inquiries from prospective new accounts. These inquiries would each be followed up by a personal call by a company salesperson. In the past the company sales representatives were responsible for developing and following up on their own leads for new customers.

The new advertising plan was directed to proprietors, office managers, and purchasing agents because they were primarily responsible for the selection of a supplier of office equipment. A budget of $30,000 was allocated for the first year. Since there was no historical precedent to go by, the budget was based primarily on the requirements of the desired media program. Two media, newspaper and direct mail, were selected. One 500-line ad per week was scheduled in the morning edition of the dominant daily newspaper in the city. All ads were placed in the business and financial section of the paper. One direct mail piece was sent each month to a list of city businesses and municipal offices with over 10 employees. Creatively, the newpaper ads were based on a "tips for successful office management" series which the company purchased from a creative services supplier. Each ad contained an office management hint and then suggested that NEOMC could be helpful in streamlining office procedures through the use of modern office machinery. Readers were invited to inquire if they wanted further information. The direct-mail advertisements followed a similar approach, but also offered a free booklet containing a collection of the office management hints. In addition to the advertising, the company sponsored a contest among sales representatives to encourage follow-up of the leads generated by the advertising. The salesperson converting the greatest percentage of leads into active accounts was eligible for a free, two-week trip for two to Bermuda.

Because the use of advertising marked a sharp departure from past practice, Mr. Alexander felt it essential to develop some measure of how well the plan was performing, whether or not it should be continued, and how it might be improved.

1. Make a list of the elements of the advertising plan that should be evaluated for effectiveness.
2. For each element to be evaluated, state what the standard should be and where the necessary information for setting the standard could be obtained.
3. Using the hierarchy-of-effects approach, indicate at what stage in the hierarchy each of the elements in (1) should be measured.

# CHAPTER 22

*Techniques for Measuring*
*Advertising Effectiveness*

LEARNING OBJECTIVES

In studying this chapter you will learn:

- Many of the advertising effectiveness measurement techniques that are in current use.

- How each of these measurement techniques is designed.

- The application of each technique to specific measurement needs.

- The strengths and weaknesses of each measurement technique.

The advertising effectiveness evaluation program in the advertising plan should contain three elements—a statement of the standard or target level of performance, specification of the means by which actual performance will be measured, and provision for corrective action. Of these elements, the selection of a measurement technique is the most difficult. In this chapter consideration turns to description and evaluation of effectiveness measurement techniques that are currently used by practicing advertisers.

## Evaluating Measurement Techniques

There are many advertising effectiveness measurement techniques that are in use—too many to examine in this chapter. Instead, measurement techniques will be divided into classes and then typical techniques in each class will be evaluated.

## Classes of Measurement Techniques

The most important difference among measurement techniques is the response that is measured. Some techniques, for example, measure how many people notice an advertisement, while other techniques attempt to measure the sales resulting from an advertisement.

As discussed in Chapter 21, the hierarchy-of-effects model suggests that advertising moves people through six steps leading to purchase of the product. The six steps are awareness, knowledge, liking, preference, conviction, and purchase. These six steps can be combined to form three basic categories of response: cognitive, affective, and conative. Advertising effectiveness measurement techniques can similarly be classified as measuring cognitive response, affective response, or conative response. A cognitive-response measurement technique evaluates changes in subjects' knowledge; an affective-response measurement technique measures changes in consumers' attitudes toward a product; and a conative-response measurement determines the action that consumers take with regard to a product. The specific measurement techniques to be examined in this chapter are classified in Exhibit 22-1 in terms of these three categories.

## Approach to Examining Measurement Techniques

The advertiser who prepares an advertising effectiveness evaluation program will specify a number of different elements and programs that should be appraised. As a consequence, a number of different measurement techniques will be required. In selecting each measurement technique, two related questions must be considered. First, does the measurement technique meet the criteria that were suggested in the previous chapter—is the technique accurate and valid, will it be acceptable to those controlled, and does it provide enough information to make correction possible? Second, the advertiser must select a technique that measures the particular element to be evaluated. Some techniques are appropriate for

Classes of advertising effectiveness measurement techniques.                                            EXHIBIT 22-1

| Cognitive (Knowledge) Tests | Affective (Attitude) Tests | Conative (Motive) Tests |
| --- | --- | --- |
| Media audience measurements | Opinion measurements | Inquiry measurements |
| Physiological measurements | Attitude measurements | Split-run tests |
| Readership measurements | | Theater tests |
| Recall measurements | | Split-cable tests |
| Awareness measurements | | Sales measurements |
| | | Market tests |

measuring creative elements, others for media or budget programs. Some can be used as pre-test instruments, others as post-tests.

The analysis of measurement techniques which follows is designed to help in answering these questions. Each technique will be discussed roughly in the order that the response measured appears in the hierarchy of effects. Each technique will be described, including its uses or applications, and then the technique will be evaluated.

## Cognitive (Knowledge) Tests

*cognitive tests*

The responses measured by **cognitive tests** are at the earliest stages of the hierarchy of effects. Some of these tests measure changes in the first or awareness stage by determining how many people were exposed to the element being tested; e.g., media audience measures or physiological or readership measurements. Other cognitive tests operate on the second or knowledge stage, determining through awareness or recall measurements what facts consumers recall from a particular test element.

### Media Audience Measurements

Techniques for measuring the audience of a medium were considered in Chapter 12 because they are an important tool in the selection of media. In addition to that function, media audience measurements serve as an important technique for evaluating the effectiveness of media programs.

DESIGN OF THE MEASUREMENT. The technique used to measure the audience of a media vehicle varies from medium to medium. For magazines and newspapers, the audience to be measured is the total number of people who read an average issue. This measurement is made by interviewing a sample of people and asking whether or not they read a particular issue. Some attempt is usually made to disguise the intent of the questions in order to overcome people's tendency to overstate the extent of their reading.

The audience of the outdoor and transit media is the number of people exposed to a showing or gross-rating-points package during some period, usually thirty days. Audiences of these media are usually measured by some form of traffic count. Broadcast measurement techniques include meters placed on television sets to record when the set is turned on and the channel selection, diaries kept by viewers to record programs watched, and telephone interviews to determine current listening or viewing activity. These techniques are sometimes used in combination, such as the combination of meters and diaries used by Nielsen in its television ratings.

USES OF AUDIENCE MEASUREMENTS. There are two sets of audience measurements made by the advertiser. As explained in the media selection chapter, one use is as a guide in evaluating alternative media vehicles. For example, in deciding which of two television programs should be sponsored, audience sizes and resulting cost per thousand prospects would be important determinants in the choice. When used in this way, audience measurements serve as a pre-test to help select among alternatives.

Audience measurements are also used for post-evaluation of broadcast media purchases. For example, when radio and television purchases are made, program and spot audiences must be estimated from past rating reports. Since programs, schedules, and audience tastes change frequently, the media buyer makes many judgments in the purchase decisions. When new rating and audience reports are issued, it is possible to check the actual efficiency of the spots and programs purchased by comparing the audience results predicted by the advertising plan (the standard) with actual audience. If this comparison can be made while the schedules are still in effect, the schedule can be improved by dropping low-rated programs or spots and purchasing better-rated positions. This control process also increases the media buyer's knowledge so that corrections can be included in subsequent advertising plans.

EVALUATION OF AUDIENCE MEASURES. Media audience measurements, though widely used, do have significant limitations.

*Sampling Error.* One limitation concerns sample size—the number of people actually questioned or measured in making the audience estimates. Sample sizes, because of the cost involved, are typically small. Nielsen's national television ratings (the Nielsen Television Index), for example, are based on data from only 1,200 homes. This means that the resulting estimates are subject to considerable sampling error (errors due to the small sample not being perfectly representative of the total population). Magazine audience studies usually have larger samples, but even with these studies, sampling error can be considerable. Audience figures, therefore, should be thought of as estimates which are subject to error.

*Distortion of Estimates.* Another problem with measurement techniques is that they may contain considerable bias or distortion resulting from incorrect answers by members in the sample. There is a danger, for example, that sample members who are asked to keep a diary on their television viewing habits will distort their normal viewing to make the report "look good;" this is termed "conditioning" the sample. There is a similar danger in magazine audience studies that sample members will exaggerate their report of magazines that they have read in order to make themselves look good in the eyes of the interviewer. Overstatement may also result from the natural tendency to confuse magazines that look alike. Television viewing diaries may also suffer from exaggerated reporting or errors due to faulty memory. The sample itself in an audience study is likely to be distorted by the unwillingness of some households to cooperate in the study—because they are too busy, or suspicious, or simply not at home when the interviewer calls. All of these factors add another element of error to the resulting audience estimates.

The existence of these errors — sampling error and bias — has been confirmed by comparisons made between competitive audience studies made at the same time from the same population. Comparison, for example, of separate television audience estimates derived from meters, from diaries, and from telephone coincidental studies have shown substantial divergencies. This comparison does not indicate which approach is best, but it does indicate that such audience figures should be treated only as approximations.

*What Is Measured?* The advertiser using audience measurements should keep clearly in mind what is and what is not being measured. Audience measurements operate at the very earliest stage of the hierarchy of effects. They ask simply how many people were exposed to a particular medium. They do not measure whether the people noticed the advertiser's ad; therefore, there is no measurement of attitude change or product purchase. In addition, audience measures do not evaluate many qualitative values of media, such as the environment offered by the medium and its creative latitude.

## Physiological Measurements

*physiological tests*

A variety of laboratory measurement devices that record physical response to stimuli have been applied as advertising evaluation measures. These **physiological tests** are most often used to evaluate creative elements — individual advertisements or components of advertisements.

DESIGN OF THE MEASUREMENT. Although a variety of physiological measurement devices has been used, the design of the test follows a common form. Sample consumers are placed in a laboratory or controlled setting and shown test and control advertisements. Their physical responses are measured by one of the laboratory measurement devices.

One measurement device is the psychogalvanometer. Electrodes are placed on the individual's skin, as with a lie detector, to record changes in electrical resistance. It is hypothesized that when the individual is exposed to an advertisement, emotional involvement, excitement, or tension caused by the advertisement will induce an increase in perspiration. This, in turn, lowers electrical resistance and is recorded by the meter.

In pupil dilation tests, changes in pupil size are recorded by an eye camera. Increased dilation upon exposure to an advertisement is thought to indicate interest or involvement. Another physiological measurement approach uses eye-tracking technology to record the movement of a reader's eyes across an advertisement, package design, billboard, or other creative material. This viewing information is stored in a computer and can later be analyzed to give diagnostic information on what was read, the order of reading, elements skipped, and the time spent on various parts of the ad.[1] Modern eye-tracking devices can be concealed so that test consumers are not aware of the equipment, thus creating a near normal viewing situation.

Another approach that has recently been applied to the evaluation of advertising, especially to the evaluation of television commercials, is brain-wave analysis.[2] By recording brain waves as test consumers view a television commercial, it is possible to measure the viewers' alertness and involvement. New techniques allow brain waves to be measured and recorded separately for the left and right hemispheres of the brain. Physiologists have demonstrated that the left hemisphere of the brain specializes in processing logical, rational information while the right hemisphere processes emotional and esthetic information. Modern technology also permits second-by-second or scene-by-scene recording of brain-wave responses to a commercial. Analysis of the test results can help to determine the level of response to various elements of a commercial and whether that response is an emotional one or a rational one.

USES OF PHYSIOLOGICAL MEASUREMENTS. The physical testing devices described here are used primarily for pre-testing alternative creative executions. An advertising agency, for example, might have developed two different layouts for a particular advertising idea. The agency might use a *tachistoscope test* to determine which layout communicates most clearly. A *psychogalvanometer test* might be used to compare two different central ideas in advertisements for a product.

EVALUATION OF PHYSIOLOGICAL MEASUREMENTS. Physiological measures of one sort or another have been available to advertisers for many years, but have never gained widespread use. Although these measures have the advantages of conceptual simplicity and ability to bypass ego defenses, they are of uncertain validity. When these measures are used, it is just not certain what is being measured. If on seeing an ad consumers' pupils dilate or their voice pitch rises or their sweat glands are activated, does this mean the ad is good or bad? And how are these responses related to sales effectiveness? There are few published studies that validate physiological testing methods although one vendor of such services claims that psychogalvanometer test results correlated well with later sales results for a number of ads.[3] Some of the physiological measures, eye-tracking and brain-wave analysis, do provide diagnostic information that can be helpful in improving executions of the advertising program.

---

[1]Bernie Whalen, "Eye Tracking Technology to Replace Day-after-recall by '84," *Marketing News* (November 27, 1981).

[2]"Advances in Brain Wave Analysis Allow Researchers to Test Effectiveness of Ads," *Marketing News* (September 17, 1982), p. 21.

[3]"Psychogalvanometer Testing 'Most Predictive'," *Marketing News* (June 16, 1978), p. 11.

## Readership Measurements

**Readership tests,** or recognition studies as they are sometimes called, attempt to measure the number of people who have actually read a particular advertisement. To be effective in influencing purchase, an advertisement must first be read. Therefore the more effectively an advertisement attracts readership, the greater the sales it can produce. Readership tests usually serve as post-tests for evaluating individual print advertisements.

DESIGN OF THE MEASUREMENT. The best known readership measurement service is the Starch Readership Service. Starch periodically measures readership of advertisements in over 100 consumer and business magazines, newspapers, and newspaper supplements. The Starch interviewing staff measures ad readership among a sample of adults. Readers of the magazine to be "Starched" are located by showing the prospective sample members the cover of the magazine. If they state that they have read that issue, the interviewer then goes through the magazine page-by-page inquiring about readership of each advertisement to be evaluated. For each ad, each sample member is recorded as either a nonreader of that ad, a "noted" reader (remembers seeing the ad), an "associated" reader (read enough to see the brand name), and a "read most" reader (read more than half of the ad).

Subscribers to the Starch service receive a copy of the test magazine with labels pasted on the tested ad pages to show the readership scores. A sample page scored in this way is shown in Exhibit 22-2. In addition, a printed listing, such as that shown in Exhibit 22-3, is provided for all advertisements tested. Readership indexes are also shown. Starch periodically publishes average readership scores (called Adnorms) for various product categories. These serve as control standards against which an advertiser can compare actual readership results.

EVALUATION OF READERSHIP MEASUREMENTS. Readership studies are popular because they are low in cost, are published frequently, and are easily understood. Readership studies, however, are subject to some rather important limitations. The sample size in most readership studies is usually small and not randomly selected. Starch, for example, uses a quota sample of 100 to 200 persons per issue measured.

Readership studies may be subject to biased responses by consumers. For example, sample members may tend to exaggerate readership of magazines and recognition of advertisements because they wish to appear knowledgeable or important. Readership scores may also be distorted by confusion on the part of the respondent. An advertisement may look familiar because it appeared in another magazine or is part of a continuing campaign of similar ads. On the other hand, it should be recognized that the readership measured in these tests takes place under normal conditions — it is not forced as in the physiological tests.

A magazine advertisement showing Starch scores.

EXHIBIT 22-2

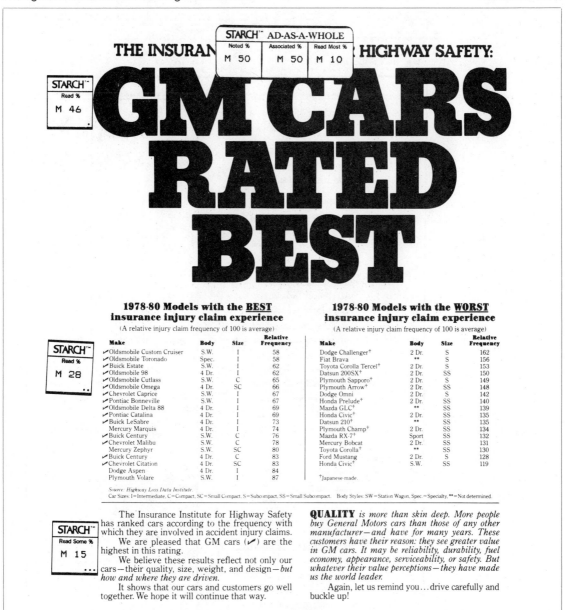

THE INSURANCE INSTITUTE FOR HIGHWAY SAFETY:

STARCH™ AD-AS-A-WHOLE

| Noted % | Associated % | Read Most % |
|---|---|---|
| M 50 | M 50 | M 10 |

STARCH™ Read % M 46

# GM CARS RATED BEST

STARCH™ Read % M 28

### 1978-80 Models with the **BEST** insurance injury claim experience
(A relative injury claim frequency of 100 is average)

| Make | Body | Size | Relative Frequency |
|---|---|---|---|
| ✔Oldsmobile Custom Cruiser | S.W. | I | 58 |
| ✔Oldsmobile Toronado | Spec. | I | 58 |
| ✔Buick Estate | S.W. | I | 62 |
| ✔Oldsmobile 98 | 4 Dr. | I | 62 |
| ✔Oldsmobile Cutlass | S.W. | C | 65 |
| ✔Oldsmobile Omega | 4 Dr. | SC | 66 |
| ✔Chevrolet Caprice | S.W. | I | 67 |
| ✔Pontiac Bonneville | S.W. | I | 67 |
| ✔Oldsmobile Delta 88 | 4 Dr. | I | 69 |
| ✔Pontiac Catalina | 4 Dr. | I | 69 |
| ✔Buick LeSabre | 4 Dr. | I | 73 |
| Mercury Marquis | 4 Dr. | I | 74 |
| ✔Buick Century | S.W. | C | 76 |
| ✔Chevrolet Malibu | S.W. | C | 78 |
| Mercury Zephyr | S.W. | SC | 80 |
| ✔Buick Century | 4 Dr. | C | 83 |
| ✔Chevrolet Citation | 4 Dr. | SC | 83 |
| Dodge Aspen | 4 Dr. | I | 84 |
| Plymouth Volare | S.W. | I | 87 |

*Source: Highway Loss Data Institute.*

### 1978-80 Models with the **WORST** insurance injury claim experience
(A relative injury claim frequency of 100 is average)

| Make | Body | Size | Relative Frequency |
|---|---|---|---|
| Dodge Challenger[+] | 2 Dr. | S | 162 |
| Fiat Brava | ** | S | 156 |
| Toyota Corolla Tercel[+] | 2 Dr. | S | 153 |
| Datsun 200SX[+] | 2 Dr. | SS | 150 |
| Plymouth Sapporo[+] | 2 Dr. | S | 149 |
| Plymouth Arrow[+] | 2 Dr. | SS | 148 |
| Dodge Omni | 2 Dr. | S | 142 |
| Honda Prelude[+] | 2 Dr. | SS | 140 |
| Mazda GLC[+] | ** | SS | 139 |
| Honda Civic[+] | 2 Dr. | SS | 135 |
| Datsun 210[+] | ** | SS | 135 |
| Plymouth Champ[+] | 2 Dr. | SS | 134 |
| Mazda RX-7[+] | Sport | SS | 132 |
| Mercury Bobcat | 2 Dr. | SS | 131 |
| Toyota Corolla[+] | ** | SS | 130 |
| Ford Mustang | 2 Dr. | S | 128 |
| Honda Civic[+] | S.W. | SS | 119 |

[+]Japanese-made.

Car Sizes: I=Intermediate, C=Compact, SC=Small Compact, S=Subcompact, SS=Small Subcompact.  Body Styles: SW=Station Wagon, Spec.=Specialty, **=Not determined.

STARCH™ Read Some % M 15 ...

The Insurance Institute for Highway Safety has ranked cars according to the frequency with which they are involved in accident injury claims.

We are pleased that GM cars (✔) are the highest in this rating.

We believe these results reflect not only our cars—their quality, size, weight, and design—*but how and where they are driven.*

It shows that our cars and customers go well together. We hope it will continue that way.

**QUALITY** *is more than skin deep. More people buy General Motors cars than those of any other manufacturer—and have for many years. These customers have their reason: they see greater value in GM cars. It may be reliability, durability, fuel economy, appearance, serviceability, or safety. But whatever their value perceptions—they have made us the world leader.*

Again, let us remind you...drive carefully and buckle up!

STARCH™ Signature % M 42

**GM**
**General Motors**

Chevrolet • Pontiac • Oldsmobile • Buick • Cadillac • GMC Truck

Courtesy:  Starch INRA  Hooper, Inc., and General Motors Corporation.

**EXHIBIT 22-3**      Sample page from a Starch Readership Report.

READERSHIP REPORT

U. S. News & World Report                      February 22 1982
Total of  25  1/2 Page or Larger Ads            Men Readers

| PAGE | SIZE & COLOR | ADVERTISER | RANK IN ISSUE BY NUMBER OF READERS | PERCENTAGES | | | READERSHIP INDEXES | | |
|---|---|---|---|---|---|---|---|---|---|
| | | | | NOTED | ASSOCIATED | READ MOST | NOTED | ASSOCIATED | READ MOST |
| | | **ALL FREIGHT** | | | | | | | |
| 48 | 1P4B | ASSOCIATION OF AMERICAN RAILROADS | 16 | 53 | 36 | 12 | 110 | 95 | 150 |
| | | **COMMERCIAL TRUCKS/LEASING** | | | | | | | |
| 65 | 1P | GMC TRUCKS CASH BONUS PLAN | 13 | 47 | 38 | 8 | 98 | 100 | 100 |
| | | **COMMUNICATION/PUBLIC UTILITY** | | | | | | | |
| 9 | 1P4B | BELL TELEPHONE SYSTEM/ TELECONFERENCING | 11 | 46 | 39 | 9 | 96 | 103 | 113 |
| 41 | 1P4B | BELL PHONE CENTER | 15 | 44 | 37 | 7 | 92 | 97 | 88 |
| | | **LIFE/GROUP/MEDICAL INSURANCE** | | | | | | | |
| 12 | 1P | METROPOLITAN LIFE INSURANCE | 13 | 51 | 38 | 6 | 106 | 100 | 75 |
| 81 | 1P | NEW YORK LIFE INSURANCE NYL-A-PLUS PLAN | 21 | 35 | 31 | 8 | 73 | 82 | 100 |
| | | **MAGAZINES/NEWSPAPERS** | | | | | | | |
| 47 | 1P | WALL STREET JOURNAL | 8 | 46 | 42 | 18 | 96 | 111 | 225 |
| 76 | 1PB | BELL SYSTEM YELLOW PAGES | 19 | 35 | 35 | 7 | 73 | 92 | 88 |
| | | **MISCELLANEOUS GENERAL PROMOTION** | | | | | | | |
| 59 | 1P | INTERNATIONAL TEL & TEL G P | 16 | 46 | 36 | 18 | 96 | 95 | 225 |
| | | **OFFICE MACHINES/EQUIPMENT** | | | | | | | |
| 2C | 1S4B | IBM COMPUTER SYSTEMS | 2 | 69 | 54 | 14 | 144 | 142 | 175 |
| 17 | 1P | RICOH FT6200 SERIES COPIERS | 24 | 39 | 25 | 7 | 81 | 66 | 88 |
| 75 | 1PB | MINOLTA EP 530R COPIERS | 11 | 48 | 39 | 9 | 100 | 103 | 113 |
| | | **PASSENGER CARS/VEHICLES** | | | | | | | |
| 2 | 1P | GENERAL MOTORS CORP G P | 4 | 50 | 50 | 10 | 104 | 132 | 125 |
| 14 | 1PB | VOLKSWAGEN RABBIT CARS | 10 | 49 | 40 | 8 | 102 | 105 | 100 |
| 42 | A1S5B | DODGE CARS | 1 | 70 | 58 | 9 | 146 | 153 | 113 |
| 83 | 1P4B | FORD MOTOR COMPANY G P | 6 | 50 | 43 | 4 | 104 | 113 | 50 |
| | | **PASSENGER TRAVEL** | | | | | | | |
| 55 | 1P | AVIS RENT-A-CAR SYSTEM | 19 | 37 | 35 | 7 | 77 | 92 | 88 |
| | | **PETROLEUM COS GENERAL PROMOTION** | | | | | | | |
| 51 | 1P4B | TEXACO INCORPORATED G P | 3 | 62 | 52 | 11 | 129 | 137 | 138 |
| | | **RESORTS/TRAVEL ACCOMMODATION** | | | | | | | |
| 3C | 1S4B | HOLIDAY INN G P | 5 | 50 | 45 | 16 | 104 | 118 | 200 |
| | | **RETAIL &/OR DIRECT BY MAIL** | | | | | | | |
| 6 | 1P | MIDAS MUFFLER SHOPS | 9 | 42 | 41 | 6 | 88 | 108 | 75 |
| | | **STATIONERY/MISC. PAPER GOODS** | | | | | | | |
| 44 | 1P | HAMMERMILL BUSINESS PAPERS | 25 | 32 | 20 | 8 | 67 | 53 | 100 |
| | | **TOBACCO/TOBACCO PRODUCTS** | | | | | | | |
| 4C | 1P4B | VANTAGE CIGARETTES | 16 | 48 | 36 | 7- | 100 | 95 | 88- |
| 10 | X1S4 | TOBACCO INSTITUTE | 23 | 48 | 27 | 10 | 100 | 71 | 125 |
| 35 | 1P4B | MARLBORO CIGARETTES | 6 | 53 | 43 | 11- | 110 | 113 | 138- |
| 70 | 1P4 | MERIT CIGARETTES | 22 | 35 | 28 | 4 | 73 | 74 | 50 |
| | | MEDIANS | | 48 | 38 | 8 | | | |

Source:  Starch Readership Report (Starch INRA  Hooper, Inc., 1982).

Perhaps the most important limitation of readership studies involves the response measured. Readership studies measure whether or not a reader recognizes an advertisement. They do not measure the effect of the ad on purchases, whether the reader's product knowledge was enhanced, or even if the reader was truly interested. Readership, in other words, reflects awareness, the first step in the hierarchy of effects. Even if readership is a prerequisite to the knowledge and purchase steps, it is still a matter of controversy whether or not high readership of an advertisement necessarily leads to increased knowledge or purchase. Experienced copywriters claim that they can modify advertisements to make them score well on Starch ratings, but they have less confidence that they have really improved the effectiveness of the advertisements.

Interpretation of Starch or other readership scores is also made difficult by the fact that readership scores in part reflect the existing popularity of products. This reverse hierarchy effect was discussed in Chapter 21.

## Recall Measurements

**Recall tests** measure effectiveness at the same level in the hierarchy of effects as do readership studies, but the technique is more rigorous. Rather than being shown advertisements and asked if they recognize them, respondents are required to recall the advertisements from memory.

*recall tests*

DESIGN OF RECALL MEASUREMENTS. Probably the best-known and most widely used recall-measurement service is Burke's Day-After Recall, a television commercial testing technique. To use the Burke service, the advertiser arranges to have the test commercial shown in one or more designated cities either by buying time or by substituting the test commercial in already purchased time. Twenty-four hours after the test commercial is aired, interviewers call a sample of consumers to find people who viewed the program in which the commercial appeared. Then, without prompting and without revealing the identity of the test commercial, consumers are asked a series of questions to determine what advertisements they recall seeing in the program. The most important measure provided is **related recall,** the percentage of program viewers who recall the test commercial and correctly identify it with the advertised brand. Because Burke recall scores are "unaided" and consumers must correctly identify the advertised brand, scores tend to be far lower than Starch "noted" scores. In addition to this score, Burke provides, for diagnostic purposes, transcripts of verbatim viewer comments on what was recalled about the test commercial.

*related recall*

Gallup and Robinson offers a similar recall-measurement service, called "In-View," for testing television commercials. Like Burke, G & R measures recall related to brand name — termed proven commercial registration or PCR — records communication of copy points, and provides verbatim reactions to the commercial. The PCR scores from an In-View report on the test of a commercial for Puffs Tissues are shown on page 621.

Gallup and Robinson also offers a recall measurement service for magazines (Magazine Impact Research Service or MIRS) that is conceptually similar to the television approach. An issue of a magazine containing the ad to be tested is placed with a geographically dispersed sample of 150 consumers who are regular readers of the test magazine. After waiting a day to allow for reading of the magazine, the sample members are contacted by telephone and questioned on recall, name registration, and idea communication. Responses are counted only if the consumer can recall a specific, identifiable feature of the advertisement and relate it to the proper brand.

G & R's Impact Service is primarily for post-testing of print ads, but the firm also offers Tip-In Service for pre-testing of print ads. In this service, which is often replicated in similar form by agencies and individual advertisers, a comprehensive ad layout or a proof is prepared in the size of a test magazine. Multiple copies of the ad are prepared and *tipped in* (individually pasted in) to test magazines. The magazines are then distributed and readers surveyed as under the Impact Service.

USE OF RECALL MEASUREMENTS. Recall testing can be used for both print and broadcast advertising, but its most widespread application is for television commercials. Recall measurements usually serve as post-tests because the commercial or print ad must be produced before the test can be conducted. However, it is possible to conduct television-commercial tests in a limited area and get results before the advertisement is placed in general use and tip-in style recall tests can be used to pre-test print advertisements.

Recall tests generally include verbatim responses that are useful in diagnosing the communications strengths and weaknesses of test advertisements. However, the verbatims are limited in depth and the tendency is to rely most heavily on the recall scores as a means of rating the test commercial. Many experienced advertisers feel that recall tests, with their heavy emphasis on the recall of specific copy points, understate the performance of emotional commercials that emphasize the use of nonverbal communication such as music and visuals. Nonetheless, recall testing is widely used today by major television advertisers. By one estimate, about one out of three tests of television commercials uses this technique.[4]

EVALUATION OF RECALL MEASUREMENTS. Recall measurements are superior in some ways to readership measurements. An attempt is made to measure recall of an advertisement after a near-normal exposure to the medium. Recall tests are more rigorous in screening sample members. These tests also attempt to control distorted or exaggerated responses by counting only that recall that can be verified through recollection of some specific features of an advertisement. Recall tests are superior to readership studies in that they provide verbatim responses that can be used in

[4]Jack Honomichl, "A 'Rough' Look at Tests of TV Commercials," *Advertising Age* (April 14, 1980), p. 32.

explaining where a particular advertisement is weak or strong. However, these verbatim replies are limited and recall tests tend to be valued for the verified recall score which tends to be relied upon as a go, no-go decision-making measure. Indeed, this reliance is seen by some as a principle weakness of recall testing.

Other limitations of recall testing are like those of readership studies. The response being measured is still at an early stage of the hierarchy of effects, and bears an uncertain relationship to the ultimate response of purchase. Recall tests, according to some, tend to favor mass-appeal ads, ads with simple ideas and specific facts, and ads presenting rational product claims. Yet, for some products, technical products for example, ultimate sale may depend upon communicating complex ideas. Recall tests may judge such ads harshly because of consumer difficulty in recalling involved copy points after only one exposure. Also a problem are ads that are designed to appeal to only a narrow market segment. The percentage of consumers that actually pay attention to and recall such an ad might be very small even though the ad might be highly effective with the intended segment. Likewise, as noted earlier, emotional appeal ads that lack product-fact copy tend to score low on recall tests.[5] A final problem with recall tests is their reliance on a single exposure. As noted in Chapter 21, valid advertising effectiveness measures should be based on results from multiple exposures.

Despite these limitations, recall testing, which is inexpensive and readily available, is widely used by advertisers. According to one recent study, single exposure, day-after recall tests are the most widely used method for testing television commercials.[6]

## Awareness Measurements

Awareness measurement differs from the tests considered thus far in that it measures the effect of an entire advertising effort rather than the sole effectiveness of a single advertisement.

DESIGN OF AWARENESS MEASUREMENTS. Some **awareness studies** are limited to measuring awareness of particular brands while others probe awareness of advertising for a product class. The studies usually involve field interviews — sometimes personal interviews, but more often telephone interviews. To be included in the sample, consumers sometimes must meet specified criteria such as age, or they may have to be consumers of a product similar to that of the advertiser. Data on socioeconomic characteristics of the respondent are frequently gathered for later cross-tabulation. Questioning then turns to awareness of specific brands. If, for

*awareness studies*

---

[5]Jack Honomichl, "FCB: Day-after-recall Cheats Emotion," *Advertising Age* (May 11, 1981), p. 2.
[6]Lyman E. Ostlund and Kevin Clancy, "Copy Test Methods and Measures Favored by Top Ad Agency and Advertising Executives," *Journal of the Academy of Marketing Science* (Winter, 1982), p. 76.

example, the advertiser's product is a soft drink, the interviewer might ask, "What brands of soft drinks can you name?" After several have been named, the interviewer may probe by asking, "Can you think of any others?" As a next step, the study may include a directly-aided question that involves reading a list of brand or company names and asking which ones the respondent recognizes. The study may terminate at this point or it may go on to a measurement of awareness of specific advertising. The interviewer may begin by going down the list of brand names remembered by the respondent and asking with regard to each one: "Can you remember any advertising for _____ brand? Describe what you remember." After this, more directly-aided questions can follow, addressing whether or not the respondent remembers specific slogans, appeals, or other elements, for example, "Do you know what brand claims '100 percent caffein-free, never had it, never will?'".

*tracking study*

USE OF AWARENESS MEASUREMENTS. Awareness measurements are usually used as part of a **tracking study,** research that monitors over time the changes taking place among consumers as a result of an advertising program. They provide little information on the effectiveness of particular elements of the program, evaluating instead the impact of all elements combined. To be of value, awareness studies need to be conducted at regular intervals, such as every six months or every year. The first study provides baseline awareness scores for the advertiser's own product and competitive products. Awareness scores from later studies are compared with these earlier scores to detect trends in brand-advertising awareness.

EVALUATION OF AWARENESS MEASUREMENTS. Like the other measurements examined prior to this one, awareness studies measure response at a very early stage in the hierarchy of effects. Consequently, there is the usual uncertainty as to how changes in awareness actually translate into changes in purchase habits.

Awareness measures differ in important ways from readership and recall studies. Because awareness tests can be conducted by telephone, larger samples can be used and often they are randomly selected to improve their representativeness. Awareness measurement is valuable as a long-term evaluation device because the most meaningful results are trends in levels of brand and advertising awareness.

One limitation of awareness measurements is that study results are difficult to interpret. Awareness studies do not provide descriptive information that would permit diagnosing problems or successes. If awareness begins to decline, it may mean, for example, that the budget is too low or the copy wrong, or that the wrong medium is being used. The awareness study results give little guidance as to which of these problems is involved.

Another reason why awareness scores are difficult to interpret is that changes in awareness may come about from something other than the advertising program. Improved distribution, putting the product within the reach of more people, may increase awareness. Unintended publicity, the decline of competition, and changes in consumer needs can all influence awareness. There is also the reverse hierarchy effect; an increase in purchases will probably lead to an increase in awareness scores.

## Affective (Attitude) Tests

The measurement devices just examined are essentially memory devices recording the brands and advertisements consumers actually remember. **Affective tests** move to the liking and preference stages in the hierarchy. The responses measured are consumers' attitudes toward companies, products, and advertisements. The rationale behind these tests is that a favorable change in attitude toward a product means that the person so affected will be more likely to buy that product. Hence, advertisements that generate improved attitudes are more effective than those that do not.

*affective tests*

### Opinion Measurements

One approach to measuring consumer attitudes toward products, companies, and advertisements is to directly ask consumers their opinion. A number of tests take this direct opinion form, but they have declined in use in recent years, having been replaced by more sophisticated techniques.

DESIGN OF OPINION MEASUREMENTS. Opinion measurements can be designed to test products, but the most widespread use of the technique has been to pre-test individual advertisements or elements of advertisements.

*Consumer Juries.* One of the earliest forms of advertising effectiveness testing, the **consumer jury technique** consists in showing proposed advertisements to a consumer and asking for an opinion of each ad. This is repeated with a number of consumers, and then the preferences are combined to give a final rating for each advertisement.

*consumer jury technique*

A variety of questions may be used to elicit the consumer's opinion. The consumer might be shown all the test advertisements at one time and asked which one was "liked" best, which one was "most interesting" or "most believable." In keeping with the consumer behavior model presented in Chapter 5, the consumer might be asked which advertisement would be "most useful" in making a purchase decision.

Another approach to opinion measurement is to have the consumer rank all the test advertisements in terms of some criterion. Thus, the consumer might be asked to arrange the test ads in order from "like best" to "like least." Another approach consists in showing the consumer only two advertisements at a time, asking that one of the two be picked according to some criterion such as "like best." This is termed a paired comparison test. The ads paired together are changed from consumer to consumer to avoid any pairing bias.

*Headline Testing.* **Headline testing** is used to pre-test alternative positionings or product benefits. The proposed benefits or positionings are written in the form of headlines with each one printed on a separate card. These cards (perhaps five or six different ones) are shown to a sample of consumers. Each consumer's opinion of these appeals is then elicited using direct questions, rankings, and paired comparisons. A similar approach is used to test other elements of advertisements such as alternative slogans, logotypes, or illustrations.

EVALUATION OF OPINION MEASUREMENTS. The two forms of opinion testing described provide fast, inexpensive information on consumer opinions of advertisements and ad elements. The central difficulty with opinion measurement has to do with the validity issue — what is it that these techniques actually measure? What is desired is a prediction of the effectiveness of alternative ads or appeals. This is approached by asking consumers a question such as "Which advertisement do you like best?" Even if the consumer answers this question accurately, there is no very good evidence that relates liking an advertisement to its effectiveness in generating sales. Note that in the hierarchy of effects, the "liking" stage refers to an increase in liking the product, not in liking the advertising itself.

In addition to this, it is not clear what criteria the consumer jury member actually uses in selecting or ranking advertisements. Selections seem, in practice, to be rather independent of the criterion suggested by the interviewer. For example, if the consumer is asked which ad is most interesting and then which one is liked best, the selection will likely be the same. This may be in response to a felt need to be consistent or it may indicate that consumers act on some unstated criterion of their own regardless of the question. In practical use, consumers seem to be attracted to clever, clean-looking, soft-sell advertisements, suggesting that they, perhaps, select "pleasant" advertisements. Pleasantness seems an unlikely criterion for measuring effectiveness.

The headline-testing approach has an additional problem not found in the testing of entire advertisements. When one element of an advertisement, such as the key benefit, is taken out of the context of the total advertisement, its effectiveness may change. For example, some benefits are particularly effective because they lend themselves to dramatic creative execution.

## Attitude Measurements

Opinion tests treat consumer reactions as a one-dimensional phenomenon — a liking or disliking of some object. **Attitude tests** take a more sophisticated approach that attempts to measure not only different dimensions of people's feelings toward objects, but also the intensity of those feelings.

DESIGN OF ATTITUDE MEASUREMENTS. Attitude measurement relies heavily on the use of rating scales. A *rating scale* is a device by which respondents can select one of several alternative answers and indicate how strongly they feel about the answer. For example, an automobile advertiser attempting to explore attitudes toward automobile makes and models might ask a sample of consumers to react to statements such as:

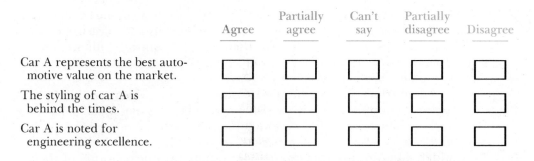

|  | Agree | Partially agree | Can't say | Partially disagree | Disagree |
|---|---|---|---|---|---|
| Car A represents the best automotive value on the market. | ☐ | ☐ | ☐ | ☐ | ☐ |
| The styling of car A is behind the times. | ☐ | ☐ | ☐ | ☐ | ☐ |
| Car A is noted for engineering excellence. | ☐ | ☐ | ☐ | ☐ | ☐ |

The use of rating scales makes it possible to combine the answers of different sample members and arrive at a composite attitude toward the product.

Many different forms of rating scales have been devised. Selection and construction of the proper form of scale is a highly technical field in which a great deal of research has been conducted, notably by psychologists.

*Semantic Differential.* One form of rating which has received widespread use in the marketing field is the semantic differential. Originally developed by psychologists to measure the meaning of difficult-to-define concepts,[7] the technique has been adapted to marketing to measure people's feelings toward products and companies.[8] The *semantic differential technique* uses a series of seven-point scales, each one of which contains a pair of bi-polar (opposite) adjectives. One of the scales might look like this:

beautiful  ugly

Subjects are asked to rate a concept or an object by marking a point on each one of a series of these scales. In marketing applications, the adjectives chosen are ones that are descriptive and meaningful in terms of the item being evaluated.

*Interview Procedures.* In gathering attitudinal data, personal interviews are usually necessary so that respondents can see the rating scales. Subjects

---

[7]The original presentation is found in C. Osgood, G. Suci, and P. Tannenbaum, *The Measurement of Meaning* (Urbana, Illinois: University of Illinois Press, 1957).
[8]Examples of its application are in William A. Mindak, "Fitting the Semantic Differential to the Marketing Problem," *Journal of Marketing* (April, 1961), pp. 28–33.

usually find rating scales easy to understand and enjoyable to fill out. For some types of rating scales, such as the semantic differential, subjects are encouraged to answer quickly, before their defenses are aroused, thereby giving the rating scales some of the characteristics of an indirect question approach.

USE OF ATTITUDE MEASUREMENTS. One difference between the attitude approach and the direct opinion approach just considered lies in the object being evaluated. Opinion measurements usually measure consumers' reactions to individual advertisements. By contrast, attitude tests are usually concerned with measuring the effect of advertising in changing consumers' feelings toward a product.

*image study*

One application of attitude measurement is in what is popularly called an **image study.** The study consists of a number of scales which inquire into various dimensions of people's attitudes toward the advertiser's product and, often, competitors' products as well. The semantic differential is widely used in this application. The results provide a profile of the way people view the product. This profile can be thought of as being the result of the total advertising effort. Usually the image study is repeated at regular intervals to see what changes have taken place in the profile of the advertiser's product. The effectiveness of the advertising effort is judged in terms of the direction and extent of attitude changes toward the product.

Another application of attitude measurement is in testing specific advertisements. These tests are usually in the form of experiments. Sample members to be included in the test are first given a set of rating scales by which they express their attitudes toward the advertiser's product. The sample group is then exposed to the advertiser's test advertisement followed by another administration of the rating scales to determine what changes took place in attitudes as a result of the exposure to the advertisement. Different groups may be exposed to different test ads to give comparative results. Efforts are usually made in these tests to disguise the advertiser's intent by asking about attitudes toward several products and by placing the test advertisement in context with other advertisements and editorial material.

EVALUATION OF ATTITUDE MEASUREMENTS. The attitude measurement techniques described here represent a substantial improvement over the direct opinion approach. The use of rating scales makes more explicit the basis on which the consumer is evaluating the advertisement or the product and provides considerably richer detail about the areas of strength and weakness that are perceived in the product.

Like any test that measures response at a stage in the hierarchy of effects prior to purchase, there is uncertainty as to whether or not an improvement in attitude will lead to an increase in sales. In the case of attitude measurement, the problem is even more complex—it is not always clear which changes in attitude constitute an improvement and which a decline. Attitude studies, in other words, measure changes in attitude, but do not evaluate their desirability.

In addition to this problem, attitude tests share some of the problems of the previous measurements. The results of image studies, while designed to measure the impact of advertising, are also influenced by many other factors such as the consumer's experience with the product and the recommendations of friends. Hence, when an attitude change occurs, it is not always clear that it was advertising that caused the change.

The use of attitude measurement to evaluate individual advertisements sometimes involves small-sized samples with subjects viewing commercials under unnatural, forced conditions. There is a substantial danger that sample members' responses will be distorted for a number of reasons. They may "play expert," they may see through the disguise and guess the company doing the testing, or their second attitude rating may be "conditioned" by the fact that they had been asked to answer the same questions just before seeing the advertisements.

## Conative (Motive) Tests

Attitude tests measure consumers' feelings toward objects. **Conative tests** move one stage further along the hierarchy of effects and measure the action that people take as a result of advertising. Sometimes the action measured is actual purchase of the product, and sometimes the measurement is of some action prior to purchase or some action that is thought to simulate purchase.

*conative tests*

### Inquiry Measurements

**Inquiry measurement** is used as a post-test of individual advertisements. The number of requests for information or responses to offers is counted for each advertisement and comparison is made between advertisements. Inquiries in this case are assumed to be indicative of sales results that would be generated by the advertisements. Inquiry tests can also be used to measure the relative effectiveness of media vehicles by comparing their ability to generate inquiries. This approach is most often used in print advertising, but can have application in radio and television also.

*inquiry measurement*

DESIGN OF INQUIRY TESTS. In order to conduct an inquiry test, an invitation to consumers to write in for further information must be included in the advertisement. This invitation might offer a booklet, a sample, or some other incentive to write in. The offer and address may be contained within the body copy of a print advertisement or included in a coupon printed in the ad. The use of a coupon, because of its visibility and ease of use, tends to increase the number of inquiries received. The offer in each advertisement must be keyed to the particular ad. This is usually done by including in the address or coupon a different department or box number for each advertisement being tested.

The inquiry test must be strictly controlled so that the difference in inquiries between two advertisements represents only differences between the ads being tested. This ideal is difficult to achieve in practice, but it means that if inquiries from two advertisements are to be comparable, the ads must appear in the same media vehicle, in the same season, and with the same offer presented in the same way. If the inquiry test is being used to compare two media vehicles instead of two advertisements, then the same advertisement would be run in the two media vehicles at the same time with the offer keyed differently in the two places.

When two advertisements are being tested, evaluation consists in a direct comparison of the number of inquiries received from each ad. In the case of a media test, some adjustment must be made to offset the fact that the two media vehicles are likely to have different circulations and different advertising rates. The adjustment is usually made by comparing cost per inquiry (cost of the space unit purchased divided by the number of inquiries) for the two media vehicles.

EVALUATION OF INQUIRY TESTS. Measurement by means of inquiries is a popular evaluation approach, particularly in the industrial advertising field. Its appeal is not difficult to see. The response being measured is a specific action which appears to be much more closely related to purchasing than is a simple change in a person's mental attitude. Inquiry tests are easy to understand and inexpensive to apply. Indeed, any advertiser who regularly receives inquiries based on advertising and makes no effort to tabulate them is wasting a valuable evaluation resource.

This method is not, however, without limitations. The validity of using inquiries as an indicator of sales effectiveness is certainly open to question. It is a valid response measure when the principal objective of the advertising is to generate inquiries as is often the case in industrial advertising where advertising serves primarily to produce leads for salespeople to follow up. By contrast, requests for a recipe booklet offered in a cake mix advertisement would provide much less direct evidence of effectiveness since the primary purpose of the ad would not be to generate inquiries.

Inquiry tests also fall short unless some special effort is made to examine the quality of inquiries received. A familiar experience in offers made in consumer magazines is to receive an overabundance of inquiries from children and lonely older people. Surely these inquiries should not be counted as heavily as inquiries from prime prospects and, yet, it is often difficult to sort these out.

Some advertisers, particularly in the industrial field, have sought to overcome this problem by tracing the ultimate sales results achieved from each inquiry. One company, after extensive investigation of their procedure for tracing sales results from inquiries, estimated that actual attributable sales were probably four times as large as the traceable sales.[9]

---

[9]"Analysis of Ads' Sales Effect Leads Haskell to Allocate More," *Advertising Age* (April 5, 1971), p. 36.

## Split-Run Tests

**Split-run tests** are a specialized form of inquiry test used to pre-test alternate versions of advertisements or elements of advertisements such as headlines, illustrations, or product benefits.

*split-run tests*

DESIGN OF SPLIT-RUN TESTS. Some large newspapers and magazines offer what is termed an "A-B split-run." (This should not be confused with a geographic split-run which is, in effect, different regional editions.) The A-B split allows an advertiser to run two different versions of an advertisement in the same newspaper or magazine issue. The insertion of each ad is handled so that every other paper coming off the press has one version of the ad while the alternate paper has the second version of the ad. This insures that the two ad versions are distributed to highly comparable samples of consumers.

Measurement of effectiveness in this test is achieved by making some form of offer in each advertisement, keying it to the ad version, and then tabulating responses for each version.

EVALUATION OF SPLIT-RUN TESTS. The principal advantage of split-run testing over regular inquiry tests is the added control — the two ads go to closely matched samples and they appear at the same time in the same environment. Beyond this, the limitations are very much like those suggested for inquiry tests.

Split-run tests, because they provide quantifiable returns, may tend to give a false sense of confidence in the results. The advertiser should consider, however, whether or not the test situation is truly representative of the situation in which the final advertising will operate. For example, for many years one of the favorite split-run vehicles was the *New York Daily News* because of its very large circulation. Advertising agencies often used it as a means for testing alternative copy approaches. Alternative key benefits were prepared in the form of headlines and appeared in small all-copy ads containing a free offer of a product sample. The actual use of the selected benefit often was sharply different from this test environment. It was often used in a different medium (television, for example), in a different area (national usage instead of New York City), combined in the ad with other visual and copy elements, and without inclusion of a free sample offer. It is difficult to be sure that the split-run test results would be indicative of the real effectiveness of the advertisement as it would finally appear.

## Theater Tests

**Theater tests,** which received their name from the practice of using converted theaters as test locations, are, according to the study noted

*theater tests*

earlier, the second most widely used method for testing television commercials.[10] They are predominantly used for pre-testing.

DESIGN OF THEATER TESTS. Several research firms offer theater test services and some of the larger advertising agencies provide similar test programs for their clients. One of the well-known services in this field is Advertising Research Service (ARS) with theater facilities in Chicago and Philadelphia. ARS draws a sample of consumers from residential telephone directories who are then invited by mail to attend a preview of new television programs at a converted downtown theater.

Upon arrival at the theater, audience members are asked to indicate their choice of brand in a number of product categories to indicate their preference for a door prize. After the door-prize drawing is held, a half-hour television pilot film is shown including three test commercials in their normal positions. After an intermission and a questionnaire on the program shown, a second television pilot is shown, with a different set of test commercials. After the second film, audience members are again asked to fill out a form indicating brand choice in a number of product categories in preparation for another door-prize drawing. The product categories in both instances are the same and include the product classes for the test commercials shown in the films. The final door-prize drawing completes the program. Three days after the showing, a sample of audience members is called to ask what commercials they recall from the viewing.

Two measures of commercial effectiveness are provided by the ARS service — recall and what ARS terms "persuasion." The recall measure, the same as that described earlier, is derived from the telephone callback. Persuasion, which appears to be the equivalent of what we termed "conviction" in the hierarchy of effects, is measured by the difference in brand preference expressed before seeing the test commercials and preference after seeing the commercials. ARS has developed norms from many years of testing to which individual test scores — both recall and persuasion — can be compared.

A variation of the theater test uses viewing facilities in a trailer located in a supermarket parking lot.[11] Shoppers are intercepted as they enter the store and given a price-off card as an incentive to cooperate. Half of the group is taken to the trailer and shown test commercials while the other half, serving as a control group, is released to the store. The price-off card is used to identify the participants when they check out their purchases and code the laser scanner that records purchases at the check out stations. The scanners record the purchases, including purchases of the products in the test commercials. Comparison of the purchases of the test and control groups provides a sales measure of the effectiveness of the test commercial.

---

[10]Ostlund and Clancy, *op. cit.*

[11]John L. Carefoot, "Scanner-based Copy-testing Methodology Links Purchase Behavior to Ad Exposure," *Marketing News* (September 17, 1982), pp. 11, 16.

EVALUATION OF THEATER TESTS. Theater tests attempt to be a more sophisticated effectiveness measure than those reviewed thus far by controlling the test situation and by measuring a response variable closer to the purchase end of the hierarchy of effects. Companies offering theater-test services have done considerable research to demonstrate the reliability of this test method. Theater testing is, of course, limited to television commercials and it is expensive — about $4,000 to $5,000 per test. To this, of course, must be added the still larger cost of producing the commercial to be tested. It is possible to conduct theater tests using inexpensively produced "rough" commercials. Research firms offering these test services claim that reliable results can be obtained by testing with rough commercials that cost perhaps $5,000 rather than with finished commercials costing up to $50,000 or more.

One problem with theater tests is that the viewing situation is not natural. Although the test commercial is viewed in the context of a program, the theater viewing situation is considerably different from what it would be in the home — there is an audience present and the audience members are generally aware that they are participating in some sort of test. This tends to force and distort viewing. The test sample is far from ideal. Only a small percentage of those invited actually attend and, of course, they are from a limited geographic area.

The validity of the response measured is also open to question. As a substitute for actual purchase, theater tests use brand preference in a door-prize drawing. It seems quite possible that preference in a give-away situation will be different from preference as exercised in the store. This objection is mitigated somewhat by the use of changes in preference rather than of absolute levels of preference. Another problem, one which is common to many other test approaches, is that the measurement of response is based on a single exposure to an advertisement. Most advertising campaigns use commercials on a repetitive basis so that the real issue is effectiveness after repeated exposure.

## Split-Cable and Split-Scan Testing

Two technological advances, cable television and laser scanning at store checkouts, have led to the development of two related advertising effectiveness measurement approaches that have great promise.

DESIGN OF SPLIT-CABLE AND SPLIT-SCAN TESTS. The originator of **split-cable testing** in 1967 was AdTel which continues as a leader in this service under the name Test Marketing Group. The split-cable system was originally established in two small (by test-market standards) markets operating independently of each other. These two markets were ones that received their television coverage exclusively by cable. Arrangements were made to split the cable into a checkerboard pattern so that half the market could receive a test commercial while the other half received at the same time a control commercial. With all other factors held constant, the result, much as in A-B split-run newspaper testing, is two very evenly matched samples.

*split-cable testing*

In order to measure the results in the test households as compared to the control households, two 1,000 household panels were formed. One panel was made up of members who were receiving the test commercial while the other was made up of members who were receiving the control commercial. Members of the panels agreed to record in diaries their purchases of household items, including the products advertised in the test commercials. By comparing purchases of the test product by the test panel with those by the control panel, the effectiveness of the test commercial could be determined in terms of sales results.

*split-scan system*

One of the weaknesses in the split-cable system is the tendency for households to record purchases inaccurately or to fail to record some items altogether. This problem is largely overcome in the split-scan system that marries scanner technology to split-cable technology. The two pioneers in this form of testing, BehaviorScan and Test Marketing Group, operate similarly.[12] The **split-scan system** is installed in medium-sized markets that receive their dominant television coverage over cable. As under the AdTel system, arrangements were made for split-cable feed to homes in the market. In addition, the research firm offering the split-scan testing equips a panel of supermarkets with scanners at their checkout stations. Two panels of households, one *test* and one *control,* are then recruited and supplied with special cards that are presented at the checkout station so that the households' sales are recorded and designated as belonging either to the test group or to the control group. Analysis of these scanner results are used in place of the diary-panel data of the split-cable test in order to provide a sales effectiveness measure of a test commercial.

EVALUATION OF SPLIT-CABLE, SPLIT-SCAN TESTS. Both the split-cable and the split-scan systems are used to test television commercials or, less frequently, levels and distribution of television budgets. Pre-testing is possible through these systems, but a finished, rather than a rough, commercial is needed. With the cost of producing the commercial, the cost of media time, and the cost of the research service, this is an expensive test method when compared to recall testing, but considerably less expensive than a full-scale market test. Test facilities are limited to a few small cities, but sample sizes are substantial.

Despite these limitations, split-cable and split-scan represent the most advanced advertising testing approach that is available today short of test marketing. Viewing of the test commercial takes place in an unforced, home environment and multiple commercial exposures can be and usually are used. The use of the split-cable results in well-matched panels with external variables affecting each panel equally. Measurement of effectiveness is made in terms of sales results, and diagnostic data can be collected through post-test interviewing.

---

[12]See Eileen Norris, "Product Hopes Tied to Cities with the 'Right Stuff'," *Advertising Age* (February 20, 1984), pp. M-10ff.

## Sales Analysis Measurements

Since the ultimate effect desired from an advertisement is purchase, sales results, if they can be related to advertising effort, represent a most valuable measure of advertising effectiveness.

DESIGN OF THE SALES-MEASUREMENT APPROACH. In its simplest form, the **sales-analysis approach** is used as a post-test of the total advertising program. The procedure involves measuring product sales or market share for the preceding planning period and relating the results to the advertising effort. If sales or market share improve, the advertising effort is judged successful; if sales decline, the advertising is deemed unsuccessful.

*sales-analysis approach*

There are some obvious difficulties with this sort of direct linkage of advertising effort and sales. First, it is obvious that in most cases changes in sales or market share result from a variety of influences, only one of which is advertising. These other influences include external factors such as competition and natural phenomena like weather, and they include all the other elements in the marketing mix such as price and personal selling. A second difficulty in directly linking sales and advertising is that sales changes often lag behind the advertising effort that causes them. Another problem is that for many companies advertising is directed to the ultimate consumer, but the company sells to middlemen. Consequently, the company's sales figures do not reflect the purchase response of consumers, but purchases by wholesalers and retailers. These latter sales figures can be heavily influenced by changes in levels of inventory held by the wholesaler or retailer.

These measurement difficulties limit the situations in which sales results can be linked directly to advertising. There are, however, some cases where it is possible. Mail order firms, for example, can directly trace sales to particular advertisements. Retailers in many lines feel that they can read response to sales-promotion advertising very directly because there is little lag and no middleman. There are also other types of products for which advertising is so dominant an element in the marketing mix that sales changes can often be attributed to advertising rather than to other elements of the mix. Heavily advertised food, drug, toiletry, and household cleaning items are examples of such products.

MEASURING CONSUMER SALES. To relate sales to advertising effort, companies that sell through middlemen (which would include most of the foods, drugs, toiletries, and household cleaners mentioned above) need to have a way to measure actual sales to consumers or, as it is frequently termed, consumer take-away. There are several research approaches to providing this information.

*Retail Audits.* One approach to determining consumer purchases is to audit the sales of a representative sample of retail stores and to project the results to get total purchases. The leading commercial service in the

**retail audit** field is A. C. Nielsen's Retail Index which provides consumer sales information from both food and drug retailers. The audit principle is simple in concept, although in practice it becomes quite complex. Nielsen has its own staff of field auditors. Every 60 days they call on each retail store in a sample of some 1,300 stores and take a physical inventory of each product on which sales are to be calculated. In addition, invoices or warehouse withdrawal records are checked to determine purchases during the preceding 60 days. Consumer sales are computed as follows: inventory at the beginning of the period (from the audit conducted in the prior period), plus purchases or warehouse withdrawals, minus inventory at the end of the period (from the current audit) gives sales for the preceding 60 days.

The information yielded by this technique can be highly detailed. Nielsen, for example, provides information on sales, inventory, distribution, retail prices, and dealer support (such as special displays). This information is cross-tabulated by brand and package size, geographic region, county size, and type of store. These figures are presented to subscribers in tabular form such as that in Exhibit 22-4.

*Warehouse Withdrawals.* An alternative approach used in the determination of consumer grocery purchases is to conduct an audit at grocery warehouses rather than in retail stores. It is contended by those who offer these services that modern food-store inventories are so small and stock turnover so rapid that the difference between warehouse withdrawal and consumer sales is negligible.

The leading firm offering warehouse withdrawal measurement is Selling Areas-Marketing, Inc. (SAMI), a subsidiary of Time Inc. The SAMI service measures grocery withdrawals in 28 individual markets which are also projected to estimate national volume. Types of information provided by warehouse-withdrawal measurements are similar to the information provided by retail audits.

*Scanner-Data Systems.* Laser scanner systems are used at the checkout stations of self-service retail outlets, such as supermarkets, to "read" the Universal Product Code (the bar symbols printed on most consumer-products packages) and to transmit transaction information to the cash register and to storage in a computer. These systems are designed to simplify and speed-up the checkout process for consumers and to provide store management with inventory and product-movement data. A by-product of these systems is their ability to provide product-movement data to marketing research firms.

The use of laser scanner systems in supermarket checkouts as a measurement technique for copy testing and new product testing has already been discussed. However, the most fundamental research application of these devices is their use in the collection of retail-sales data as part of or as a substitute for retail audits or warehouse withdrawal measurements. The use of laser scanner systems in retail outlets is still a relatively new research

Example of data contained in the Nielsen Retail Index Report. EXHIBIT 22-4

SHARE OF CONSUMER SALES
BY BRAND

Drug, Grocery,
Mass Merchandiser Comb.
(Total U.S. — Pint Basis)

| PRODUCT CLASS A | JF | MA | MJ | JA | SO | ND | JF | MA |
|---|---|---|---|---|---|---|---|---|
| ALL OTHERS | 19.0 | 18.5 | 17.9 | 17.3 | 17.0 | 16.8 | 16.7 | 16.2 |
| BRAND 5 | 6.2 | 6.1 | 6.0 | 6.0 | 6.0 | 6.1 | 6.0 | 6.0 |
| BRAND 4 | 6.1 | 7.3 | 8.4 | 9.0 | 9.5 | 9.5 | 9.7 | 9.9 |
| BRAND 3 | 24.2 | 23.7 | 23.1 | 22.9 | 22.7 | 22.5 | 22.5 | 22.5 |
| BRAND 2 | 11.0 | 10.5 | 10.0 | 9.7 | 9.3 | 9.1 | 8.7 | 8.5 |
| BRAND 1 | 33.5 | 33.9 | 34.6 | 35.1 | 35.5 | 36.0 | 36.4 | 36.9 |
| BI-MO. PERIODS | JF | MA | MJ | JA | SO | ND | JF | MA |

application, but it is growing rapidly, especially in larger supermarket chains. It is estimated that by 1985 stores accounting for 50 percent of food-store volume will be scanner equipped.[13] As more stores install scanners, the potential of auditing product movement by scanner will increase.

Unlike the situation in the copy-testing and new-product testing fields, the firms offering scanner-based store-audit data are the same as the firms offering the more traditional services — retail audits and warehouse-withdrawal data. Up to the present, these firms, such as Nielsen, SAMI, and Towne-Oller, have offered scanner data as a supplement rather than as a substitute for the more traditional services. Nielsen's National Scantrack service is, perhaps, typical of the state of the art. This service gathers scanner data from a national panel of 120 food stores (as compared to 1,300 stores in their Retail Index). The sales data from this panel of stores is projected so as to represent the sales of all supermarkets with a weekly volume of over $80,000. Because the sample size is small, the precision of the results of this scanner measurement service is considerably under that of Nielsen's normal store audit. However, scanner reports like Nielsen's Scantrack provide data very much like that found in the retail-audit reports. The Scantrack biweekly reports contain consumer sales and share by product class, brand, and item as well as price, distribution, and sales-promotion data for the purchased product class.

*Consumer Panels.* A quite different approach to the measurement of consumer purchases is to go directly to the consumers themselves and record what they have actually purchased. One method is the diary panel approach. The panel is made up of homemakers who agree to record their daily purchases of specified products in a diary. These diaries are collected periodically and the results tabulated and projected to the total population. Consumer diaries list consumer purchases, package sizes, prices paid, special deals utilized, and type of store from which purchased. An important difference between panel data and audit data is that the panel reports can include information on the characteristics of the purchaser — demographic characteristics such as age, income, family size, and also media usage characteristics. However, panel data do not include in-store information such as inventories, distribution, display, and out-of-stock conditions. A leading panel measurement service is Market Research Corporation of America (MRCA) which retains a continuous panel of 10,000 families.

There are also other methods of making direct consumer purchase measurements. The pantry check method uses interviewers who physically check what products are in the home. Direct interviews are sometimes used to ask what products people have purchased in a product category for some recent period.

---

[13]Nancy Giges, "Nielsen, SAMI Co-exist with Scanners," *Advertising Age* (November 9, 1981), p. 40.

EVALUATION OF CONSUMER SALES MEASURES. In the final analysis the type of consumer sales measure selected is determined by the type of information needed. All of the methods suffer in some degree from sample deficiencies — size, representativeness, and bias due to conditioning of sample members. The services are very expensive, representing a major research expenditure for even large firms. In the consumer products field, however, marketers find these services indispensable tools in evaluating the effectiveness of their advertising programs.

## Market Tests, Controlled Store Tests, and Simulated Test Markets

Market tests and their close relatives, controlled store tests and simulated test markets, can be used to measure consumer purchase response to advertising in a controlled yet natural purchase situation. In many respects, these techniques represent the ultimate and ideal effectiveness measurement device. Both the design and evaluation of these three measurement techniques are discussed in detail in Chapter 20 because of their use in evaluating new-product introduction programs. That discussion will not be repeated here, but the applicability of these three forms of testing to the measurement of advertising effectiveness will be considered.

Market tests, controlled store tests, and simulated test markets are experimental test designs and as such have special power to validly determine cause and effect. They are able, for example, to measure the effect on sales of a change in advertising copy and to give assurance that the change in sales was due to the change in advertising and not due to some other factor.

These market experiments can be used to test any single advertising program element or they can be used to evaluate the overall effectiveness of the total advertising plan. In either case, market experiments serve as pre-tests of contemplated changes in the advertising plan. Elements commonly evaluated through market tests, controlled store tests, and simulated test markets include alternative positionings, budget levels, media, and creative approaches. Proposed sales promotions can also be tested through these experimental techniques.

Effectiveness measurement techniques can be classified in terms of which response is measured as cognitive, affective, and conative techniques. Cognitive tests operate at the earliest stages of the hierarchy of

*CHAPTER SUMMARY*

effects, measuring the number of people exposed to the advertising or what people remember from the exposure. Media audience measurements are used to evaluate media programs by measuring the audience of the media vehicles used. Physiological measurement devices record physical response to advertising stimuli. Devices include psychogalvanometers, eye-tracking cameras, and brain-wave analysis. These devices are used primarily to pre-test alternative creative executions. Readership or recognition studies measure the number of people who have read a particular ad. They serve as post-tests for evaluating individual print ads. Recall tests are similar to readership tests, but the technique is more rigorous because consumers must recall specific ads without prompting. Awareness tests track over time the effect of an entire advertising plan by asking consumers what brand names and advertising they remember in specified product categories.

Affective tests measure consumers' attitudes toward companies, products, and advertisements. These tests operate at the liking and preference stages of the hierarchy of effects. Opinion measurements such as consumer juries and headline tests directly ask consumers' opinions of advertisements or elements of advertisements. Attitude tests provide a more sophisticated measure than opinion tests, measuring several dimensions of people's feelings toward advertisements or products as well as the intensity of those feelings.

Conative tests operate at the last two stages of the hierarchy of effects, measuring the action that people take as a result of advertising. Inquiry tests measure the effectiveness of individual advertisements by counting the number of persons who respond to an offer made in the ad. Split-run tests are a specialized form of inquiry test in which alternative versions of a test advertisement appear in alternate copies of a magazine or newspaper. Theater tests are experimental studies of the change in product choice resulting from exposure to a test advertisement. They are used primarily to pre-test television commercials. Split-cable and split-scan tests are newer measurement techniques for television commercials that combine the characteristics of split-run and theater testing. Direct measurement of the sales effect of advertising requires, for those advertisers that sell through middlemen, a measure of sales to consumers. Retail audits, warehouse withdrawals, scanner data, and consumer panels are four approaches for estimating consumer sales. Market tests, controlled store tests, and simulated test markets are field experimental approaches to measuring consumer purchase response to advertising. These tests can be used to test a single element in an advertising program or a total plan for a product.

1. Local market television ratings are recorded only for selected weeks *QUESTIONS* during the year. The rating services announce in advance when their *FOR* rating or "sweep" weeks will be and, in response, the networks try to *DISCUSSION* schedule high audience specials in those weeks to "hypo" their ratings. Does this practice invalidate the ratings results?

2. Television Audience Assessment, Inc., is attempting to develop a new form of television rating service that will measure not only how many people watch a television program, but also how they respond to the programs that they do watch. The new service would have two qualitative measures — program appeal, a measure of viewer loyalty to the program and program impact, a measure of viewer involvement while viewing the program. How might this new service be used in the evaluation of advertising effectiveness?

3. Looking at the Starch Message Report scores in Exhibit 22-3, do you see any tendency for some product classes to score generally higher than others? What would cause this? Does this tendency invalidate the readership test results?

4. What is the difference between aided and unaided methods of measuring recall? For a given advertisement, how would recall test scores differ on an aided basis as compared to an unaided basis? Which method provides the better results?

5. One of the most talked-about advertising campaigns in recent times has been the Wendy's "Where's the beef?" series. After the introduction of the ads, a national survey to determine advertising awareness, the Wendy's commercial scored first with more than twice the mentions of the second place ad, the also much talked-about Pepsi ad with Michael Jackson.[14] At the same time, one critic suggested that the Wendy's "commercial has committed the gravest sin in advertising. It doesn't sell Wendy's fast food. It sells the ad agency, the author, director, and, most of all, Clara Peller." It is possible that the Wendy's advertising could have such high awareness and yet not be effective in selling the product?

6. Numerous city, regional, and national advertising associations annually make awards for outstanding advertisements, frequently presented at a gathering of advertising executives and with considerable fanfare. Selection of the winners is usually made by a panel of advertising experts. Is this selection process the equivalent of an opinion test? Would such awards provide a good measure of advertising effectiveness?

7. On-Air Lab offers a variation in recall testing approach from Burke's Day-After Recall. On-Air Lab places the test commercial always in the first-commercial position and always in a regularly scheduled situation comedy in the test city. Consumers are pre-recruited and asked to watch the television program, but no mention is made of the advertising. The evening after the program, the test consumers are called and asked, after verification of program viewership, questions on commercial recall, copy-point playback, and intention to buy.

   a. In what ways does this test differ from Burke's Day-After Recall?
   b. What are the advantages and disadvantages of the On-Air Lab approach?

8. It is easy to heighten the number of inquiries received from an ad in an inquiry test by giving prominence in the ad to the offer, by providing a coupon to make it easy to write in, and by making the offer free rather than requiring payment. In conducting an inquiry test, is it better to use ads that encourage inquiry or ads in which the offer is placed without special prominence in the body of the ad copy?

9. Warner Communications has introduced a two-way cable television system called Qube in Columbus, Ohio, that allows viewers to respond to questions that are asked over television by pressing buttons on a special in-home terminal. The responses are collected and tabulated by a central computer. What potential do you think this system would offer for testing television commercials?

---

[14]Scott Hume, "It's Everywhere, It's Everywhere," *Advertising Age* (March 26, 1984), pp. 3, 74.

10. Two television commercials for Puffs Tissues were evaluated by Gallup and Robinson's In-View, an on-air recall test.[15] Both commercials used a slice-of-life format with the primary benefit being softness. In the first commercial, the subject uses the product while suffering from a head cold. In the second, the product is used by a woman who is crying after seeing a sad movie. Test results were as follows:

|  | Score in Percentages | | | | | |
|---|---|---|---|---|---|---|
|  | Head cold | | Crying | | Norm | |
|  | Men | Women | Men | Women | Men | Women |
| Recall (PCR) | 29 | 43 | 27 | 35 | 27 | 33 |
| Persuasiveness |  |  |  |  |  |  |
|    Recallers | 47 | 48 | 18 | 32 | 33 | 37 |
|    Total Sample | 14 | 21 | 5 | 11 | 9 | 12 |

a. Based on the test scores, what is your evaluation of the two commercials?

b. What do you think accounts for the difference between the two scores?

---

*PROBLEM*

The advertising manager for the Mid City National Bank, Anne Stevens, is considering how to set up measurements to evaluate a forthcoming sales promotion designed to increase the bank's savings deposits. Mid City National is the largest commercial bank in a city of 300,000. It has a single downtown location, branch banks not being permitted by state law. Mid City National has had a strong growth record through the years, but recently several new federal savings and loan associations have provided increasing competition for savings accounts. It was in response to the S&L competition that Stevens designed the sales promotion.

The basic idea in the bank's sales promotion was to offer a free gift, a brand-name electric blanket, to anyone opening a new savings account with $300 or more during the two-month period of the offer. Advertising for the promotion would appear in the daily city newspaper which dominated Mid City National's market area. Three 1,000-line ads were to be scheduled each week for the first six weeks of the promotion period. Stevens did not utilize an advertising agency, but with the assistance of the retail advertising department of the newspaper she was able to come up with an advertisement for the sales promotion. Creatively the ad attempted to tie together the electric blanket gift and the act of opening a savings account

---

[15]Gallup and Robinson, Inc., Advertising and Marketing Research, "Puffs Tissues: 1980 Cold Problem/Solution versus 1981 Softness Emphasis," *Gallup and Robinson Television Impact Report IN-VIEW* (Princeton, N.J.).

with the headline "You'll sleep better with a Mid City savings account." Copy went on to explain the security benefits of a savings account and also the value of the free gift. In addition to these ads, Stevens had obtained a number of signs to be placed in the bank using the same promotional appeal, stuffers on the promotion were used in checking account statements, and all bank floor personnel were given large "You'll sleep better" buttons. A sales meeting of all customer personnel was scheduled in advance of the promotion.

Mid City National had traditionally been conservative in their advertising and it was only because of the inroads made by the savings and loan institutions that Stevens had been able to convince the president that a sales promotion should be tried. Despite the president's approval, Stevens knew that the results would be most critically scrutinized. Because of this and because it was her first sales promotion experience, Stevens was anxious to establish a complete evaluation-of-effectiveness program for the sales promotion. She hoped that it would be possible to pre-test parts of the promotion—the choice of gift and possibly the newspaper ad. Since the bank operated in only a single city, it did not seem feasible to test-market the promotion. However, Stevens did wish to have a complete set of post-evaluation measures from which she could decide whether or not further promotions of this sort were desirable.

1. Define the elements in the sales promotion that you feel should be evaluated.
2. For each element to be evaluated, describe one or more measurement techniques that you would recommend. Be sure to describe fully how the measurement would be made and its timing.

# CHAPTER 23

## Assuring Advertising's Contribution to the Consumer

**LEARNING OBJECTIVES**

In studying this chapter you will learn:

- What consumers think of advertising.

- The advertising manager's responsibilities toward the consumer.

- The basic elements of a consumer responsibility advertising program.

The advertising manager, like other business managers, has a primary responsibility to create profitable sales for the business and its owners. Most of our attention to this point has been devoted to helping the advertising manager fulfill that responsibility.

However, business people today should recognize that their responsibilities extend beyond their immediate companies to consumers themselves. Advertising managers in particular should feel a responsibility toward the consumer because advertising is highly visible and it directly interacts with consumers.

How does the advertising manager assure that this responsibility to consumers is met? We should stress that the advertising planning process discussed thus far is a highly consumer-responsible one. Recall that advertising planning stresses understanding the needs of target consumers and then creating advertising that directs useful information to them. This is a consumer-responsible process.

In addition, however, the advertising manager needs a review and evaluation program to assure that the end result is consumer responsive. This chapter outlines a positive program that evaluates the consumer contribution of the advertising for a product or service. This control program should stand equal in importance with the effectiveness evaluation program described in the two preceding chapters and the legal evaluation program described in the next chapter.

How Consumers
Perceive Advertising

In order to develop a consumer responsibility program, the advertising manager needs to understand how consumers feel about advertising and what they expect of it.

## How Consumers Feel About Advertising

Advertising plays a variety of roles in the consumer's life. In some cases consumers see advertising as beneficial and useful; in other cases they see it as falling short.

A number of large-scale surveys have been conducted through the years to measure consumer attitudes toward advertising. One study sponsored by the American Association of Advertising Agencies (4As) was reported by Bauer and Greyser in 1968.[1] Louis Harris conducted a survey on consumer attitudes toward advertising in 1971,[2] and the 4As again sponsored a study that was reported by Bartos and Dunn in 1975.[3] Most recently, Selection Research, Inc., conducted in 1983 an advertising-image study commissioned by *Advertising Age*.[4] Although these studies were separated by several years, the results show remarkable consistency. They undoubtedly remain true today.

Surveys of consumer attitudes toward advertising consistently reveal that the thing liked most about advertising is the information it provides. From the consumer's standpoint, advertising's primary function is to provide information that can be used in evaluating products.

ADVERTISING AS A SOURCE OF INFORMATION. Consumers use and value advertising for its information, which allows them to make comparisons of products or to gain knowledge about products in which they are interested. However, consumers are often critical of advertising's information deficiencies.

*Does Advertising Provide Useful Information?* In the first 4As national study of the consumer view of advertising, Bauer and Greyser reported as a major finding that "far and away the most popular type of reason offered for liking advertising was that in one way or another *advertising is information*." When in the same survey consumers were asked what they disliked about advertising, lack of useful information was not even listed as

---

[1]Raymond A. Bauer and Stephen A. Greyser, *Advertising in America: The Consumer View* (Boston: Division of Research, Graduate School of Business Administration, Harvard University, 1968).

[2]Reported in John Revett, "Consumers Endorse More Restrictions on Business: Harris," *Advertising Age* (October 25, 1971), p. 98.

[3]Rena Bartos and Theodore F. Dunn, *Advertising and Consumers—New Perspectives* (New York: American Association of Advertising Agencies, n.d.).

[4]Nancy Millman, "The Image of Advertising," *Advertising Age* (October 24, 1983), pp. 1, 18.

a response. In the survey by Louis Harris, 80 percent of the respondents mentioned informational value as the thing they liked most about advertising. This included learning about new products, help in making choices, and learning about sales, prices, and bargains. Bartos and Dunn reported that "the essential function of advertising as a benefit to the consumer in making him aware of or helping him find out about products was the most frequently volunteered reason for positive opinion of advertising." In the 1983 SRI study, 34 percent of respondents felt that, compared to the previous year, advertising was supplying better or much better information while only 7 percent found it worse.

*Is Advertising Information Misleading?* While consumers value advertising because of the useful information that it delivers, they criticize it at the same time for providing misleading information. In the Bauer-Greyser survey the second leading reason for disliking advertising (26 percent) was that it was untruthful or exaggerated. In the Harris survey 44 percent complained of misrepresentation, and in the Bartos-Dunn study the most frequently mentioned negatives toward advertising (50 percent) were that it was misleading or deceptive or not believable. A hopeful sign is provided by a series of studies by Opinion Research Corporation that found a trend over the past ten years of decreasing complaints about false and misleading advertising.[5]

While advertisers might correctly argue that material falsification of facts in advertising is rare, this would be missing the true meaning of this consumer complaint. Consumers appear to feel that a great deal of advertising is exaggerated and makes claims that are both excessive and not well balanced by revealing negatives as well as positives. As a result, the believability and hence the effectiveness of advertising is seriously diminished. In the Harris survey consumers were asked to rank their confidence in 16 institutions; advertising was ranked 16th and last. Lewis Engman, Federal Trade Commission chairman, reflecting on this stated, "the constant bombardment of excessive claims is little by little innoculating the consumer against credence."[6] The most recent study, the one by SRI in 1983, indicates little change in the credibility of advertising. In that study, nearly half of the respondents disagreed with the statement "Advertising is generally honest and trustworthy," and only 26 percent of the sample felt that the honesty of advertising had improved in the course of the previous year.

Clearly, if advertising is to serve the consumer, it must provide useful information, but that information must also be provided in a balanced, unexaggerated way if it is to be believed.

ADVERTISING—ENTERTAINMENT OR ANNOYANCE. Beyond its informational value, consumers have other feelings and attitudes toward

---

[5]"Consumer Complaints over Misleading Ads Drop," *Advertising Age* (October 15, 1979), p. 20.
[6]"FTC's Engman: 'Bad Ads May Breed Generation of Skeptics'," *Marketing News* (June 1, 1974), p. 1.

advertising. Some consumers consider advertising to be entertaining, but more, apparently, consider it to be annoying.

*Advertising as Entertainment.* Both of the 4As surveys found that advertising is liked by some consumers because it is entertaining. In the Bauer-Greyser survey, entertainment value was the third leading reason for liking advertising with mention by 14 percent. Bartos and Dunn found "surprising" strength in the consumer opinion that advertising is entertaining. In describing this feeling toward advertising, consumers used such terms as amusing, clever, colorful, and artistic.

*Advertising as an Annoyance.* Opinions that advertising is entertaining appear to be far outweighed by feelings that it is annoying. Bauer and Greyser found that the leading reason for disliking advertising was its repetitiveness and interruptive nature. While consumers approved of advertising for filling its informational role, they faulted it as being unpleasant and intrusive. The Bartos-Dunn study confirmed this finding, although annoyance factors placed second to lack of credibility as a criticism.

The surveys reveal several specific sources of consumer annoyance with advertising, some of which are controllable by the individual advertiser, while some are not. Perhaps the number one source of annoyance for consumers is that there is simply too much advertising and too much repetition. A second and related complaint is that advertising is too intrusive and too interruptive of the entertainment. It appears that the intrusiveness complaint and probably the repetition complaint relate primarily to broadcast media. In a 1979 survey, three out of four people said they were annoyed by too many ads and 60 percent of these referred specifically to television.[7] While advertisers consider the intrusiveness of television to be a major advantage of the medium, they, like consumers, are concerned about the clutter on television.

BAD TASTE IN ADVERTISING. In addition to finding advertising annoying, consumers find some advertising to be in poor taste. According to a study conducted by Warwick, Welsh & Miller advertising agency through Home Testing Institute, television advertising in particular is criticized as being less tasteful than television programming.[8] Specific charges of bad taste were directed to advertising for sensitive product classes like feminine hygiene, laxatives, bras, and girdles and for product classes that tend to be distastefully presented like women's jeans and panty hose.

ADVERTISING AND CHILDREN. Government regulators are attempting to determine whether or not advertising to children should be limited or eliminated because it is inherently unfair. Critics charge that children are

---

[7]Colby Coates, "TV Clutter Rankles Public Most, Survey of Media Ads Shows," *Advertising Age* (February 12, 1979), p. 3.
[8]"More Find TV Tasteful Than Not: Study," *Advertising Age* (April 12, 1982), p. 48.

unable to evaluate advertising and its intent to sell them products. The legal case pro and con will be examined in the next chapter, but here we shall examine consumers' attitudes toward advertising and children.

Bauer and Greyser found that advertising's influence on children was cited by consumers as a reason why they did not like advertising. However, only 8 percent volunteered this concern. The Bartos-Dunn survey asked consumers several specific questions concerning the role of advertising to children, but the responses revealed such a low level of concern that the authors classified the subject as a "non-issue."

Other researchers who have conducted special surveys more directly focused on the children-television issue have found a greater level of concern. For example, a recent *Woman's Day* nationwide survey found that 60 percent of the respondents were in favor of stopping television advertising to children even if it meant fewer children's programs.[9] Professor Barry reviewed a number of surveys on consumer opinions of advertising to children. It appears that if guided to the issue by the survey, consumers express concern that advertising to children is troublesome and misleading. On the other hand, without prompting, the issue does not seem to be a highly important one to consumers. Barry concludes that parents in their concern "are somewhere in the middle," between the very vocal consumer activists and the advertisers.[10]

THE ECONOMIC AND SOCIAL VALUE OF ADVERTISING. Consumers recognize that in addition to affecting them as individuals, advertising as an institution has economic and social impact. In general, consumers are more approving of advertising's economic role than its social role. Bauer and Greyser, for example, found that consumers tended to respond favorably to the ideas that advertising is essential to the economy, that it raises the standard of living, and that it results in better products. On the other hand, consumers responded unfavorably to social aspects of advertising, feeling that it tends to be untruthful, tends to persuade people to buy things they should not buy, and tends to insult one's intelligence.

Bartos and Dunn examined similar issues in their study with much the same results. They found that consumers were "strong in their endorsement of the economic value of advertising," but were negative as regards its social qualities. Consumers responded to the ideas that ads work on people's emotions or weaknesses and that advertisements make people want things they do not really need.

The American Association of Advertising Agencies, reacting to consumer criticisms of advertising, has developed an advertising response to the most popular economic and social arguments against advertising. One of the Four As advertisements from this campaign, shown in Exhibit 23-1, summarizes the counter-arguments in favor of advertising.

[9]"Majority Against Advertising to Children," *Advertising Age* (May 8, 1978), p. 88.
[10]Thomas E. Barry, *Children's Television Advertising* (Chicago: American Marketing Association, Monograph Series #8, 1977), pp. 32–35.

EXHIBIT 23-1      An advertisement by the Four As in support of the value of advertising.

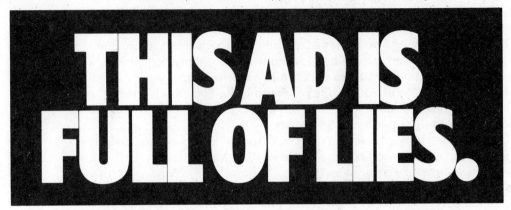

### LIE #1: ADVERTISING MAKES YOU BUY THINGS YOU DON'T WANT.

Advertising is often accused of inducing people to buy things against their will.

But when was the last time you returned home from the local shopping mall with a bag full of things you had absolutely no use for? The truth is, nothing short of a pointed gun can get *anybody* to spend money on something he or she doesn't want.

No matter how effective an ad is, you and millions of other American consumers make your own decisions. If you don't believe it, ask someone who knows firsthand about the limits of advertising. Like your local Edsel dealer.

### LIE #2: ADVERTISING MAKES THINGS COST MORE. Since advertising

costs money, it's natural to assume it costs *you* money. But the truth is that advertising often brings prices down.

Consider the electronic calculator, for example. In the late 1960s, advertising created a mass market for calculators. That meant more of them needed to be produced, which brought the price of producing each calculator down. Competition spurred by advertising brought the price down still further.

As a result, the same product that used to cost hundreds of dollars now costs as little as five dollars.

### LIE #3: ADVERTISING HELPS BAD PRODUCTS SELL.

Some people worry that good advertising sometimes covers up for bad products.

But nothing can make you like a bad product. So, while advertising can help convince you to try something once, it can't make you buy it twice. If you don't like what you've bought, you won't buy it again. And if enough people feel the same way, the product dies on the shelf.

In other words, the only thing advertising can do for a bad product is help you find out it's a bad product. And you take it from there.

### LIE #4: ADVERTISING IS A WASTE OF MONEY. Some people wonder why

we don't just put all the money spent on advertising directly into our national economy.

The answer is, we already do.

Advertising helps products sell, which holds down prices, which helps sales even more. It creates jobs. It informs you about all the products available and helps you compare them. And it stimulates the competition that produces new and better products at reasonable prices.

If all that doesn't convince you that advertising is important to our economy, you might as well stop reading.

Because on top of everything else, advertising has paid for a large part of the magazine you're now holding.

And that's the truth.

## ADVERTISING.
**ANOTHER WORD FOR FREEDOM OF CHOICE.**
American Association of Advertising Agencies

ADVERTISING AND THE MEDIA. In both of the 4As studies (Bauer and Greyser and Bartos and Dunn), consumers without prompting mentioned that one reason they liked advertising was that it supported the media, providing free television and affordable magazines and newspapers.

The level of these unprompted responses was relatively low. However, Bartos and Dunn reported that consumers, when they were asked directly, expressed highly favorable feelings toward advertising's support of the media. This attitude is supported by a series of consumer surveys by the Roper Organization. In the latest results, 84 percent of those questioned felt that television commercials were a fair price to pay for being able to watch television.[11] The percentage agreeing has steadily climbed since 1964 when the first survey was made.

## The Advertising Manager's Responsibility Toward the Consumer

The surveys of consumer attitudes toward advertising present a mixed picture. Consumers appear to see several benefits from advertising, while at the same time being critical of several of its characteristics. How important are these consumer criticisms and who is responsible for dealing with them?

CONSUMER CRITICISM — HOW IMPORTANT? The discussion thus far about consumer attitudes toward advertising may seem to suggest that consumers feel advertising to be an important factor in their lives and that its shortcomings overwhelm its benefits. The well-publicized views of consumer advocates seem to reinforce that level of importance. The facts, however, suggest a more moderate view.

Although several consumer criticisms of advertising have been mentioned, both of the 4As surveys show that consumers' overall evaluation of advertising is favorable. Bauer and Greyser asked consumers how they felt about advertising and found 41 percent favorable, 34 percent mixed, and 14 percent unfavorable. Bartos and Dunn more recently used a somewhat different rating scale, but found 56 percent favorable and 41 percent unfavorable. Both surveys compared overall consumer attitudes toward advertising with attitudes toward other institutions. Bartos and Dunn, for example, found that attitudes toward advertising were less favorable than those toward the press, but were more favorable than those toward labor unions, big business, and the federal government.

If consumers have this generally favorable attitude toward advertising, what accounts for the volume of complaints noted earlier? One clue is given by the Bauer and Greyser survey finding that advertising ranked high as an issue that people say they "enjoy complaining about but are not serious in their complaints." This reaction, however, should not make

---

[11]"Majority Feels Ads Are 'Fair Price' for TV: Roper," *Advertising Age* (April 21, 1975), p. 26.

advertisers complacent. The reason that people do not look upon their advertising complaints as serious may be that they do not take advertising itself seriously. Recall that the leading complaint about advertising concerns its credibility. Unless business restores credibility in advertising, its effectiveness will be seriously diminished.

IS THE ADVERTISING MANAGER RESPONSIBLE TO CONSUMERS? Most business managers — advertising managers included — have been conditioned and trained to believe that their primary responsibility is to earn a return on their investors' capital. This primary responsibility assures that owners will continue to invest in the business and thus assures its continued vitality and growth.

Today, however, managers must recognize that their responsibilities extend beyond their company to society. Managers have a responsibility to respect the environment, to support democratic ideals, and most of all to contribute to consumer satisfaction.

Some people in advertising have expressed concern that responsibility to the consumer may conflict with responsibility to the company for which they work. For example, if the advertising manager believes that an exaggerated product claim will benefit product sales, but injure the consumer, what course of action should be taken? In this instance the ethical and legal responsibility is clear — the consumer's interest should be protected by assuring that the advertising accurately portrays product benefits.

But is there really a conflict between consumer interests and those of the advertiser? Or is the notion of conflict a crutch for those who are uncertain as to how to react to such situations? One of the central themes of this book is that advertisers are successful when they serve the informational needs of their target consumers. This means that advertiser's needs and consumers' needs are not in conflict, but parallel. Advertising is successful when it provides useful information. When advertising is exaggerated or unsupported, it will be discredited by consumer reaction. Many supposed notions of conflict disappear when consumers are perceived, as they should be, as reasoning, discerning shoppers. In the long run certainly, and in the short run usually, the advertiser serves the company's needs by serving those of the consumer.

## A Program for Evaluating the Consumer Responsibility of Advertising

How is the advertising manager to fulfill the firm's advertising responsibility to consumers? Clearly the solution that is consistent with the planning approach recommended thus far is to build and implement a consumer responsibility control program.

*consumer responsibility program*

The basic elements of a **consumer responsibility program** are like those of any control program — standards of desirable performance must be set, actual performance must be measured against the standards, and then corrective action must be taken to bring performance up to par. The consumer responsibility program should be a written portion of the advertising plan describing each of the elements of the control program and who is to carry them out.

## Setting Consumer Responsibility Standards

The responsibility for setting standards of responsibility to consumers rests squarely with the advertising manager. Higher management may have enunciated broad policies or standards of conduct in the marketing areas or in dealings with consumers that can provide a foundation for the advertising standards. The American Advertising Federation has developed principles of responsible advertising as follows:

1. *Good advertising* aims to inform consumers and help them to buy more intelligently.
2. *Good advertising* tells the truth, avoiding misstatements of facts as well as possible deception through implication or omission. It makes no claims which cannot be met in full without further qualifications. It uses only testimonials of competent witnesses.
3. *Good advertising* conforms to the generally accepted standards of good taste. It seeks public acceptance on the basis of the merits of the product or service advertised, rather than by the disparagement of competing goods. It tries to avoid practices that are offensive or annoying.
4. *Good advertising* recognizes both its economic responsibility to help reduce distribution costs and its social responsibility in serving the public interest.

Such broad guidelines need to be translated by the advertising manager into a specific and detailed list of legal and consumer responsibility standards. Some of the areas in which the advertising manager should consider the need for standards are discussed below.

CLAIM SUPPORT. From the consumer's standpoint, probably the most important deficiency of advertising is its inability or failure to support benefit claims. This leads to mistrust of the advertising which, as noted earlier, consumers want to use as a guide to shopping.

To maintain credibility the advertiser should set standards stringent enough to require full substantiation of all claims. But in order to meet this standard the advertising manager must think beyond literal truth and its substantiation. In years past, deliberate inflation of claims (termed "puffery") was excused on the grounds that it was harmless because consumers understood it to be an exaggeration. A claim, for example, that a detergent makes clothes smell "like a fresh spring day" is an obvious exaggeration that is perhaps harmless. What the advertiser must decide is whether such a claim detracts from the credibility of the advertising.

A related problem is the advertising claim that is literally true, but nonetheless creates a false impression. A recent ad for Ajax dishwashing detergent, for example, claimed that "They squeeze real lemon juice in

New Ajax...Watch Ajax lemon up suds, level this mound of dishes covered with greasy spaghetti sauce..."[12] While it was literally true that the detergent contained lemon juice, the ad was criticized as implying that the lemon made the detergent a more effective cleaner rather than simply serving as a scent. The claim was modified to clarify the real role of the lemon ingredient.

FULL DISCLOSURE. In addition to assuring that claims are truthful and substantiated, the advertising manager should establish a standard that deals with what must be disclosed in the advertising about a product. Historically, it has been the practice to reveal only the positive attributes of a product in advertising. However, today some argue that consumers have a right to be informed of both the strengths and the weaknesses of a product. The Federal Trade Commission, for example, once proposed a trade rule that would have forced used-car dealers to publicize to buyers the defects in the used cars that they were selling. This ruling was overturned. However, it has for many years been required that pharmaceutical marketers publish in their advertisements for drug products the contraindications and side effects of the products.

In some instances, such as interest rate charges and drug side effects, full disclosure is required by law. In most cases, however, full disclosure is not required by law, but may be necessary for the consumer to make an intelligent choice. A well-balanced presentation of product facts may enhance the credibility of the advertising and the product.

COMPARATIVE ADVERTISING. Advertising that names competitors and compares one product to another presents both legal and creative complications. For this reason, some advertisers have a policy that prohibits or discourages such advertising. The advertiser should consider, however, that such a policy may not serve consumer needs. Consumers, after all, have to make comparisons in selecting products. If advertising can provide accurate information that aids the comparison process, then it serves consumers' needs. In spite of the difficulties, the advertiser should consider the potential consumer benefits in setting a standard that permits comparative advertising. Clearly the standard should insist on accurate comparisons. The more subtle danger to be guarded against is implying that a product that is superior to its competition in one characteristic is therefore superior overall. Perhaps it is more responsible to point out to consumers competitive differences, leaving the consumers to judge superiority.

GOOD TASTE. It is clear from the previous section that repetitive, tasteless ads that talk down to consumers are a major consumer complaint.

---

[12]"Ajax Gold Ad Claims Top NAD Dec. List," *Advertising Age* (January 18, 1982), p. 10.

They are also a problem that the advertiser can avoid by providing adequate variety and by offering substantial information in the ads. Sensitive products, as discussed earlier, are particularly susceptible to charges of bad taste. Both the manner in which they are to be presented and the medium in which they will be advertised should be carefully considered with a view to minimizing appearances of bad taste or inappropriateness. The use of sexual themes in advertising also raises questions of good taste. The importance of relevance in using sexual themes was discussed in Chapter 16. Beyond this, the advertising manager should recognize that overtly sexual themes offend many consumers, especially when the advertisement appears in a family-use medium. The responsible advertising manager avoids such advertising.

MEDIA CONTENT. For most media, advertisers have no direct influence on the content of the medium in which they advertise. Yet, the advertiser can indirectly bring pressure on a medium to change its content by withholding advertising dollars from the medium. In most cases, advertisers are reluctant to become involved as arbiters of consumer taste in the media. However, if the advertiser believes that media content will reflect unfavorably on the company's product or works against consumer interest, some action may be both warranted and justifiable. Media output that contains violence, profanity, and sex has come under heavy criticism in recent years; the advertiser should probably set a responsibility standard in this area.

In recent years, conservative religious groups, such as the Moral Majority, have been outspoken in criticizing violence, profanity, and sex in television programming and have attacked advertisers whose advertising appears in such programs. Most recently, the Coalition for Better Television, directed by Rev. Donald Wildmon, threatened to organize a consumer boycott against television networks programming violence or sex as well as against products advertised on such programs. Although the threatened boycott did not develop, the publicity given to the issue did appear to have impact. A survey of leading advertisers at the time of the boycott threat revealed that 86 percent were concerned about the amount of sex, violence, and profanity in television programming and nearly half felt that major changes in television were needed.[13] Advertisers generally felt that the consumer protests had resulted in significant changes in television programming.[14]

TREATMENT OF MINORITIES AND WOMEN. The increased concern with fairness toward minorities and women cuts across all sectors of society.

[13]Janet Neiman, "Advertisers Want 'Major Change' in TV," *Advertising Age* (March 8, 1982), pp. 1, 67.
[14]"Advertisers Confirm TV 'Morality' Impact," *Advertising Age* (November 16, 1981), pp. 3, 107.

Because advertising is so visible to the public, it often finds itself a center of concern in this fight for equal treatment.

There are some specifics that the advertising manager should consider in setting standards in this area. Advertisers have widely adopted the practice of using minorities as models and spokespersons in advertising. Care must be taken that minorities are not shown in stereotyped roles. Care should also be taken that unintended racial slurs do not appear in ads. In addition care must be taken that advertising directed to or portraying women does so in a fair and balanced way. A review of evidence by a panel of the National Advertising Review Board suggests that many women resent much of the advertising directed to women today as being demeaning and offensive. Based on this study, the panel suggested the checklist shown in Exhibit 23-2 for use in evaluating women-related advertising. The checklist attempts to help the advertising manager in two areas: in avoiding portrayals of women in advertising that present undesirable stereotypes or are degrading, and in avoiding copy appeals that insult women's intelligence or play upon stereotyped insecurities.[15]

---

**EXHIBIT 23-2**       Checklist for evaluating women-related advertising.

---

**Checklist: Destructive Portrayals**

● Am I implying in my promotional campaign that creative, athletic, and mind-enriching toys and games are not for girls as much as boys? Does my ad, for example, imply that dolls are for girls and chemistry sets are for boys, and that neither could ever become interested in the other category?

● Are sexual stereotypes perpetuated in my ad? That is, does it portray women as weak, silly, and over-emotional? Or does it picture both sexes as intelligent, physically able, and attractive?

● Are the women portrayed in my ad stupid? For example, am I reinforcing the "dumb blonde" cliché? Does my ad portray women who are unable to manage a household without the help of outside experts, particularly male ones?

● Does my ad use belittling language? For example, "gal Friday" or "lady professor"? Or "her kitchen" but "his car"? Or "women's chatter" but "men's discussions"?

● Does my ad make use of contemptuous phrases? Such as "the weaker sex," "the little women," "the ball and chain," or "the War Department."

● Do my ads consistently show women waiting on men? Even in occupational situations, for example, are women nurses or secretaries serving coffee, etc., to male bosses or colleagues? And never vice versa?

● Is there a gratuitous message in my ads that a women's most important role in life is a supportive one, to cater to and coddle men and children? Is it a "big deal" when the reverse is shown,

---

[15]"Advertising Portraying or Directed to Women," *Advertising Age* (April 21, 1975), pp. 72–76.

that is, very unusual and special—something for which the woman must show gratitude?

• Do my ads portray women as more neurotic than men? For example, as ecstatically happy over household cleanliness or deeply depressed because of their failure to achieve near perfection in household tasks?

(A note is needed here, perhaps. It is not the panel's intention to suggest that women never be portrayed in the traditional role of homemaker and mother. We suggest instead that the role of homemaker be depicted not in a grotesque or stereotyped manner, but be treated with the same degree of respect accorded to other important occupations.)

• Do my ads feature women who appear to be basically unpleasant? For example, women nagging their husbands or children? Women being condescending to other women? Women being envious or arousing envy? Women playing the "oneupmanship" game (with a sly wink at the camera)?

• Do my ads portray women in situations that tend to confirm the view that women are the property of men or are less important than men?

• Is there double entendre in my ads? Particularly about sex or women's bodies?

## Checklist: Negative Appeals

• Do my ads try to arouse or play upon stereotyped insecurities? Are women shown as fearful of not being attractive to men or to other women, fearful of not being able to keep their husbands or lovers, fearful of an in-law's disapproval, or, for example, of not being able to cope with a husband's boss coming for dinner?

• Does my copy promise unrealistic psychological rewards for using the product? For example, that a perfume can lead to instant romance.

• Does my ad blatantly or subtly suggest that the product possesses supernatural powers? If believed literally, is the advertiser unfairly taking advantage of ignorance? Even if understood as hyperbole, does it insult the intelligence of women?

## Checklist: Constructive Portrayals

• Are the attitudes and behavior of the women in my ads suitable models for my own daughter to copy? Will I be happy if my own female children grow up to act and react the way the women in my ads act and react?

• Do my ads reflect the fact that girls may aspire to careers in business and the professions? Do they show, for example, female doctors and female executives? Some women with both male and female assistants?

• Do my ads portray women and men (and children) sharing in the chores of family living? For example, grocery shopping, doing laundry, cooking (not just outdoor barbecuing), washing dishes, cleaning house, taking care of children, mowing the lawn, and other house and yard work?

• Do the women in my ads make decisions (or help make them) about the purchase of high-priced items and major family investments? Do they take an informed interest, for example, in insurance and financial matters?

• Do my ads portray women actually driving cars and showing an intelligent interest in mechanical features, not just in color and upholstry?

• Are two-income families portrayed in my ads? For example, husband and wife leaving home and returning from work together?

• Are the women in my ads doing creative or exciting things? Older women, too? In social and occupational environments? For example, making a speech, in a laboratory, or approving an ad?

**Checklist: Positive Appeals**

● Is the product presented as a means for a women to enhance her own self-esteem, to be a beautiful human being, to realize her full potential?

● Does my advertisement promise women realistic rewards for using the product? Does it assume intelligence on the part of women?

Reprinted with permission from the April 21, 1975, issue of *Advertising Age*. Copyright 1975 by Crain Communications, Inc.

ADVERTISING TO CHILDREN. There is no more controversial area in advertising than advertising directed to children, particularly television advertising. The reason for special concern is the belief that young children may be unusually susceptible to advertising and may not recognize its purpose. This means that the responsible advertiser to children will exercise caution in several areas. Care should be taken that advertising is not only truthful, but avoids exaggeration, supports claims, and does not imply benefits that raise false expectations. Advertising to children should not attempt to supplant parental judgment in what is best for a child. Particular care is needed in advertising food products so that unsound nutritional ideas are not fostered. Toys and other products should be shown used in a safe way.

The National Advertising Division of the Council of Better Business Bureaus has published an extensive set of guidelines for children's advertising. The principles on which these guidelines are based are shown in Exhibit 23-3. Those who advertise to children should consult the detailed guidelines in preparing their own standards.

EXHIBIT 23-3    Principles for advertising to children.

1. Advertisers should always take into account the level of knowledge, sophistication, and maturity of the audience to which their message is primarily directed. Younger children have a limited capability for evaluating the credibility of what they watch. Advertisers, therefore, have a special responsibility to protect children from their own susceptibilities.
2. Realizing that children are imaginative and that make-believe play constitutes an important part of the growing-up process, advertisers should exercise care not to exploit that imaginative quality of children. Unreasonable expectations of product quality or performances should not be stimulated either directly or indirectly by advertising.
3. Recognizing that advertising may play an important part in educating the child, information should be communicated in a truthful and accurate manner with full recognition by the advertiser that the child may learn practices from advertising which can affect his or her health and well-being.
4. Advertisers are urged to capitalize on the potential of advertising to influence social behavior by developing advertising that, wherever possible, addresses itself to social standards generally regarded as

positive and beneficial, such as friendship, kindness, honesty, justice, generosity, and respect for others.

5. Although many influences affect a child's personal and social development, it remains the prime responsibility of the parents to provide guidance for children. Advertisers should contribute to this parent-child relationship in a constructive manner.

Source:   Self-Regulatory Guidelines for Children's Advertising, 1983 (New York: Children's Advertising Review Unit, National Advertising Division, Council of Better Business Bureaus, Inc., 1983)

CONSUMER SAFETY. Both publicity and government regulation appear to have made consumers more aware of product safety. Although there is no evidence that advertising makes products more or less safe, advertisers should be careful that their communications encourage safe use of products.

Certain product categories are particularly susceptible to safe usage problems. Examples include bicycles, lawn mowers, drugs, power tools, and appliances. Products used by or attractive to children are an additional concern. Advertisers of such products should be careful that unsafe uses are not suggested by the copy and, in particular, that illustrations or video do not show the product being used in an unsafe manner. For example, an advertisement for a power saw should show it in use with its protective hood and the user should be wearing safety goggles.

Advertisers with products in sensitive categories should consult the guidelines prepared by the National Advertising Review Board.[16]

## Measuring and Correcting the Consumer Responsibility Program

After standards of responsibility to the consumer in advertising have been set, a procedure for evaluating whether or not advertising meets the standards should be established. Responsibility for correcting ads that are deficient in meeting consumer responsibility should also be clearly established.

THE IMPORTANCE OF PRE-MEASUREMENT. What does "measurement" mean in controlling the consumer responsibility of advertising? It means that ads are evaluated against consumer responsibility standards to see if they conform.

It is important that this measurement or evaluation take place before the advertising is run. This permits ads to be corrected before they are exposed to consumers. Remedying the harm done after the fact is often impossible.

Responsibility for initiating corrective action clearly lies with the advertising manager. If it is determined that an ad does not meet consumer responsibility standards, the advertising manager should issue clear

---

[16]The National Advertising Review Board, 845 Third Avenue, New York, NY 10022.

instructions regarding the changes required and should follow up to see that those changes are implemented.

ESTABLISHING A CONSUMER PRE-AUDIT. Conducting an objective review of the consumer responsibility of individual advertisements is a difficult task for the advertising manager. Generally the advertising manager has been closely involved in an ad from its conception to its final production. It is difficult after this long involvement for the advertising manager to then decide that the ad is not acceptable because it does not serve the consumer. Further, it is not easy for an advertising manager to objectively view an ad from the consumer's point of view when by training and responsibility the advertising manager is also expected to represent the company's interests.

A better alternative to having the advertising manager evaluate the responsibility to the consumer of the company's ads is to form an independent panel to perform this service. The panel members should have no other connection with the firm's advertising. Members might be drawn from within the company, but greater objectivity might be achieved by using members from the outside community to which the company advertises.

The panel's criteria for evaluating the advertising for a product would be the consumer responsibility standards established in the advertising plan. The panel would be asked to review each piece of advertising for the firm's products and/or services and consider whether or not it meets the advertiser's standards of consumer responsibility. Advertising that does not meet these standards would be returned to the advertising manager or ad agency for revision.

## CHAPTER SUMMARY

There are a number of demands that consumers place on advertising. Most important, if advertising is to serve consumer needs, it must provide useful, unexaggerated information. Although they value the information in advertising, consumers find its repetitiveness and intrusiveness annoying, especially in broadcast media. Some consumers are particularly concerned because they feel that advertising directed to children is inherently unfair, but other parents find this an unimportant issue. Consumers feel strongly that advertising fulfills an important economic role and they appreciate the fact that it provides financial support to the media. Although consumers have, in general, a favorable attitude toward advertising, it is the responsibility of the advertising manager to be responsive to the shortcomings of the advertising from the consumer's point of view, so that advertising does not lose its credibility and usefulness.

To carry out these responsibilities, the advertising manager should establish a consumer responsibility control program. Standards should be set for acceptable consumer advertising performance. Areas in which the advertising manager should consider setting standards include the substantiation of claims, decisions regarding the extent to which both strengths and weaknesses of the product should be revealed, and how comparative advertising should be handled. In addition, the advertiser must decide how much responsibility the firm will assume for presenting tasteful and enjoyable advertising and the extent to which the firm will accept responsibility for the content of the media in which the advertising appears. The advertiser's standards should also deal explicitly with the treatment of minorities and women in the advertising. If advertising is directed to children or deals with products that have safety problems, then standards should be defined that set consumer responsibility guidelines in these areas.

All advertisements should be evaluated against these standards before being exposed to consumers. Probably the best way to determine objectively whether the ads meet the consumer responsibility standards is to establish an independent audit panel to advise the advertising manager who is then responsible for corrective action.

Consumer responsibility program                                          *KEY TERM*

1. Critics of advertising directed to children, led by Action for Children's *QUESTIONS*
   Television (ACT), have called for an outright ban on advertising to *FOR*
   children. The arguments in favor of such a ban have been widely com- *DISCUSSION*
   municated by activist groups, but the trade-offs have not. What would
   consumers stand to lose if advertising to children were eliminated?

2. Considering the susceptibility of children to candy and sweet foods, do
   you think that it is socially responsible to advertise pre-sweetened
   breakfast cereals to children? Is it consistent with the *Children's Advertising Guidelines* shown on pages 636 and 637.

3. As an occupational group, advertisers tend to be very self-conscious
   about the reputation of their profession. In a recent consumer survey
   sponsored by advertisers, 93 percent of the sample agreed that advertising was important to the economy, 90 percent agreed that advertising
   was a highly professional occupation, and 53 percent said they would
   like to have their children employed in advertising. However, in another
   study, when consumers were asked to rank advertising with other
   professions, they ranked advertising next to last, just above used-car
   sales.[17]

---

[17]Nancy Millman, "Consumers Rate Advertising High," *Advertising Age* (October 24, 1983), pp. 1, 18.

a. What might account for the differing results as between the two surveys?

b. From your own experience, what do you think the reputation of the advertising profession is? What accounts for that reputation?

4. In a recent national survey about distasteful advertising, one of the commercials cited as being most objectionable was for Underalls panty hose.[18] Underalls commercials feature shots of women's backsides while the announcer says "Okay, America, show us your Underalls!" In the same survey, 55 percent of those questioned said that they avoided buying brands with objectionable advertising. When confronted with these figures, the vice-president in charge of marketing for Underalls said that he was more impressed by the fact that 27 million pairs of Underalls are sold each year.

a. Does distasteful advertising hurt sales or help sales?

b. Should an advertiser avoid distasteful advertising?

5. From the same survey discussed in question 4, the researchers developed a measure of "net impression" for various product categories by subtracting the percent that found ads for each category to be in poor taste from the percentage that found them to be in good taste.[19] The results are shown below.

| Product Category | In Good Taste | In Poor Taste | Net Impression |
|---|---|---|---|
| Feminine hygiene | 12% | 70% | −58 |
| Laxatives | 18% | 51% | −33 |
| Bras and girdles | 18% | 50% | −32 |
| Jeans | 24% | 48% | −24 |
| Panty hose | 26% | 39% | −13 |
| Antacids | 34% | 27% | + 7 |
| Island resorts | 38% | 19% | +19 |
| Cosmetics | 43% | 18% | +25 |
| Perfumes | 43% | 18% | +25 |

a. Is it preferable for a company's product to be in a class at the top of the list or at the bottom of the list?

b. Examining the "net impression" ranking, can you suggest what may cause some product categories to fall in the negative net-impression class and others to have positive net impressions?

6. Andrew Kershaw, formerly president of Ogilvy and Mather advertising agency, stated, "Advertising *can* tell the truth, *can* tell nothing but the

---

[18]Bill Abrams, "Poll Suggests TV Advertisers Can't Ignore Matters of Taste," *The Wall Street Journal* (July 23, 1981), p. 25.
[19]*Ibid.*

truth, but should not be required to tell the whole truth." What does Kershaw mean? Do you feel that this is a consumer-responsible position to take?

7. Suppose that you were the advertising manger for a bank in your hometown and you decided to form a consumer panel to oversee the consumer responsibility of the bank's advertising. Assuming your panel was to have five members, identify whom you would invite to sit on the panel.

8. In a survey of advertising executives to determine attitudes toward television programming, 57 percent of those answering and 70 percent of the larger advertisers disagreed with the statement: "Programming quality is not as important as cost-per-thousand target audience considerations."[20]

   a. What responsibility does the advertiser have toward the quality of television programming?
   b. What steps can the advertiser take to improve the quality of television programming?

9. The results of a ten-year study by the National Institute of Mental Health stated that there was overwhelming evidence to suggest "a causal relationship between television violence and later aggressive behavior."[21] The study found that heavy television viewers can be influenced by television violence even if they have no predisposition toward violence.

   a. Do you think that placing ads on programs containing violence can hurt sales of that product?
   b. Regardless of that, do you think that the advertiser has a social responsibility to avoid placing commercials on programs containing violence?

*PROBLEM*

Recently the advertising agency handling the tourism account for the city of Miami, Florida, developed a poster as part of a new campaign to attract tourists to that city.[22] The four-color poster featured the back of an attractive young woman clad only in a snorkel mask and a bikini bottom. The poster, 25,000 of which had been distributed, was greeted with a storm of protest. The Commission of the Status of Women protested to the Dade

---

[20]"Corporate Ad Execs: We Care About the Quality of TV Programs," *Marketing News* (November 27, 1981), p. 8.

[21]Jane Mayer, " 'Causal' Link Drawn Between Television and Acts of Violence," *The Wall Street Journal* (October 22, 1981), p. 38.

[22]This problem is based on "Miami Poster Fires Up Locals," *Advertising Age* (December 3, 1979), p. 44.

County Commission which funded the campaign. In turn, three of eight members of the Commission (including two women) disapproved of the poster. One said she felt that the poster was offensive and represented Miami poorly. "We're a major urban center where you can go shopping, dine out, attend cultural events and so on—not just an extension of the sands of Miami Beach."

In defense of the poster, the account supervisor for the advertising agency that had prepared the advertising said, "It's sexy, but in a tasteful way, and it wasn't intended to be exploitative." He added that the poster had generated a great deal of publicity with stories in newspapers all over the country. He explained that the poster was intended to reach a younger audience "to convince people that we're not all old people and Latins." A representative of the County Manager's Office stated that he was very pleased with the overall results of the campaign, noting that in the last two weeks his office had received 2,600 requests for information about the Miami area.

Members of the County Commission were considering what action to take.

1. If you were a member of the County Commission, would you vote to terminate distribution of the poster?
2. Do you feel that the poster represents socially responsible advertising?
3. Do your feelings about the poster's social responsibility conflict with your beliefs about its effectiveness?
4. As a result of this experience, would you recommend any further action?

# CHAPTER 24

*Meeting Advertising's
Legal Responsibilities*

**LEARNING OBJECTIVES**

In studying this chapter you will learn:

- The governmental and non-governmental agencies that regulate advertising.

- The acceptability standards set by the media themselves.

- The advertising industry's attempts at self-regulation.

- The basic legislation that regulates advertising.

- That an advertiser should have a legal responsibility program.

In addition to social responsibility to consumers, the advertising manager is responsible for meeting the regulatory requirements of the advertising industry. Legal requirements are not, of course, entirely separable from the interests of consumers because most regulation in this field is designed to provide protection for the consumer and to maintain competition.

To meet these legal responsibilities, the advertising manager must know the many governmental and non-governmental agencies that regulate advertising and, most importantly, must develop an understanding of the legal ground rules that apply to advertising. Surprisingly, advertising legislation changes frequently and quickly. This chapter provides a foundation of legal ground rules, but the advertising manager must update this information continuously by reading reports of current legislation in trade and professional publications. The advertising manager needs to address legal problems by framing a legal responsibility program, a topic covered at the close of this chapter.

The Agencies that
Regulate Advertising

Advertising is regulated at the federal, state, and local levels. In addition, there are a variety of industry groups that exercise important control over advertising through voluntary self-regulation. The scope and responsibility of the major regulatory bodies are described in this section.

### The Federal Trade Commission

The most important force in the regulation of advertising, despite recent actions to reduce its jurisdiction, is the Federal Trade Commission or FTC.

*Wheeler-Lea Amendment*

FTC JURISDICTION. The commission was established as an independent regulatory body by the Federal Trade Commission Act of 1914. The focus of the FTC when it was established was to prevent trade practices that would cause injury to competition or, as the bill stated, to regulate "unfair methods of competition (and) unfair or deceptive acts or practices in commerce." The **Wheeler-Lea Amendment** of 1938 extended the powers of the FTC from the regulation of anti-competitive trade practices to the protection of consumers from "unfair or deceptive acts or practices." The Amendment specifically extended the FTC's jurisdiction to the regulation of advertising, charging the Commission to protect consumers from deceptive or unfair advertising. In recent years, the FTC's jurisdiction over advertising has been alternatively strengthened and weakened in clashes between legislative and administrative philosophies over the role of regulation. The current status of the law will be examined in a later section, but despite the on-going changes, the FTC remains the most important regulator of advertising, especially on a national level.

COMMISSION PROCEDURE. In most instances of deceptive advertising the FTC proceeds by charging individual advertisers and trying civil cases before the commission. The commission staff monitors advertising for infractions and also acts on complaints received from companies and consumers. If the situation warrants, the commission issues a complaint against the offending advertiser. These complaints may be settled by negotiation, sometimes resulting in issuance of a cease and desist order (an order to stop the unlawful practice) or a consent decree (an agreement to stop the practice in question without agreement as to its illegality). If the advertiser wishes to contest the FTC's complaint, a hearing is held before a trial examiner who is a member of the commission's staff. The findings of the hearing examiner are considered by the full commission, whereupon the commission issues a decision and an order for remedial action. The decision of the commission can be appealed by the advertiser through the federal court system — the Circuit Courts of Appeal and the Supreme Court.

COMMISSION REMEDIES. The primary remedy resulting from FTC hearings is a cease and desist order prohibiting further use of the misleading advertising. In some severe cases, charges can be brought against responsible individuals and fines or jail terms imposed. This remedy, however, is seldom sought. A relatively new remedy imposed by the commission has been **corrective advertising** designed to explain to consumers that previous advertising may have been misleading. The Supreme Court in the case of Listerine antiseptic mouthwash recently upheld the FTC's authority to order corrective advertising. The use of corrective advertising as a remedy, because of controversy over its effectiveness, appears to be declining.

*corrective advertising*

RULES FOR REGULATION OF TRADE. The **Magnuson-Moss Act** of 1975 enabled the FTC to issue Trade Regulation Rules (TRR) when changes were needed for an entire class of advertising or when uniform marketing practices were needed for all companies in an industry. TRRs are issued by the FTC after hearings and study of a problem area. After the FTC announces its intention to consider making a rule, extensive hearings are held to gather information from affected businesses and experts in the field. After the hearings, the FTC issues the rule in its final form. TRRs have the force of law, but can be appealed through the courts.

*Magnuson-Moss Act*

After passage of the Magnuson-Moss Act in 1975, the FTC was very active in promulgating rules. Rules were proposed, for example, in advertising to children, in the making of nutritional claims, and the advertising of eyeglasses. Many of these proposed rules became highly controversial and in 1980, the **FTC Improvement Act** was passed which substantially limited the FTC's rule-making authority. Many of the proposed rules were dropped as the FTC reverted to greater emphasis on a case-by-case approach.

*FTC Improvement Act*

## Other Federal Regulatory Agencies

There are several other federal agencies involved in regulating some phase of advertising activity.

FOOD AND DRUG ADMINISTRATION. The Food and Drug Administration (FDA) regulates the labeling and packaging of foods, drugs, medical devices, and cosmetics. The FDA controls misleading statements on labels or other materials that accompany the package. It also administers regulations concerning statements such as warnings and cautions that must appear on labels. The FDA has developed detailed rules regulating cents-off and similar sales promotions utilizing promotional labeling. The power of the FDA was broadened by the passage in 1966 of the "truth in packaging" bill.

The FDA's authority over advertising and its relationship to the FTC has long been a matter of contention. From time to time, the FDA has attempted to link its authority over label copy to the claims allowable in advertising. This has occurred in both food advertising and in drug advertising. For the most part, these attempts at regulation of advertising have been turned back. The Congress recently restricted the FDA's authority to determine what nutritional information should appear in food ads.

THE BUREAU OF ALCOHOL, TOBACCO, AND FIREARMS. Advertising of alcoholic beverages is a special and very complex case regulated in part by this agency of the Treasury Department. Recently the Treasury Department ordered this unit to be disbanded and its regulatory responsibilities to be absorbed by other departments. In addition, each state usually has its own regulatory agency and rules for alcoholic beverage advertising.

THE FEDERAL COMMUNICATIONS COMMISSION. The Federal Communications Commission or FCC regulates the broadcast media and this has some impact on broadcast advertisers, mostly through the power of the FCC to regulate programming. In connection with this, the FCC for many years regulated the number of commercial minutes allowable on radio and on television. As part of a major deregulation program at the FCC, commercial time limits were eliminated in radio and it is proposed that the guideline of 16 commercial minutes per hour in television also be scrapped, along with other programming requirements.[1] The result will be considerably less FCC authority over advertising.

### State Regulation

Most states have regulations that attempt to control dishonest advertising. Most state laws are based on the *Printers' Ink* model statute which was proposed in 1911 by the now discontinued advertising trade magazine. Many states have also passed additional consumer protection legislation most of which contains regulation directed at advertising.

Perhaps more significant than new state legislation has been the rapid growth in the number of new agencies designed to enforce existing regulations. Nearly half the states have consumer protection agencies in operation.

### Local Regulation

In addition to increasing advertising regulatory activity at the state level, many cities and counties have established advertising regulations and consumer affairs agencies to enforce these regulations. Most such agencies are in more populous cities and counties. New York City, for example, has established a Department of Consumer Affairs. A new consumer protection act gives the department wide authority to act against many forms of deceptive selling practices, including false advertising.

### Media Acceptability Standards

In addition to regulation by governmental authorities, advertising must often go through an approval process exercised by the medium in which it is to appear. Individual media vehicles have the right to reject

---

[1]"FCC Outlines TV Deregulation Plan," *Advertising Age* (July 4, 1983), p. 3.

advertising that does not meet the standards of honesty or good taste that have been established by the medium. In some cases these standards are surprisingly stringent.

BROADCAST CONTINUITY CLEARANCE. Broadcast advertising is screened for acceptability at both the network and the individual station level. The television networks are most demanding in this respect and maintain sizeable staffs of editors who review every commercial before it is aired. Usually advertisers submit commercials at the storyboard stage so that revisions can be made before final production. Considering that television networks are dependent upon advertisers for income, network continuity departments are notoriously demanding. One agency executive told of arguing for hours about "how much of a toilet can be shown in a toilet-cleaner ad and whether the mother in a detergent commercial could talk about her daughter's 'murdering' her clothes."[2] Networks frown on ethnic stereotypes and sexual innuendo, and they are insistent that claims be fully documented. Networks have become so demanding that at least one FTC official has raised questions about the process. "Networks may be burdening advertisers by demanding more than the FTC would require, and if this is so, it is conceivable that the FTC might eventually want to issue a report expressing its concern."[3]

Individual broadcast stations also screen commercials for acceptability. For many years individual stations used the television and radio continuity codes of the National Association of Broadcasters to judge the acceptability of commercials. The codes defined such things as products not acceptable for advertising (liquor and fortune-telling, for example), types of advertising prohibited (bait and switch), and gave guidelines for presentation to special groups (children) or for presentation of sensitive products (feminine hygiene items). In addition, the codes set standards for the number of commercials allowed per time period and regulated the use of **piggyback commercials** (two commercials sharing a single commercial time period.)

*piggyback commercials*

It was these two latter items that spelled the end of the NAB code. In 1982, to settle an antitrust suit brought by the Justice Department, the NAB agreed to eliminate its time standards and piggybacking rules. Later, fearing additional legal problems, the NAB suspended all code enforcement and dissolved its code authority staff. Although the formulation of a new code has been discussed, no action has been taken to date.[4]

---

[2]Bill Abrams, "The Networks Censor TV Ads For Taste and Deceptiveness," *The Wall Street Journal* (September 30, 1982), p. 33.
[3]Richard L. Gordon, "Net Censors Worse: FTC Aide," *Advertising Age* (December 13, 1982), pp. 2, 57.
[4]Stanley E. Cohen, "NAB Studies Future of Code," *Advertising Age* (November 29, 1982), pp. 1, 68.

PRINT ACCEPTABILITY STANDARDS. The print media also establish standards of advertising acceptability although the strictness and the thoroughness of their application vary widely. One expert suggests that newspapers and magazines, unlike the broadcast media, have easy-going media standards much like 20 years ago before government and consumerists advocated a raising of standards.[5] The larger newspapers and magazines tend to have the best developed standards. As an example, the *St. Petersburg Times* offers advertisers a thirty-page book defining its advertising standards. The table of contents lists over sixty specific advertising subjects covered by the standards.[6]

## Advertising Self-Regulation

In recent years, the advertising industry has made important strides in industry self-regulation of deceptive advertising. Implementation takes place both on a local and on a national level.

BETTER BUSINESS BUREAUS. Important self-regulation of advertising practices comes from Better Business Bureaus (BBBs) in local communities. These business-supported agencies, established in about 140 cities, concern themselves with a wide variety of unfair advertising and selling practices. Better Business Bureaus (BBBs) are mostly concerned with local practices, the type likely to escape the notice of federal and state regulatory authorities.

In the 1970s many local advertising self-regulation units, independent of BBBs were set up. However, a lawsuit by a local advertiser in Denver against the local self-regulation unit, went to the U.S. Supreme Court with a threat of personal liability judgments against the panel members. This led not only to the disbanding of the Denver unit, but also meant the end of many more local units around the country.

Recently local advertising self-regulation units have been making a comeback, this time as advisory bodies to local Better Business Bureaus so that members can enjoy the liability insurance protection of the BBB.[7] Under this system, Better Business Bureau staff members make the initial decision in an advertising case, with the advisory committee being called in to advise the staff or to hear an appeal from the advertiser.

Compliance with the BBB decision is voluntary, but if the advertiser refuses to comply with suggestions for corrective action, the BBB can publicize the name of the offender and turn the evidence over to law enforcement agencies.

---

[5]Stanley E. Cohen, "Publishers Face Stronger Reaction for Failure to Call Fraudulent Ads," *Advertising Age* (July 1, 1974), p. 4.

[6]*Advertising Standards of Acceptability* (St. Petersburg, Fl.: Times Publishing Co., September, 1978).

[7]"Local Ad Review Units Try Again," *Advertising Age* (April 27, 1981), pp. 1, 90.

NATIONAL ADVERTISING REVIEW BOARD. The most important industry-wide attempt at self-regulation of advertising is the **National Advertising Review Board (NARB)** established in 1971.

*National Advertising Review Board (NARB)*

*Organization of the NARB.* The NARB is sponsored by the Council of Better Business Bureaus together with the three leading advertising trade associations. The organization was built around the existing facilities and resources of the Better Business Bureau by establishing within it a new unit called the National Advertising Division (NAD). The staff of this division monitors advertising to detect unfairness and processes complaints of unfair advertising from consumers or others. The National Advertising Review Board acts as an appeal body for NAD decisions. The NARB is made up of 50 volunteer members: 30 from companies, 10 from advertising agencies, and 10 from the public. The NARB is financed by the Council of Better Business Bureaus, Inc.

*Scope of NARB Activities.* The NARB's self-regulation effort is directed primarily at untruthful advertising, although it sometimes offers suggestions on the more subjective issues of good taste and social responsibility. The NARB set forth as its primary purpose "to render judgments on individual matters of truth and accuracy in advertising."[8] In recent years, by far the largest number of cases have concerned the substantiation of claims.[9] A separate unit, the **Children's Advertising Review Unit of NAD (CARU)** handles cases concerning advertising to children.

*Children's Advertising Review Unit of NAD (CARU)*

In addition to examining specific cases of truth in advertising, the NARB has formed special consultive panels to develop position papers on issues having broadly applicable social implications. Position papers have been developed on such topics as the portrayal of women in advertising and the safe portrayal of product use.

*Advertising Review Procedures.* Cases concerning truth in advertising come to the NARB in a variety of ways — through the NAD's monitoring program, from complaints by competitors, from referrals by local Better Business Bureaus, and from consumer complaints. As shown in Exhibit 24-1, NAD monitoring and competitive challenges are the leading sources of cases. The NAD maintains a system that tapes commercials off the air for study by staff members. In addition, major print media are reviewed for possible infractions.

Regardless of the source of the complaint, the case is assigned to the NAD staff for investigation. After gathering information and substantiation from the advertiser, the NAD analyzes the situation and decides either to dismiss the case or to pursue corrective action. If the case is continued, a staff member goes directly to the advertiser, without publicity, to attempt to

---

[8]*A Review and Perspective on Advertising Industry Self-Regulation* (New York: National Advertising Review Board, 1978), p. 5.

[9]Stanley E. Cohen, "FTC Memo Hits Ad Self-Regulation" *Advertising Age* (February 7, 1983), p. 39.

EXHIBIT 24-1      Sources of NARB Self-regulation Cases

|  | 1983 | |
|---|---|---|
| Sources | # | % |
| NAD monitoring | 41 | 37 |
| Competitor challenges | 46 | 42 |
| Local BBBs | 12 | 11 |
| Consumer complaints | 6 | 5 |
| Reopened cases | — | — |
| Other | 5 | 5 |
| Total | 110 | 100% |

Source: *NAD Case Report*, (January 16, 1984), Vol. 13, No. 12, p. 43.

get the advertisement corrected or discontinued. If the advertiser and the NAD find that they cannot agree on the issue, either party has the right to request a review by a five-member NARB panel. The NARB panel then reexamines the evidence and renders a judgment. Compliance with a request to effect change in the advertisement is voluntary, but if the panel cannot bring about a voluntary change on the part of the advertiser, the findings in the case can be publicized and turned over to the appropriate regulatory agency. Exhibit 24-2 diagrams the NARB/NAD self-regulatory procedure.

EVALUATION OF THE NARB PROGRAM. It is difficult to evaluate with certainty the level of success that the NARB self-regulation program has achieved, but by most measures it appears successful. Certainly the longevity of the program exceeds that of any comparable effort. The program has been active since 1971. The system has also processed a significant number of cases. In the first 12 years of its life, 1,757 cases have been decided, not including about 200 additional cases handled by the Children's Advertising Review Unit.[10] Examination of the outcome of NAD decisions indicates that the system does not owe its life to being lenient with advertisers. Of the 1,757 cases, 907, or more than half, resulted in either modification or discontinuation of the advertising under examination. Interestingly, of all the cases heard by the NAD, in only 38 was there an appeal to an NARB panel. Perhaps most encouraging is the fact that during its first 12 years, there has not been a single case in which the advertiser refused to comply with the decision of one of these NARB panels.

Two potential problems pose a threat to this industry self-regulation effort. The program is dependent on volunteer assistance from industry members and on voluntary financial support from advertisers. Throughout its life the NARB has been constrained by a shortage of funds. A more potent danger comes from government regulators who from time to time

---

[10]NAD Case Report, July 15, 1983 (New York: National Advertising Division, Council of Better Business Bureaus, Inc.), pp. 20–23.

The NARB/NAD Self-Regulatory Process **EXHIBIT 24-2**

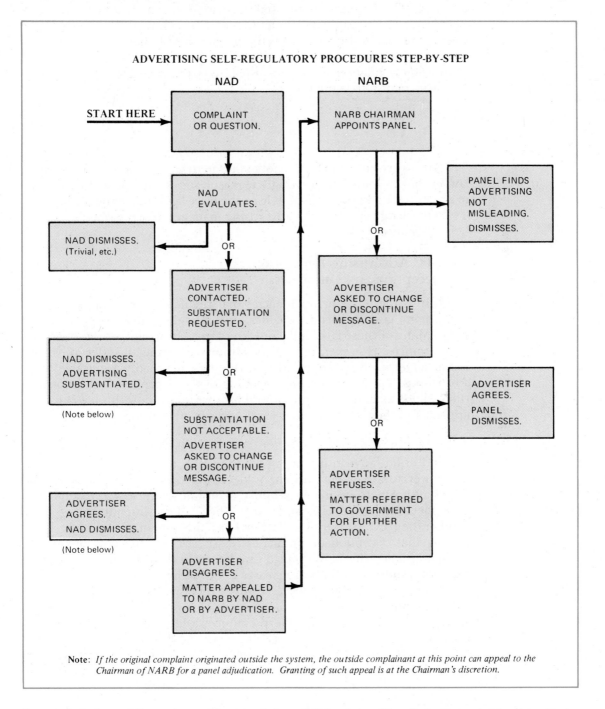

**ADVERTISING SELF-REGULATORY PROCEDURES STEP-BY-STEP**

NAD                NARB

START HERE → COMPLAINT OR QUESTION.

NARB CHAIRMAN APPOINTS PANEL.

NAD EVALUATES.

PANEL FINDS ADVERTISING NOT MISLEADING. DISMISSES.

NAD DISMISSES. (Trivial, etc.)

OR

ADVERTISER CONTACTED. SUBSTANTIATION REQUESTED.

OR

ADVERTISER ASKED TO CHANGE OR DISCONTINUE MESSAGE.

NAD DISMISSES. ADVERTISING SUBSTANTIATED.

OR

ADVERTISER AGREES. PANEL DISMISSES.

(Note below)

SUBSTANTIATION NOT ACCEPTABLE. ADVERTISER ASKED TO CHANGE OR DISCONTINUE MESSAGE.

OR

ADVERTISER REFUSES. MATTER REFERRED TO GOVERNMENT FOR FURTHER ACTION.

ADVERTISER AGREES. NAD DISMISSES.

OR

(Note below)

ADVERTISER DISAGREES. MATTER APPEALED TO NARB BY NAD OR BY ADVERTISER.

**Note**: *If the original complaint originated outside the system, the outside complainant at this point can appeal to the Chairman of NARB for a panel adjudication. Granting of such appeal is at the Chairman's discretion.*

Source: *A Review and Perspective on Advertising Industry Self-Regulation*, (New York: National Advertising Review Board, 1978), p. 12.

threaten to attack the legality of the self-regulation activity. A recent study by the FTC charged that the self-regulation system was being used by advertisers to harass their competitors and recommend that the NAD be sued for restraint of trade.[11] Whether or not this will happen is a matter of conjecture, but the threat, coupled with the legal action taken against local advertising regulation and against the NAD code, may lead to a restriction of this form of self-regulation.

## Legal Ground
## Rules in Advertising

An advertising manager is not expected to have the legal expertise of a lawyer, but in today's increasingly legalistic society, it is essential that the manager have a knowledge of at least the basic laws regulating advertising. This knowledge will help the advertising manager to know when to call for legal assistance.

### FTC Advertising Regulation:
### Deception and Unfairness

Just as there are many agencies that regulate advertising, so too are there many laws, regulations, codes, and guidelines that apply to advertising. Many of these laws apply only to particular products or in restricted circumstances. However, the FTC's authority to act against deceptive and unfair advertising is a fundamental rule that is broadly applicable to all advertising. The evolution and meaning of the deception and unfairness rules will be examined first, followed by a review of how this law has been applied and then of some other legal issues in advertising.

ORIGINS OF DECEPTION AND UNFAIRNESS. Prohibitions against deceptive and unfair advertising began with the FTC in 1914 when it was given the power to act against unfair or deceptive competitive practices. The FTC's authority to regulate deceptive or unfair practices was extended to consumers and to advertising by the Wheeler-Lea Amendment of 1938. Neither the FTC Act nor the Wheeler-Lea Amendment provide criteria for finding that deception or unfairness exist. Instead, the development of definitions and criteria was left to case law or to the precedents developed through trying and adjudicating cases in the courts.

Through FTC and court cases over a period of some forty years, a working definition of deception emerged. That interpretation held that an act or a practice (including advertisement) was deceptive if it had the tendency or capacity to mislead substantial numbers of consumers in a material way. The meaning of unfairness is much less well developed because it has very seldom been invoked as the basis for complaints against advertising

---

[11]Stanley E. Cohen, *op. cit.*

and, hence, few precedents exist.[12] In instances where unfairness has been charged in an advertising case, it has generally been linked to deception, with deception being the primary charge. As will be discussed later, the primary use of the concept of unfairness has been in developing trade regulation rules.

THE NEW FTC POLICY ON DECEPTION. In the early 1980s, with a new administration committed to deregulation in control in Washington and with the appointment of a new chairman for the FTC, the authority of the FTC came under serious attack. Both Congress and the Administration were critical of the FTC's regulatory excesses and its non-productive selection of cases. One step in the reining in of the FTC was the FTC Improvement Act of 1980. Although that bill dealt mostly with the unfairness issue, it did also result in further hearings and debate about the future direction of the FTC.

In later hearings before congressional committees, the chairman of the FTC proposed statutory changes in order to define criteria in terms of which to judge whether or not advertising was deceptive. He argued that a more specific definition of deception would both improve the procedure by which the FTC selected cases for prosecution and uncertainty in advertisers' minds as to what constituted legally acceptable advertising. While the Congressional committee did not elect to change the statute dealing with deceptive advertising, it did invite the FTC to conduct an "analysis of the law" of deception. The FTC conducted this analysis and, as an outcome, adopted, after some controversy and dissent, a policy statement that defined deception. Although this definition does not have the force of law, the FTC announced that the new deception policy would be used as a basis for selecting and prosecuting suits involving allegations of deception in advertising. Indeed, the FTC, shortly after announcing the new policy, used it as the basis for decision in a deceptive advertising suit brought against a mail-order company. If this or subsequent decisions are upheld by the courts, the precedent would become established.

What is the new standard for deception? The old definition, if you will recall, held that an advertisement was deceptive if it had "the tendency or capacity to mislead substantial numbers of consumers in a material way." The new standard states that an advertisement will be found deceptive if "there is a misrepresentation, omission, or other practice, that misleads the consumer, acting reasonably in the circumstances, to the consumer's detriment."[13]

It will take some time before the implications of the new policy on deception are clear. Proponents of the new policy feel that it will provide a

---

[12]Dorothy Cohen, "Unfairness in Advertising Revisited," *Journal of Marketing* (Winter, 1982), pp. 73–80.

[13]Letter from the Federal Trade Commission to the U.S. Senate Committee on Commerce, Science, and Transportation, dated October 14, 1983.

safeguard against the bringing of frivolous and unwinnable suits and provide advertisers with a clearer definition of unlawful advertising. The new standard defines three criteria for determining that unlawful deception exists:

1. The advertisement contains a claim or omits information so that consumers are likely to be misled. This portion of the standard represents little change from the previous one.
2. The advertising claim must be considered "from the perspective of a reasonable consumer." This standard substitutes for the "reasonable numbers of consumers" language in the old standard. It is designed to relieve the advertiser from extreme interpretations of an advertisement by a small group of consumers, but makes the advertiser liable for reasonable interpretations by a reasonable member of the group to whom the advertising was addressed.
3. The misrepresentation or the omission of information must be material. A representation is judged to be material when it is likely to affect the consumer's choice of product. The objective of this element of the standard is to steer the FTC away from trivial cases in which the consumer is unlikely to sustain any injury.[14]

The new standard of deception has been highly controversial. Critics charge that the new standard is a misreading of precedents set in the courts over a period of forty years, that it will make accusations of deception more difficult to prove, and that the rule is circular and confusing. Most criticism seems to be focused on the "reasonable consumer" concept which some fear will lead to lessened protection for the gullible or those least able to care for themselves. Others fear that the requirement of material injury will mean that consumers will first have to be injured before action can be taken.[15]

CHANGES IN THE FAIRNESS STANDARD.. Unlike the case of deception, controversy over the use of the fairness standard arose not because of its case-by-case application, but because of its use in setting trade regulation rules (TRRs). Following enactment of the Magnuson-Moss Act in 1975, the FTC moved toward consideration and issuance of TRRs as a major advertising regulation device. Some of these TRRs were very controversial. Included were a rule on advertising to children, a rule on sales of used cars, a rule on nutrition advertising, and a rule nullifying state laws that limited advertising of eyeglasses.

In 1980, the FTC Improvement Act was passed in response to criticism of the FTC's TRR activity and to a general sentiment to narrow the Commission's scope. The most important change made by this new law was to limit the FTC's use of the concept of unfairness, prohibiting its use as a basis for formulating trade regulation rules, at least until such time as

---

[14]*Ibid.*
[15]See Patricia P. Bailey, "It's a Matter of Definition," *Advertising Age* (February 13, 1984), pp. M-27, 28.

unfairness could be adequately defined. However, despite major efforts by advertisers, the Act left undisturbed the Commission's authority to use unfairness in bringing individual suits against advertisers.

The standards or the criteria by which advertising is ruled unfair are much less developed than those for deception because far fewer cases have been tried under the concept of unfairness and thus precedents are few. After the passage of the 1980 Act, however, the FTC issued a policy statement defining the criteria that the Commission intended to use in bringing and evaluating suits for unfairness in advertising. The policy suggests that unfairness exists when:

1. The consumer is unjustifiably injured. (The injury must be substantial, must not be outweighed by offsetting benefits, and must not have been reasonably avoidable by the consumer.)
2. There is a violation of public policy, as, for example, a violation of other statutes or the First Amendment.[16]

It is clear that the concept of unfairness is still not well defined and not well tested in the courts. As a result, its future application to advertising remains uncertain. Advertising managers, however, should not overlook its importance. Despite heavy industry pressure, the Congress decided to leave unfairness in the statute as an FTC enforcement standard. Unfairness appears likely to be of concern to advertisers for many years to come.

## Applications of Deception and Unfairness Standards

There are many additional legal ground rules that concern the advertising manager. Many, if not most, of these are based on application of the deception and unfairness standards.

TRADE REGULATION RULES. The purpose and procedure for issuance of TRRs by the FTC has been covered in some detail. TRRs were authorized by and stimulated by the Magnuson-Moss Act of 1975, but substantially curtailed by the FTC Improvement Act of 1980 and events which followed upon it. Most of the TRRs issued by the FTC were based on unfairness. Consequently, when the 1980 Act forbade use of unfairness as a criterion for TRRs, the issuance of these rules was drastically reduced. Instead, the FTC decided to reverse its approach to regulation, reverting to a case-by-case approach.[17]

The FTC's rulemaking was further reduced by the courts, the Congress, and the FTC's own actions. Several TRRs were overturned by the courts — for example, the rule disallowing state control over eyeglass advertising. In the FTC Improvement Act of 1980, the Congress gave itself a legislative veto over proposed TRRs. This veto power has been used to

---

[16]Cohen, *op. cit.*
[17]"Back to Cases at the FTC," *Business Week* (July 5, 1982), p. 90.

eliminate several proposed rules, including the one that was to cover used-car sales. In the face of this opposition, the FTC itself voluntarily dropped some of the TRRs that it was considering, including a highly controversial one that would have regulated nutritional claims in food ads and another that would have regulated advertising to children. However, in 1983 the Supreme Court ruled that the Congressional legislative veto was unconstitutional. Despite this, it seems likely that for the immediate future, Trade Regulation Rules will play a much less important role in the regulation of advertising.

SUBSTANTIATION OF CLAIMS. In 1972, The Federal Trade Commission in a case brought against Pfizer's Unburn decided that claims made for that product were unfair because the advertiser did not have substantiation of the claims in hand before the advertising was run. Court confirmation of that decision established the precedent that advertisers must have prior substantiation of advertising claims. The reasoning of the FTC and of the court is that it is an unreasonable and uneconomical expectation that consumers will individually conduct their own testing of advertising claims. The responsibility, therefore, is incumbent upon the advertiser.

After that decision, the FTC began a program of going to groups of advertisers and requiring that they submit for examination substantiation for advertising that was then running. If, in the judgment of the FTC the substantiation was not adequate, the advertising was declared to be deceptive and unfair. Although this procedure was loudly criticized by advertisers, it was continued until 1980 when, with a new administration, a new FTC chairman, and a critical Congress, numerous changes took place in the Commission's regulatory approach.

Shortly thereafter, the chairman of the FTC called for a full review of the FTC's substantiation policy. In the light of other changes that had taken place in advertising regulation, advertisers were apprehensive about major changes in the substantiation policy. However, when the results of the review and the new substantiation policy were announced in early 1984, industry leaders were relieved that the changes in the policy were minor. The FTC policy that was announced and put into effect reaffirms the principle that advertisers are expected to have substantiation for advertising claims in hand before the advertising is run. In addition, the new policy clarifies the prior substantiation policy in three areas:

1. Some additional guidance has been given to advertisers on the amount of substantiation that is needed to support a claim. For example, if an ad claims that "survey results show that...," then the survey results must be available in advance and must support the claim.
2. In some cases, the FTC has agreed that it will consider substantiation developed after the advertising has run, although not as a substitute for prior substantiation.

3. Finally, the FTC acknowledges that it anticipates no more use of the procedure of collecting substantiation information from groups of companies to check on compliance with the prior substantiation policy.[18]

For the future, it seems clear that the necessity for prior substantiation of claims remains, but compliance will be checked only in connection with specific deception cases. There is some indication that application of the substantiation policy will be somewhat more flexible than has been true in the past.

TESTIMONIALS. Ads in which celebrities, experts, or consumers endorse products have for some time attracted regulatory attention. In 1975, the FTC issued a guideline on the use of endorsements and testimonials in advertising and a revision to the guideline in 1980. The guideline covers three areas:

1. Celebrities or experts who are represented as using the product must actually do so and must continue to use it during the time when the advertising is being used. The endorser's opinion of the product must not be misrepresented and the advertiser must be able to substantiate claims that are made, even if they are stated by the endorser.
2. When the endorsement is made by a consumer, the advertiser must be able to show that an average consumer will get the same performance from the product as the endorser.
3. If there is a material connection between the endorser and the advertiser that would affect the endorser's credibility and would not be expected by the consumer, the advertiser must reveal the connection.[19]

A further caution based on prior cases is in order. Regulatory authorities are likely to challenge endorsements by celebrities who are not by training or experience competent to make the advertised statements. The FTC, for example, recently challenged testimonials in which famous athletes told why they thought milk was good for their health on the grounds that they were not qualified to give such advice.[20]

DEMONSTRATIONS. Advertisers using demonstrations in television commercials should exercise special care that their ads are not deceptive. In a celebrated case, a Colgate Rapid Shave commercial was judged deceptive because the demonstration used a mock-up. In the commercial, Rapid Shave was applied to what looked like sandpaper to show that even sandpaper could be shaved using Rapid Shave. However, the "sandpaper" was actually sand glued onto Plexiglass. From this case the rule emerged that a mock-up is not permitted in a commercial if it is central to the demonstration of the product claim.

---

[18]Richard L. Gordon, "Miller Stands Behind Prior Substantiation," *Advertising Age* (March 26, 1984), pp. 1, 77.
[19]Dorothy Cohen, "FTC Issues Guidelines on Endorsements, Testimonials," *Marketing News* (March 21, 1980), p. 3.
[20]"FTC Says Everybody Doesn't Need Milk," *Advertising Age* (April 15, 1974), pp. 1, 59.

This rule permits the common practice in television commercials of using wine in place of coffee (because it photographs more like coffee) and mashed potatoes instead of ice cream (they won't melt under studio lights) as long as those substitutes are incidental to the commercial situation.

In more recent cases it has been ruled that demonstrations are misleading if they are too removed from ordinary experience. The demonstration may be factually correct, but if it does not represent the way that the product is normally used, it is unfair. A Vicks Sinex Nasal Spray commercial showing the ability of Sinex vapor to penetrate a glass tube filled with cotton was charged as misleading because nasal sprays are not actually used this way.[21]

TEST AND SURVEY RESULTS. Advertisers frequently wish to quote survey or test results in advertising. If this is done, the advertiser must, of course, have the test or survey results before the advertising is run, and the results must be accurately represented. Past FTC suits against test and survey users provide three other guidelines for this type of advertising:

1. Test results must not be distorted by using them selectively. The FTC acted against a claim that "Fleischmann's is the margarine most recommended by doctors" when test results revealed that 15 percent of the doctors surveyed recommended Fleischmann's while 67 percent did not recommend any brand.
2. When experts are surveyed, they must indeed be experts with regard to the product and product attribute being advertised. They must also base their statements on actual use or testing of the product.
3. The surveys or tests quoted must be based on a large enough sample to give projectable results and the survey must be less than three years old unless there is evidence that the data are still valid.[22]

## Comparative Advertising

We have considered comparative advertising as a creative technique in Chapter 17 and as a matter of responsibility to consumers in Chapter 23. Here we must consider it again in a legal sense, for there is probably no more legally contentious area in advertising today than comparative ads, particularly those that name competitors.

LEGAL STATUS OF COMPARATIVE ADVERTISING. There is nothing inherently illegal about comparative advertising, even when competitors are named, as long as the comparison is not deceptive or unfair. In fact, the recent resurgence of comparative advertising came about when the FTC, trying to encourage advertisers to provide more useful information to consumers, convinced the television networks to drop their ban on comparative ads.

---

[21]*How to Keep Your Ads Out of Court* (New York: J. Walter Thompson Co., n.d.).
[22]"FTC Consent Pacts Set Test, Survey Guides," *Advertising Age* (January 12, 1981), p. 10.

Nonetheless, the increase in comparative ads has brought with it a flurry of legal disputes. One frequent charge has been that the comparison between competitors has been inaccurate. Alberto-Culver filed a multi-million dollar suit against Gillette Co. charging that commercials for its Tame cream rinse "disparaged" the Alberto-Culver product, Alberto Balsam, resulting in destruction of the brand. In the commercial Tame and Alberto Balsam were compared side by compared side by side to show that Alberto Balsam left an oily residue on the hair, while Tame did not. Copy, in part, read "Tame rinses clean." The commercial was based on Gillette's finding that Alberto Balsam contained mineral oil while Tame did not. In their suit Alberto executives charged that the demonstration was disparaging because in order to be effective, rinse products had to leave something on the hair. They claimed that the inference of the Tame commercial was so strong that it had virtually destroyed the brand.[23]

A second legal problem has been with comparative ads that demonstrate superiority over a competitive product in only one characteristic, but imply from this that the product has overall superiority. In a case handled by the NARB, Drackett Company's commercial for Behold furniture polish was ruled to be deceptive in its comparison with S. C. Johnson's Pledge. In the commercial's demonstration Behold was compared to Pledge in its ability to remove greasy wax marks. Copy, in part, read "Cleaning is one important way to judge a furniture polish." The NARB ruled that the comparison was deceptive because "it is insufficient to establish proof of one characteristic in such a way that the consumer can be led to conclude overall superiority."[24]

LEGAL STANDARDS FOR COMPARATIVE ADVERTISING. The advertiser considering comparative advertising should set strict legal standards to avoid these and related problems. In doing this, a set of guidelines developed by the continuity clearance department of the National Broadcast Company (NBC) might prove helpful. (It was NBC that pioneered clearance of comparative advertising at the request of the FTC.) The guidelines are as follows:

1. Products identified in the advertising must actually be in competition with one another.
2. Competition shall be fairly and properly identified.
3. Advertisers shall refrain from discrediting, disparaging, or unfairly attacking competitors, competing products, or other industries.
4. The identification must be for comparison purposes, and not simply to upgrade by association.
5. The advertising should compare related or similar properties or ingredients of the product, dimension to dimension, feature to feature, or wherever possible by a side-by-side demonstration.

---

[23]Nancy F. Millman, "Gillette Parries Alberto Suit in Court," *Advertising Age* (March 19, 1979), pp. 1, 91.
[24]"NARB Toughens Comparative Ad Rules," *Advertising Age* (December 1, 1975), pp. 1, 76.

6. The property being compared must be significant in terms of value or usefulness of the product to the consumer.
7. The difference in properties must be measurable and significant.[25]

## Other Legal Ground Rules

While deception and unfairness are the most important legal problems that advertisers face, there are also other legal pitfalls that can bring them to grief.

LOTTERIES. Advertisers using contests as part of a sales promotion should be careful that the contest is not a lottery, which would be illegal in many states. In order that a contest not be considered a lottery, it is necessary in most jurisdictions that any consideration (a purchase requirement) be eliminated. To do this, customers must be allowed to enter the contest without payment or purchase of the advertiser's product. This is why most advertisers' contests carry the disclaimer, "no purchase required,"[26] or permit the use of facsimile proofs of purchase. (Chapter 19, p. 519, provides more detail on this issue.) Legal counsel should be involved in contest development since rules are complex and vary by state.

FLAGS AND MONEY. Use of the American flag in commercials is prohibited unless it is an incidental part of a scene. Coins can be used in ads, but paper money, postage, and revenues stamps cannot.[27]

NEW PRODUCTS. By FTC rule, a product can be advertised as "new" for only six months.

COPYRIGHTED MATERIALS. Use of copyrighted materials in an advertisement without permission constitutes infringement and is illegal. Most people realize that books and magazines are usually protected by copyright. More often infringement problems occur in the use of cartoon characters or music which is copyrighted and cannot be used without permission. Gaining permission, of course, frequently requires payment of substantial sums to the copyright owner. Advertisers can also copyright an advertisement and warn competitors or others from stealing ideas from the ad by placing the copyright symbol © in the ad. In fact, many advertisers place the copyright symbol in the advertisement without ever going through the formal copyright process. Often this is enough to warn off competitors.[28]

---

[25]Based on Maurine Christopher, "NBC Spells Out New Formal Guides for Comparative Spots," *Advertising Age* (January 28, 1974), pp. 1, 61.
[26]*How to Keep Your Ads Out of Court, op. cit.*
[27]*Ibid.*
[28]Richard C. Douglas, "Ad Symbols Warn, Protect, Muddle," *Advertising Age* (March 30, 1981), p. 50.

TRADEMARKS. Companies frequently attempt to protect product names by registering the name with the U.S. Patent Office. A product name can be registered only if the company can demonstrate that it was the first to use it in a product category. If the registration is granted, the owner of the name can use the ® symbol to indicate that it is protected. The protection against others using the mark extends only to the owner's industry or product class unless the name is a very well-known one.[29] If a firm has applied for registration, but it has not yet been received, they can use the trademark symbol ™ (or the service-mark symbol Ⓢⓜ for a service) to indicate that a registration application has been filed.

Trademark owners must be careful that their brand name does not become a generic name for the product category. If that occurs, the name is declared public property and the registration protection is lost. The names cellophane and thermos, for example, were once brand names, but have now been declared generic. Advertisers attempt to protect their trademarks by using the ® or ™ symbols with the name and by stressing in ads that the name is a brand. Thus the use "Scotch Brand" tape and "Jello Brand" gelatin dessert. Parker Brothers recently lost Monopoly as a protected trademark because the court found that the name had lost its consumer identity with the corporation name Parker Brothers. Advertisers found this novel attack on trademarks to be unsettling.[30]

MODEL RELEASES. Neither a person's name nor picture should be used in an advertisement without a written release from the individual. Failure to get a release runs the risk of an invasion of privacy charge. The release should specify the use for which permission is granted. If a new or modified use is planned, a new release should be obtained. Many privacy problems occur because the user goes beyond the scope of the release.[31]

## Other Legal Issues in Advertising

It should be clear from the discussion thus far that the regulation of advertising is in a period of great change. The general direction of that change has been toward less regulation and greater governmental focus on specifics in its regulatory efforts. There are several other current issues in advertising regulation that appear to be pointed in the same direction.

ADVERTISING AND THE FIRST AMENDMENT. In a series of decisions starting in 1975, the Supreme Court overturned a precedent of over 30 years that "commercial speech" (advertising) was not fully protected under the First Amendment.

The first hint of a reversal was contained in a case (*Bigelow* vs. *Virginia*) in which the court overturned the conviction of a Virginia newspaper

---

[29]Douglas, *op. cit.*
[30]"No Monopoly on Monopoly," *Business Week* (March 7, 1983), p. 36.
[31]Sidney A. Diamond, "Many Violations of Privacy Cases Claim Use Went Beyond Written Release," *Advertising Age* (August 8, 1974), p. 34.

editor for publishing an ad for an abortion referral and placement service. The court ruled that the law under which Bigelow was convicted unconstitutionally infringed on the First Amendment because the ad contained information of public interest and value.[32]

Because the content of this ad clearly contained more than commercial information, it was not established until the *Virginia Pharmacy* case in 1976 that First Amendment protection extended to advertising dealing with purely commercial matters. In that case the court ruled that a Virginia statute prohibiting pharmacy advertising of prescription drug prices was unconstitutional under the First Amendment. The court ruled that commercial speech is protected by the First Amendment because advertising provides information that is vital to the operation of the free enterprise marketplace.

The *Virginia Pharmacy* case left many questions unanswered that are only slowly being addressed by additional court cases. The Supreme Court refused to interfere in a lower-court decision overturning the FTC ban of an advertising slogan on "instant tax refunds" even though the court felt that the slogan was misleading. The court felt that the slogan was protected by the First Amendment and that copy could be written that would clarify the slogan.[33]

Later the Supreme Court struck down on First Amendment grounds a ban on contraceptive advertising. They ruled that the possibility of offense or embarrassment does not justify overriding First Amendment protection.[34]

However, the Supreme Court refused to intervene in a lower-court decision ordering corrective advertising for Listerine antiseptic mouthwash to counteract previous misleading advertising asserting that Listerine was effective in cold prevention. The makers of Listerine had claimed that the corrective advertising order violated their First Amendment rights, but they were not upheld[35]

Recently, the Supreme Court considered a lower court decision that upheld the right of the state of Oklahoma to ban the advertising of alcoholic beverages. Opponents of the ban contended that it infringed on freedom of speech as protected by the First Amendment. However, the state contended that the Twenty-First Amendment, which gives states broad powers over the alcoholic beverage trade, takes precedence over the First Amendment.[36] The Supreme Court ruled against the advertising ban, but it failed to directly address the free-speech issue.[37]

---

[32]Dorothy Cohen, "Advertising and the First Amendment," *Journal of Marketing* (July, 1978), p. 60.

[33]"Ad Slogan Held Protected by First Amendment," *Advertising Age* (May 2, 1977), p. 4.

[34]"First Amendment Rights of Ads Get Strong High Court Support," *Advertising Age* (June 13, 1977), p. 2.

[35]"FTC Upheld in Listerine's Ads," *New York Times* (April 4, 1978), p. 37.

[36]Richard L. Gordon, "Liquor Case Spurs 1st Amendment Fears," *Advertising Age* (November 21, 1983), p. 6.

[37]Stanley E. Cohen, "Cable Ruling Leaves Issues Unanswered," *Advertising Age* (June 21, 1984), pp. 1, 47.

IMPLICATIONS FOR ADVERTISING REGULATION. While the implications of First Amendment protection for advertising are only slowly becoming clear, there have been some predictions as to what changes might be expected:

1. It may be more difficult for the FTC to establish broad trade-rule regulations constraining the advertising of companies that have violated no laws.
2. Although the Listerine ruling was upheld, the FTC may be less likely to order corrective advertising.
3. When ordering affirmative disclosures in advertising (for example, to warn of dangers to health or safety) more of the burden to prove necessity will rest with the regulators.
4. Requirements that advertisers be able to substantiate all ad claims, especially subjective claims which are difficult to prove objectively, are less likely to be upheld.
5. It will be more difficult to restrict advertising for products that are suspected of being harmful yet can be legally sold. Advertising of sugar-rich products to children may fall into this category.[38]

DEREGULATION OF PROFESSIONAL ADVERTISING. Another strong trend toward deregulation has been a series of successful attacks on restrictions by state and by professional associations on advertising by the professions. Supported by a Supreme Court First Amendment case prohibiting the states from suppressing truthful price advertising, the FTC issued a trade rule barring states from restricting ads for eyeglasses. The FTC felt that eyeglass advertising would benefit consumers by helping them to make better informed, more economic choices. However, a circuit court overturned the eyeglass rule on the grounds that it constituted an infringement on the right of the states to regulate in that area. At the same time, the same court noted that under the protection of the First Amendment, a total ban on eyeglass advertising was not permissible either.[39]

Only two years later, the Supreme Court furthered the deregulation of professional advertising by upholding an FTC order that allowed doctors and dentists to advertise. Although professional associations are allowed to monitor advertising in order to detect false or misleading ads, they are not allowed to prohibit advertising by these professions.[40] In the same case, the Supreme Court confirmed the FTC's jurisdiction over professional associations.

PROBLEMS IN CORPORATE ADVERTISING. Corporate advertising that takes a position on controversial issues has a long history of regulatory difficulty. Although the picture is still far from clear, it appears that the

---

[38]Based on "Courts Taking Ad Powers from FTC, Elman Says," *Advertising Age* (October 31, 1977), p. 4, and Stanley E. Cohen, "Supreme Court Adds Broad Protection of Advertising," *Advertising Age* (May 31, 1976), pp. 1, 2.
[39]"Court Zaps Eyeglass Ad Rule," *Advertising Age* (February 11, 1980), p. 3.
[40]Pravat Choudhury, "Top Court Upholds FTC Order Okaying Doctors', Dentists' Ads," *Marketing News* (May 28, 1982), p. 16.

trend toward less regulation may apply to this form of corporate advertising.

Corporate advertising on controversial issues has never been popular with Congress. A Senate subcommittee recently subpoenaed vast amounts of data from businesses as a part of an investigation into corporate advertising. The investigation appeared aimed particularly at oil companies and food processors. At the same time, a House subcommittee was critically investigating the tax treatment of the cost of issue and corporate image advertising.

In the face of these negative actions, corporate advertising received strong support when in 1978 the Supreme Court held that the protection of the First Amendment extended to this form of advertising. The ruling came about when the Court declared unconstitutional a Massachusetts law that prohibited corporate advertising on public referendum issues that did not directly relate to the company's business.[41]

The Court's ruling appeared to substantially clear the way for "issue" advertising by corporations, but advertisers in this area should note two restrictions. First, under Internal Revenue Service rules, corporate expenditures for issue ads are not deductible business expenses. Second, the First Amendment protection of political issue advertising does not extend to support by corporate advertising of political candidates, which is specifically prohibited by law. In addition, advertisers should recognize that issue ads are themselves controversial. Ralph Nader, the consumer advocate, continues to argue that corporate issue ads represent imprudent expenditure of stockholders' funds, should not be protected by the First Amendment, and should be more closely monitored by the FTC for accuracy.[42] Issue advertisers should recognize that the result of such advertising may be to make the company the issue.

## The Legal Responsibility Program

Just as there is a control program to assure the responsibility of consumer advertising so too there should be a program to assure that legal standards are met. Legal standards should be set that provide guidance in areas where legal difficulties can be anticipated. The discussion in the preceding sections should be helpful in defining standards.

### Defining Responsibility for the Program

Clearly the advertising manager is responsible for assuring that the

---

[41]Richard L. Gordon, "Corporate Ads Get High Court Boost," *Advertising Age* (May 1, 1978), pp. 1, 104.

[42]Ralph Nader, "Challenging the Corporate Ad," *Advertising Age* (January 24, 1983), pp. M-12, 14.

company's advertising is within the law. To do this, the advertising manager should accept the responsibility for assuring that advertisements are thoroughly checked for legality before they become public.

Ordinarily, however, the advertising manager is not qualified by either training or experience to evaluate the legality of advertising. The advertising manager's responsibility is to assure that adequate legal counsel is made available at the proper place and at the proper time in the creative process. In larger firms, corporate legal staffs can sometimes serve this need. More often, however, companies rely on attorneys who specialize in advertising law.

### The Timing of Legal Evaluation

To be effective, the legal evaluation of advertising must take place before the advertising is exposed to the public and to regulatory authorities. To avoid long delays, the acceptability of ads should also be evaluated before they are submitted to the media for clearance.

The most acceptable approach to legal evaluation is to involve legal counsel with the creative members of the agency account team at the beginning of the creative process. This means that counsel should be involved in the preparation of the creative program and at the early stages of ad creation. Through involvement early in the creative process, legal counsel is able to show "how" creative objectives can be legally met. When participation is not offered until the ads are in a finished form, the contribution of legal counsel is limited to saying "no" to those ads that do not meet standards.

---

Advertising is regulated at the federal, state, and local levels, but the most important advertising regulator is the Federal Trade Commission. The FTC is charged with protecting consumers from deceptive or unfair advertising and acts either by prosecuting individual complaints of law violation or by issuing trade regulation rules for an entire industry or product class to follow. Advertising is also regulated by other federal, state, and local agencies. In addition, there is self-regulation by the advertising industry itself. The most important self-regulation is that effected by the individual media which set standards and screen advertisements for acceptability under those standards. The key industry self-regulation effort is through the National Advertising Review Board that seeks voluntary compliance in settling issues of truth and accuracy in advertising.

The most basic legal ground rule for advertising is that it cannot be deceptive or unfair. The meanings of deception and unfairness have evolved over many years through case law, but recent administrative and legislative changes appear to have set new standards for both deception and unfairness. Most additional legal ground rules in advertising are based on the application of the deception and unfairness standards. Generally,

*CHAPTER SUMMARY*

advertisers are required to have substantiation for claims in hand before the advertising containing them is run. Product testimonials must be by actual users of the product; the endorser's claims must not misrepresent, and claims must be substantiated. Test and survey results can be used in advertising, but they must be accurately represented. Comparative advertising that names competitors is also permissible, but the comparison must not be deceptive.

The Supreme Court has ruled that advertising is protected under the First Amendment and cannot be infringed upon by state or local laws. Laws and association restrictions on professional advertising have been largely overturned. Likewise, corporate "issue" advertising is permissible although it remains a controversial area.

The advertising manager is responsible for assuring that the company's advertising meets legal standards by utilizing legal counsel during the formation of creative programs.

---

*KEY TERMS*

Wheeler-Lea Amendment
Corrective advertising
Magnuson-Moss Act
FTC Improvement Act
Piggyback commercials

National Advertising Review
  Board (NARB)
Children's Advertising Review
  Unit of NAD (CARU)

---

*QUESTIONS
FOR
DISCUSSION*

1. The FCC is planning to eliminate its controls over the time devoted to commercials in television programs, and the National Association of Broadcasters has eliminated its guidelines on commercial time slots as a result of court challenges. With this regulation eliminated, what is to keep television broadcasters from packing their popular viewing hours with commercials at the expense of programming?

2. In preparing its revised policy statement on deception in advertising, the FTC was attempting to avoid bringing unreasonable cases. Three cases that were brought under the former deception policy are summarized below. Do you feel that the charges of deception were unreasonable?

   a. Milk Board case: charged that the phrase "everybody needs milk" was false because some people are allergic to milk.

   b. Westinghouse case: charged deception in the use of the word "new" to describe television tubes made with recycled glass.

   c. Quaker case: charged that use of the description "hickory-kissed flavor" for charcoal briquets was deceptive because the briquets were made from corncobs.[43]

---

[43]"FTC 'Deception' Language Hit," *Advertising Age* (March 5, 1984), p. 6.

3. A complaint brought to the NARB charged that Hardee's Food Systems, Inc., misled consumers by advertising that the hamburgers served in its restaurants were "Charco-Broiled," which implied broiling over charcoal when, in fact, the hamburgers were cooked over ceramic briquettes heated by gas flames. If you were a member of the NARB panel hearing this complaint, how would you rule?[44]

4. In the first ten years of its life, the five product categories that generated the most NAD advertising case reviews were (a) food, (b) cosmetics, (c) automotive, (d) household products, and (e) leisure, in that order. Can you detect any pattern that suggests why these product categories are more subject to advertising complaints?[45]

5. At the urging of the FTC, the American Bar Association rewrote its advertising code for lawyers so as to make it less restrictive. The Supreme Court had ruled that professional organizations could not ban advertising by professionals if it was truthful. However, the ABA remained concerned, in particular, about direct mail, fearing that lawyers might use it to solicit known family members of the victims of collisions or other accidents. It therefore stated in its code that direct mail could be used only when it was generally distributed, not when it was directed to persons known to need the particular kind of legal service offered by that lawyer.[46]

   a. Do you think that this provision of the code meets the Supreme Court's ruling?
   b. Does this section of the code make good advertising sense?

6. Ralph Nader, the well-known consumer advocate, has long opposed corporate "advertorials": advertisements that promote a position on social or political issues. He suggests that, in order to counterbalance the economic power of large corporations, such advertorials should be subject to the "equal time" rule that governs broadcast media. Under that rule, stations that accept political statements by one advocacy group or party must give equal and free time to opposition views.

   a. Do you think it fair and responsible for corporations to use corporate funds to take and promote stands on political and social issues?
   b. Do you feel it fair for opposition views to be given free media time or space so as to respond to advertorials?

7. A complaint to the Children's Advertising Review Unit charged that television commercials for Great Adventure showed passengers waving their hands while riding on a rollercoster. The complaint alleged that children might attempt to imitate this dangerous action while on the

[44]*Ibid.,* p. 17.
[45]*Ibid.,* p. 6.
[46]"Lawyers Ease ABA Ad Code," *Advertising Age* (August 8, 1983), p. 14.

ride and thus endanger themselves. If you were a CARU panel member assigned to this case, what decision would you make concerning this advertising?

8. The American Hospital Association has issued guidelines for hospital advertising that require all ads (a) to be accurate, (b) to be fair, (c) to avoid comparisons, (d) to avoid claims of prominence, and (e) to avoid promotion of individuals.[47] Do you think this set of guidelines violates the First Amendment?

9. In filming a television commercial, one of the technically difficult problems is to film a television set in operation so that the picture on the screen looks as it does in a home situation. To make the TV picture look natural, it is necessary to take an actual television program film and optically transfer it to the TV set in the commercial. Under the rules of deception and unfairness, is it permissible to do this?

---

*PROBLEM*

Recently the National Advertising Division of the Council of Better Business Bureaus took the rarely used step of referring a controversial and unresolved case to a National Advertising Review Board panel for a decision.[48] The suit arose originally when RCA complained that claims in two television commercials for Sony's Trinitron color television were false. One of the claims in question was: "Nobody else has a system with a picture so extraordinary it can't be duplicated. And nobody else has won an Emmy for its picture. Something no other TV could have done." RCA charged that the Emmy had been awarded more than ten years before the claim was made in the commercial, too long ago to be used as current evidence of superior performance. Sony responded that no other television receiver had won an Emmy since Sony's and that therefore the claim was still valid.

In examining the issue, the NAD found that both RCA and Sony had won Emmys for technical achievement and that thus the claim "nobody else has won an Emmy for its picture" was inaccurate. The NAD also decided that, in order to prevent misunderstanding, Sony's ads should disclose the year in which the award was won. Sony proposed the addition of the "super" on its television commercials to state "Awarded 1972–73. Nobody else has ever won one." The NAD did not feel that this response was sufficient and referred the case to the NARB.

1. What do you feel is the true issue in this case?
2. If you were the advertising manager for Sony, how would you have responded to the NAD complaint?

---

[47]Stanley E. Cohen, "Next Target: Lawyer, Doctor Ad Codes," *Advertising Age* (September 5, 1977), p. 55.

[48]This problem is based on Gay Jervey, "NAD Taking Sony TV Set Case to NARB," *Advertising Age* (April 16, 1984), p. 6.

3. If you were an NARB panel member hearing this case, would you support the NAD or Sony? Would you request any further changes of Sony?

---

Albion, Mark S. and Paul W. Farris. *The Advertising Controversy: Evidence on the Economic Effects of Advertising.* Boston: Auburn House Publishing Company, 1981. A reexamination of economic and marketing evidence concerning the economic effects of advertising. Examines macroeconomic effects as well as micro issues of advertising's economic effectiveness.

Smith, Robert E. and William R. Swinyard, "Information Response Models: An Integrated Approach," *Journal of Marketing* (Winter, 1982), pp. 81–93. This article reviews evidence concerning the hierarchy of effects and develops a revised model that takes into account the low credibility given to advertising as compared to other sources.

Stone, Alan. *Regulation and Its Alternatives.* Washington, D.C.: Congressional Quarterly Press, 1982. An examination of the regulatory process as practiced in the U.S., alternatives to regulation, and recent changes in the regulatory process. Examines the social, economic, and political basis for regulation with a major section on the FTC.

Dalbey, Homer M., Irwin Gross, and Yoram Wind. *Advertising Measurement and Decision Making.* Boston: Allyn and Bacon, Inc., 1968. An analysis of the problems of evaluating advertising effectiveness and a review of alternative measurement techniques. Includes criteria (Ideal Measurement Procedure) for evaluating measurement approaches.

Bartos, Rena and Theodore F. Dunn. *Advertising and Consumers, New Perspectives.* New York: American Association of Advertising Agencies, n.d. A report on the findings of a national study of consumers' attitudes toward advertising — what they like about it, what they dislike, and what issues underlie these attitudes.

Oathout, John D. *Trademarks.* New York: Charles Scribners Sons, 1981. The author draws upon extensive experience in business to provide us with a description of how to create, use, and protect trademarks.

Rohrer, Daniel Morgan. *Mass Media, Freedom of Speech, and Advertising: A Study in Communication Law.* Dubuque, Iowa: Kendall-Hunt Publishing Company, 1979. A detailed analysis, with summaries of relevant court cases, of communications law and the application of the first amendment to advertising.

*PART FOUR:*

*SELECTED READINGS*

# GLOSSARY

**Account executive.** The advertising manager's counterpart and the client's direct representative within the client contact unit of an advertising agency.

**Account group.** A task team in an advertising agency that is made up of members from various functional areas who work together on a particular advertising account.

**Advertising.** A paid message that appears in the mass media for the purpose of informing or persuading people about particular products, services, beliefs, or actions.

**Advertising agency.** A business service organization that plans, creates, places, and researches advertising for client organizations.

**Advertising manager.** An advertising generalist who, through use of advertising specialists, plans, implements, and controls advertising programs.

**Advertising media.** The channels through which a product's advertising is carried to prospective consumers.

**Advertising objectives.** Statements of what the advertiser hopes to accomplish with advertising in order to overcome problems facing the product. Goals that must be attained by the advertising program if the advertising is to contribute to the successful marketing of a product.

**Advertising plan.** A detailed schedule of advertising activities to be carried out for a product, including advertising content, media, and budget programs, each directed by advertising objectives.

**Advertising-related-to-sales budgeting approach.** A method of setting the ad-vertising budget in which a fixed proportion of expected sales is set aside for advertising.

**Advertising researcher.** An advertising specialist whose work focuses on the pre- and post-measurement of advertising effectiveness.

**Advertising specialties.** Utilitarian items containing a brief advertising message that are given, usually without charge, to prospects by an advertiser.

**Advertising-to-sales (A to S) ratio.** The percentage of sales spent on advertising. A measure of advertising expenditure weight.

**Affective tests.** Advertising effectiveness tests that measure response at the liking, preference, or attitude stages in the hierarchy of effects.

**AIDA formula.** A formulation of the steps that consumers pass through in making a purchase decision. The acronym stands for Attention, Interest, Desire, and Action.

**A la carte advertising approach.** A do-it-yourself approach to advertising in which the advertiser contracts with independent specialists for various agency-type services.

**Animated commercial.** A television commercial that uses hand- or computer-drawn cartoon or stylized figures and settings.

**Answer print.** A final step in the editing process that combines the film or tape, optical effects, and sound track to provide a finished commercial for review purposes.

**A *priori* segmentation studies.** Segmentation studies in which the researcher uses research to verify assumed market segments.

**Area of dominant influence (ADI).** A geographic market area made up of counties whose predominant television viewership originates from the same metropolitan area.

**Art director.** A creative services unit member responsible for design and illustration in print advertising and for designing video action in television commercials.

**As-it-falls approach.** An approach to the problem of translating the introductory marketing program budget into the test markets that results in the percentage of the test market budget to the total budget being made equal to the percentage of the test market population to the total population.

**Association tests.** An indirect question form used to determine connotations or attitudes attached to products or ideas.

**Attitude tests.** In advertising effectiveness research, an approach that measures, through use of attitude scales, the dimensions and intensity of consumers' feelings toward companies, products, or advertisements.

**Audience.** The total number of persons who have read a particular issue of a print publication or viewed/listened to a particular broadcast program or time period.

**Audience distribution.** The apportionment of total readers or viewers over a media schedule, usually measured in terms of reach and frequency.

**Audience studies.** Services that measure the readership of print media such as newspapers and magazines.

**Audit report.** A publisher's statement that has been verified by one of the independent circulation auditing services.

**Availabilities.** Broadcast programs or spots that are available for purchase.

**Average paid circulation.** The number of copies of a newspaper or magazine sold for an average issue.

**Awareness studies.** An advertising effectiveness test that measures the level of recall or awareness of a brand or of an advertising program.

**Basic offer.** The incentive offered in a sales promotion to the consumer or to the trade in order to encourage response.

**Bleed pages.** Print publication pages that permit an illustration to extend without a border to the edge of the page.

**Brand manager.** Also called a product manager. A manager, usually in a large, multi-product, consumer-goods firm, who has marketing responsibility for a single brand, often with focus on advertising and sales promotion activities.

**Business administration unit.** A functional department in an advertising agency that is responsible for the financial, personnel, and other administrative needs of the agency.

**Central idea.** A verbal or visual device or a situation used in an advertisement to provide a context for expressing the copy content.

**Centralized advertising department.** An organizational alternative that pools all advertising personnel and resources at a single location to take advantage of opportunities for specialization.

**Children's Advertising Review Unit of NAD (CARU).** A special unit with the National Advertising Review Board that handles cases concerning advertising to children.

**Circulation.** The number of copies of a newspaper or magazine distributed in an average issue.

**Client contact unit.** An advertising agency functional department that receives and supervises action on client requests and serves as the channel through which agency work and recommendations flow to the client and through which client feedback flows back to the agency.

**Closing dates.** The dates by which advertising materials must be supplied to a publication for inclusion in a particular issue.

**Clutter.** The crowding of a medium with many advertisements that compete for viewer attention.

**Cognitive tests.** Advertising effectiveness tests that measure response at the awareness or knowledge stage.

**Color preprints.** Color advertisements prepared on a continuous roll in a repeating pattern to be cut off and inserted in newspapers.

**Combination rate.** A discounted newspaper space rate granted for using more than one newspaper (usually a morning-evening combination) owned by the same publisher.

**Competitive-parity budgeting approach.** A method of setting the advertising budget that establishes the size of the budget based on a relationship to competitive advertising expenditures.

**Conative tests.** Advertising effectiveness tests that measure the actions that people take as a result of advertising.

**Concept board.** A stimulus, usually in the form of a dummy advertisement, used in a concept test.

**Concept statement.** A description of a proposed new product used as a stimulus in concept testing.

**Concept test.** A test to evaluate proposed products or product changes by asking respondents their reaction to a short product description, drawing, or dummy advertisement.

**Concept testing.** The process of evaluating a new product idea before the physical product is available, usually by exposing prospects to a written or visual representation of the product.

**Consumer goals.** Tangible, achievable targets that consumers set as steps to fulfillment of underlying needs.

**Consumer jury technique.** An advertising pretesting technique in which consumers are shown advertisements and their opinion is asked about each advertisement.

**Consumer needs.** The complex of underlying needs, goals, and problems that make up an individual's need structure.

**Consumer problems.** The obstacles that consumers face and must overcome if goals are to be reached.

**Consumer responsibility program.** A section within the advertising plan that specifies how the advertising effort will be controlled to assure that it meets acceptable standards in its dealings with consumers.

**Consumer take-away.** Sales of a manufacturer's product at the retail level.

**Consumer use (home use) test.** A product test in which consumers are asked to evaluate the product after using a sample supply in their home under normal conditions.

**Controlled or non-paid circulation publication.** A publication that is distributed free of charge to target audience members in the field served by the publication.

**Controlled store testing (minimarket testing).** A form of market test in which distribution of the test product into retail outlets in the test area is arranged contractually in advance by a research firm.

**Cooperative advertising.** An arrangement under which a manufacturer pays a designated proportion of a dealer's or retailer's advertising expenditure on the manufacturer's product.

**Cooperative advertising allowance.** An element in an advertising program by which the manufacturer offers to pay a portion of a retailer's advertising expenditures on behalf of the manufacturer's product.

**Copy platform.** A statement, in consumer language, of the claims, supporting evidence, and information that advertising for a product is to present to consumers.

**Copywriter.** A creative services unit member responsible for conceptualizing advertising and for writing the words used in print and broadcast advertising and related materials.

**Corporate operating plan.** The consolidated departmental plans from all operating departments of the firm, providing firm-wide objectives and programs for reaching objectives, usually for a one-year period.

**Corporate or institutional advertising.** Advertising with the objective of creating a favorable attitude toward an entire company rather than a particular product.

**Corporate strategy.** A decision, based on a matching of the firm's strengths with the opportunities in the marketplace, that defines how a company will compete.

**Corrective advertising.** A remedy imposed by the Federal Trade Commission that requires advertisers to run ads designed to explain to consumers that previous advertising may have been misleading.

**Cost per thousand.** The cost of a media purchase unit times 1,000 divided by the number of prospects reached by that unit.

**Coupon misredemption.** The cashing of a price reduction coupon without purchasing the specified product.

**Creative integration.** The process of tying together the creative elements of an advertising program both visually and verbally.

**Creative review board.** An advertising agency committee, usually made up of senior creative personnel, that reviews the creative output of the agency.

**Creative services unit.** An advertising agency functional department that is responsible for writing, designing, and supervising the production of advertising and related materials.

**Cultural variables.** Traditional, learned responses to individual needs, goals, and problems. Problem-solving approaches that are shared by the members of a society.

**Customer-organized advertising department.** An advertising department whose work is divided up and assigned by customer or class of customer.

**Decentralized advertising department.** An organizational alternative that distributes advertising personnel and resources to the various users of advertising services in order to bring those services closer to other product marketing decisions.

**Demographically selective medium.** A medium whose audience is concentrated among people with certain common demographic characteristics.

**Depth interview.** An unstructured interview technique in which the subject is encouraged to talk freely about a topic.

**Designated market area (DMA).** See Area of dominant influence.

**Diary study.** A technique for measuring product sales by analysis of purchase information provided by a panel of consumers who agree to maintain a diary of purchases by product category.

**Direct advertising.** The medium and the communication intended for direct marketing prospects.

**Direct marketing.** A marketing system, fully controlled by the marketer, that develops products, promotes them directly to the end consumer, accepts orders direct from consumers, and distributes the products directly to the consumer.

**Duplication.** The overlap in circulation or audience between two media or media vehicles.

**Emotional benefits.** Promises contained in advertisements to satisfy consumers' social or psychological needs.

**Environmental factor.** A force external to a market that is an underlying cause of change in market size, growth, and distribution.

**Fear appeal.** An emotion-arousing advertising approach designed to raise anxiety concerning a dangerous or harmful problem facing the consumer.

**Flat rate.** A newspaper advertising space rate without a discount for quantity purchases.

**Flighting or pulsing.** Constructing a broadcast advertising schedule in such a way that commercials are concentrated in waves with a hiatus between waves.

**Focus-group interview.** A form of depth interview conducted by a moderator with a group of persons rather than with an individual.

**Free-standing insert.** A pre-printed, multipaged newspaper section containing the advertising of one advertiser that is inserted into and distributed with a daily newspaper.

**Frequency.** The average number of print media issues read (for those who have read at least one issue) in a print media schedule during a specified time period. The average number of programs or station time periods heard or viewed (for those who have heard or viewed at least one) in a broadcast media schedule.

**FTC Improvement Act.** An act of 1980 that limited the FTC's rule-making authority.

**Functionally organized advertising department.** An advertising department whose work is divided up and assigned by advertising subfunction.

**Gatefold.** An oversized magazine page which the reader can fold out to full size.

**Geographically organized advertising department.** An advertising department whose work is divided up and assigned by geographic area.

**Geographically selective medium.** A medium whose audience is concentrated in a particular geographic area.

**Geographic index of market sales.** An index that describes the variation in sales of a product class by geographic territory.

**Gross-rating points (GRP).** The sum of the rating points for the individual programs or announcements in a broadcast media schedule. In print media, the sum of the reach percentages for each advertisement scheduled. In outdoor, the percentage of the gross market population exposed daily to an outdoor showing.

**Habitual purchase.** A purchase, that because of prior experience, can be made with little forethought.

**Headline testing.** A technique for pretesting advertising benefits or product positionings that uses headline statements as stimuli for eliciting consumer opinions.

**Hierarchy of effects.** An approach to measuring advertising effectiveness that utilizes progress along the steps intermediate to sales as measures of effectiveness.

**High impact.** A term used to describe a media program that quickly reaches the total target audience.

**Homes using television (HUT).** The total number of television homes with television sets turned on during a particular time period.

**House agency.** An advertising agency formed by an advertiser for the purpose of preparing advertising for the company's own products.

**Ideal measurement procedure (IMP).** A list of seven attributes that can be used to evaluate the technical quality and validity of advertising effectiveness measurement techniques.

**Image study.** An attitude study that uses scales, such as the semantic differential, to provide a profile of consumer attitudes toward particular products.

**Indirect research techniques.** An approach to soliciting responses in which the intent of the researcher is hidden from the respondent.

**Information usefulness concept.** Consumers select the information that they will perceive, including advertising, in terms of its usefulness to them in meeting current or anticipated needs.

**Informercials.** In-depth informational commercials up to ten minutes in length, sometimes used on the new electronic media.

**In-pack premium.** A sales promotion basic offer in the form of a gift included in the product package.

**Inquiry measurement.** A method of post-testing the effectiveness of advertisements by tabulating the number of requests for information or responses to offers resulting from an advertisement.

**Layout.** A design showing the size and spatial arrangement of the elements of a print advertisement.

**Line.** A standardized measure of advertising space one column wide and 1/14th of an inch deep.

**Little U.S. approach.** An approach to the problem of translating the introductory marketing program budget into test markets that results in media weight (usually in terms of gross rating points) in the test markets being made equivalent to the average weight called for by the introductory plan.

**Live action commercial.** A television commercial that utilizes actors and actresses filmed or taped in a studio or on location.

**Logotype.** A company or product name having a distinctive style of type or art treatment or both.

**Magnuson-Moss Act.** An act of 1975 that empowered the Federal Trade Commission to issue Trade Regulation Rules.

**Mail-order catalog advertising.** A multi-product advertising booklet sent through the mail to direct marketing prospects.

**Management by exception.** A method of management under which subordinates are provided with a plan to implement and are expected to report back to their superior only if some unforeseen circumstance requires an exception to the plan or if results turn out to be different from those projected.

**Market segments.** Subgroups of consumers each with some common characteristic that influences that group's demand for a product.

**Market share.** The percentage of product category sales realized by a specified product or brand.

**Market test.** A field experiment that introduces advertising programs into a limited number of representative markets; used to evaluate advertising program elements or to evaluate the interactions in a total advertising plan.

**Marketing concept.** To be successful in the marketplace, producers must design a product to meet consumer needs rather than try to reshape consumer needs to fit existing products.

**Marketing department plan.** The consolidated marketing plans, usually in condensed form, for all of the products for which the marketing department is responsible.

**Marketing plan.** A detailed set of marketing objectives and programs for achieving them for a particular product. Wider in scope than an advertising plan because it contains programs for all marketing functional areas, including personal selling, product development, and pricing.

**Marketing services unit.** An advertising agency functional department that is responsible for the media, merchandising, and research functions.

**Mass media.** Public advertising carriers such as television, radio, magazines, and newspapers.

**Media buyer.** An advertising specialist, usually employed in an advertising agency, who plans and purchases media schedules.

**Media buying service.** A specialized advertising service organization that plans and implements media buys, particularly in the field of television.

**Media department.** A marketing services unit in an advertising agency that is responsible for planning the media program for client products and negotiating for and purchasing advertising time and space on behalf of clients.

**Media life.** The average length of time that a particular media vehicle is actively used by a consumer.

**Media sales representative.** An employee or agent of an advertising media firm who sells advertising time or space.

**Media selectivity.** The ability of a medium to deliver an audience that is limited to people with certain common characteristics.

**Media spill-in.** The percentage of media coverage in a test market originating from outside the test market.

**Media vehicle.** A particular publication or program in a media class.

**Merchandising department.** A marketing services unit in an advertising agency that is responsible for planning sales promotions, conducting marketing studies, and gathering data for marketing decisions.

**Merchandising the advertising.** Promotion of a product's consumer advertising program to trade intermediaries to influence their efforts on behalf of the product.

**Merchandising value of the medium.** The influence of an advertising medium with trade intermediaries and the sales force.

**Milline rate.** The cost of one line of newspaper space times one million divided by the number of prospects reached by that unit.

**Mixing session.** A step in the process of editing a commercial in which audio elements such as music or sound effects are added to the voice track.

**Narrowcasting.** The selective audience delivery capability of the new electronic media.

**National Advertising Review Board (NARB).** An industry-wide, advertising self-regulatory body sponsored by the Council of Better Business Bureaus.

**New product.** A product can be termed "new" when the change over prior products is sufficient to require a new positioning.

**Nondirective technique.** An interview technique which uses nonevaluative comments to encourage the respondent to talk fully and nondefensively about a topic. Used in depth interviewing.

**Open rate.** A newspaper advertising space rate that offers a discount based on the predicted amount of space to be purchased in some specified time period, usually a year.

**Original research.** Data, needed to solve a problem, that is collected specifically for that use.

**Painted bulletins.** Large outdoor advertisements painted one at a time with an advertiser's design.

**Pass-along circulation or secondary audience.** For a print medium, the difference between circulation and audience.

**Physiological tests.** Advertising effectiveness tests that utilize laboratory measurement devices to record physical response to stimuli.

**Piggyback commercial.** Two commercials for different products, but usually from the same company, that share a single commercial position.

**Plans board.** An advertising agency committee, usually made up of senior executives, that reviews advertising plans to be presented to clients.

**Point-of-purchase advertising.** An advertising medium consisting of signs and display materials placed inside retail stores where the advertiser's product is available.

**Positioning.** The decision that matches a product attribute with a consumer need or consumer segment in such a way as to gain competitive advantage.

**Positioning description.** See Positioning.

**Poster panels.** Large metal frames to which outdoor advertisements are pasted.

**Preemptible spot.** A broadcast advertising position that is sold to an advertiser on the condition that it can be resold to another advertiser who is willing to pay a higher nonpreemptible rate.

**Preference tests.** Product tests in which respondents are asked their reaction to a product or product feature after sampling the product.

**Price-off.** A temporary price reduction widely used as a basic offer in sales promotions.

**Primary-demand advertising.** Advertising that attempts to stimulate sales for a total product category rather than of a particular brand.

**Problem-solving objective.** See Advertising objectives.

**Producer.** In advertising, a specialist who brings advertising from the design stage to the physical form required by the medium for publication or broadcast.

**Product (brand) image.** The sum of consumer perceptions of, impressions of, or predispositions toward a product or brand.

**Product-organized advertising department.** An advertising department whose work is divided up and assigned by product class.

**Product positioning.** See Positioning.

**Production department.** A creative services unit, usually in an advertising agency, that contracts for and supervises the physical preparation of advertising material for use by the media.

**Projective question.** An indirect question form in which respondents are allowed to express their own feelings through another person.

**Prospect profile.** A tabular presentation of prospects, market segments, and demographic descriptions of each.

**Psychographics.** A description of consumers or groups of consumers in terms of their activities, interests, and opinions.

**Psychological needs.** The class of needs that is concerned with the development and projection of oneself as an individual.

**Publisher's statement.** A document supplied by the publisher of a newspaper or magazine containing circulation and related data on the publication.

**"Pull" marketing operation.** A product marketing operation in which advertising is directed to end-consumers to pre-sell them before they come to the retail outlet.

**"Push" marketing operation.** A product marketing operation in which advertising is directed to channel members in order to encourage and support their selling efforts.

**Push money.** A basic offer in a trade sales promotion that provides cash payments to retail sales clerks as an incentive to push the promoted items. Also termed "PM's" or "spiff."

**Qualitative research.** In-depth research conducted with small numbers of respondents, usually to probe consumer needs and attitudes.

**Rating points.** The percentage of total television- or radio-equipped homes with sets tuned to a particular program or station time period.

**Rating reports.** Reports issued by services that measure the audience of broadcast stations and programs. They are used in the evaluation of broadcast media.

**Rational benefits.** Promises contained in advertisements to satisfy consumers' utilitarian needs.

**Reach.** The total number of people who read one or more of the print media issues included in a media schedule during a specified time period, or the total number of persons who heard or viewed one or more of the programs or station time periods included in a broadcast media schedule.

**Readership tests.** Advertising effectiveness measurement tests that measure the number of people who have actually read a particular advertisement. Also called *recognition studies*.

**Recall tests.** Advertising effectiveness measurement tests that ask consumers to report from memory on advertisements that they have seen.

**Recent-reading technique.** A magazine audience measurement technique in which respondents are shown a list of magazine titles and asked for which titles they have read the current issue.

**Related recall.** A measure in a recall test of the percentage of viewers who recall a commercial and correctly identify it with the advertised brand.

**Response-based segmentation studies.** Segmentation studies in which the researcher does not assume in advance how the market is segmented, but applies multivariate techniques to consumer survey responses so as to define potential segments.

**Retail audit.** A technique for measuring retail sales or consumer takeaway of consumer products through auditing the sales and inventory of a sample of retail stores.

**Reuse payments.** The amounts paid to broadcast commercial talent for broadcast of a commercial after the initial use period (usually 13 weeks).

**Roll-out.** A new product introduction that spreads out gradually from one area to another.

**ROP color.** Color printing carried out by a newspaper on its own presses using the normal paper stock on which the entire newspaper is printed.

**Sales-analysis approach.** An approach to post-testing an advertising program measuring product sales and relating those sales to the advertising effort.

**Sales audit.** A measure of retail sales of designated products calculated from an audit of purchase records and inventories in a sample of retail outlets.

**Sales effect of advertising.** An approach to measuring advertising effectiveness that considers that the only valid measurement of effectiveness is sales response.

**Sales promotion.** A limited-time, special-offer advertising program directed to consumers, to the trade, or to both, which is designed to achieve fast response.

**Sales-response-to-advertising curve.** A graphic plot of the sales volume generated by various levels of advertising expenditure.

**Scatter plan.** A network television advertising schedule in which commercial positions change each week.

**Seasonal sales index.** An index that describes the expected periodic variation in sales of a product category.

**Secondary source information.** Data used in solving a problem that was originally collected for some other purpose.

**Segmentation.** The process of dividing prospects into subgroups or segments.

**Segmentation studies.** Research designed to define effective dimensions for seg-

menting a market and describing the resulting segments.

**Segmenting the market.** Dividing a market into subgroups of consumers or segments.

**Selective-demand advertising.** Advertising designed to stimulate the sales of a particular brand.

**Self-liquidating premium.** A sales promotion basic offer that makes available to purchasers a gift item for which the consumer must pay part of the cost.

**Semantic differential.** A seven-interval rating scale marked with a pair of bi-polar adjectives that is used, in advertising, to evaluate attitudes toward products, brands, and companies.

**Sequential budget-setting procedure.** An approach to setting the advertising budget that utilizes several variables, each one considered in sequence.

**Share of audience.** The percentage of homes using television or radio that are tuned to a particular program or station time period.

**Short-rate bill.** A newspaper charge to an advertiser whose actual space purchases do not meet the quantity necessary to qualify for the discount rate charged during the period.

**Showing.** A unit of purchase in outdoor advertising, usually expressed as 100, 50, or 25 showings with a 100 showing being the equivalent of 100 GRP.

**Signature line.** A standardized closing copy line designed to provide integration and continuity among different advertisements for the same product.

**Social needs.** The class of needs that is concerned with getting along with and being accepted by other persons and groups.

**Social variables.** Influences on the individual from friends, experts, and admired figures or from groups such as family, work groups, or groups to which the individual aspires to belong.

**Solo direct mail.** Individual advertisements sent to prospects through the mail.

**Sound-on-film commercial.** A television commercial in which the audio portion will be recorded simultaneously with the filming or videotaping.

**Spectaculars.** Large, illuminated outdoor displays, often with animation or other special effects, usually placed in high traffic metropolitan areas.

**Speculative presentation.** A method of evaluating a prospective advertising agency by requiring that the agency staff prepare, usually without payment, requested elements of an advertising program for a specified product.

**Split-cable testing.** A technique for testing television commercials utilizing cable transmission that permits matched samples of households to receive test and control commercials.

**Split-run tests.** A form of inquiry test of advertising effectiveness in which two different versions of an advertisement are alternated in an issue of a newspaper or magazine.

**Split-scan system.** A technique for evaluating advertising effectiveness that utilizes split-cable testing and measures household response to the test product by collecting purchase data through supermarket scanner systems.

**Spot.** A broadcast advertising purchase that is not scheduled as part of a program.

**Standard Advertising Units (SAU).** A system of 56 uniform newspaper advertising purchase units using the column inch as a unit of depth measurement and basing width on a standard newspaper page format.

**Supers.** Statements about type of product benefit, brand name, or other information, superimposed on the video of television commercials to lend emphasis, often coordinated with an audio statement.

**Take-ones.** Display cards holding reply cards, order forms, pamphlets or the like for consumers.

**Test market.** A selected representative market into which market test programs are introduced.

**Test market laboratory (simulated test market — STM).** An approach to testing new product introduction programs that brings consumers to central laboratory locations so as to expose them to product concepts and measure their reactions through simulated buying situations and interviews.

**Theater tests.** A technique for pre-testing television commercials in which a sample of consumers is brought to a central location to view a test television program with test commercials. Response to the test commercials is measured through survey and simulated purchase.

**Through-the-book technique.** A magazine audience measurement technique in which respondents are shown skeletonized versions of magazines and asked if they have read those issues.

**Tracking study.** In advertising, an advertising effectiveness evaluation test that monitors over time the changes taking place in response to an advertising program.

**Trade shows.** Events held in major cities, often in conjunction with industry conventions, where business firms can display, demonstrate, and sell their products.

**Trade survey.** An approach to gathering competitive and other market data by interviewing trade intermediaries in the subject product class.

**Traffic department.** An advertising agency creative services unit that is concerned with the internal routing and scheduling of creative work and with the delivery and scheduling of the advertising materials used by the media.

**Transit advertising.** An advertising medium consisting of paper advertising posters placed on mass transit vehicles and in transit stations.

**Underlying needs.** Deep-lying, inborn, permanent human requirements that, when not satisfied, motivate individuals to act in order to find satisfaction.

**Utilitarian needs.** The class of needs that is concerned with coping with the physical environment.

**Values and Life Style (VALS) Program.** A study that produced a description of nine American life styles or psychographic profiles.

**Voice-over commercial.** A television commercial in which the announcer's voice is heard but the announcer is not seen.

**Wheeler-Lea Amendment.** An amendment to the Federal Trade Commission Act of 1914 that extended the powers of the FTC by extending the FTC's powers to the protection of consumers.

**Word-of-mouth communication.** Verbal information gained from private, individual sources like family, friends, or expert acquaintances.

**Zero-base budgeting approach.** A method of setting the advertising budget that is based on the sum of each individual decision package or advertising task, with the cost of each task being determined without reference to the prior year's expenditures.

# INDEX